HOLLYWOOD STYLE ICONS

ANNALEE HODGES

Published by Hinkler Pty Ltd in 2026
45-55 Fairchild St
Heatherton VIC 3122
www.hinkler.com

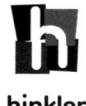

hinkler

President: Sean Moore
Production Director: Adam Moore
Editorial Director: Lisa Purcell
Art Direction: Nicola Plumb

Premedia Production Partner: DataWorks.co.in

ISBN: 978-1-4889-7510-3
Printed and bound in China

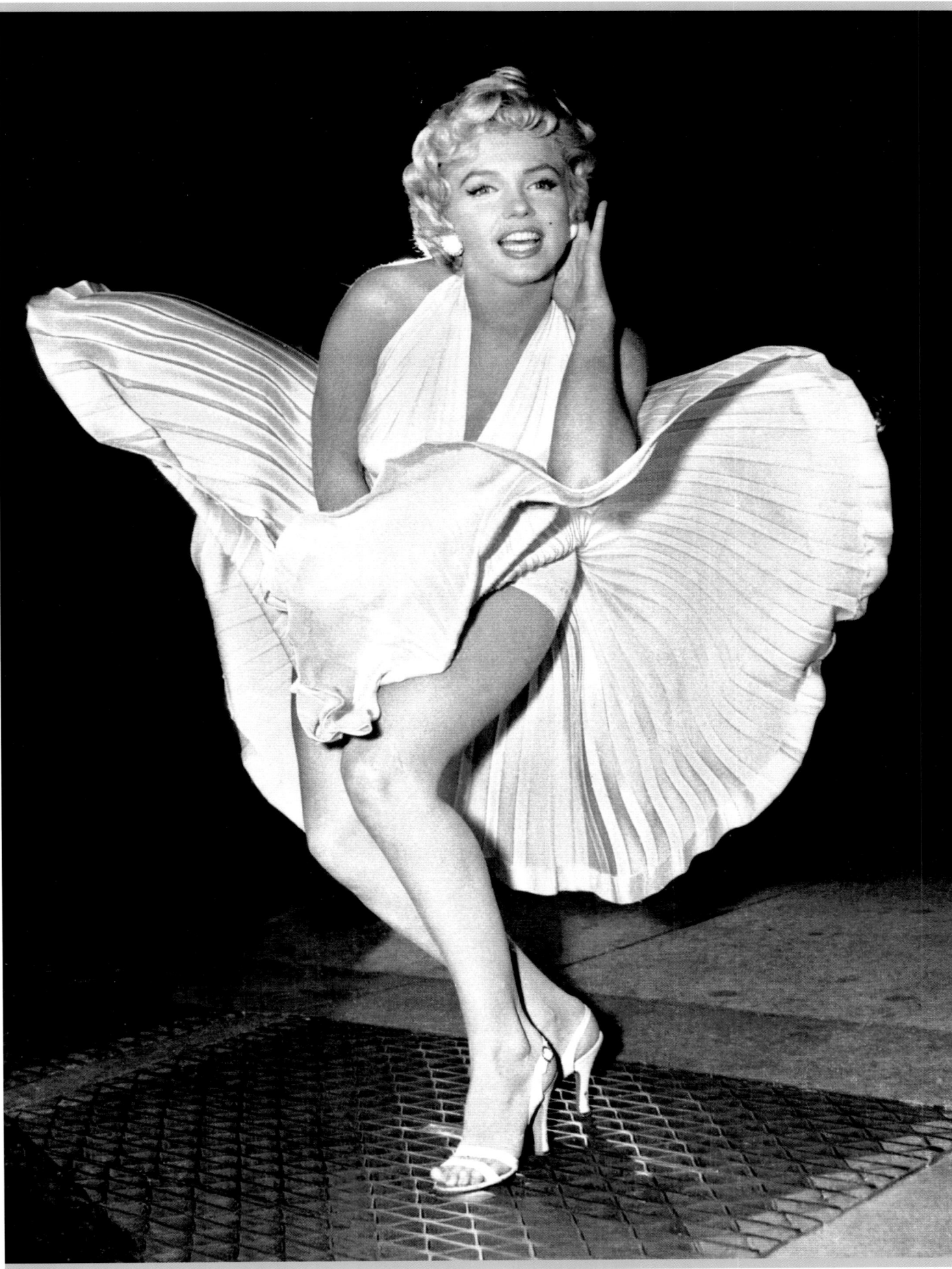

CONTENTS

CONTENTS

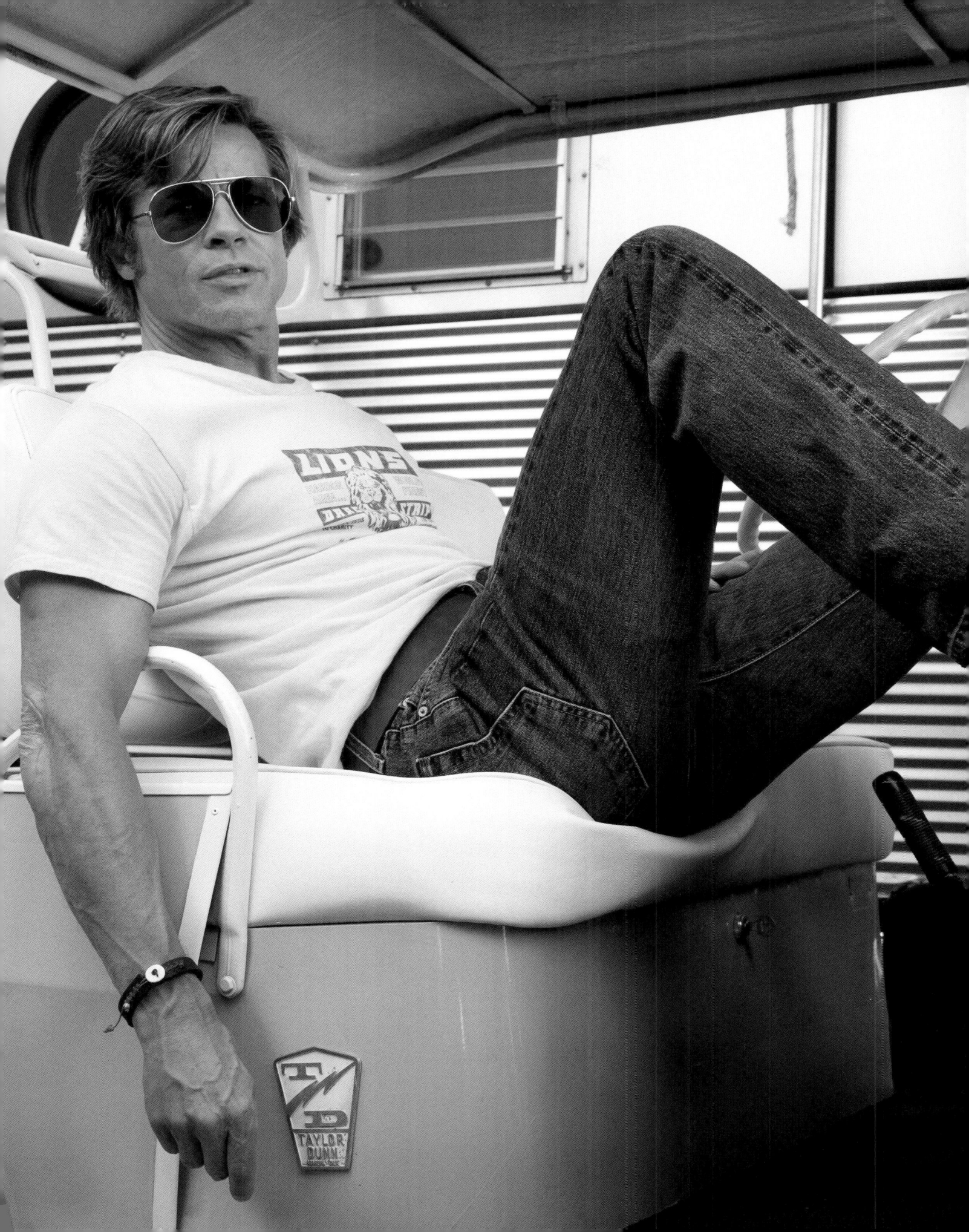

THE ORIGINS OF HOLLYWOOD STYLE

Hollywood's emergence as a fashion capital wasn't premeditated. It unfolded organically, driven by visual storytelling, public fascination, and the expanding scale of the film industry. As movies transitioned from short reels to full-length features in the 1910s and 1920s, a revolution in style quietly took root—one that would eventually rival the influence of Paris.

The industry's effect on fashion lay not only in its reach but also in its intimacy. For the first time, American women could study glamorous clothing in motion, up close, from their theater seats. No magazine or store display could match the fluid spectacle of a gown gliding across the screen. Early studios didn't intend to influence public style. Costumes were often pulled from actors' wardrobes or rented from supply houses. But as characters turned more complex and narrative demands became more nuanced, clothing evolved from an afterthought into an essential storytelling tool.

The shift was economic as well as artistic. Producers noted that on-screen style shaped consumer preferences. When Pearl White wore a sharply tailored black-and-white outfit in *The Perils of Pauline*, young women rushed to imitate it. Suddenly, fashion wasn't confined to couture—it was being crafted on soundstages.

This marked the birth of the studio costume designer, a role that fused research, artistry, and visual narrative. Clare West, considered one of the first professional designers, introduced structure and artistry to the wardrobe process on films such as *Intolerance*. Designers stopped improvising and began sketching, sourcing, and constructing with a clear purpose. Studios also recruited European names such as Paul Iribe and Erté to boost fashion credibility. But by the 1920s, American designers were forging their path—balancing historical reference with the demands of lighting and cinematography.

The rise of studio costume departments mirrored Hollywood's transformation into a dream factory. Clothing, perhaps more than sets or lighting, was what audiences copied most fervently. Designers such as Gilbert Adrian helped define the quintessential Hollywood look: bold, glamorous, and tailored to enhance star personas.

Design had to adapt to changing technologies. In silent film, designers relied on contrast and silhouette to communicate engaging content visually. The arrival of Technicolor in the 1930s forced a total rethink. Colors that looked appealing in person often failed to display the same shades on film. Designers navigated this new terrain through trial and experimentation.

Before formal departments existed, costuming was chaotic. Garments were often hastily constructed, borrowed, or dismantled within days. Today, costume design is a collaborative effort involving

BELOW
———
Gloria Swanson, steely and elegant in a military-style coat, faces Walter Byron's ardent Prince in *Queen Kelly* (1929)—a silent-era tableau of passion, power, and doomed romance.

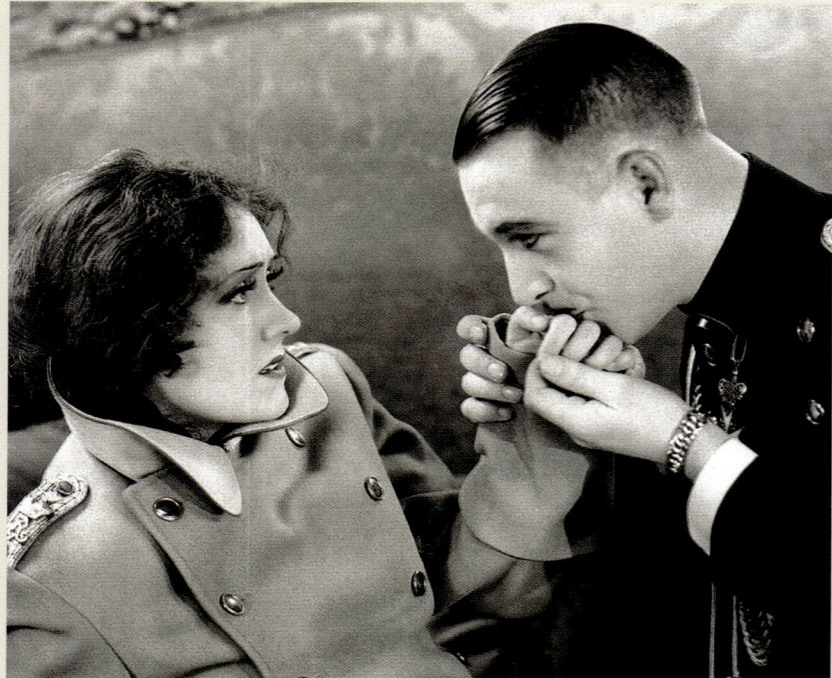

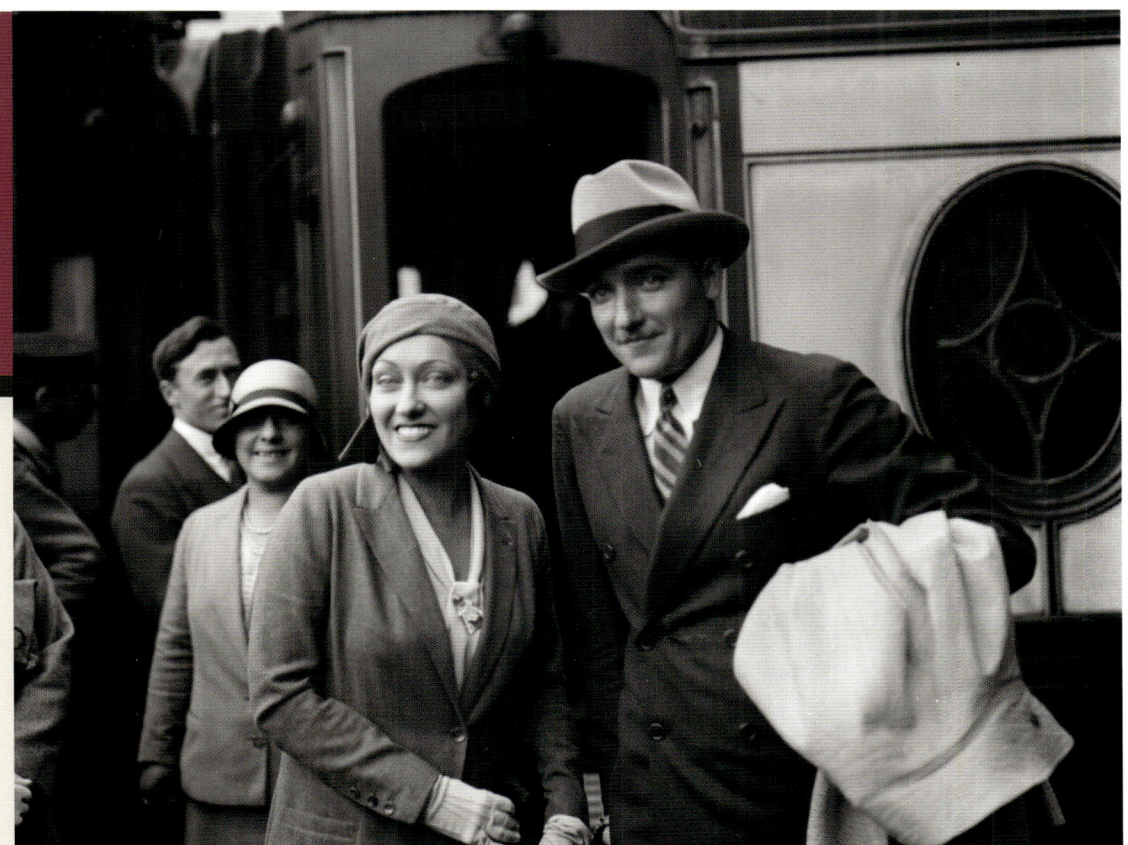

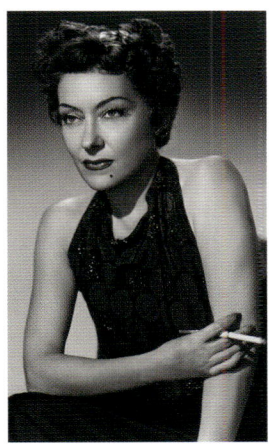

In difficult times, fashion is always outrageous.

ELSA SCHIAPARELLI

directors, cinematographers, and lighting teams to ensure a unified visual world.

Economic potential added further momentum. Studios realized clothing had market power beyond the screen. Film-inspired outfits were turned into mass-produced patterns and ready-to-wear lines. Joan Crawford's puff-sleeved gown in *Letty Lynton* sparked a national craze, with Macy's reportedly having sold tens of thousands of replicas—one of the earliest examples of Hollywood costume influencing mass-market retail.

At the same time, Hollywood offered an alternative to Parisian dominance. America had no centralized fashion authority in the 1930s and 1940s, but Hollywood filled that gap. Film promoted individuality over couture elitism, speaking directly to consumers. Magazines such as *Photoplay* and *Modern Screen* picked up on this, giving on-set wardrobe choices equal weightage as red-carpet appearances. Designers such as Edith Head and Adrian became household names.

Wartime shortages in the 1940s challenged designers to do more with less. Fabrics were rationed, but creativity flourished. Strong shoulders, narrow skirts, and sharp tailoring weren't just aesthetic choices—they were cinematic solutions to real-world constraints.

Men's fashion also evolved. Characters such as Douglas Fairbanks and Humphrey Bogart helped define iconic masculine styles—from swashbuckling romanticism to trench-coated noir. Male costumes became as central to storytelling as female ones.

By the postwar era, the line between costume and fashion had blurred. Hollywood became both archive and oracle, preserving the past while forecasting the future.

The collapse of the studio system in the 1950s marked a turning point. In-house departments closed, and designers became freelancers. While the loss of structure meant fewer resources, it also offered creative freedom. Costume designers moved between studios, genres, and even media, bringing their vision to television, theater, and independent film.

Today, costume design is an art form that blends historical research, trend forecasting, and character development. Although never intended as a style authority, Hollywood's fashion legacy endures. It has influenced global couture, redefined beauty standards, and permanently altered how clothing tells a story. Costume design has played a major role in defining eras and influencing fashion trends of Hollywood, significantly shaping culture—one unforgettable costume at a time.

ABOVE

Gloria Swanson, poised and enigmatic in a sequined halter gown, smolders with classic Hollywood elegance in this 1927 Los Angeles portrait—a timeless icon at the height of her stardom.

TOP LEFT

Gloria Swanson arrives in style at London's Victoria Station on 3 September 1929, alongside her husband, the Marquis de la Falaise. Dressed in tailored elegance and a cloche hat, the silent screen icon beams ahead of the world premiere of her first talking picture, *The Trespasser*.

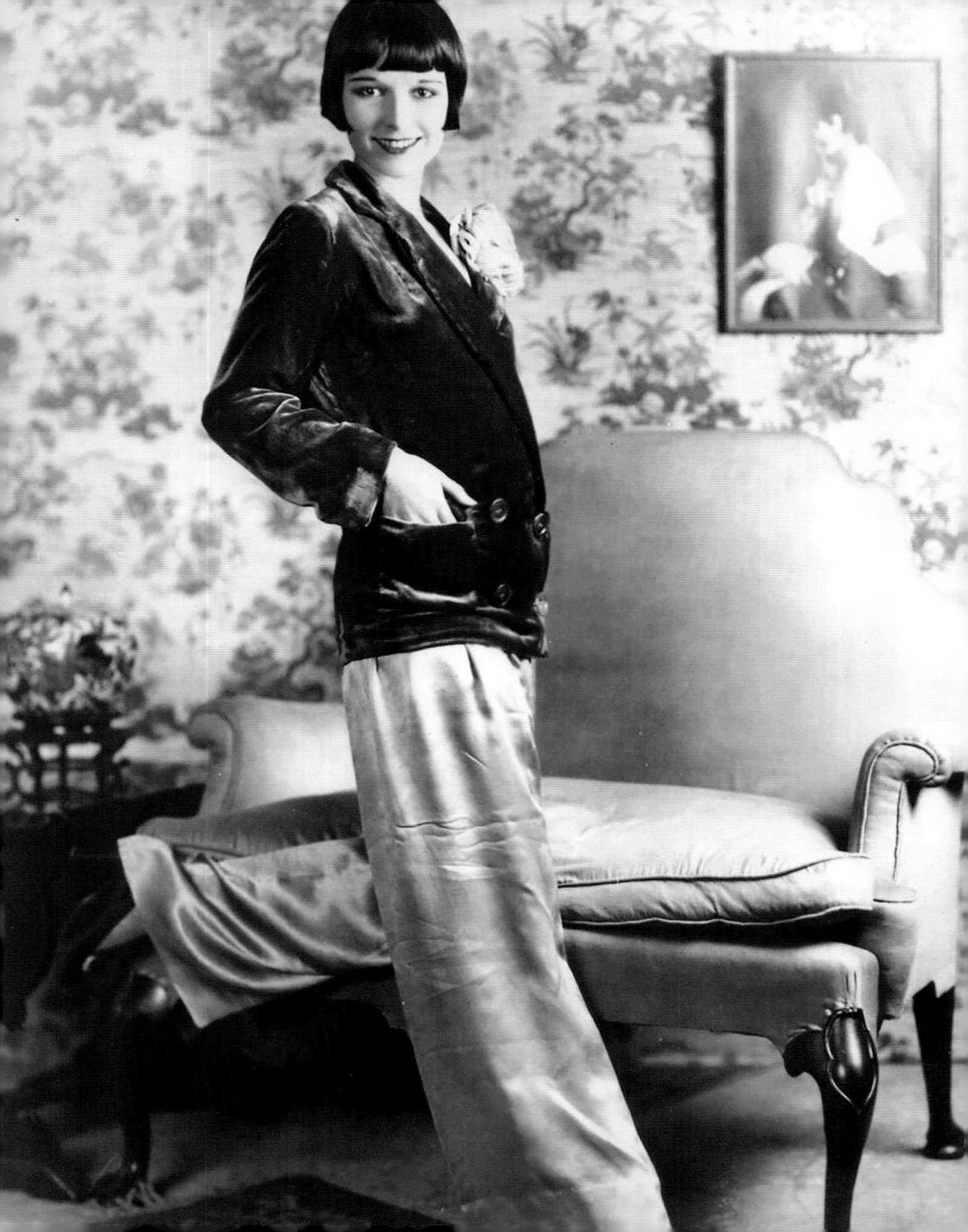

NINETEEN TWENTIES

The 1920s were the formative years of Hollywood fashion—an era when the silver screen began to dictate trends rather than simply reflect them. With the expansion of full-length feature films and the arrival of new cinematic genres, the movie industry experienced a burst of creative and commercial energy. This was also the decade when the studio system took root and stars became household names. Glamor, once an occasional element of film storytelling, became a requirement, and costume designers emerged as vital creative forces behind the camera. As filmmakers experimented with lighting and framing, clothing became part of the visual language of storytelling. Characters needed wardrobes that matched not only the period or plot, but their public image—especially with fan magazines beginning to spotlight star fashion both on and off the screen.

More than any decade before, the 1920s solidified Hollywood's role in shaping popular taste. Actresses such as Clara Bow, Mary Pickford, and Gloria Swanson became fashion icons, setting off waves of imitation among American women. Costume departments grew in size and prestige, and designers began to develop distinct styles for their stars. Whether portraying flappers, ingénues, or screen vamps, the leading women of the decade were dressed to define an era. In this dazzling decade of cinematic expansion, Hollywood didn't just entertain—it began to lead the fashion parade.

VILMA BÁNKY

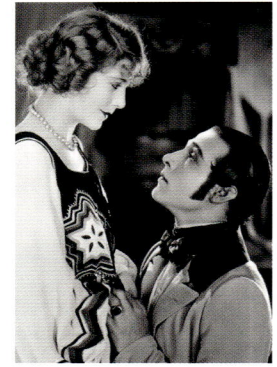

Graceful and enigmatic, Vilma Bánky captivated silent film audiences with her refined beauty and romantic screen presence.

Vilma (1901–1991) was born in Hungary and began her acting career in European films before being discovered by Hollywood producer Samuel Goldwyn in the mid-1920s. Without any prior English language skills, she was brought to America, where her delicate features and serene charm quickly won over audiences. Goldwyn promoted her as "The Hungarian Rhapsody," and she was soon cast opposite some of the era's most famous leading men.

Bánky achieved major stardom costarring with Rudolph Valentino in *The Eagle* (1925) and *The Son of the Sheik* (1926), where her graceful elegance perfectly complemented Valentino's smoldering magnetism. She also starred alongside Ronald Colman in a series of romantic dramas, including *The Dark Angel* (1926) and *The Winning of Barbara Worth* (1926). These roles solidified her reputation as one of the screen's great romantic heroines.

With the arrival of sound, Bánky's career slowed down, in part due to her accent. After marrying actor Rod La Rocque in 1927, she gradually retired from film and lived a quiet life away from Hollywood's spotlight. Although her career was brief, her performances remain a testament to the allure of silent cinema's Golden Age.

ABOVE

Vilma Bánky captivates in *The Eagle* (1925), her expressive poise and aristocratic charm matching Valentino's intensity in Clarence Brown's lavish tale of love and disguise.

RIGHT

Bánky as Yasmin in *The Son of the Sheik* (1926), radiating desert allure and silent-era elegance in George Fitzmaurice's sweeping tale of passion and peril.

The Bánky Look

Ethereal and feminine, Bánky favored flowing gowns, delicate embroidery, and soft curls that emphasized her graceful, aristocratic appeal.

- Soft, waved hair
- Romantic, draped dresses
- Feathered hats
- Long lashes and porcelain complexion

FASHION FEATURES

THE EAGLE (1925)
THE SON OF THE SHEIK (1926)
THE DARK ANGEL (1926)
THE WINNING OF BARBARA WORTH (1926)

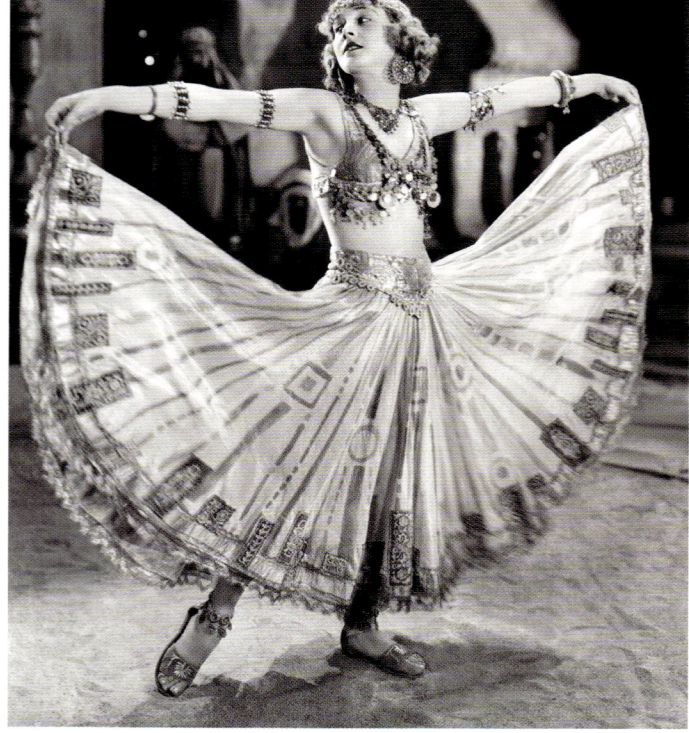

THEDA BARA

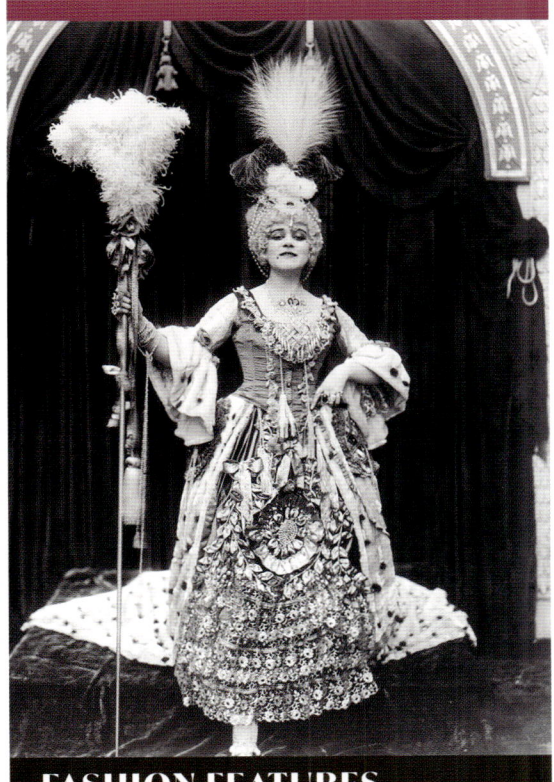

FASHION FEATURES

A FOOL THERE WAS (1915)
CLEOPATRA (1917)
SALOMÉ (1918)
MADAME MYSTERY (1926)

The Bara Look

Sensual and theatrical, Bara's look featured exotic fabrics, dramatic silhouettes, and mystical accessories that amplified her dangerous allure.

- Kohl-rimmed eyes
- Headscarves and shawls
- Snake and scarab jewelry
- Dark lips and cascading curls

Theda Bara, cinema's original "vamp," transformed early Hollywood with her dark mystique and magnetic screen presence.

Theda (1885–1955), born Theodosia Burr Goodman in Cincinnati, Ohio, rose to fame in the 1910s as one of silent film's most sensational stars. She was rebranded by Fox Studios as an exotic femme fatale, supposedly born in the Sahara and raised in occult knowledge—an entirely fabricated backstory. Her screen name, an anagram of "Arab Death," fed into this persona, and her image as a dangerous seductress captivated audiences and scandalized censors.

Bara's breakthrough role came in A Fool There Was (1915), where her portrayal of a predatory "vampire woman" introduced the archetype of the vamp—an alluring woman who lured men to ruin. Her success launched a wave of similar roles in films such as Cleopatra (1917), Salomé (1918), and Madame Mystery (1926). Although many of her films are now lost, Bara's reputation as Hollywood's first dark goddess endures.

Unlike many stars of her time, Bara's appeal lay not in innocence but in power and mystery. Her elaborate costumes, including serpent jewelry, headscarves, and heavily lined eyes, became a hallmark of silent film glamor. Although her career faded with the advent of sound, her influence on cinematic archetypes and screen fashion remains iconic.

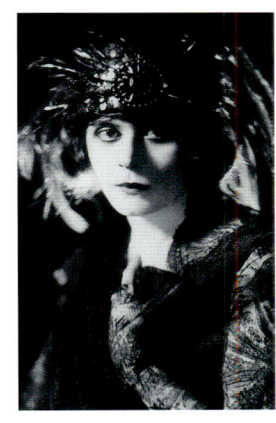

ABOVE

Theda Bara, seen here in ornate costume, pioneered Hollywood's "vamp" archetype and starred in over 40 films.

LEFT

Bara commands the screen in Madame Du Barry (1920), embodying the infamous courtesan with dark allure, opulent gowns, and the magnetic presence that made her silent cinema's original vamp.

CLARA BOW

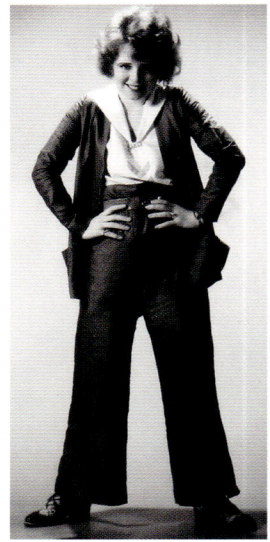

The original "It Girl," Clara Bow defined the flapper era with her uninhibited energy and magnetic screen presence.

Clara Bow (1905–1965) became one of the most iconic actresses of the 1920s, capturing the spirit of the Jazz Age like no other. Born in Brooklyn, New York, she overcame a difficult childhood marked by poverty and family instability to win a national acting contest, launching her film career. Bow's breakthrough came with the smash hit *It* (1927), where her portrayal of a vivacious department store clerk established her as a symbol of modern, carefree femininity. "It Girl" was coined specifically to describe her irresistible charisma.

At the height of her career, Bow was one of the most bankable stars in Hollywood, with films such as *Wings* (1927)—winner of the first Academy Award for Best Outstanding Picture—cementing her status. She transitioned to talkies but struggled with the pressures of fame and with mental health issues, and retired in 1933.

Bow's impact on film and fashion was lasting. With bobbed hair, expressive eyes, and a bold attitude, she represented a new kind of woman—independent, playful, and truly unforgettable.

ABOVE

With a confident stance and tousled curls, Clara Bow shattered conventions—her performance in *Wings* (1927) helped the film win the first-ever Academy Award for Best Picture.

RIGHT

Clara Bow radiates bold glamor in shimmering sequins. As the original "It Girl," she captured 1920s flapper spirit which influenced both women's attitudes and their style.

FASHION FEATURES

IT (1927)
WINGS (1927)
MANTRAP (1926)

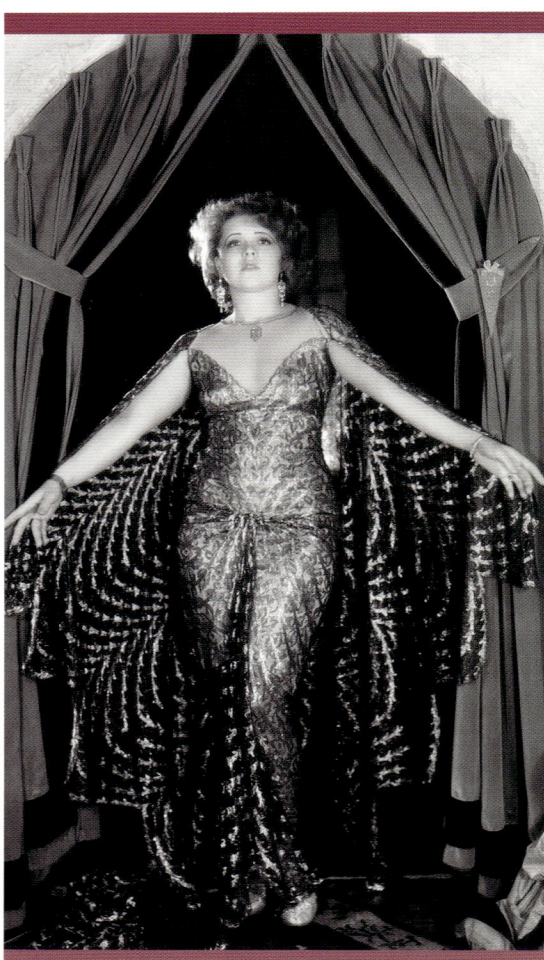

The Bow Look

Flirty and effortlessly modern, Clara Bow embraced cloche hats, above-the-knee skirts, and curve-skimming silhouettes that echoed her free-spirited persona, setting trends for the generation of young women eager to embody the new, liberated flapper style.

• Bobbed hair with finger waves
• Cupid's bow lips
• Cloche hats
• Bold eye makeup and slim dresses

LOUISE BROOKS

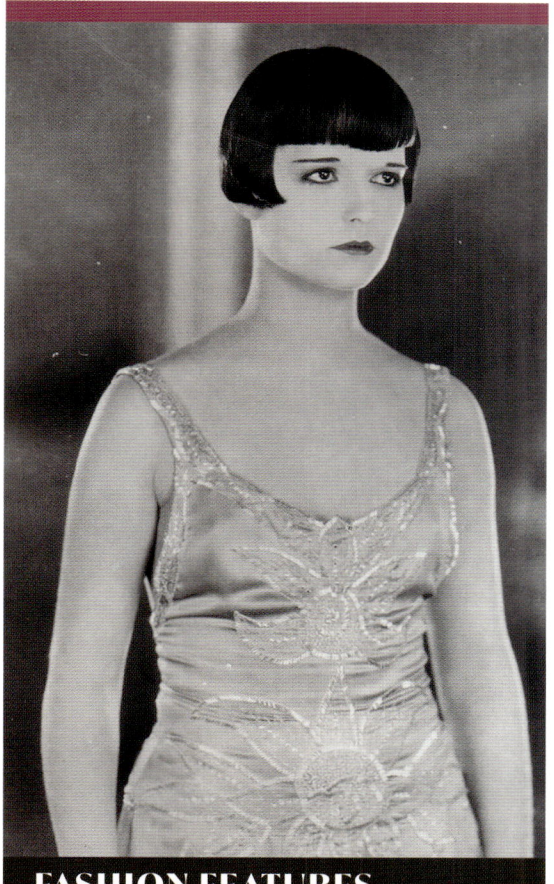

FASHION FEATURES

A GIRL IN EVERY PORT (1928)
BEGGARS OF LIFE (1928)
PANDORA'S BOX (1929)
DIARY OF A LOST GIRL (1929)

The Brooks Look

Minimalist and sharp, Brooks favored clean lines, pearls, and dark dresses that framed her iconic hair and expressive face.

• Sleek, blunt-cut bob
• Dark lipstick
• Fur wraps
• Simple, elegant silhouettes

Effortlessly modern and fiercely independent, Louise Brooks became a lasting symbol of 1920s sophistication and rebellion.

Louise Brooks (1906–1985), originally from Cherryvale, Kansas, started her performing career as a dancer with the Denishawn Company before making her way to Broadway.

Her striking features, confident presence, and iconic bob haircut quickly drew attention, leading to a film contract with Paramount Pictures in the mid-1920s. Brooks brought a cool detachment and emotional realism to her roles, setting her apart from her more theatrical contemporaries.

She appeared in silent films such as *A Girl in Every Port* (1928) and *Beggars of Life* (1928), but her most acclaimed performances came in Europe. Director G.W. Pabst cast her in *Pandora's Box* (1929) and *Diary of a Lost Girl* (1929), where she played complex, sexually liberated women with rare depth and vulnerability. Although her career in Hollywood faded quickly due to conflicts with studios and her refusal to conform, her artistry was rediscovered in the 1950s by French critics who hailed her as a true auteur performer.

Brooks' style—sharp, elegant, and ahead of its time—helped shape the image of the flapper and continues to influence fashion and film aesthetics today.

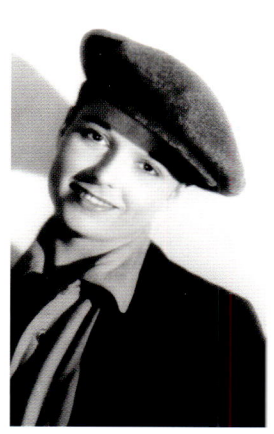

ABOVE

Louise Brooks, a silent film rebel, rejected Hollywood norms and found acclaim in German cinema classics like *Pandora's Box* (1929).

LEFT

Brooks popularized the sleek bob hairstyle and the modern attitudes of the flapper.

LEADING MEN
RUDOLPH VALENTINO

> **I am beginning to look forward to the time when I shall be just a memory.**
>
> RUDOLPH VALENTINO

Rudolph Valentino, born Rodolfo Pietro Filiberto Raffaello Guglielmi di Valentina d'Antonguolla in 1895 in Castellaneta, Italy, became one of silent cinema's most iconic figures— an international sex symbol whose impact on fashion and masculine identity reverberated far beyond the silver screen. His career may have lasted just a decade, but his style and mystique remain immortal.

Valentino emigrated to the United States in 1913, working various odd jobs before finding his way to Hollywood. After gaining attention in supporting roles, he rose to superstardom with *The Four Horsemen of the Apocalypse* (1921), followed by his signature performance in *The Sheik* (1921). These films established him as the quintessential Latin Lover—mysterious, smoldering, and dangerously alluring. He captivated audiences with his dark features, expressive eyes, and a fashion sense that set new standards for men in cinema.

Rudolph's personal style was refined, exotic, and carefully curated. He popularized slicked-back hair, impeccably tailored suits, silk cravats, and cologne—then considered overly dandyish for men. He wore tuxedos with elegance and often favored bold accessories such as signet rings, canes, and patterned scarves. In a time when masculine fashion leaned toward conservative or rugged styles, Valentino introduced European sophistication and flair to American audiences. His off-screen wardrobe often featured custom-made Italian suits, and he was among the first major male celebrities to be as invested in fashion as his female co-stars.

Even in casual wear, Valentino maintained an aura of luxury. Linen trousers, fitted sweaters, and leather shoes became essentials in his downtime

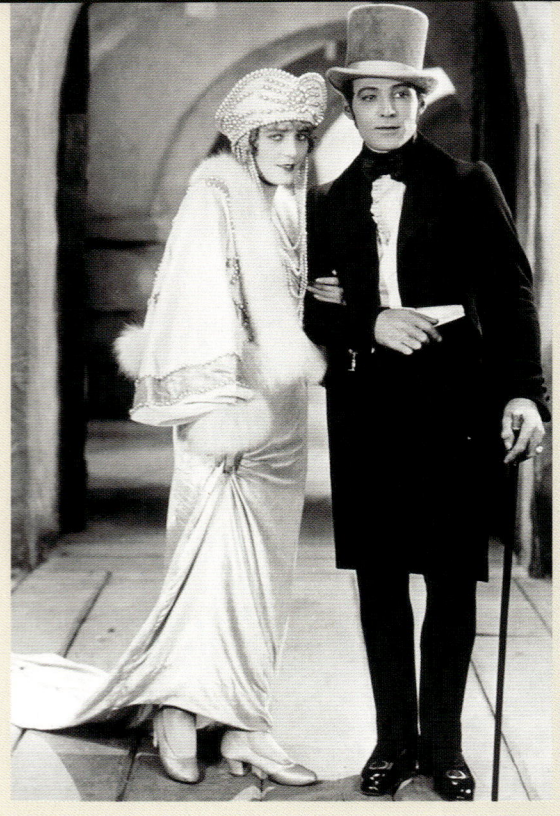

TOP RIGHT

Vilma Bánky and Rudolph Valentino dazzle in *The Eagle* (1925), dressed in opulent evening attire—an iconic silent-era pairing of elegance, mystery, and irresistible screen chemistry.

look. His costuming in films also contributed to his legendary status. In *The Sheik*, he wore flowing robes and desert gear that made the "orientalist" aesthetic style both cinematic and seductive—an image forever tied to his identity.

Despite his immense popularity, Valentino often battled critics who questioned his masculinity, partly due to his polished appearance and refined manner. Rather than retreat from these challenges, he confronted them with confidence. Famously, he even wrote a response to a newspaper column accusing him of promoting "effeminacy," defending his individuality and reshaping the cultural conversation around male glamor and strength.

Tragically, Valentino died in 1926 at the age of 31 from complications following surgery. His sudden death shocked the world, triggering mass hysteria

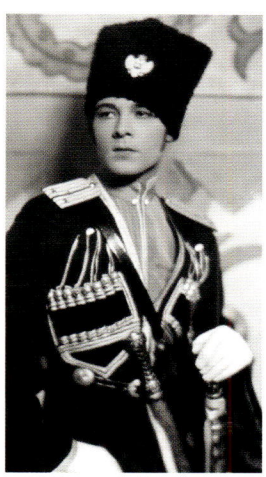

and public mourning rarely seen before or since. Over 100,000 people crowded the streets of New York City for his funeral. Fans fainted, fights broke out, and the frenzy became a testament to his unprecedented fame and emotional hold on audiences.

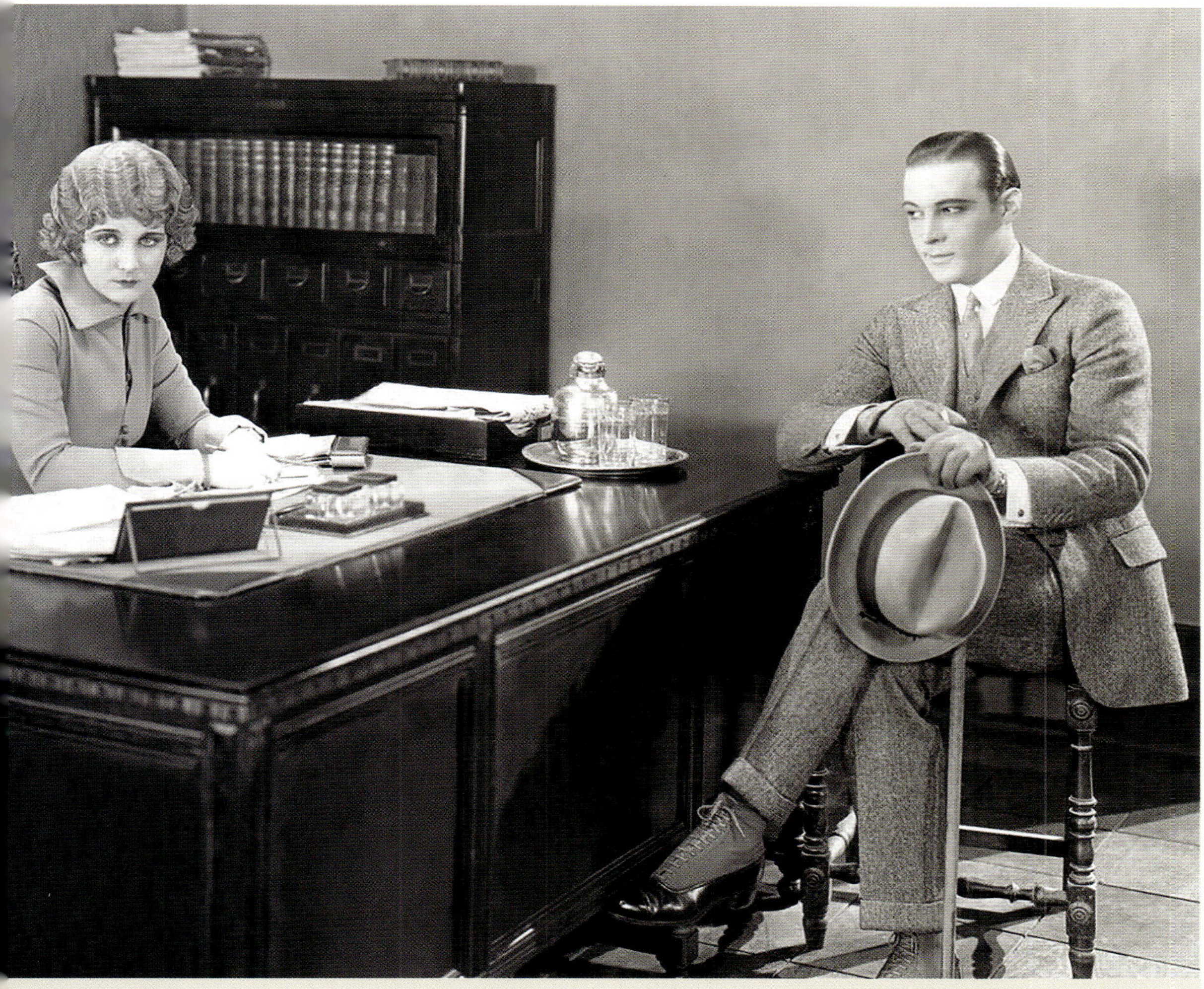

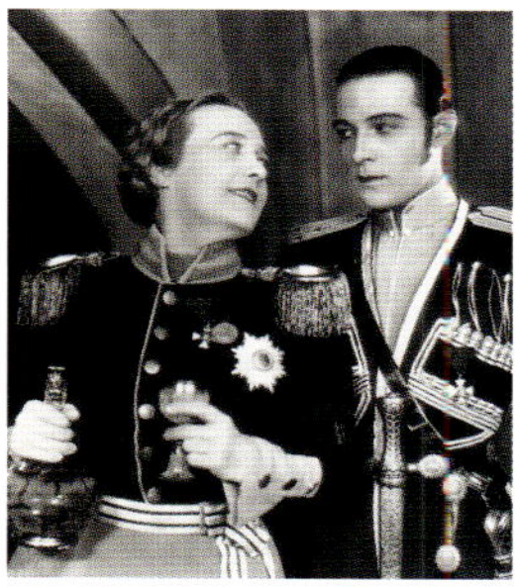

Although Valentino did not write a full-length autobiography during his lifetime, he authored a book titled *My Private Diary*, written during a trip to Europe, which was published posthumously. In it, he offered personal reflections on fame, identity, and the loneliness that often accompanied his public image. The diary reveals a man torn between the romantic persona he portrayed and the quieter, introspective self he often yearned to express.

Rudolph Valentino remains one of Hollywood's earliest and most enduring fashion icons. Through his daring style, graceful charisma, and refusal to conform to rigid norms, he helped redefine male beauty and star power in the 20th century—setting a glamorous standard that echoes through modern fashion and cinema.

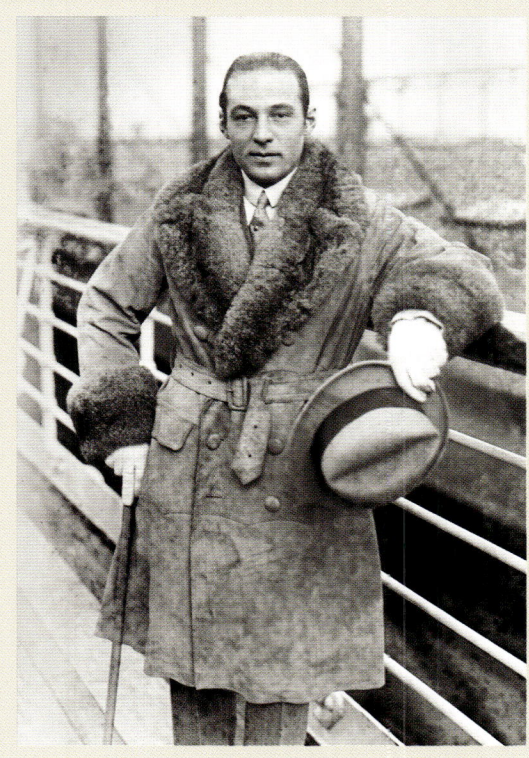

TOP RIGHT

Louise Dresser and Rudolph Valentino in *The Eagle* (1925), dressed in ornate military regalia, share a scene laced with intrigue and tension in this silent swashbuckling classic.

ABOVE

Rudolph strikes a commanding pose in *The Eagle* (1925), clad in an ornate Cossack uniform— embodying silent-era heroism with romantic flair and brooding intensity.

TOP LEFT

Gertrude Olmstead and Rudolph Valentino share a charged moment in *Cobra* (1925), with Valentino sharply dressed in a tailored suit— capturing the elegance and tension of this silent-era drama.

LEFT

Valentino, the Italian-born silent film icon, cuts a striking figure in a belted fur-trimmed coat, effortlessly embodying 1920s matinee idol style and sophistication.

DOLORES DEL RÍO

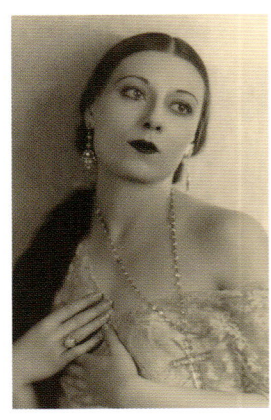

With regal poise and magnetic beauty, Dolores del Río became the first major Latin American actress to conquer Hollywood—and later became a legend in Mexican cinema.

Dolores del Río (1904–1983) was born into an aristocratic family in Durango, Mexico. Following the Mexican Revolution, she relocated to Los Angeles, where her striking features and graceful presence drew the attention of Hollywood producers. Her American film debut came in the silent era with *Joanna* (1925, now lost), and by the late 1920s, she had achieved star status with roles in *What Price Glory?* (1926), *Ramona* (1928), and *Resurrection* (1927). Her performances combined elegance and emotion, captivating audiences and critics alike.

In the early sound era, del Río was often cast in "exotic" roles that highlighted her beauty but limited her range. Still, she left a lasting impression in films such as *Bird of Paradise* (1932) and *Flying Down to Rio* (1933). Frustrated by Hollywood's stereotypes, she returned to Mexico in the 1940s and helped launch the Golden Age of Mexican cinema, starring in classics such as *María Candelaria* (1943).

Beyond her screen work, del Río was known for her impeccable style, characterized by sleek silhouettes, dramatic jewelry, and flawless tailoring. She remains a timeless icon of cross-cultural elegance and cinematic influence.

ABOVE
—
Dolores del Río, captured in a 1927 portrait by Benjamin Strauss and Homer Peyton, exudes timeless poise—her sculpted features and serene gaze marking her as a luminous figure of early Hollywood.

RIGHT
—
Mexican film star Dolores del Río departs for Paris after observing London's underworld types—composed and curious, she moves with the poise of a star drawn to real-world drama.

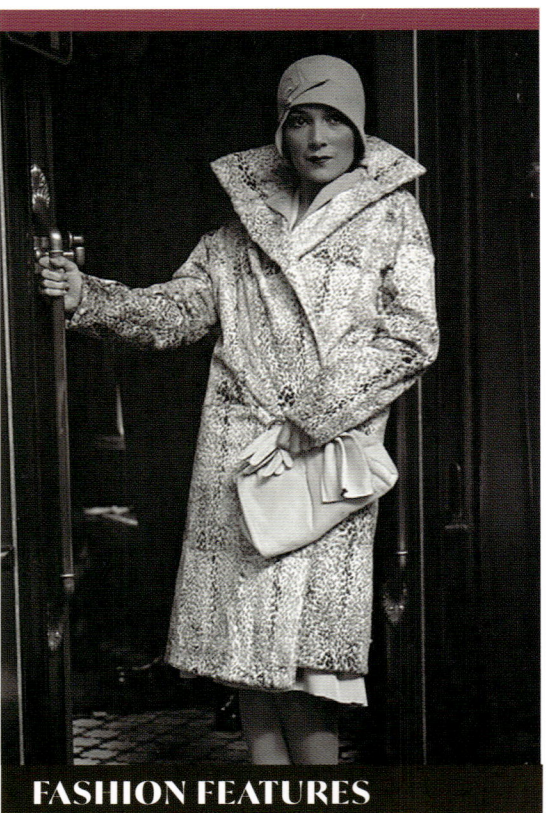

FASHION FEATURES

RAMONA (1928)
RESURRECTION (1927)
BIRD OF PARADISE (1932)
FLYING DOWN TO RIO (1933)
MARÍA CANDELARIA (1943)

The Del Río Look

Polished and glamorous, del Río favored bias-cut gowns, fine tailoring, and statement accessories that reflected Hollywood sophistication and her Mexican heritage.

• Sleek, waved hair
• Floor-length gowns
• Dramatic earrings and necklaces
• Bold lips and sculpted brows

JANET GAYNOR

The Gaynor Look

Innocent and sweet, Gaynor's wardrobe featured soft fabrics, delicate collars, and romantic silhouettes that reflected her tender on-screen persona.

- Short, wavy hair
- Soft organdy gowns
- Ruffled collars and bows
- Modest hats and delicate accessories

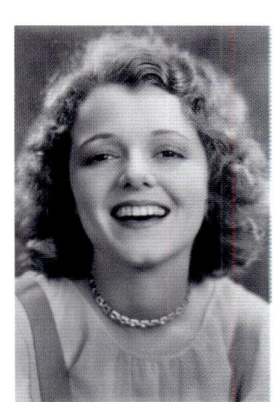

Soft-spoken yet determined, Janet Gaynor charmed early film audiences with her expressive vulnerability and became the first-ever winner of the Academy Award for Best Actress.

Janet Gaynor (1906–1984), born Laura Augusta Gainor in Philadelphia, moved to San Francisco as a child and later pursued acting in Los Angeles while working as a secretary. After appearing in bit parts, she landed her breakthrough role in *The Johnstown Flood* (1926), which led to a contract with Fox Film Corporation. Her gentle presence, emotional range, and wholesome charm made her an immediate star.

In 1929, Gaynor won the first Academy Award for Best Actress for her performances in three films: *Seventh Heaven*, *Street Angel*, and *Sunrise: A Song of Two Humans*. Her naturalistic acting style helped define the transition from silent to sound films. Throughout the 1930s, she remained a box-office favorite with roles in *State Fair* (1933), *Small Town Girl* (1936), and the original *A Star is Born* (1937).

Gaynor's image was modest, feminine, and emotionally sincere, often portraying resilient women facing hardship with quiet strength. She retired from film in 1939 and focused on painting and family life, but returned briefly to the screen and stage in the 1950s and 1960s.

Her legacy endures as one of Hollywood's first great leading ladies.

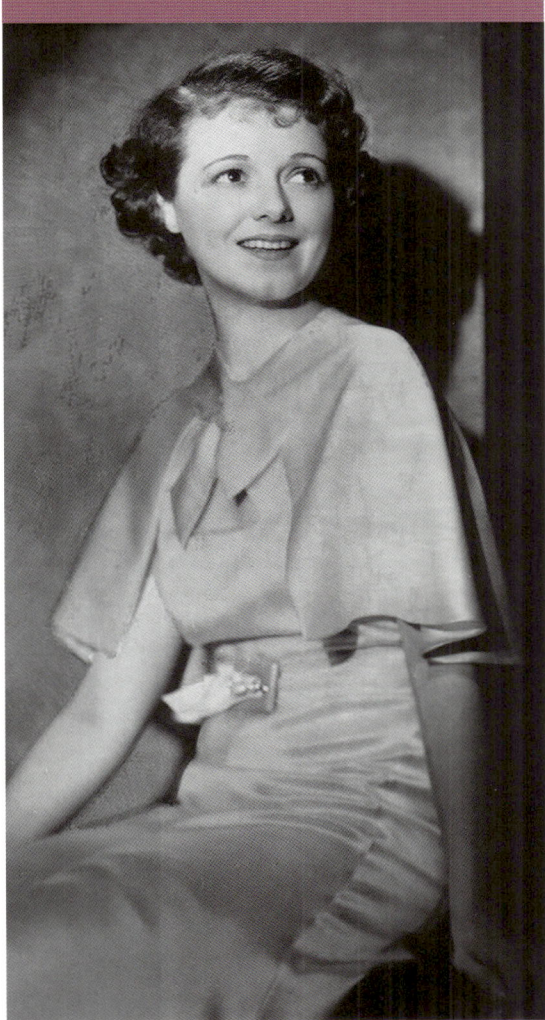

FASHION FEATURES

SEVENTH HEAVEN (1927)
SUNRISE (1927)
STREET ANGEL (1927)
A STAR IS BORN (1937)

ABOVE
—
With a radiant smile, Janet Gaynor showcases the easy, American-girl charm that led to her film success.

LEFT
—
Janet Gaynor made history as the first woman to win Best Actress Oscar in 1929.

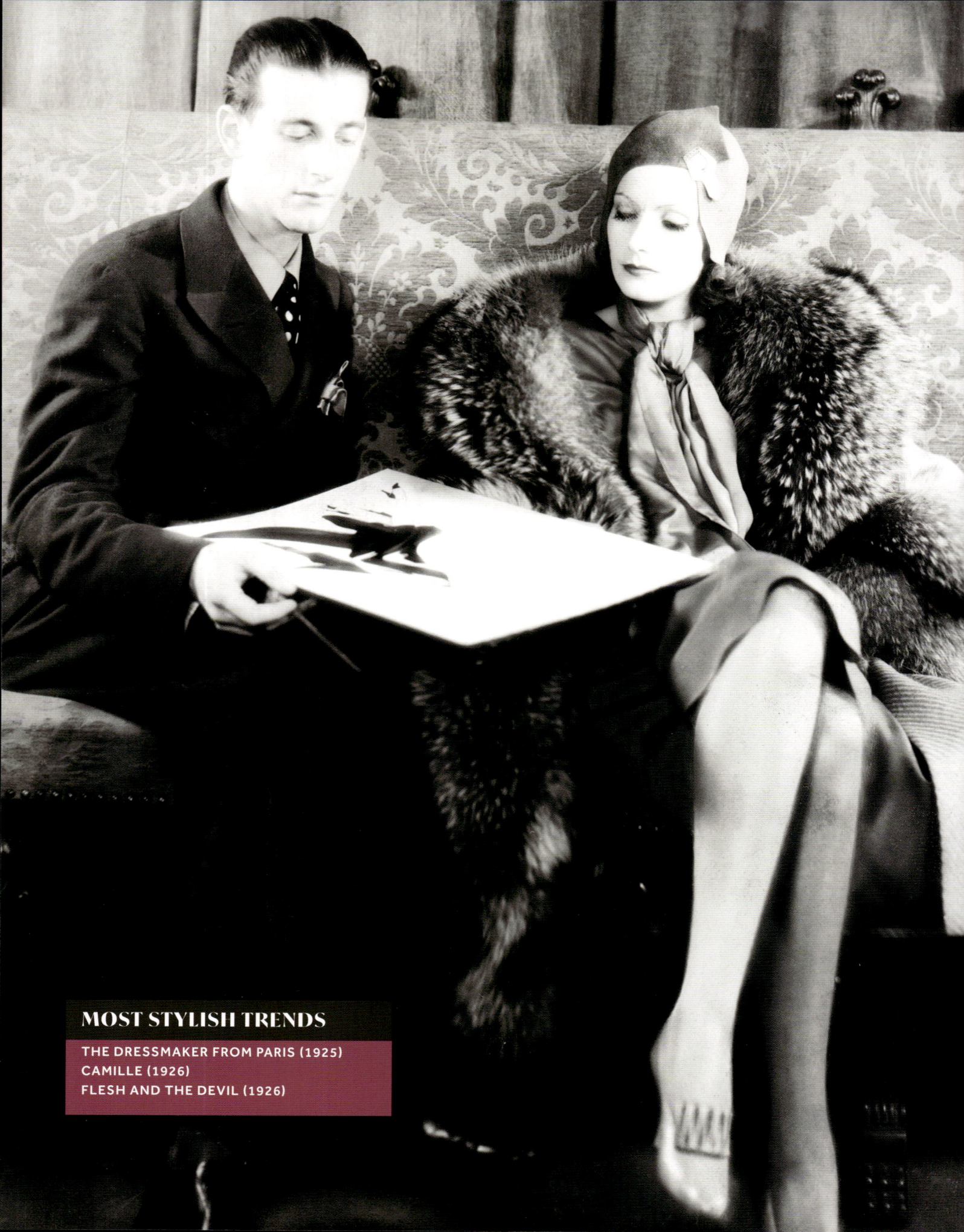

DESIGN SENSE
ADRIAN

Visionary, precise, and boldly original, Gilbert Adrian helped define the Golden Age of Hollywood glamor and transformed costume design into cinematic art.

Adrian Adolph Greenburg, from Naugatuck, Connecticut, began his artistic studies at the Parsons School of Design in New York and continued his training in Paris. His early training in fine art and theater design gave him a unique foundation, combining structural understanding with dramatic flair. His career took off when Broadway impresario Irving Berlin noticed his work and brought him into the world of stage production. This exposure eventually led Adrian to Hollywood, where his striking visual sensibility and innovative designs made an immediate impact.

He joined MGM in 1928 and quickly rose to become the studio's chief costume designer.

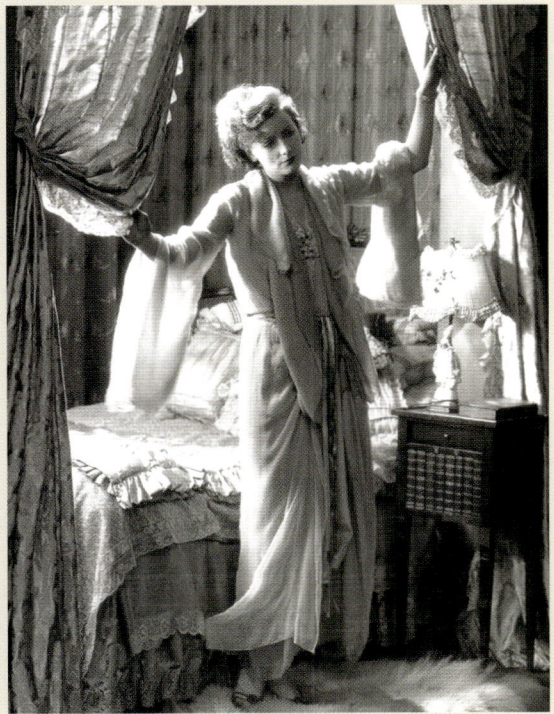

He remained in that role until 1941, creating more than 250 film wardrobes during his tenure. Adrian's influence was immense; he crafted the screen identities of many of MGM's top stars, including Greta Garbo's sleek androgyny, Jean Harlow's bias-cut glamor, Katharine Hepburn's aristocratic cool, and Joan Crawford's sharp-shouldered modernism.

The costumes they sported were more than clothing—they were character. Adrian believed a wardrobe should not only enhance a film's visual impact but also deepen the audience's understanding of the character. His design for Crawford's structured suits in *Letty Lynton* (1932) sparked a retail phenomenon, with thousands of imitations sold in department stores. His work for *Marie Antoinette* (1938) displayed elaborate 18th-century opulence, whereas *The Women* (1939) featured a rare all-color fashion show within a black-and-white film.

His most iconic achievement remains *The Wizard of Oz* (1939), for which he designed Dorothy's gingham dress and the ruby slippers—costume elements that have become fixtures of American pop culture.

In 1942, Adrian left MGM to launch his fashion label, Adrian Ltd., where he continued to bring Hollywood elegance to American women through ready-to-wear collections. His designs remained bold, geometric, and theatrical. He retired in 1952 due to a heart condition but left behind a design legacy that shaped both costume design and American fashion.

Although he never won an Academy Award, Adrian is remembered as one of the most inventive and influential designers in film history. His ability to combine story, personality, and silhouette changed how costumes were used in cinema—and how audiences saw their favorite stars.

LEFT

Greta Garbo exudes languid sensuality in a flowing peignoir designed by Adrian, whose work defined 1920s cinematic elegance. The sheer, soft layers and trailing sleeves evoke intimacy and opulence, perfectly capturing Garbo's magnetic screen presence. Adrian's early mastery of draped silhouettes and romantic textures laid the groundwork for his iconic career—and helped elevate Garbo to the status of screen goddess.

FULL PAGE

Greta Garbo and Adrian in 1928, in a rare behind-the-scenes moment of style collaboration. Garbo lounges in a tailored ensemble, complete with a cloche hat, fur-trimmed coat, and silk scarf—quintessential hallmarks of her cool, aloof elegance. Adrian presents a fashion sketch during filming of *Wild Orchids* (1929).

GRETA GARBO

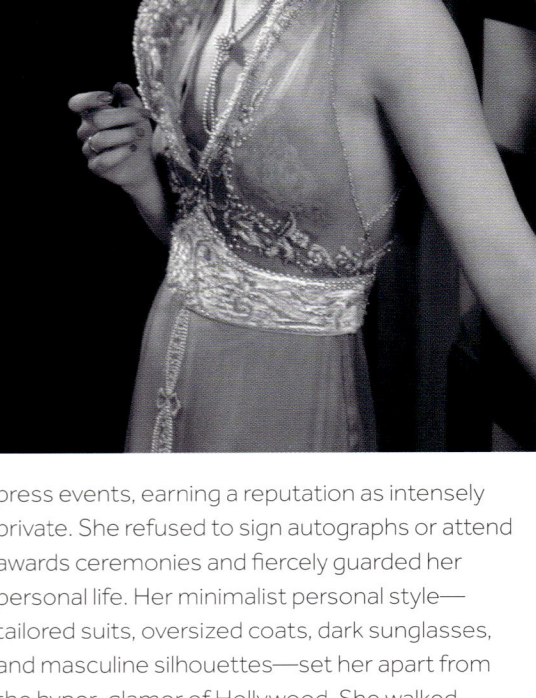

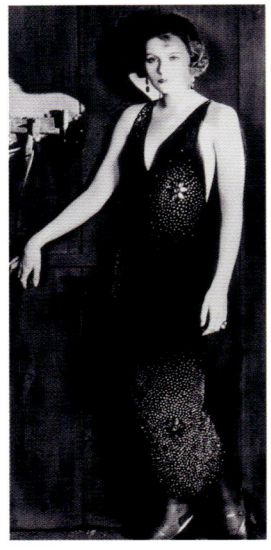

Mysterious, magnetic, and utterly unforgettable, Greta Garbo became one of cinema's most elusive and revered legends.

Greta Garbo (1905–1990), a native of Stockholm, Sweden, began her career as a department store clerk and commercial model before securing a scholarship to the Royal Dramatic Theater. Her striking features and commanding screen presence led to early film roles in Sweden, where she caught the attention of director Mauritz Stiller. He became her mentor, shaped her image and guided her career. In 1925, Stiller brought Garbo to Hollywood under a contract with MGM, where she was quickly embraced by audiences. Although she spoke little English and had no prior exposure to American cinema, Garbo's debut in *Torrent* (1926) and breakout in *Flesh and the Devil* (1926) marked the arrival of a formidable new talent. Her expressive face and magnetic silence captivated viewers during the Golden Age of silent film.

When sound arrived, Garbo transitioned effortlessly. Her first talkie, *Anna Christie* (1930), was marketed with the tagline "Garbo Talks!". Her deep, husky voice and European accent only enhanced her mystique. Over the next decade, she delivered a series of unforgettable performances in *Mata Hari* (1931), *Grand Hotel* (1932), *Queen Christina* (1933), *Camille* (1936), and *Ninotchka* (1939), demonstrating both dramatic depth and comedic flair. Her roles often embodied inner conflict, restrained passion, and tragic grandeur, which became her hallmark. She worked closely with MGM's top costume designers, including Adrian, whose designs for Garbo helped elevate her to fashion icon status. Her regal bearing and ability to command the screen made her the studio's top box office draw through much of the 1930s.

Offscreen, Garbo cultivated an aura of mystery. She famously avoided interviews, premieres, and

press events, earning a reputation as intensely private. She refused to sign autographs or attend awards ceremonies and fiercely guarded her personal life. Her minimalist personal style—tailored suits, oversized coats, dark sunglasses, and masculine silhouettes—set her apart from the hyper-glamor of Hollywood. She walked the streets of New York anonymously, often recognized but rarely disturbed, and became a fashion icon known for her understated elegance and enigmatic charm.

After *Two-Faced Woman* (1941), which received poor reviews, Garbo retired abruptly. Disillusioned with Hollywood's expectations and uninterested in fame for its own sake, she declined numerous comeback offers. She spent the rest of her life in seclusion, focusing on art collecting, travel, and close friendships. Although she accepted an honorary Academy Award in 1955 for her "unforgettable screen performances," she did not attend the ceremony.

Garbo's legacy remains singular. She defined the art of cinematic restraint and projected an emotional intensity that remains unmatched. She redefined modern femininity in both film and fashion—not by revealing herself, but by refusing to. She remains one of the most influential and enduring icons in the history of cinema.

ABOVE

Greta mesmerizes as Elena in *The Temptress* (1926), her poised expression and sculpted silhouette embodying the allure and danger of silent-era femme fatales.

RIGHT

Seen in glamorous attire, Greta Garbo captivated audiences with her enigmatic presence and won acclaim in *Anna Christie* (1930)—her first talkie, famously marketed with the tagline "Garbo Talks!".

FULL PAGE

Garbo in *The Single Standard* (1929), a romantic drama directed by John S. Robertson, portrays a modern woman challenging the double standards of love and freedom.

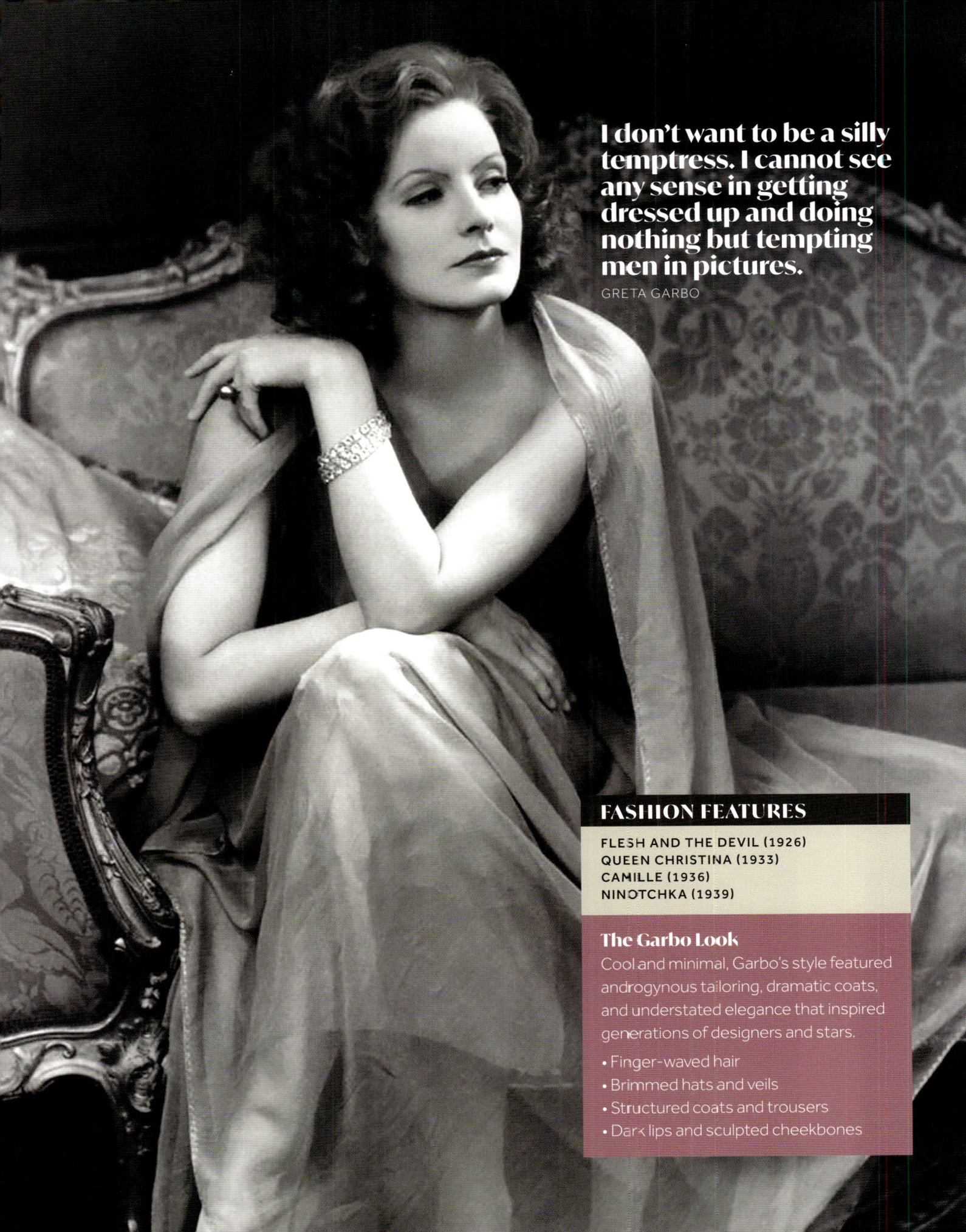

I don't want to be a silly temptress. I cannot see any sense in getting dressed up and doing nothing but tempting men in pictures.

GRETA GARBO

FASHION FEATURES

FLESH AND THE DEVIL (1926)
QUEEN CHRISTINA (1933)
CAMILLE (1936)
NINOTCHKA (1939)

The Garbo Look

Cool and minimal, Garbo's style featured androgynous tailoring, dramatic coats, and understated elegance that inspired generations of designers and stars.

• Finger-waved hair
• Brimmed hats and veils
• Structured coats and trousers
• Dark lips and sculpted cheekbones

LILLIAN GISH

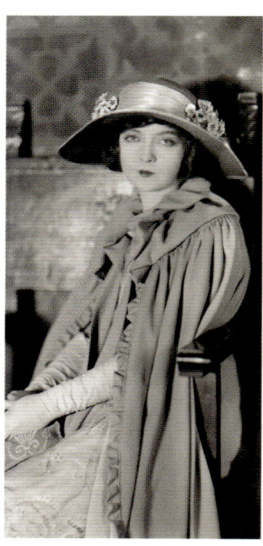

Lillian Gish combined delicate beauty with quiet strength, creating some of silent cinema's most enduring performances and setting the tone for generations of screen actresses to follow.

Gish (1893–1993) was one of the most revered figures in early cinema and is widely known as the "First Lady of the Silent Screen." Born Lillian Diana de Guiche in Springfield, Ohio, she began acting in touring theater productions in 1902. Her film debut came in 1912 in *An Unseen Enemy*, directed by D. W. Griffith.

Over the next two decades, she appeared in over 60 silent films, including *The Birth of a Nation* (1915), *Intolerance* (1916), *Broken Blossoms* (1919), and *Orphans of the Storm* (1921), shaping the language of cinematic acting through her emotionally resonant performances.

Lillian was known for her artistic integrity and commitment to realism—she endured actual ice storms for *Way Down East* (1920) and starved herself for roles. She transitioned to sound films and stage work in the 1930s and, in later years, appeared in *The Night of the Hunter* (1955) and *The Whales of August* (1987). She received an honorary Academy Award in 1971 and an AFI Lifetime Achievement Award in 1984.

ABOVE

With soft curls and serene poise, Lillian Gish earned fame as the "First Lady of the Silent Screen" through haunting performances

RIGHT

In flowing nightdress and curls, Lillian Gish pioneered emotional realism in silent cinema's earliest masterpieces

FASHION FEATURES

THE BIRTH OF A NATION (1915)
BROKEN BLOSSOMS (1919)
ORPHANS OF THE STORM (1921)
LA BOHÈME (1926)

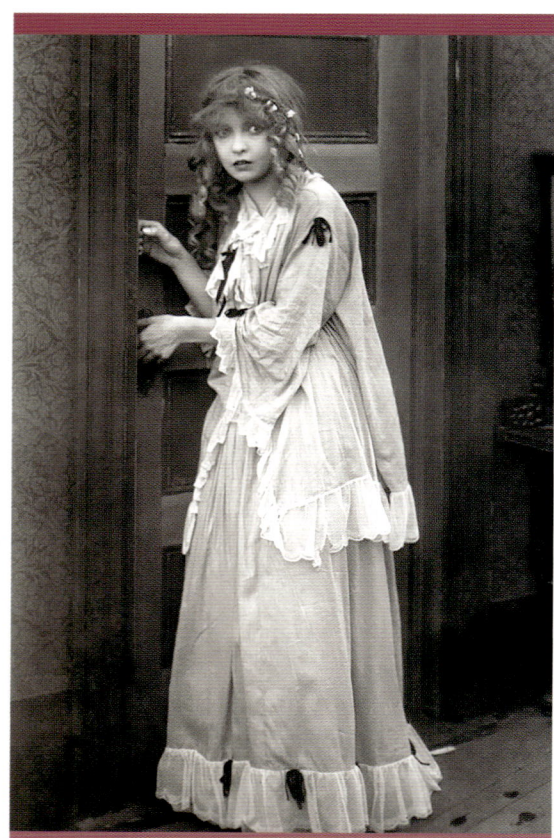

The Gish Look

Gish favored delicate, flowing garments that emphasized grace over glamor. Her costumes often featured sheer fabrics, lace, and light colors, aligning with her portrayals of gentle, tragic heroines. She avoided contemporary trends, instead choosing timeless silhouettes that enhanced her ethereal presence on screen and stage.

- Soft, sheer gowns
- Natural curls
- Minimal makeup
- Delicate accessories such as pearl chokers and ribbons

MARY PICKFORD

FASHION FEATURES

REBECCA OF SUNNYBROOK FARM (1917)
THE POOR LITTLE RICH GIRL (1917)
POLLYANNA (1920)
LITTLE LORD FAUNTLEROY (1921)
COQUETTE (1929)

The Pickford Look

Romantic, youthful silhouettes with carefully crafted innocence—feminine dresses, picture hats, and cascading curls that mirrored her screen persona and reinforced her status as "America's Sweetheart."

- Waist-length curls
- Picture hats
- Frilly pinafores and dresses
- Ribbons and lace trims

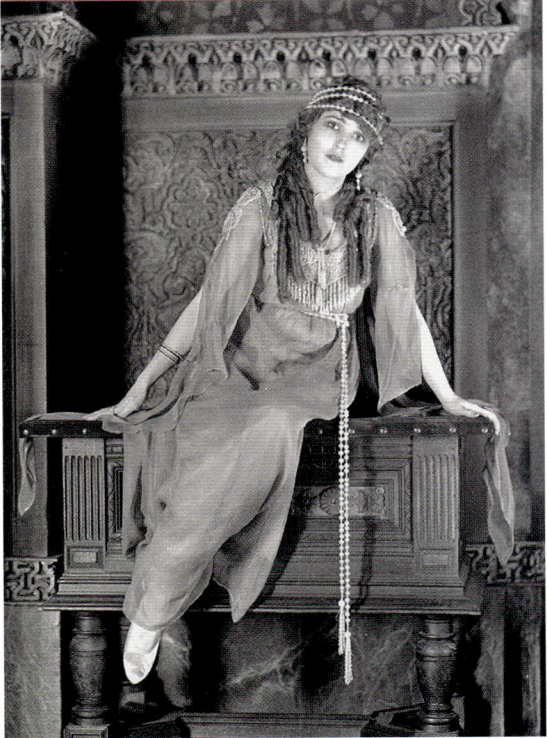

America's golden-haired sweetheart, famed for her "luminous tenderness," was also a trailblazing businesswoman who co-founded United Artists and helped shape how female stars gained creative and contractual power in Hollywood.

Mary Pickford (1892–1979), born Gladys Marie Smith in Toronto, was Hollywood's original sweetheart and a central figure in both film and fashion. She entered show business early, touring in stage plays before transitioning to silent cinema. By 1909, she was under contract at Biograph Studios with director D. W. Griffith, quickly rising to prominence in dozens of short films. Audiences adored her expressive face, flowing curls, and feisty, youthful roles. With films such as *Rebecca of Sunnybrook Farm* (1917), *The Poor Little Rich Girl* (1917), and *Pollyanna* (1920), Pickford became the symbol of American girlhood.

Her wardrobe—lace-trimmed pinafores, ribbons, and picture hats—was crafted to highlight innocence without appearing artificial. Offscreen, she maintained her image with meticulous styling and custom clothing. Behind the scenes, she was a powerhouse. In 1919, she joined Chaplin, Fairbanks, and Griffith to form United Artists, gaining rare creative control. She also helped establish the Academy of Motion Picture Arts and Sciences. Although she retired in 1933, Pickford's legacy as a performer, businesswoman, and fashion icon remains foundational in Hollywood history.

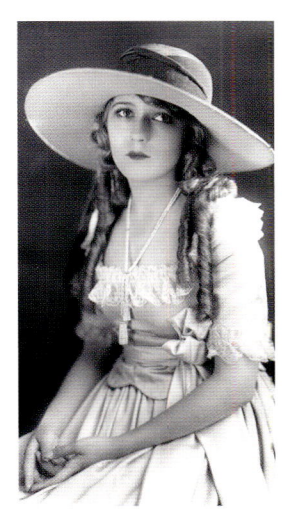

ABOVE

With her cascading curls and signature picture hats, Mary Pickford charmed audiences worldwide and co-founded United Artists in 1919—becoming one of Hollywood's first major female powerhouses both on and off screen.

LEFT

Mary Pickford in *Suds* (1920), adorned in sheer chiffon and pearls, framed by ornate arches—silent era elegance in a moment of poised melancholy.

GLORIA SWANSON

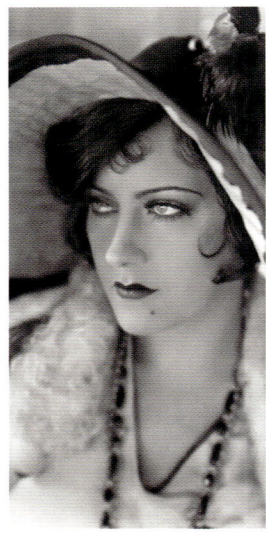

> **By the time I was 15, my mother had turned me into a real clotheshorse.**
>
> GLORIA SWANSON

One of silent cinema's most glamorous stars, Gloria Swanson embodied the rise, fall, and reinvention of Hollywood stardom.

Gloria Swanson (1899–1983) rose to prominence in the 1920s as one of the era's most celebrated actresses, known for her dramatic roles, regal presence, and opulent fashion. Born in Chicago, she began working at Essanay Studios in her teens and soon moved to Keystone, where she starred in comedies under Mack Sennett. Her transition to drama came under director Cecil B. DeMille, who cast her in lavish productions such as *Male and Female* (1919) and *Don't Change Your Husband* (1919). These films transformed her into a fashion icon and symbol of sophisticated womanhood.

Swanson's silent-era stardom peaked with critically acclaimed performances in *Sadie Thompson* (1928) and *The Trespasser* (1929), the latter marking her successful transition to sound. Despite this, her career declined in the 1930s as public tastes shifted and Hollywood evolved. After a period away from film, she returned triumphantly in Billy Wilder's *Sunset Boulevard* (1950), portraying Norma Desmond, a faded silent star haunted by past fame. The role earned Swanson an Academy Award nomination and remains one of the most iconic performances in film history.

Throughout her life, Swanson was admired for her screen talent as much as for her commanding style and resilience in the spotlight.

ABOVE

With her smoldering gaze and feathered hat, Gloria Swanson became Hollywood's first true fashion icon, flaunting custom couture on screen.

RIGHT

Gloria Swanson in *Why Change Your Wife?* (1920), portraying a sharp-witted woman caught between tradition and transformation in this early Hollywood marital comedy.

FASHION FEATURES

MALE AND FEMALE (1919)
SADIE THOMPSON (1928)
THE TRESPASSER (1929)
SUNSET BOULEVARD (1950)

The Swanson Look

Swanson's look blended high glamor and Art Deco elegance, with ornate gowns, turbans, and statement jewelry defining her screen image.

- Beaded evening gowns
- Dramatic headpieces
- Sculpted eyebrows
- Bold lipstick and fur wraps

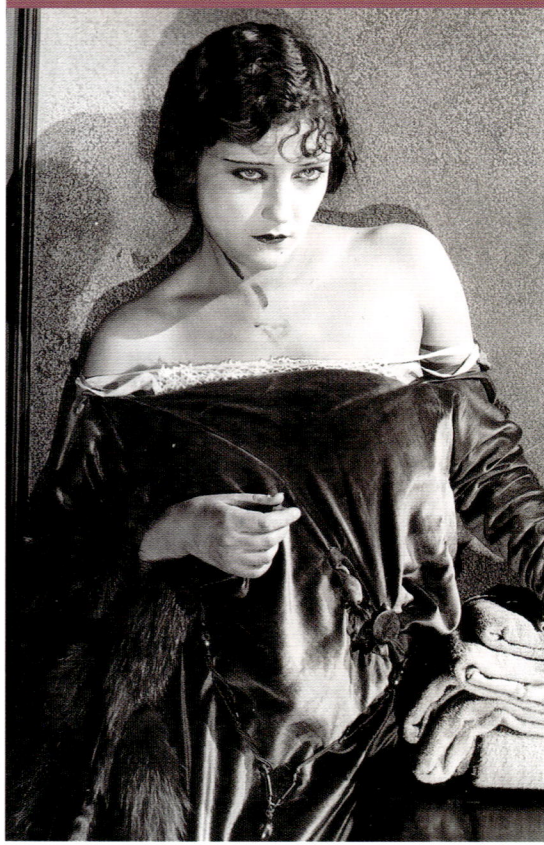

ANNA MAY WONG

FASHION FEATURES

THE TOLL OF THE SEA (1922)
THE THIEF OF BAGDAD (1924)
PICCADILLY (1929)
SHANGHAI EXPRESS (1932)

The Wong Look

Elegant and modern, Wong fused traditional Chinese motifs with Hollywood chic, using silk gowns, bold prints, and sleek silhouettes.

- Straight bangs and finger waves
- High-collared cheongsams
- Embroidered silk and brocade
- Dramatic brows and dark lips

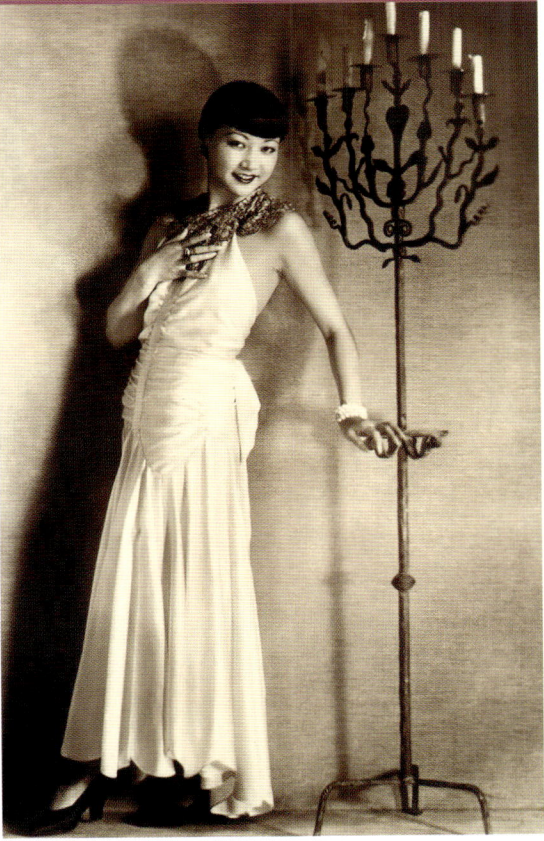

Poised and trailblazing, Anna May Wong was the first Chinese American movie star and a pioneer for representation in Hollywood.

Anna May Wong (1905–1961), born Wong Liu Tsong in Los Angeles, grew up near film sets and was drawn to the screen from a young age. She began acting in silent films as a teenager and earned her first lead role in *The Toll of the Sea* (1922), which showcased her talent and beauty. Her breakthrough came with *The Thief of Bagdad* (1924), where she starred alongside Douglas Fairbanks, cementing her status as a rising international star.

Despite her success, Wong was repeatedly typecast in stereotypical or supporting roles, often denied lead parts due to anti-miscegenation laws and widespread racial prejudice. Frustrated, she moved to Europe, where she found more fulfilling opportunities in German and British films, including *Piccadilly* (1929) and *Pavement Butterfly* (1929). She returned to the United States in the 1930s and starred in *Daughter of the Dragon* (1931) and *Shanghai Express* (1932), becoming a fashion icon and symbol of Asian American resilience.

Wong's style blended Hollywood glamor with Eastern elegance, and her legacy paved the way for future generations of Asian American performers.

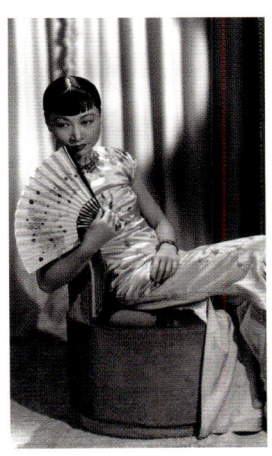

ABOVE

Anna May Wong, Hollywood's first Chinese-American star, challenged racial stereotypes on screen.

LEFT

Anna May Wong, a radiant presence in 1920s Hollywood, became a silent-era style icon—her sleek bob, embroidered silks, and smoldering gaze capturing the decade's fascination with exoticism and elegance.

LEADING MEN
CHARLIE CHAPLIN

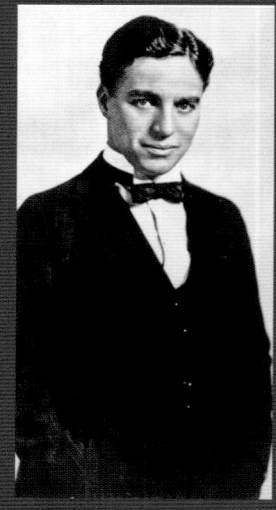

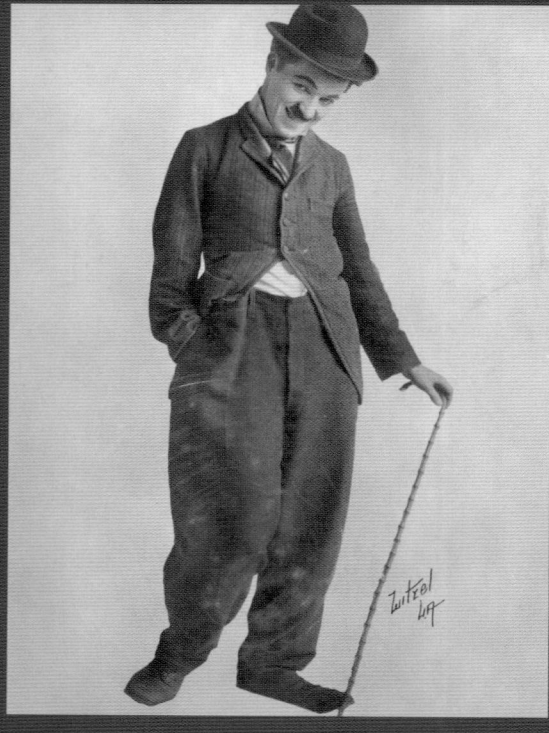

In the annals of Hollywood fashion, few looks are as instantly recognizable—or as deliberately constructed—as Charlie Chaplin's Tramp. With his ill-fitting suit, bowler hat, oversized shoes, and signature cane, Chaplin created not only one of cinema's most iconic characters but also a silhouette that remains etched in the cultural imagination. While it may appear accidental or comedic, the Tramp's wardrobe was carefully composed to serve both form and function—emphasizing physical comedy, emotional nuance, and social commentary through every stitch.

Chaplin developed the look in 1914, during his early days at Keystone Studios. As legend has it, he assembled the costume from various studio wardrobe pieces: Fatty Arbuckle's baggy pants, a tight jacket from a slimmer actor, an undersized bowler hat, and shoes two sizes too large—borrowed from Ford Sterling. The contradictions of the outfit mirrored the contradictions of the character: a tramp with the manners of a gentleman, a misfit with surprising grace. By the time Chaplin entered the 1920s, the look had crystallized into a global symbol, one he would refine but never abandon.

Though the outfit remained essentially the same, Chaplin's increasing control over his productions throughout the 1920s—particularly with the establishment of United Artists—allowed for greater attention to detail in his costume and its presentation on screen. The suit, while still comically ill-proportioned, was often tailored for maximum physical effect, emphasizing Chaplin's tightrope balance between elegance and absurdity. The bowler hat, perched precisely, became almost a character in itself, a prop in both slapstick routines and poignant moments. His

shoes, so central to his walk and comedic timing, were carefully chosen—and famously edible, at least in *The Gold Rush* (1925), where licorice versions were made for a scene in which the starving Tramp boils and eats one.

Despite the lack of a single named costume designer—Chaplin often had final say over his wardrobe—his look bears the influence of early Hollywood costume departments, which were then run largely by anonymous tailors and stylists. Some credit goes to Charles D. Hall, Chaplin's longtime production designer, who helped coordinate the visual world around the Tramp's costume. The effectiveness of the outfit was not merely in its comedic shape but in its emotional accessibility; it humanized Chaplin and offered audiences, many of whom were themselves struggling through postwar economic hardship, a figure of resilience and grace.

ABOVE

Offscreen, Charlie Chaplin's personal style was sharply tailored and unmistakably refined. Often seen in impeccably cut suits, crisp white shirts, and bow ties, Chaplin embraced a classic Edwardian elegance that stood in stark contrast to his Tramp persona.

TOP RIGHT

Charlie Chaplin as *The Tramp* —a masterclass in visual storytelling through costume. With his tight jacket, baggy trousers, floppy shoes, bowler hat, and bamboo cane, Chaplin crafted a look that was at once comedic, poignant, and universally relatable. First assembled in 1914 from mismatched wardrobe pieces, the outfit was deliberately absurd in proportion yet meticulously styled. It became a symbol of resilience, wit, and the human spirit.

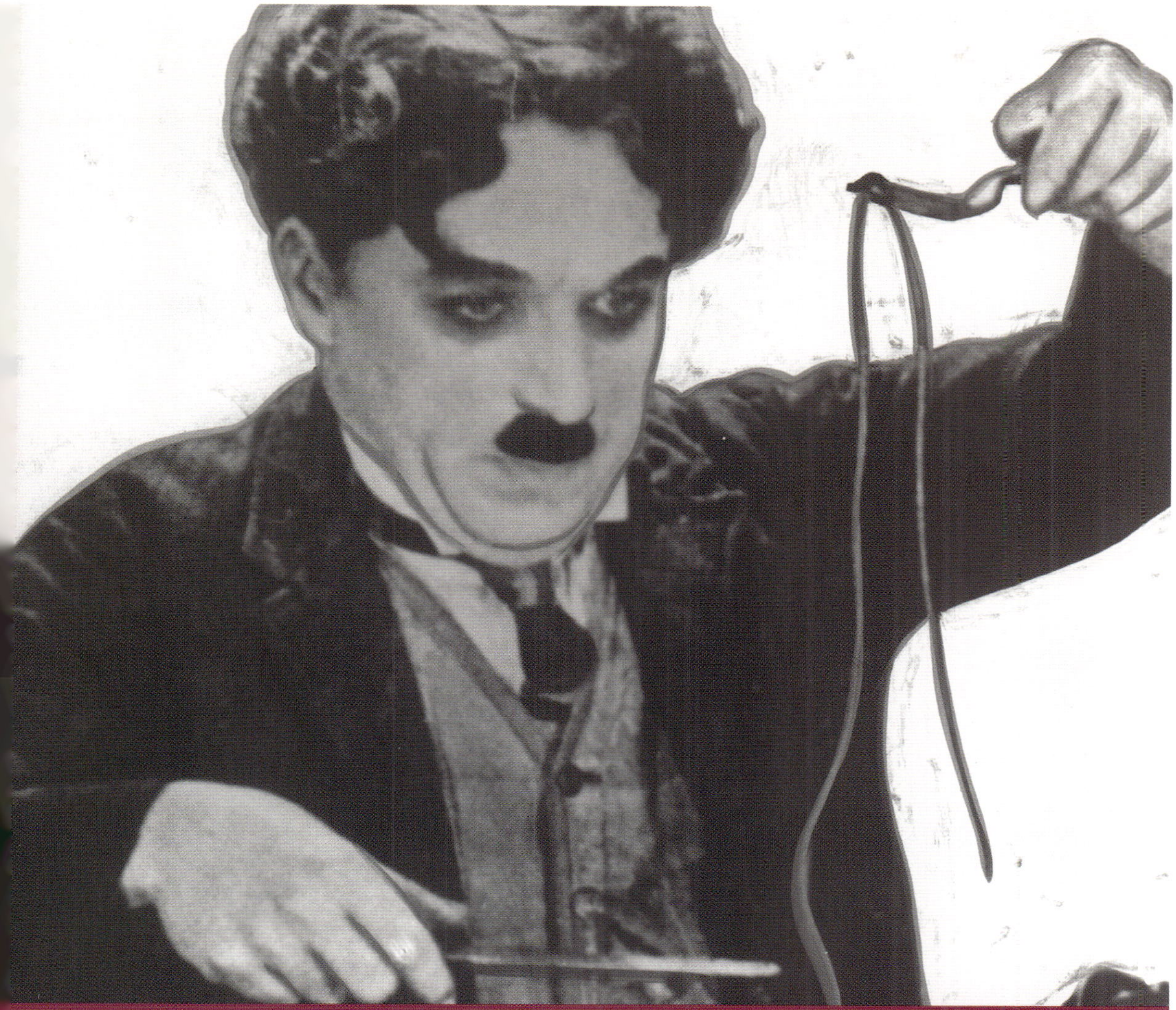

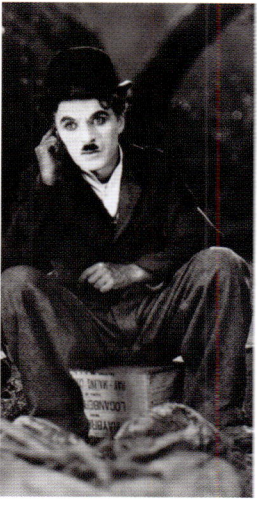

By the end of the 1920s, Chaplin's look was more than fashion—it was folklore. His Tramp became a visual shorthand for Hollywood's silent era, a study in how costume can transcend the screen to become part of the collective memory.

On the way to the wardrobe I thought I would dress in baggy pants, big shoes, a cane, and a derby hat. I wanted everything a contradiction: the pants baggy, the coat tight, the hat small and the shoes large... I added a small moustache, which I reasoned would add age without hiding my expression.

CHARLIE CHAPLIN

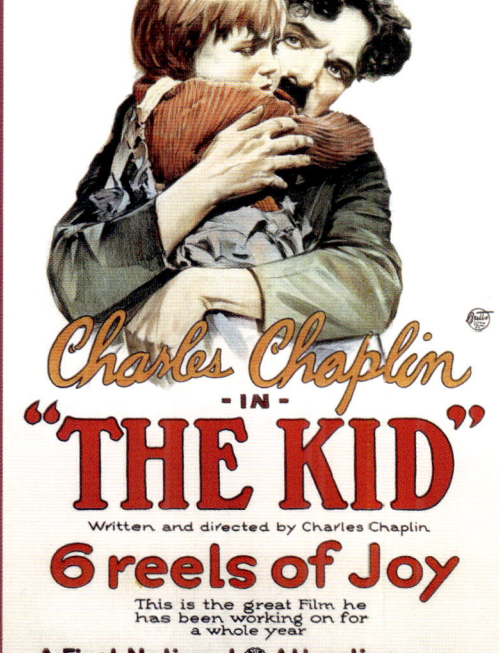

ABOVE

The Circus (1928)—Chaplin's Tramp costume had by now reached its most refined form. The ill-fitting trousers, tightly buttoned jacket, and ever-tilted bowler hat remained unchanged, but the details had sharpened. His silhouette was cleaner, the fabric more deliberate, and his gestures more nuanced—reflecting over a decade of performance evolution.

TOP LEFT

Chaplin's Tramp in this unforgettable scene, where he delicately dines on a boiled shoe. Chaplin's attention to costume detail extended even to props: the shoe was made of licorice and gelatin.

LEFT

In *The Kid*, this tender landmark of silent cinema, Chaplin's Tramp is paired with the equally tattered garb of young co-star Jackie Coogan.

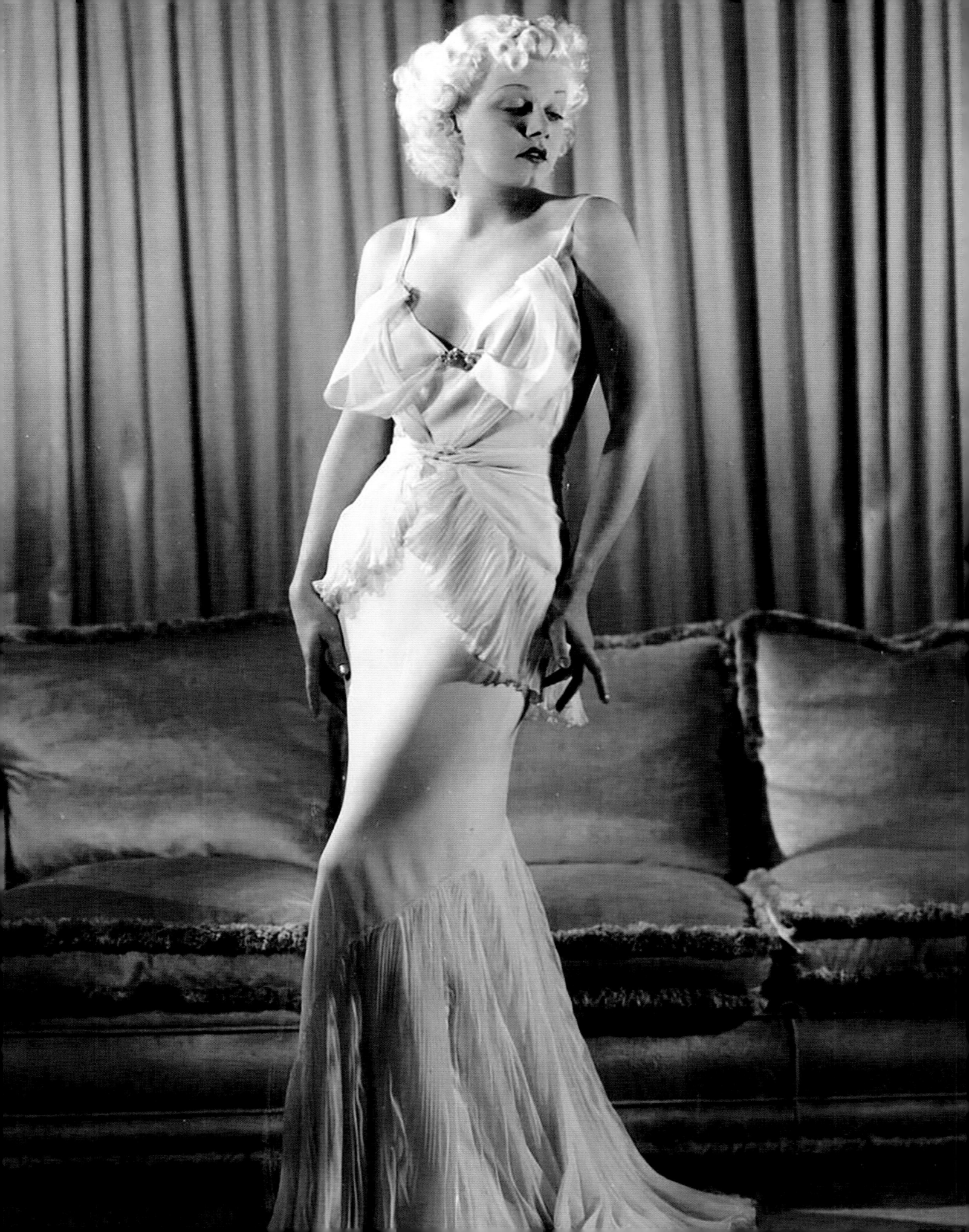

NINETEEN THIRTIES

The 1930s marked a new era of Hollywood fashion, an era shaped by glamor, resilience, and reinvention. As the nation experienced the Great Depression, a period of severe economic hardship, the film industry responded with a dazzling display of escapism. Movie palaces filled with audiences seeking relief from economic hardship, and Hollywood delivered spectacle in the form of musicals, screwball comedies, costume dramas, and romantic fantasies. Wardrobe departments flourished, and the studio designer was no longer a behind-the-scenes artisan but a credited creative force whose work often rivaled that of top fashion houses.

Sound had fully arrived, transforming both performance and presentation. Stars no longer acted in silence; they spoke, sang, and danced. As a result, clothing had to serve a dual function: flattering the performer while accommodating choreography and dialogue scenes. Enter a new generation of costume legends such as Travis Banton, Orry-Kelly, and Adrian, who tailored wardrobes not just to characters, but to the unique silhouettes and personas of each star.

This was also the decade when fashion and film began to influence one another more directly. Gowns worn by Jean Harlow, Greta Garbo, and Carole Lombard were imitated in department stores across the country. Hollywood didn't just reflect the trends of the time, it set them. Bias cuts, shoulder pads, and satin halter gowns filtered from the silver screen into everyday wardrobes. The movies of the 1930s didn't just help audiences forget their troubles; they gave them something to aspire to, with style that shimmered against the gloom of the times

JEAN ARTHUR

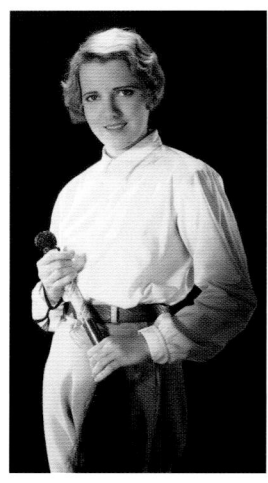

Known for her distinctive voice, comedic charm, and quiet strength, Jean Arthur became one of the most beloved actresses of the 1930s and 1940s Hollywood, especially in screwball comedies and Frank Capra classics.

Born Gladys Georgianna Greene in Plattsburgh, New York in 1900, Jean Arthur began her film career in silent movies during the 1920s. Although her early roles were modest, she found her true footing with the arrival of sound, thanks to her uniquely husky voice and natural comic timing. Arthur rose to fame in the mid-1930s with standout performances in films such as *Mr. Deeds Goes to Town* (1936), *You Can't Take It with You* (1938), and *Mr. Smith Goes to Washington* (1939)—all directed by Frank Capra.

Arthur's career spanned several decades and she was still playing saucy working girls into her 40s. She became known for playing smart, independent women who could mix vulnerability with wit. In the 1940s, Arthur continued to shine in films like *The More the Merrier* (1943), earning an Academy Award nomination for Best Actress. Arthur's Hollywood career longevity was aided by her natural beauty, which allowed her to play plucky working girls into her 40s.

Despite her onscreen appeal, Arthur was famously shy and intensely private, often avoiding publicity and interviews. She eventually transitioned to teaching drama and left behind a legacy of wit, warmth, and unforgettable performances.

ABOVE

Jean Arthur, a prominent American actress of the Golden Age of Hollywood, in a sporty tailored ensemble typical of her low-key style.

RIGHT

Famed for her husky voice and girl-next-door charm, Jean Arthur rose to stardom in Frank Capra classics such as *Mr. Deeds Goes to Town* and *Mr. Smith Goes to Washington*.

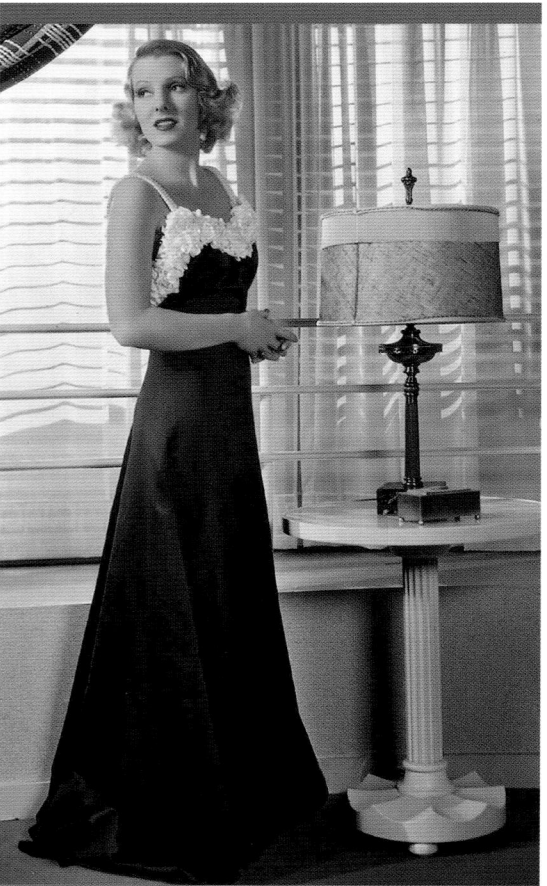

The Arthur Look

Practical yet feminine, Arthur's style featured modest tailoring, soft blouses, and ladylike accessories that suited her roles as working-class heroines.

• Curled blonde bob
• Tweed suits and blouses
• Delicate collars
• Natural makeup with rosy lips

FASHION FEATURES

MR. DEEDS GOES TO TOWN (1936)
THE MORE THE MERRIER (1943)
THE DEVIL AND MISS JONES (1941)

CLAUDETTE COLBERT

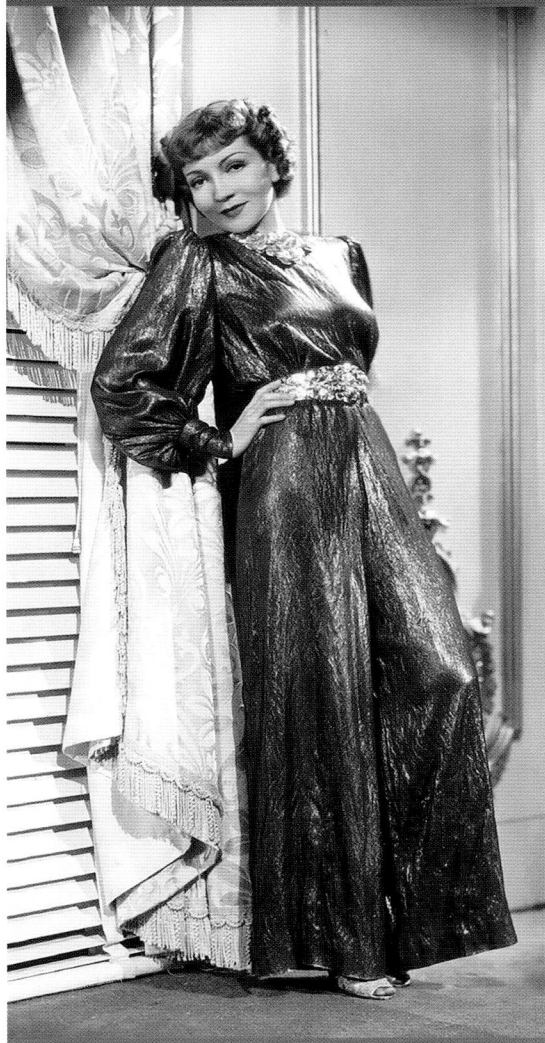

Born Émilie Claudette Chauchoin in France, in 1903, Colbert moved to the United States as a child and studied acting in high school and at college. She began her career on the Broadway stage before transitioning to film in the late 1920s. Colbert made a successful leap from silent films to talkies, quickly establishing herself as a leading lady known for both sophistication and warmth.

Witty, elegant, and effortlessly versatile, Claudette Colbert was one of Hollywood's most enduring stars, known for her sparkling screen presence and impeccable comic timing.

Her breakthrough came with *It Happened One Night* (1934), in which she starred opposite Clark Gable. The film became a critical and commercial success, winning five Academy Awards including Best Actress for Colbert. She followed it with standout roles in *Cleopatra* (1934), *The Palm Beach Story* (1942), and *Since You Went Away* (1944), which showcased her skill in both drama and comedy.

Offscreen, Colbert was known for her professionalism and attention to image, always working to present herself in the most flattering light. She remained active in television and theater well into the 1950s and 60s.

Claudette Colbert's legacy endures as a pioneer of the screwball comedy and a symbol of timeless screen sophistication.

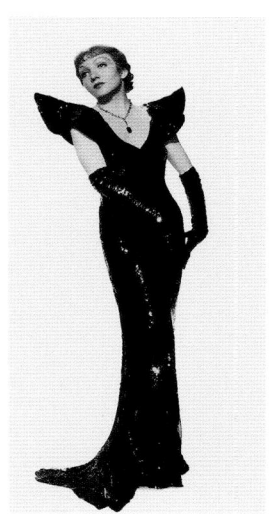

The Colbert Look

Feminine yet sharp, Colbert favored draped gowns, sleek silhouettes, and costumes that emphasized her elegance and profile.

- Arched brows and cupid's bow lips
- Side-parted bob
- Bias-cut dresses
- Fur-trimmed evening wear

FASHION FEATURES

IT HAPPENED ONE NIGHT (1934)
CLEOPATRA (1934)
THE PALM BEACH STORY (1942)

ABOVE

Claudette Colbert, known for her elegance and versatility, won an Oscar for *It Happened One Night* (1934) and was a major star of the 1930s and 1940s.

LEFT

Claudette Colbert was the first actress to win an Academy Award for a screwball comedy, *It Happened One Night* (1934), earning legendary status in Hollywood's Golden Age.

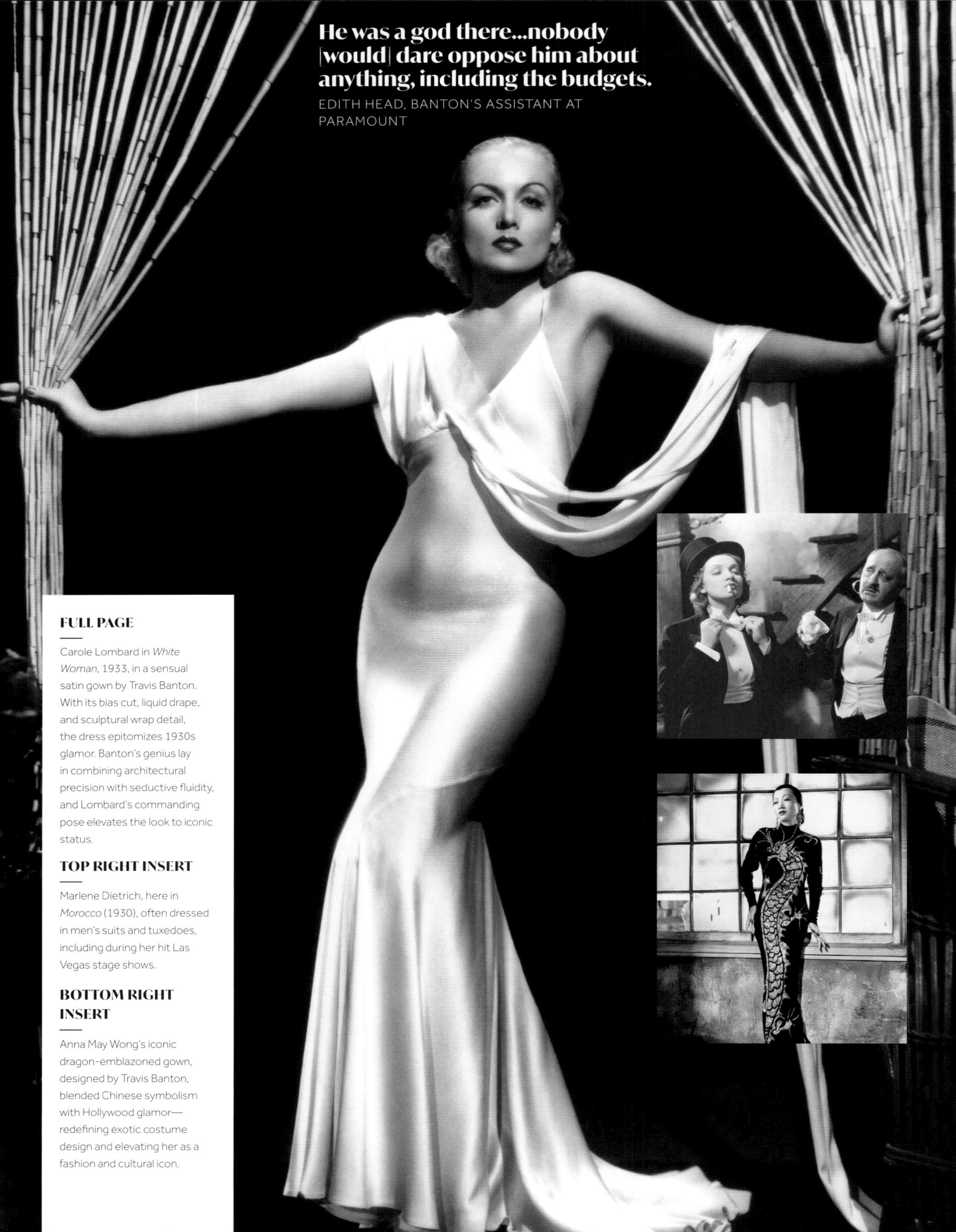

He was a god there...nobody [would] dare oppose him about anything, including the budgets.

EDITH HEAD, BANTON'S ASSISTANT AT PARAMOUNT

FULL PAGE

Carole Lombard in *White Woman*, 1933, in a sensual satin gown by Travis Banton. With its bias cut, liquid drape, and sculptural wrap detail, the dress epitomizes 1930s glamor. Banton's genius lay in combining architectural precision with seductive fluidity, and Lombard's commanding pose elevates the look to iconic status.

TOP RIGHT INSERT

Marlene Dietrich, here in *Morocco* (1930), often dressed in men's suits and tuxedoes, including during her hit Las Vegas stage shows.

BOTTOM RIGHT INSERT

Anna May Wong's iconic dragon-emblazoned gown, designed by Travis Banton, blended Chinese symbolism with Hollywood glamor—redefining exotic costume design and elevating her as a fashion and cultural icon.

DESIGN SENSE
TRAVIS BANTON

Elegant, opulent, and technically masterful, Travis Banton was one of Hollywood's most celebrated costume designers of the 1930s. His glamorous creations shaped the public image of some of the era's greatest stars and helped to define the visual language of the Golden Age cinema.

Born in Waco, Texas, in 1894, Banton studied art at Columbia University and fashion design at the Art Students League in New York. He began his career designing custom garments for New York's elite and later created gowns for the stage, eventually drawing the attention of Hollywood. Hired by Paramount Pictures in the mid-1920s, he initially worked under the head designer Howard Greer. When Greer left in 1929, Banton was promoted and quickly became Paramount's chief designer, leading the studio's wardrobe department through its most glamorous decade.

Elegant, opulent, and technically masterful, Travis Banton was one of Hollywood's most celebrated costume designers of the 1930s. His glamorous creations shaped the public image of some of the era's greatest stars and helped to define the visual language of the Golden Age cinema.

Banton's design philosophy prioritized elegance, sensuality, and dramatic visual impact. He favored luxurious materials like satin, silk, chiffon, and velvet, and was admired for his expert draping and precision in tailoring. His mastery of the bias cut gave his gowns a fluid movement, which translated beautifully on screen. He designed for many of Hollywood's biggest female stars, including Marlene Dietrich, Carole Lombard, Mae West, Claudette Colbert, Kay Francis, and Sylvia Sidney.

His collaboration with Marlene Dietrich—particularly in her films directed by Josef von Sternberg—remains one of cinema's most iconic designer-star pairings. For *Shanghai Express* (1932) and *Blonde Venus* (1932), Banton crafted extravagant gowns, fur-lined cloaks, and glittering headpieces that reinforced Dietrich's powerful, mysterious screen image. Their combined aesthetic married sensuality with aristocratic polish and redefined cinematic glamor.

Banton also delivered unforgettable work for Claudette Colbert in *Cleopatra* (1934), merging historical fantasy with modern flair. His contemporary designs for screwball comedies such as *My Man Godfrey* (1936) and *Nothing Sacred* (1937) introduced chic, wearable looks that influenced American fashion trends far beyond the theater.

Despite his extraordinary artistry, Banton's career at Paramount came to an end in 1938. Increasing tensions within the studio, combined with his personal struggles with alcoholism, led to his departure. His protégé, Edith Head, succeeded him and later credited him as a formative influence on her style and success.

Although Banton continued designing for stage and occasional films throughout the 1940s, it was his Paramount years that solidified his place in Hollywood's history. His legacy endures through the silhouettes, innovations, and timeless glamor he brought to the screen. His designs were not merely costumes—they were character, mood, and fantasy in motion.

Signature Look

- Sleek, streamlined silhouettes
- Bias-cut gowns
- Satin and lamé fabrics
- Beads, furs, and feathers

FASHION FEATURES

IT and WINGS (1927)
I'M NO ANGEL (1933)
THE SCARLET EMPRESS (1934)
MY MAN GODFREY (1936)
NOTHING SACRED (1937)

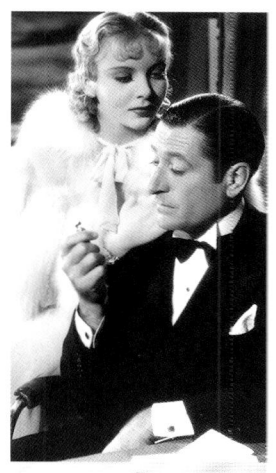

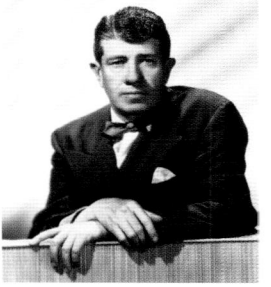

TOP

Ida Lupino, playing a British aristocrat opposite Arthur Treacher in *Anything Goes* (1936), finds her white, fur-edged cape is the perfect lure for a high-seas romance with Bing Crosby.

ABOVE

Travis Banton, Paramount's legendary costume designer, defined 1930s Hollywood glamor. He crafted stunning ensembles for Marlene Dietrich and Claudette Colbert, blending sophistication, sensuality, and luxurious fabrics with unmatched flair.

LEADING MEN
RONALD COLMAN

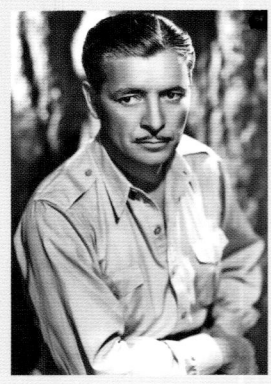

The screen's ultimate English gentleman, Ronald Colman, began his career in silent films and became one of early Hollywood's most respected and admired stars. Known for his graceful charm, thoughtful presence, and rich, melodic voice, Colman made a lasting impression on generations of filmgoers and helped define the image of the suave, sensitive leading man.

Ronald Charles Colman was born on February 9, 1891, in Richmond, Surrey, England. He was the son of Charles Colman, a silk merchant. Ronald was educated in boarding schools and originally hoped to study engineering at Cambridge University. However, when his father died unexpectedly in 1907, financial constraints forced him to abandon those plans and seek work instead.

Colman's life took a dramatic turn during World War I. He joined the London Scottish Regiment and served in the British Army until he was badly injured at the Battle of Messines in 1917. A serious wound to his ankle left him with a limp—an injury he would successfully conceal throughout his acting career. After the war, he pursued acting in earnest, appearing on stage in London and later in British silent films. His breakout moment came in 1923 when he starred opposite Lillian Gish in *The White Sister*. The film's success brought him to Hollywood and launched a flourishing career in American cinema.

He quickly rose to fame in silent films, winning audiences over with romantic and heroic roles in movies like *Beau Geste* (1926) and *The Winning of Barbara Worth* (1926). When sound arrived, Colman's deep, cultured voice only added to his appeal. He starred in *Bulldog Drummond* (1929)

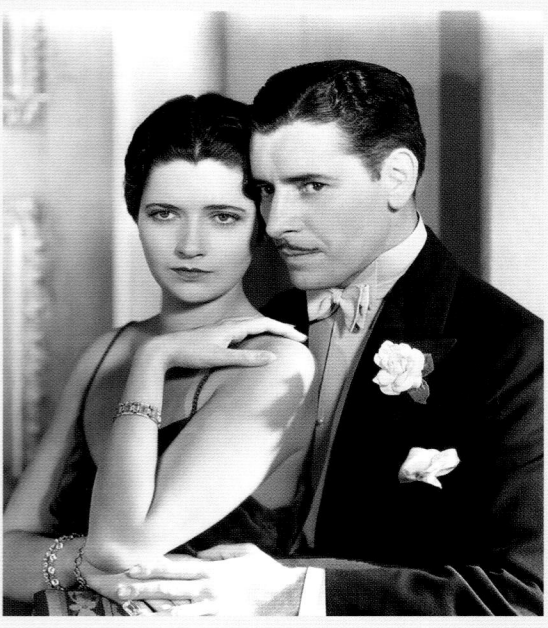

and *Condemned* (1929), earning his first two Academy Award nominations for Best Actor.

Throughout the 1930s and 1940s, Colman continued to shine in high-profile films such as *A Tale of Two Cities* (1935), *Lost Horizon* (1937), and *The Prisoner of Zenda* (1937). In *Random Harvest* (1942), he played a shell-shocked veteran struggling with amnesia—a performance that brought him yet another Oscar nomination. He finally won the Academy Award for Best Actor in 1947 for *A Double Life*, portraying an actor who becomes dangerously entangled in his stage role as Othello. The film was widely praised for its psychological complexity and Colman's haunting performance.

Outside of film, Colman enjoyed a successful radio career with his wife, actress Benita Hume, in the popular series *The Halls of Ivy*, which later became a television show. During World War II, he also supported Allied efforts by participating

ABOVE
—
Ronald Colman, renowned for his velvety voice and refined charm, won the Academy Award for *A Double Life* (1947), solidifying his place in cinematic history.

ABOVE RIGHT
—
Kay Francis and Ronald Colman in *Raffles* (1930), a suave pairing of wit and intrigue, as high society meets high-stakes crime in this stylish pre-Code caper.

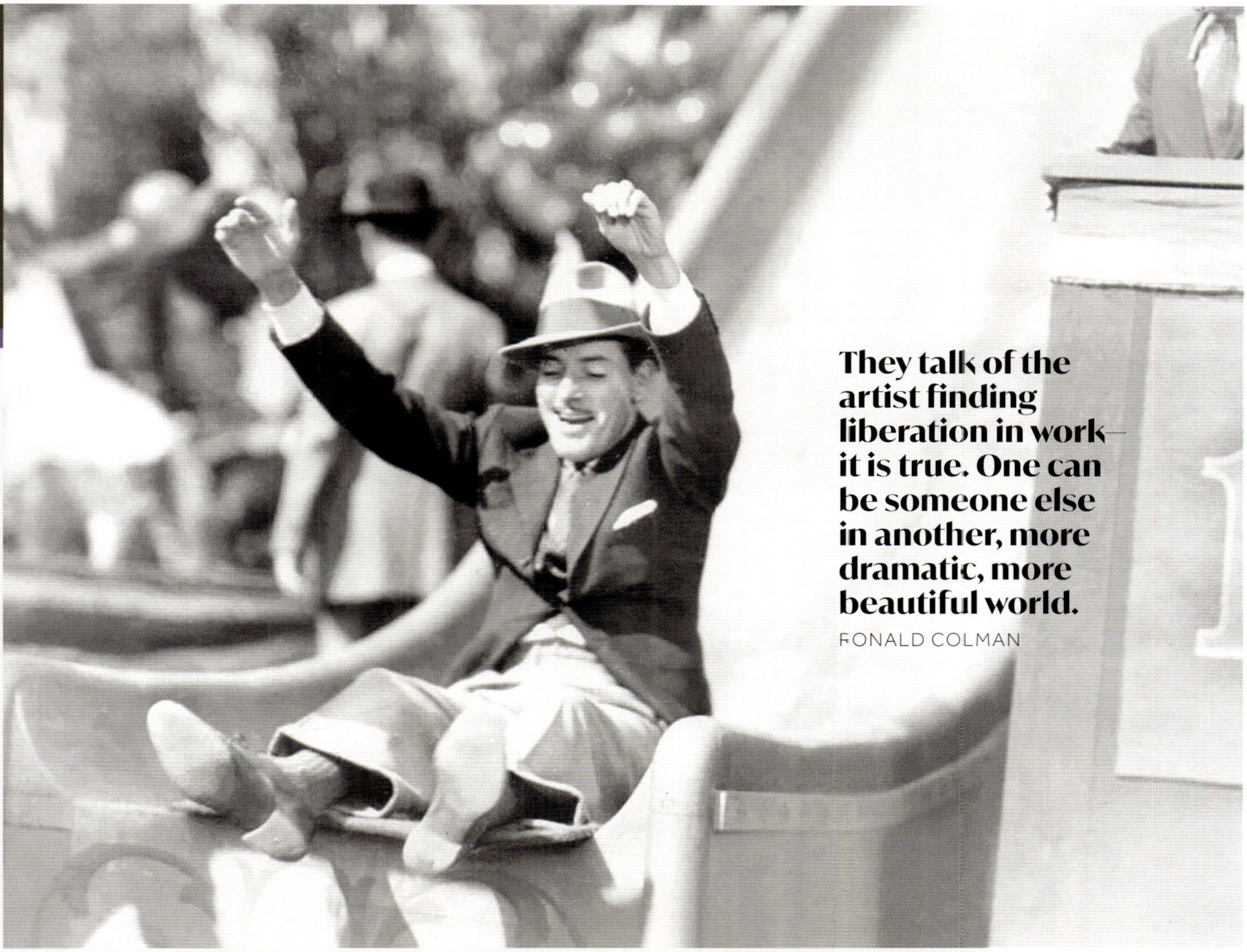

> **They talk of the artist finding liberation in work—it is true. One can be someone else in another, more dramatic, more beautiful world.**
>
> RONALD COLMAN

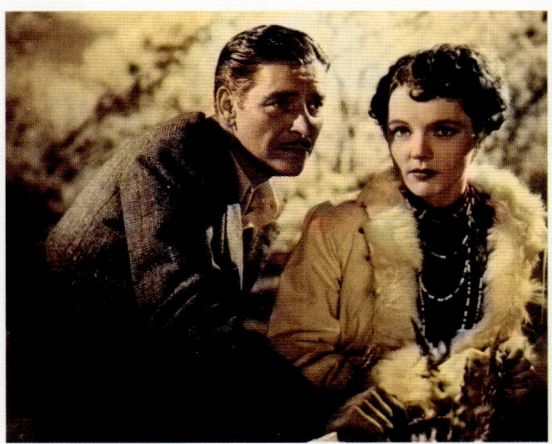

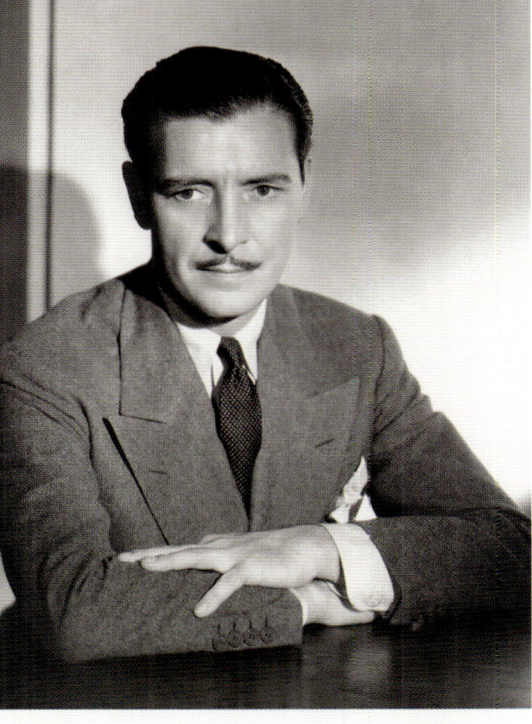

in wartime broadcasts, public events, and cultural diplomacy campaigns that reached audiences across the globe.

Colman was honored with two stars on the Hollywood Walk of Fame—one for motion pictures and one for television. He died of emphysema on May 19, 1958, in Santa Barbara, California, at the age of 67.

ABOVE

In *The Devil to Pay!* (1930), Ronald Colman is, effortlessly debonair as a charming rogue navigating love, scandal, and society in this early talkie romance.

LEFT

Ronald transitioned from silent films to talkies with ease, becoming a beloved leading man of classic Hollywood cinema.

FAR LEFT

Ronald was a distinguished British actor, known for his debonair screen persona and distinctive voice, earning an Academy Award for Best Actor.

37

MARLENE DIETRICH

FASHION FEATURES

THE BLUE ANGEL (1930)
SHANGHAI EXPRESS (1932)
THE SCARLET EMPRESS (1934)
DESTRY RIDES AGAIN (1939)
WITNESS FOR THE PROSECUTION (1957)

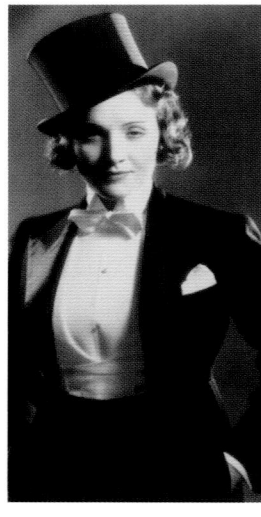

Marlene Dietrich (1901–1992) was born in Berlin, Germany, and began her career on the German stage and in silent films before gaining international attention in the late 1920s. Her breakout came with The *Blue Angel* (1930), in which she played the alluring cabaret singer Lola Lola. Her performance and iconic rendition of "Falling in Love Again" launched her to stardom and caught the eye of director Josef von Sternberg, who brought her to Hollywood.

Sultry, stylish, and endlessly enigmatic, Marlene Dietrich captivated audiences with her smoky voice, commanding screen presence, and daring approach to fashion, both on and off the screen.

Under von Sternberg's direction, Dietrich starred in a string of visually stunning films for Paramount Pictures, including *Morocco* (1930), *Shanghai Express* (1932), and *The Scarlet Empress* (1934). These films helped to shape her mystique as a cool, seductive femme fatale. With her androgynous style, she challenged gender norms by wearing tuxedos and men's suits both onscreen and in public—choices that caused a stir in the 1930s but made her a lasting icon of empowered individuality.

Although her popularity waned in the late 1930s, Dietrich revitalized her career with roles in *Destry Rides Again* (1939), where she showcased her comedic side, and later in *Witness for the Prosecution* (1957). During World War II, she toured extensively with the USO, entertaining American troops overseas and receiving the Medal of Freedom in recognition of her contributions.

In the postwar years, Dietrich transitioned to live performance, headlining sold-out cabaret shows in Las Vegas, Paris, and London. Her stage persona—gowned in glittering dresses, bathed in theatrical lighting—continued to reinforce her image as an

The Dietrich Look

Elegant and provocative, Dietrich embraced tuxedos, satin gowns, and glittering embellishments that emphasized her bold silhouette and defiant glamor.

• Pencil-thin arched brows
• Men's suits and tuxedos
• Backlit satin and sequins
• Defined lips and smokey eyes

ageless symbol of glamor and sophistication. She worked with top designers such as Jean Louis and Edith Head to craft her stage wardrobe, often enhancing her presence with long gloves, dramatic capes, and form-fitting gowns.

Beyond her cinematic and musical contributions, Dietrich was also a vocal critic of fascism and a proud anti-Nazi figure throughout the war. Her refusal to perform in Hitler's Germany, despite lucrative offers, demonstrated her courage and conviction. She later became a U.S. citizen and remained outspoken on global issues. Her influence extended into the realm of gender identity, as her open embrace of masculine attire and bisexuality challenged norms long before it was culturally accepted. Her daughter, Maria Riva, later wrote a memoir that offered deeper insight into her mother's complex personal life, revealing the discipline, intelligence, and vulnerability behind the legend.

Offscreen, Dietrich was known for her intellect, political awareness, and fiercely guarded privacy. She maintained lifelong friendships with notable figures such as Ernest Hemingway and Jean Cocteau, and her Berlin apartment later became a museum exhibit. She died in Paris in 1992 at the age of 90, having spent much of her final years out of the public eye.

ABOVE

In *Morocco* (1930), Marlene Dietrich broke cinematic and sartorial boundaries in a tuxedo and top hat—an androgynous look that redefined glamor and remains one of Hollywood's most iconic fashion moments.

FULL PAGE

Marlene Dietrich, pictured in a dazzling flapper ensemble, rose to fame in *The Blue Angel* (1930) and became known for her sultry voice and androgynous style.

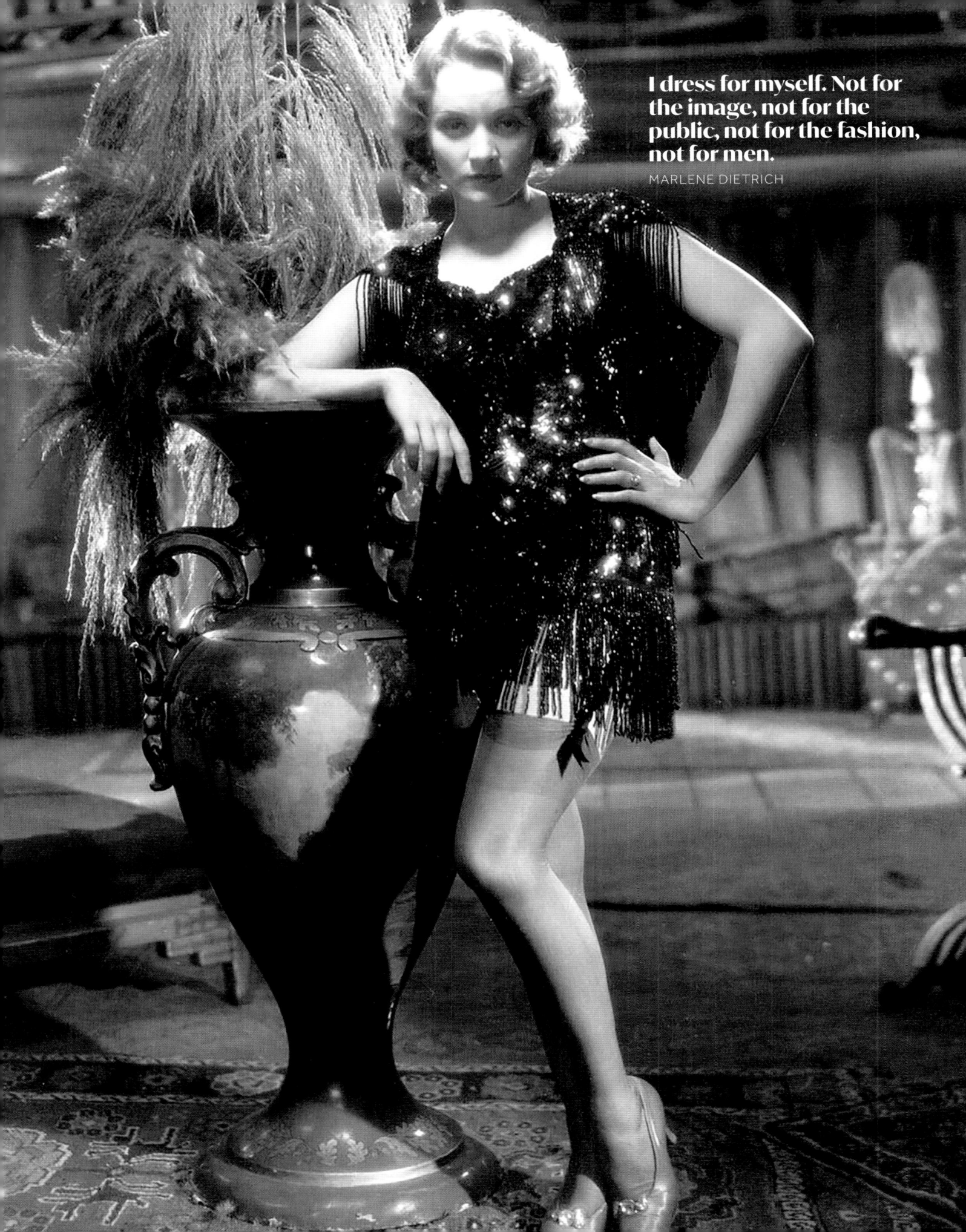

I dress for myself. Not for the image, not for the public, not for the fashion, not for men.

MARLENE DIETRICH

SETTING TRENDS
BLONDE BOMBSHELLS

From Jean Harlow's shimmering curls to Brigitte Bardot's effortless sensuality and Grace Kelly's cool perfection, blonde actresses have defined the look of glamor for nearly a century.

Their pale hair and luminous screen presence made them unforgettable—symbols of allure, confidence, and control. Hollywood directors understood their power.

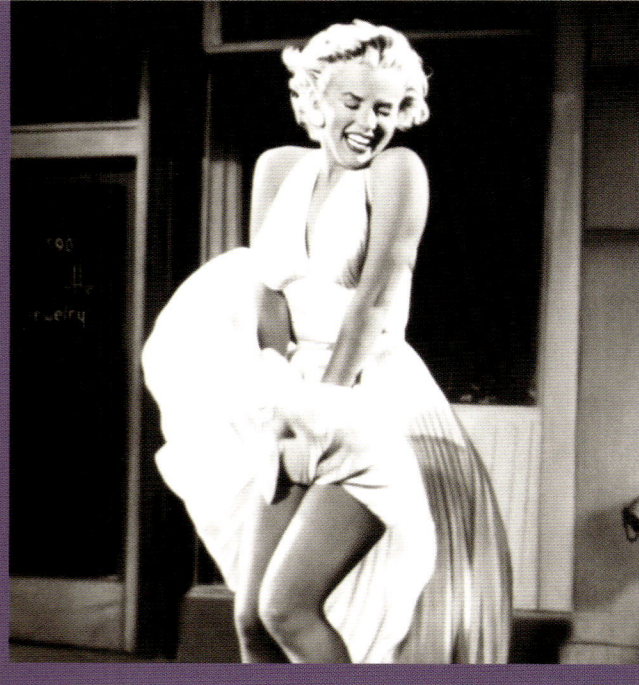

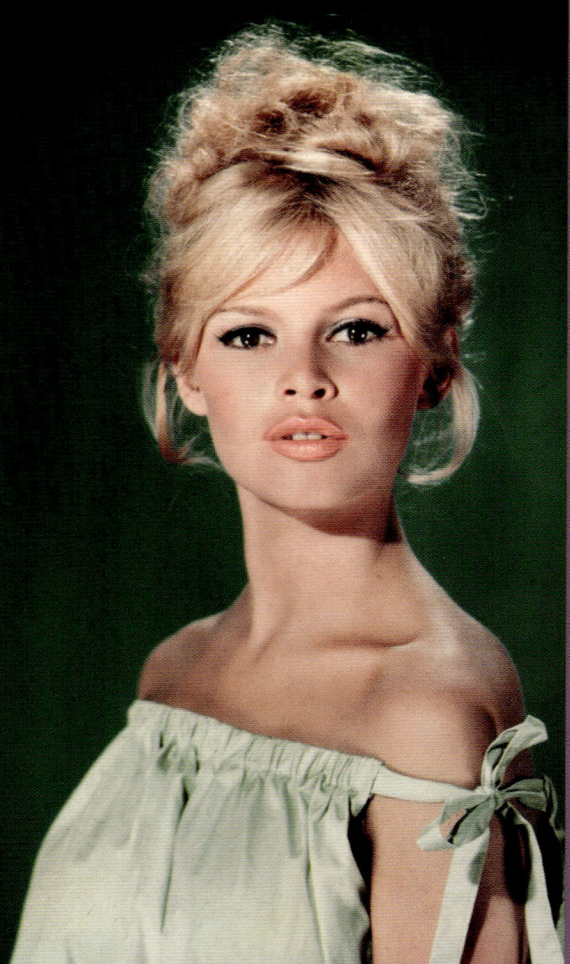

RIGHT

Brigitte Bardot's tousled hair and self-assured gaze redefined what it meant to be a modern woman on screen.

ABOVE RIGHT

Marilyn Monroe in *The Seven Year Itch* (1955), in one of film's most famous moments, captured the spirit of the ultimate blonde bombshell—playful, iconic, and instantly recognizable.

BOTTOM RIGHT

Scarlett Johansson in *Match Point* (2005), her understated beauty and quiet allure proving that blonde mystique still captivates today.

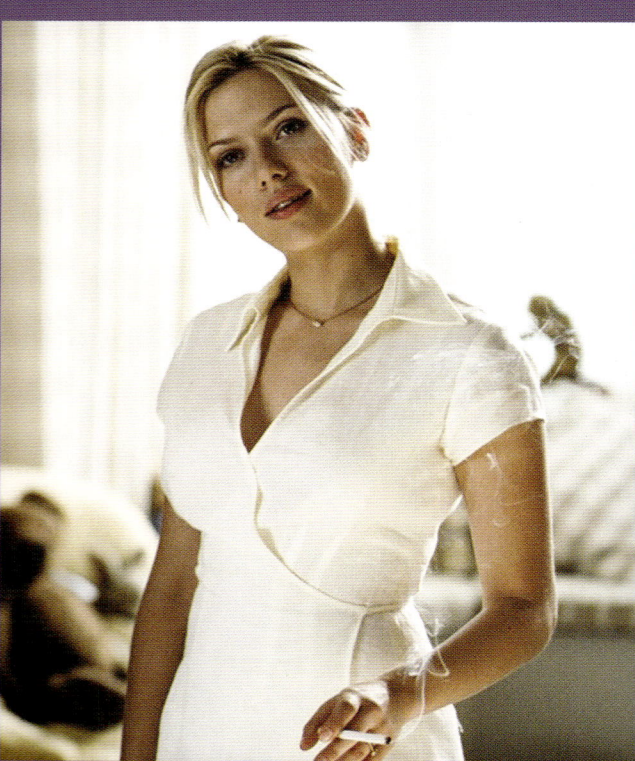

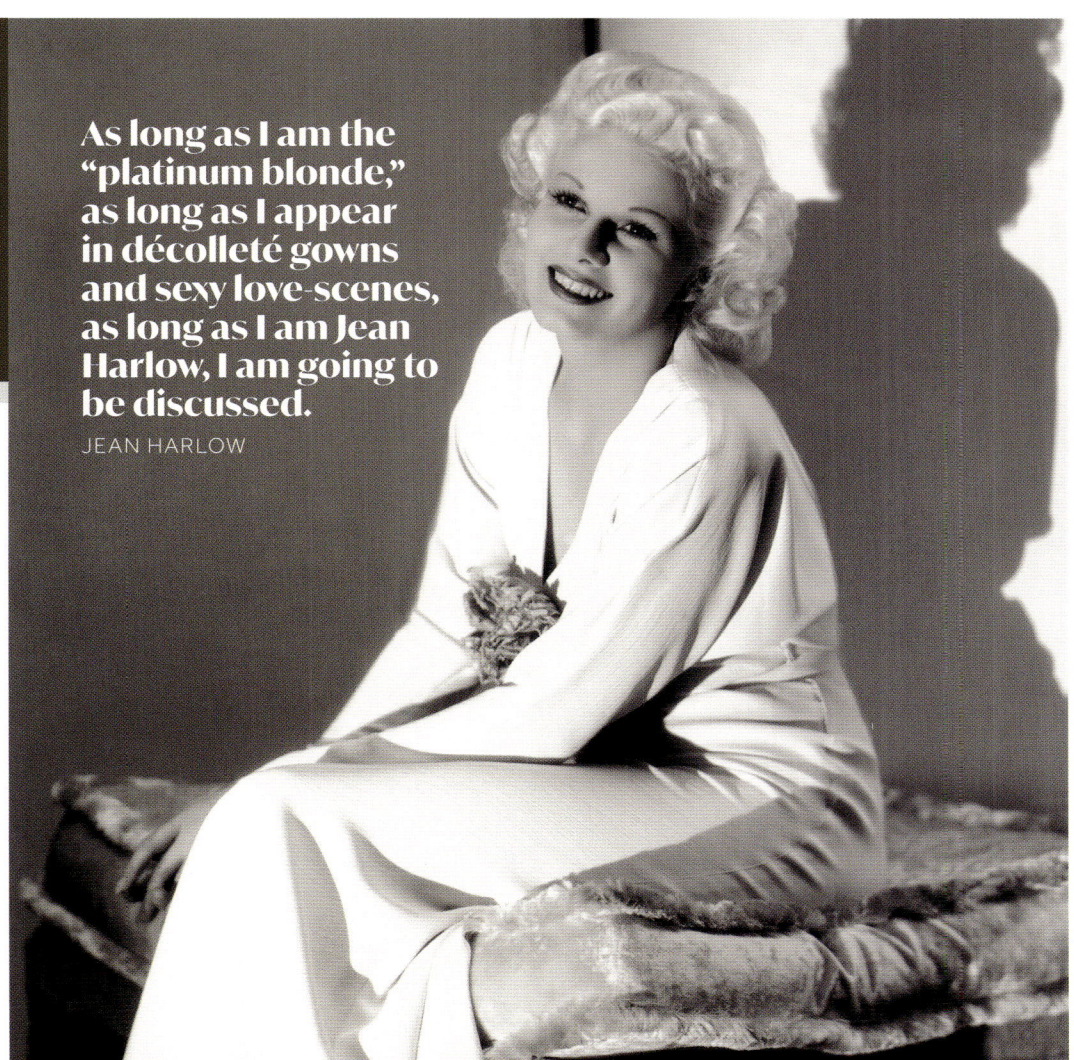

> As long as I am the "platinum blonde," as long as I appear in décolleté gowns and sexy love-scenes, as long as I am Jean Harlow, I am going to be discussed.
>
> JEAN HARLOW

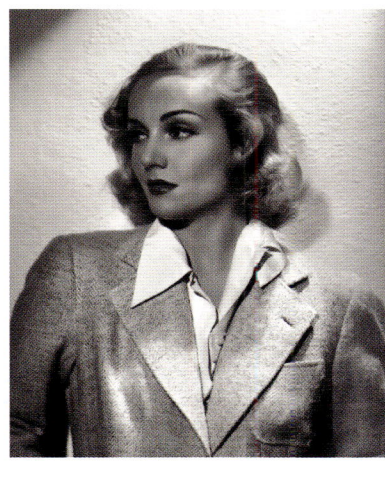

ABOVE

Carole Lombard was one of Hollywood's most gifted comedians—quick-witted, radiant, and fearless on screen. Her timing, intelligence, and natural charm made her the perfect blend of glamor and substance, defining the smart blonde for a generation.

LEFT

Jean Harlow, Hollywood's original platinum blonde, set the standard for screen glamor in the 1930s and made peroxide a symbol of power.

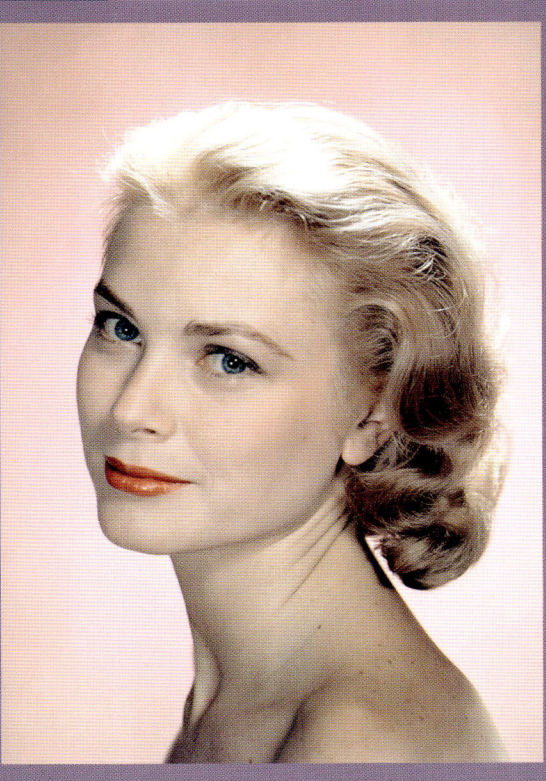

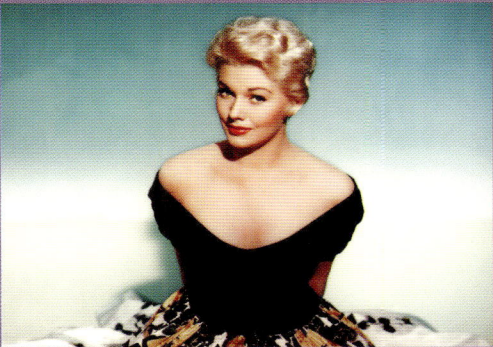

Hitchcock turned blondes like Grace Kelly and Kim Novak into the embodiment of mystery and desire —serene on the surface, complex underneath. Bardot, meanwhile, gave the archetype a new edge: rebellious, modern, and entirely her own.

The blonde bombshell continues to evolve, reinvented by stars such as Charlize Theron, Scarlett Johansson, and Naomi Watts. Whether icy, playful, or seductive, the blonde remains one of cinema's most enduring and magnetic icons.

LEFT

Kim Novak in *Phffft!* (1954), years before *Vertigo*, already exuded the cool confidence that made her one of cinema's most enduring blondes.

FAR LEFT

Grace Kelly's poise and precision made her Hitchcock's ideal heroine—elegant, enigmatic, and seemingly untouchable.

4

JEAN HARLOW

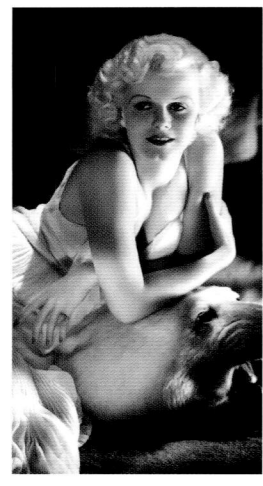

Hollywood's original blonde bombshell, Jean Harlow, set the template for screen seduction before her life was tragically cut short.

Jean Harlow (1911–1937) emerged as one of Hollywood's most iconic and influential stars of the 1930s, known for her bold screen presence, comedic timing, and platinum blonde hair that became her signature. Born Harlean Harlow Carpenter in Kansas City, Missouri, she moved to Los Angeles in her teens and was drawn into the film industry almost by chance. Although she first appeared in uncredited bit parts, it was her role in *Hell's Angels* (1930), directed by Howard Hughes, that made her a sensation. Her performance, paired with her striking hair and sultry screen persona, helped define a new image of modern, unapologetic femininity.

Dubbed the "Platinum Blonde" and "Blonde Bombshell," Harlow became a top box-office draw for Metro-Goldwyn-Mayer (MGM), where she starred in a series of successful films including *Red-Headed Woman* (1932), *Dinner at Eight* (1933), *Bombshell* (1933), and *Libeled Lady* (1936). Her characters were often wisecracking, street-smart women with a mix of sex appeal and approachability. Harlow's screen roles challenged conventional ideas of propriety, embracing independence, sexuality, and wit in equal measure. Offscreen, however, she was said to be reserved and down-to-earth, known for her kindness and professionalism.

Harlow's fashion influence was immense. Costume designer Adrian crafted her iconic silk gowns, which clung to her figure in shimmering bias-cut perfection. Her bleached blonde hair, pencil-thin eyebrows, and glamorous style inspired a generation of women and helped cement the look of the decade.

Tragically, Harlow's life and career were cut short when she died at the age of 26 due to kidney failure. At the time of her death, she was one of MGM's

ABOVE

Hollywood's first platinum blonde, Jean Harlow, known for her sensual satin-clad screen presence.

RIGHT

Harlow's satin gown, designed by Adrian, became iconic, defining 1930s Hollywood glamor and her bombshell image.

FULL PAGE

Jean Harlow revolutionized Hollywood glamor in the 1930s with her platinum blonde hair, bias-cut satin gowns, and bold attitude. She became MGM's top star before her untimely death at just 26.

FASHION FEATURES

PLATINUM BLONDE (1931)
RED-HEADED WOMAN (1932)
DINNER AT EIGHT (1933)
BOMBSHELL (1933)
LIBELED LADY (1936)

The Harlow Look

Harlow's style redefined screen glamor with slinky satin gowns, curve-hugging silhouettes, and daring necklines that emphasized her figure. She popularized bias-cut dresses and exuded a provocative elegance that became synonymous with 1930s Hollywood.

- Platinum blonde curls
- Low-cut satin gowns
- Pencil-thin eyebrows
- Glossy lips and sculpted cheekbones

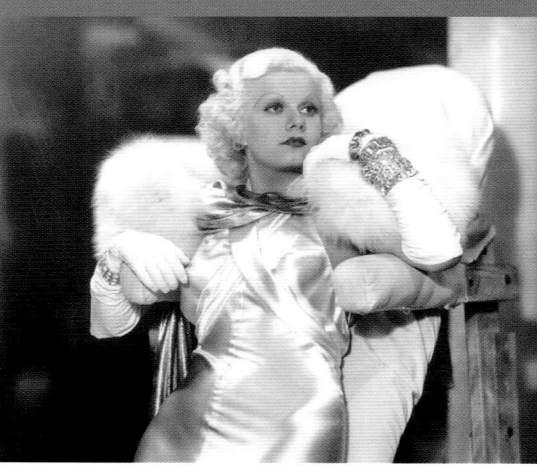

biggest stars, and her unexpected passing shocked the film world. Despite her brief career, Harlow left an enduring mark on Hollywood. She redefined the image of the screen siren and helped pave the way for later stars such as Marilyn Monroe. Jean Harlow's blend of charisma, sensuality, and comedic skill made her one of the first truly modern movie stars.

Must I always wear a low-cut dress to be important?
JEAN HARLOW

LEADING MEN
LESLIE HOWARD

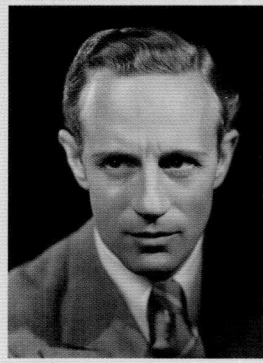

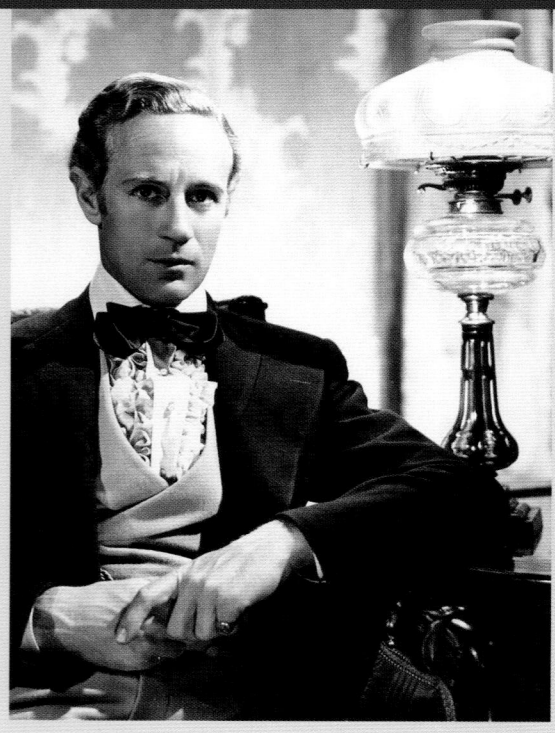

The screen's beloved Ashley Wilkes was a two-time Oscar nominee, a dedicated artist, and a wartime patriot—but his life ended under mysterious circumstances over the Atlantic.

Leslie Howard (1893–1943) gained fame for playing introspective, principled Englishmen, bringing quiet intensity to roles that blended intellect and emotion. Born Leslie Howard Steiner in Forest Hill, London, he was the son of a Hungarian-Jewish father and an English mother. Before acting, Howard worked as a bank clerk, but the trauma of World War I—where he served and was discharged for shell shock—pushed him toward the stage. He debuted as an actor in 1917, and soon became a respected presence on the London stage and on Broadway.

By the 1930s, Howard was a prominent figure in Hollywood. He received Academy Award nominations for his performances in *Berkeley Square* (1933) and *Pygmalion* (1938), where he also took on directing duties. In *The Scarlet Pimpernel* (1934), he embodied a hero leading a double life with elegance and wit. His role in *The Petrified Forest* (1936) was pivotal—not only for him but for Hollywood—since he demanded that studio executives cast a struggling stage actor named Humphrey Bogart in a role that would ultimately make Bogart a star.

Howard's most recognized screen appearance came in *Gone with the Wind* (1939), where he portrayed the gentle and conflicted Ashley Wilkes. Although he reportedly felt too old for the role, his nuanced performance left a lasting impression on audiences worldwide.

Outside of acting, Howard was devoted to Britain's cultural and wartime efforts. He directed and starred in patriotic wartime films such as

Pimpernel Smith (1941) and *The First of the Few* (1942), which honored the designer of the Spitfire aircraft. He also worked behind the scenes in anti-Nazi propaganda and is believed to have collaborated with British intelligence, using his fame as a tool in support of the Allies.

On June 1, 1943, while returning from a diplomatic and possibly intelligence-related mission in Portugal, Howard was aboard BOAC Flight 777 when it was shot down by German fighters over the Bay of Biscay. His death at the age of 50 shocked the world, fueling theories that he had been deliberately targeted.

His influence lives on through his pivotal role in shaping British wartime cinema and for helping launch Humphrey Bogart's film career with *The Petrified Forest*.

ABOVE

Leslie was a distinguished British actor and director, best known for *Gone with the Wind*, and also served in WWII intelligence before his tragic death in 1943.

RIGHT

Howard, best remembered as Ashley Wilkes in *Gone with the Wind*, was also a wartime hero. He died when his plane was shot down during a WWII diplomatic mission.

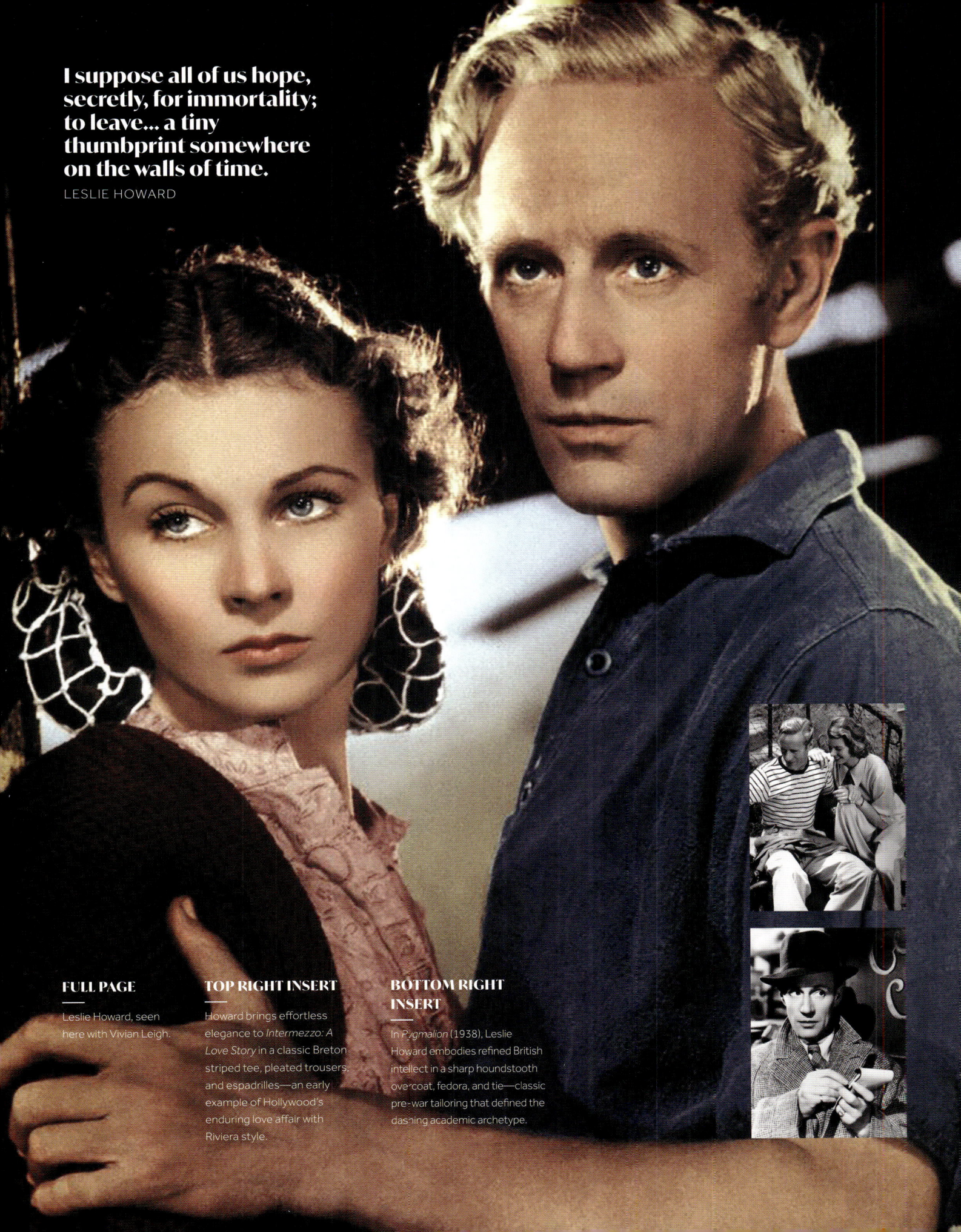

> I suppose all of us hope, secretly, for immortality; to leave... a tiny thumbprint somewhere on the walls of time.
>
> LESLIE HOWARD

FULL PAGE

Leslie Howard, seen here with Vivian Leigh.

TOP RIGHT INSERT

Howard brings effortless elegance to *Intermezzo: A Love Story* in a classic Breton striped tee, pleated trousers, and espadrilles—an early example of Hollywood's enduring love affair with Riviera style.

BOTTOM RIGHT INSERT

In *Pygmalion* (1938), Leslie Howard embodies refined British intellect in a sharp houndstooth overcoat, fedora, and tie—classic pre-war tailoring that defined the dashing academic archetype.

VIVIEN LEIGH

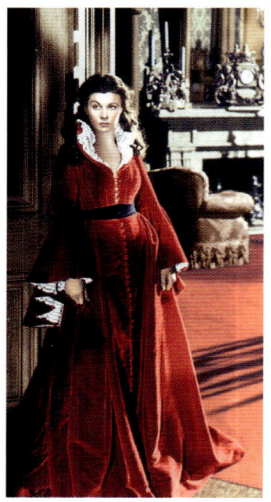

Born Vivian Mary Hartley in Darjeeling, India in 1913, Leigh moved to England at a young age and developed an early passion for theater. She studied acting at the Royal Academy of Dramatic Art and began appearing on stage and in British films in the 1930s. Her breakthrough came when she was cast as Scarlett O'Hara in *Gone with the Wind* (1939), a role that would define her career. Chosen from among hundreds of actresses, Leigh captivated audiences with her portrayal of the complex, headstrong Southern belle. Her performance earned her an Academy Award for Best Actress.

Graceful, intense, and magnetically expressive, Vivien Leigh became one of the most iconic actresses of the 20th century, known for her breathtaking beauty and emotionally rich performances.

In 1940, Leigh married British actor Laurence Olivier, and together they became one of the most celebrated couples of theater and film. She balanced her film work with a respected stage career, often performing Shakespearean roles. In 1951, she won her second Oscar for her portrayal of the fragile Blanche DuBois in *A Streetcar Named Desire*, a role she had played to acclaim on stage.

Behind the scenes, Leigh battled bipolar disorder and chronic illness, which affected her health and work. She died in 1967 at the age of 53. Despite her struggles, Vivien Leigh's legacy endures as a brilliant, passionate actress who brought unforgettable depth to every role she had played.

ABOVE

Pictured as Scarlett O'Hara in *Gone with the Wind* (1939), Vivien Leigh won her first Academy Award for this role. Renowned for her beauty and poise, Leigh captivated audiences with her emotional depth and intensity, later earning a second Oscar for *A Streetcar Named Desire* (1951), solidifying her legacy as one of cinema's finest actresses.

RIGHT

As Scarlett O'Hara in *Gone with the Wind* (1939), a role that earned her an Academy Award and cemented her legacy as one of cinema's most iconic leading ladies.

The Leigh Look

Romantic and regal, Leigh favored structured gowns, nipped waists, and rich fabrics that complemented her classical beauty and stage-trained poise.

- Delicate curls
- Bold brows and defined lips
- Victorian-inspired dresses
- Elegant tailoring and lace details

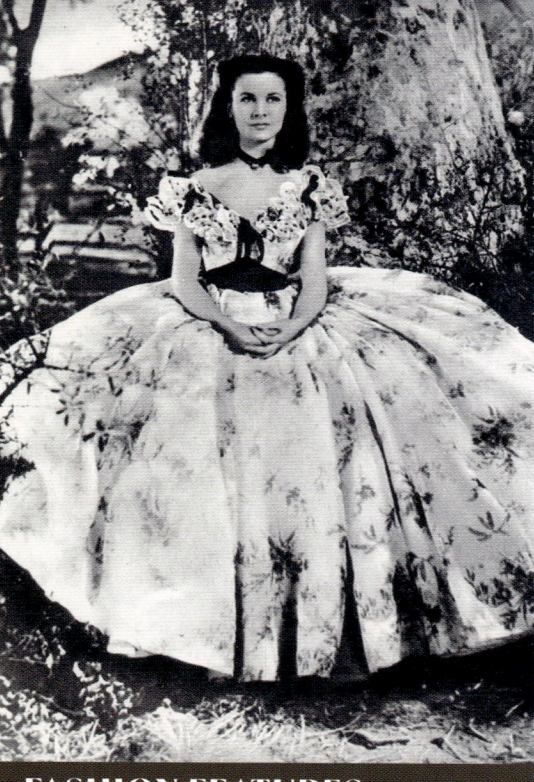

FASHION FEATURES

GONE WITH THE WIND (1939)
WATERLOO BRIDGE (1940)
A STREETCAR NAMED DESIRE (1951)
THE ROMAN SPRING OF MRS. STONE (1961)

CAROLE LOMBARD

FASHION FEATURES

NO MAN OF HER OWN (1932)
TWENTIETH CENTURY (1934)
RUMBA (1935)
MY MAN GODFREY (1936)
NOTHING SACRED (1937)

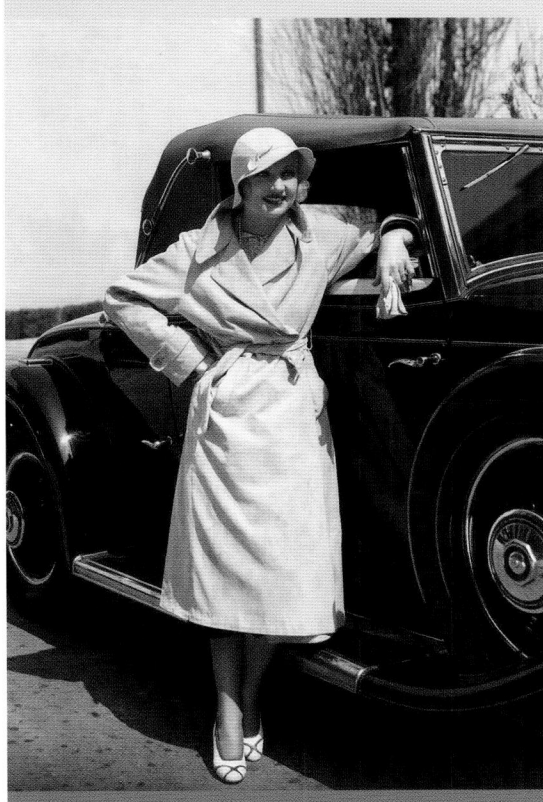

The Lombard Look
Sophisticated and polished, Lombard favored bias-cut gowns, soft silks, and elegant tailoring that emphasized her sleek, modern silhouette.

• Blonde finger waves
• Cowl-neck evening dresses
• Minimal jewelry
• Clean, classic Hollywood glamor

Born Jane Alice Peters in Fort Wayne, Indiana, in 1908, Lombard moved to Los Angeles as a child and began acting in silent films as a teenager. She gained early attention for her lively screen presence and comedic instincts. After a car accident left a scar on her face, she transitioned to roles that leaned on her charm and wit rather than conventional beauty. By the early 1930s, she had emerged as a leading actress, signing with Paramount Pictures and starring in a string of successful films.

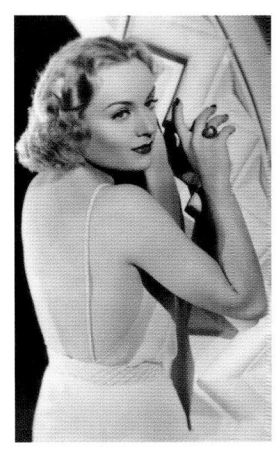

Witty, radiant, and effortlessly modern, Carole Lombard became one of the most beloved actresses of 1930s Hollywood, known for her dazzling beauty and impeccable comedic timing.

Lombard's true breakthrough came with the screwball comedy *Twentieth Century* (1934), followed by standout performances in *My Man Godfrey* (1936)—for which she received an Academy Award nomination—and *Nothing Sacred* (1937). She was celebrated for playing sharp-tongued, fast-talking heroines who could hold their own in any situation, often stealing scenes from her male costars.

Offscreen, Lombard was known for her down-to-earth personality, charitable work, and whirlwind romance with actor Clark Gable, whom she married in 1939. Tragically, her life was cut short in a plane crash in 1942 while returning from a World War II bond rally.

Although her career lasted just over a decade, Carole Lombard left an indelible mark on American film, helping to shape the screwball comedy genre and redefine the role of women in comedy.

ABOVE
Carole Lombard, a leading lady of 1930s screwball comedies, was known for her wit, glamor, and marriage to Clark Gable. She tragically died in a 1942 plane crash.

LEFT
Carole Lombard was a versatile actress who always brought a touch of down-to-earth realism to her comedic roles.

DESIGN SENSE
ORRY-KELLY

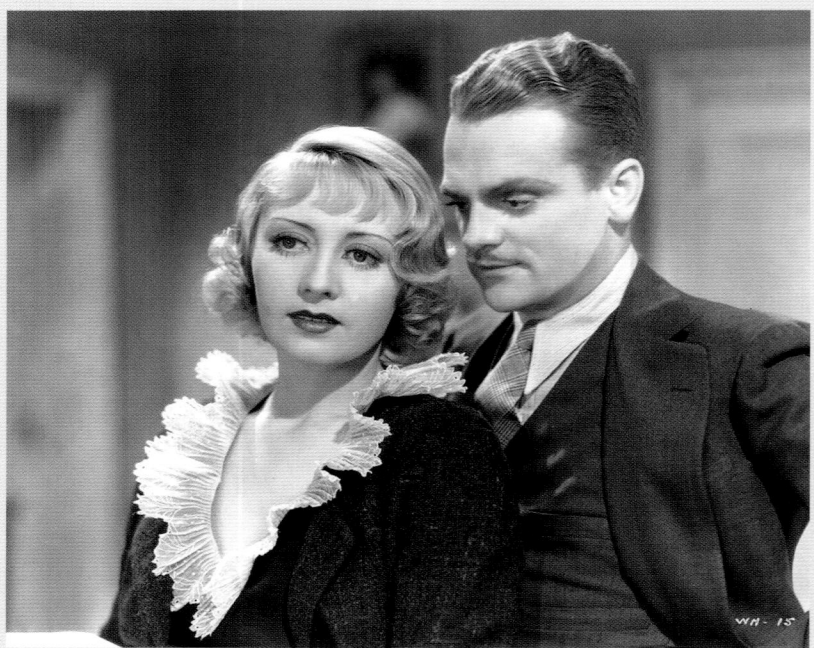

ABOVE

James Cagney wore Orry-Kelly's sharp, structured suits that emphasized his tough persona, notably in *The Public Enemy*, defining the gangster style of 1930s Hollywood cinema.

Orry-Kelly, born Orry George Kelly on December 31, 1897, in the coastal town of Kiama, New South Wales, Australia, was one of the most influential costume designers in Hollywood's Golden Age. The son of a gentleman tailor, he was exposed to fashion from a young age. At 17, he moved to Sydney to study banking, but his interest soon shifted to the performing arts. In 1921, he relocated to New York City with his dreams of becoming an actor. There, he lived with future screen legend, Cary Grant. While supporting himself by painting murals in nightclubs, he eventually found work designing title cards for silent films at Fox's East Coast studios, and soon transitioned to creating costumes for Broadway revues.

Kelly moved to Hollywood in 1932, and was soon hired as the head costume designer at Warner Bros., a position he held until 1944. His Hollywood career spanned multiple studios, including Universal, RKO, MGM, and 20th Century Fox. Over the course of three decades, he designed costumes for more than 300 films, lending his talent to cinematic classics such as *42nd Street*, *Now Voyager*, *The Maltese Falcon*, *Arsenic and Old Lace*, *Oklahoma!*, *Auntie Mame*, and *Some Like It Hot*.

Renowned for his intuitive grasp of character and form, Orry-Kelly had a particular genius for enhancing an actress's on-screen presence. His designs often cleverly disguised perceived imperfections while amplifying a star's charisma. He dressed many of Hollywood's greatest actresses, including Bette Davis, Kay Francis, Ruth Chatterton, Marilyn Monroe, Olivia de Havilland, Katharine Hepburn, Dolores del Río, Ava Gardner, Ann Sheridan, Barbara Stanwyck, and Merle Oberon.

His remarkable work was recognized with three Academy Awards for Best Costume Design for *An American in Paris* (1951), *Les Girls* (1957), and *Some Like It Hot* (1959). He also earned a nomination for *Gypsy* (1962). In addition to his artistry, he was admired for his wit, resilience, and unapologetic authenticity in an often-conformist industry.

Orry-Kelly was also notable for living as an openly gay man during an era when such openness was rare in Hollywood. His posthumously published memoir, *Women I've Undressed*, was released in 2015, alongside the acclaimed documentary *Women He's Undressed* by director Gillian Armstrong.

He died of liver cancer on February 27, 1964, in Los Angeles. Among his pallbearers were Cary Grant, Tony Curtis, Billy Wilder, and George Cukor, with a eulogy delivered by Jack L. Warner. Orry-Kelly's legacy continues to shine through his iconic designs and lasting impact on film costume history.

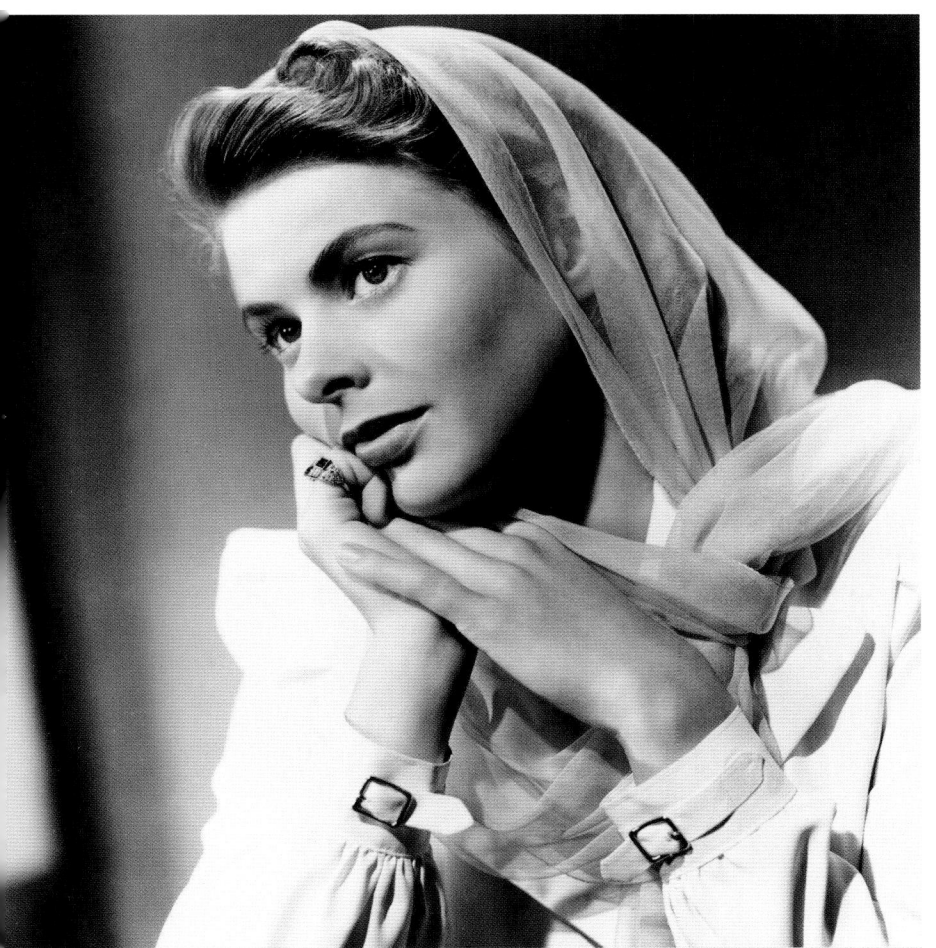

FASHION FEATURES

42ND STREET (1933)
THE MALTESE FALCON (1941)
CASABLANCA (1942)
AN AMERICAN IN PARIS (1951)
SOME LIKE IT HOT (1959)

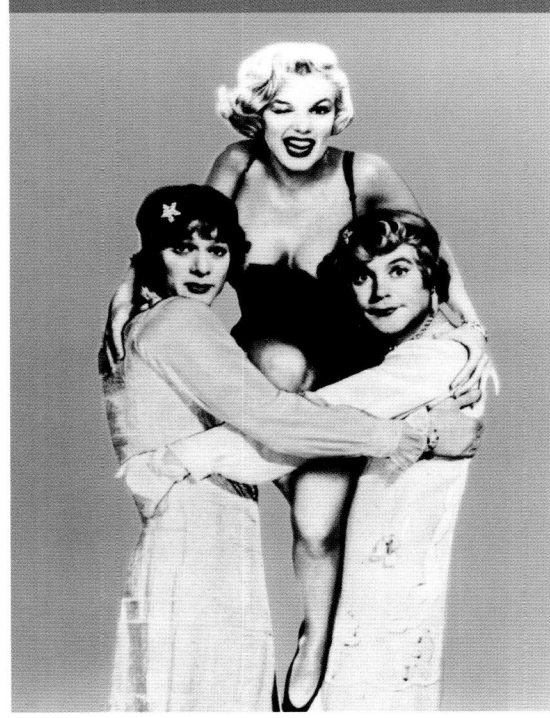

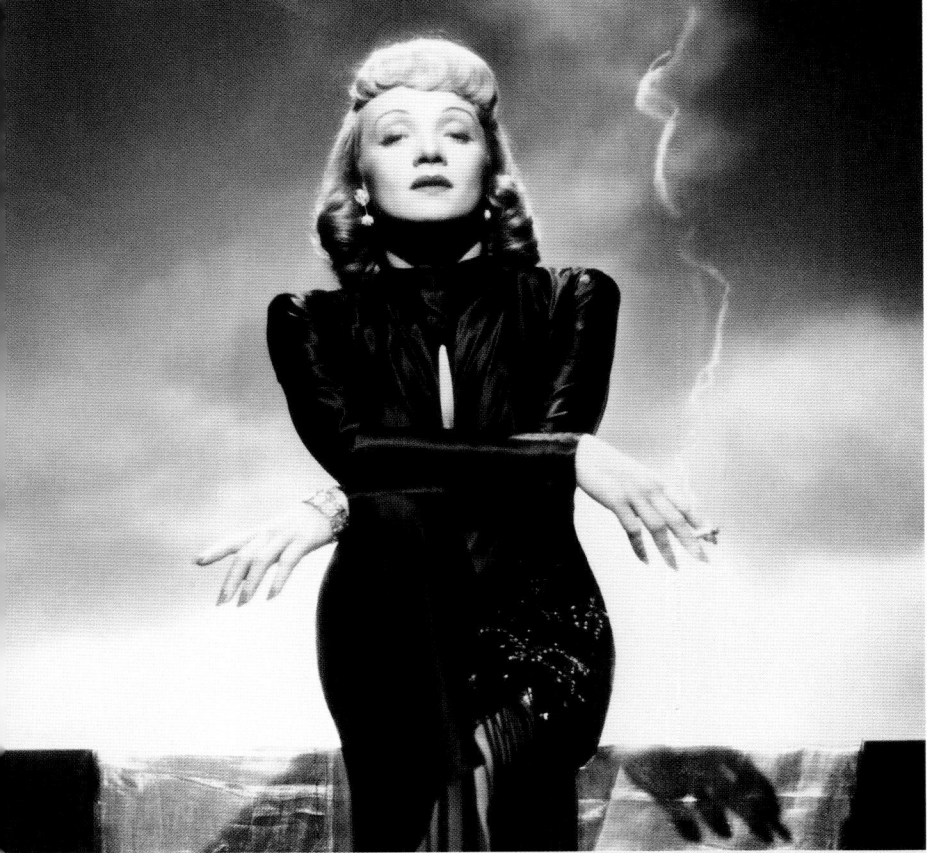

I wish I had a dime for every time that's been copied.

ORRY-KELLY ON INGRID BERGMAN'S
JUMPER DRESS FROM *CASABLANCA*

ABOVE LEFT

In *Casablanca*, Ingrid Bergman radiates timeless elegance in soft lighting and softer fabrics—a sheer headscarf and tailored blouse capturing the poise, grace, and quiet strength of classic Hollywood style.

LEFT

Marlene Dietrich in *Manpower* (1941), wearing a sharp, black satin gown by Orry-Kelly. Clean lines, fringe details, and bold presence—Hollywood style with unmistakable authority

ABOVE

Marilyn Monroe, flanked by Tony Curtis and Jack Lemmon in drag, strikes a playful pose for *Some Like It Hot* (1959)—a classic comedy of disguise, desire, and perfectly timed chaos.

MYRNA LOY

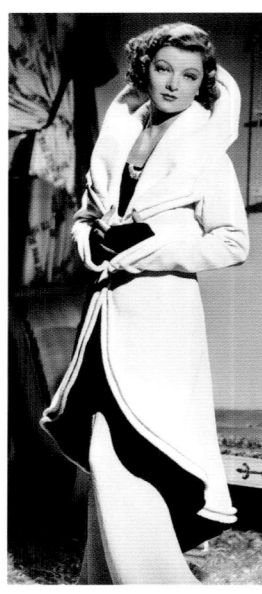

Myrna Loy (1905–1993), born Myrna Adele Williams in Montana, began her film career in the silent era after working as a dancer and model in Los Angeles. With her striking features and exotic looks, she was often cast in vamp or femme fatale roles early on, including in films such as *The Mask of Fu Manchu* (1932). However, it wasn't until she was cast as Nora Charles in *The Thin Man* (1934) that Loy found her true niche. Her performance, opposite William Powell, showcased her impeccable timing, natural charm, and the relaxed intelligence that would come to define her screen persona.

Graceful, clever, and endlessly composed, Myrna Loy became the quintessential sophisticated woman of 1930s and 1940s Hollywood, beloved for her wit, elegance, and quiet strength.

Loy and Powell went on to make several more *Thin Man* films together, becoming one of Hollywood's most iconic screen pairings. She was also celebrated for her roles in *The Best Years of Our Lives* (1946) and *Libeled Lady* (1936), where she demonstrated a wide range of drama and comedy.

Beyond the screen, Loy was politically active, serving as a member of the U.S. National Commission for UNESCO and supporting civil rights efforts. She received an honorary Academy Award in 1991 for her lifetime contribution to film. Loy remains a symbol of intelligence, style, and enduring Hollywood sophistication.

ABOVE

Myrna Loy, known as the "Queen of Hollywood" during the 1930s, became beloved for her role as Nora Charles in *The Thin Man* series and was awarded an honorary Oscar in 1991.

RIGHT

William Powell, best known for his role as detective Nick Charles in *The Thin Man* series, starred opposite Loy—and fox terrier Asta—in 14 successful films.

FASHION FEATURES

THE THIN MAN (1934)
LIBELED LADY (1936)
THE BEST YEARS OF OUR LIVES (1946)

The Loy Look

Chic and tailored, Loy favored smart suits, bias-cut gowns, and sleek lines that emphasized her refined elegance and urbane screen image.

- Finger-waved hair
- Silk blouses and skirts
- Structured evening dresses
- Subtle, polished makeup

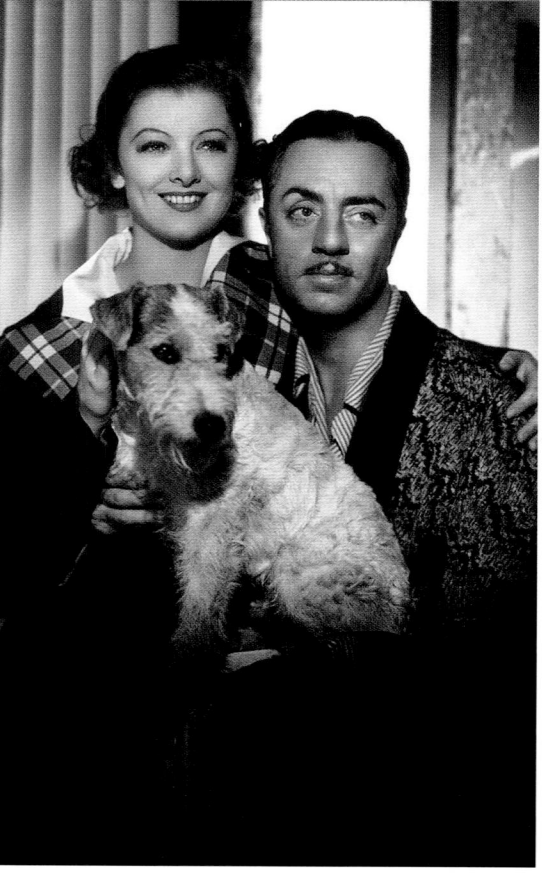

GINGER ROGERS

TOP HAT (1935)
SWING TIME (1936)
KITTY FOYLE (1940)

The Rogers Look

Ginger Rogers' style blended Old Hollywood glamor with graceful functionality. Her wardrobe featured flowing chiffon gowns, feather-trimmed skirts, and sleek satin dresses designed to enhance her dance movements. Offscreen, she favored tailored suits, wide-legged trousers, and crisp blouses, combining elegance with ease in a look that was timeless and polished.

- Blonde waves
- Flowing satin gowns
- Halter necklines
- Polished heels made for dancing

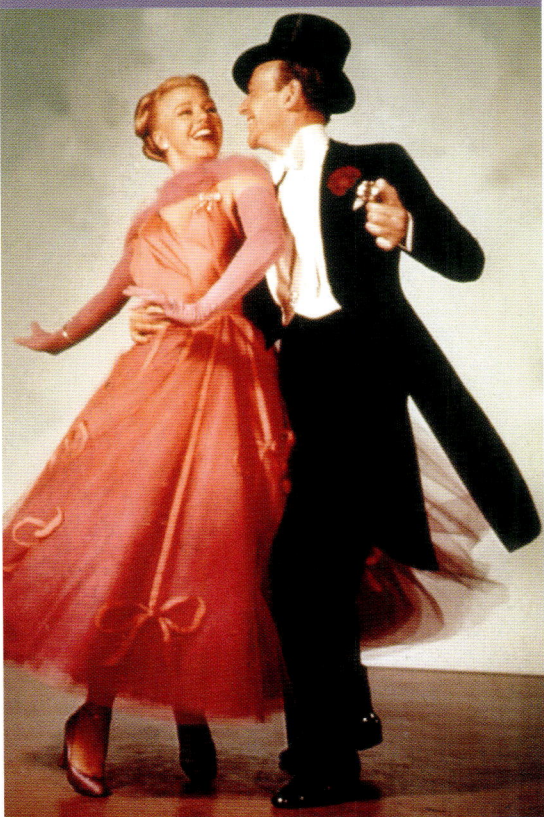

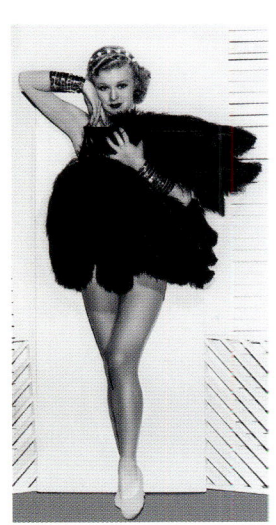

Born Virginia Katherine McMath in Independence, Missouri, in 1911, Ginger Rogers began her performing career in vaudeville before transitioning to Broadway and eventually film. She rose to international fame in the 1930s when she was paired with Fred Astaire in a series of now-iconic RKO musicals. Their first film together, *Flying Down to Rio* (1933), was followed by a string of hits including *Top Hat* (1935), *Swing Time* (1936), and *Shall We Dance* (1937). Their graceful routines and onscreen chemistry helped to define the Golden Age of the Hollywood musical.

Graceful, quick-witted, and radiantly charismatic Ginger Rogers danced, acted, and sang her way into film history as one of Hollywood's most versatile and enduring stars.

Although best known for her dancing, Rogers proved herself a capable dramatic actress as well. She won the Academy Award for Best Actress for her performance in *Kitty Foyle* (1940), playing a working-class woman with emotional complexity and determination. She went on to star in dramas, comedies, dramas, and musicals throughout the 1940s and 1950s.

Beyond her screen talents, Rogers became a style icon, frequently wearing elegant, flowing gowns designed to complement her movement. Her combination of glamor, relatability, and charm made her a beloved figure for decades.

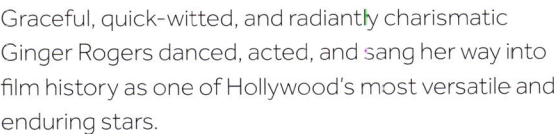

I believe in dressing for the occasion. There's a time for sweater, sneakers, and Levis, and a time for the full-dress jazz.

GINGER ROGERS

ABOVE

Ginger Rogers, shown here in a dramatic feathered costume, won an Oscar for *Kitty Foyle* and famously danced alongside Fred Astaire in ten classic musicals.

RIGHT

Fred Astaire and Ginger Rogers dazzle in timeless elegance—he in a classic black tux and top hat, she in a twirl-ready pink tulle gown adorned with bows—a picture-perfect duo in Hollywood's Golden Age of dance.

NORMA SHEARER

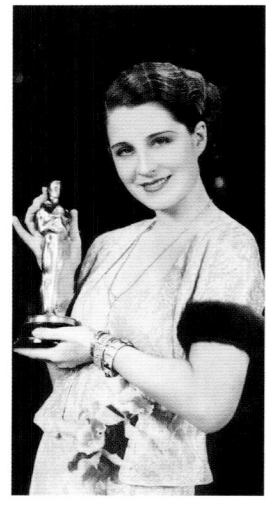

Refined, intelligent, and effortlessly elegant, Norma Shearer rose from modest beginnings to become one of MGM's most bankable and respected stars of the 1930s.

Born in Montreal, Canada, in 1902, Norma Shearer began her film career in the silent era, moving to Hollywood with her mother and sister in pursuit of stardom. After a series of small roles, she caught the attention of MGM and quickly ascended the studio ranks. Her talent, combined with striking beauty and charisma, earned her leading roles and eventually a long-term contract. She was often cast as modern, self-assured women who challenged traditional roles—a reflection of her own quiet ambition.

Refined, intelligent, and effortlessly elegant, Norma Shearer rose from modest beginnings to become one of MGM's most bankable and respected stars of the 1930s.

Shearer married Irving Thalberg, MGM's influential head of production, in 1927. With his support, she secured roles that showcased her dramatic range, most notably in *The Divorcee* (1930), for which she won the Academy Award for Best Actress. Throughout the 1930s, she starred in successful films such as *A Free Soul* (1931), *The Barretts of Wimpole Street* (1934), and *Marie Antoinette* (1938), often portraying women of depth and emotional complexity.

Following Thalberg's death in 1936, Shearer's influence at MGM gradually declined. She retired from acting in 1942 but left behind a legacy of sophistication, subtlety, and female empowerment that continues to resonate.

ABOVE
———
Norma Shearer proudly displays her Best Actress Oscar awarded in 1930 for her role in *The Divorcee*.

RIGHT
———
Shearer, the Canadian-American actress, poses for a captivating portrait, showcasing her iconic smile and elegant style.

FASHION FEATURES

THE DIVORCEE (1930)
MARIE ANTOINETTE (1938)
THE WOMEN (1939)

The Shearer Look

Polished and regal, Shearer favored rich fabrics, dramatic gowns, and structured silhouettes that matched her dignified screen image.

- Sculpted waves
- Embellished evening wear
- High collars and sweeping skirts
- Bold lips and refined poise

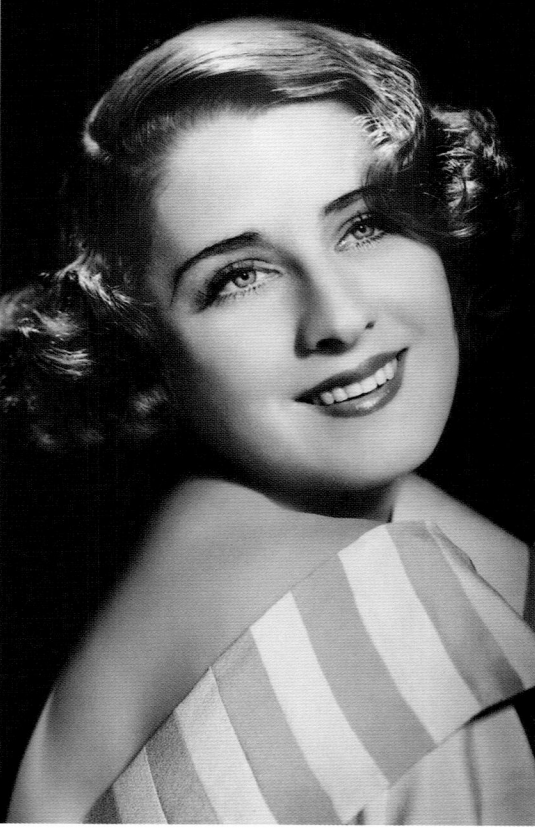

MAE WEST

The West Look

Her lavish costumes made the most of her exaggerated curves, while corseted gowns, feathered hats, and sparkling jewels enhanced her commanding presence on the stage. Her fashion choices further elevated her five-foot frame with platform heels hidden beneath the sweeping hems.

• Form-fitting gowns
• Blonde curls piled high
• Dramatic boas and furs
• Heavy-lidded eyes and red lips

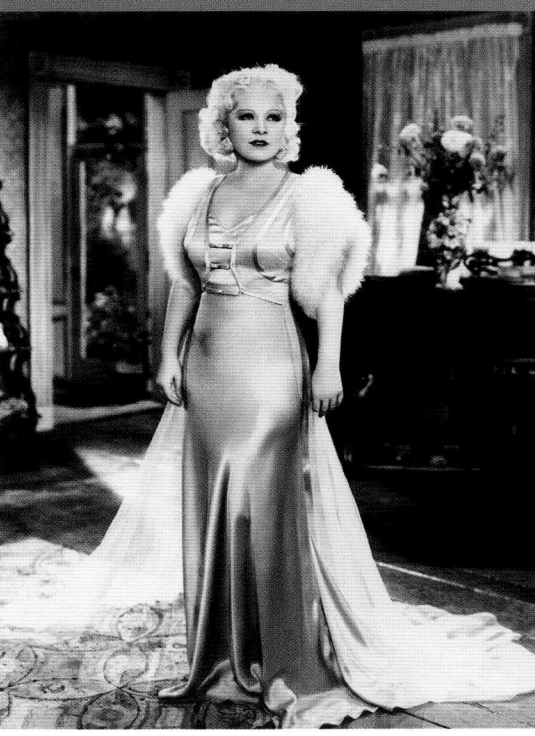

Mae West (1893–1980), born in Brooklyn, New York, began performing in vaudeville as a teenager and soon made her mark on Broadway as both a performer and playwright. Her 1926 play *Sex*, which she wrote, produced, and starred in, led to a jail sentence for "corrupting the morals of youth"—an incident that only added to her fame.

West had a unique ability to mix humor with innuendo, and her sharp, self-aware dialogue became her trademark. Bold, brassy, and unapologetically provocative, Mae West became one of early Hollywood's most iconic figures, celebrated for her wit, boundless confidence, and extraordinary charm.

She transitioned to Hollywood in her late thirties, an age when many actresses struggled for roles, and immediately made a splash with films like *She Done Him Wrong* (1933) and *I'm No Angel* (1933), both of which helped save Paramount Pictures from financial ruin during the Great Depression.

Known for her hourglass figure, sultry walk, and razor-sharp one-liners, West redefined the image of female sexuality on screen.

More than a movie star, Mae West was a cultural force who used humor and style to challenge norms around gender, age, and power—on her terms. Defying Hollywood's expectations, she became a star in her late thirties and retained control over her image. Even under censorship, her wit and double entendres endured, cementing her as a trailblazer who redefined female independence and sexuality on screen.

Cultivate your curves—they may be dangerous but they won't be avoided.

MAE WEST

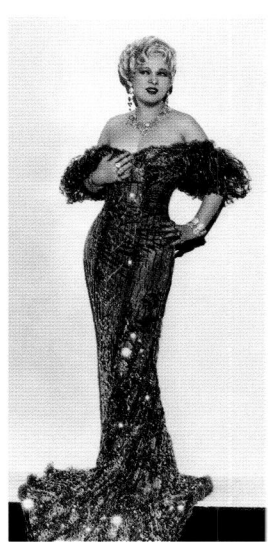

ABOVE
———
West, seen here in a dazzling gown, revolutionized Hollywood with her sharp wit, seductive confidence, and unapologetic sexuality—becoming a trailblazer for female screenwriters and a censorship-era icon.

LEFT
———
West, known for her sultry wit and bold style, wrote many of her own films and famously defied censors with double entendres and daring screen presence.

LEADING MEN
SUAVE, STALWART, OR SINISTER

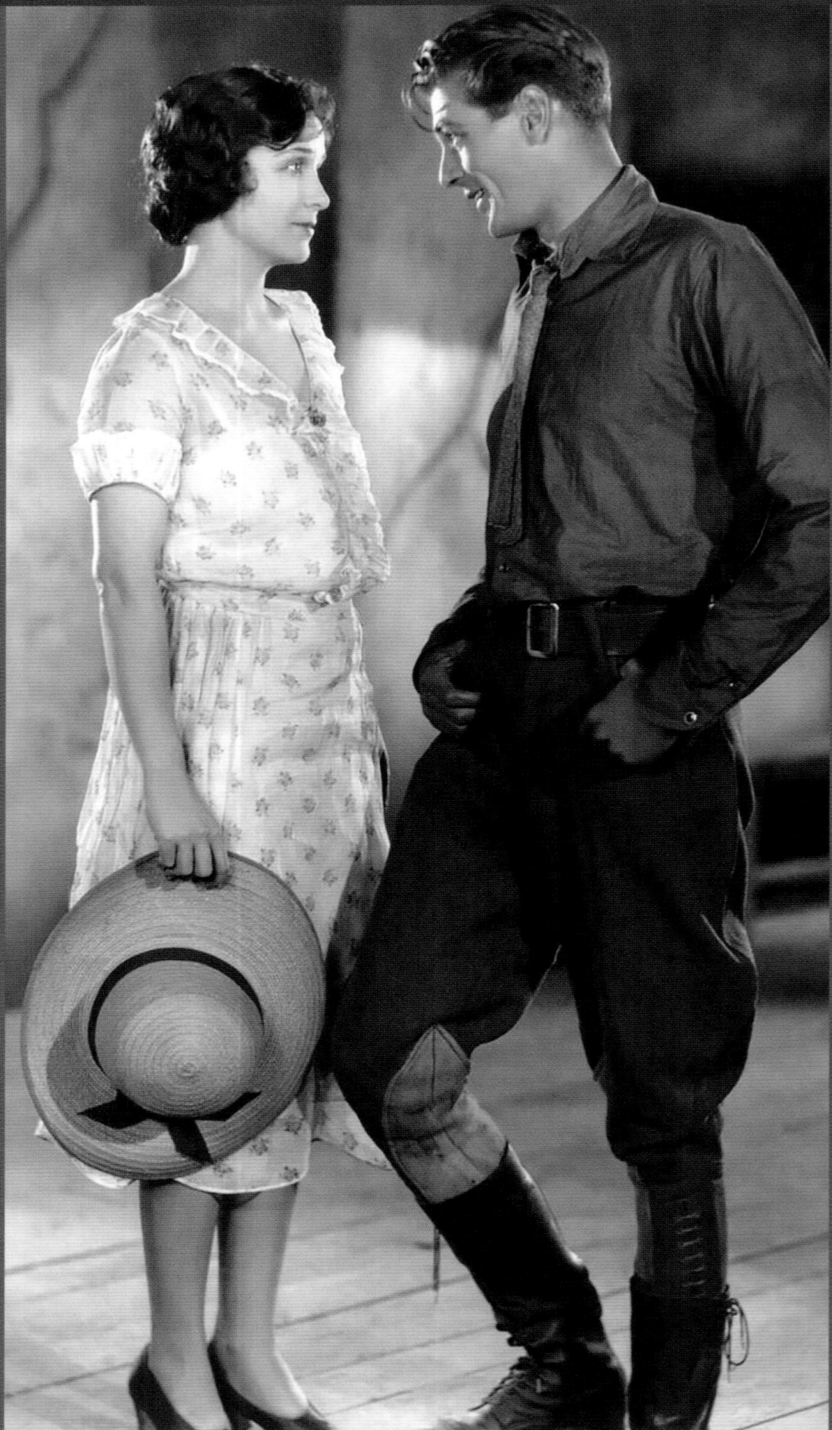

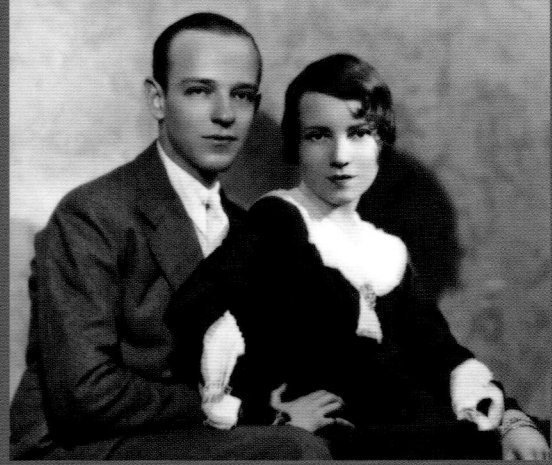

The 1930s marked a pivotal decade in cinema, with the advent of sound reshaping the silver screen and defining new masculine archetypes. As studios churned out a steady stream of genre films, male leads emerged as either smooth operators, righteous crusaders, or brooding rebels. This era saw the rise of clearly defined cinematic styles—from the charm of urbane comedies to the grit of crime dramas and the rhythmic dazzle of musicals.

Suave Charmers

Stars such as Cary Grant, William Powell, Robert Montgomery, and Melvyn Douglas headlined screwball comedies, trading sharp banter with powerhouse actresses like Rosalind Russell, Claudette Colbert, and Irene Dunne. Films such as *The Awful Truth*, *Libeled Lady*, *Midnight*, and *Ninotchka* reflected the sophistication and playfulness of Depression-era escapism. These actors were typically outfitted in tuxedos, crisp three-piece suits, and stylish sportswear, epitomizing elegance even in comic chaos.

Everyman Heroes

As economic hardship deepened, moviegoers gravitated toward principled protagonists. Spencer Tracy, Henry Fonda, and Gary Cooper embodied moral integrity in films like *Boys Town*, *Young Mr. Lincoln*, and *Mr. Deeds Goes to Town*. Their wardrobe choices were intentionally plain—worn suits, working-class jackets, and humble hats—to reflect their outsider status or homespun ideals. These "good men" often stood alone against corruption—their understated clothing emphasizing character over class.

Menacing Mavericks

Meanwhile, gangster films offered audiences a more dangerous allure. Edward G. Robinson, Humphrey Bogart, and James Cagney dominated this genre, portraying ruthless figures in titles such as *Little Caesar*, *The Public Enemy*, and *Angels with Dirty Faces*. Their costumes—double-breasted suits, wide lapels, fedoras, and flashy ties—set trends that extended beyond the screen. The "gangster chic" look became synonymous with power and defiance.

Frontier Legends

The Western, long a staple of American cinema, flourished in the late 30s. John Wayne

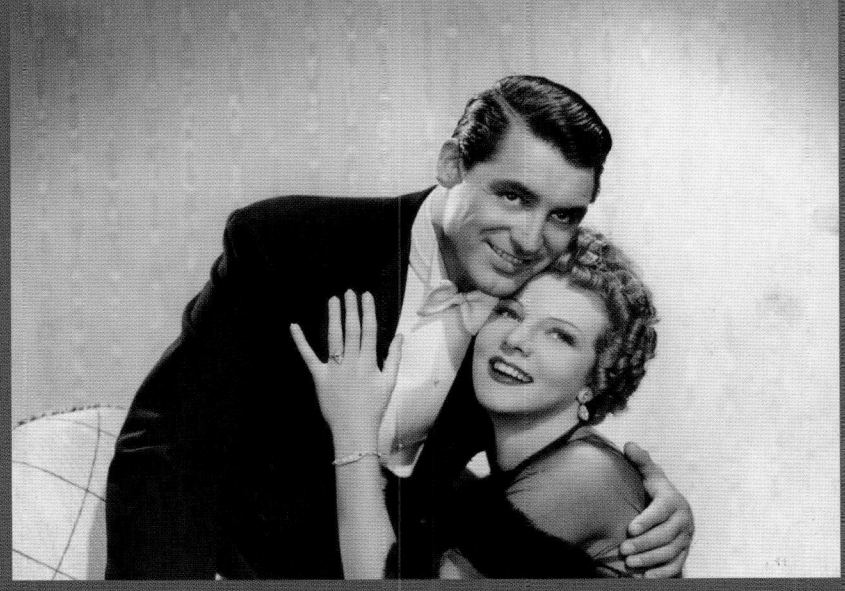

gained national recognition with *Stagecoach*, while Joel McCrea and Randolph Scott played laconic cowboys in films like *Wells Fargo* and *When the Daltons Ride*. Their rugged attire—denim, flannel, leather, and wide-brimmed hats—helped shape enduring symbols of American masculinity.

Entertainers in Motion

Musicals captivated Depression-era audiences with escapist glamor and rhythmic spectacle. Fred Astaire redefined screen sophistication in films like *Top Hat* and *Swing Time*, while Gene Raymond, Dick Powell, and Nelson Eddy showcased their vocal and dancing chops in everything from jazzy revues to lavish operettas. Vaudeville veterans like Eddie Cantor and dynamic performers like Paul Robeson brought a rich variety to the genre. Costumes ranged from tap shoes and tails to period uniforms and minstrel garb—each enhancing the magic of music on film.

ABOVE

Cary Grant, known for his effortless charm and debonair screen presence, became a Hollywood icon starring in classics like *Bringing Up Baby* and *North by Northwest*.

FAR LEFT

Gary Cooper in a still from the 1928 silent film "Doomsday." He gained early fame in silent Westerns before his successful transition to "talkies."

FAR TOP LEFT

Fred Astaire, pictured here with sister Adele, revolutionized film musicals with his graceful choreography, timeless elegance, and groundbreaking dance routines that redefined Hollywood's Golden Age of song and dance.

STYLE SIGNIFIERS

- Herringbone or stippled suit fabrics
- Glen and other plaids
- London cut or London drape suits
- Windsor or Kent double-breasted suit
- "Palm Beach" suit (made of seersucker, silk, or linen)
- Suntans
- Blazers
- Fedoras

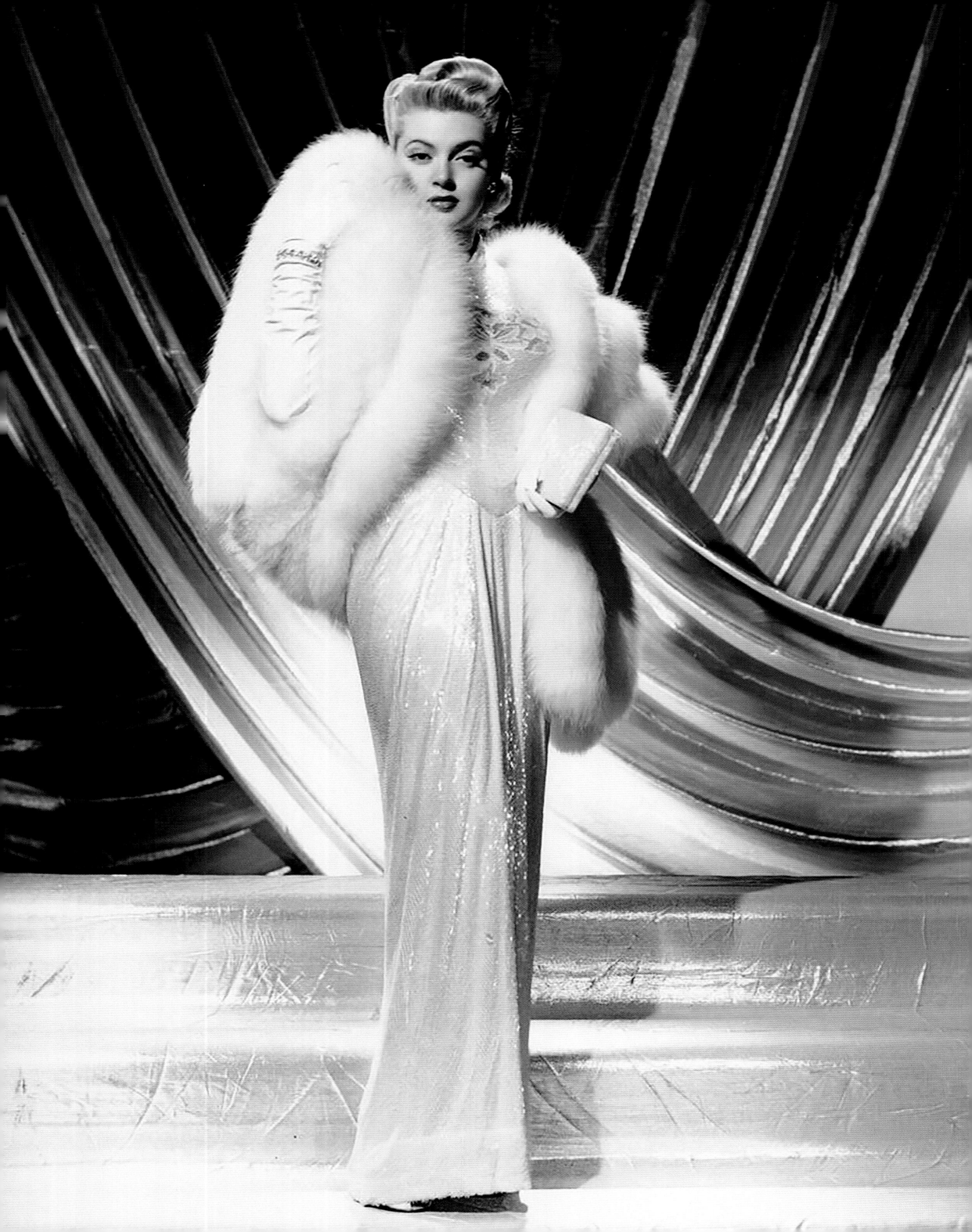

NINETEEN FORTIES

The 1940s were a defining decade for Hollywood fashion, shaped by global conflict, patriotic spirit, and postwar reinvention. As World War II reshaped life across the world, it also transformed what appeared on screen. With fabric rationing, wartime shortages, and many designers and actors joining the war effort, practicality and restraint replaced the extravagant glamor of the previous decade. Sharp-shouldered suits, tailored silhouettes, and military-inspired details became common, both in costume and in daily wear.

Despite these limitations, Hollywood remained a source of inspiration and fantasy. Costume designers such as Edith Head and Irene adapted brilliantly, creating memorable looks that balanced realism with allure. Onscreen, women were strong, resourceful, and fashionable even in adversity—reflected in the wardrobes of stars such as Bette Davis, Barbara Stanwyck, and Lauren Bacall. Films of the era championed working women, patriotic heroines, and noir femme fatales, each with a distinct visual identity.

As the war ended, fashion softened. Full skirts, romantic gowns, and Technicolor musicals brought glamor back into the spotlight. The 1940s proved that style could endure—and evolve—even in the face of global upheaval.

KATHARINE HEPBURN

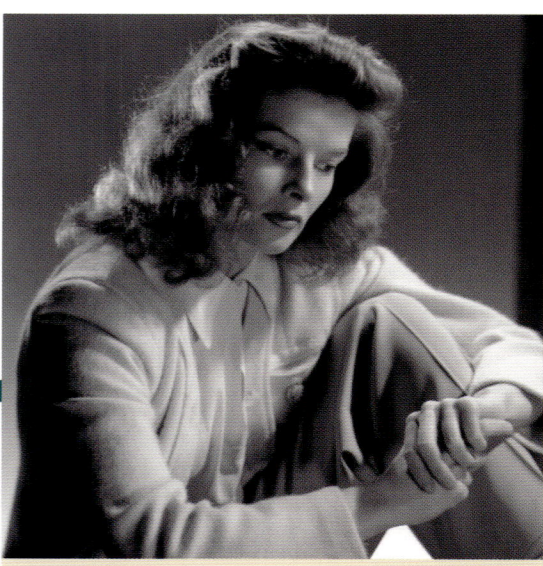

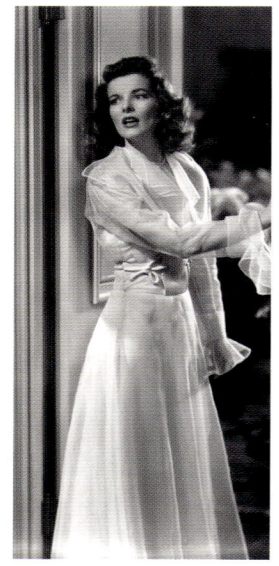

A fearless individualist, Katharine Hepburn broke every rule of Hollywood femininity and became one of its most enduring icons.

Katharine Hepburn (1907–2003) was known for her fiercely independent spirit, quick wit, and unwavering sense of self, which together contributed to a remarkable career spanning more than sixty years. Born in Hartford, Connecticut, she was raised by forward-thinking parents who instilled in her a deep respect for individuality, education, and athleticism. These early influences helped shape the strong, no-nonsense women she later portrayed on screen. After graduating from Bryn Mawr College, Hepburn pursued theater in New York, and her commanding stage presence soon caught the attention of Hollywood.

She debuted in *A Bill of Divorcement* (1932), and just a year later, won her first Academy Award for *Morning Glory* (1933). Yet, Hepburn's refusal to conform to Hollywood norms—eschewing makeup, wearing trousers, and avoiding the press—clashed with studio expectations. By the late 1930s, she was labeled "box office poison," a stigma that might have ended a lesser career.

Instead, she orchestrated her comeback by securing the film rights to *The Philadelphia Story* (1940), a play written specifically for her. The film's success reestablished her star status and showcased her blend of intelligence, humor, and emotional complexity. She would go on to win three more Oscars for *Guess Who's Coming to Dinner* (1967), *The Lion in Winter* (1968), and *On Golden Pond* (1981)—a record that still stands.

Her long-standing partnership with Spencer Tracy, both personal and professional, became legendary, producing nine beloved films. Even in her later years, Hepburn challenged traditional ideas about aging, continuing to portray dynamic, independent women into her eighties. She never shied away

ABOVE

In private life, Hepburn preferred a more practical look, but her willowy frame was the perfect vehicle for costume designers to show off their expertise. Here she looks lovely in a chiffon confection designed by Adrian for *Philadelphia Story* (1940).

TOP RIGHT

Known for her rebellious style, Katharine Hepburn famously refused to wear skirts off-camera, helping normalize trousers for women in Hollywood and beyond.

FULL PAGE

A 1949 publicity shot shows Hepburn in an impeccably tailored suit with a high contrast between the skirt and jacket.

The Hepburn Look

Hepburn's style was modern, minimalist, and unapologetically androgynous, setting her apart from the glamor-driven image of most leading ladies of her time. She favored high-waisted slacks, button-down shirts, blazers, and relaxed tailoring that allowed ease of movement and projected quiet confidence. Offscreen, she rejected Hollywood opulence in favor of clean lines and functionality, creating a fashion legacy that celebrated individuality, practicality, and timeless sophistication over fleeting trends.

- Wide-legged trousers
- Button-up blouses
- Structured jackets
- Natural makeup and swept-back hair

from complex roles and maintained complete control over her public image.

In recognition of her unmatched contributions, she received the Kennedy Center Honors in 1990 and was named the greatest female star in Hollywood history by the American Film Institute in 1999. Hepburn's influence stretched far beyond performance. She redefined what a Hollywood leading lady could be—not dependent on beauty or conformity, but rooted in strength, intelligence, and authenticity. Her legacy is not just in the roles she played, but in the unapologetic way she lived and worked on her terms.

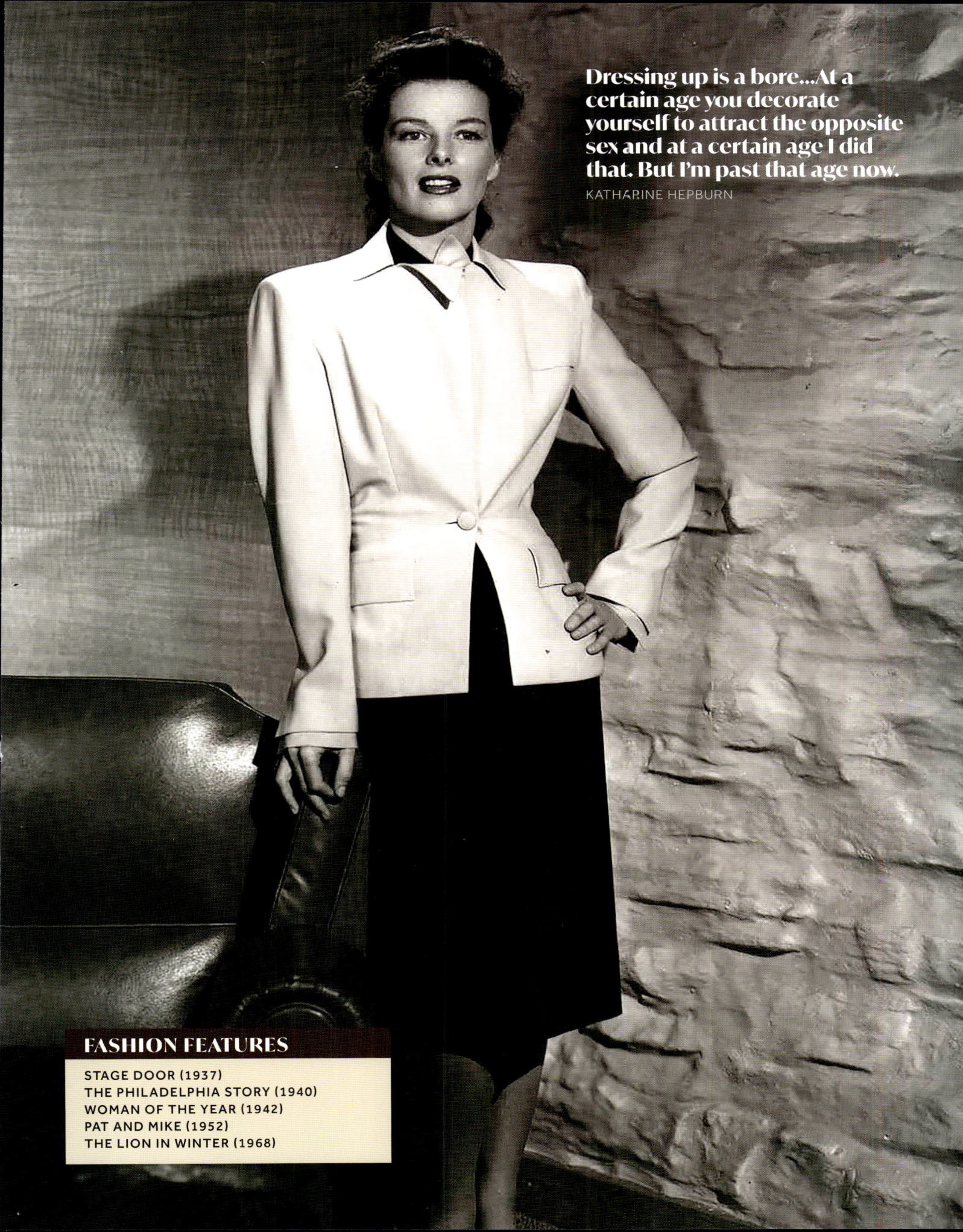

Dressing up is a bore...At a certain age you decorate yourself to attract the opposite sex and at a certain age I did that. But I'm past that age now.

KATHARINE HEPBURN

FASHION FEATURES

STAGE DOOR (1937)
THE PHILADELPHIA STORY (1940)
WOMAN OF THE YEAR (1942)
PAT AND MIKE (1952)
THE LION IN WINTER (1968)

JUNE ALLYSON

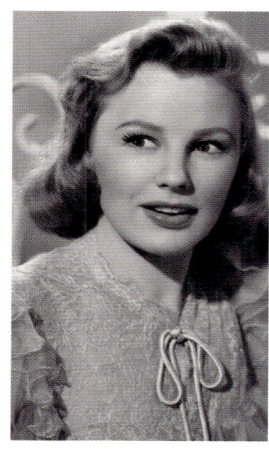

Known for her wholesome charm and raspy voice, June Allyson (1917–2006) became one of the most beloved stars of Hollywood's postwar era. Often cast as the optimistic, resilient woman-next-door, she brought warmth and energy to a wide range of musicals, comedies, and dramas. Born Eleanor Geisman in the Bronx, New York, Allyson faced serious hardship early in life. Her father abandoned the family, and after a childhood accident left her temporarily paralyzed, she spent years in a steel brace before learning to walk again.

Despite her difficult beginnings, Allyson rarely spoke of her past, preferring to let her screen image reflect cheerful perseverance. Inspired by Ginger Rogers, she studied dance and began performing in nightclubs and on Broadway, eventually landing chorus roles. Her big break came when she replaced Betty Hutton in *Panama Hattie* and caught the attention of Broadway director George Abbott. He cast her in *Best Foot Forward*, which led to the MGM film adaptation and a long-term studio contract.

Allyson became a musical favorite in hits such as *Two Girls and a Sailor* (costumes by Irene), *Good News* (gowns by Helen Rose), and a notable role in *Little Women* (1949). She frequently starred opposite Van Johnson and formed a memorable screen partnership with James Stewart in *The Stratton Story* (1949), *The Glenn Miller Story* (1954), and *Strategic Air Command* (1955).

Married to actor and producer Dick Powell from 1945 until he died in 1963, Allyson stepped back from film afterward, later making only select appearances on television and in guest roles.

ABOVE

In *Two Girls and a Sailor* (1944), the costume designer Irene dressed Allyson in lots of soft and sheer fabrics, trimmed with lace and ribbons.

RIGHT

In 1947's collegiate musical *Good News*, Allyson's costumes were a 1940s' take on fashion of the 1920s. Far from authentic, they nonetheless worked well for Allyson's girl-next-door film persona.

FASHION FEATURES

BEST FOOT FORWARD (1943)
TWO GIRLS AND A SAILOR (1944)
GOOD NEWS (1947)
THE STRATTON STORY (1949)
THE GLEN MILLER STORY (1954)

The Allyson Look

June Allyson's wardrobe was crafted to emphasize her girl-next-door appeal. Studios often dressed her in soft pastels, delicate fabrics, and feminine details such as bows and ruffles, highlighting her youthful innocence over high fashion sophistication.

- Crisp white blouses with Peter Pan collars
- Light, full-skirted gowns with a prom-dress feel
- Soft, curly bangs framing her face

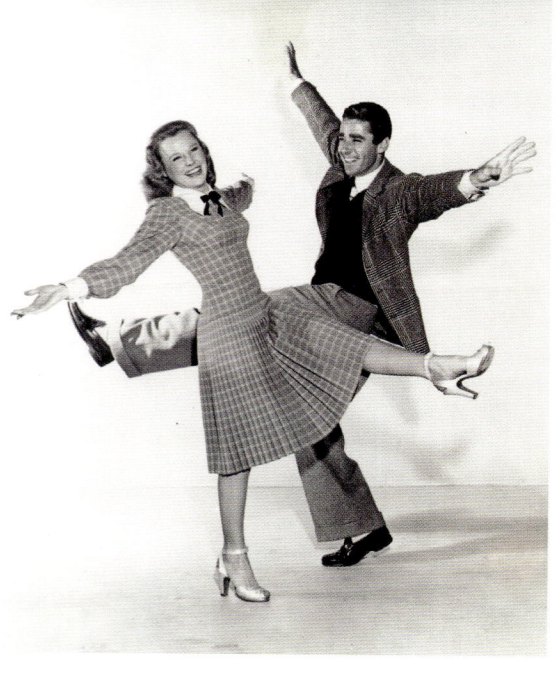

LAUREN BACALL

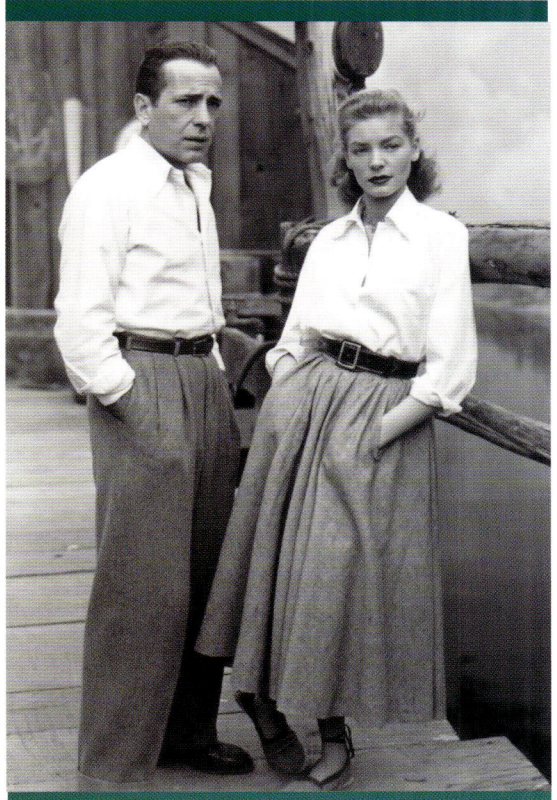

The Bacall Look

With a fashion sense that transcended decades—whether on screen or in editorial photos—Bacall's style blended classic tailoring with relaxed elegance, always polished yet effortlessly cool.

• Honey-blonde pageboy hairstyle
• Sleek, tailored tweed suits
• Flowy ethnic skirts with blouses and espadrilles

FASHION FEATURES

TO HAVE AND HAVE NOT (1944)
THE BIG SLEEP (1946)
KEY LARGO (1948)
DESIGNING WOMAN (1957)

Bogart's husky-voiced "Baby" blended sharp acting talent with the polished elegance of a seasoned fashion model.

Lauren Bacall (1924–2014), known for her cool confidence and effortless glamor, captivated audiences with her smoky voice, piercing gaze, and commanding presence, becoming a defining figure of Hollywood's Golden Age. Born Betty Joan Perske in New York City, she began as a fashion model, gracing the cover of *Harper's Bazaar* in 1943. This exposure led to a screen test arranged by director Howard Hawks, who transformed her into "Lauren Bacall" and cast her opposite Humphrey Bogart in *To Have and Have Not* (1944). Their on-screen chemistry ignited a real-life romance, culminating in marriage in 1945.

Bacall's early film roles, including *The Big Sleep* (1946), *Dark Passage* (1947), and *Key Largo* (1948), solidified her status as a film noir icon. She later showcased her versatility in comedies such as *How to Marry a Millionaire* (1953) and *Designing Woman* (1957). Following Bogart's death in 1957, Bacall continued to evolve, earning two Tony Awards for her performances in the musicals *Applause* (1970) and *Woman of the Year* (1981).

In her later years, Bacall remained active in film and television, earning an Academy Award nomination and a Golden Globe win for *The Mirror Has Two Faces* (1996). She also lent her distinctive voice to the animated film *Howl's Moving Castle* (2004). Beyond her screen achievements, Bacall was known for her political activism and candid memoirs, including *By Myself* (1978). She passed away in 2014 at the age of 89, and is remembered for her strength, intelligence, and unforgettable style.

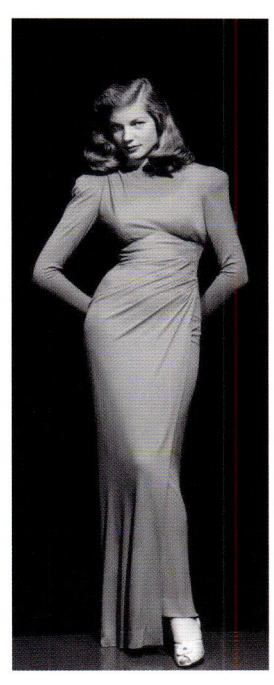

ABOVE

Lithe and leggy, Lauren Bacall embodies 1940s Hollywood allure wearing a slinky knit gown in this moody 1944 publicity shot.

LEFT

With outfits echoing the other's in a publicity shot for *Key Largo* (1948), Bogie and Bacall are the epitome of noir sangfroid. The full skirt—a key style note of the postwar 40s—adds a feminine touch, along with Bacall's iconic espadrilles

INGRID BERGMAN

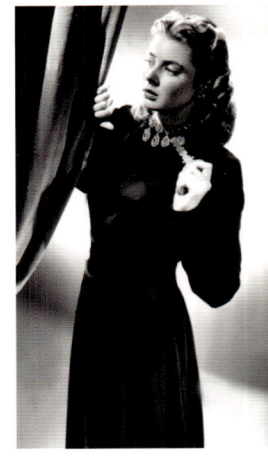

Ingrid Bergman's path to Hollywood stardom began not with a signature line but with performances that left a lasting impact.

Her portrayal of Ilsa Lund in *Casablanca* (1942) remains one of cinema's most iconic, securing her legacy as a screen legend. Following the success of Garbo and Dietrich, American studios sought European actresses with elegance and depth—Bergman, brought to the United States in 1939 by producer David O. Selznick, was a perfect match. She debuted in *Intermezzo* (costumes by Travis Banton and Irene), launching a career defined by grace and emotional intelligence.

Bergman won her first Academy Award for *Gaslight* (1944) and starred in hits such as *The Bells of St. Mary's* (1945) and *For Whom the Bell Tolls* (1943). Her work with Alfred Hitchcock in *Spellbound* (1945) and *Notorious* (1946) showcased her versatility. In *Casablanca*, opposite Humphrey Bogart and dressed by Orry-Kelly, she delivered one of her most moving performances. She later won Oscars for *Anastasia* (1956) and *Murder on the Orient Express* (1974), proving her brilliance endured for decades.

The Bergman Look
Bergman's style was quiet and refined—soft, simple, and effortlessly classic. Her natural beauty and unadorned looks made her both relatable and timeless.
- Soft waves and natural brows
- Tailored suits and modest gowns
- Minimal makeup with full lips
- Gloves and classic pumps

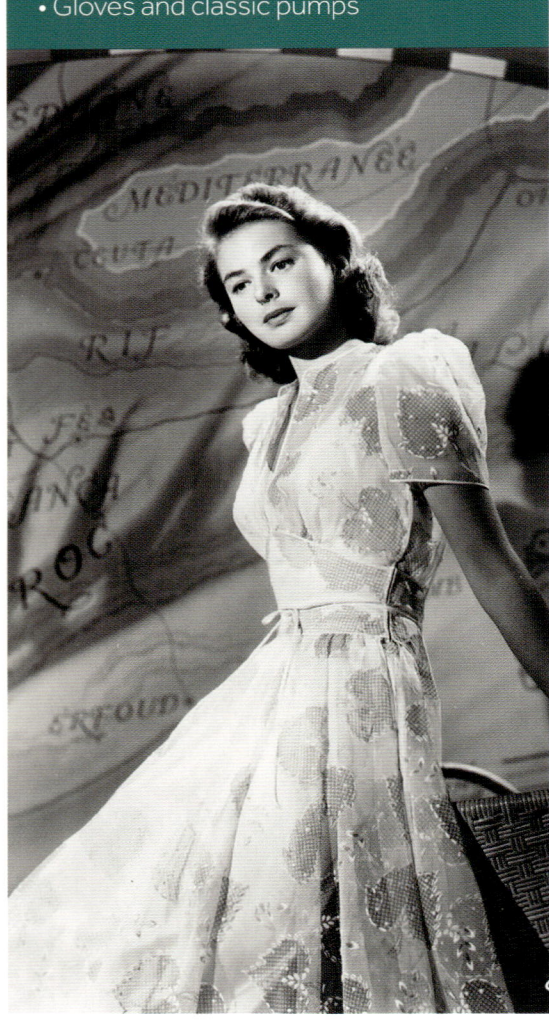

FASHION FEATURES

CASABLANCA (1942)
GASLIGHT (1944)
ANASTASIA (1956)
SPELLBOUND (1945)
NOTORIOUS (1946)

Her clothes must have simplicity, skillful design and practically no ornamentation. This is elegance in the subtlest sense.

EDITH HEAD

ABOVE

Bergman exudes understated elegance in a simple dark dress set off with a statement necklace in Alfred Hitchcock's 1946 noir spy film *Notorious*, also starring Cary Grant and Claude Rains.

RIGHT

Bergman, luminous in organza and shadow, leans pensively before a map of Morocco in a studio still from *Casablanca* (1942), a timeless icon of wartime longing.

IRENE DUNNE

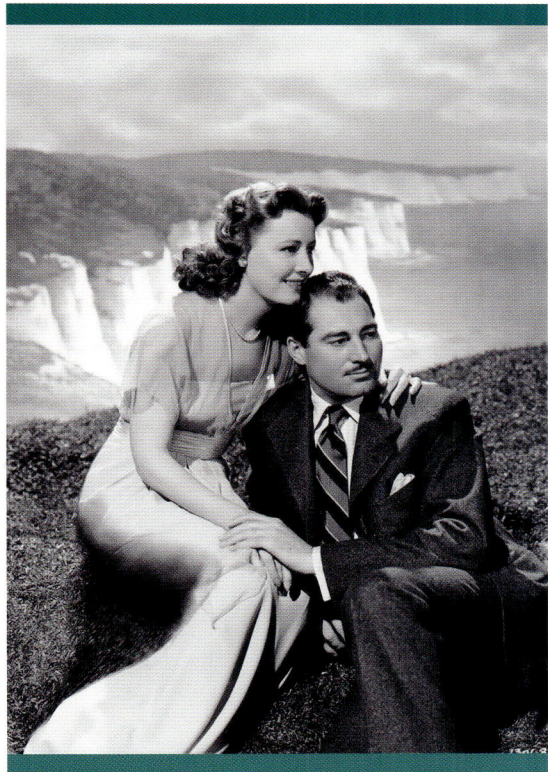

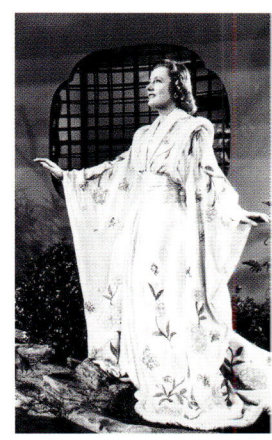

Poised, versatile, and effortlessly charming, Irene Dunne (1898–1990) was one of Hollywood's most respected and graceful leading ladies. Known for her warmth and intelligence, she moved seamlessly between comedy, drama, and musical films—earning five Academy Award nominations across a career that spanned over two decades.

Born in Louisville, Kentucky, Dunne trained as a singer and initially aspired to a career in opera. She made her Broadway debut in the 1920s before transitioning to film in the early 1930s. Her breakthrough came with *Cimarron* (1931), which earned her first Oscar nomination. She soon established herself as a romantic lead and comedian in classics such as *Theodora Goes Wild* (1936) and *The Awful Truth* (1937) opposite Cary Grant, where her impeccable comic timing made her a standout of the screwball era.

Dunne also shined in dramatic roles, most notably in *Love Affair* (1939) and *I Remember Mama* (1948). Her characters were often dignified, emotionally rich, and deeply relatable, which helped her maintain a loyal fan base throughout her career.

Offscreen, Dunne was known for her elegance, modesty, and charitable work. She largely retired from acting in the 1950s but remained active in public life. Irene Dunne's legacy endures as a symbol of grace, talent, and timeless screen appeal.

The Dunne Look

Timeless and refined, Dunne favored soft tailoring, bias-cut gowns, and polished silhouettes that highlighted her refinement on and off screen.

- Side-parted waves
- Flowing gowns with defined waists
- Feminine blouses
- Delicate accessories
- Graceful, composed presence

FASHION FEATURES

ROBERTA (1935)
THE AWFUL TRUTH (1937)
LOVE AFFAIR (1939)
WHEN TOMORROW COMES (1939)
ANNA AND THE KING OF SIAM (1946)

ABOVE

In a publicity still, Dunne shows off a flowing Japanese-inspired costume for *Penny Serenade*, a 1941 melodrama that saw her play opposite Cary Grant.

LEFT

Irene Dunne and Alan Marshal share a tender moment, captured against the iconic Cliffs of Dover, from the 1944 wartime romance *The White Cliffs of Dover*.

JOAN CRAWFORD

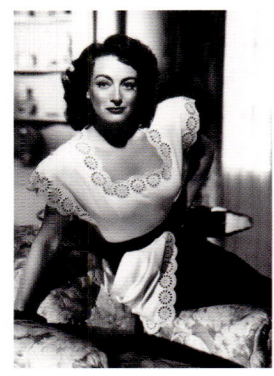

Crawford's fierce ambition and unwavering determination propelled her from a carefree dancing flapper to Hollywood's reigning queen.

Joan Crawford, born Lucille Fay LeSueur on March 23, 1904 (though some sources cite 1905), in San Antonio, Texas, emerged from a challenging upbringing to become one of Hollywood's most enduring and complex stars. Her early years were marked by instability, with her parents separating before her birth and subsequent hardships during her education. Despite these obstacles, Crawford's determination led her to pursue a career in entertainment, initially dancing in nightclubs under the name Billie Cassin.

By 1924, Crawford was performing in Broadway musicals, and a year later, she transitioned to film with MGM. Her breakthrough came with the 1928 film *Our Dancing Daughters*, where she captivated audiences as a vivacious Jazz Age flapper. This role solidified her status as a symbol of modern femininity and propelled her to stardom.

Throughout the 1930s, Crawford became known for portraying hardworking young women who found romance and success, resonating with Depression-era audiences. Her performances in films such as *Grand Hotel* (1932) and *Dancing Lady* (1933) showcased her versatility and screen presence; however, by the late 1930s, her popularity waned, and she was labeled "box office poison" in a 1938 advertisement by the Independent Theatre Owners Association.

Crawford's career experienced a resurgence after she left MGM and signed with Warner Bros. Her portrayal of the titular character in *Mildred Pierce* (1945) earned her an Academy Award for Best Actress. This role, depicting a woman who rises from waitress to successful business owner, showcased Crawford's depth and range

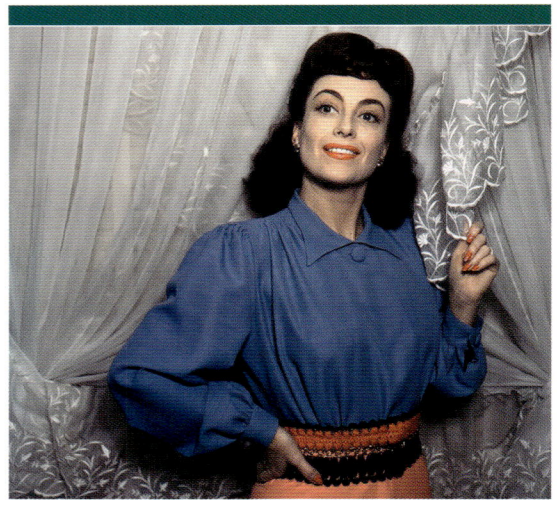

ABOVE

With her dark curls somewhat softened and wearing a delicate cutwork-embroidered blouse, Crawford conveys a more vulnerable aspect for her portrayal of the tragic lead in *Humoresque* (1946).

ABOVE RIGHT

Exemplifying the 1940s signature trends of wide shoulders and pompadour hair, Crawford also shows that although Hollywood in that decade was mostly black and white, the clothing color palettes were actually vibrant

FULL PAGE

In a publicity still for 1940's *Susan and God*, Crawford dons a flowing gown with intricate sleeve details that echo the Art Deco–inspired décor. Her softer looks of the 1920s and 30s would soon give way to the more structured styles of her 1940s heyday.

as an actress. She continued to deliver compelling performances in films such as *Humoresque* (1946), *Possessed* (1947), and *Sudden Fear* (1952), earning additional Academy Award nominations.

In the later stages of her career, Crawford took on roles that reflected her evolving screen persona. Her performance in the psychological thriller *What Ever Happened to Baby Jane?* (1962), alongside Bette Davis, was both a critical and commercial success, revitalizing her career once more. She continued to act in films and television until her retirement in the early 1970s.

Beyond her acting career, Crawford was known for her involvement in various charitable causes and her role as a director of the Pepsi-Cola Company, following the death of her fourth husband, Alfred Steele. Her personal life, however, became the subject of controversy after the publication of her adopted daughter Christina Crawford's best-selling memoir, *Mommie Dearest* (1978), which portrayed her as an abusive mother.

She passed away on May 10, 1977, in New York City. Despite the controversies surrounding her personal life, her contributions to cinema remain significant. Her performances continue to be studied and celebrated for their intensity and complexity, solidifying her place in the annals of Hollywood history.

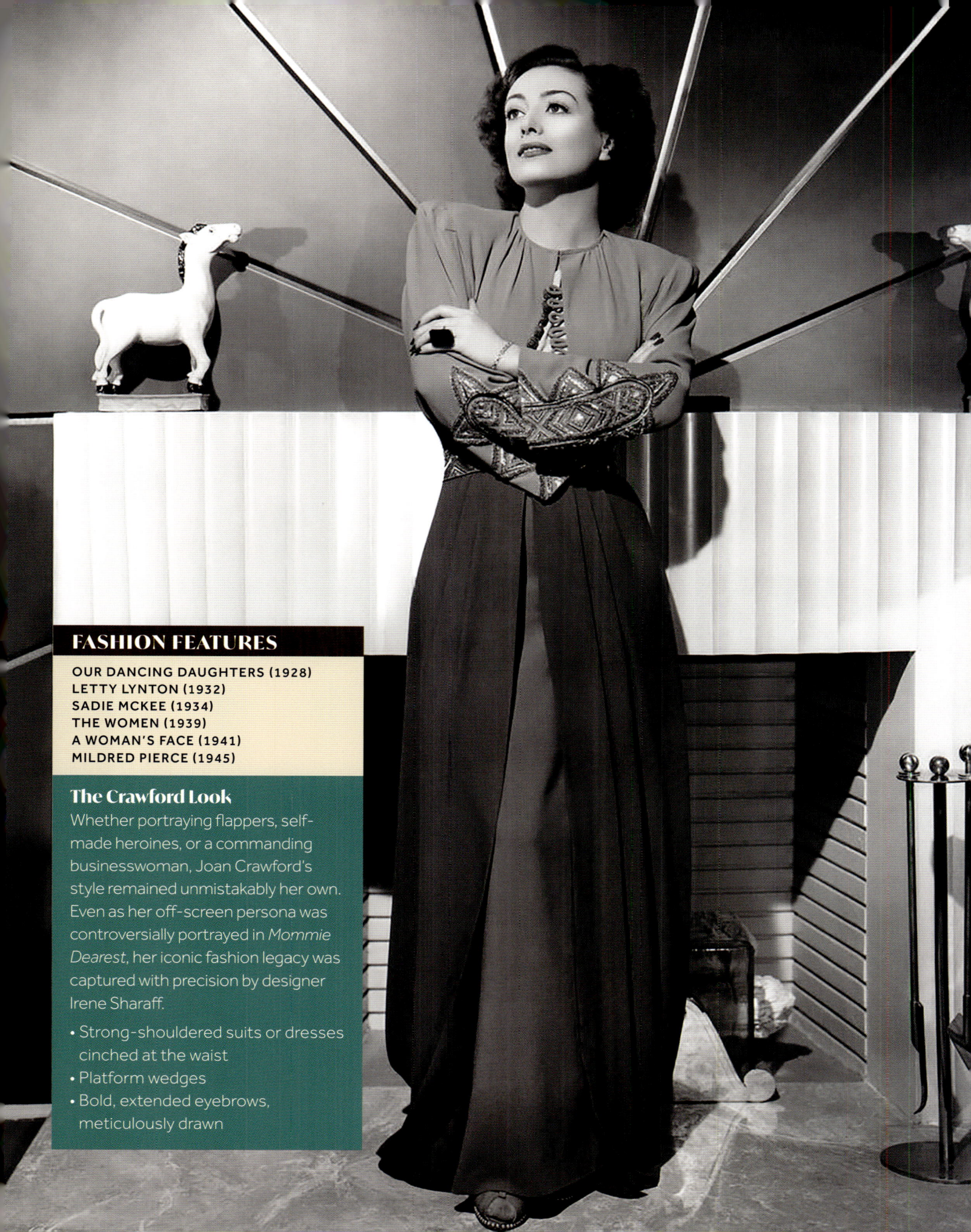

FASHION FEATURES

OUR DANCING DAUGHTERS (1928)
LETTY LYNTON (1932)
SADIE MCKEE (1934)
THE WOMEN (1939)
A WOMAN'S FACE (1941)
MILDRED PIERCE (1945)

The Crawford Look

Whether portraying flappers, self-made heroines, or a commanding businesswoman, Joan Crawford's style remained unmistakably her own. Even as her off-screen persona was controversially portrayed in *Mommie Dearest*, her iconic fashion legacy was captured with precision by designer Irene Sharaff.

- Strong-shouldered suits or dresses cinched at the waist
- Platform wedges
- Bold, extended eyebrows, meticulously drawn

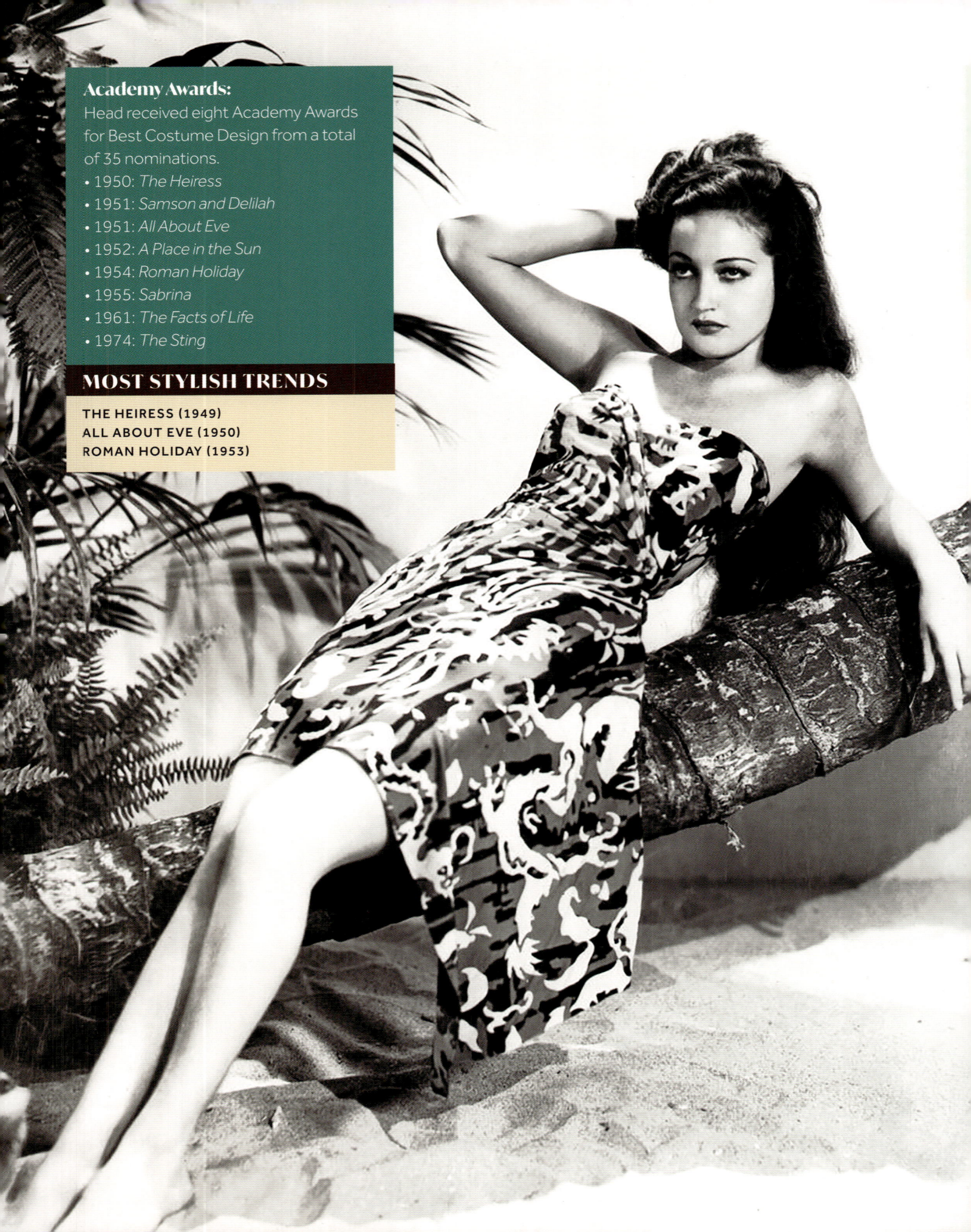

Academy Awards:
Head received eight Academy Awards for Best Costume Design from a total of 35 nominations.
- 1950: *The Heiress*
- 1951: *Samson and Delilah*
- 1951: *All About Eve*
- 1952: *A Place in the Sun*
- 1954: *Roman Holiday*
- 1955: *Sabrina*
- 1961: *The Facts of Life*
- 1974: *The Sting*

MOST STYLISH TRENDS

THE HEIRESS (1949)
ALL ABOUT EVE (1950)
ROMAN HOLIDAY (1953)

DESIGN SENSE
EDITH HEAD

In a field filled with extraordinary talent, Edith Head distinguished herself as the most celebrated costume designer in Hollywood history. With a career that spanned over 50 years, she won eight Academy Awards—more than any other woman in Oscar history—and was nominated 35 times. Her work defined the look of generations of film icons and helped elevate costume design from a background craft to a central storytelling tool in cinema.

Edith Claire Posener was born in San Bernardino, California, in 1897. She pursued higher education at the University of California, Berkeley, and Stanford University, where she studied letters and romance languages. Initially a schoolteacher, she entered the film industry in 1923 by securing a job as a sketch artist at Paramount Pictures. Although she lacked formal fashion training, she quickly rose through the ranks, demonstrating a keen eye for detail, a tireless work ethic, and an instinctive understanding of character through costume. By 1938, she had become Paramount's head designer, overseeing one of the largest costume departments in the industry and working with many of the era's most prominent stars.

Head believed the costume should serve the story first. She was known for collaborating closely with actors—especially actresses—helping them feel confident and authentic in their roles. Among her most memorable creations were Dorothy Lamour's sarong in *The Jungle Princess* (1936), Audrey Hepburn's wardrobe in *Roman Holiday* (1953), and the sleek, stylish looks of *Sabrina* (1954). Her long-standing collaboration with Alfred Hitchcock further highlighted her range, as seen in the suspenseful elegance of *Notorious* (1946), *Rear Window* (1954), and *To Catch a Thief* (1955).

In 1967, after more than four decades at Paramount, Head moved to Universal Pictures, where she continued to work prolifically on both film and television productions. She even designed official women's uniforms for the U.S. Coast Guard, a contribution that earned her the Meritorious Public Service Award. Her influence also reached beyond the studio lot through her books *The Dress Doctor* (1959) and *How to Dress for Success* (1967), which shared her insights into fashion, dressing for body type, and the psychological impact of clothing.

She passed away on October 24, 1981, in Hollywood. Her designs are still studied, replicated, and revered. Known for her signature round glasses, pragmatic approach, and trademark professionalism, Head set the gold standard in costume design. Her work continues to inspire new generations of designers, directors, and actors who understand that wardrobe can tell a story before a single word is spoken.

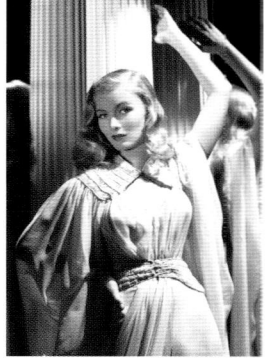

You can have anything you want in life if you dress for it.

EDITH HEAD

ABOVE

Bathed in shadow and silk, Veronica Lake poses in an Edith Head design. The dress evokes the mystery that defined Lake's roles in 1940s film noir classics.

LEFT

Posed outside a boutique window, a starlet in an Edith Head–designed peplum jacket and tilted hat captures the sharp elegance of 1940s Hollywood street fashion at its peak.

FULL PAGE

A publicity shot for *Road to Singapore* (1940) shows Dorothy Lamour lounging against a palm trunk costumed by Edith Head in a boldly patterned sarong. This was the first of Paramount's popular "Road to…" series starring Lamour with Bob Hope and Bing Crosby.

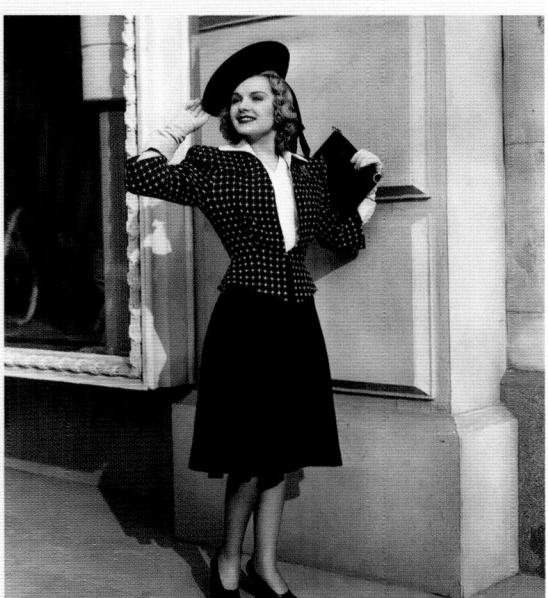

BETTE DAVIS

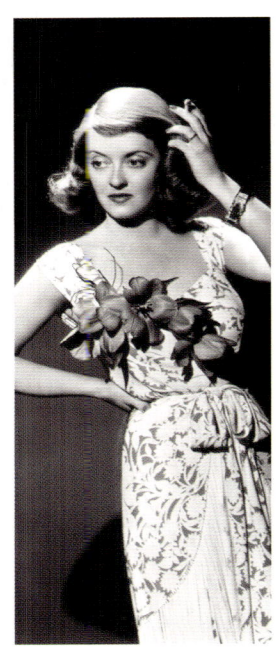

Bette Davis (1908–1989) was a groundbreaking American actress celebrated for her fierce performances, expressive eyes, and commanding presence on screen. Born Ruth Elizabeth Davis in Lowell, Massachusetts, she developed a passion for acting early in life. After studying drama in New York, she made her stage debut and quickly gained recognition for her talent. In 1930, she moved to Hollywood, where her career took flight.

Her breakthrough role came in *Of Human Bondage* (1934), where she played a troubled waitress in a performance so powerful that it earned her a rare write-in nomination for the Academy Award for Best Actress. Davis won her first Oscar for *Dangerous* (1935) and a second for *Jezebel* (1938), establishing herself as one of the era's top stars. Throughout the 1930s and 1940s, she delivered a string of acclaimed performances in *Dark Victory* (1939), *The Letter* (1940), *The Little Foxes* (1941), and *Now, Voyager* (1942), becoming known for playing fiercely independent and emotionally complex women.

In 1950, she starred in one of her most iconic roles as Margo Channing, the aging theater diva in *All About Eve*. The film was a critical triumph and earned Davis yet another Oscar nomination. Over the following decades, she continued to challenge expectations, notably in *What Ever Happened to Baby Jane?* (1962), where her chilling performance as a deranged former child star earned her a tenth Academy Award nomination.

Off-screen, Davis broke barriers as well. She became the first female president of the Academy of Motion Picture Arts and Sciences and co-founded the Hollywood Canteen during World War II, providing food and entertainment to Allied servicemen. Fearlessly outspoken and often combative with studio executives, she was unafraid to demand stronger roles for women—both for herself and others.

Her career spanned more than fifty years and included over 100 film, television, and stage appearances. Known for her sharp wit and unwavering dedication to her craft, Davis was a trailblazer who reshaped the image of the Hollywood leading lady. She never shied away from unflattering or difficult roles, proving that strength and vulnerability could coexist on screen.

Bette Davis died on October 6, 1989, in Neuilly-sur-Seine, France. She continues to inspire actors and audiences alike, marking her as one of cinema's most enduring and influential icons.

ABOVE

A publicity still for 1941's screwball comedy *The Bride Came C.O.D.* shows a softer side of Davis, who wears a floral-patterned gown festooned with a cascade of blossoms.

FULL PAGE

Bette Davis in *The Little Foxes* (1941), dressed in a sculpted black gown with a sheer shawl that echoes the film's tone of elegance and control. The look is sharply tailored and dramatically lit, reinforcing her character's cold authority and calculating charm. Every detail—from the beaded bodice to the swept-up hair—contributes to a portrait of power cloaked in refinement.

FASHION FEATURES

JEZEBEL (1938)
DARK VICTORY (1939)
THE LITTLE FOXES (1941)
NOW, VOYAGER (1942)
ALL ABOUT EVE (1950)

The Davis Look

According to designer Orry-Kelly, Bette Davis didn't adhere to a consistent fashion identity on screen—her characters always dictated her wardrobe choices. Whether she wore a fiery red gown in *Jezebel* or embraced Dior's New Look in *June Bride*, Davis brought authority and flair to every outfit.

- Sleek bobs, soft waves, or neat up-dos
- Structured fur jackets and coats
- Bold, brimmed hats with attitude

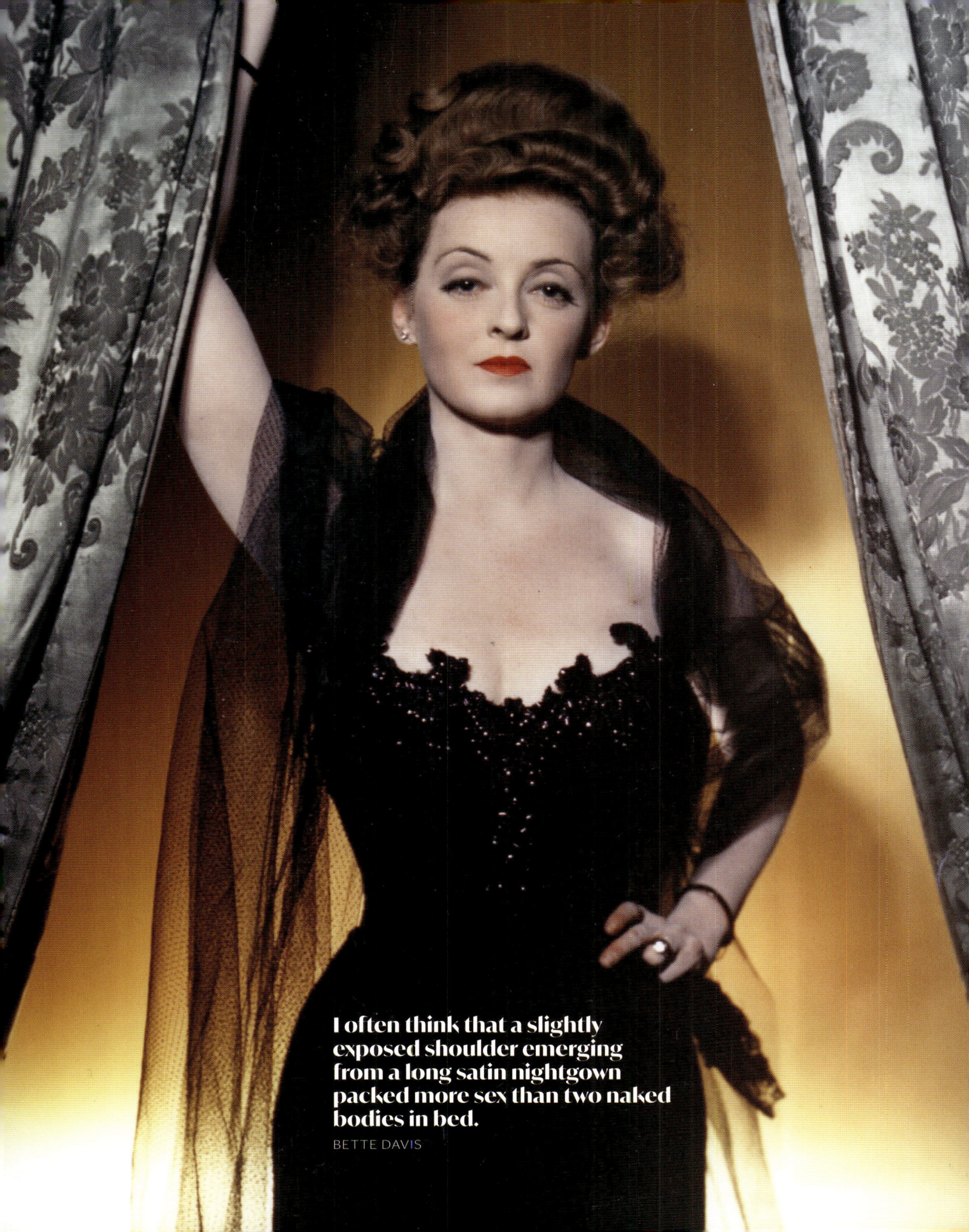

I often think that a slightly exposed shoulder emerging from a long satin nightgown packed more sex than two naked bodies in bed.

BETTE DAVIS

JUDY GARLAND

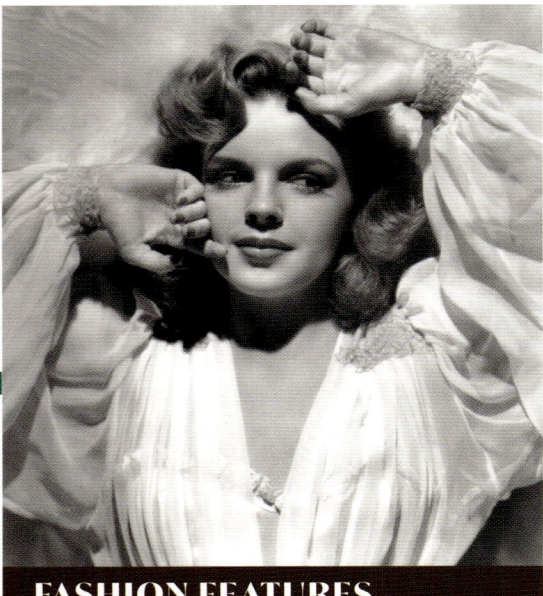

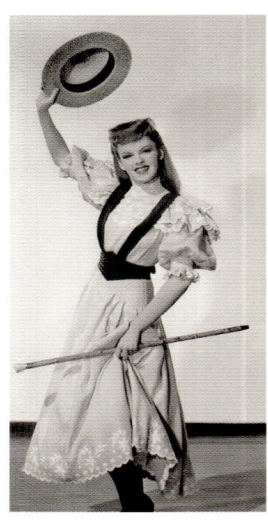

ABOVE

Judy and her castmates cycled through a series of stunning costumes in 1944's *Meet Me in St. Louis*. The clothing, designed by Irene Sharaff, does give off a true turn-of-the-last-century feel, but the hair and makeup is all 1940s glamor.

ABOVE RIGHT

The 1940s saw Judy transition from a winsome child star to a lovely young woman. In 1943's *Presenting Lily Mars*, her costumes reflect that growing maturity.

FULL PAGE

A vibrant period costume festooned with lace and set off with a wide-brimmed hat lends Judy a lively air in the 1948 Technicolor musical *The Pirate*. Costume designers of this period often relied more on the fashionable silhouettes of the day rather attempting historical accuracy.

Judy Garland (1922–1969) remains one of the most iconic and emotionally resonant performers in American entertainment history. Born Frances Ethel Gumm on June 10, 1922, in Grand Rapids, Minnesota, she was the youngest child of vaudeville performers Frank and Ethel Gumm. She first took the stage with her sisters as part of the family act, "The Gumm Sisters," making her debut at just two and a half years old. By the age of ten, she was already drawing critical praise, including from Variety. In 1934, comedian George Jessel suggested the name "Garland," and she soon adopted "Judy" as her first name, reportedly inspired by a popular Hoagy Carmichael tune.

Garland's career launched in earnest when she signed with MGM in 1935—without a screen test. Her breakthrough came in 1939 as Dorothy in *The Wizard of Oz*, where her rendition of "Over the Rainbow" became an instant classic. The role earned her a special Juvenile Academy Award and catapulted her into stardom. During the 1940s, she headlined hit musicals such as *Meet Me in St. Louis* (1944), *Easter Parade* (1948), and *Summer Stock* (1950), admired for her extraordinary voice and emotional depth.

Behind the scenes, Garland's life was marked by intense personal challenges. From a young age, she was subject to the harsh demands of the studio system, including pressure to lose weight and maintain an idealized image, which led to a dependency on prescription drugs. She faced ongoing struggles with self-esteem, mental health, and finances—issues that shadowed her throughout her life.

FASHION FEATURES

THE WIZARD OF OZ (1939)
MEET ME IN ST. LOUIS (1944)
THE HARVEY GIRLS (1946)
EASTER PARADE (1948)
A STAR IS BORN (1954)

In the 1950s, Garland shifted her focus to live performance and found renewed success on stage. Her concerts at the London Palladium and New York's Palace Theatre were major events, culminating in her legendary 1961 concert at Carnegie Hall—widely hailed as one of the greatest nights in show business. The live recording, *Judy at Carnegie Hall*, earned her four Grammy Awards, including Album of the Year. That same decade, she returned to film in *A Star Is Born* (1954), earning an Academy Award nomination for Best Actress.

Her personal life was complex. She was married five times and had three children, including Liza Minnelli, who would go on to achieve stardom in her own right. Despite the turmoil, Garland's talent never waned. She continued performing through the 1960s, though her health deteriorated. On June 22, 1969, she died of an accidental barbiturate overdose in London at the age of 47. Her funeral in New York drew tens of thousands of mourners, reflecting the depth of public admiration for her.

Judy's life was filled with both dazzling highs and heartbreaking lows, but her artistry left an unforgettable mark. Her ability to channel raw emotion into song and character continues to influence generations of performers. More than half a century after her death, she remains a symbol of extraordinary talent, vulnerability, and resilience.

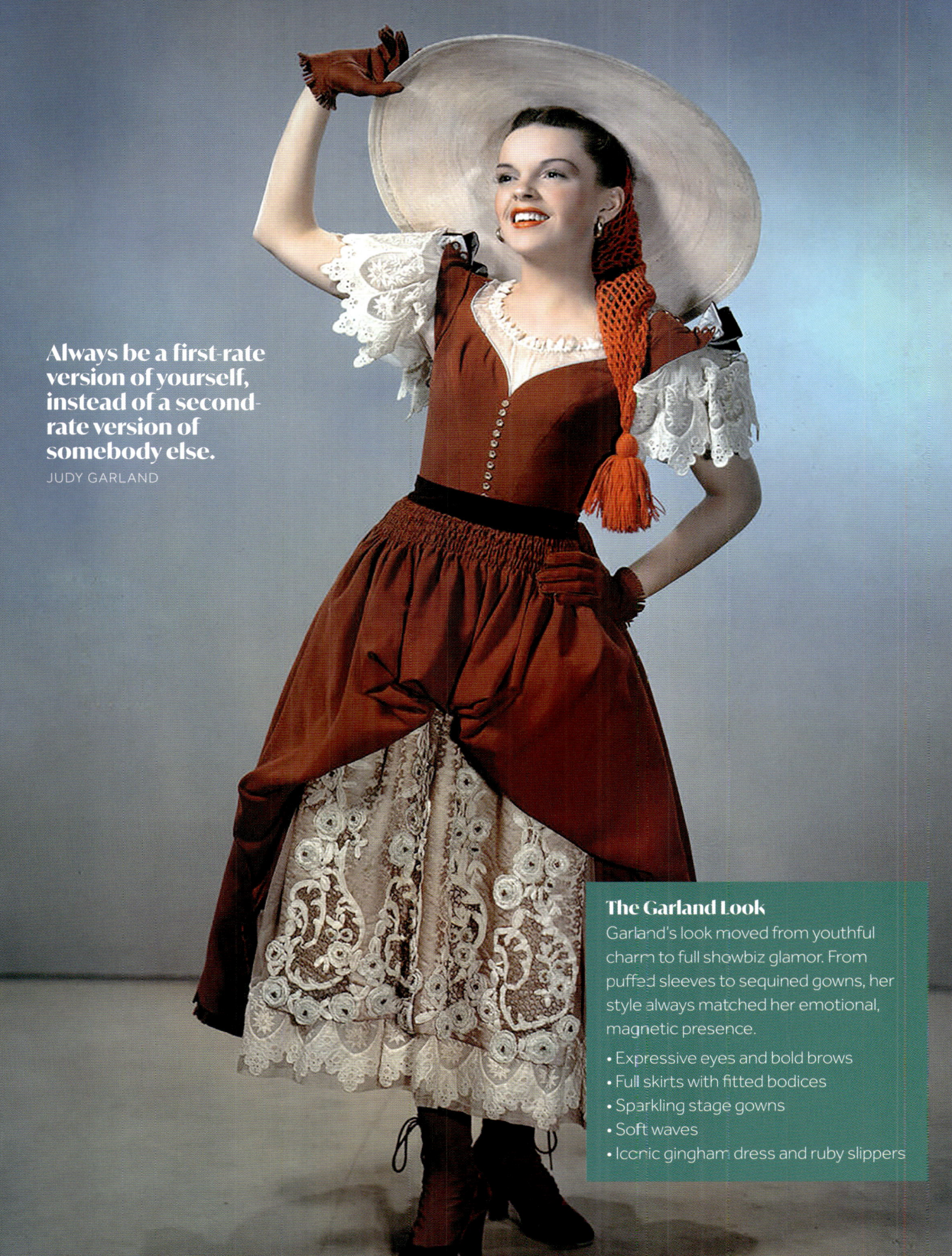

Always be a first-rate version of yourself, instead of a second-rate version of somebody else.

JUDY GARLAND

The Garland Look

Garland's look moved from youthful charm to full showbiz glamor. From puffed sleeves to sequined gowns, her style always matched her emotional, magnetic presence.

- Expressive eyes and bold brows
- Full skirts with fitted bodices
- Sparkling stage gowns
- Soft waves
- Iconic gingham dress and ruby slippers

BETTY GRABLE

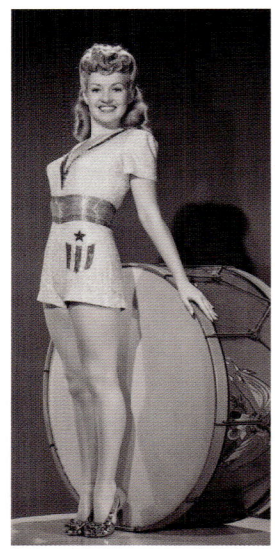

I became a star for two reasons, and I'm standing on them.

BETTY GRABLE

ABOVE
—
The cover of a June 1943 issue of Yank, *the Army Weekly Magazine*, featured a pin-up photo of shorts-clad Betty Grable showing off her celebrated legs.

RIGHT
—
Grable dazzles in this extravagant Travis Banton design in a publicity shot for *Tin Pan Alley* (1940). Even with its volume, it allows Grable to show off one of her "million dollar legs."

Dubbed the "quicksilver blonde," Betty Grable (1916–1973) rose from small dance roles to become the top box-office draw in Hollywood. Born Elizabeth Ruth Grable in St. Louis, Missouri, she was pushed toward stardom by her ambitious stage mother. Trained in ballet and tap, she began appearing in films by age 13, but it wasn't until 1940 that she found real success. Her breakthrough came in *Down Argentine Way*, a Technicolor musical from 20th Century Fox starring Don Ameche, featuring vibrant Latin-inspired costumes by Travis Banton.

Grable's charm and upbeat persona made her a natural fit for musical comedies, and she followed up with hits such as *Moon Over Miami* (1941), again with Ameche and costumes by Banton, *Springtime in the Rockies* (1942) alongside bandleader Harry James—whom she married in 1943—and *Coney Island* and *Sweet Rosie O'Grady*, both released that same year. During World War II, Grable became an icon: her pin-up photo was a favorite among soldiers, and her famously shapely legs were reportedly insured by 20th Century Fox with Lloyd's of London.

By 1947, she was Hollywood's highest-paid star, earning $300,000 annually. She continued to headline hits including *Mother Wore Tights* (1947, costumes by Orry-Kelly), *Wabash Avenue* (1950, costumes by Charles LeMaire), and *How to Marry a Millionaire* (1953, costumes by Travilla). Grable retired from film in 1955, in part due to a decline in quality roles—many of which had become uninspired remakes of her earlier successes.

The Grable Look

Betty Grable had an unmatched ability to make a fitted sweater and a pair of shorts look iconic. With her dancer's legs and curvy silhouette, she effortlessly carried off both modern and vintage-inspired fashion on screen.

- Bright tropical-print playsuits
- Satin loungewear and tap pants
- Figure-hugging sweaters paired with silk scarves

FASHION FEATURES

MILLION DOLLAR LEGS (1939)
DOWN ARGENTINE WAY (1940)
MOON OVER MIAMI (1941)
HOW TO MARRY A MILLIONAIRE (1953)

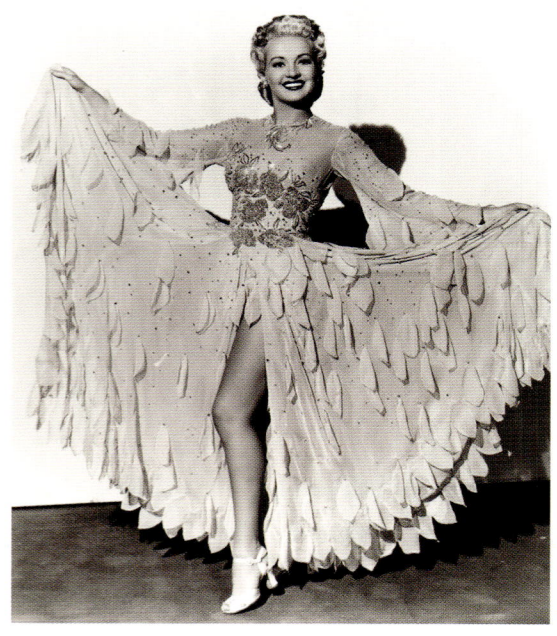

RITA HAYWORTH

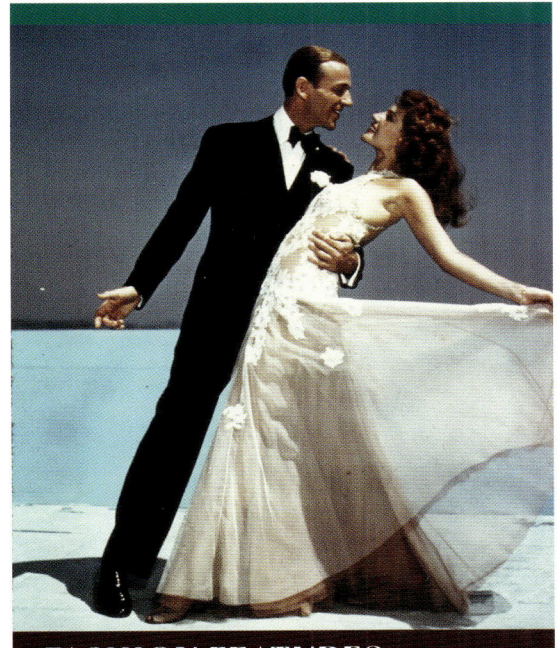

FASHION FEATURES

YOU WERE NEVER LOVELIER (1942)
COVER GIRL (1944)
GILDA (1946)
THE LADY FROM SHANGHAI (1947)
THE LOVES OF CARMEN (1948)

The Hayworth Look

Off-screen, Rita Hayworth favored relaxed, unfussy fashion—often seen in trousers, loafers, and a simple knit sweater. She was especially proud of her graceful hands, which she considered her best feature.

- Strapless gowns paired with opera-length gloves
- Voluminous, cascading waves
- Flattering necklines such as V-necks and sweetheart cuts

This iconic pin-up started as a dancer, dazzled as a leading lady, and ultimately became Hollywood royalty—both on- and off-screen.

Rita Hayworth (1918–1987) was an American film actress and dancer who rose to glamorous stardom in the 1940s and 50s. Born Margarita Carmen Cansino in Brooklyn, New York, she was the daughter of Spanish-born dancer Eduardo Cansino and his partner, Volga Hayworth. As a child, she performed in her parents' nightclub act called *Dancing Cansinos*. In the mid-1930s, she began appearing in films under her given name, Rita Cansino. On the advice of her first husband and manager, Edward Judson, she changed her name to Rita Hayworth and dyed her hair auburn, cultivating a sophisticated glamor that first registered with her role in *Only Angels Have Wings* (1939).

Her role in *Only Angels Have Wings* led to notable performances in *Blood and Sand* (1941), *You Were Never Lovelier* (1942), and *Cover Girl* (1944), establishing her as Columbia's top star. In *Gilda* (1946), she delivered a memorable performance, famously performing a striptease in a Jean Louis–designed strapless gown.

In 1943, she married actor-director Orson Welles. For *The Lady from Shanghai* (1947), Welles had her hair cut and dyed blond, a change that surprised fans. Following their divorce, she married Prince Aly Khan, son of Shia Muslim leader Aga Khan III. Their daughter, Yasmin Khan, cared for Hayworth in the 1980s when she was diagnosed with early-onset Alzheimer's disease, which led to her death in 1987.

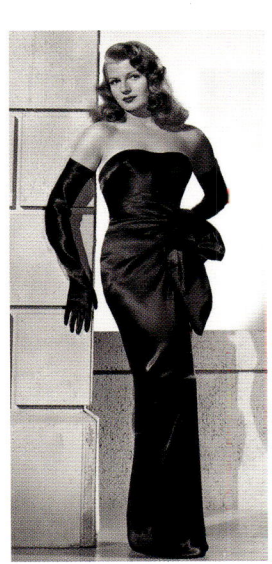

ABOVE

Rita Hayworth smolders in a satin gown and opera gloves for *Gilda* (1946), capturing the femme fatale allure that cemented her as Hollywood's ultimate screen siren.

LEFT

Hayworth had a chance to show off her dancing skills when paired with Fred Astaire in *You Were Never Lovelier* (1942). The diaphanous gown covered with appliqué flowers shows off the figure that made her the envy of women and a top pin-up for GIs.

LEADING MEN
GREGORY PECK

> Greg was true to himself to the last. He wasn't seduced by trends, not just in a fashion sense, but in life as well. He was a good father, a good husband, and a good citizen.
>
> ANTHONY PECK (GREGORY PECK'S SON)

Gregory Peck didn't just play noble characters—he made virtue compelling. In an era that often celebrated rebels and rogues, Peck's calm dignity and moral strength made him stand out.

Gregory Peck was born Eldred Gregory Peck in 1916 in La Jolla, California, and originally pursued medical studies at the University of California, Berkeley. But after discovering a love for acting, he moved to New York and trained at the Neighborhood Playhouse, making his stage debut in 1942.

Two years later, he entered film with *Days of Glory* (1944), followed by his breakout role in *The Keys of the Kingdom*, which earned him his first Oscar nomination. His early roles in *The Yearling* (1946), *Gentleman's Agreement* (1947), and *Twelve O'Clock High* (1949) showed his ability to carry stories with emotional depth and integrity. In *Gentleman's Agreement*, he took on the risky subject of anti-Semitism, playing a journalist who pretends to be Jewish to expose social prejudice.

His most famous role came in *To Kill a Mockingbird* (1962), where his portrayal of Atticus Finch—a principled lawyer in the segregated South—won him the Academy Award for Best Actor. It remains one of cinema's most admired performances.

RIGHT

Peck, in plaid shirt and red neckerchief, as the troubled but charismatic Lewt McCanless opposite Jennifer Jones as Pearl Chavez in *Duel in The Sun* (1946), King Vidor's Technicolor western melodrama.

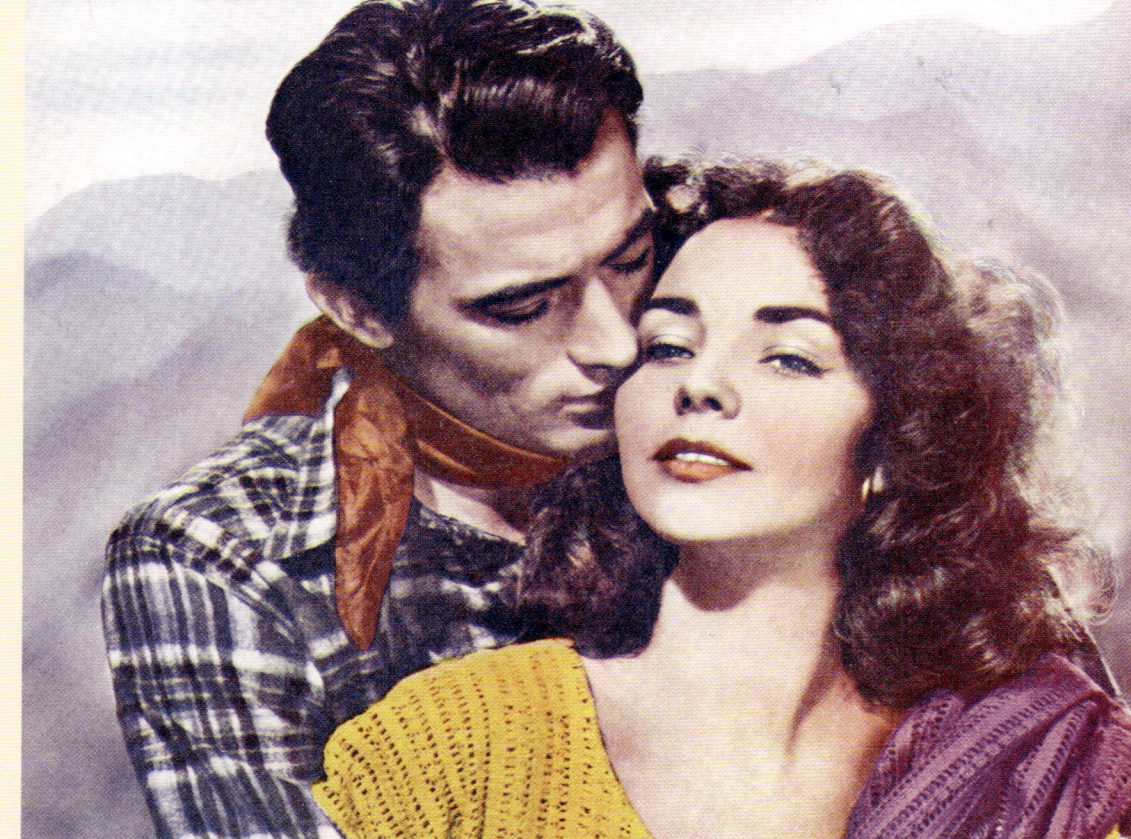

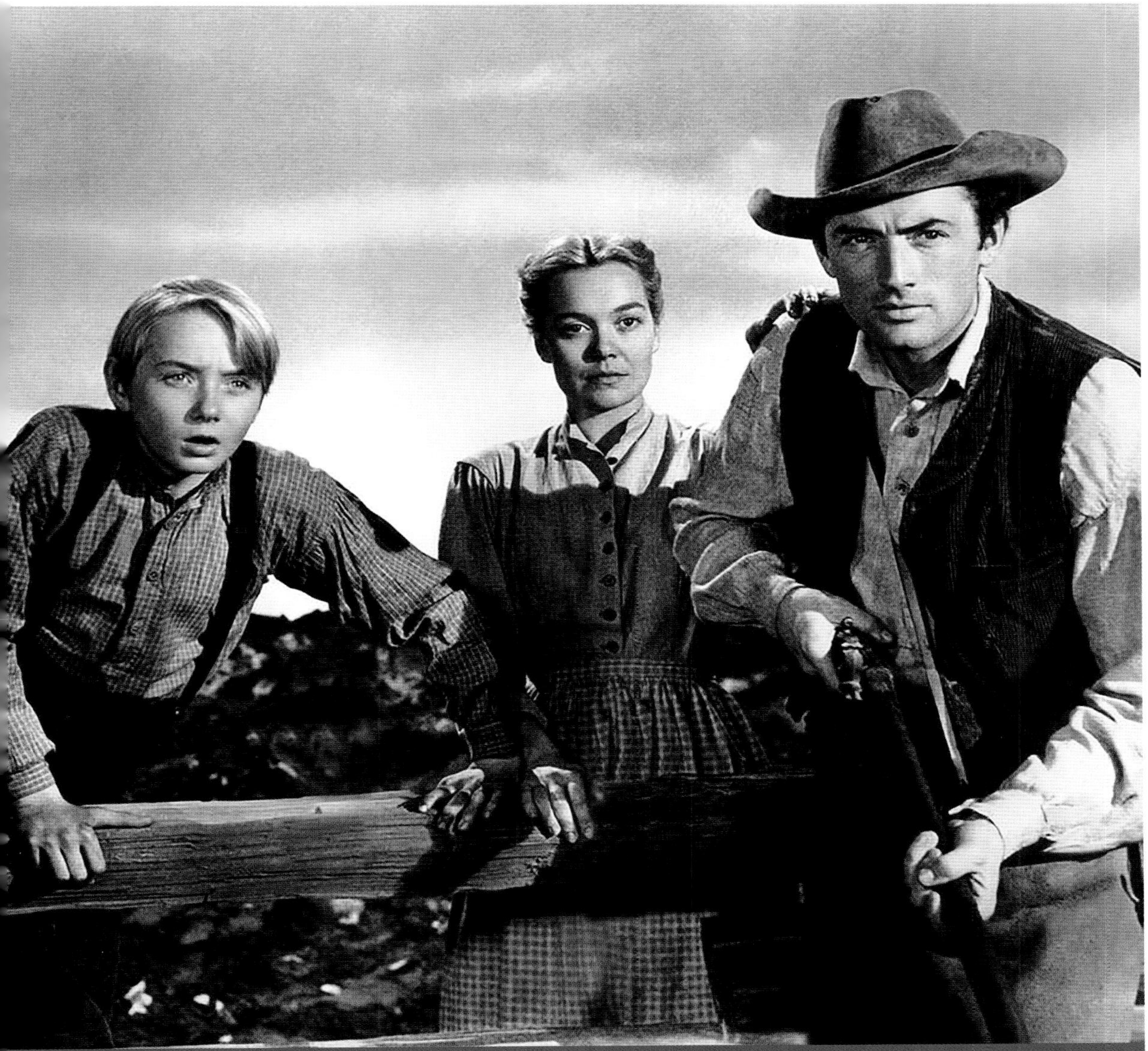

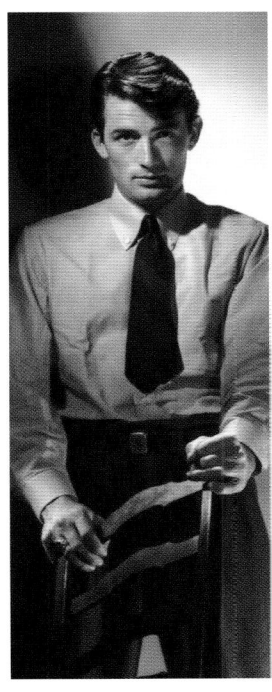

Peck also starred in the romantic classic *Roman Holiday* (1953), the war adventure *The Guns of Navarone* (1961), and the psychological thriller *Cape Fear* (1962).

Off-screen, he supported social causes, co-founded the La Jolla Playhouse, and served as president of the Academy of Motion Picture Arts and Sciences. He was honored with the Presidential Medal of Freedom in 1969 and the National Medal of Arts in 1998.

Gregory Peck died in 2003 at age 87. His performances continue to resonate as examples of strength, integrity, and timeless artistry.

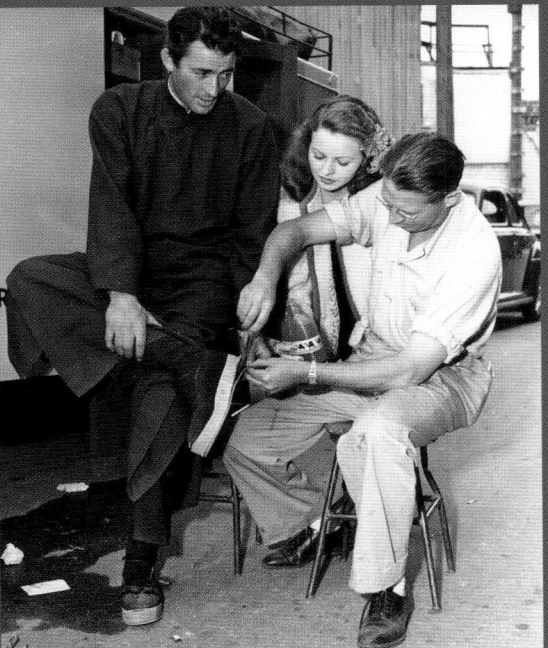

ABOVE LEFT

In *The Yearling* (1946), Peck looked every inch the rugged pioneer in homespun shirt and sturdy vest.

ABOVE

A publicity still from Alfred Hitchcock's *Spellbound* (1945). Very tall and lean, Peck made even everyday menswear look elegant.

LEFT

Peck receives some wardrobe adjustments on the set of *The Keys of the Kingdom* (1944). This film gained Peck his first Oscar nomination.

LENA HORNE

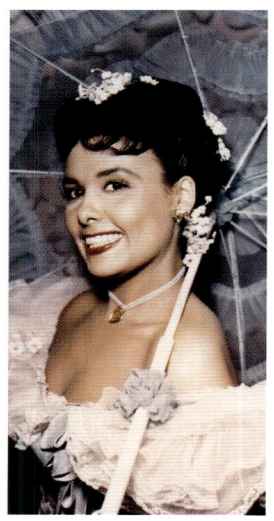

Lena Horne (1917–2010) was a trailblazing performer whose influence reached far beyond the stage and screen. Born in Brooklyn, New York, she began her career as a teenager at Harlem's legendary Cotton Club, performing in segregated venues—an experience that sparked her lifelong fight against racial injustice.

Horne made history in the 1940s as the first African American woman to sign a long-term contract with a major Hollywood studio, MGM. She appeared in films such as *Cabin in the Sky* and *Stormy Weather* (1943), delivering a stunning performance of the title song. Yet even with her talent and presence, she was often limited to musical numbers that could be easily cut when shown to segregated audiences in the South.

Determined not to be boxed into stereotypical roles, Horne spoke out against Hollywood's discrimination and became a powerful voice in the civil rights movement. She worked closely with the National Association for the Advancement of Colored People, performed at rallies, and refused to sing for segregated military audiences during World War II—opting instead to perform for Black troops and even German prisoners of war.

As film roles faded, Horne's career flourished in nightclubs and on stage. Her 1957 live album *Lena Horne at the Waldorf-Astoria* became a bestseller, and her acclaimed Broadway show *Lena Horne: The Lady and Her Music* earned her both a Grammy and a special Tony Award.

She passed away in 2010 at the age of 92, remembered as a fierce, elegant force who reshaped American entertainment.

ABOVE
Horne was garbed in ruffles, ribbons, and lace for her part in the 1946 MGM film *Till the Clouds Roll By.*

RIGHT
The austere style of the 1940s that sought to limit fabric consumption were enlivened by bold prints. Horne's peep-toe sling-back platforms were the peak of style.

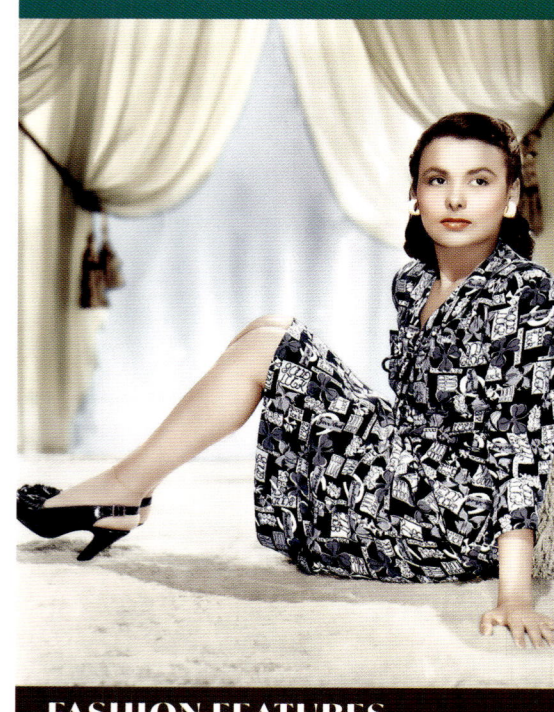

FASHION FEATURES

STORMY WEATHER (1943)
BROADWAY RHYTHM (1944)
ZIEGFELD FOLLIES (1946)

The Horne Look
Lena Horne combined classic glamor with fierce conviction, making her not just a screen icon but a style inspiration for generations of young Black women.

- Strapless, curve-hugging mermaid gowns
- Halter-top sundresses
- Soft, cropped hairstyles with delicate tendrils

ROSALIND RUSSELL

The Russell Look

Rosalind Russell never relied on traditional glamor—instead, she embraced a distinctive blend of sharp tailoring and understated elegance. Her signature style was a confident mix of masculine lines and feminine flair, often featuring practical yet fashionable pieces.

- Smart tweed suits with crisp tailoring
- Strong-shouldered evening gowns
- Capri pants paired with embellished tops

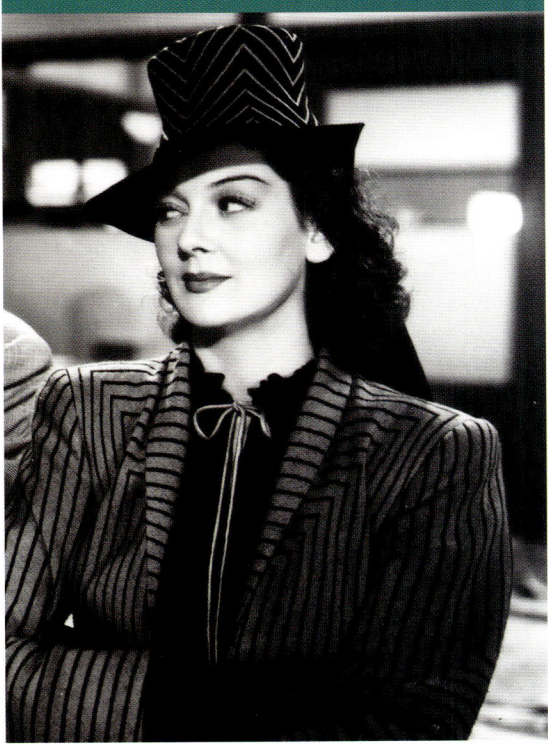

Rosalind Russell (1907–1976) was a dynamic American performer known for her sharp comedic timing, strong on-screen presence, and portrayals of smart, independent women. Born in Waterbury, Connecticut, she studied at the American Academy of Dramatic Arts before launching her acting career on Broadway in 1930. Hollywood soon noticed her, and she took the leap to film in the mid-1930s, quickly becoming a standout in both comedy and drama.

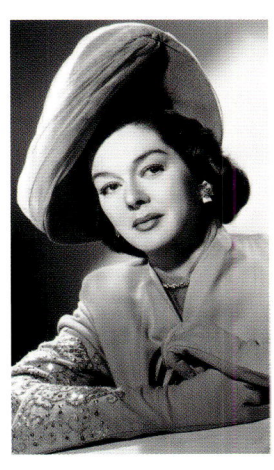

Her rise to fame began with *The Women* (1939), but it was her iconic role as Hildy Johnson, the fast-talking reporter in *His Girl Friday* (1940), that secured her place as a leading figure in screwball comedy. Russell earned four Academy Award nominations for standout performances in *My Sister Eileen* (1942), *Sister Kenny* (1946), and *Mourning Becomes Electra* (1947).

She also thrived on stage, winning a Tony Award for *Wonderful Town* (1953), and captivated film audiences again in *Auntie Mame* (1958). Honored with five Golden Globes and the Jean Hersholt Humanitarian Award, Russell remained a beloved and influential presence in entertainment.

> **It takes time to develop taste in anything, and clothes are no exception. It takes observation, analysis, and experience.**
>
> ROSALIND RUSSELL

ABOVE

An embellished ensemble and dramatic hat convey elegance but have a slight touch of whimsy that captures the wit and sophistication of Rosalind Russell's signature screen persona.

LEFT

To play fast-talking ex-reporter Hildy Johnson in 1940's *His Girl Friday*—originally a man's role—Russell donned sharp-looking striped suits designed by Kalloch that evoke a menswear feel.

SETTING TRENDS
STUNNING REDHEADS

I dyed my hair this crazy red to bid for attention. It has become a trademark and I've got to keep it this way.

─LUCILLE BALL

REDHEADS

The arrival of color film revolutionized how redheaded actresses were seen on screen. Although their fair skin and light eyes often looked subdued in black-and-white, Technicolor gave them a dazzling new dimension. Hues of auburn and strawberry blonde suddenly came alive, turning red hair into a cinematic spectacle. Nicknamed "Queens of Technicolor," stars such as Rhonda Fleming, Maureen O'Hara, and even the occasionally flame-haired Maria Montez embodied the full power of color on film. But the title could just as easily belong to any actress whose fiery locks became a signature part of her screen allure.

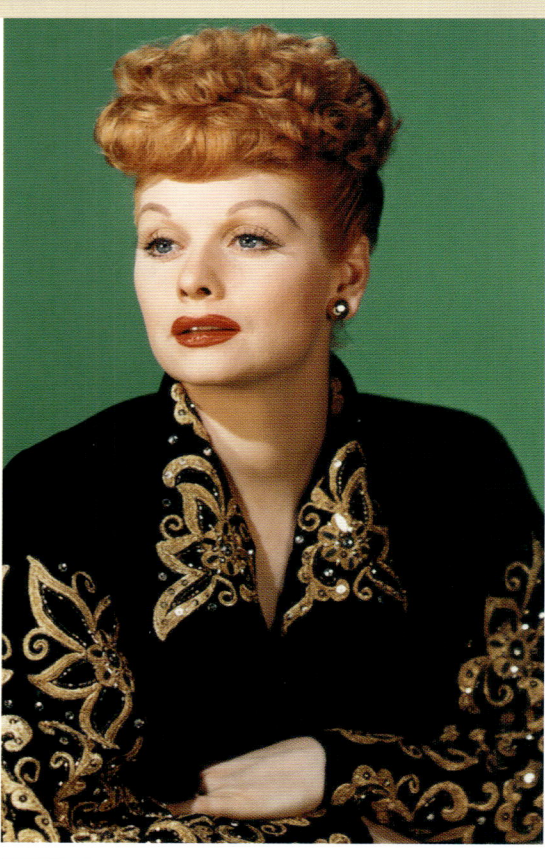

RIGHT

Elsa Martinelli in a 1962 Hollywood publicity still for *Hatari!*—her soft auburn hair styled in a chic, voluminous bob that frames her face with effortless precision. Wearing a delicate white lace slip, she stands in striking contrast to the snarling black panther behind her. It's a bold image of poised femininity with an undercurrent of wildness.

ABOVE RIGHT

Lucille Ball, radiant in embroidered velvet and signature red curls, captured in a 1950s studio portrait that reveals the poised glamor behind America's queen of comedy.

BELOW RIGHT

Julianne Moore dazzles in emerald green at the Venice Film Festival; her radiant smile and auburn waves embodying timeless grace with a modern red carpet flourish.

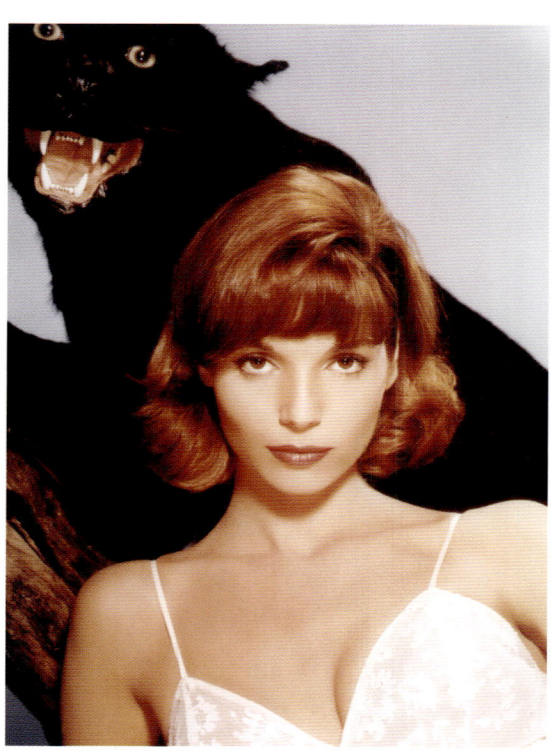

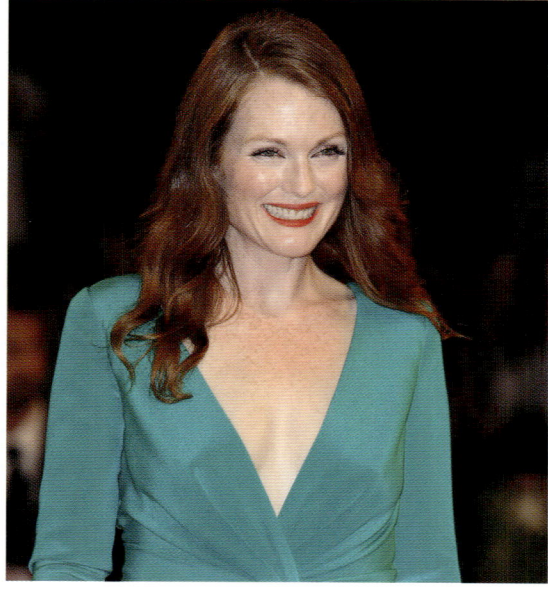

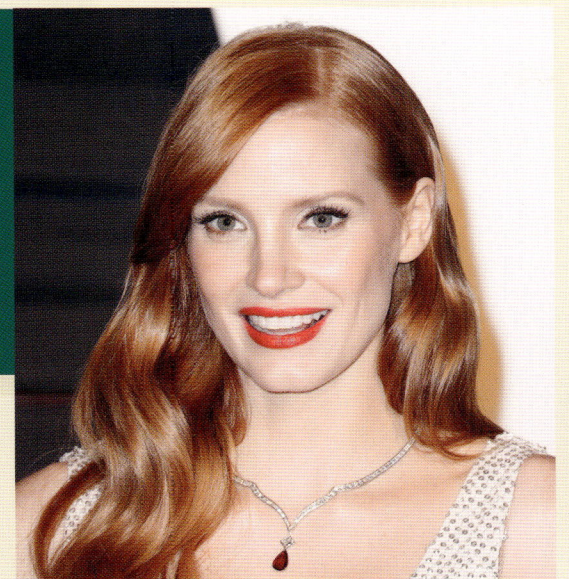 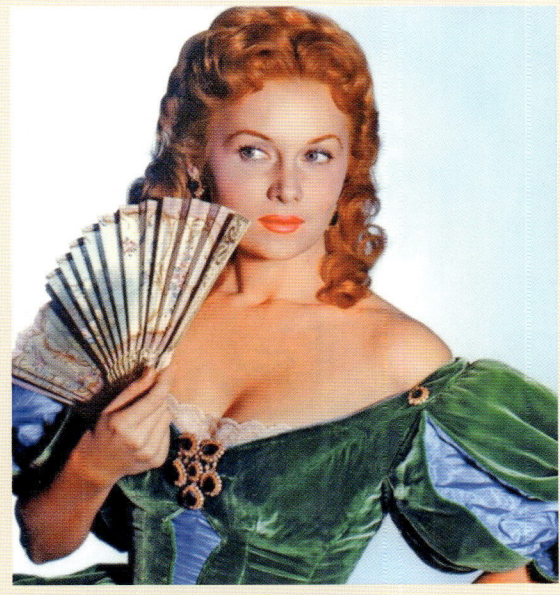

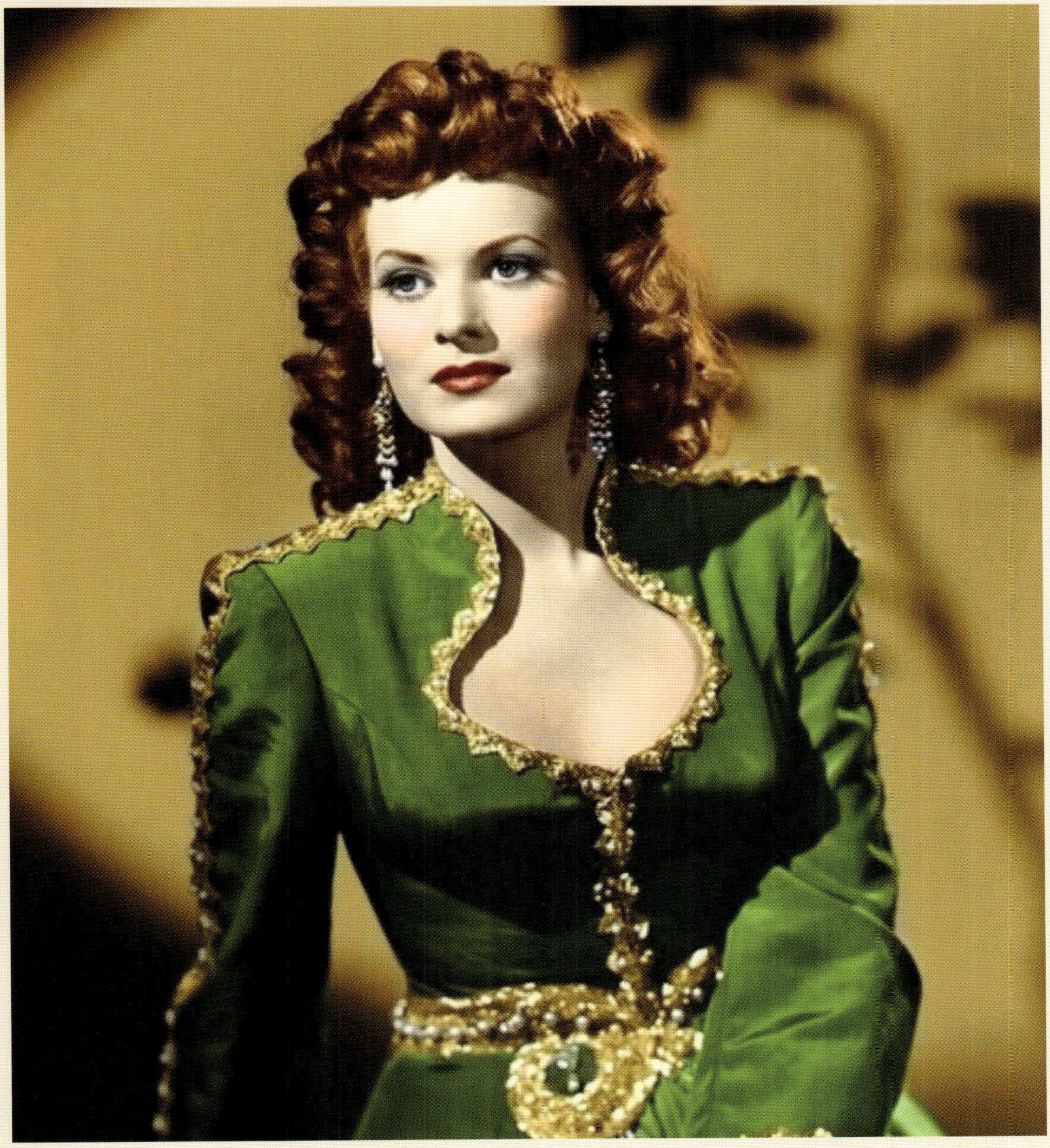

TOP LEFT

Jessica Chastain at the 2015 Vanity Fair Oscar Party, glowing in a shimmering silver gown that catches the light with every angle. Her signature red hair cascades in soft Hollywood waves, perfectly complemented by a diamond necklace with a striking red drop pendant

TOP RIGHT

Embodying the radiant glamor of 1950s Technicolor, Rhonda Fleming wears an emerald green gown made of velvet with cerulean taffeta inserts that complements her signature flaming red hair in a press shot for *The Golden Hawk* (1952).

LEFT

Known for her portrayal of fiery redheads, Irish-American Maureen O'Hara glows in a gold-embellished green silk gown in a Technicolor-era portrait that captures her poised radiance and timeless appeal.

BARBARA STANWYCK

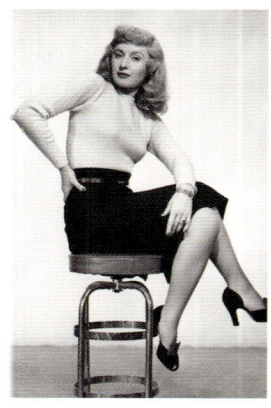

Tough, magnetic, and endlessly compelling, Barbara Stanwyck was one of Hollywood's most respected and versatile actresses. With her smoky voice, commanding screen presence, and emotional depth, she flourished across genres—shining in gritty pre-Code dramas, sparkling screwball comedies, tense noir thrillers, and rugged Westerns.

Raised in Brooklyn as Ruby Stevens, she faced adversity early in life. Orphaned before age five, she grew up in foster homes and worked a variety of jobs before finding her way to the stage. Beginning as a Ziegfeld chorus girl, she transitioned to Broadway and quickly attracted attention for her natural talent and striking presence.

Her film breakthrough came with *Ladies of Leisure* (1930), directed by Frank Capra, who became a key supporter throughout her career. Stanwyck delivered a string of acclaimed performances, most notably in *Stella Dallas* (1937), where she portrayed a self-sacrificing mother, and *Double Indemnity* (1944), in which she redefined the femme fatale archetype with chilling precision.

Stanwyck kept audiences enthralled with standout roles in *The Lady Eve* (1941) and *Ball of Fire* (1941) and later found success on television in *The Big Valley*, where she won multiple Emmy Awards. Renowned for her discipline, independence, and enduring charisma, she was admired as much for her craft as for her down-to-earth character off-screen.

The Stanwyck Look

Polished and tailored, Stanwyck's fashion leaned toward structured silhouettes, dark tones, and sleek, fuss-free elegance that reflected her confident screen presence.

- Sharp-shouldered blouses and skirts
- Glossy, waved hair
- Strong brows and sculpted lips
- Simple yet commanding evening gowns

FASHION FEATURES

BABY FACE (1933)
BALL OF FIRE (1941)
DOUBLE INDEMNITY (1944)
THE LADY EVE (1941)

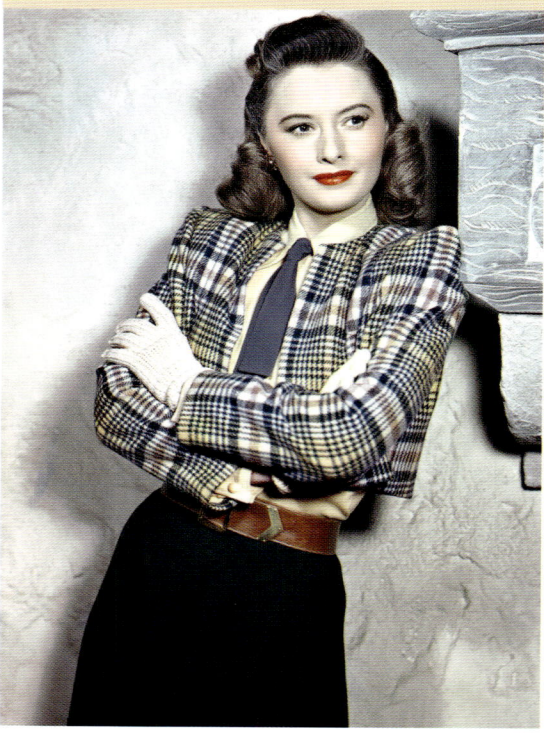

ABOVE

Donning a brassy blonde wig in *Double Indemnity* (1944), Barbara Stanwyck epitomizes the noir femme fatale in a form-fitting sweater over a simple skirt. The look is subtly sexy, just hinting at the danger this woman will bring to the men in her life.

RIGHT

A no-nonsense suit complete with a tie and a plaid bolero jacket topping a navy skirt was a perfect ensemble to convey Stanwyck's plain-speaking screen persona.

GENE TIERNEY

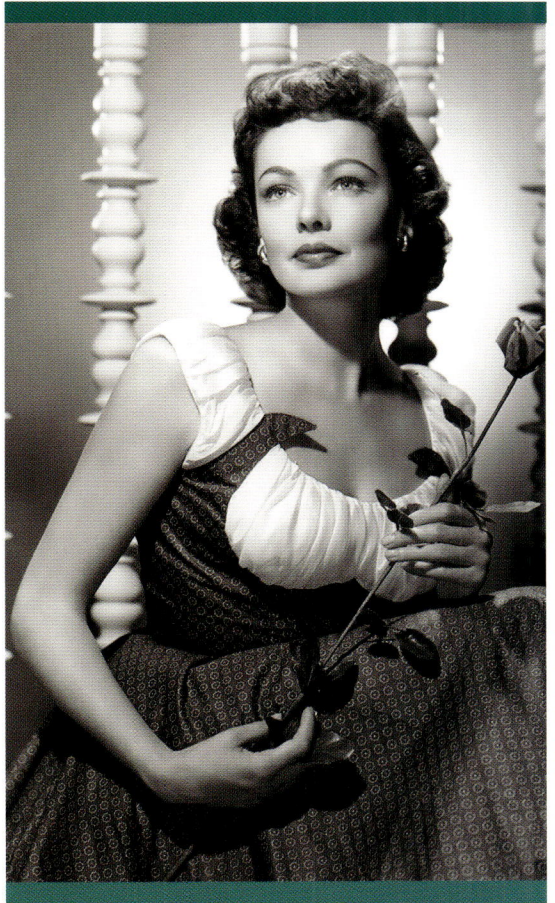

The Tierney Look

Graceful and refined, Tierney favored structured silhouettes, soft curls, and timeless details that reflected her poised, quietly captivating presence both on and off screen.

- Tailored suits with nipped waists
- Monogrammed blouses and pleated skirts
- Sculpted brows and bold red lips
- Glossy waves framing her porcelain complexion

With a unique look that seemed sculpted for the screen, Gene Tierney captivated audiences in the 1940s and quickly became one of Hollywood's most unforgettable stars.

Born in Brooklyn in 1920 to a wealthy family, she was educated in finishing schools before discovering a passion for the stage. Her career began on Broadway, but it wasn't long before her striking looks and poise caught the attention of 20th Century Fox executives.

Her breakthrough came with the role of Laura Hunt in *Laura* (1944), a haunting film noir that established her as a new kind of screen siren—cool, composed, and undeniably magnetic. The following year, she took a daring turn as Ellen Berent in *Leave Her to Heaven* (1945) playing a woman whose obsessive love spirals into chilling territory. The performance earned Tierney an Academy Award nomination for Best Actress and proved her dramatic range.

Tierney's screen presence was matched by her impeccable fashion sense—both on and off camera. Designers admired her regal bearing and symmetrical features, which made her an ideal canvas for elegant, tailored styles. Her wardrobe in *Leave Her to Heaven*, designed by Kay Nelson, set a new bar for cinematic glamor and remains one of the era's most memorable costume collections.

FASHION FEATURES

LAURA (1944)
LEAVE HER TO HEAVEN (1945)
THE GHOST AND MRS. MUIR (1947)
WHIRLPOOL (1950)

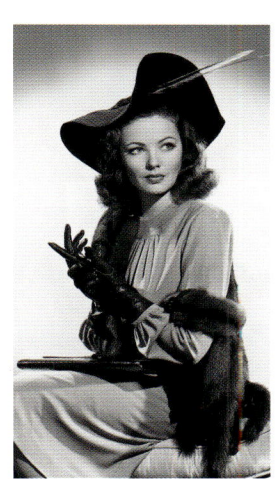

ABOVE

Gene Tierney radiates poised sophistication in a feathered hat and fur stole—an iconic 1940s portrait echoing the polished allure she brought to *Laura* (1944).

LEFT

The peasant/ethnic style was a popular trend of the 1940s and suits Gene Tierney's idiosyncratic beauty. She wears a patterned dress with a gathered white bodice in this publicity still for *Tobacco Road* (1941).

LEADING MEN
ROBERT TAYLOR

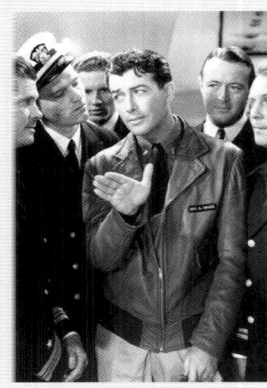

Robert Taylor (1911–1969), born Spangler Arlington Brugh in the small town of Filley, Nebraska, rose to become one of the most recognizable leading men in Hollywood's Golden Age. Known for his chiseled features and polished screen presence, Taylor starred in more than 70 films over a career that spanned more than three decades.

Before his film success, Taylor's early aspirations were musical. He studied the cello at Doane College in Nebraska, inspired by his artistic inclinations rather than dreams of stardom. It wasn't until he transferred to Pomona College in California that his interest in acting took hold. Joining the school's theater company, he quickly gained attention for his natural charisma onstage. MGM scouts discovered him there, and by 1934, he had a studio contract and a name change—Robert Taylor.

His breakthrough came in *Magnificent Obsession* (1935), quickly followed by major roles in *Camille* (1936) opposite Greta Garbo and *A Yank at Oxford* (1938). These films made him a bankable star, often cast in romantic or dramatic roles that capitalized on his good looks and refined demeanor. But Taylor sought more depth as an actor, especially after serving in World War II.

During the war, Taylor was commissioned as a lieutenant in the U.S. Naval Air Forces. He trained pilots and appeared in instructional military films, adding a new level of discipline and purpose to his life. When he returned to Hollywood, he chose more psychologically demanding roles in *Undercurrent* (1946) and *High Wall* (1947), showing critics he could do more than play the romantic lead.

Perhaps his most iconic post-war role came in *Quo Vadis* (1951), where he played the Roman

ABOVE

In *Flight Command* (1940), Taylor wears a bomber jacket, a look that will become a classic for both men and women in the ensuing decades.

RIGHT

There was no style more influential than that of military uniforms during the war years. Taylor donned uniforms for both film and real life. Here, then-wife Barbara Stanwyck walks with Lt. Robert Taylor to the car as the screen star leaves for active Navy duty in 1943.

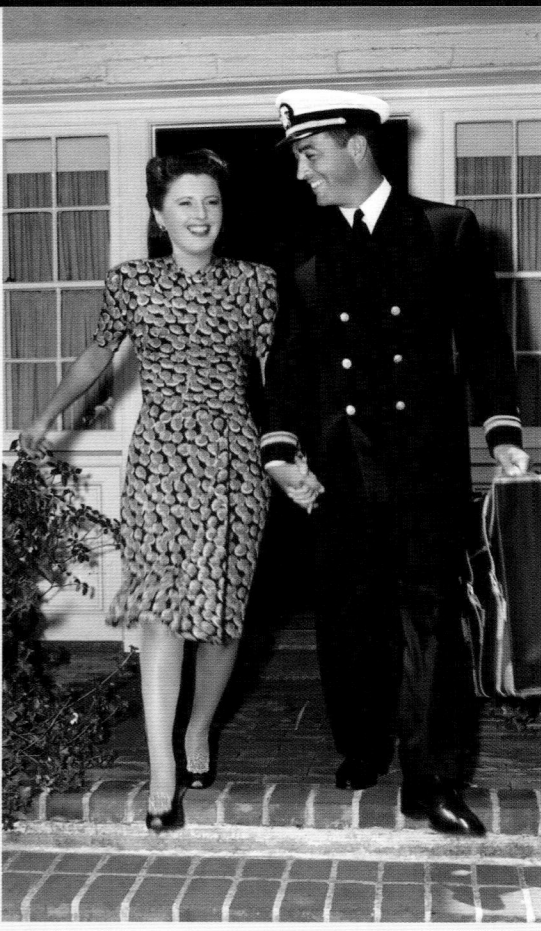

officer Marcus Vinicius in a lavish production that became a massive box-office success. The film demonstrated his ability to anchor historical epics with authority and appeal. In the 1950s, Taylor increasingly gravitated toward Westerns, a genre he both enjoyed and excelled in. Films such as *Many Rivers to Cross* (1955) and *The Law and Jake Wade* (1958) reflected his growing comfort with rugged, stoic characters.

Taylor was also a familiar face on television. From 1959 to 1962, he starred in *The Detectives Starring Robert Taylor*, and later took over as the host of *Death Valley Days* from 1966 until his death. These roles helped him remain a household name even

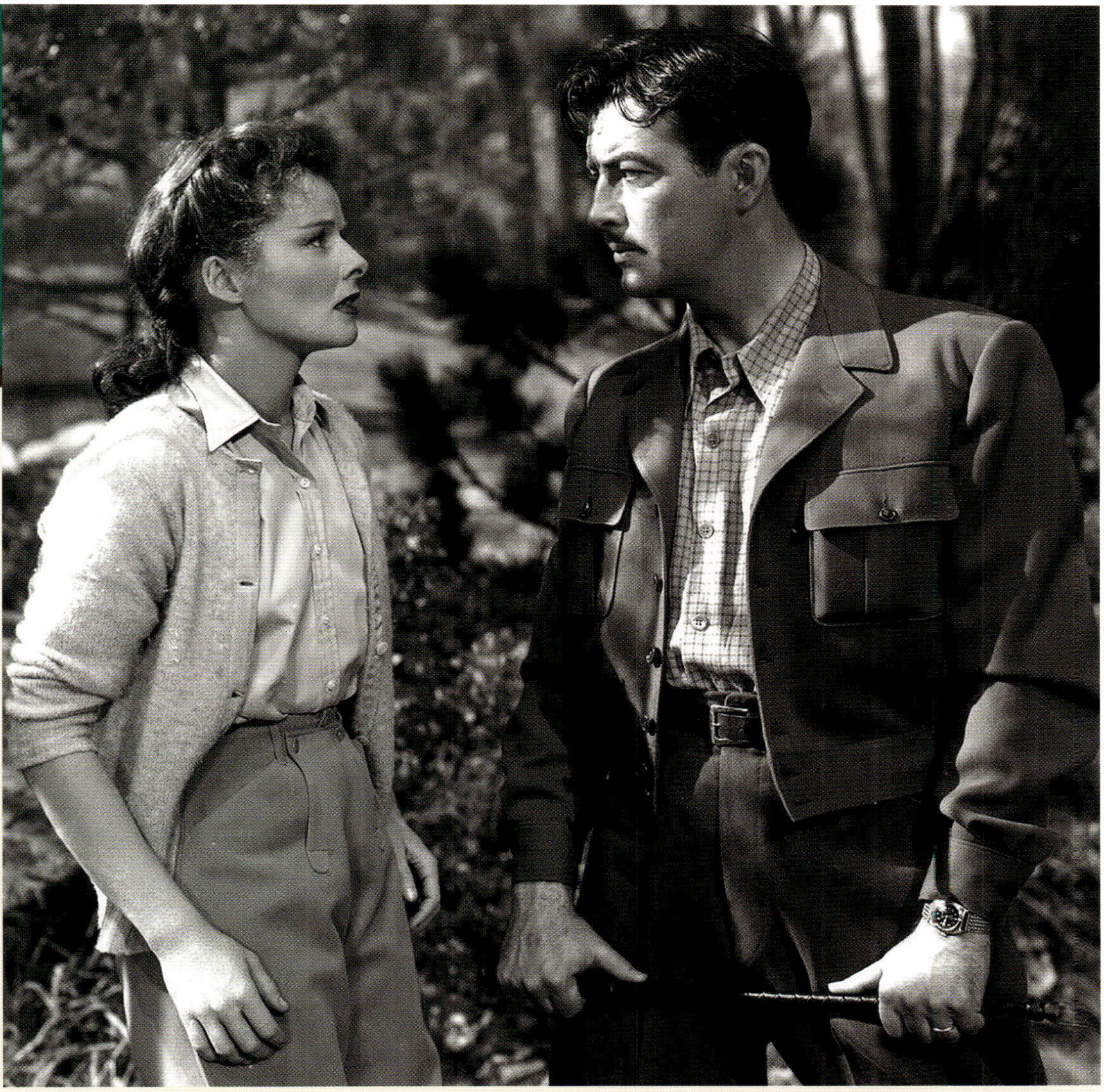

Robert Taylor was not only a splendid actor in a wide variety of roles but one of the most handsome men in the western world.

AUDREY MEADOWS

as the studio system that launched his career began to fade.

Off-screen, Taylor's personal life drew frequent media attention. He married actress Barbara Stanwyck in 1939, and although the couple divorced in 1951, they were considered one of Hollywood's golden couples during their marriage. In 1954, he married German actress Ursula Thiess, with whom he had two children.

He also made headlines for his political views. In 1947, he testified before the House Committee on Un-American Activities, aligning himself with the anti-communist sentiment of the era. His testimony was controversial, but it underscored the conviction with which he approached both his public and private life.

Sadly, Taylor's health declined in the late 1960s. A lifelong smoker, he was diagnosed with lung cancer in 1968 and passed away on June 8, 1969, at age

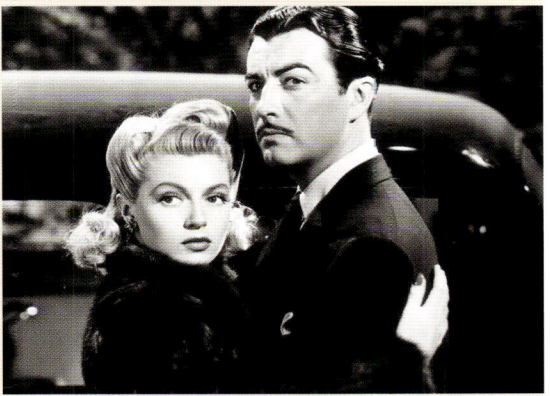

57. His funeral was attended by many, including the then-Governor Ronald Reagan. Today, Taylor is remembered not only for his iconic roles and film contributions but also for a career that mirrored the evolution of classic American cinema. His star still shines on the Hollywood Walk of Fame—a quiet testament to his lasting impact.

ABOVE

Tension brews in the wilderness as Katharine Hepburn and Robert Taylor face off in *Undercurrent* (1946), their tailored riding attire mirroring the film's elegant yet simmering suspense.

LEFT

Robert Taylor and Lana Turner lock into a tense embrace in *Johnny Eager* (1941), their noir chemistry framed by fur, suspicion, and the gleam of postwar deceit.

LANA TURNER

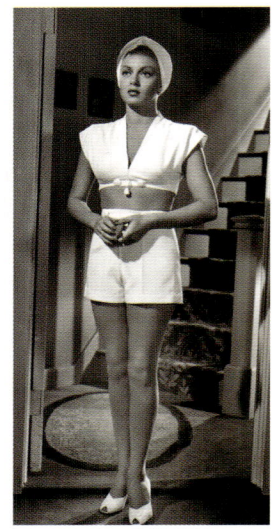

Hollywood lore claims Lana Turner was discovered sipping a soda at a drugstore counter, but the truth was far less glamorous and far more determined. Lana Turner (1921–1995), known as the original "Sweater Girl," built her career on beauty, sex appeal, and tenacity—while surviving a life filled with real-life scandal and personal hardship.

After her father was murdered when she was a child, Turner and her mother relocated to California. She began seeking work in films as a teenager, landing her first major role in *They Won't Forget* (1937). But it was her appearance in *Love Finds Andy Hardy* (1938) that turned her into a pin-up sensation, with tight sweaters and figure-hugging silhouettes earning her instant fame.

By the 1940s, Turner was more than a novelty—she starred in films such as *Johnny Eager* (1941), *Dr. Jekyll and Mr. Hyde* (1941), and the sultry, noir-defining *The Postman Always Rings Twice* (1946), where she dazzled in Irene's iconic white ensembles. She continued to headline dramatic hits in the 1950s, including *The Bad and the Beautiful* (1952), *Peyton Place* (1957), and *Imitation of Life* (1959).

Turner's off-screen life was infamous—seven marriages, ties to gangsters, and the 1958 killing of her boyfriend Johnny Stompanato by her teenage daughter Cheryl, in what was ruled self-defense. Through it all, Turner remained a star—glamorous, controversial, and unforgettable.

ABOVE

One of the most iconic looks in film history is the white midriff-baring top, shorts, peep-toe shoes, and turban worn by Lana Turner in the quintessential film noir, *The Postman Always Rings Twice* (1946).

RIGHT

Turner, a vision of 1940s casual chic in a polka-dot skirt and white blouse, poses elegantly with a bicycle.

FASHION FEATURES

ZIEGFELD GIRL (1941)
SLIGHTLY DANGEROUS (1943)
THE POSTMAN ALWAYS RINGS TWICE (1946)
THE MERRY WIDOW (1952)
IMITATION OF LIFE (1959)

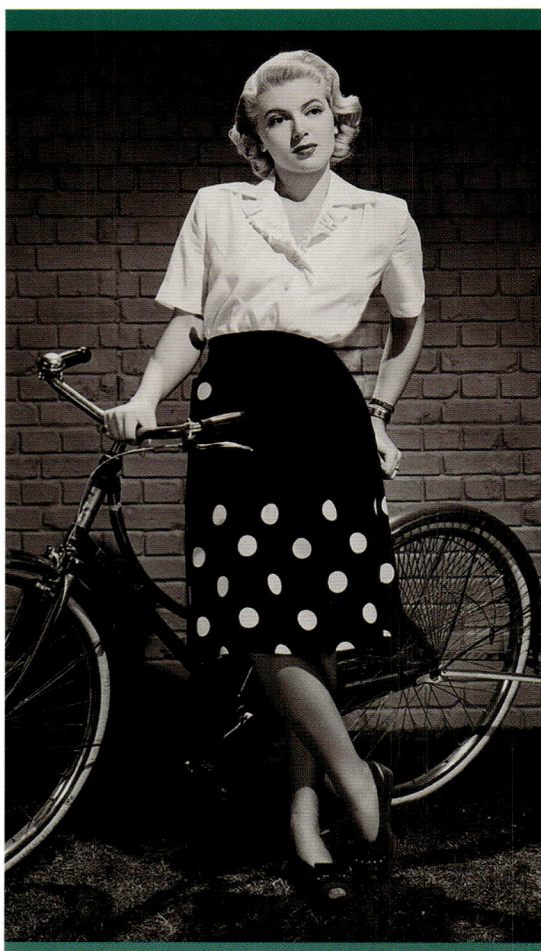

The Turner Look

Turner loved to dress in head-to-toe white, pairing high-waisted garments with luxurious fur and heels. With nearly 700 pairs of shoes, she epitomized old-school glamor and unapologetic femininity.

- White satin gowns
- Tight sweaters and high-waisted shorts
- Dramatic fur stoles and bold lipstick

LORETTA YOUNG

The Young Look

During her television years, Loretta Young upheld her status as a style icon, famously opening each episode with a dramatic entrance in a flowing gown. Her wardrobe choices reflected refined glamor and timeless charm.

- Soft, face-framing waves
- Dresses with strong shoulders and graceful draping
- Full-skirted gowns that created elegant silhouettes

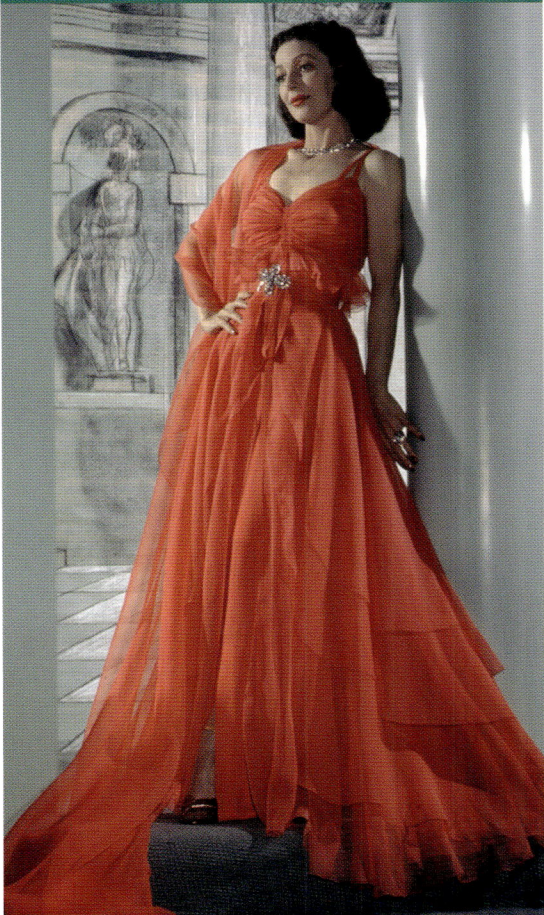

One of Hollywood's most poised and admired stars, Loretta Young (1913–2000) defined grace and charm throughout her extensive career.

Originally named Gretchen Young and raised in Salt Lake City, she moved with her family to Hollywood at an early age. Her entry into film was unexpected—she answered a call meant for her sister and landed the role instead. Starting in silent films, she quickly transitioned into talkies and became a leading lady in the 1930s.

Her breakthrough came alongside Clark Gable in *Call of the Wild* (1935), followed by memorable performances in *Suez* (1938), *Along Came Jones* (1945) with Gary Cooper, and *The Bishop's Wife* (1947) with Cary Grant. In 1947, she won an Academy Award for *The Farmer's Daughter*—with costumes by Edith Head—and earned another nomination for *Come to the Stable* (1949).

Young made a successful shift to television in the 1950s with *The Loretta Young Show*, which ran from 1953 to 1961 and earned her three Emmy Awards. Off-screen, she was deeply spiritual and widely respected for her charitable work, remaining a symbol of integrity and screen professionalism throughout her life.

FASHION FEATURES

HE STAYED FOR BREAKFAST (1940)
THE MEN IN HER LIFE (1941)
THE FARMER'S DAUGHTER (1947)
THE BISHOP'S WIFE (1947)
KEY TO THE CITY (1950)

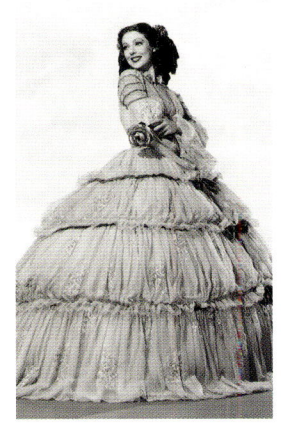

Glamor is something you can't bear to be without once you're used to it.

LORETTA YOUNG

ABOVE

Loretta Young, captivating in a period gown with intricate lace and a voluminous skirt, epitomizes historical romance in *The Men in Her Life* (1941).

LEFT

Layers of scarlet chiffon create an ethereal effect in an exquisite gown that shows Young's sophisticated beauty.

LEADING MEN
HOLLYWOOD HEROES

Style is knowing who you are, what you want to say, and not giving a damn.

ORSON WELLES

RIGHT

In a still from *Citizen Kane* (1941), Orson Welles as Charles Foster Kane wears a fedora, gray cuffed flannels, and a sports jacket and scarf—all style notes of the early 1940s.

TOP RIGHT

Even as the World War II ground down, the public has an appetite for films that focused on the combatants. Here, Dennis O'Keefe and John Wayne stand in front of back projection screen wearing the hard hats of the construction unit of the U.S. Navy in 1944's *The Fighting Seabees*.

BOTTOM RIGHT

When not immersing themselves in the gritty reality of battle films, wartime move-goers looked the studios to offer escapist fantasy, such as *Arabian Nights* (1942), Universal's inaugural Technicolor spectacle starring Sabu and Jon Hall.

World War II dominated the cultural and cinematic landscape of the 1940s, and Hollywood not only rallied behind the war effort, but kept telling those stories even after the guns fell silent. John Wayne took the battlefield to the screen in films such as *The Fighting Seabees*, *Back to Bataan*, *They Were Expendable*, and *The Sands of Iwo Jima*. Director William Wyler shifted focus to life after war in *The Best Years of Our Lives*. The influence of military life and war films left a lasting imprint on men's style, introducing structured tailoring and uniform-inspired fashion that endures today—epaulets, frogging, piping, and garments such as the army greatcoat, the bomber jacket, and the naval pea coat all became civilian staples.

Hollywood wasn't just about heroics. Social issues took center stage in a number of conscience-driven dramas. *Gentleman's Agreement* tackled anti-Semitism, *The Lost Weekend* explored the grip of alcoholism, and *Citizen Kane* exposed the rot behind the American dream. In *The Third Man*, postwar Europe's black market served as a shadowy backdrop. These weightier stories demanded toned-down wardrobes, prompting designers such as Kay Nelson (*Gentleman's*

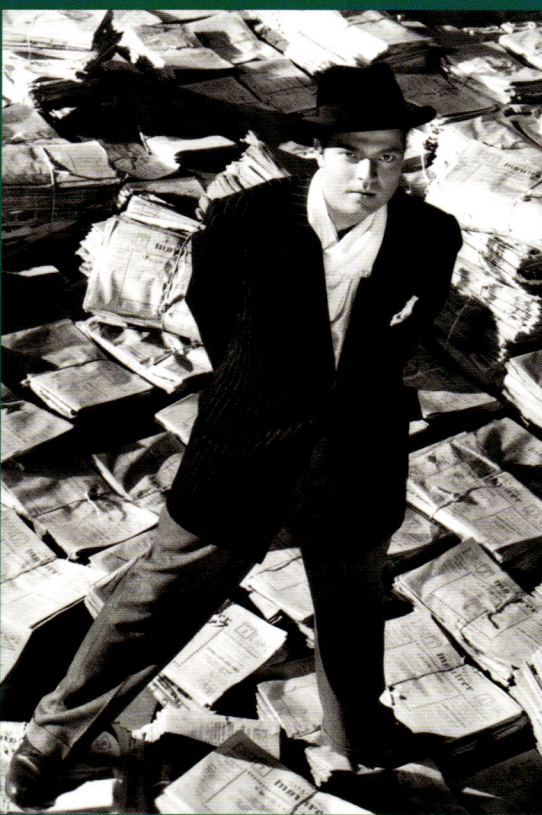

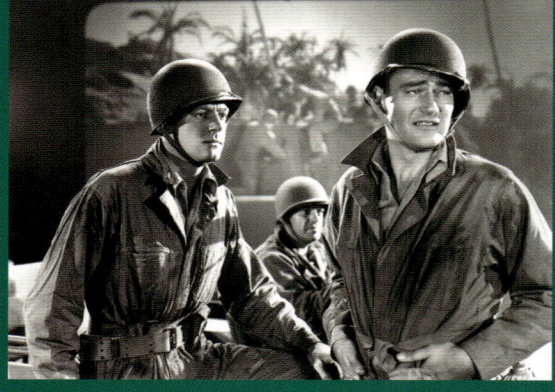

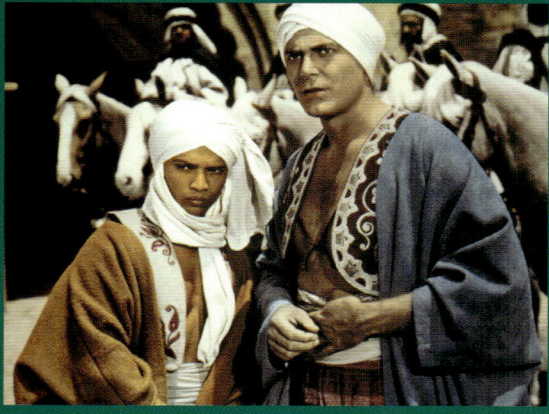

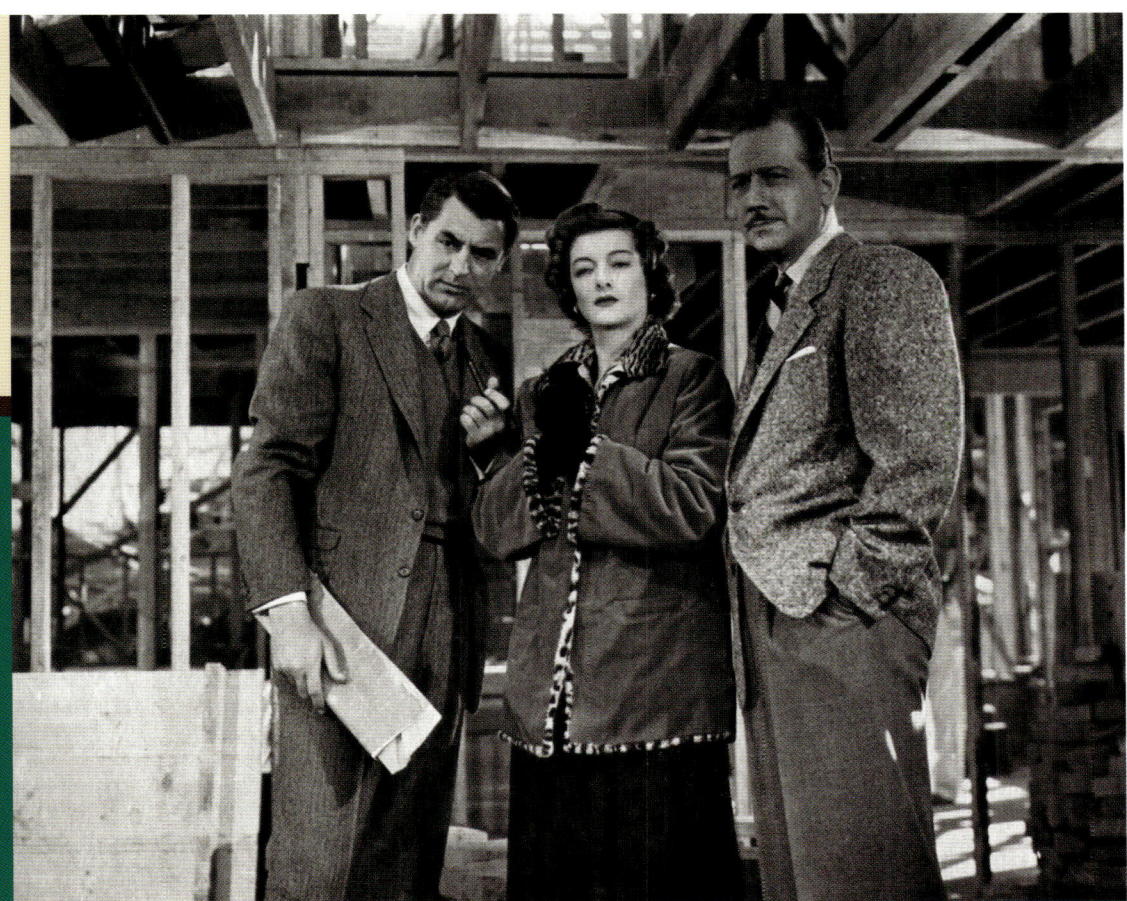

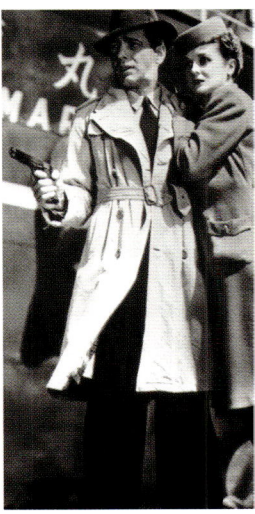

Key 1940s Menswear Trends

Wartime Looks:

- Slim, practical suits without pocket flaps or cuffs
- Notched lapels on single-breasted jackets
- High-waisted trousers
- Bold, short ties with Windsor knots
- Tie pins, suspenders, and zoot suits for rebellious flair
- Trench coats and wingtip shoes
- Wide-brimmed fedoras

Postwar Style:

- Hand-painted novelty ties featuring pin-ups or Western motifs
- Long overcoats
- Hawaiian shirts and more casual sportswear

Agreement), Edith Head (The Lost Weekend), and Edward Stevenson (Citizen Kane) to create somber "Victory Suits"—sparse, cuffless, pleat-free outfits made up of synthetic blends.

Meanwhile, audiences flocked to light-hearted escapism. Tyrone Power charmed as Zorro, Errol Flynn swashbuckled through The Sea Hawk, and Gene Kelly took up swords in The Three Musketeers. The Thief of Bagdad, a fantasy adventure featuring Sabu, borrowed from the magic of Arabian Nights and influenced both fashion and interior design trends. Iconic figures such as Sherlock Holmes and Tarzan also returned to the screen, becoming costume party favorites for a new generation.

Bing Crosby and Bob Hope emerged as two of the decade's biggest stars. Their popular "Road" comedy films, alongside Dorothy Lamour in her signature sarongs, provided much-needed comic relief and exotic escapism for wartime audiences.

On the darker side of cinema, film noir flourished. Humphrey Bogart hunted for The Maltese Falcon, whereas Alan Ladd brooded through This Gun for Hire and The Glass Key. The trench coat, once a standard military issue, found a new identity as the uniform of the private detective—and soon, everyday men adopted it as part of their wardrobe, proving just how closely fashion and film were entwined.

ABOVE

Humphrey Bogart and Mary Astor in The Maltese Falcon (1941). The rumpled trench coat is the perfect outwear from a world-weary PI, such as Sam Spade.

TOP LEFT

Cary Grant, Myrna Loy, and Melvyn Douglas in 1948's Mr. Blandings Builds His Dream House. Even as the decade ticked down, traces of wartime austerity lingered in the narrower cuts and single breast of suit jackets. At this time, men's more "casual" wear still consisted of less formal suits, such as the tweeds shown here.

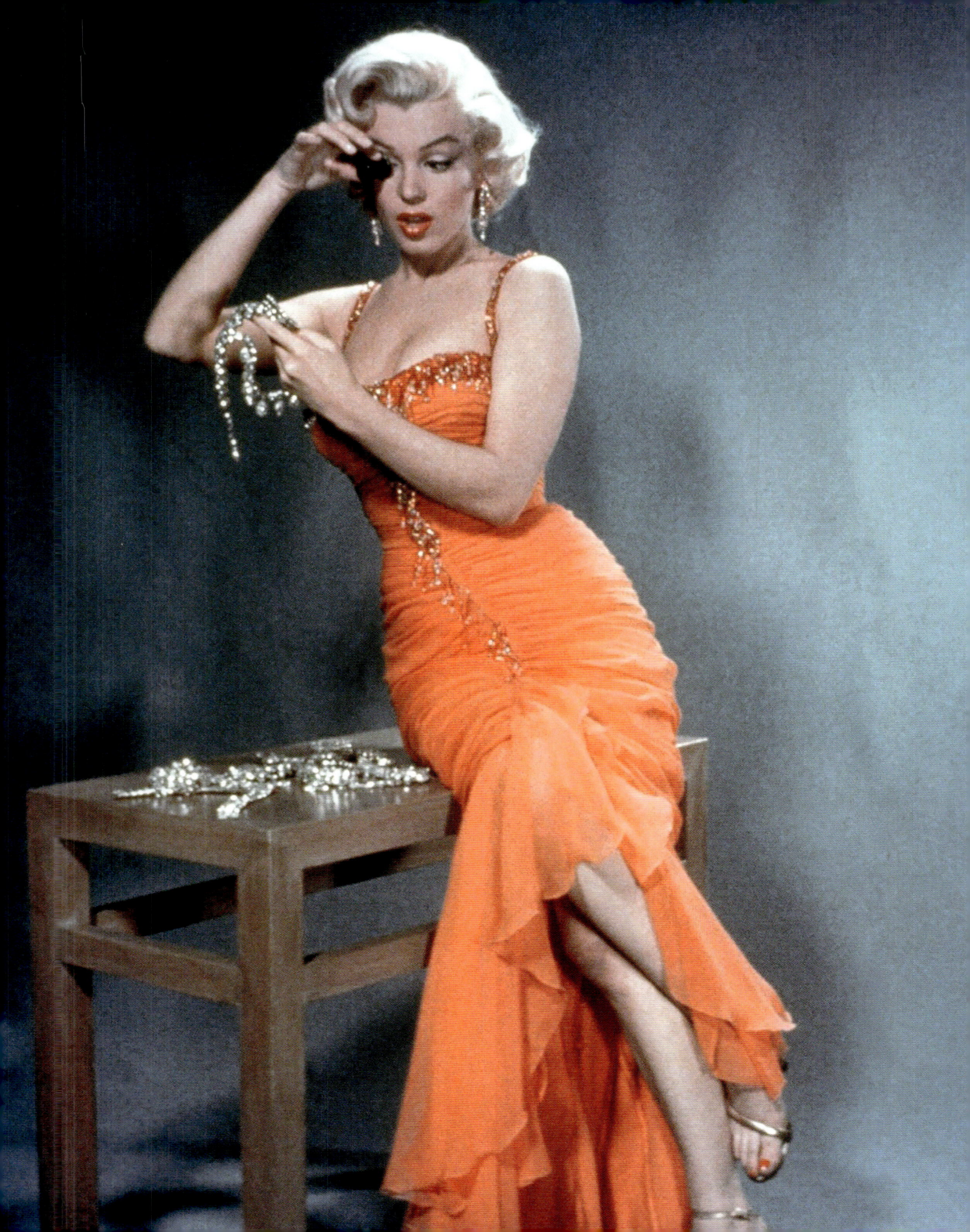

NINETEEN FIFTIES

The 1950s ushered in a new wave of glamor in Hollywood, shaped by postwar optimism, the rise of television, and a renewed appetite for spectacle. With the hardships of World War II behind them, American audiences sought escapism in full color, widescreen epics, lavish musicals, and high-fashion dramas. The studio system, though beginning to show cracks, still had the power to craft stars and shape public taste. Costume designers such as Helen Rose, Walter Plunkett, and Edith Head produced some of their most iconic work during this decade, defining the look of an era driven by polished sophistication.

This was a time when fashion and femininity were reimagined in technicolor. Gowns flowed with tulle, satin, and embellishment, whereas daywear embraced structure and grace. Dior's "New Look" silhouette—cinched waists, full skirts, and soft shoulders—translated seamlessly onto the screen, reinforcing a hyper-feminine ideal that audiences embraced. Leading ladies such as Grace Kelly, Audrey Hepburn, and Elizabeth Taylor became global style icons, admired as much for their off-screen elegance as their on-screen roles.

The 50s also brought new themes to the forefront. Teen culture began influencing style through films featuring Sandra Dee, James Dean, and Marilyn Monroe, whose casual sex appeal marked a shift from the demure glamor of earlier stars. As the decade progressed, fashion in film became more diverse, reflecting both tradition and rebellion. It was a golden age of costume design—refined, bold, and unforgettable.

SANDRA DEE

FASHION FEATURES

GIDGET (1959)
A SUMMER PLACE (1959)
IMITATION OF LIFE (1959)

Sweet, sunny, and eternally youthful, Sandra Dee captured the hearts of 1950s and 1960s audiences as the epitome of American innocence and girl-next-door charm.

Sandra Dee (1942–2005), born Alexandra Zuck in New Jersey, began her career as a child model, quickly rising in popularity due to her fresh-faced beauty, photogenic charm, and innate poise. Her early success in modeling led naturally to acting, and she made her film debut in *Until They Sail* (1957), showcasing a promising screen presence. Just two years later, her performance in *Imitation of Life* (1959) earned widespread praise for its emotional depth and vulnerability, firmly establishing her as a rising star.

Dee's stardom soared with *Gidget* (1959), where she charmed audiences as a spirited teen surfer. Her role in *A Summer Place* (1959) further defined her as the wholesome ingénue, a persona that would become her signature throughout the early 1960s. Her appeal lay in her ability to embody innocence and optimism while conveying genuine feeling, making her a beloved figure for an entire generation.

In 1960, she married teen idol Bobby Darin, forming one of Hollywood's most celebrated young couples. Their romance, although brief, added to her allure and media fascination. As the decade progressed, however, shifting cultural tastes led to a decline in her film roles, and she gradually retreated from the spotlight.

ABOVE
—
Sandra Dee, the beloved blonde bombshell of the 1960s, captivated audiences with her wholesome image in popular films such as *Gidget* and *Tammy and the Doctor*.

RIGHT
—
Sandra Dee, known for her wholesome screen persona, rose to fame in the late 1950s and starred in *Gidget* and *A Summer Place*, becoming a teenage icon of the era.

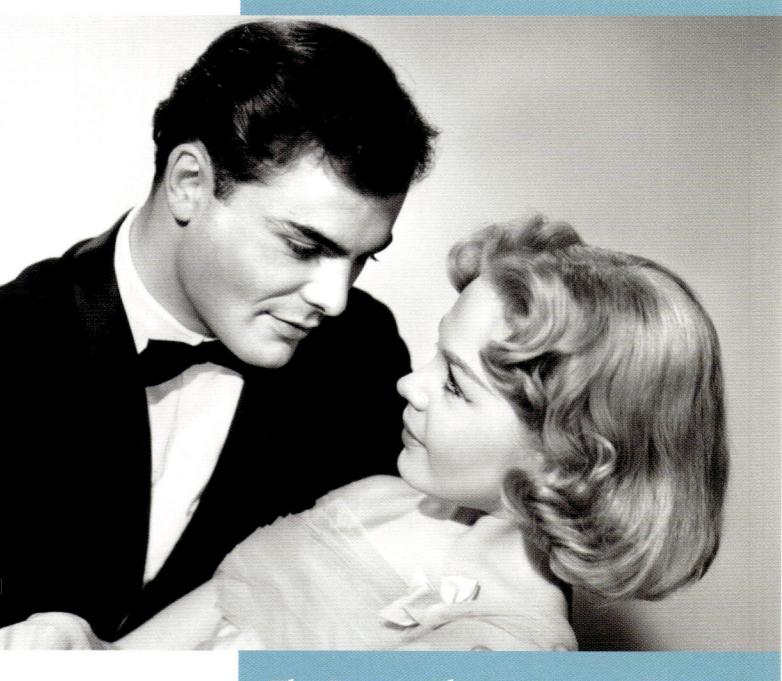

The Dee Look

Effortlessly sweet and youthful, Dee's look featured clean silhouettes, soft pastels, and playful touches that reflected her on-screen innocence.

- Flipped bob or ponytail
- Peter Pan collars
- Cardigans and circle skirts
- Natural, fresh-faced makeup

Behind her sunny image, Dee faced personal challenges, including struggles with anorexia, alcoholism, and depression. In later years, she spoke candidly about these experiences, bringing attention to issues of mental health and the pressures of fame. Despite her hardships, Sandra Dee remains a lasting symbol of innocence, beauty, and the Golden Age of teen cinema.

JANET LEIGH

FASHION FEATURES

SCARAMOUCHE (1952)
MY SISTER EILEEN (1955)
PSYCHO (1960)
BYE BYE BIRDIE (1963)

The Leigh Look

Known for her 21-inch waist and hourglass silhouette, Leigh dazzled in form-fitting fashions of the 1950s.

- Tight sweaters
- Black lingerie and bustiers
- Illusion-neckline gowns

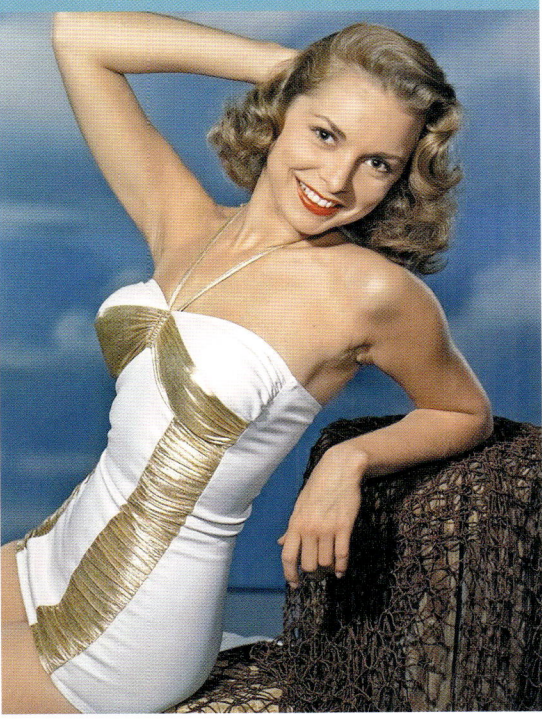

With her girl-next-door radiance and ability to play both sweetness and steel, Janet Leigh carved out a unique place in Hollywood's Golden Age, becoming a style icon and enduring screen presence.

Janet Leigh (1927–2004), born Jeanette Helen Morrison in California, began her Hollywood journey in a true fairy-tale fashion. Discovered from a photograph by actress Norma Shearer, Leigh soon found herself under contract at MGM and made her screen debut in *The Romance of Rosy Ridge* (1947). She quickly proved her versatility in costume dramas such as *Little Women* (1949) and *Scaramouche* (1952), where her beauty, grace, and classic features made her a favorite of both audiences and studio stylists.

She starred opposite her then-husband Tony Curtis in several films, including *Houdini* (1953) and *The Vikings* (1958), where her on-screen charm and ability to convey vulnerability added emotional depth to period epics and romantic tales. But her defining moment came in 1960, when she played Marion Crane in Alfred Hitchcock's *Psycho*. Her performance—and the infamous shower scene—redefined horror and suspense, earning Leigh a Golden Globe and an Academy Award nomination.

Outside of thrillers, she demonstrated range in musicals such as *Bye Bye Birdie* (1963) and political dramas such as *The Manchurian Candidate* (1962). Her legacy lives on through her daughter, Jamie Lee Curtis, and through one of cinema's most unforgettable screen moments.

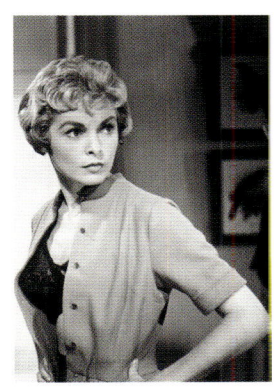

ABOVE

Janet in *Psycho* (1960), unforgettable as Marion Crane in Alfred Hitchcock's chilling masterpiece—her performance and that iconic shower scene redefining suspense and screen history.

LEFT

Leigh, best known for her iconic role in Alfred Hitchcock's *Psycho*, earned a Golden Globe and an Oscar nomination for the film's unforgettable shower scene that redefined horror cinema.

LEADING MEN
JAMES DEAN

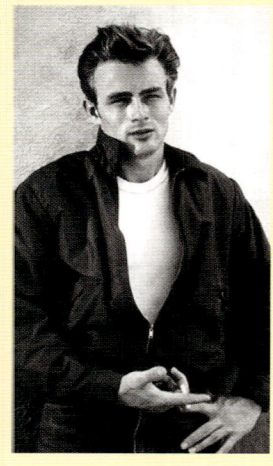

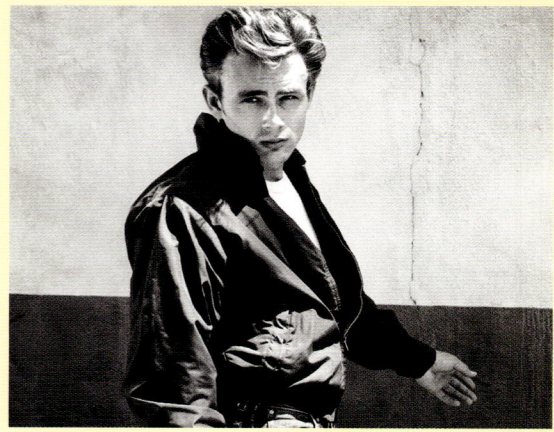

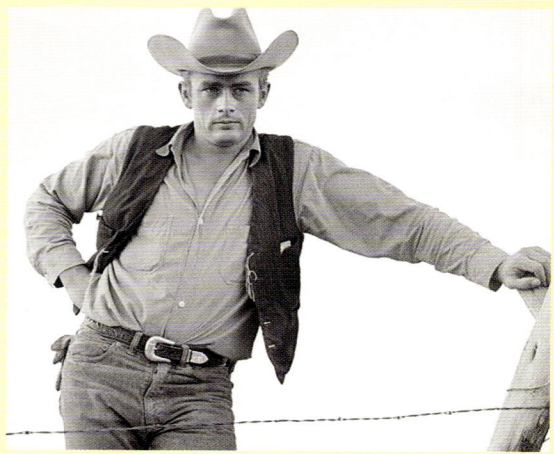

Rebellious, magnetic, and achingly vulnerable, James Dean became the eternal symbol of youthful angst and defiant cool, revolutionizing Hollywood's portrayal of masculinity in just three films before his life was tragically cut short.

James Dean (1931–1955), born James Byron Dean in Marion, Indiana, spent much of his early life on a farm in Fairmount after his mother's death because of cancer when he was just nine years old. Raised by his aunt and uncle, Dean developed a deep emotional sensitivity and introspective nature that would later infuse his performances with haunting realism. In high school, he excelled in drama, debate, and sports, hinting at the complex, multidimensional persona he would later bring to the screen.

After a brief stint studying prelaw at Santa Monica College, Dean transferred to the University of California, Los Angeles, where he majored in drama and starred in several stage productions. Recognizing his talent, he left college in 1951 and moved to New York City, immersing himself in the world of method acting. At the Actors Studio, under the guidance of Lee Strasberg, Dean refined his emotionally driven craft, earning roles in live television dramas and gaining a reputation for his commitment and intensity.

Dean's cinematic breakthrough came with *East of Eden* (1955), directed by Elia Kazan. Cast as Cal Trask, a troubled youth yearning for his father's love, Dean delivered a performance of raw emotional power that earned him his first posthumous Academy Award nomination. His ability to channel vulnerability and rage in equal measure marked him as an actor of rare depth and immediacy.

Later that same year, he starred in *Rebel Without a Cause* (1955), portraying Jim Stark, a

ABOVE/TOP RIGHT

Wearing cuffed jeans and a torn shirt, James Dean defined brooding rebellion in *East of Eden* (1955). He was the first actor to receive a posthumous Oscar nomination, setting a precedent in Hollywood history. His style inspired generations, and *Rebel Without a Cause* solidified his legacy as the face of 1950s youth rebellion and timeless cinematic allure.

BOTTOM RIGHT

Leaning against a fence in cowboy gear, James Dean channels rugged charisma in *Giant* (1956). It was his final film role, released posthumously, earning him a second consecutive Oscar nomination and solidifying his iconic Hollywood legacy.

tormented teenager navigating the confusing terrain of adolescence. With his slouched posture, pleading eyes, and iconic red jacket, Dean captured the anguish and defiance of a generation. The film resonated deeply with postwar youth who felt misunderstood and alienated, turning Dean into a voice for the disenchanted and emotionally restless.

His final film, *Giant* (1956), released after his death, featured Dean as Jett Rink, a lonely outsider whose rise to wealth exposes his emotional emptiness. Acting alongside Rock Hudson and Elizabeth Taylor, Dean's performance displayed remarkable maturity, securing him a second posthumous

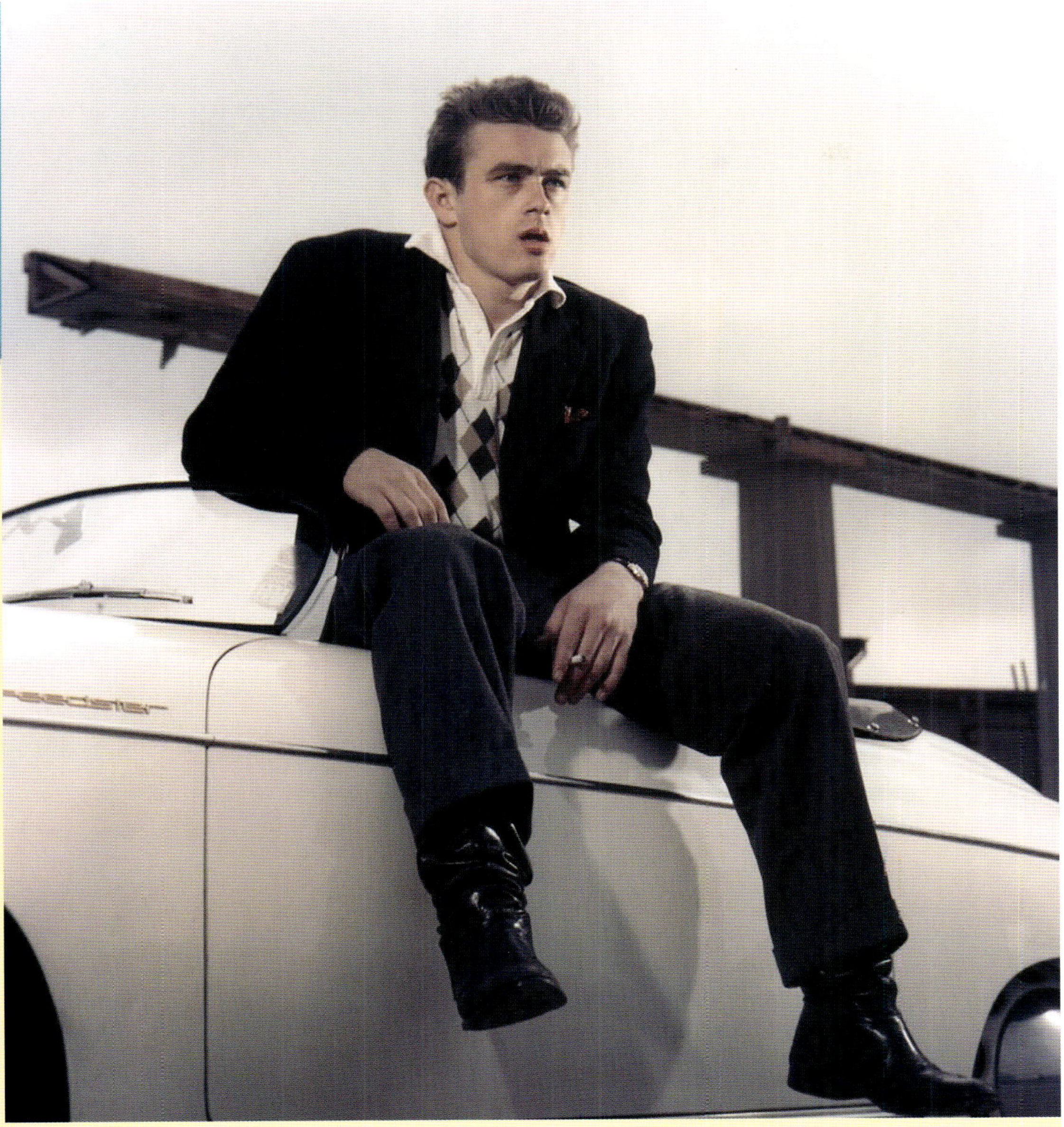

Oscar nomination. He brought subtle nuance and layered vulnerability to a role that demanded bravado and quiet pain. His haunting gaze and tense physicality remain unforgettable.

On September 30, 1955, at just 24 years of age, Dean died in a high-speed car crash while driving his Porsche 550 Spyder. The tragedy shocked the world and instantly elevated him to legendary status. In just three major films, Dean redefined masculinity on screen—fusing sensitivity, rebellion, and emotional authenticity in a way that still resonates. His untimely death sealed his image as the eternal outsider, and his legacy continues to shape film, fashion, and youth culture. James Dean remains a timeless symbol of promise, rebellion, and tragic brilliance—an enduring figure whose impact far exceeds the brevity of his life and whose myth continues to evolve.

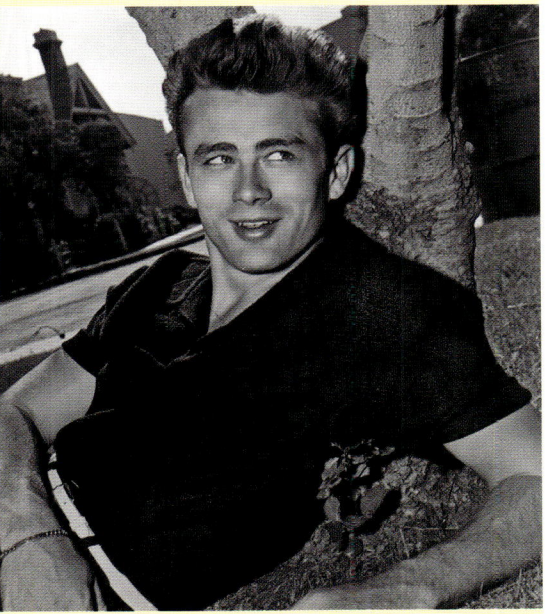

TOP LEFT

Pictured here with his Porsche Speedster, Dean was a keen motorsports fan, and competed in his first professional racing event in March 1955.

LEFT

Although Dean's career included only three films, his influence on fashion, film, and youth culture remains profound and enduring. Images of him sporting his iconic leather jacket still define teen angst to this day.

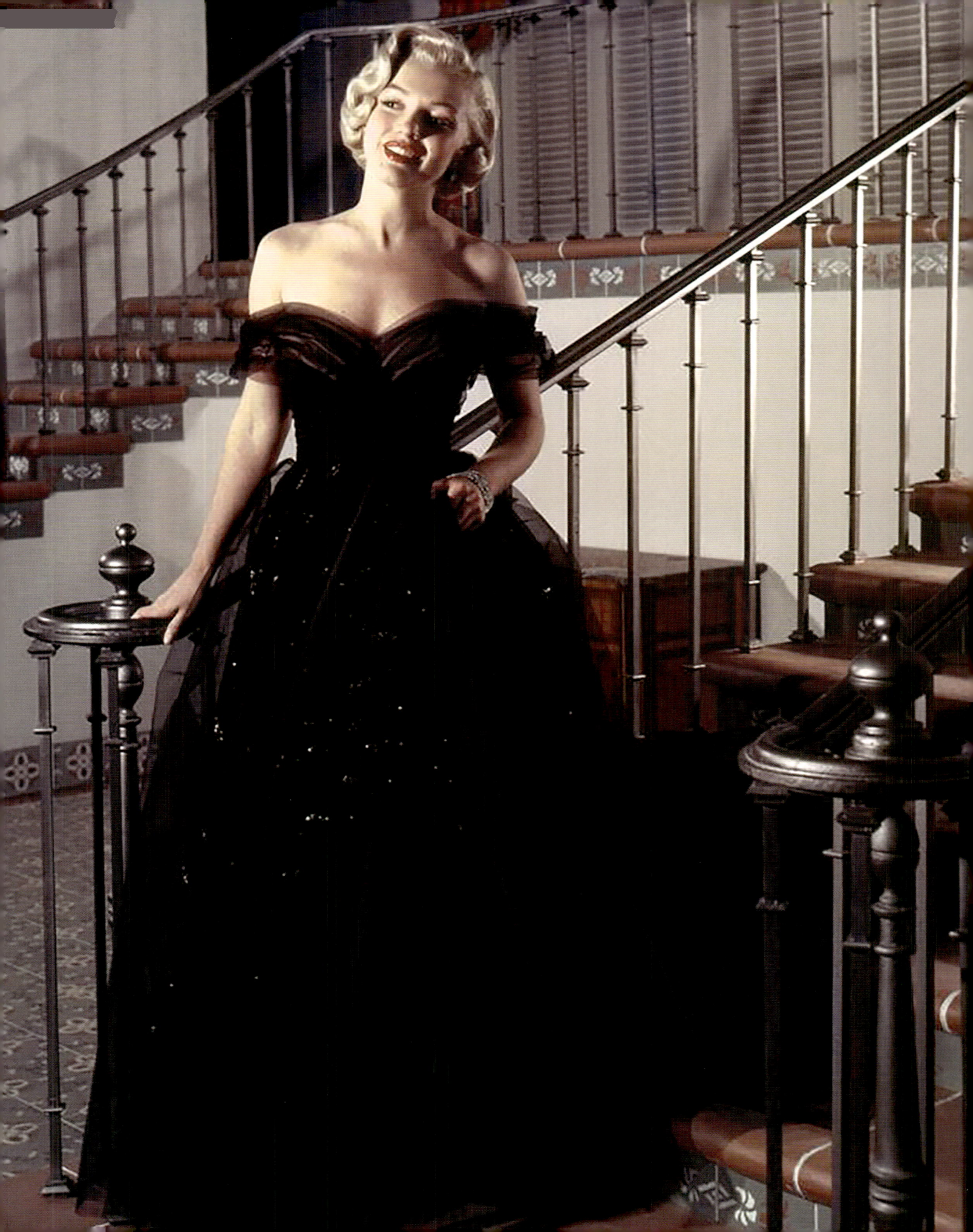

MARILYN MONROE

The ultimate screen siren, Marilyn Monroe turned vulnerability and sensuality into global stardom and became the most iconic face of 1950s Hollywood.

Marilyn Monroe (1926–1962), born Norma Jeane Mortenson in Los Angeles, lived a life shaped as much by reinvention as by talent. Raised in foster homes and orphanages, her early years were marked by instability and hardship. In her teens, she began modeling, quickly catching the attention of photographers for her photogenic charm and approachable beauty. Her success as a model led to a film contract with 20th Century Fox in the mid-1940s, though she initially appeared in minor or uncredited roles.

Her breakthrough came in 1950 with small but impactful performances in *The Asphalt Jungle* and *All About Eve*, where her luminous presence stood out amid star-studded casts. By 1953, Monroe had catapulted to full stardom. Films such as *Gentlemen Prefer Blondes* and *How to Marry a Millionaire* showcased her signature blend of childlike innocence, sultry charisma, and comic timing. She became synonymous with the "dumb blonde" archetype, but her portrayals often layered charm with self-awareness and vulnerability.

Frustrated by the limits of her typecasting, Monroe took bold steps to redefine her career. In 1955, she founded Marilyn Monroe Productions, one of the first female-led production companies in Hollywood. She also enrolled at the Actors Studio in New York to study method acting under Lee Strasberg. Her later roles, especially in *Bus Stop* (1956) and *Some Like It Hot* (1959), reflected her growth as a performer. The latter earned her a Golden Globe for Best Actress and remains one of her most celebrated performances.

Monroe's personal life, meanwhile, was tumultuous. She endured three marriages, most famously to

The Monroe Look

Monroe's signature hip-swinging walk, famously described by Jack Lemmon as "like Jello on springs," was achieved by wearing mismatched heels. Her iconic look was completed by makeup artist Whitey Snyder, who developed her trademark face during the filming of *Niagara* (1953).

- Platinum blonde curls
- Red lips and cat-eye liner
- Backless or halter satin gowns
- High heels and figure-hugging silhouettes

baseball legend Joe DiMaggio and playwright Arthur Miller, as well as long-standing struggles with anxiety, depression, and substance dependency. Despite these difficulties, Monroe maintained a captivating public persona that combined fragility with glamor.

Her image became iconic: platinum curls, radiant skin, red lips, and curve-hugging dresses that highlighted her hourglass figure. She was a muse to photographers, designers, and artists and helped shape the visual language of modern celebrity. Monroe appeared on countless magazine covers, endorsed major fashion and beauty brands, and became a global symbol of feminine allure. She also used her fame to challenge the power structure of Hollywood, demanding better roles and greater creative control.

Tragically, Monroe died in 1962 at the age of 36 from a barbiturate overdose. Her untimely death shocked the world and contributed to her enduring mythos. Today, Marilyn Monroe remains a symbol of both Hollywood's Golden Age and its human cost. Her life was marked by contradiction, fame, loneliness, desire, and vulnerability, but her impact on film, fashion, and pop culture is timeless.

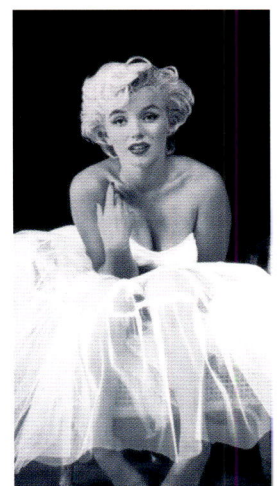

ABOVE

This iconic image of Marilyn Monroe in a white tulle dress was captured by photographer Milton H. Greene during one of their 50 collaborations—she later made him vice president of her production company.

FULL PAGE

Marilyn Monroe descends in style, radiant in a black off-the-shoulder evening gown—her signature blend of Old Hollywood glamor and effortless star power captured in a timeless moment.

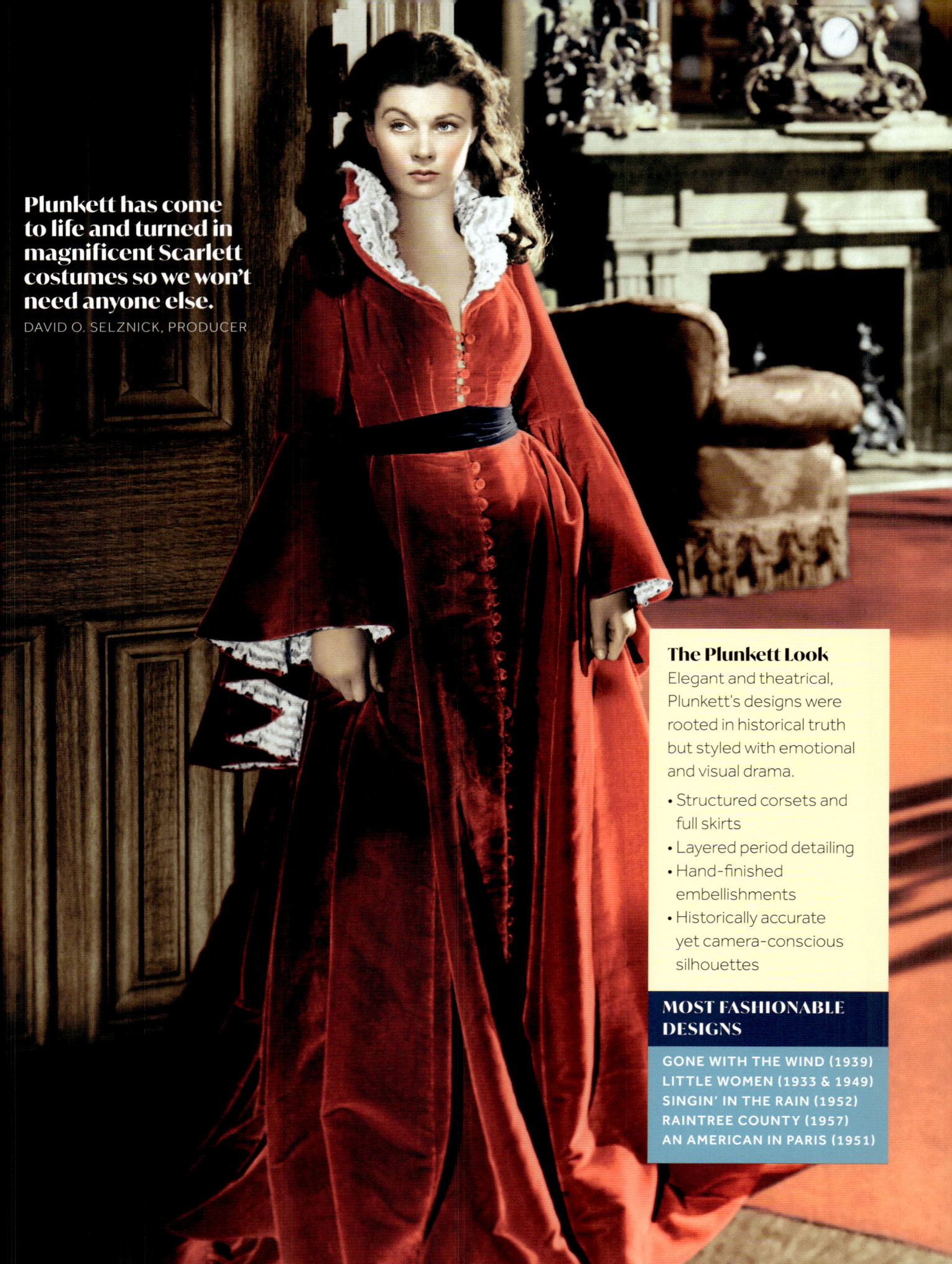

> **Plunkett has come to life and turned in magnificent Scarlett costumes so we won't need anyone else.**
> DAVID O. SELZNICK, PRODUCER

The Plunkett Look

Elegant and theatrical, Plunkett's designs were rooted in historical truth but styled with emotional and visual drama.

- Structured corsets and full skirts
- Layered period detailing
- Hand-finished embellishments
- Historically accurate yet camera-conscious silhouettes

MOST FASHIONABLE DESIGNS

GONE WITH THE WIND (1939)
LITTLE WOMEN (1933 & 1949)
SINGIN' IN THE RAIN (1952)
RAINTREE COUNTY (1957)
AN AMERICAN IN PARIS (1951)

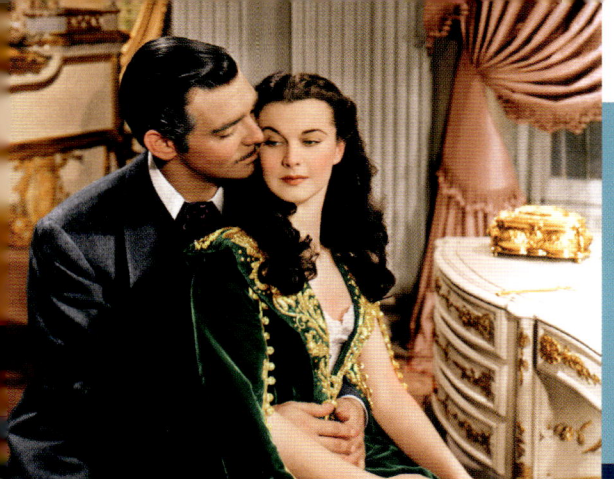

DESIGN SENSE
WALTER PLUNKETT

Meticulous, visionary, and dramatically attuned to narrative, Walter Plunkett was a titan of historical costume design in Hollywood's Golden Age, revered for his scholarship, theatricality, and deep commitment to storytelling through wardrobe.

Walter Plunkett (1902–1982), born in Oakland, California, originally studied law and fine arts at the University of California, Berkeley. But his passion for theater and design led him down a creative path. After working as an actor and scenic designer in New York, Plunkett transitioned to Hollywood in the early 1920s, where he found his true calling—not in front of the camera, but behind the scenes, designing costumes that would become central to the visual language of classic American cinema.

Plunkett joined RKO Pictures in 1927 and quickly rose to prominence as the head of its costume department. His affinity for period detail, rooted in intense research and a love of history, set him apart. He approached design as a fusion of scholarship and showmanship, believing that costumes should serve both character and era. Plunkett often spent weeks studying fashion plates, paintings, and cultural context before sketching. Yet, he also possessed an innate flair for theatrical elegance—his designs never felt like museum pieces but always brought characters to life with vibrancy and authenticity.

Perhaps his most famous achievement is the extraordinary costume design for *Gone with the Wind* (1939), where he created more than 5,000 individual costumes. Scarlett O'Hara's green velvet gown—repurposed from drapes—is still considered one of the most iconic garments in film history. Plunkett's ability to blend historical authenticity with emotional storytelling gave his costumes a cinematic power that helped define

characters before they spoke a word. His designs didn't just reflect the period—they enhanced the psychology, status, and emotional arc of the characters who wore them.

In addition to *Gone with the Wind*, Plunkett designed for a wide array of films, including *Little Women* (1933 and 1949), *The Hunchback of Notre Dame* (1939), *Pride and Prejudice* (1940), *Singin' in the Rain* (1952), and *Raintree County* (1957). His work often required recreating complex historical periods—from Civil War ball gowns to Regency-era empire silhouettes—yet he made them functional for actors and flattering for contemporary audiences. He was especially skilled at tailoring period looks to the specific figure and personality of each actress, making stars such as Vivien Leigh, Katharine Hepburn, and Elizabeth Taylor shine on screen. His intuitive understanding of how costume informed performance made him a favorite among directors and actors alike.

In 1951, Plunkett won the Academy Award for Best Costume Design (Color) for *An American in Paris*, sharing the honor with Irene Sharaff and Orry-Kelly. Despite numerous Oscar nominations throughout his career, he remained modest and focused, always prioritizing storytelling over personal acclaim. His humility and dedication to the craft left an indelible mark on Hollywood.

Plunkett eventually retired in the early 1960s but left behind a legendary body of work that continues to inspire designers and filmmakers. His gowns are preserved in archives and museum collections, and his influence can be seen in the historical precision and elegance of today's period films. He is widely credited with elevating costume design from a background trade to a vital storytelling art form, forever changing how audiences understand character through clothing.

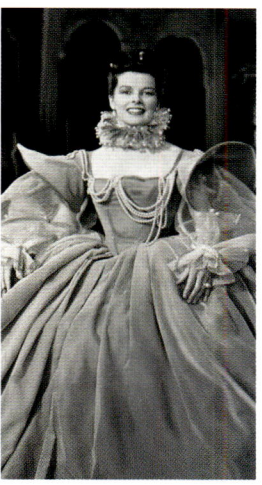

ABOVE

Walter Plunkett was a master of period costume design, creating lavish, historically inspired wardrobes for stars such as Katharine Hepburn in *Mary of Scotland* (1936) and *Little Women* (1933).

TOP LEFT

Vivien Leigh, as Scarlett O'Hara in *Gone with the Wind* (1939), wears the unforgettable green velvet gown fashioned from curtains, designed by Walter Plunkett. With its gold tassels and lavish embroidery, the costume became a symbol of Scarlett's resourcefulness and one of cinema's most iconic fashion moments.

FULL PAGE

Vivien Leigh as Scarlett O'Hara in *Gone with the Wind* (1939), wearing Walter Plunkett's lavish, character-defining costumes—each gown capturing Scarlett's fiery spirit and the sweeping grandeur of Hollywood's Golden Age.

LEADING MEN
CARY GRANT

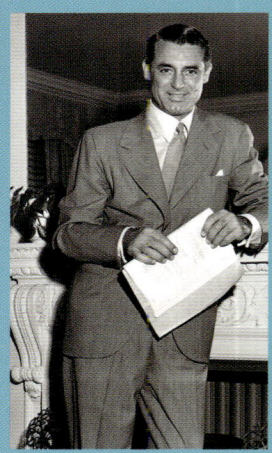

ABOVE

Looking debonair in a tailored suit, Grant epitomized classic Hollywood sophistication. Although never awarded a competitive Oscar, he received an Honorary Academy Award in 1970 for his unique mastery of the art of screen acting.

TOP RIGHT

Embracing Cary Grant in *Crisis*, Paula Raymond transitioned from modeling to Hollywood.

BOTTOM RIGHT

Holding a vintage press camera with suave precision, Cary Grant showcases his screen-ready charm. Known for his impeccable timing and debonair style, Grant starred in over 70 films and never won a competitive Oscar—despite being Hollywood royalty.

Charming, debonair, and endlessly refined, Cary Grant defined the archetype of the sophisticated leading man, effortlessly blending humor, elegance, and emotional depth into one of Hollywood's most iconic personas.

Cary Grant (1904–1986), born Archibald Alexander Leach in Bristol, England, overcame a turbulent childhood and modest beginnings to become one of the most cherished and influential stars in the history of American cinema. Raised in a working-class family marked by hardship—his mother was institutionalized when he was just a boy—Grant found refuge in performance. He ran away from home at a young age and joined a traveling acrobatic troupe, which helped him develop the athleticism and stage presence that would define his screen career. After a successful stint in vaudeville, he emigrated to the United States, eventually becoming a citizen and signing with Paramount Pictures in the early 1930s.

With his chiseled features, transatlantic accent, and effortless sophistication, Grant quickly ascended the Hollywood ranks. His early roles in romantic and screwball comedies such as *The Awful Truth* (1937), *Bringing Up Baby* (1938), and *His Girl Friday* (1940) displayed his dazzling comic timing, refined charm, and physical agility. These films not only solidified his status as a leading man but also helped shape the genre. Audiences adored his ability to project both lightness and gravitas, often within the same scene.

As he progressed, Grant took on more varied and complex roles in suspense thrillers and romantic dramas. His collaborations with Alfred Hitchcock—*Suspicion* (1941), *Notorious* (1946), *To Catch a Thief* (1955), and *North by Northwest* (1959)—revealed a darker, more mysterious edge beneath his polished

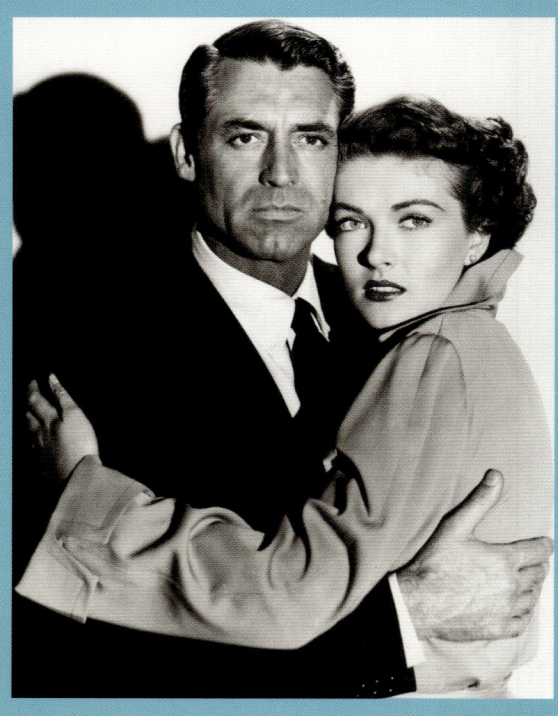

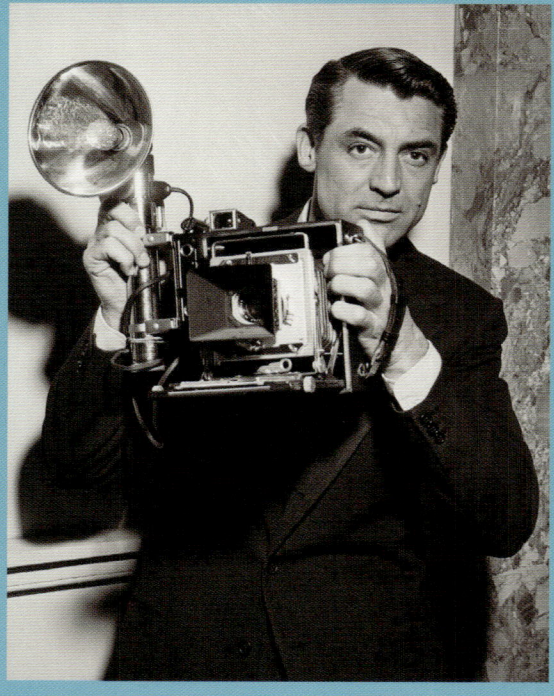

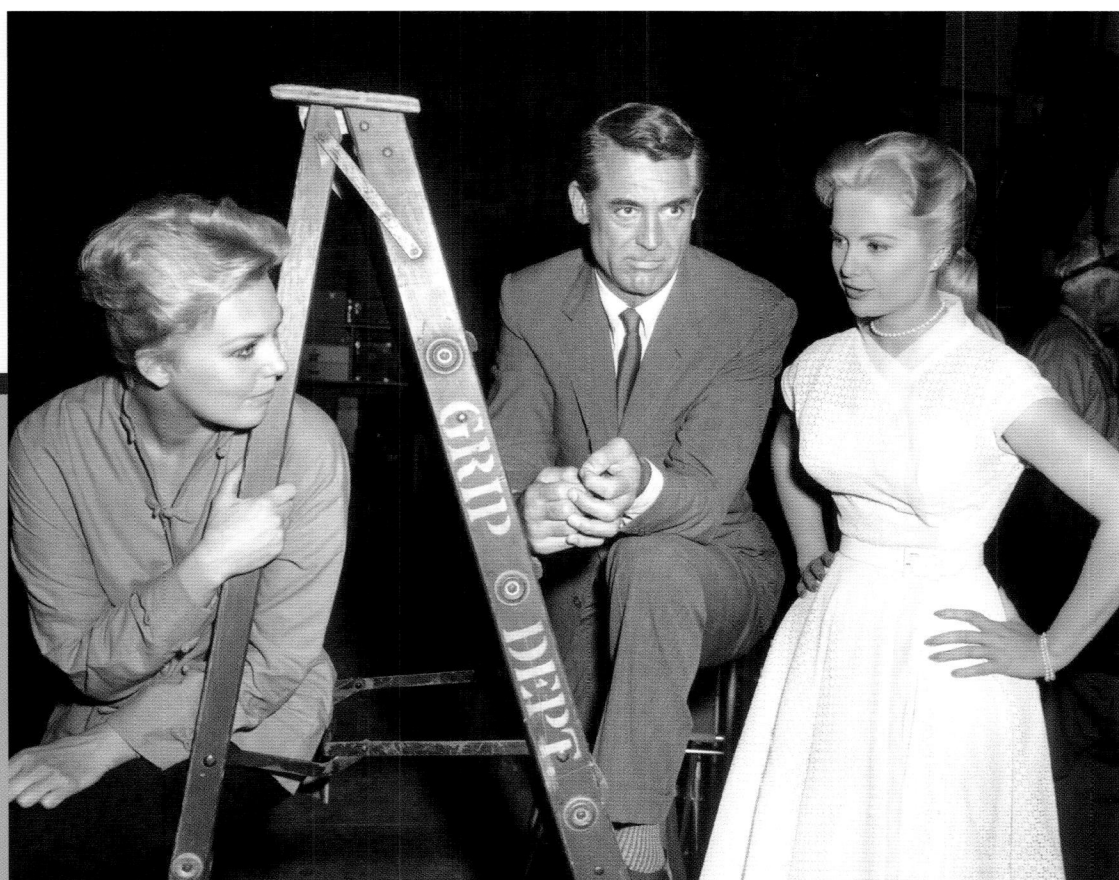

I pretended to be somebody I wanted to be until finally I became that person. Or he became me.

CARY GRANT

exterior. These performances combined elegance with emotional nuance, enhancing his reputation as a box office draw and a formidable actor. Grant's work with leading ladies such as Katharine Hepburn, Ingrid Bergman, Grace Kelly, and Audrey Hepburn produced some of Hollywood's most iconic screen pairings, notable for their chemistry and sophistication.

Off-screen, Grant became a fashion icon whose clean-cut tailoring and signature suiting influenced generations of men's style. He was also known for his integrity and professionalism in an often unpredictable industry. Despite two Academy Award nominations, he never won competitively, but in 1970, he received an Honorary Oscar celebrating his lifetime contributions to film.

Grant retired from acting in 1966 but remained a beloved public figure until his death. In later years, he pursued business interests and spent time with his family, becoming a devoted father in his fifties. He also participated in one-man shows and public appearances, always exuding the same charm that made him a star. Known for his dry wit and intelligence, he became a sought-after presence on lecture circuits, sharing reflections on his career and personal growth.

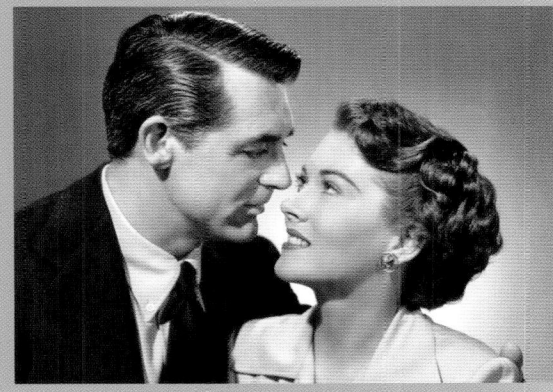

His legacy endures not only in the unforgettable characters he portrayed but in the very notion of cinematic elegance and charisma. Cary Grant remains, without question, one of Hollywood's most enduring legends—with his films, style, and persona as captivating today as they were at the height of his fame. His influence is felt in every actor who values subtlety, grace, and enduring screen presence. A master of understatement, Cary proved that true star power lies not in volume or flash, but in confidence, restraint, and authentic charm. His timeless appeal continues to resonate, influencing modern cinema and redefining what it means to be a leading man.

TOP LEFT

On the set with Kim Novak and Cary Grant, Martha Hyer exudes grace in a belted white dress.

BOTTOM LEFT

Sharing an intimate gaze with Cary Grant, Paula Raymond complements his signature style. Grant's perfectly tailored suit, crisp pocket square, and immaculate grooming epitomize the elegance of 1940s menswear, setting the standard for Hollywood sophistication.

JUDY HOLLIDAY

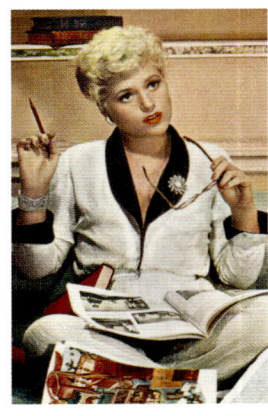

> **People have a hard time making me dress up to look like a classy gal.**
>
> JUDY HOLLIDAY

Clever, sharp-tongued, and irresistibly funny, Judy Holliday brought a unique blend of comedic brilliance and unexpected depth to 1950s Hollywood, carving out a niche for intelligent, endearing women with a comic edge.

Judy Holliday (1921–1965), from New York City, began her entertainment career with nightclub acts and radio performances before earning recognition on Broadway. Her breakthrough came with the stage play *Born Yesterday*, where she played Billie Dawn—a seemingly ditzy blonde who reveals surprising intellect and moral clarity. Holliday's portrayal won her the Academy Award for Best Actress when she reprised the role in the 1950 film adaptation, triumphing over more established stars and firmly establishing herself as a leading actress in Hollywood.

Holliday's gift for comedic timing and her distinctive, slightly nasal voice set her apart, especially in films such as *It Should Happen to You* (1954), opposite Jack Lemmon, and *The Solid Gold Cadillac* (1956), where she once again played a woman underestimated by those around her. Although she often portrayed naïve characters, Holliday imbued them with warmth, authenticity, and a keen intelligence that subtly critiqued gender expectations of the era.

Off-screen, her career was briefly interrupted during the McCarthy era due to suspicions about her political associations, though she was eventually cleared of any wrongdoing. Despite her relatively short film career and life—tragically cut short by cancer at the age of 43—Judy Holliday left an indelible mark on Hollywood. Her legacy persists as a symbol of comedic brilliance, intellectual depth, and enduring charm.

ABOVE

With her signature platinum curls and comedic timing, Judy Holliday won an Oscar for *Born Yesterday* (1950), proving brains and wit could outshine bombshell looks

RIGHT

Holliday beams in this radiant portrait, her platinum curls, coral shawl, and dazzling smile capturing the wit and warmth that made her a beloved star of 1950s Hollywood comedies.

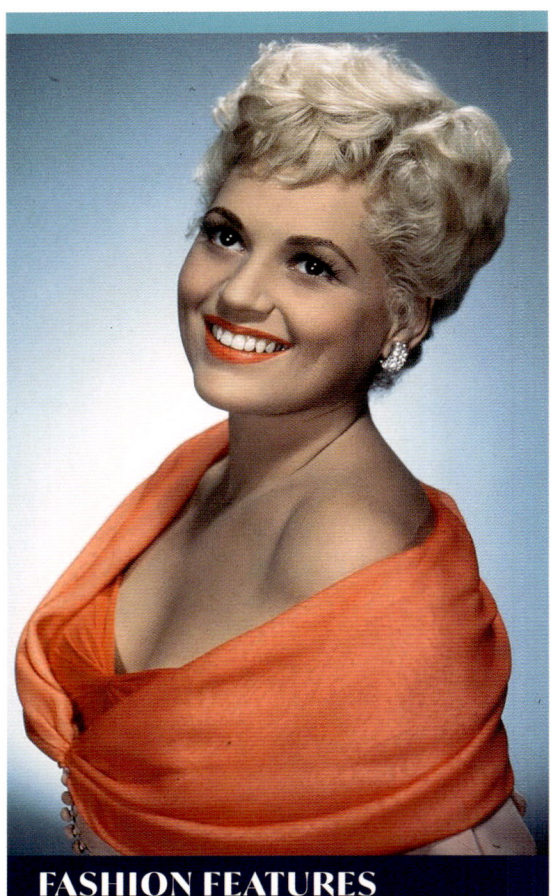

FASHION FEATURES

BORN YESTERDAY (1950)
IT SHOULD HAPPEN TO YOU (1954)
THE SOLID GOLD CADILLAC (1956)

The Holliday Look

Playful yet poised, her wardrobe combined soft, feminine silhouettes with quirky accessories, echoing her on-screen charm and off-screen intelligence.

- Curled blonde bob
- Fit-and-flare dresses
- Peep-toe heels
- Sweetheart necklines

DEBORAH KERR

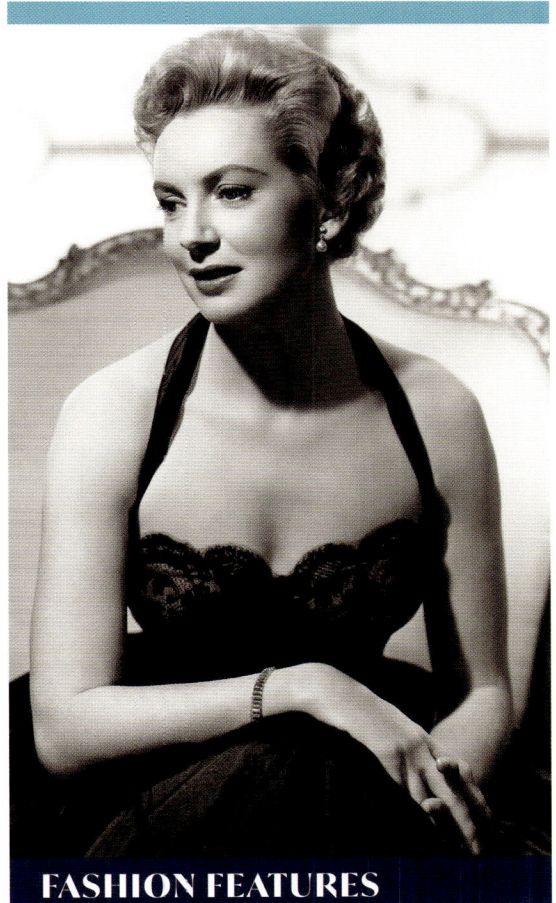

Refined, radiant, and consistently graceful, Deborah Kerr was the epitome of poise in classic cinema, seamlessly moving between British drama and Hollywood romance while earning acclaim for her dignified yet deeply human portrayals.

Deborah Kerr (1921–2007) was born in Helensburgh, Scotland, and trained in ballet before turning to acting in the 1930s. She began her career on stage and quickly gained popularity in British films during World War II, earning recognition for her sincerity, poise, and emotional intelligence. Kerr made a major impression in *The Life and Death of Colonel Blimp* (1943), portraying three different characters and showcasing her ability to embody intelligence, empathy, and quiet strength across eras and through different roles.

Her transition to Hollywood in the late 1940s was smooth and successful, aided by her refined demeanor, lyrical voice, and expressive eyes that conveyed emotional depth beneath an exterior of classic grace. She became known for playing composed, morally upright women, though her performance in *From Here to Eternity* (1953) challenged that typecasting—her passionate beach scene with Burt Lancaster remains one of the most unforgettable moments in film history.

Kerr received six Academy Award nominations for Best Actress, with standout performances in *The King and I* (1956), *Heaven Knows, Mr. Allison* (1957), *Tea and Sympathy* (1956), and *Separate Tables* (1958). Although she never won a competitive Oscar, she was honored with an Academy Award for lifetime achievement in 1994.

Kerr retired from feature films in the late 1960s but continued acting on stage and television into the 1980s. She remains revered for her emotional range, quiet dignity, and enduring screen presence

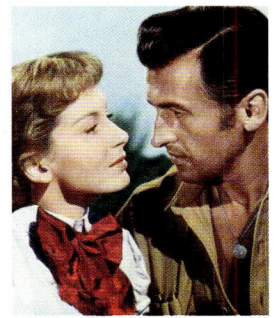

I don't think anyone knew I could act until I put on a bathing suit.

DEBORAH KERR ON HER ROLE IN *FROM HERE TO ETERNITY*

FASHION FEATURES

**THE KING AND I (1956)
FROM HERE TO ETERNITY (1953)
AN AFFAIR TO REMEMBER (1957)
TEA AND SYMPATHY (1956)**

The Kerr Look

Elegant and demure, Kerr's fashion sense exuded sophistication, with tailored gowns and graceful silhouettes that suited her classic beauty.

- Crisp evening dresses
- Full skirts and fitted waists
- Soft updos and natural makeup
- Delicate gloves and pearls

ABOVE

Kerr, known for her elegance and emotional depth, earned six Oscar nominations without a win. Her versatility shone in dramas, romances, and epics such as *King Solomon's Mines*.

LEFT

Deborah Kerr was celebrated for her poise and grace, often portraying refined women. She starred in classics such as *The King and I*, showcasing her talent across romantic dramas and epic musicals.

GRACE KELLY

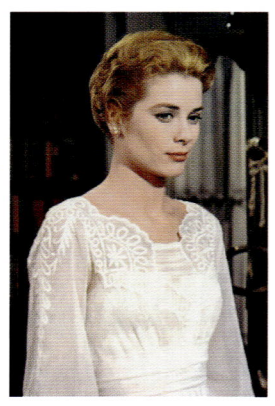

Cool, refined, and radiantly poised, Grace Kelly captivated audiences with her serene beauty and understated elegance, leaving behind a legacy that bridges Hollywood stardom and European royalty.

Grace Kelly (1929–1982), born into a prominent Philadelphia family, pursued acting against her parents' wishes, graduating from the American Academy of Dramatic Arts in New York. She began her career on stage and live television before transitioning to film, where her luminous presence and poised demeanor quickly drew critical acclaim. Kelly's film debut in *Fourteen Hours* (1951) led to a breakthrough role opposite Gary Cooper in *High Noon* (1952), setting the stage for her rapid ascent in Hollywood.

Her collaborations with director Alfred Hitchcock—*Dial M for Murder* (1954), *Rear Window* (1954), and *To Catch a Thief* (1955)— highlighted her enigmatic screen persona and her innate ability to project mystery, elegance, and emotional restraint. Although known for her cool and sophisticated image, Kelly delivered emotionally resonant performances in dramatic roles such as *Mogambo* (1953) and *The Country Girl* (1954), the latter earning her the Academy Award for Best Actress. She became a symbol of 1950s glamor, praised for her beauty, talent, and magnetic screen presence.

In 1956, at the peak of her career, Kelly retired from acting to marry Prince Rainier III of Monaco. As Princess Grace, she seamlessly transitioned into royal life, dedicating herself to philanthropy, promoting the arts, and raising her three children. Her wedding gown, designed by Helen Rose, became one of the most iconic bridal looks ever, further elevating her global

ABOVE

Kelly won an Academy Award for *The Country Girl* (1954) and starred in classic Hitchcock films before retiring from acting at 26 to become Princess of Monaco after marrying Prince Rainier III.

TOP RIGHT

Grace Kelly, poised in casual elegance, was the epitome of Hollywood royalty before becoming actual royalty.

FULL PAGE

Grace Kelly, draped in ethereal white, embodied timeless elegance. She starred in Hitchcock classics such as *Rear Window* and *To Catch a Thief*, earning global admiration.

The Kelly Look

Minimal yet regal, Grace Kelly's fashion sense combined classic lines with luxe materials, effortlessly elevating simplicity into high glamor.

- Silk blouses and midi skirts
- Chic scarves and structured handbags
- Tailored suits and clean silhouettes

fashion status. Her elegance, grace, and style made her a beloved figure worldwide.

Although she never returned to acting, Kelly remained active in public life and humanitarian efforts, supporting causes related to children, culture, and the environment. Her tragic death in a car accident in 1982 at age 52 shocked the world and deepened the mystique surrounding her.

Grace Kelly is remembered not only for her cinematic brilliance and royal dignity but for her enduring legacy as a fashion icon, humanitarian, and timeless embodiment of beauty, compassion, and poise. Her influence continues to inspire generations of actors, designers, and admirers across the globe.

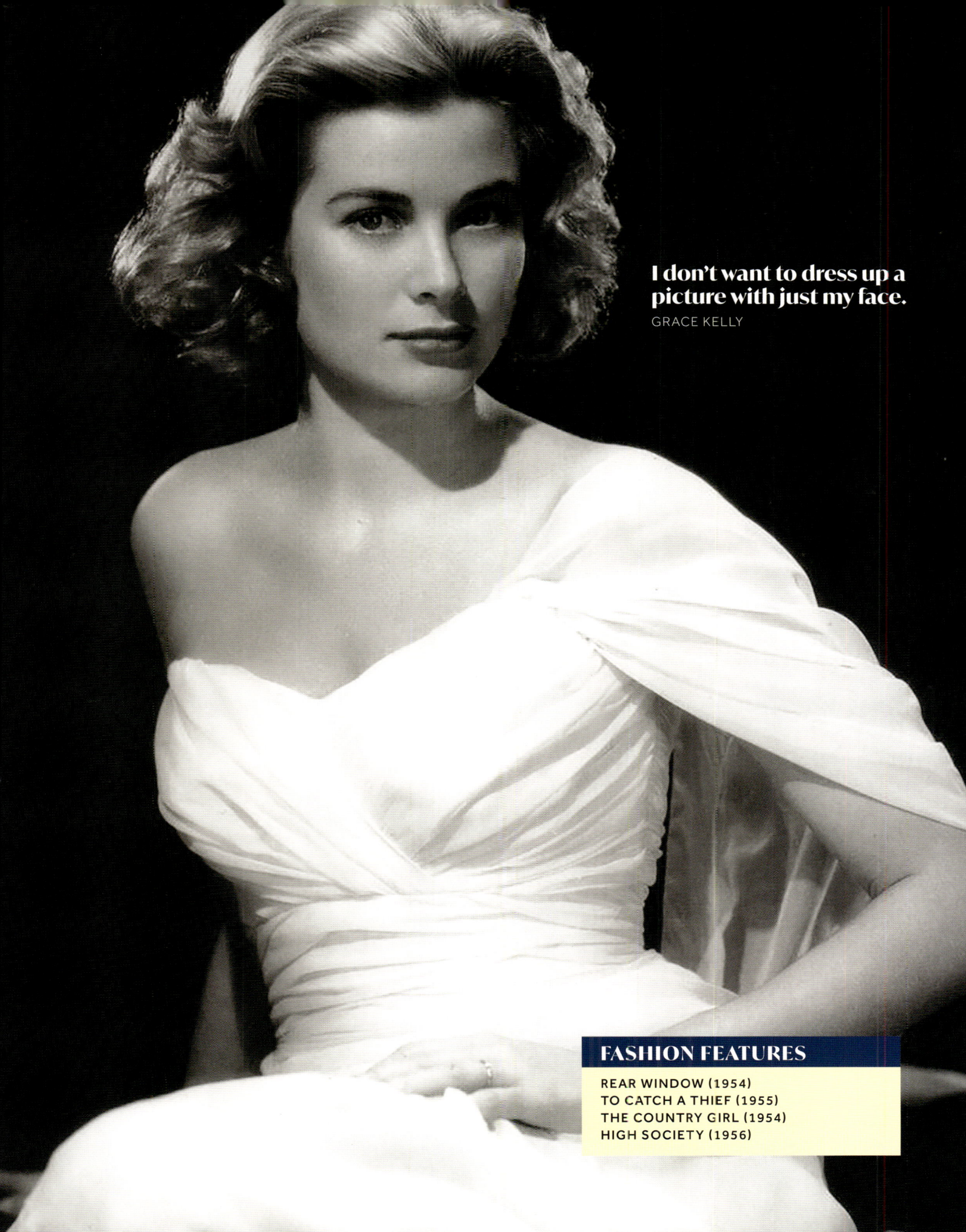

I don't want to dress up a picture with just my face.
GRACE KELLY

FASHION FEATURES

REAR WINDOW (1954)
TO CATCH A THIEF (1955)
THE COUNTRY GIRL (1954)
HIGH SOCIETY (1956)

LEADING MEN
YOUNG TYROS

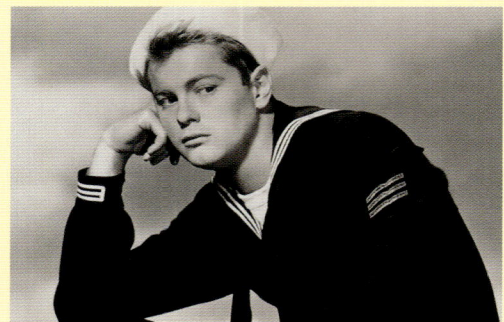

Fresh-faced, rebellious, and undeniably cool, the teenagers of the 1950s redefined American youth culture, establishing the style, sound, and spirit that would influence generations to come.

The 1950s teenagers came of age in a unique era—one marked by postwar prosperity, the birth of rock 'n' roll, and the emergence of a distinct youth identity. For the first time, adolescents were no longer expected to blend into adult society but instead celebrated their subculture with fashion, music, and attitudes that broke from tradition. This was the age of jukeboxes, soda fountains, sock hops, and Saturday night drive-ins. With Elvis Presley on the radio and James Dean on the screen, teens cultivated a sense of autonomy that was previously unheard of. They weren't just growing up—they were shaping a cultural revolution from behind the wheel of their parents' cars and under the glow of neon diner lights, fueled by soda pop, fast food, and teenage dreams.

Fashion played a pivotal role in this teenage transformation. Boys gravitated toward cuffed jeans, white T-shirts, and slicked-back hair—a look immortalized by Marlon Brando and the "greaser" subculture. Leather jackets and ducktail haircuts became synonymous with teen cool. Girls donned poodle skirts, saddle shoes, and angora sweaters, accessorizing with bobby socks, pastel lipstick, and ponytails tied in colorful scarves. For many, style was as much about belonging as it was about rebellion. Being seen in the right clothes, at the right hangout, with the right music was everything. Your image wasn't just a fashion choice—it was a declaration of identity and independence.

High school life revolved around dances, pep rallies, sports games, and sock hops, often soundtracked

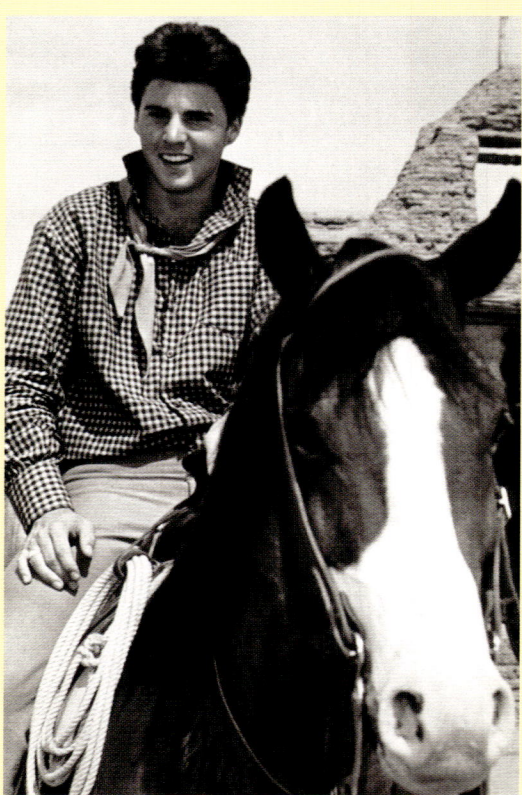

by doo-wop groups or early rock hits played on portable record players. Shopping centers became central teen hangouts, and the rise of the suburban family meant teens had access to cars, giving them the freedom to roam far from parental supervision. Dating rituals began to evolve as well. Going steady became a teenage rite of passage, marked by the exchanging of class rings, ID bracelets, and varsity jackets.

With more teens spending money than previous generations, they became a powerful consumer force, prompting businesses to cater directly to their tastes—whether in records, fashion, food, or films. They were no longer just younger versions of adults; they were cultural tastemakers, setting trends and driving entire industries. The American teenager had officially arrived—and the world would never look the same.

ABOVE

The "dreamy" blond Troy Donahue ushered in an era of preppy or West Coast styles that would later be reflected in the music of the Beach Boys.

TOP RIGHT

Ricky Nelson's checkered shirt and neckerchief in *Rio Bravo* (1959) reflected the relaxed, youthful take on classic Western wear, blending 1950s teen appeal with frontier authenticity.

FULL PAGE

In the 1950s, Elvis Presley's rebellious style and music revolutionized teen culture, influencing fashion trends such as slicked-back hair, pegged pants, and the rise of rock 'n' roll fandom.

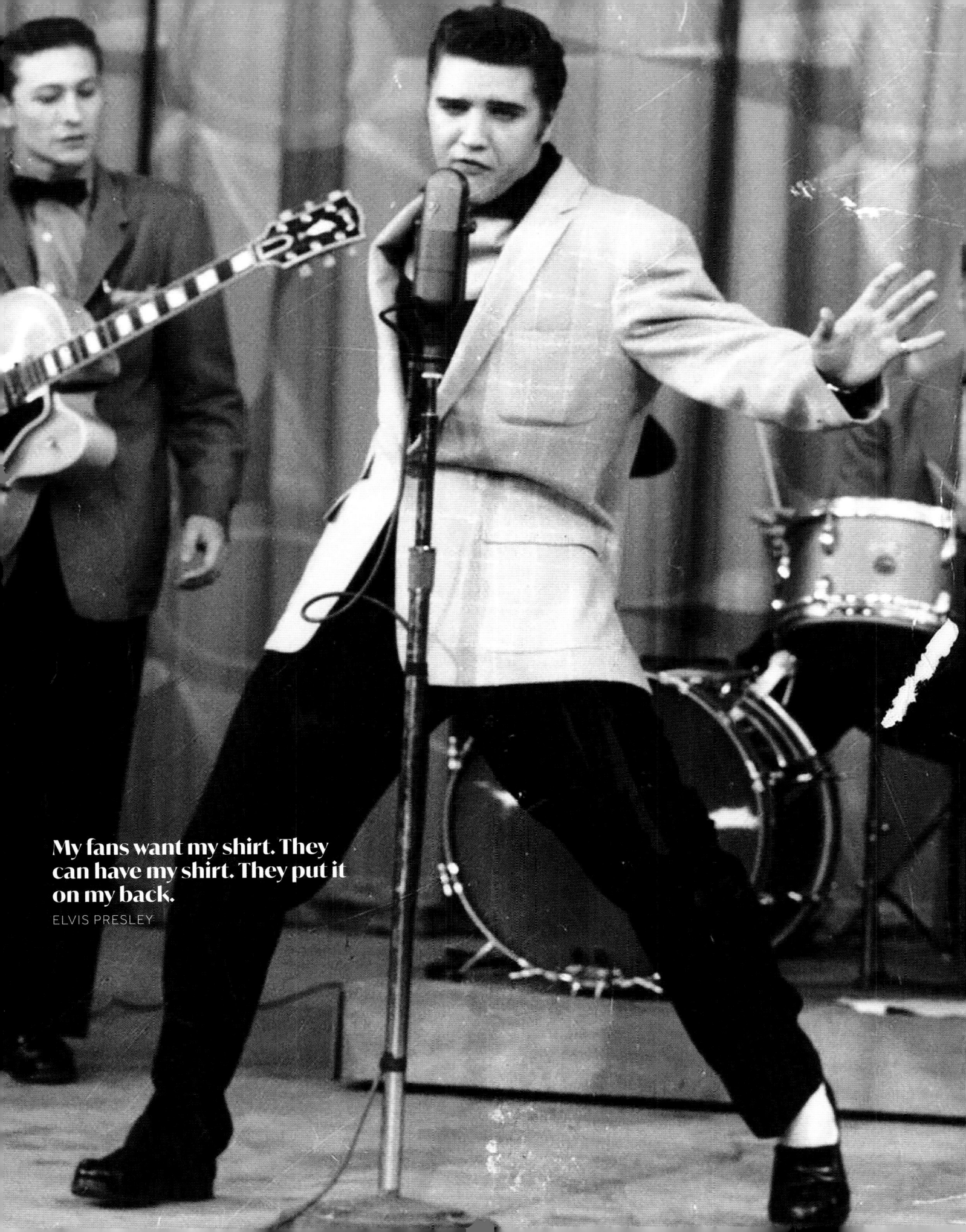

My fans want my shirt. They can have my shirt. They put it on my back.

ELVIS PRESLEY

SOPHIA LOREN

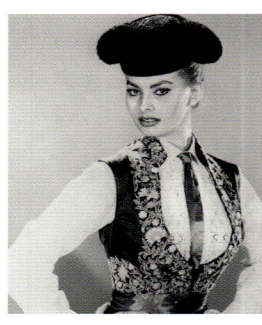

> **A woman's dress should be like a barbed-wire fence: serving its purpose without obstructing the view.**
>
> SOPHIA LOREN

ABOVE

Sophia Loren, one of Italy's most celebrated actresses, became the first performer to win an Academy Award for a foreign-language film with *Two Women* (1960), marking a milestone in international cinema.

RIGHT

Wearing a cinched bodice and full skirt, Sophia Loren embodied Mediterranean sensuality.

Fiery, statuesque, and unapologetically glamorous, Sophia Loren became a global icon of sensuality and strength, embodying a uniquely Mediterranean blend of passion, elegance, and cinematic gravitas.

Sophia Loren (1934–), raised in the impoverished town of Pozzuoli near Naples after her early years in Rome, overcame a challenging start to become one of the most iconic and beloved figures in international cinema. Growing up during wartime and raised by a single mother, Loren's early life shaped the resilience and strength that would define her screen presence.

She began her film career with small roles in the early 1950s, but her magnetic beauty, expressive eyes, and natural talent soon attracted the attention of producers and audiences alike. A key turning point came with her professional and personal partnership with producer Carlo Ponti, who helped shape her career and introduce her to international audiences.

Loren gained widespread acclaim with standout roles in *The Gold of Naples* (1954), *Boy on a Dolphin* (1957), and *Houseboat* (1958), where her chemistry with Cary Grant captivated viewers. Her most celebrated role was in *Two Women* (1960), a searing wartime drama directed by Vittorio De Sica. Her powerful performance as a mother enduring the horrors of war earned her the Academy Award for Best Actress, making her the first performer to win an Oscar for a foreign-language film.

Throughout the 1960s and 1970s, she balanced glamorous Hollywood films with emotionally rich Italian cinema, appearing in *El Cid* (1961), *Yesterday, Today and Tomorrow* (1963), and *A Special Day* (1977). With a career spanning over seven decades, Loren remains a timeless symbol of beauty, grace, and cinematic excellence, influencing generations of actors and filmmakers worldwide.

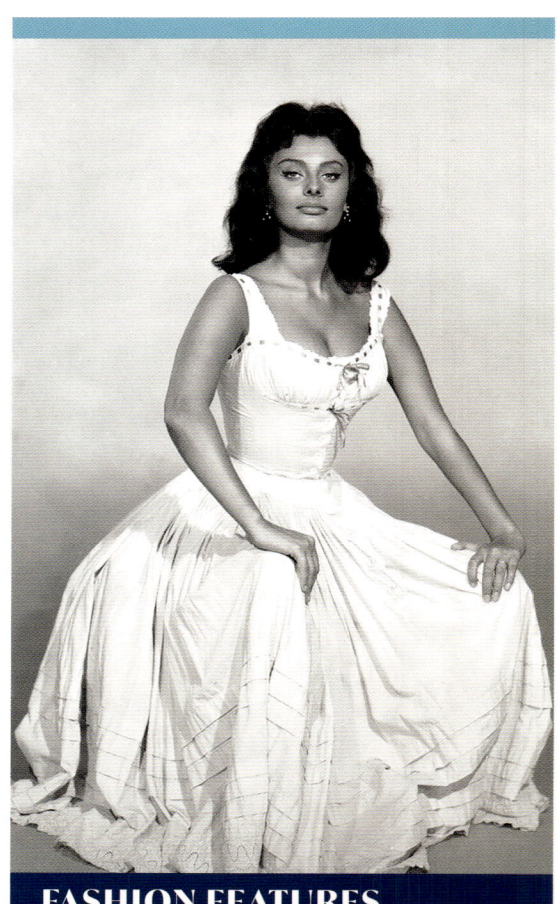

FASHION FEATURES

BOY ON A DOLPHIN (1957)
EL CID (1961)
YESTERDAY, TODAY AND TOMORROW (1963)
TWO WOMEN (1960)

The Loren Look

Commanding and womanly, Loren's fashion mirrored her screen roles— sultry, sophisticated, and distinctly European.

- Plunging necklines and cinched waists
- Voluminous hairstyles
- Bold jewelry and winged eyeliner

KIM NOVAK

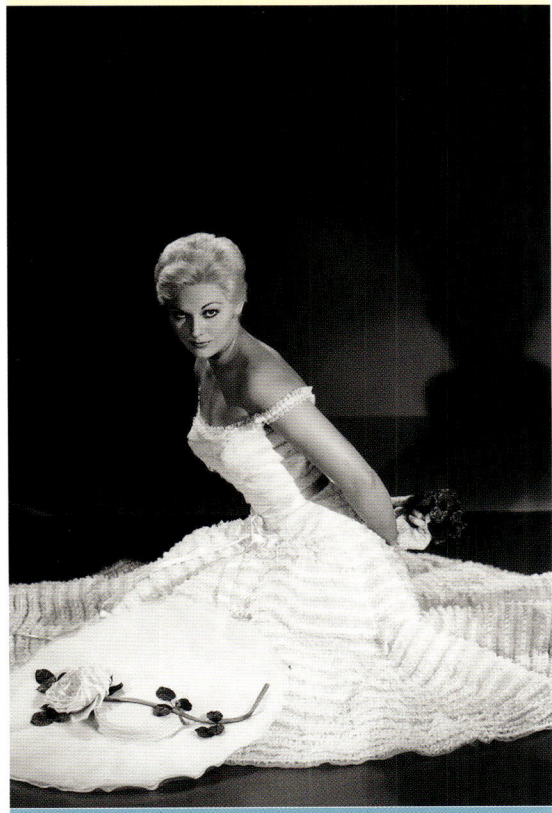

The Novak Look

Understated yet striking, Novak favored elegant silhouettes and soft textures that complemented her cool, introspective style—one that defined her roles in films such as *Vertigo* and *Picnic*.

• Honey-blonde hair styled in soft waves
• Pencil skirts and V-neck sweaters
• Swing coats and dramatic collars

Graceful and enigmatic, Kim Novak defined cool allure in mid-century Hollywood. Known for her sultry screen presence and quietly powerful performances, she left an indelible mark on American cinema.

Kim Novak (1933–), born Marilyn Pauline Novak in Chicago, Illinois, began her career as an art student and model before being signed by Columbia Pictures in the early 1950s. Studio head Harry Cohn promoted her as Columbia's answer to Marilyn Monroe, but Novak quickly carved out her own identity with a more introspective, enigmatic presence. With a quiet, magnetic screen appeal, she stood apart from the bubbly blonde archetype dominating the era.

Her breakthrough role came in *Picnic* (1955), opposite William Holden, where she played a yearning small-town girl trapped in conformity—an emotional tone she would refine throughout her career. Novak's most iconic performance came in Alfred Hitchcock's *Vertigo* (1958), where she played the dual role of Madeleine and Judy. Her haunting portrayal blended seductive mystery with aching vulnerability, and the film has since become a landmark in cinematic history.

She also excelled in *Pal Joey* (1957) alongside Frank Sinatra and in *Bell, Book and Candle* (1958), showcasing her ability to handle both dramatic and comedic roles with subtlety. In *Middle of the Night* (1959), she took on more complex material, affirming her dramatic depth. Although her career slowed in the 1960s, Novak continued to choose roles on her own terms, often stepping away from the spotlight to pursue painting and a more private life.

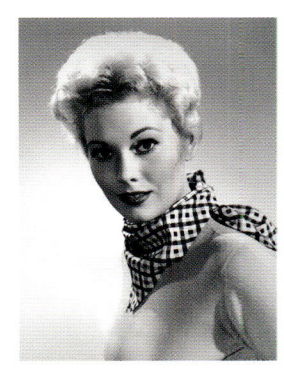

ABOVE

Known for her signature "peekaboo" hairstyle, Kim Novak helped popularize minimalist glamor, often favoring sleek silhouettes and subtle sensuality.

LEFT

Kim Novak rose to fame in the 1950s and is best known for her dual role in Alfred Hitchcock's *Vertigo* (1958), a film now considered one of cinema's greatest masterpieces.

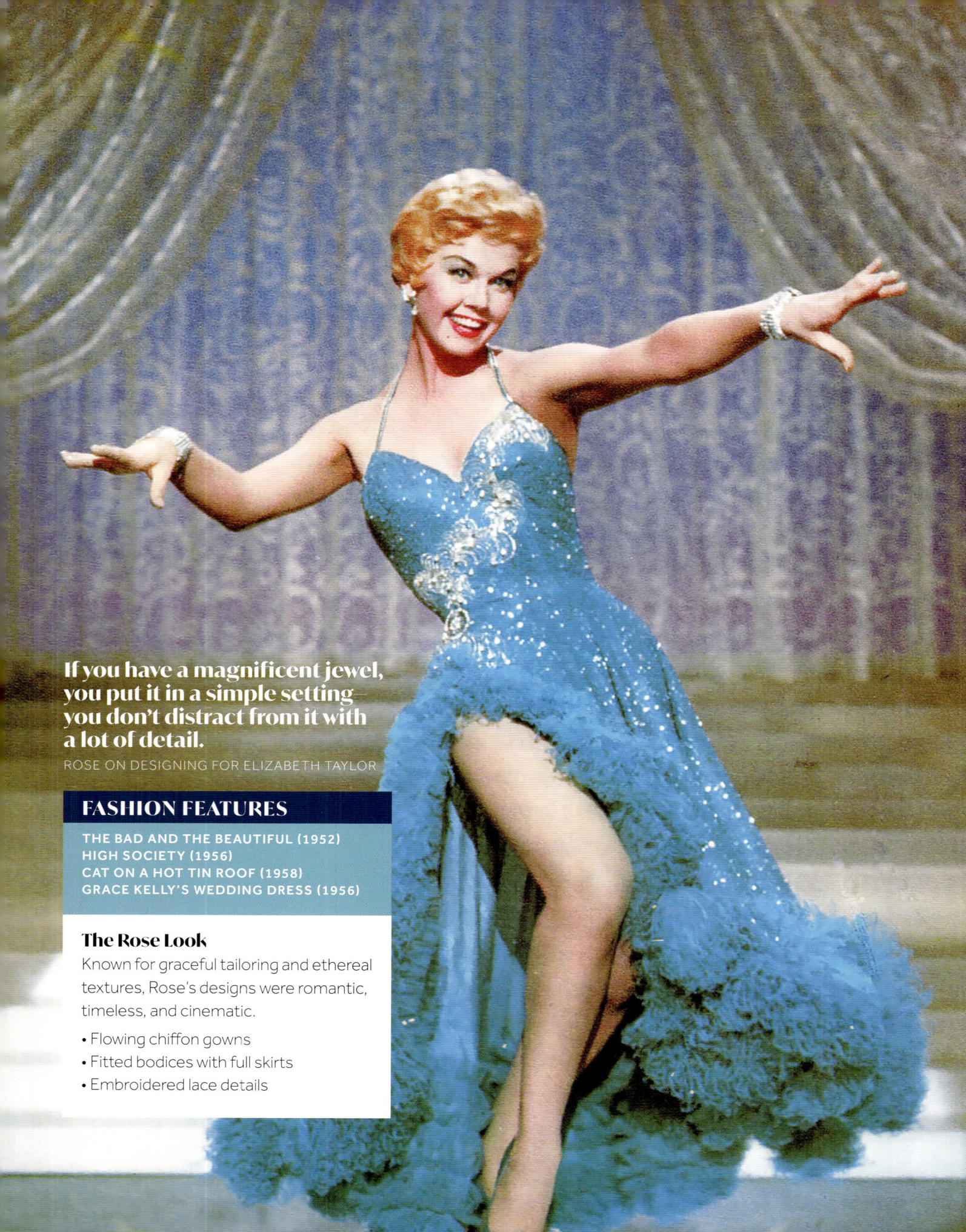

> If you have a magnificent jewel, you put it in a simple setting — you don't distract from it with a lot of detail.

ROSE ON DESIGNING FOR ELIZABETH TAYLOR

FASHION FEATURES

THE BAD AND THE BEAUTIFUL (1952)
HIGH SOCIETY (1956)
CAT ON A HOT TIN ROOF (1958)
GRACE KELLY'S WEDDING DRESS (1956)

The Rose Look

Known for graceful tailoring and ethereal textures, Rose's designs were romantic, timeless, and cinematic.

- Flowing chiffon gowns
- Fitted bodices with full skirts
- Embroidered lace details

DESIGN SENSE
HELEN ROSE

Elegant, prolific, and attuned to the nuances of feminine glamor, Helen Rose became one of Hollywood's most influential costume designers, known for her ability to enhance a star's persona while shaping postwar fashion for the everyday woman.

Helen Rose (1904–1985) was born in Chicago and studied at the Chicago Academy of Fine Arts, where she laid the foundation for a career that would influence both Hollywood and global fashion. She began designing costumes for nightclubs, Las Vegas stage revues, and the Ice Follies—work that helped her develop a flair for dramatic movement and glamorous silhouettes. After a brief period at 20th Century Fox, she joined MGM in 1943, a studio known for its lavish productions and star-studded roster.

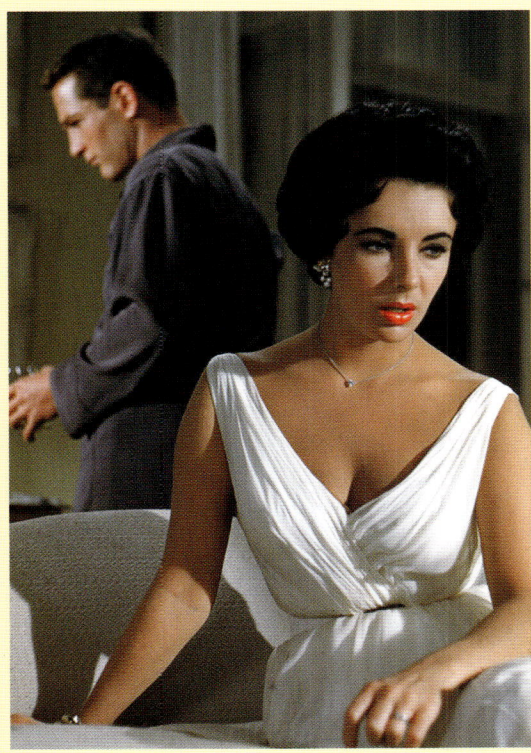

Rose quickly distinguished herself with her exquisite attention to detail and ability to accentuate a woman's beauty without overshadowing her personality. When MGM's then-head designer Irene Lentz left the studio, Rose was promoted to chief designer, where she remained one of the most influential costume artists of her time and shaped the studio's signature aesthetic for over two decades.

Her creations adorned some of Hollywood's biggest stars, including Elizabeth Taylor, Grace Kelly, Lana Turner, Judy Garland, and Debbie Reynolds. Rose was especially praised for her romantic use of chiffon, satin, and organza—soft, luxurious fabrics that moved elegantly on screen. Her costumes flattered and framed the actresses, emphasizing femininity with elegance and sophistication.

She won two Academy Awards for Best Costume Design: *The Bad and the Beautiful* (1952) and *I'll Cry Tomorrow* (1955), and was nominated ten more times. Her notable film credits include *High Society* (1956), *Cat on a Hot Tin Roof* (1958), and *The Last Time I Saw Paris* (1954).

Outside of film, Rose achieved international fame by designing Grace Kelly's wedding gown for her 1956 royal marriage to Prince Rainier of Monaco. The timeless silk taffeta and lace design, featuring a high neckline and long sleeves, became a gold standard for bridal fashion and continues to influence bridal designers today.

Later in her career, she launched her fashion label, offering ready-to-wear collections that brought the glamor of the silver screen into women's everyday wardrobes. She also authored a memoir, *Just Make Them Beautiful*, which chronicled her life in costume design and her intimate experiences dressing Hollywood royalty. Rose's legacy endures as a symbol of elegance, innovation, and timeless style in both fashion and film.

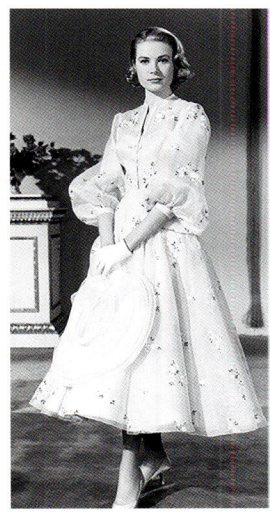

ABOVE

Rose and Grace Kelly were busy with *High Society* when Kelly asked her to design the gown for Kelly's wedding with Prince Rainier. Rose used one of the ball gowns from *High Society* as a starting point.

LEFT

In 1958's *Cat on a Hot Tin Roof*, Elizabeth Taylor tries to entice husband Paul Newman by donning a series of seductive gowns, including this stunning low-cut white dress with a draped, crossover bodice.

FULL PAGE

Doris Day proved her mettle playing real-life jazz-age singer Ruth Etting in 1958's *Love Me or Leave Me*. Here, she struts her stuff in a glittering turquoise stage costume trimmed with ostrich feathers.

LEADING MEN
FRANK SINATRA

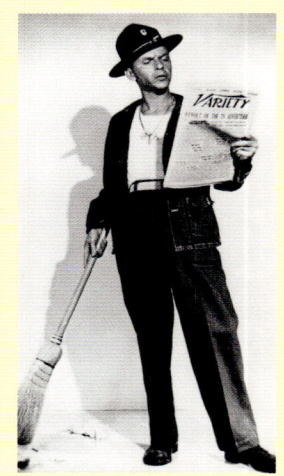

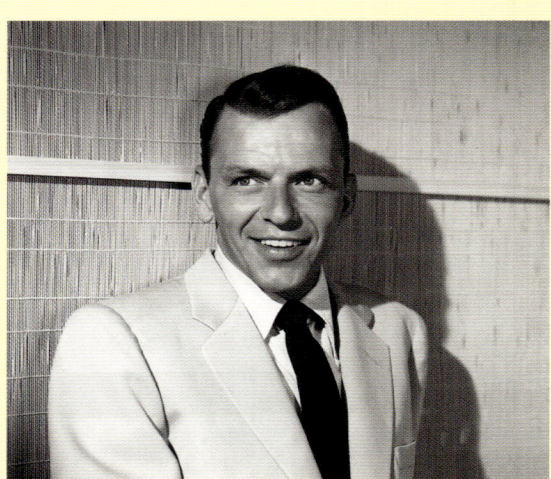

Magnetic, moody, and unmistakably iconic, Frank Sinatra defined 20th-century cool with his rich voice, brooding charisma, and timeless sense of style that transcended the stage and screen.

Frank Sinatra (1915–1998), born Francis Albert Sinatra in Hoboken, New Jersey, rose from humble beginnings to become one of the most influential entertainers of all time. The son of Italian immigrants, Sinatra was drawn to music early on, captivated by the smooth crooning of Bing Crosby. He began singing as a teenager and honed his craft in local nightclubs and radio stations. His big break came when he joined the big bands of Harry James and later Tommy Dorsey, where he learned the importance of breath control, phrasing, and timing—skills that would become his trademarks. Sinatra's emotional delivery and smooth, nuanced voice quickly won over audiences, and by the early 1940s, he had achieved solo stardom, igniting a fan frenzy dubbed "Sinatramania."

Sinatra's early fame was defined by his romantic ballads and lush orchestral arrangements, but the 1950s saw him reinvent himself both musically and personally. After facing a career slump and vocal strain, he staged one of the most celebrated comebacks in entertainment history with a powerful performance in *From Here to Eternity* (1953), earning an Academy Award for Best Supporting Actor. This triumph marked a turning point, revitalizing his career and ushering in a period of creative depth. Albums such as *In the Wee Small Hours* (1955) and *Songs for Swingin' Lovers!* (1956) demonstrated a new artistic maturity, where Sinatra fully inhabited the roles of the introspective romantic, the suave swinger, and the heartbroken loner.

In the 1950s and the 60s, Sinatra became the ultimate symbol of American cool. As the unofficial leader of the Rat Pack—a group of entertainers that included Dean Martin, Sammy Davis Jr., and Peter Lawford—he projected an image of confidence, wit, and effortless charm. He starred in a string of stylish films, including *Ocean's 11* (1960), *The Man with the*

ABOVE

Dressed as a janitor with a Variety paper in hand, Frank Sinatra parodied fame. He won an Oscar for *From Here to Eternity* (1953), reviving his film career.

TOP RIGHT

Frank Sinatra, dressed in a crisp light suit, was a legend of music and film. He won nine Grammy Awards and an Oscar for acting.

RIGHT

At Columbia Records in 1951, Rosemary Clooney shares a laugh with Sinatra during a publicity shoot for their duet 'If Only I Had a Match.'

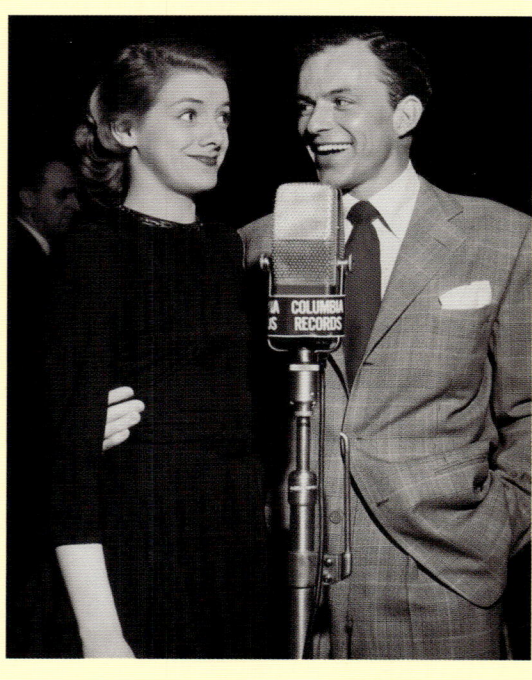

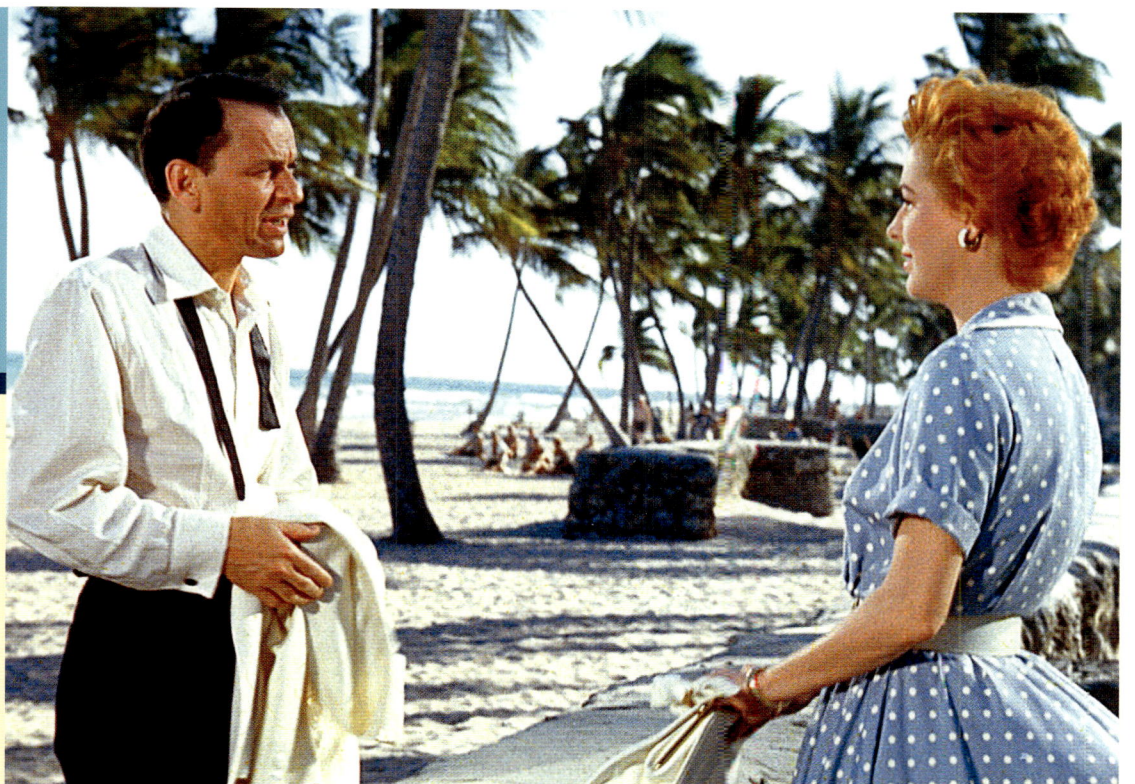

Clothes don't make the man. But they help. I've always believed in looking sharp. If you feel good in what you wear, you carry yourself better.

FRANK SINATRA

Golden Arm (1955), and *Pal Joey* (1957), all of which reinforced his persona as the urbane, streetwise leading man. His musical output remained prolific, filled with swing anthems, torch songs, and jazzy standards that defined mid-century sophistication. Whether in a smoky Vegas lounge or on a world stage, he commanded attention.

Outside the spotlight, Sinatra was deeply engaged in political and social issues. He championed civil rights, demanding integrated audiences at his shows and supporting causes for racial equality. Politically, he evolved—initially a vocal supporter of Democratic figures such as Franklin D. Roosevelt and John F. Kennedy, and later aligning with Republicans, including close friend Ronald Reagan. He used his fame to influence culture not only through entertainment but also through civic engagement and philanthropy.

Throughout his extraordinary career, Sinatra earned nine Grammy Awards, a Presidential Medal of Freedom, and the Congressional Gold Medal. He founded his record label, Reprise Records, which gave him creative control and allowed him to continue shaping his legacy on his terms. A master of reinvention, he remained artistically relevant into the 1990s. His legacy spans over six decades, touching countless genres and generations, from jazz to pop to big band swing.

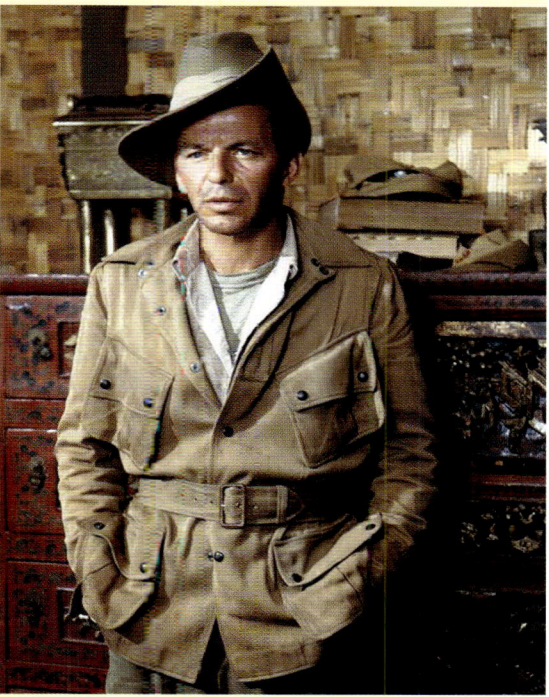

To this day, Frank Sinatra remains a cultural icon—a timeless representation of style, talent, and magnetic presence. His music and image continue to define what it means to be effortlessly cool, proving that true charisma never fades. For millions around the world, Sinatra isn't just a voice from the past—he's a mood, a memory, and an enduring emblem of American elegance.

TOP LEFT

Frank Sinatra shares a beachside moment in classic cool—loosened bow tie and jacket in hand—effortlessly embodying mid-century charm against a breezy palm-lined backdrop.

LEFT

Sinatra in rugged adventure mode, sporting a belted safari jacket and fedora—captured in a rare offbeat moment that blends Hollywood charisma with a world-weary edge.

DEBBIE REYNOLDS

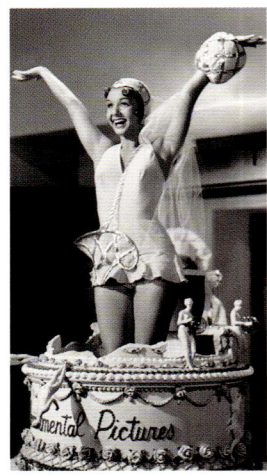

Sunny, spirited, and endlessly charming, Debbie Reynolds captivated audiences with her wholesome appeal, sparkling energy, and versatile talent as one of Hollywood's most beloved stars of the postwar era.

Debbie Reynolds (1932–2016), hailing from El Paso, Texas, was discovered by Warner Bros. and quickly rose to stardom. After winning a beauty contest at age sixteen, she soon moved to MGM, where her girl-next-door charm, comic timing, and strong singing voice made her a standout in musicals and romantic comedies. Her breakout role came in *Singin' in the Rain* (1952), where she starred opposite Gene Kelly and Donald O'Connor in what would become one of the most iconic musicals ever. Despite having no formal dance training, Reynolds rehearsed tirelessly to match Kelly's choreography, earning both acclaim and respect from her peers.

Reynolds continued her success throughout the 1950s and 1960s with roles in light-hearted romances and family-friendly comedies. She starred in *Tammy and the Bachelor* (1957), which introduced the hit song "Tammy," showcasing her sweet, lilting vocals. In *The Unsinkable Molly Brown* (1964), she portrayed the fiery, real-life *Titanic* survivor, a role that earned her an Academy Award nomination for Best Actress. Other highlights included *The Singing Nun* (1966) and *How Sweet It Is!* (1968), cementing her status as one of Hollywood's most versatile and beloved stars.

Beyond the screen, Reynolds advocated for film preservation, amassing one of the largest private collections of Hollywood costumes and memorabilia. She also enjoyed a prolonged stage career in Las Vegas and on Broadway. Her daughter, actress, and writer Carrie Fisher, carried on her legacy in entertainment, and their close relationship remained central to both women's public lives.

ABOVE

Debbie Reynolds stole hearts as Kathy Selden in *Singin' in the Rain* (1952), mastering dance routines despite no prior training—showcasing her determination, charm, and emerging star power.

RIGHT

Reynolds balanced stardom with resilience, raising daughter Carrie Fisher while thriving in film and music. Her wholesome charm made her one of Hollywood's most beloved post war actresses.

FASHION FEATURES

SINGIN' IN THE RAIN (1952)
TAMMY AND THE BACHELOR (1957)
THE UNSINKABLE MOLLY BROWN (1964)
THE SINGING NUN (1966)

The Reynolds Look

Fresh-faced and feminine, Reynolds favored youthful silhouettes that matched her lively screen persona.

- Sweetheart necklines
- Full skirts and nipped waists
- Soft curls and radiant smile
- Classic, demure dresses

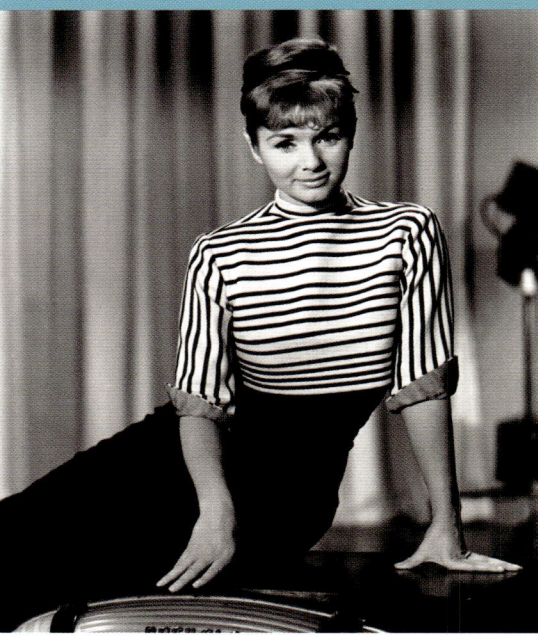

Debbie is one of the few women I know who can take a gown that might seem conservative and put sex into it.

EVA GABOR

NATALIE WOOD

FASHION FEATURES

WEST SIDE STORY (1961)
SPLENDOR IN THE GRASS (1961)
GYPSY (1962)

The Wood Look

Romantic and feminine, Wood favored fitted bodices, soft necklines, and timeless silhouettes that reflected her youth and grace.

- Winged eyeliner
- Full-skirted dresses
- Soft curls
- Pastel knits and coats

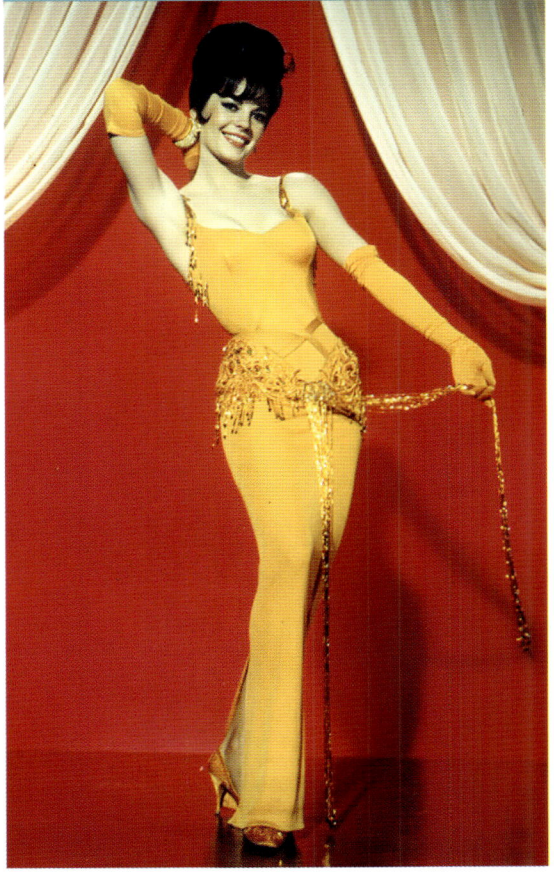

Sensitive, dazzling, and precociously talented, Natalie Wood embodied the complexities of youth and femininity on screen, leaving behind a poignant legacy of beauty, vulnerability, and emotional depth.

Natalie Wood (1938–1981), born Natalia Nikolaevna Zakharenko in San Francisco to Russian immigrant parents, began acting as a child and rose to fame early with her role in *Miracle on 34th Street* (1947). Her transition from a child star to a serious actress was marked by her Oscar-nominated performance in *Rebel Without a Cause* (1955), where she captured the restless spirit of postwar American youth. With her large, expressive eyes and earnest presence, Wood became a beloved screen figure throughout the 1950s and 1960s.

She starred in a string of memorable films, including *Splendor in the Grass* (1961), *West Side Story* (1961), and *Love with the Proper Stranger* (1963), each showcasing her emotional range, luminous beauty, and magnetic vulnerability. Wood was especially admired for portraying women in psychological conflict, often caught between societal expectations and personal desire—a theme that resonated powerfully with audiences of the era.

Her performances combined technical skill with an intuitive understanding of complex emotion, allowing her to inhabit roles that were both tender and raw. Off-screen, her personal life—including her high-profile marriages to actor Robert Wagner—captivated the public as much as her work. Her untimely and mysterious death in 1981 only deepened the fascination with her life and legacy. Natalie Wood remains an enduring symbol of Hollywood glamor, sensitivity, and tragic mystique.

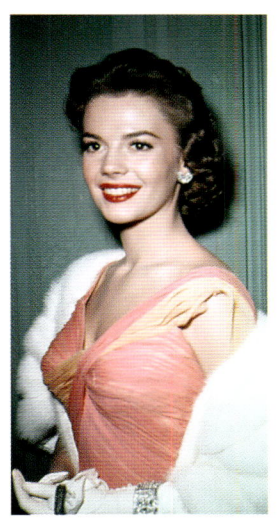

ABOVE

Natalie Wood in the 1950s, radiant in a blush-toned gown, diamond earrings, and white fur stole—capturing the polished glamor and poised charm of Hollywood's golden era.

LEFT

Wood dazzles in *Gypsy* (1962), portraying burlesque star Gypsy Rose Lee in a whirlwind of feathers, sequins, and transformation—brought to life through Warner Bros. glamor and dazzling costume design.

LEADING MEN
REBELS WITH A CAUSE

In 1950s Hollywood, the image of masculinity was shifting. Gone were the purely stoic heroes of wartime dramas, replaced by brooding, conflicted young men who seemed to be searching for identity in a rapidly changing world. Nowhere was this more powerfully embodied than in Nicholas Ray's 1955 film *Rebel Without a Cause*, a cultural landmark that redefined the American male archetype.

Starring James Dean as Jim Stark, the film captured the disillusionment and restlessness of postwar youth. Jim is the quintessential 1950s rebel—not a criminal, but a sensitive outsider alienated from his parents and struggling to find meaning and connection. Dean's performance, with its raw emotional vulnerability and understated intensity, became a touchstone for a new kind of masculinity: wounded, expressive, and unpredictable.

Rebel Without a Cause wasn't just a portrait of teenage angst—it was a mirror of broader social tensions. The postwar years brought prosperity, but also strict conformity.
Men were expected to be breadwinners, emotionally restrained, and loyal to traditional roles. But the boys in *Rebel*—Jim, Plato (Sal Mineo), and Buzz—pushed back against those expectations. Their rebellion wasn't political, but deeply personal, rooted in emotional neglect, broken families, and a yearning to be seen.

The film's popularity helped usher in a wave of similar characters in American cinema—men who wore leather jackets, spoke in fragmented thoughts, and carried the weight of invisible battles. These "rebels with a cause" questioned authority, challenged societal norms, and expressed their pain in ways both explosive and quiet. Marlon Brando in *The Wild One* (1953) and Montgomery Clift in *A Place in the Sun* (1951)

RIGHT

Marlon Brando, here sporting a plaid bomber jacket, takes on dockyard corruption in Elia Kazan's hard-hitting *On the Waterfront* (1954).

FAR RIGHT

In Mark of the Hawk (1957), Sidney Poitier redefined heroism for a new era—intelligent, principled, and unshakably dignified. As Obam, a Western-educated activist caught between colonial rule and native unrest, Poitier brought moral strength and emotional depth to the screen. Dressed in traditional West African attire within the setting of a colonial courtroom, he stood not just as a character, but as a symbol of emerging African-American independence and modern identity.

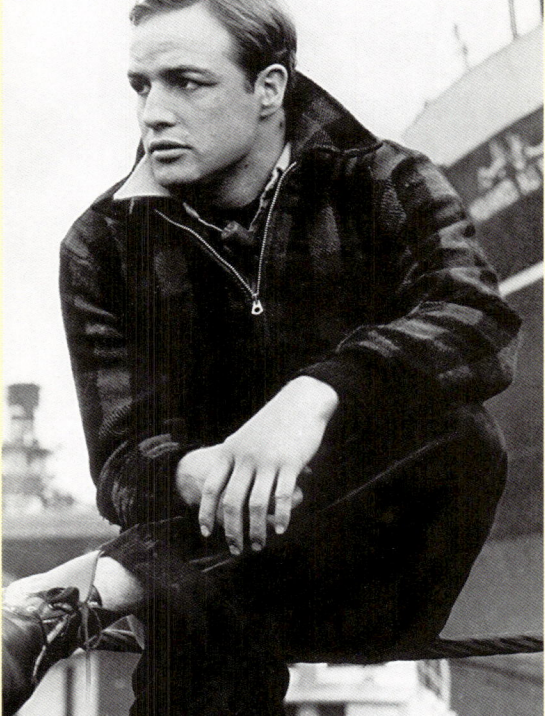

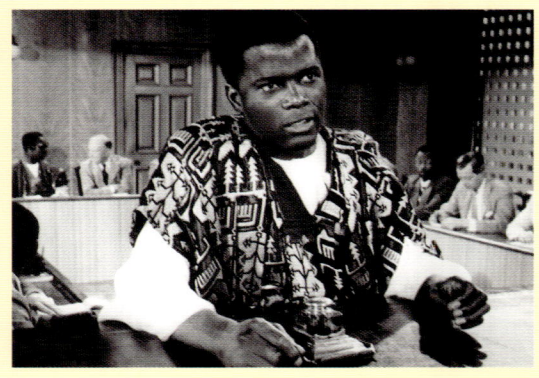

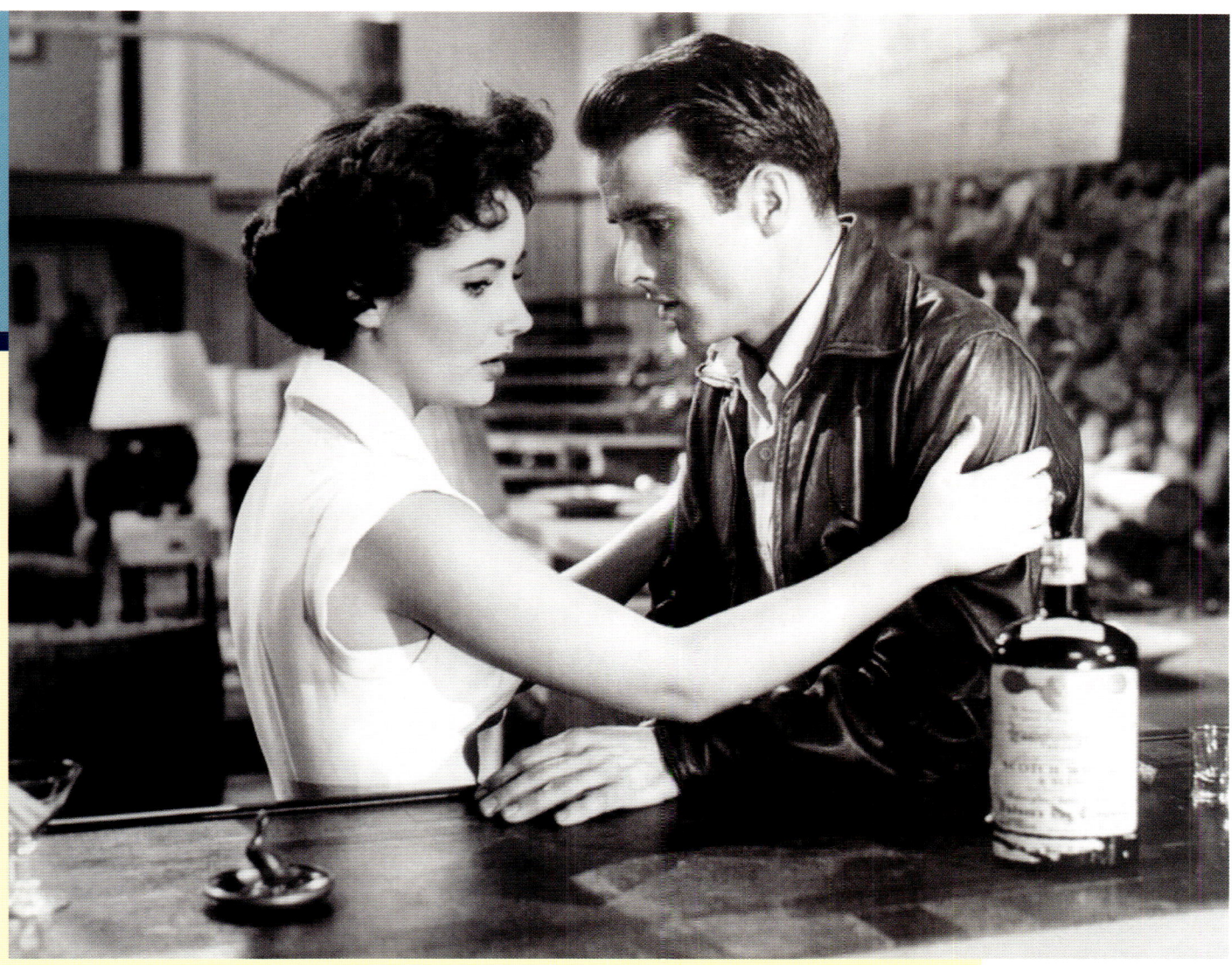

similarly portrayed men caught between rebellion and vulnerability.

James Dean, with his tragic death shortly after *Rebel's* release, became an immortal figure—his red jacket, anguished gaze, and slouched posture defining the tortured young man for generations. He wasn't just acting—he was channeling the fears and desires of a generation of men who felt misunderstood in their own homes and communities.

By breaking from the emotionally repressed male leads of the past, *Rebel Without a Cause* helped open the door to more nuanced portrayals of masculinity in Hollywood. It gave space for sensitivity, for sorrow, and for male characters who weren't superheroes, but simply young men trying to make sense of the world. These 1950s rebels, with their contradictions and complexity, left a legacy that still shapes how manhood is portrayed onscreen today.

STYLE SIGNIFIERS

- Less-structured suits without shoulder pads
- Polo shirts
- Hawaiian shirts
- White T-shirts, blue jeans, and sneakers
- Patterned sports jackets
- Penny loafers
- Crew-cut hair or pompadours
- Beat styles: ankle boots, black turtlenecks, berets

ABOVE
—

Montgomery Clift's brooding rebel persona is underscored by his leather jacket and open-collar shirt—an unpolished, modern look that broke from Hollywood's tailored tradition and set a new standard for effortless cool.

ELIZABETH TAYLOR

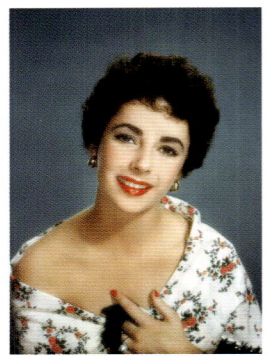

Dazzling, defiant, and eternally iconic, Elizabeth Taylor epitomized the height of Hollywood glamor while forging a path as one of the most influential actresses—and public figures—of the 20th century.

Elizabeth Taylor (1932–2011) was born in London to American parents and moved to Los Angeles during World War II. As a child star by the age of ten, she gained early fame with *Lassie Come Home* (1943), but her radiant performance in *National Velvet* (1944) catapulted her to stardom. With her luminous violet eyes, flawless beauty, and poised screen presence, Taylor became a defining figure of classic Hollywood glamor. Her transition to adult roles was seamless, with her innate elegance and growing emotional depth matched by increasingly complex characters that matured with her.

In the 1950s, Taylor earned critical acclaim for her performances in *A Place in the Sun* (1951), *Giant* (1956), and *Raintree County* (1957). Her role as the sultry Maggie in *Cat on a Hot Tin Roof* (1958) confirmed her status as a powerful dramatic actress. Taylor received her first Academy Award for *Butterfield 8* (1960), and in 1963, she made headlines worldwide by becoming the highest-paid actress of her time to star in *Cleopatra*. The film's extravagant production and her scandalous affair with co-star Richard Burton fueled endless media coverage.

Taylor and Burton became one of Hollywood's most legendary and scrutinized couples, starring together in *The V.I.P.s* (1963), *The Sandpiper* (1965), and *Who's Afraid of Virginia Woolf?* (1966). Her performance as the bitter, emotionally explosive Martha earned her a second Oscar and is still hailed as one of the bravest portrayals in cinematic history. The volatile intensity she brought to the screen made her performances unforgettable, reflecting her passion and willingness to embrace imperfection and vulnerability in front of the camera.

Off-screen, Taylor was a trailblazer. She set fashion trends with her glamorous style, launched a successful perfume line, and redefined celebrity philanthropy. In the 1980s, she became one of the first stars to publicly advocate for HIV/AIDS awareness, co-founding The Foundation for AIDS Research or amfAR and later establishing The Elizabeth Taylor AIDS Foundation. Her outspoken activism helped destigmatize the disease and fund critical research. She used her fame not just for promotion but for progress, devoting her time and resources to causes others ignored and giving a voice to those who had none.

Despite personal losses, numerous health issues, and eight high-profile marriages, Taylor remained a symbol of resilience and compassion. Until her death in 2011, she embodied grace under pressure, enduring fame, and fearless individuality—an icon whose influence transcended film and whose legacy continues to inspire. She was not only a star but a force, leaving behind a life that was as bold and brilliant as the diamonds she loved. Her memory lives on as a testament to glamor with purpose and passion with impact.

ABOVE

Blessed with legendary violet eyes and double eyelashes, Elizabeth Taylor captivated audiences for decades. She won two Academy Awards for Best Actress and became as famous for her acting talent as for her dazzling jewelry and tumultuous love life.

TOP RIGHT

Elizabeth Taylor became a Hollywood legend with her striking beauty and acting talent, winning two Academy Awards and famously marrying eight times, including twice to actor Richard Burton.

FULL PAGE

Lounging with playful elegance, Elizabeth Taylor radiates mid-century glamor. Renowned for her stunning beauty and passionate performances, she was also a humanitarian, co-founding amfAR and becoming a leading voice in the fight against HIV/AIDS.

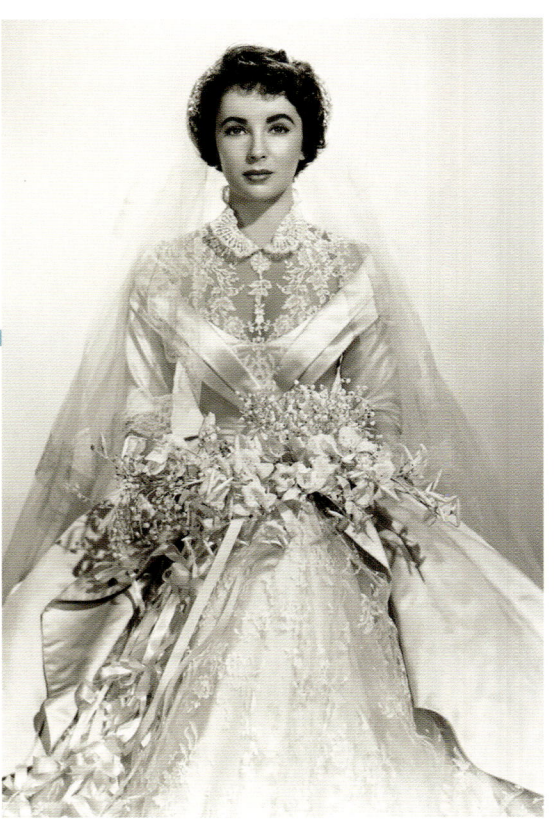

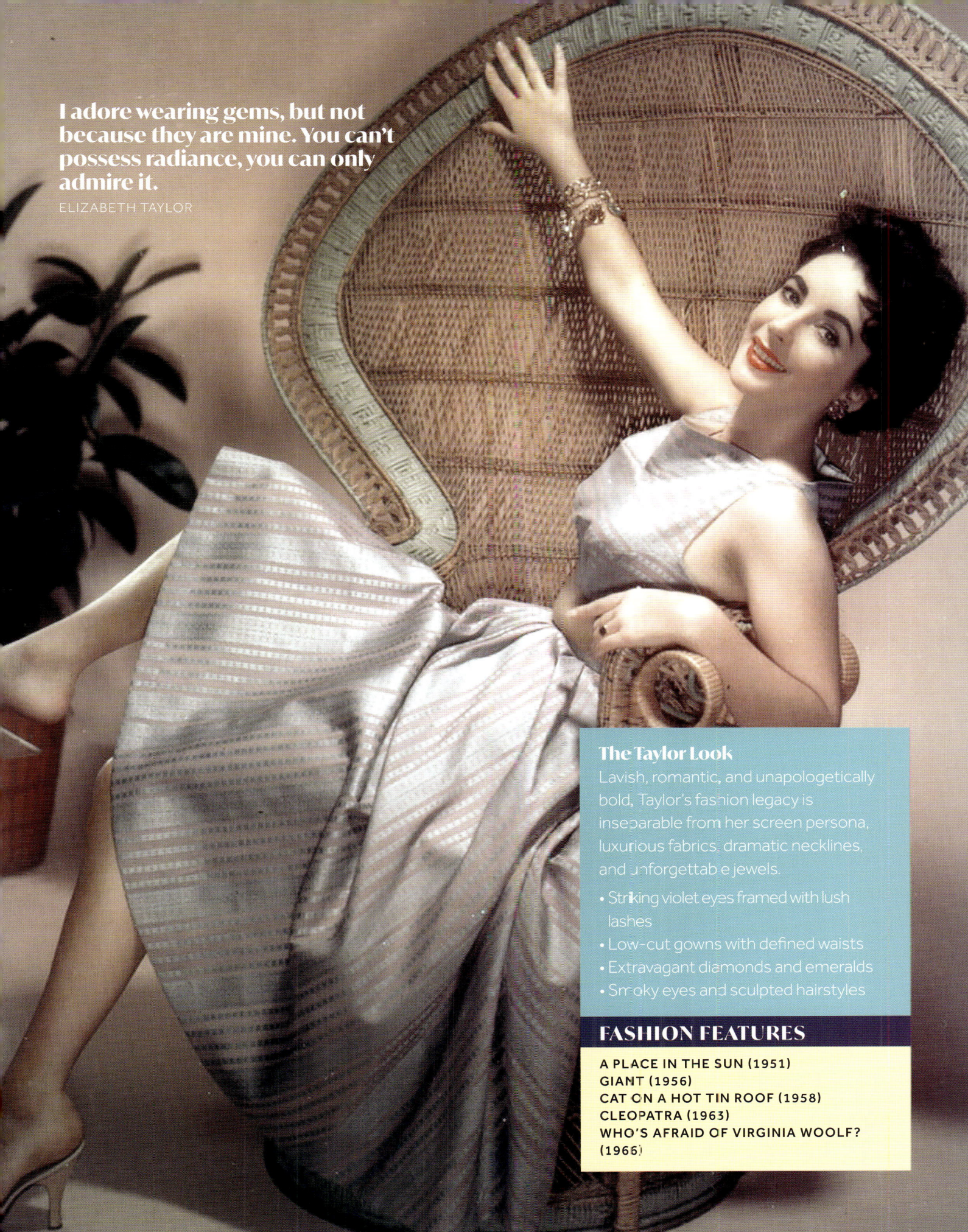

I adore wearing gems, but not because they are mine. You can't possess radiance, you can only admire it.

ELIZABETH TAYLOR

The Taylor Look

Lavish, romantic, and unapologetically bold, Taylor's fashion legacy is inseparable from her screen persona, luxurious fabrics, dramatic necklines, and unforgettable jewels.

• Striking violet eyes framed with lush lashes
• Low-cut gowns with defined waists
• Extravagant diamonds and emeralds
• Smoky eyes and sculpted hairstyles

FASHION FEATURES

A PLACE IN THE SUN (1951)
GIANT (1956)
CAT ON A HOT TIN ROOF (1958)
CLEOPATRA (1963)
WHO'S AFRAID OF VIRGINIA WOOLF? (1966)

LEADING MEN
NOIR STYLE

The noir hero is a knight in blood-caked armor. He's dirty and he does his best to deny the fact that he's a hero the whole time.

FRANK MILLER, ARTIST/WRITER/ DIRECTOR

Emerging in the 1940s, Hollywood film noir cast a long, moody shadow over cinema. Drawing from hard-boiled crime fiction and German expressionism, these gritty films were defined by stark black-and-white visuals, morally ambiguous characters, and stories steeped in fatalism. The term "film noir," or "black film," was coined by French critics who recognized the dark undercurrents running through American postwar movies.

Iconic examples such as *Double Indemnity* (1944), *The Maltese Falcon* (1941), and *Out of the Past* (1947) showcase twisted plots, doomed romance, and cynical anti-heroes caught in webs of crime and deception. Private detectives, corrupt cops, and femmes fatales ruled the screen—often trapped by desire, guilt, and/or greed.

Lighting was essential to noir's visual language— deep shadows, Venetian blinds, rain-slick streets, and cigarette smoke became signature elements. Directors such as Billy Wilder, Otto Preminger, and Fritz Lang mastered the genre's atmospheric tension, whereas stars such as Humphrey Bogart, Barbara Stanwyck, and Robert Mitchum embodied its style.

Although its classic era faded in the 1950s, film noir's influence endures through neo-noir revivals in films such as *Chinatown* (1974), *Blade Runner* (1982), and *L.A. Confidential* (1997). Its legacy remains—a mirror to society's darker truths and cinema's most haunting style.

FAR RIGHT

Humphrey Bogart in *The Enforcer* (1951), dressed in a sharply tailored single-breasted suit and fedora—a pared-back noir aesthetic that underscored his quiet intensity.

RIGHT

Fred MacMurray and Edward G. Robinson in *Double Indemnity* (1944)—a smoky office, pressed suits, and moral tension define this noir landmark of betrayal and sharp dialogue.

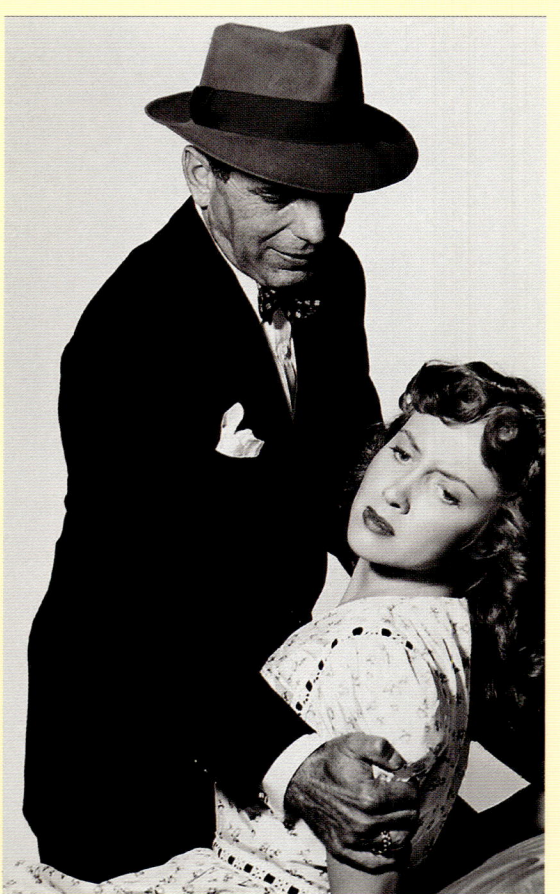

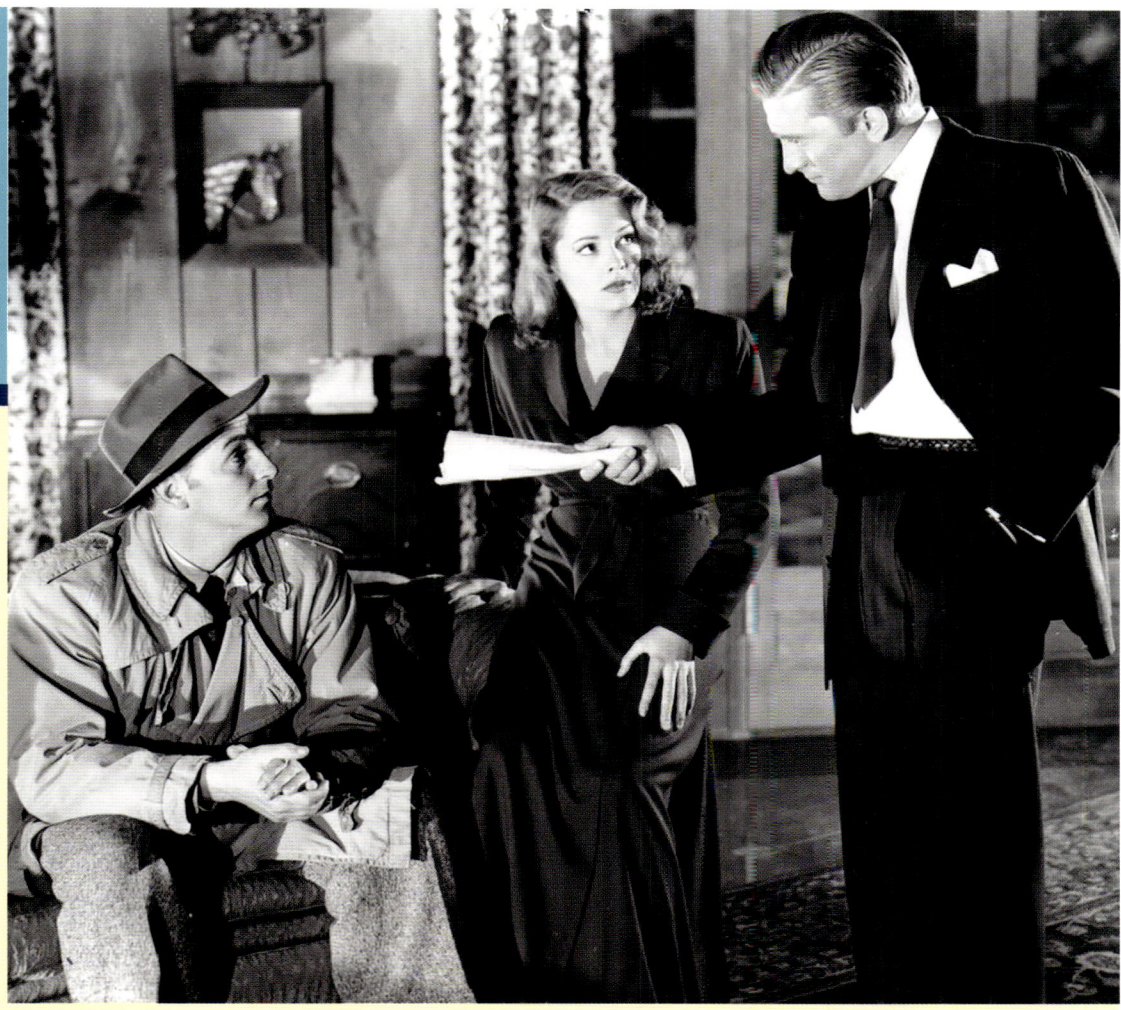

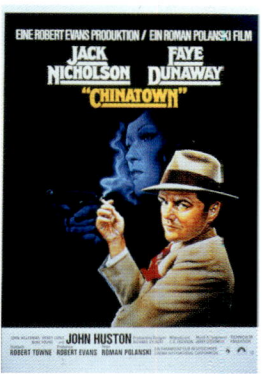

STYLE SIGNIFIERS

- Longer hair and sideburns, facial hair
- Latin- and Italian-influenced business suits
- Suit vests worn without jackets
- Collarless suit jackets
- Narrow ties
- Flared suit trousers
- Bell-bottom jeans
- Tie-dye shirts
- Mixing and matching colors and patterns
- Peace medallions and chunky chain necklaces
- Desert boots

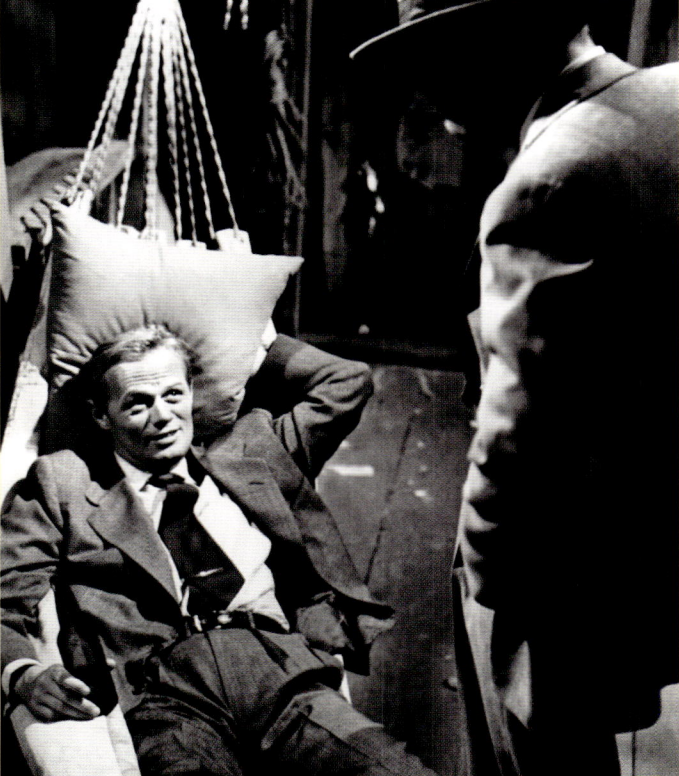

TOP LEFT

Robert Mitchum, Jane Greer, and Kirk Douglas in *Out of the Past* (1947)—a taut standoff framed in Venetian shadows, sharp suits, and classic film noir tension.

TOP RIGHT

In *Chinatown* (1974), Jack Nicholson embodies the modern noir antihero, channeling the cynicism, moral ambiguity, and trenchcoat cool of classic 1940s noir. Roman Polanski's haunting vision draws heavily from the genre's shadowy aesthetics and fatalistic tone—proving that even decades later, noir's influence still looms large

LEFT

Richard Widmark's rumpled suit and loosened tie in *Pickup on South Street* (1953) reflect the raw, unvarnished style of noir's antiheroes—sharp tailoring undone by moral ambiguity and street-level grit.

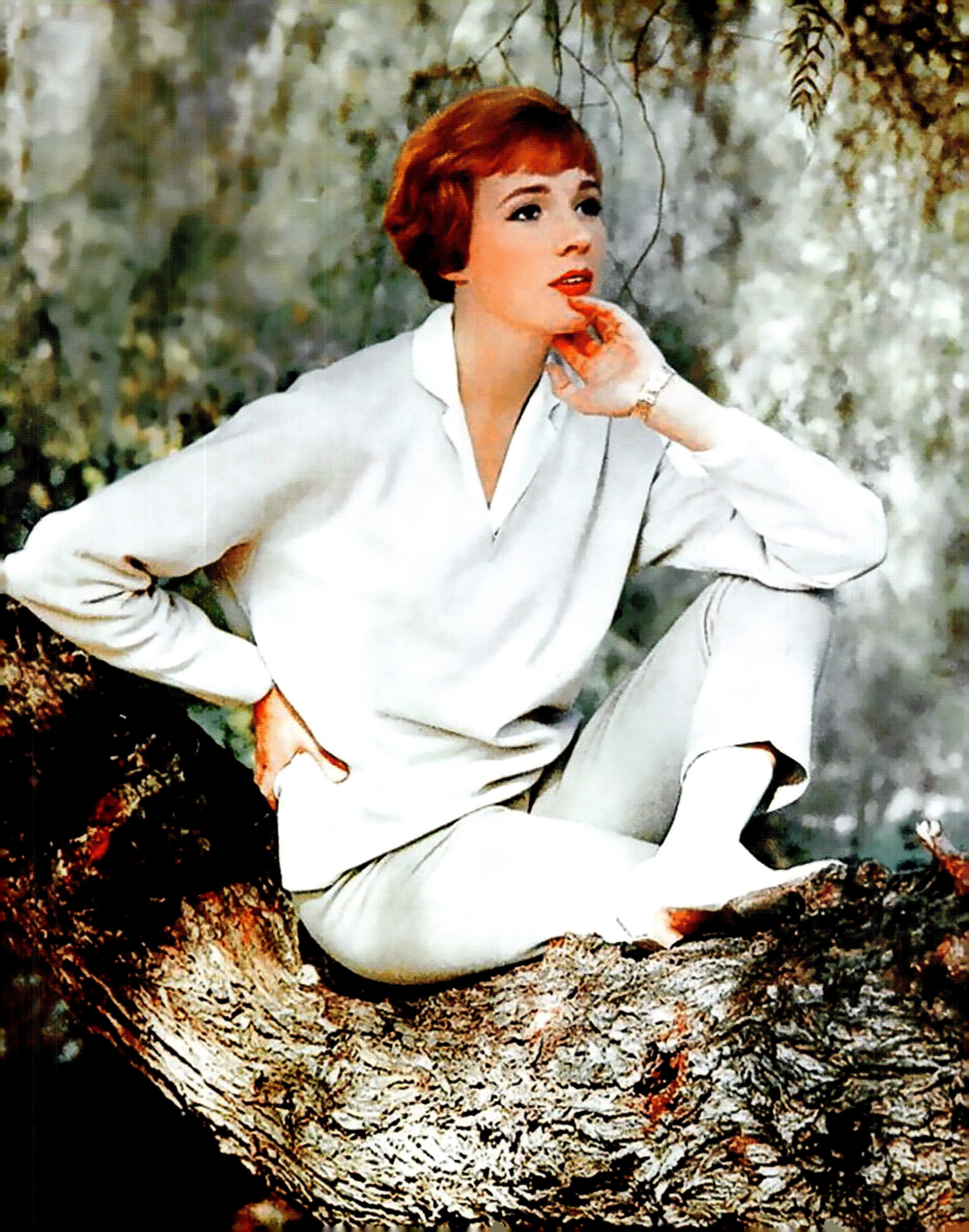

NINETEEN SIXTIES

The 1960s brought seismic cultural shifts, and Hollywood fashion evolved to reflect the changing spirit of the era. In a decade defined by social movements, political unrest, and youth rebellion, traditional glamor gave way to more experimental and diverse expressions of style. Costume design in film mirrored the collision between old Hollywood elegance and the bold aesthetics of a new generation. As the studio system declined and independent filmmaking rose, wardrobe choices became more relaxed, more character-driven, and increasingly influenced by global trends.

Stars such as Audrey Hepburn and Elizabeth Taylor carried forward the grace of the previous decade, whereas newcomers such as Jane Fonda, Nancy Kwan, and Julie Christie introduced modern silhouettes, shorter hemlines, and freer attitudes. Designers embraced mod fashion, minimalist lines, psychedelic prints, and bold color palettes that spoke to a younger, more politically aware audience. Even period films such as *Cleopatra* (1963) and *The Lion in Winter* (1968) delivered high-impact costume spectacles that resonated with contemporary sensibilities.

The emergence of counterculture, rock and roll, and sexual liberation also influenced how women and men were dressed on screen. From the polished sheath dresses of *Breakfast at Tiffany's* to the bohemian fringe of *Easy Rider*, 1960s Hollywood offered a wide spectrum of fashion identities. No longer just aspirational, fashion in film began to feel personal, political, and grounded in the social currents of the time—a visual evolution that echoed the revolution happening far beyond the studio gates.

JULIE ANDREWS

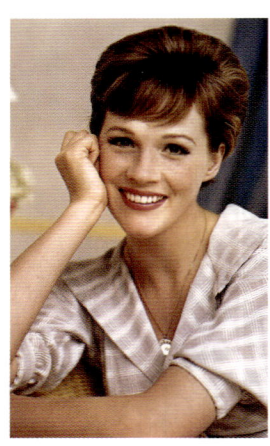

Poised, golden-voiced, and imbued with innate dignity, Julie Andrews became one of the most beloved figures in cinematic and stage history, known for her crystalline soprano, warm screen presence, and enduring elegance.

Julie Andrews (born 1935), raised in England, began performing as a child prodigy with a remarkable vocal range that stunned audiences and professionals alike. Trained in classical voice by her stepfather, she possessed near-perfect pitch and incredible control. By her early teens, she was already dazzling crowds in London's West End. Her Broadway breakthrough came with starring roles in *The Boy Friend* (1954), *My Fair Lady* (1956), and *Camelot* (1960), where her crystalline soprano and luminous stage presence made her a favorite of both critics and theatergoers.

Although controversially passed over for the film version of *My Fair Lady*, Andrews triumphed in her Hollywood debut as the magical nanny in *Mary Poppins* (1964), a role that showcased her versatility, charm, and vocal brilliance—earning her an Academy Award for Best Actress. She cemented her screen legacy the following year with *The Sound of Music* (1965), portraying Maria von Trapp with a radiant blend of humor, warmth, and strength.

Andrews' film career thrived in the following decades, with standout performances in *Thoroughly Modern Millie* (1967), *Victor/Victoria* (1982), and, later, *The Princess Diaries* franchise. Despite a 1997 vocal surgery that significantly altered her singing ability, she continued to act, write bestselling children's books, and narrate film and television with her signature grace.

Honored with numerous accolades, including Kennedy Center Honors and the title of Dame in 2000, Julie Andrews remains a symbol of enduring talent, elegance, and heartfelt artistry.

ABOVE
———
Andrews turned Broadway stardom into a celebrated cinema career. Today, she is still a beloved icon of musical films and charming comedies.

RIGHT
———
Julie Andrews enchanted audiences as the practically perfect nanny in *Mary Poppins* (1964), a role that earned her an Academy Award and made her an enduring figure in cinematic history.

FASHION FEATURES

MARY POPPINS (1964)
THE SOUND OF MUSIC (1965)
VICTOR/VICTORIA (1982)

The Andrews Look
Classic and poised, she favored structured silhouettes, high necklines, and elegant tailoring that mirrored her graceful persona.

- Soft pixie cuts
- High-collared dresses
- Velvet and brocade ensembles
- Understated, luminous makeup

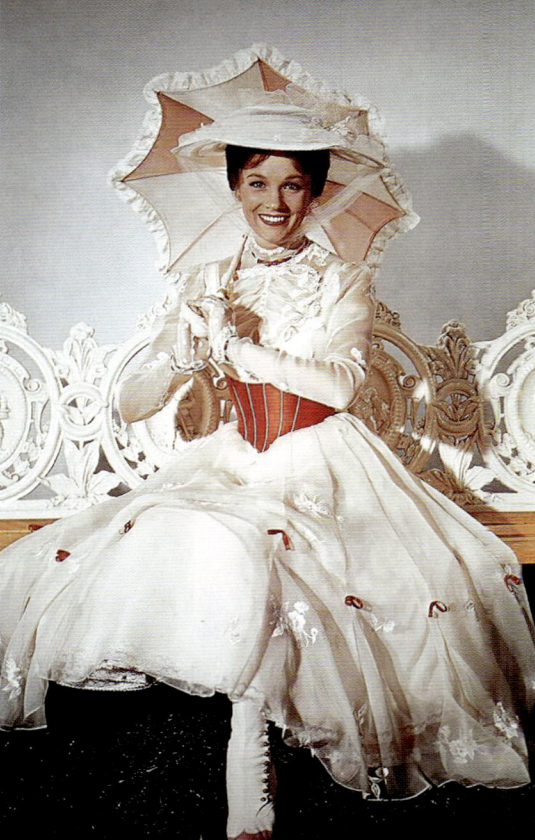

ANN-MARGRET

BYE BYE BIRDIE (1963)
VIVA LAS VEGAS (1964)
THE SWINGER (1966)

The Ann-Margret Look

Her figure and dancer's poise made her the queen of skimpy chic:

• Hot pants and fitted capris
• Colorful crop tops
• Flirty, youthful silhouettes

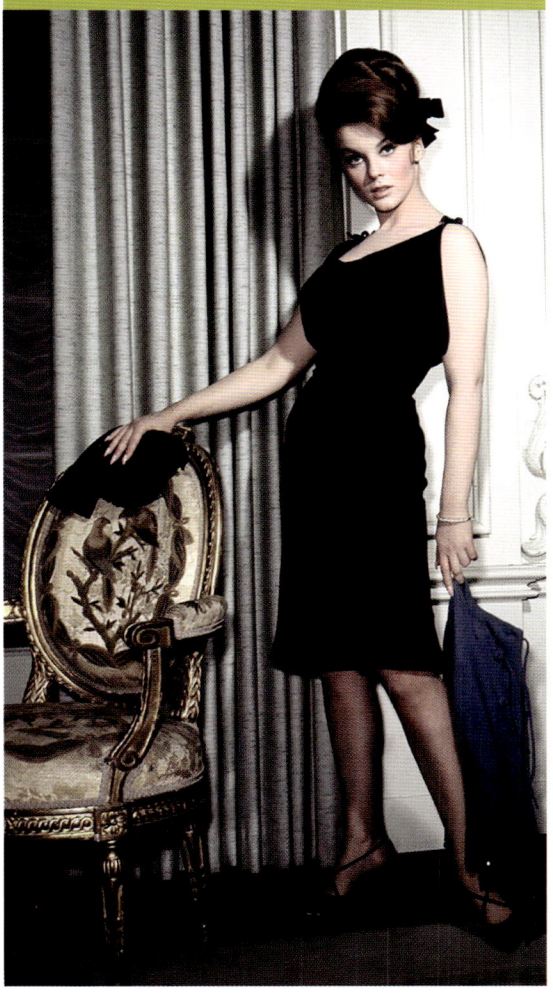

Vivacious, electric, and impossible to ignore, Ann-Margret burst onto the Hollywood scene in the early 1960s as a flame-haired force of nature, bringing a unique blend of sex appeal, musicality, and charm to every performance.

Ann-Margret Olsson (1941–), born in Sweden and raised in Illinois demonstrated a flair for performance from an early age. A natural dancer and singer, she made her television debut at 16, studied at Northwestern, and was discovered by George Burns. A record deal with RCA and a movie contract with 20th Century Fox followed swiftly. She rocketed to fame with her role in *Bye Bye Birdie* (1963), where her energy and charisma made her an instant teen idol. Her dynamic turn in *Viva Las Vegas* (1964), opposite Elvis Presley, solidified her stardom.

Throughout the 1960s, she became known for playing playful, sultry characters in films such as *The Swinger* and *Kitten with a Whip*. However, she was more than just a sex symbol. Her talent was undeniable, and in the 1970s, she shifted into more serious roles, earning her an Oscar nomination for *Carnal Knowledge* (1971). A near-fatal fall in 1972 didn't stop her—she was back onstage just weeks later, showing her signature resilience. She also earned praise for her performances in television films and continued to work steadily across genres.

Ann-Margret's bold beauty and daring style—short shorts, midriff-baring tops, and curve-hugging pants—made her a 1960s fashion icon. Her signature red hair, dazzling stage presence, and timeless appeal have kept her in the cultural spotlight for decades. She continues to inspire with her blend of grit, glamor, and boundless energy.

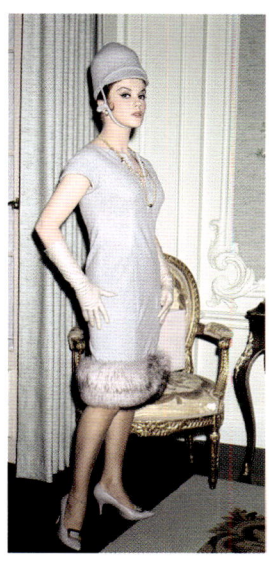

ABOVE

Ann-Margret played Maggie Scott in the 1966 fashion-focused romantic comedy film *Made in Paris*.

LEFT

Ann-Margret, known for her sultry screen presence, starred alongside Elvis Presley in *Viva Las Vegas* (1964), a film that showcased not only her charisma but also her dynamic dancing talent and fashion sense.

SETTING TRENDS
AT THE OSCARS
1930s – 1960s

Glamor, drama, and cinematic brilliance converged at the Academy Awards between the 1930s and 1960s, defining decades of Hollywood fashion. This era was foundational— where red carpet appearances became a critical style moment, not just for the films, but for the actors who brought them to life.

The 1930s saw the debut of the Oscars at the Hotel Roosevelt, with stars such as Bette Davis turning heads in regal silhouettes—most famously in the red gown from *Jezebel* (1938) by Orry-Kelly. As film went from silent to talkies, fashion also evolved, with sharply tailored suits, flowing gowns, and dazzling accessories taking the center stage. Edith Head, who later dominated the costume design category, began shaping public taste during this formative time.

In the 1940s and 50s, Hollywood stars fully embraced the Oscars as a fashion platform. Grace Kelly's ice-blue satin gown in 1955 and Audrey Hepburn's floral Givenchy masterpiece in 1954 elevated fashion to high art. Meanwhile, male stars such as Humphrey Bogart and Marlon Brando made the tuxedo a cultural standard.

The 1960s embraced more experimental and bold fashion choices, reflecting the shifting social landscape. Elizabeth Taylor, draped in violet chiffon and diamonds, stunned in 1961, whereas Barbra Streisand turned heads in a sheer, sequined pantsuit in 1969—a boundary-pushing look that echoed her singular persona.

This era cemented the Oscars as the ultimate fashion runway—where cinematic royalty showcased elegance, innovation, and unmistakable star power. From regal gowns to iconic suits, the red carpet was no longer just a walk—it was a legacy of glitter, glamor, golden-age prestige, storytelling, influence, identity, attitude, artistry, and unforgettable fashion.

RIGHT

Clark Gable won the Academy Award for Best Actor in 1935 for *It Happened One Night*. His suave presence and charisma made him the quintessential leading man of Hollywood's Golden Age.

ABOVE RIGHT

Bette Davis, seen here holding her Oscar for *Jezebel*, was the first woman to receive ten Academy Award nominations. Known for fierce roles and sharp wit, she redefined female stardom in Hollywood.

BOTTOM RIGHT

Marlon Brando won for *On the Waterfront* and Grace Kelly won for *The Country Girl*. Kelly wore a green silk dress by Edith Head. It was reported to be the most expensive Oscar dress up to that time.

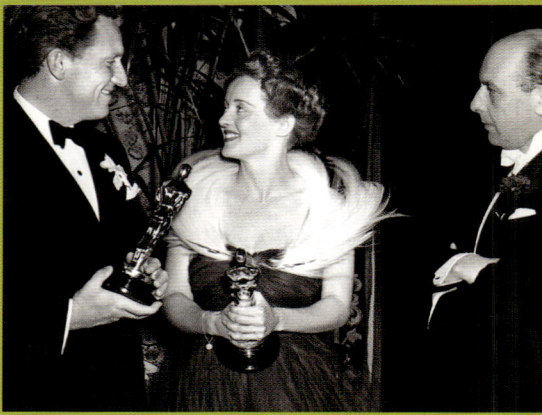

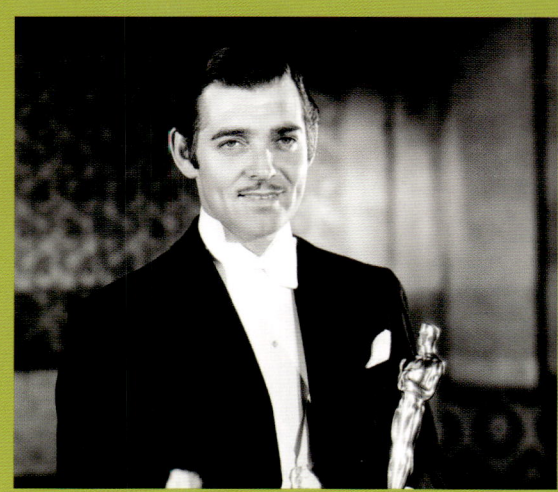

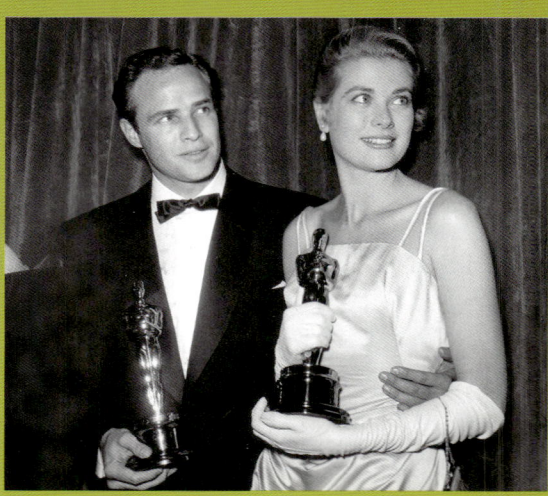

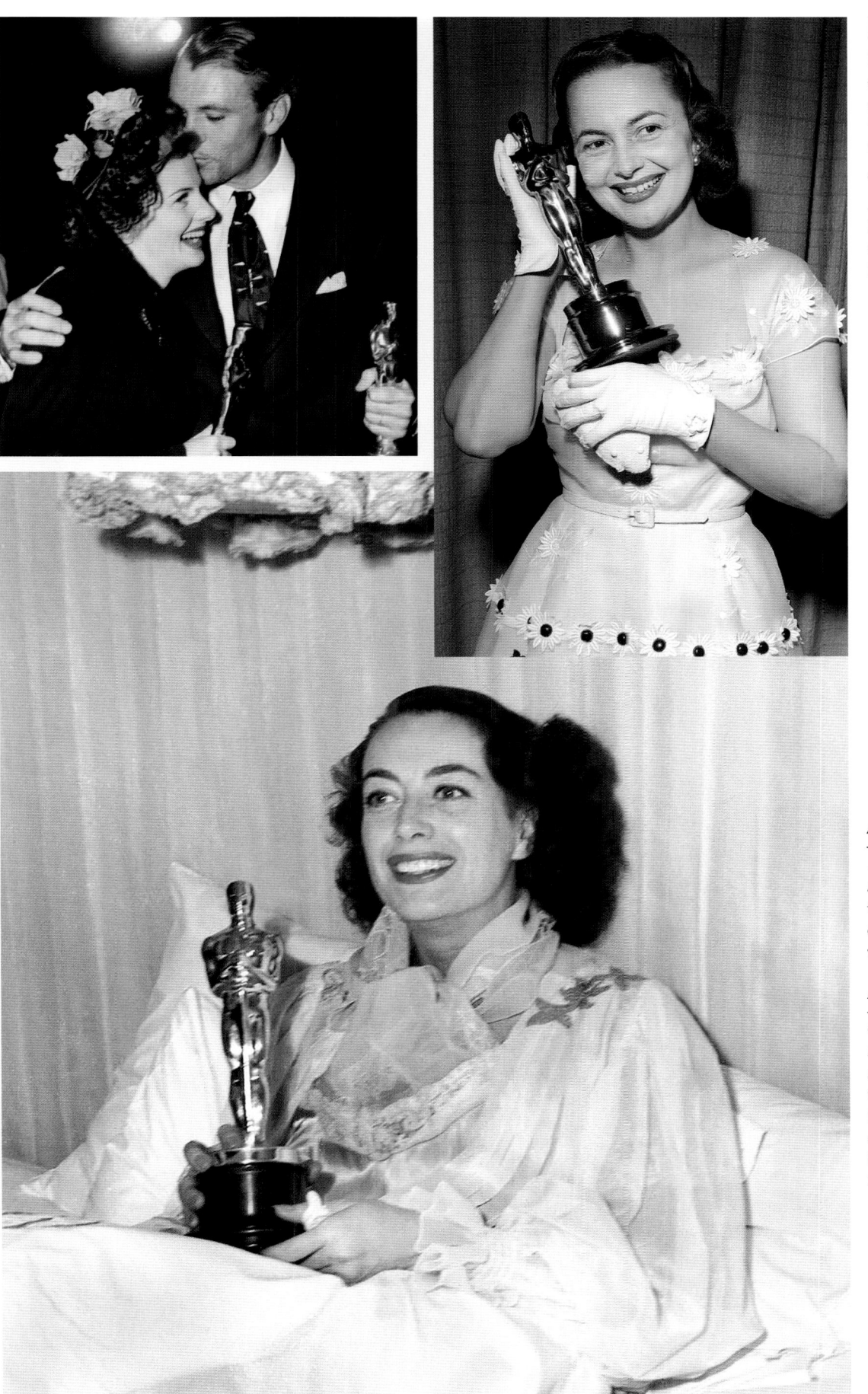

If I'd known this was all it would take, I'd have put that eyepatch on 40 years ago.

JOHN WAYNE,
UPON WINNING AS
ROOSTER COGBURN
IN **TRUE GRIT**

ABOVE LEFT

At the 1941 Academy Awards, Joan Fontaine won for *Suspicion*. Here, she is congratulated by Gary Cooper, who won for Sergeant York.

ABOVE RIGHT

Olivia de Havilland won the Academy Award for Best Actress twice, including for *The Heiress* (1949). Her elegance and strength onscreen made her one of Hollywood's most enduring leading ladies.

LEFT

Joan Crawford famously accepted her 1946 Oscar for *Mildred Pierce* from her bed, citing illness. The dramatic moment became one of the most iconic and discussed in Academy Awards history.

JULIE CHRISTIE

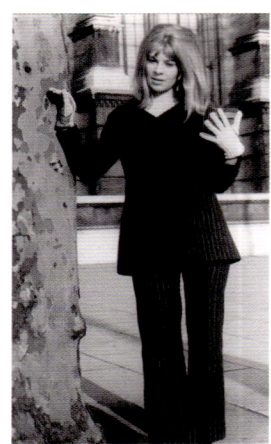

Radiant, cerebral, and effortlessly modern, Julie Christie emerged as a defining face of 1960s cinema, embodying the glamor and introspection of her era with grace and complexity.

Julie Christie (born 1941), raised in rural Wales and India, trained in theater before gaining national attention in *Billy Liar* (1963). Her breakthrough came with *Darling* (1965), where she portrayed a stylish, self-involved model navigating the shallows of Swinging London. The role earned her the Academy Award for Best Actress and positioned her as a fashion icon and an emblem of the era's evolving femininity. That same year, she starred opposite Omar Sharif in David Lean's *Doctor Zhivago* (1965), further elevating her international acclaim and securing her place among cinema's most captivating leading women.

With a luminous screen presence and keen emotional intelligence, Christie brought authenticity to each role. In François Truffaut's *Fahrenheit 451* (1966), she played dual roles with subtle nuance. Her performance in *Petulia* (1968) was hailed for its raw emotional depth, and in Robert Altman's *McCabe & Mrs. Miller* (1971), embodied a brothel madam with both grit and grace, earning her an Oscar nomination.

Throughout her career, Christie remained fiercely independent, turning down roles that didn't align with her values or vision. She reemerged in the 1990s and 2000s with critically acclaimed performances in *Afterglow* (1997) and *Away from Her* (2006), the latter earning her a fourth Academy Award nomination.

Preferring a quiet life in the countryside over the spotlight of celebrity, Christie has been advocating for environmental causes and human rights. As a performer and public figure, she continues to represent a rare combination of beauty, intellect, and conviction—an icon of timeless artistry and subtle defiance.

ABOVE

Christie won an Academy Award for *Darling* (1965), becoming a defining face of 1960s cinema.

RIGHT

Julie became a fashion icon of the 1960s, known for her effortlessly chic style both on and off screen.

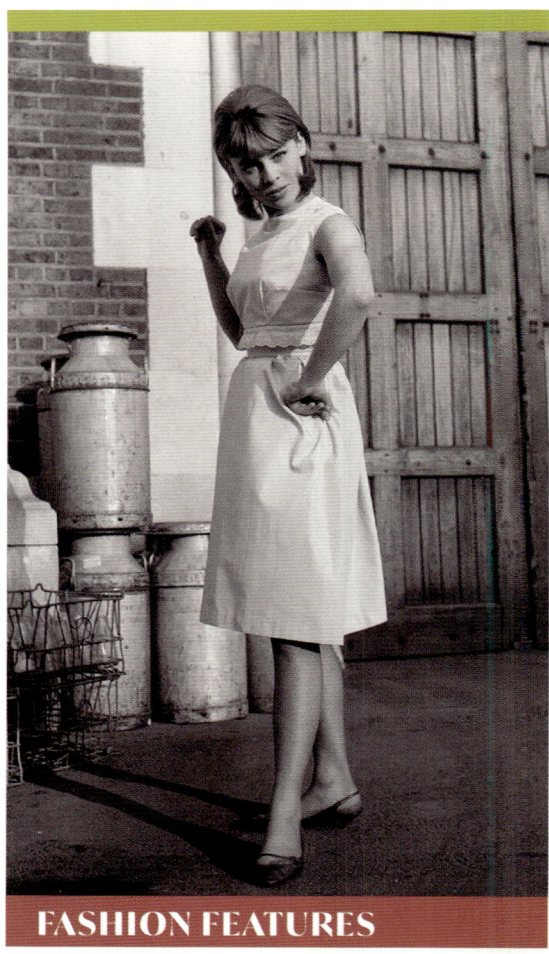

FASHION FEATURES

DARLING (1965)
DOCTOR ZHIVAGO (1965)
PETULIA (1968)

The Christie Look

Mod, sharp, and effortlessly chic, she favored bold silhouettes, tailored coats, and clean lines—always tinged with a rebellious spirit.

- Tousled blonde hair
- Minimalist makeup
- Swinging sixties shift dresses
- Statement coats with luxe textures

DORIS DAY

FASHION FEATURES

CALAMITY JANE (1953)
PILLOW TALK (1959)
LOVER COME BACK (1961)

The Day Look

Crisp, classic Americana—shirtwaist dresses, capri pants, and neat pastels that mirrored her fresh-faced appeal.

- Soft blonde bob
- Button-up blouses
- Pedal pushers
- Natural, radiant makeup

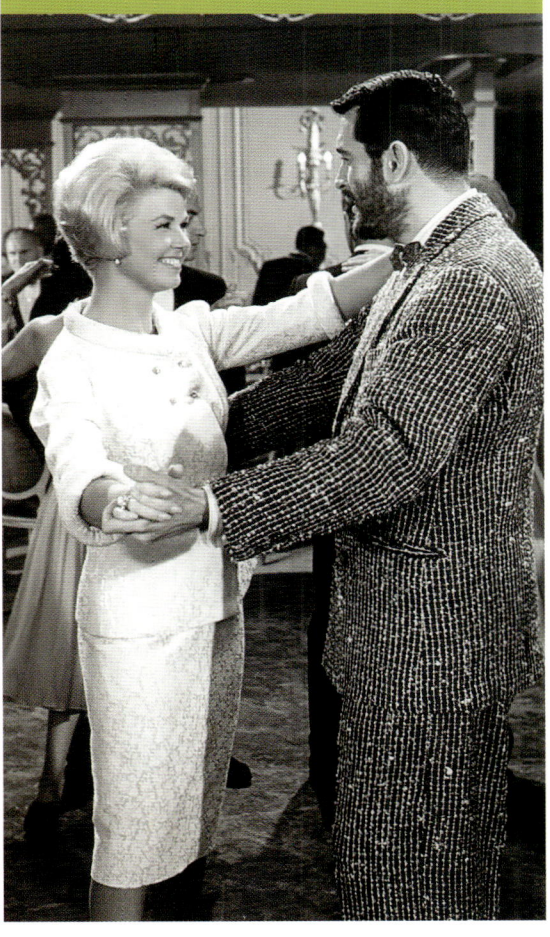

Sunny, sincere, and effortlessly charming, Doris Day embodied the wholesome allure of mid-twentieth century American cinema, blending girl-next-door sweetness with an undeniable star presence.

She was the golden girl with a golden voice—Doris Day (born Doris Mary Ann Kappelhoff 1922) seemed destined for the stage from a young age. Growing up in Cincinnati, she trained as a dancer until fate intervened. A near-fatal car accident changed the course of her life, putting an end to her dance aspirations but opening a door she hadn't expected: singing. As she recovered, her voice—light, clear, and full of feeling—began to shine. It wasn't long before she made a name for herself with big bands; her rendition of "Sentimental Journey" capturing the hearts of returning World War II soldiers and establishing her as a national sweetheart.

Hollywood soon came calling. In 1948, Day made her film debut in *Romance on the High Seas*, and her career took flight. With a warm screen presence and effortless charm, she quickly became one of the most popular stars of the era. Her roles in musicals such as *Calamity Jane* and *Love Me or Leave Me* blended her vocal gifts with real acting depth, hinting at an emotional range that often went underappreciated.

By the 1960s, Day was redefining romantic comedy. Paired famously with Rock Hudson, she brought intelligence, humor, and elegance to box office hits such as *Pillow Talk* and *Lover Come Back*. Audiences loved her, and so did critics.

Off-camera, Day's life was less carefree. She endured personal losses and financial betrayal but never lost her sense of purpose. Later in life, she diverted her energy toward animal rights, founding a well-respected nonprofit and stepping away from the spotlight.

She never chased fame—fame chased her. With honors such as the Presidential Medal of Freedom and a Grammy Lifetime Achievement Award, Doris Day remains not just a star, but an American original.

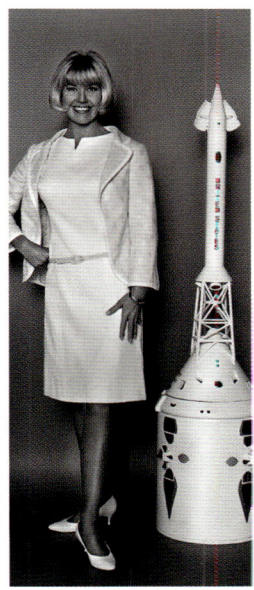

ABOVE

Doris Day poses with U.S. rocket models during the 1960s, reflecting America's space-age optimism—just as her film *The Glass Bottom Boat* (1966) spoofed Cold War espionage.

LEFT

Advertising executive Doris Day dances with Rock Hudson (masquerading as an eccentric scientist) in *Lover Come Back*. The comedic duo appeared in several other hit films.

SETTING TRENDS
BOLLYWOOD: GLAMOR, GRANDEUR, AND THE POWER OF STYLE

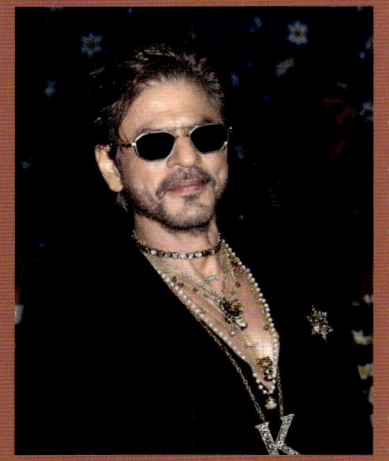

Bollywood isn't just a film industry—it's a spectacle of fashion, a cultural touchstone where clothing speaks as loudly as dialogue. For decades, it has shaped how millions view beauty, glamor, and tradition, while increasingly captivating Hollywood and the global fashion elite. From the flowing saris and embroidered sherwanis of its golden age to today's haute couture gowns and edgy streetwear, Bollywood style has mirrored India's rapid modernization and its growing influence on international red carpets. At its heart, it reflects a cinematic tradition as dynamic and dazzling as Hollywood itself—one that now shares its stars, designers, and visual language with the world.

During the 1950s and 60s, heroines like Madhubala and Waheeda Rehman embodied elegance with their silk saris, winged eyeliner, and bouffant hair—an Indian take on Hollywood glamor that wouldn't have looked out of place alongside Audrey Hepburn or Elizabeth Taylor. (Taylor herself famously wore saris at Hollywood galas, helping spark a fascination with Indian fashion in the West.) Heroes such as Raj Kapoor and Dev Anand made Nehru jackets, slim suits, and scarves aspirational for generations of men, with Dev Anand's slick coiffure and tailored looks earning him comparisons to Gregory Peck. Even in this era, films like *Awara* (1951) found unexpected audiences in Russia and the Middle East, laying the groundwork for Bollywood's later global appeal.

The 1970s brought disco fever to Indian screens, with sequins, bell-bottoms, and bold prints defining stars like Zeenat Aman and Amitabh Bachchan. This era of flamboyance resonated abroad too: Madonna famously adopted Bollywood-inspired looks in her 1998 Ray of Light tour, and designers like Jean Paul Gaultier drew on Indian embroidery and silhouettes. Hollywood also began experimenting onscreen, from *Gandhi* (1982) to *Indiana Jones and the Temple of Doom* (1984), which—though controversial—highlighted Bollywood's aesthetic excesses.

By the 1990s and 2000s, Bollywood fashion entered a fully global phase. Aishwarya Rai's Cannes debut in 2002, where she paired a Neeta Lulla sari with Cartier diamonds, announced Bollywood's couture credentials to the West. Priyanka Chopra's leap from Bollywood superstar to Hollywood lead in *Quantico* (2015) and films like *Baywatch* brought a new kind of

ABOVE

Shah Rukh Khan brings Bollywood flair to the 2025 Met Gala in New York, celebrating "Superfine: Tailoring Black Style." His layered chains, embellished blazer, and oversized "K" pendant exude effortless cool, marking a rare and striking appearance by Bollywood's King Khan on fashion's most prestigious global stage.

RIGHT

Former Miss World Aishwarya Rai Bachchan dazzles in an emerald Elie Saab gown at the gala premiere of *Carol* during the 68th Cannes Film Festival, May 17, 2015. The intricate beadwork and flowing silhouette cemented her status as a global style icon, effortlessly blending Bollywood glamor with haute couture elegance.

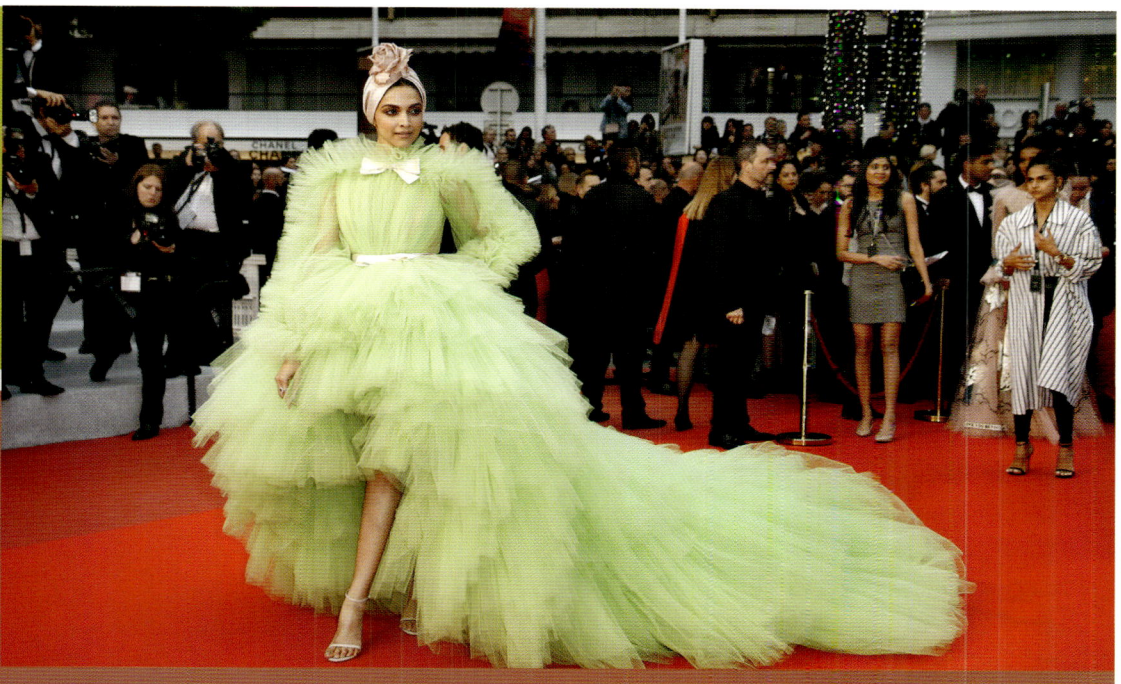

Saris are eternally graceful and can rival the most modern fashion statements... knowing oneself and dressing with purpose and pride is what truly defines personal style.

REKHA JI

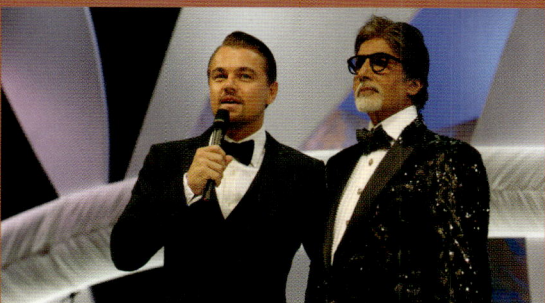

cross-cultural fashion diplomacy; her Ralph Lauren Met Gala trench gown in 2017 remains a defining red-carpet moment. Designers such as Manish Malhotra and Sabyasachi Mukherjee became household names worldwide, influencing collections from New York to Paris.

Today's stars—deeply plugged into international fashion circuits—move effortlessly from Met Gala couture to on-screen traditional wear that still inspires millions. Deepika Padukone's appearances at Louis Vuitton shows and her custom Zac Posen gown at the 2019 Met Gala signal a new era where Bollywood and Hollywood fashion are part of the same conversation. Meanwhile, films like *Slumdog Millionaire* (2008) brought Bollywood's visual language to Western audiences, with AR Rahman's music and Shiamak Davar-inspired choreography paired with Indian-inspired costumes that captivated the world. In Bollywood, fashion has never been passive. It's narrative, symbolic, and spectacular—whether in a slow-motion sari twirl or the swagger of a hero's perfectly tailored suit—and now it's a dialogue with Hollywood itself.

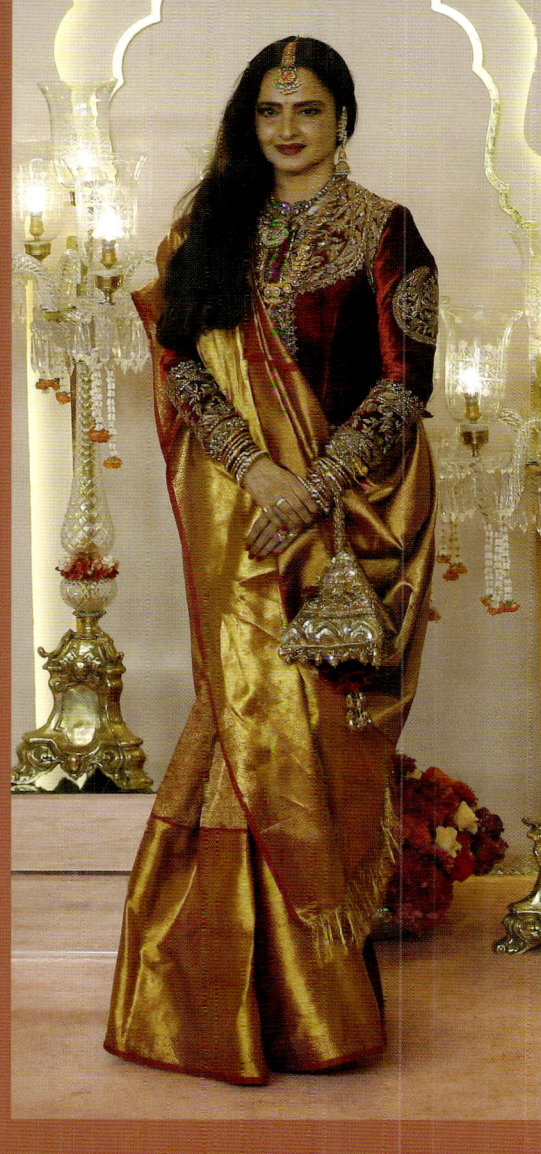

TOP

Deepika Padukone makes a dramatic statement in a voluminous lime-green Giambattista Valli couture gown at the premiere of *Pain and Glory* during the 72nd Cannes Film Festival, May 17, 2019. The sculptural tulle layers and satin headwrap showcased her fearless approach to fashion and cemented her as a global style risk-taker.

ABOVE LEFT

Leonardo DiCaprio and Bollywood legend Amitabh Bachchan share the stage at the opening ceremony of the 66th Cannes Film Festival, May 15, 2013. Bachchan's sequined black tuxedo and oversized glasses brought a bold touch of Bollywood flair to Cannes' classic red-carpet elegance, marking a rare East-meets-West fashion moment.

RIGHT

Rekha radiates timeless elegance in a golden Kanjeevaram sari with a richly embroidered velvet blouse at the wedding of Anant Ambani and Radhika Merchant in Mumbai, July 12, 2024. With her signature red lips, sindoor, and intricate jewelry, she embodies the enduring glamor of Bollywood's most iconic style muse.

FAYE DUNAWAY

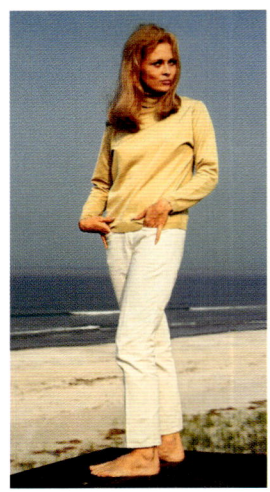

Magnetic, enigmatic, and often daringly intense, Faye Dunaway carved a niche as the embodiment of fierce femininity, bringing intelligence and edge to Hollywood's golden era of modern cinema.

Faye Dunaway (1941–), born Dorothy Faye Dunaway in Bascom, Florida, launched her career on Broadway before electrifying the screen in 1967 as Bonnie Parker in *Bonnie and Clyde*. Her fashion-forward portrayal helped spark a craze for 1930s-inspired style, with tilted berets, tweed skirts, and slim sweaters flooding boutiques. The film's success not only redefined cinematic storytelling but also cemented Dunaway as a fashion icon of the era.

Whether the glam accomplice in *The Thomas Crown Affair*, the haunted heroine of *Chinatown*, or the cold, ambitious producer in *Network*—which won her a Best Actress Oscar—Dunaway was known for her ability to dive deep into complex, flawed characters with an unsettling realism and magnetic presence.

She reigned in the 1970s, her screen persona oscillating between vulnerable and ruthless, culminating in her infamous turn as Joan Crawford in *Mommie Dearest*. Her commanding performances were matched by a commanding sense of style, influencing everything from gangster chic to corporate couture.

One of Hollywood's most chiseled and expressive beauties, Dunaway was never just a pretty face— her voice, gaze, and defiant grace turned every role into an unforgettable force. Her legacy remains etched in both fashion and film history.

ABOVE
Dunaway, pictured in a relaxed beachside moment, rose to stardom in the late 1960s with roles in *Bonnie and Clyde* and *The Thomas Crown Affair*, cementing her status as a screen icon and fashion trendsetter.

RIGHT
In *Bonnie and Clyde* (1967), Faye Dunaway gained international fame for her role as Bonnie Parker. Her performance, style, and fierce charisma helped redefine the modern screen heroine and 1960s fashion.

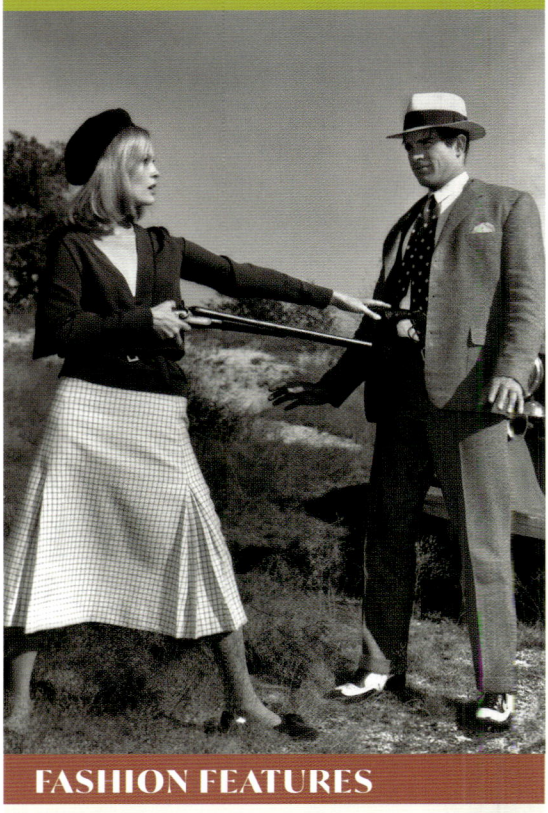

FASHION FEATURES

BONNIE AND CLYDE (1967)
THE THOMAS CROWN AFFAIR (1968)
CHINATOWN (1974)
THREE DAYS OF THE CONDOR (1975)

The Dunaway Look
Chic yet sharp, Dunaway favored sleek lines, luxe separates, cinematic boldness, and unmistakably commanding elegance.

• Pencil skirts with tall boots
• Fitted trousers with feminine blouses
• Wind-tossed, sun-streaked hair

MIA FARROW

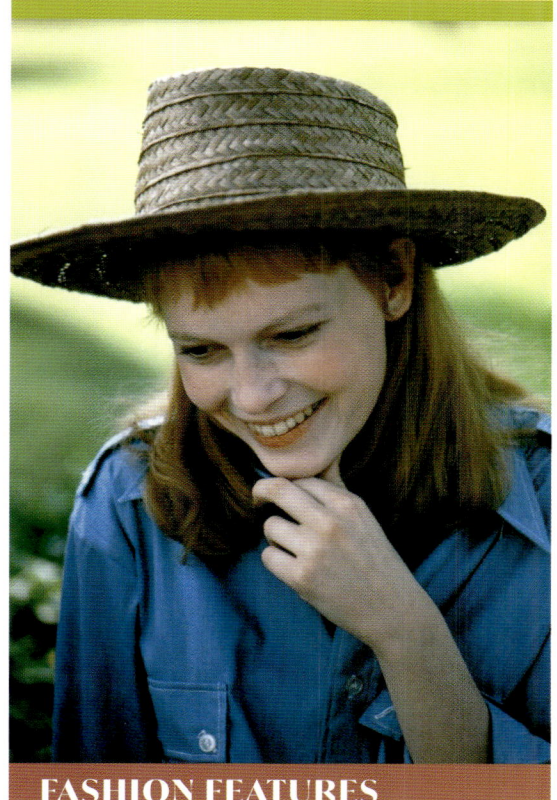

FASHION FEATURES

ROSEMARY'S BABY (1968)
THE GREAT GATSBY (1974)
THE PURPLE ROSE OF CAIRO (1985)

The Farrow Look

Mod and minimalist, she favored shift dresses, clean lines, and a fresh-faced aesthetic that defined 1960s cool.

- Pixie haircut
- Shift dresses
- Soft knits and flats
- Natural, glowing makeup

Waiflike, ethereal, and fiercely principled, Mia Farrow emerged as one of Hollywood's most enigmatic and resilient stars, known as much for her onscreen vulnerability as for her offscreen convictions.

Mia Farrow (b. 1945), born Maria de Lourdes Villiers Farrow in Los Angeles, came from Hollywood royalty as the daughter of director John Farrow and actress Maureen O'Sullivan. She began her acting career with stage work before achieving fame on the television series *Peyton Place* (1964–66). Farrow's pixie-cut charm, ethereal beauty, and delicate features soon made her a style icon of the 1960s and caught the attention of director Roman Polanski, who cast her in the chilling psychological thriller *Rosemary's Baby* (1968). Her subtle, terrified performance as a woman manipulated by a satanic cult earned her widespread acclaim and lasting cultural resonance.

Farrow's film career included collaborations with acclaimed directors, particularly Woody Allen in the 1980s, with standout roles in *The Purple Rose of Cairo* (1985) and *Hannah and Her Sisters* (1986). She also appeared in *Broadway Danny Rose* and *Crimes and Misdemeanors*, further showcasing her talent. Her portrayals often balanced sensitivity with steely intelligence, embodying a complex emotional honesty.

Beyond acting, Farrow became a passionate humanitarian, working with UNICEF and advocating for human rights across Africa and Asia. She traveled extensively, raised awareness of global crises, and was honored for her work. Her personal life, including her high-profile relationships and family, often made headlines, but Farrow remained focused on her activism and artistic contributions.

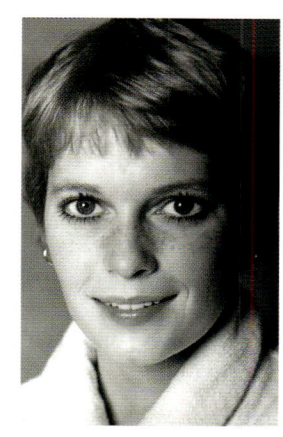

ABOVE

For her haunting performance in *Rosemary's Baby* (1968) Mia Farrow gained international acclaim, and her pixie haircut—styled by Vidal Sassoon—became a defining fashion moment of the decade.

LEFT

Farrow played the titular role in the 1969 film adaptation of Mervyn Jones' *John and Mary*, opposite Dustin Hoffman. She later starred in another popular film adaptation, 1974's *The Great Gatsby*, opposite Robert Redford.

JANE FONDA

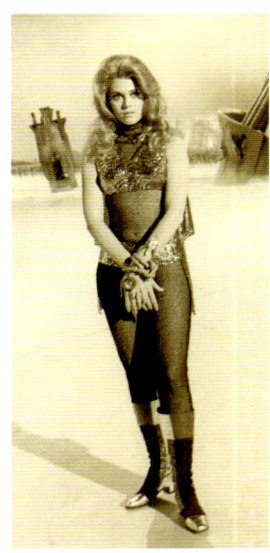

Bold, transformative, and deeply committed, Jane Fonda emerged as one of Hollywood's most fearless and multifaceted actresses, gaining acclaim not only for her artistry but also for her outspoken activism and cultural influence.

Jane Fonda (born 1937), daughter of screen legend Henry Fonda, was born in New York City and began her career in the late 1950s. Initially known for light romantic comedies such as *Barefoot in the Park* (1967), she soon defied typecasting by embracing more challenging and unconventional roles. Her Oscar-winning performance in *Klute* (1971), portraying a deeply layered call girl, marked a turning point in her career, earning critical acclaim for her emotional intensity and psychological depth. She went on to win a second Academy Award for *Coming Home* (1978), where she played the wife of a Vietnam War veteran who falls in love with a paraplegic former soldier, once again demonstrating her fearless dedication to complex material.

Fonda's off-screen presence was equally impactful. In the 1970s, she became a prominent voice in the antiwar movement, famously opposing the Vietnam War, a stance that drew both admiration and sharp criticism. In the 1980s, she redefined herself yet again, becoming a fitness icon through her bestselling home workout videos, which helped shape the era's exercise culture and empowered women everywhere.

Still active today, Fonda stars in projects such as *The Newsroom* and *Grace and Frankie*, showcasing her enduring talent. A bold force in film and an advocate for social justice, Jane Fonda continues to inspire through her artistry, activism, and unapologetic voice.

ABOVE
—
Fonda starred as *Barbarella* in 1968, becoming a futuristic fashion icon in Paco Rabanne's designs.

RIGHT
—
Jane as *Barbarella* (1968), clad in Paco Rabanne's sci-fi armor and go-go boots, redefined space-age seduction with cosmic defiance and pop-futurist flair.

FASHION FEATURES

BAREFOOT IN THE PARK (1967)
KLUTE (1971)
COMING HOME (1978)

The Fonda Look

Edgy and effortless, Fonda's fashion ranged from 1970s jumpsuits to power suits and graceful gowns, often with a rebellious twist.

- Shag haircut
- Turtlenecks and trench coats
- Workout leotards
- Statement sunglasses and activist buttons

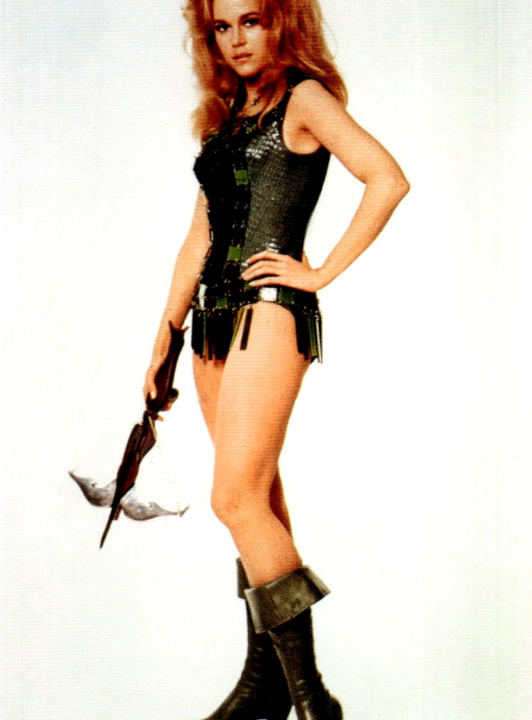

GOLDIE HAWN

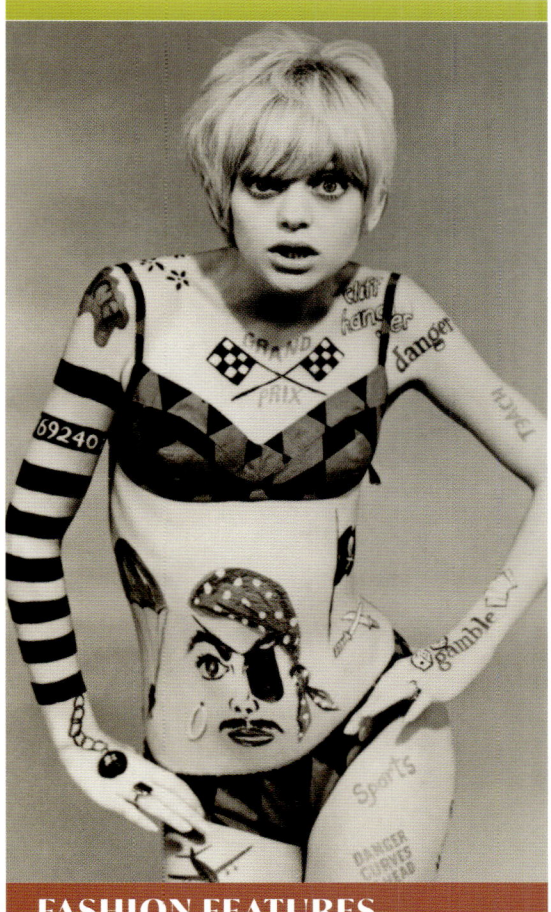

FASHION FEATURES

CACTUS FLOWER (1969)
SHAMPOO (1975)
PRIVATE BENJAMIN (1980)

The Hawn Look

Flirtatious yet chic, Hawn embraced a style marked by flowing fabrics, retro silhouettes, and a carefree glamor that defined her sunny screen image.

- Soft, feathered blonde hair
- Flared pants and crop tops
- Sequined dresses and bold prints
- Fresh, glowing complexion

Radiant, effervescent, and endlessly endearing, Goldie Hawn charmed her way into the hearts of moviegoers with a blend of breezy humor and heartfelt sincerity, establishing herself as a mainstay of American film.

Goldie Hawn (born 1945), hailing from Washington, D.C., began her career as a dancer and found early success on the popular comedy show *Rowan & Martin's Laugh-In* in the late 1960s. Her effervescent laughter, expressive eyes, and quirky persona quickly caught the public's attention. Hawn made an impressive leap to film, earning an Academy Award for Best Supporting Actress for her role in *Cactus Flower* (1969), where her blend of innocence, comic timing, and emotional nuance won critical praise.

In the decades that followed, she starred in box office successes such as *Shampoo* (1975), *Private Benjamin* (1980), and *Overboard* (1987), often portraying smart, spirited women navigating complex personal journeys with warmth and humor. With *Private Benjamin*, she not only starred but also stepped behind the scenes as a producer, proving her creative acumen and business savvy.

Beyond acting, Hawn has championed children's well-being through her MindUP foundation, blending science, emotional learning, and mindfulness. Her ability to stay relevant while remaining true to her lighthearted essence has made her a timeless and influential figure in Hollywood history.

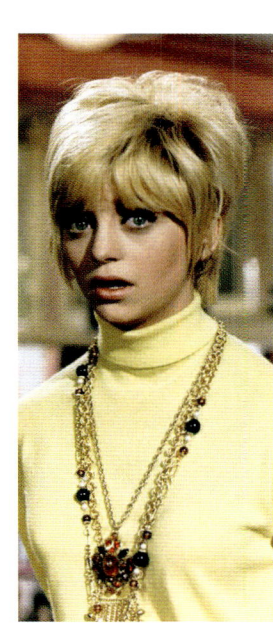

ABOVE

Hawn became a breakout star in the late 1960s with *Rowan & Martin's Laugh-In*, winning an Oscar soon after for *Cactus Flower* and embodying the era's quirky charm.

LEFT

Goldie pushed boundaries with her playful, unconventional image in the 1960s. Known for her comedic brilliance, she redefined female stardom with bold fashion and a fearless screen presence.

LEADING MEN
PAUL NEWMAN

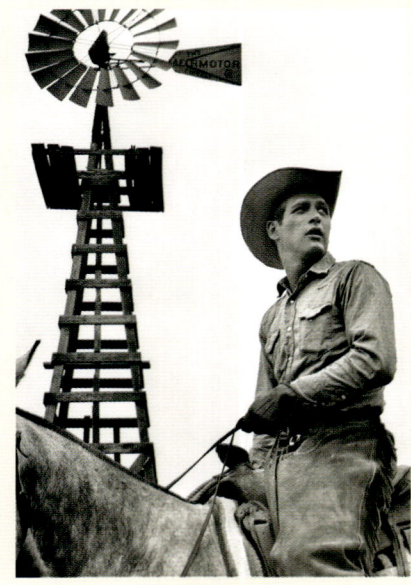

Cool, charismatic, and profoundly committed, Paul Newman was the epitome of classic Hollywood charm with a conscience—an actor of striking talent and integrity who also became a philanthropist and cultural icon.

Paul Newman (1925–2008), born in Shaker Heights, Ohio, grew up in a middle-class Jewish family and began acting in grade school plays. After graduating from high school, he enlisted in the U.S. Navy during World War II, serving as a radioman in the Pacific theater. Following his military service, he pursued higher education at Kenyon College, where he became involved in theater. His passion for acting led him to further refine his craft at the Yale School of Drama and the prestigious Actors Studio in New York City, where he studied method acting alongside future legends.

Newman made his Broadway debut in 1953 in *Picnic*, quickly attracting the attention of film studios. Although his first film, *The Silver Chalice* (1954), was critically panned, his breakthrough came with *Somebody Up There Likes Me* (1956), in which he played real-life boxer Rocky Graziano. With piercing blue eyes, a strong screen presence, and a quiet intensity, Newman captivated both audiences and critics, setting the stage for an exceptional career in Hollywood.

He soon cemented his reputation as a leading man with a string of powerful performances. In *Cat on a Hot Tin Roof* (1958), he starred opposite Elizabeth Taylor, delivering a brooding and nuanced portrayal that earned him his first

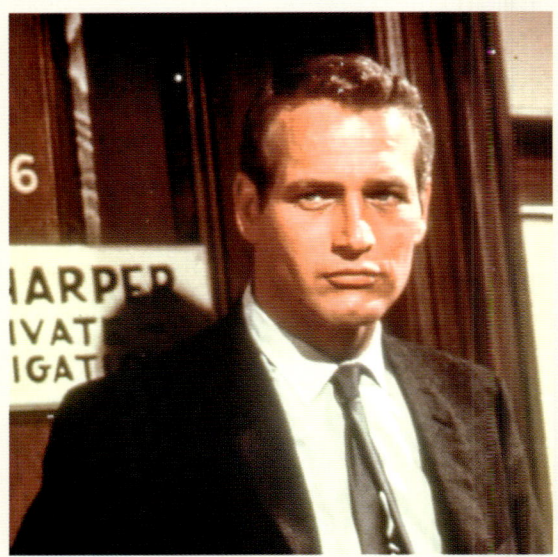

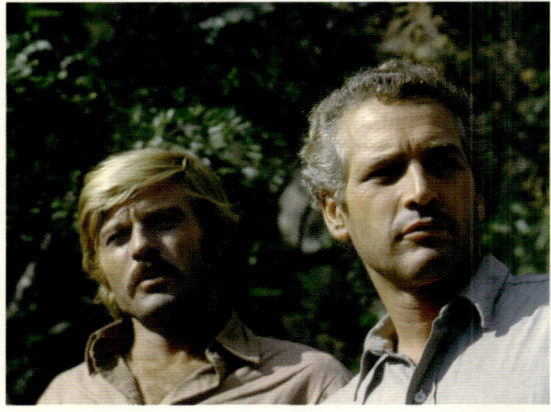

ABOVE

In *Hud* (1963), Paul Newman portrayed a morally complex antihero. The role earned him an Oscar nomination and cemented his image as a brooding, modern Western icon.

TOP RIGHT

Paul Newman played the sharp, wisecracking private detective Lew Harper in *Harper* (1966), a role that revitalized the noir genre. His cool charisma and modern edge helped redefine the screen detective for a new era.

BOTTOM RIGHT

Paul Newman starred alongside Robert Redford in *Butch Cassidy and the Sundance Kid* (1969), a film that cemented their legendary on-screen partnership.

Academy Award nomination. He followed this with *The Hustler* (1961), where his role as the complex and charismatic pool hustler "Fast" Eddie Felson showcased his remarkable emotional range. Many of Newman's characters wrestled with inner conflict and a sense of disillusionment, mirroring the shifting cultural landscape of postwar America.

During the 1960s and 1970s, Newman became one of Hollywood's most bankable and versatile stars. He headlined a series of critically acclaimed films that displayed his charm, intelligence, and

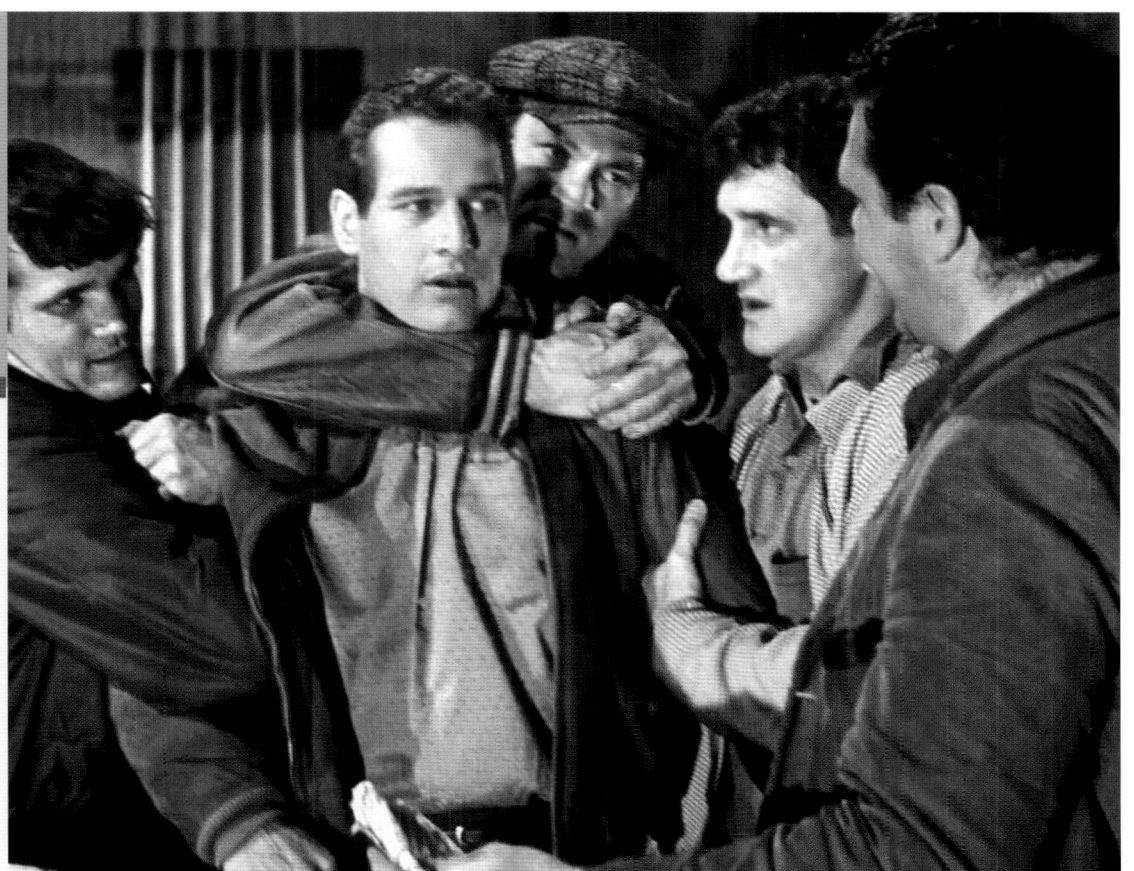

I'm not a clothes horse, but I have my own style.

PAUL NEWMAN

subtle rebellion. Standout roles in *Cool Hand Luke* (1967), *Butch Cassidy and the Sundance Kid* (1969), and *The Sting* (1973)—the latter two with Robert Redford—further solidified his legacy. His collaboration with Redford became one of cinema's most beloved partnerships, blending humor, tension, and deep camaraderie.

Newman also made his mark behind the camera, directing several films, including *Rachel, Rachel* (1968), which starred his wife, Joanne Woodward. Their marriage, enduring for five decades, was rare in the entertainment industry and admired for its depth and mutual respect. In 1982, he launched Newman's Own, a food company that donates 100% of its profits to charitable causes—demonstrating his deep commitment to philanthropy.

In his later years, Newman continued to deliver acclaimed performances. His return as "Fast Eddie" in *The Color of Money* (1986) earned him an Academy Award for Best Actor after years of nominations. He received additional praise for *Nobody's Fool* (1994) and *Road to Perdition* (2002), and charmed a younger audience by voicing Doc Hudson in Pixar's *Cars* (2006).

A passionate race car driver and team owner, Newman also championed numerous social

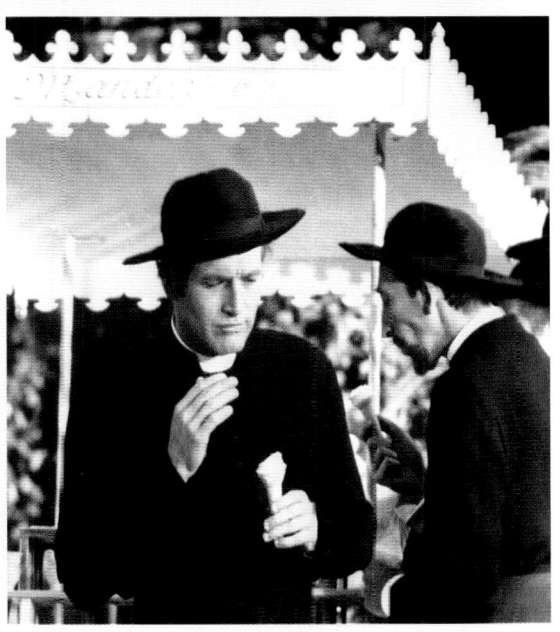

and humanitarian causes, including camps for seriously ill children and advocacy for education and justice. His life embodied generosity, authenticity, and grace.

Newman remains a timeless figure—an actor of rare talent and a man of uncommon principle whose legacy continues to inspire across generations.

TOP LEFT

Newman starred as boxer Rocky Graziano in *Somebody Up There Likes Me* (1956), a breakthrough role that launched him to Hollywood stardom.

LEFT

In *The Secret War of Harry Frigg* (1968), Paul Newman starred as Father Chuck O'Malley blending comedy and war drama while disguised as a priest during a quirky World War II escape mission.

AUDREY HEPBURN

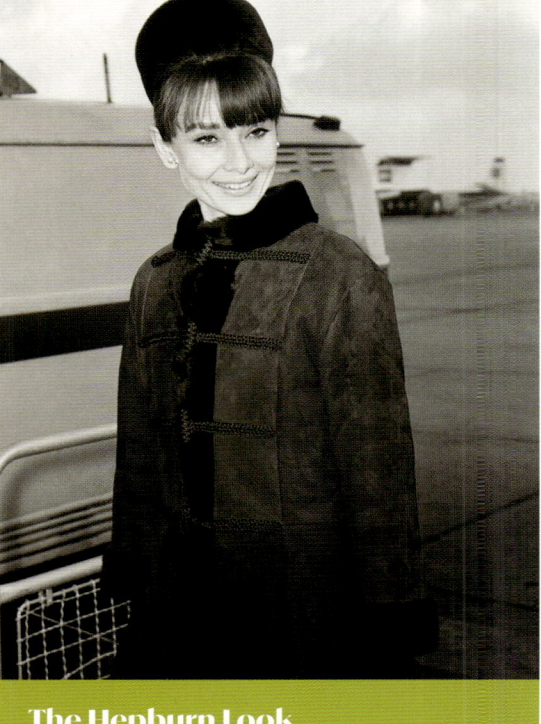

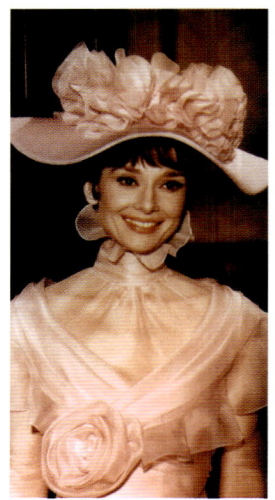

Effortlessly elegant, disarmingly graceful, and innately stylish, Audrey Hepburn captured hearts and defined an era as one of Hollywood's most iconic stars, admired equally for her charm, talent, and humanitarian spirit.

Audrey Hepburn was more than just a movie star—she was the embodiment of grace, both on and off the screen. Born Audrey Kathleen Ruston in Brussels in 1929, her early life was marked by the shadows of war. As a teenager in the Netherlands during World War II, she witnessed suffering firsthand, experiences that would quietly shape the compassion she carried for the rest of her life.

Although she dreamed of becoming a ballerina, her height and the aftereffects of wartime malnutrition redirected her path. After studying dance in Amsterdam and London, she was drawn into the worlds of modeling and theater. Her break came in the most fairy-tale of ways: the famed French writer Colette spotted her and insisted she star in the Broadway production of *Gigi* in 1951. The stage, it turned out, was merely a stepping stone.

Hollywood soon took notice. In *Roman Holiday* (1953), her first major film role, Hepburn enchanted audiences with her portrayal of a princess yearning for freedom. It earned her an Academy Award and a place in the hearts of millions. What followed was a career steeped in iconic roles—*Sabrina, Funny Face, Breakfast at Tiffany's,* and *My Fair Lady*—each performance revealing a woman who could light up a scene with a glance, a smile, or a subtle gesture.

But Hepburn wasn't just a muse for the camera. With Hubert de Givenchy as her designer and dear friend, she redefined elegance for generations. Her style—simple, poised, and impossibly chic— was not about extravagance but refinement. She wore fashion the way she acted: with grace,

ABOVE

Hepburn dazzles in a rose-organza ensemble and floral hat as Eliza Doolittle in *My Fair Lady* (1964)—a vision of Edwardian elegance in transformation.

TOP RIGHT

At Heathrow Airport in 1965, Audrey Hepburn radiates winter chic in a suede and fur toggle coat—blending jet-set sophistication with timeless European elegance.

FULL PAGE

Audrey Hepburn in *Breakfast at Tiffany's* (1961), wearing the now-legendary black Givenchy gown, long gloves, and pearls—an ensemble that redefined modern glamor. Effortlessly poised behind a decorative screen, Hepburn embodies a minimalist sophistication.

The Hepburn Look

Minimalist and poised, Hepburn's look fused Parisian chic with a gamine allure—slim silhouettes, crisp lines, and understated elegance defined her wardrobe.

- Little black dress
- Cropped trousers and ballet flats
- Oversized sunglasses
- Soft updos and natural makeup

authenticity, and a deep understanding of character. Her wardrobe staples—little black dresses, cropped trousers, and ballet flats— remain enduring inspirations in fashion to this day.

In the final chapter of her life, she turned toward service. As a UNICEF goodwill ambassador, she dedicated her energy to advocating for children in need across the globe. She traveled tirelessly, speaking not as a celebrity but as someone who understood hardship and believed deeply in kindness, healing, and dignity.

Audrey Hepburn passed away in 1993, but her spirit lingers in film, in fashion, and in the hearts of those inspired by her example. She remains a symbol of timeless beauty—not just for how she looked, but for the life she chose to live: one of elegance, empathy, and quiet strength.

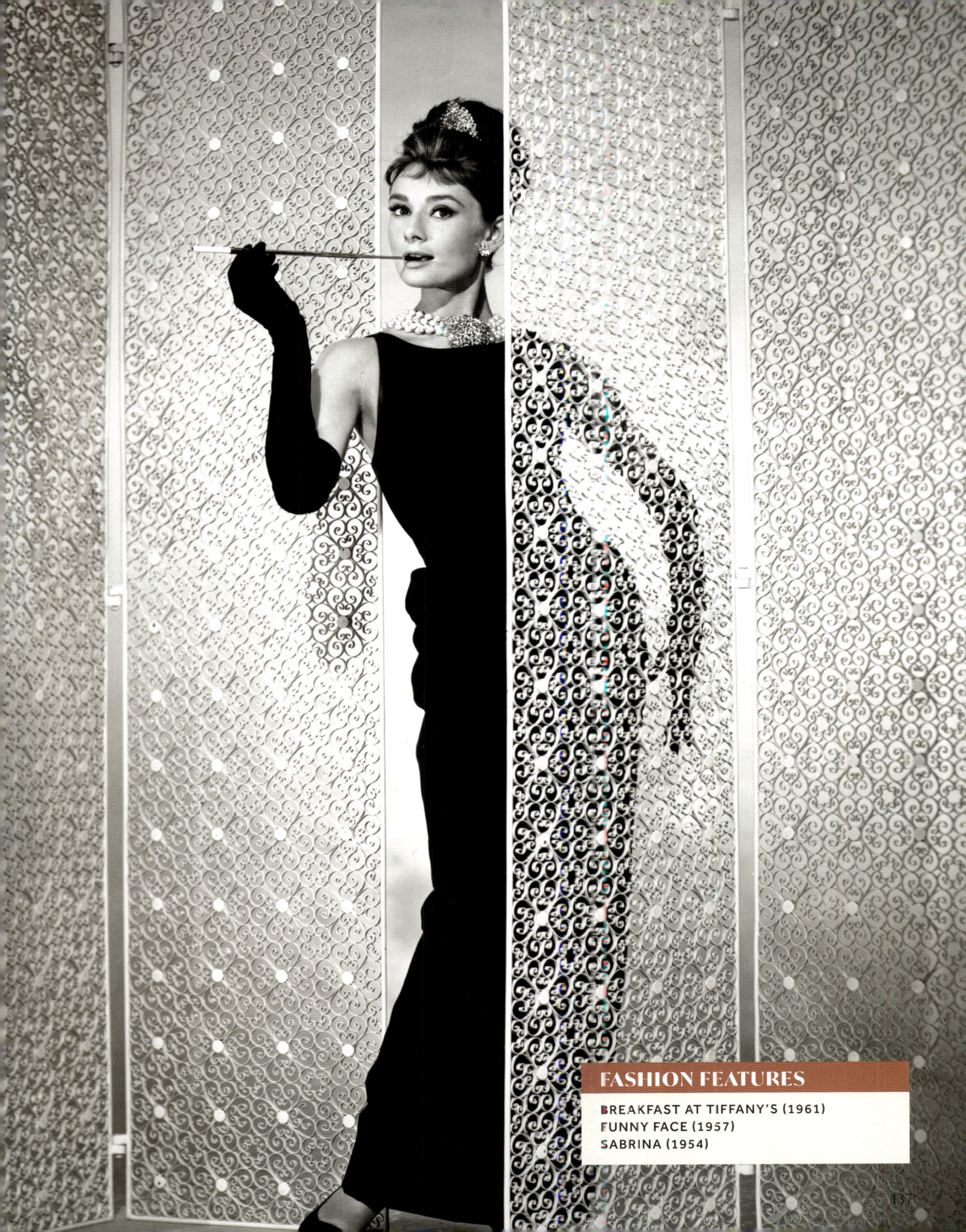

LEADING MEN
MARLON BRANDO

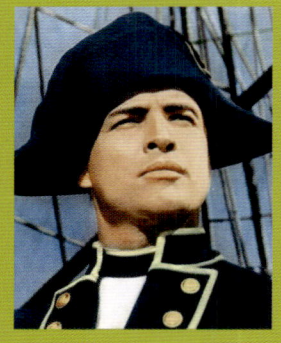

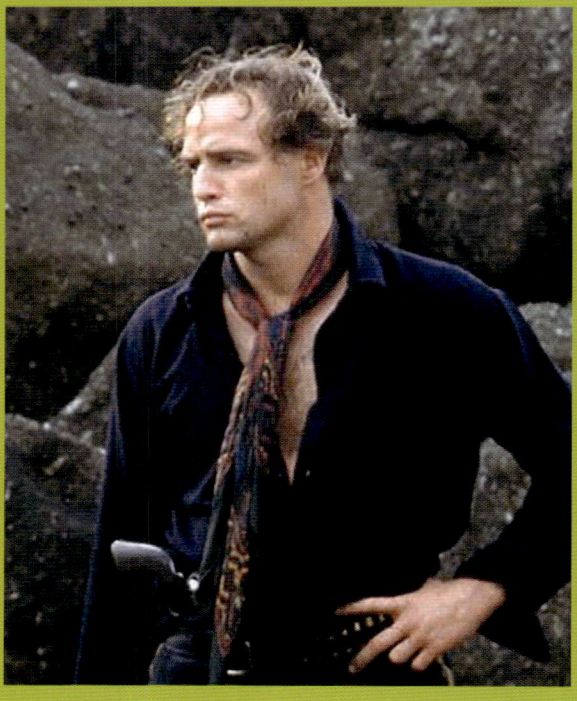

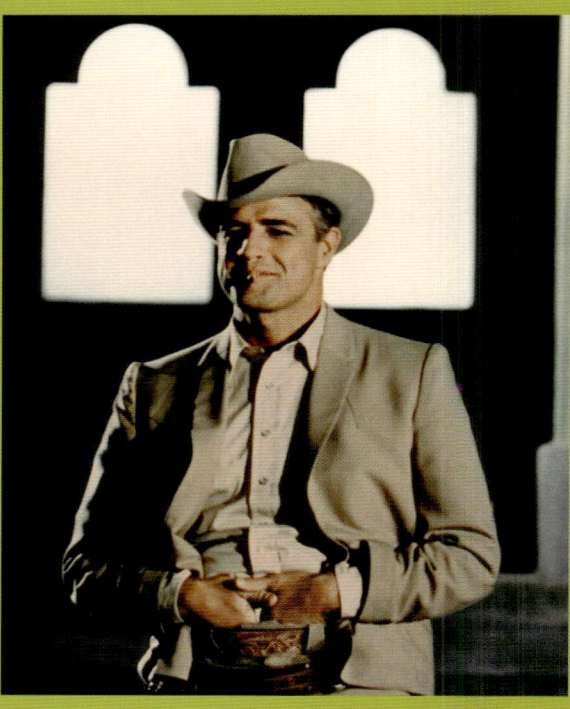

ABOVE

Brando portrayed Fletcher Christian in *Mutiny on the Bounty* (1962), a role that showcased his charisma and marked a turning point in his career's trajectory.

TOP LEFT

In *One-Eyed Jacks* (1961), Marlon Brando framed by rugged terrain, exudes brooding defiance—shirt open, pistol at his side, and the restless wind of the frontier in his hair.

TOP RIGHT

Marlon played Sheriff Matt Morgan in *The Appaloosa* (1966), a Western that explored themes of justice and revenge. Shot in rugged landscapes, it showcased Brando's stoic intensity and his evolving interest in stories rooted in cultural tension and personal redemption—offering a subtler, introspective contrast to the genre's more traditional cowboy heroes.

Gritty, unpredictable, and effortlessly cool, Marlon Brando defined the 1950s male rebel—a brooding figure who upended tradition with a leather jacket, slouched stance, and a scowl that said everything.

Marlon Brando (1924–2004), born in Omaha, Nebraska, electrified the screen with his raw intensity, visceral performances, and emotional vulnerability. Rising to fame with *A Streetcar Named Desire* (1951), Brando signaled a profound shift in American masculinity. He was rough around the edges yet deeply expressive, grounded in a personal truth that challenged the polished, stoic archetypes of the postwar era. His portrayal of Johnny Strabler in *The Wild One* (1953) immortalized the image of the 50s rebel—complete with cuffed jeans, engineer boots, and the now-iconic Schott Perfecto leather motorcycle jacket. When asked,

"What are you rebelling against?", his offhand reply— "Whaddya got?"—perfectly captured the simmering restlessness and generational disillusionment of the time.

Brando wasn't alone in channeling this new, untamed masculinity. James Dean and Montgomery Clift also embodied the outsider—a sensitive, restless figure who rejected traditional ideals and embraced a sense of inner conflict. These men wore their rebellion not just in attitude but in their wardrobes: open-collared shirts, plain white tees, knit polos, slacks with relaxed tailoring, rugged boots, and worn-in denim. They embraced utilitarian fashion, emphasizing functionality and durability, designed considering their practicality—an intentional departure from the neat, composed silhouettes of previous decades. Their style said, "I don't follow the rules." and it resonated with a generation that sought authenticity over appearance and individuality over

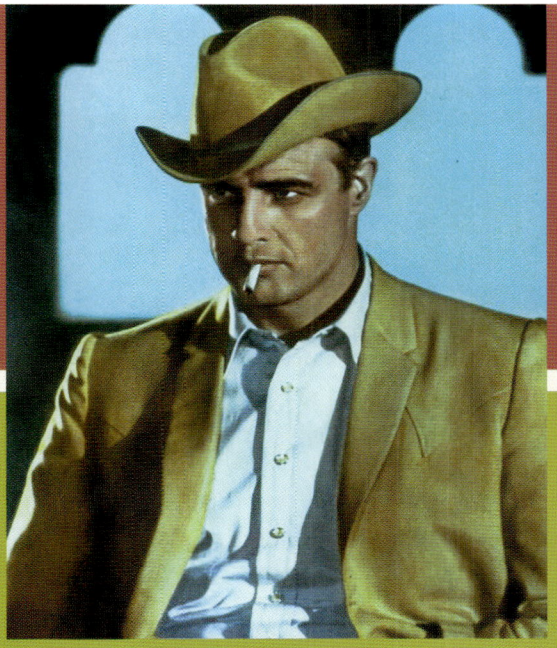

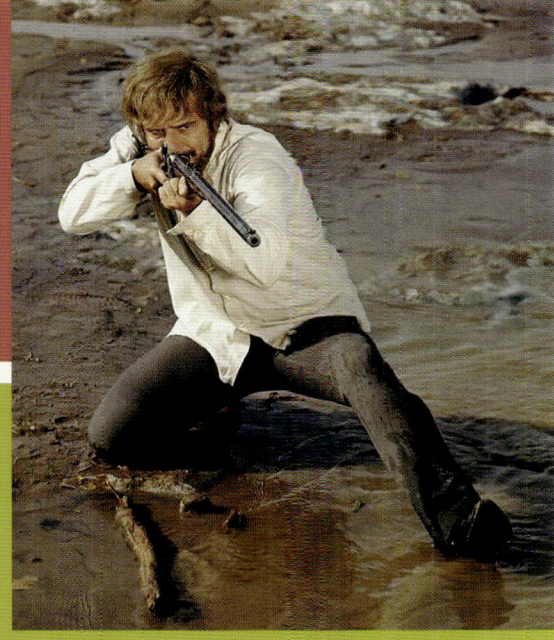

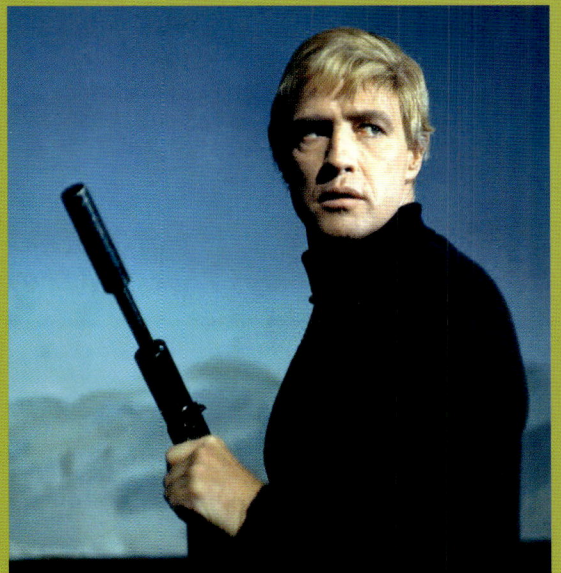

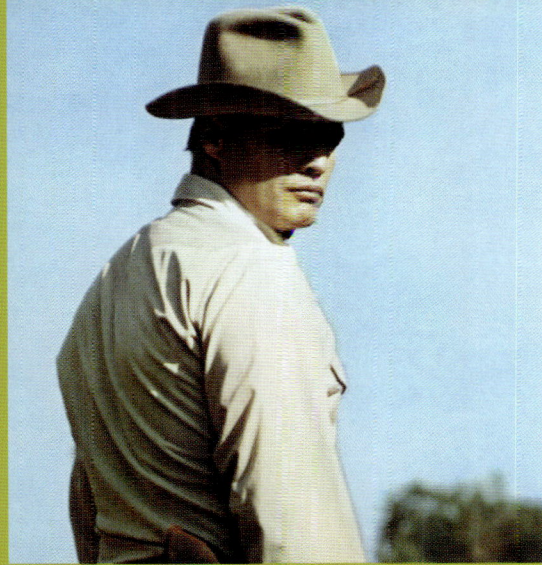

mass conformity, echoing the changing social undercurrents of mid-century America.

Meanwhile, the Ivy League look—crisp button-downs, chino pants, loafers, and letterman sweaters—offered a polished yet preppy counterpoint to the rebel image. Still, even in this clean-cut sphere, echoes of rebellion appeared: ties were worn loosened, sport coats lost their rigidity, and hairstyles shifted from heavily pomaded to more relaxed and natural. The lines between rebellion and refinement began to blur, especially among young men who sought a balanced identity between tradition and individuality.

Brando, Dean, and their counterparts didn't just influence fashion—they rewrote the cultural

script. The gentleman in a three-piece suit was no longer the only aspirational figure. Instead, youth idolized the loner in a leather jacket, who rode motorcycles, smoked Marlboros, read Jack Kerouac, and stared through the haze of postwar optimism with a look of unresolved longing and quiet defiance.

Off-screen, Brando's legacy expanded. He used fame to advocate for civil rights, oppose injustice, and champion Native American causes. Often refusing awards or roles that clashed with his principles, Brando rebelled not only through his image but also through deeply personal convictions—leaving behind a legacy as provocative, disruptive, and enduring as his unforgettable screen presence and cultural footprint.

TOP LEFT

Brando brought brooding charisma to *One-Eyed Jacks* (1961), the only film he ever directed.

TOP RIGHT

In *Burn!* (1969), a political drama set on a Caribbean island, where Marlon Brando played a British agent—a role reflecting his growing interest in activism and colonial critique.

LEFT

In *The Night of the Following Day* (1969), Marlon Brando played a mysterious chauffeur involved in a kidnapping, marking one of his lesser-known but stylistically bold crime thrillers.

RIGHT

Marlon in *The Chase* (1966), tense and dust-covered in a sheriff's uniform, embodies small-town pressure and moral turmoil in a Southern gothic powder keg ready to ignite.

NANCY KWAN

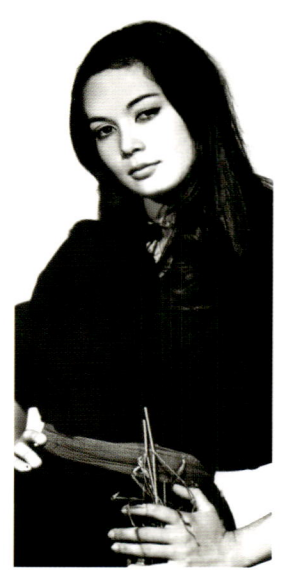

Stylish, trailblazing, and quietly subversive, Nancy Kwan broke barriers in 1960s Hollywood, bringing grace, authenticity, and cultural complexity to roles that had long been filtered through a white lens.

Nancy Kwan (born in 1939) was born in Hong Kong to a Chinese father and a Scottish mother and rose to international stardom with her debut in *The World of Suzie Wong* (1960). Her luminous screen presence and ballet-trained poise challenged narrow industry notions of Asian womanhood, even as she was often cast in roles that reinforced harmful stereotypes. Despite her groundbreaking success—especially as the lead in *Flower Drum Song* (1961), one of the first major Hollywood musicals to feature an Asian-American cast— Kwan was both celebrated and confined by an industry that rarely allowed Asian actors to move beyond cliché or caricature.

Kwan's impact, however, extended far beyond her on-screen performances. In her 2019 autobiography, *A Celebration of Life: Memories of My Son*, she offers deeply personal reflections not only on her career but also on the ways she navigated Hollywood's limiting portrayals of Asian characters. She candidly addresses how her work challenged and was constrained by enduring tropes such as the "Dragon Lady" and "Lotus Blossom." With clarity, sorrow, and pride, she explores the complexities of being a cultural pioneer—an icon both embraced and marginalized in a system built on exclusion.

Although she later stepped back from leading film roles, Nancy Kwan's legacy lives on as a symbol of progress and perseverance in Asian-American representation. Her blend of elegance, resilience, and subtle defiance paved the way for future generations of actors seeking fuller, more authentic portrayals on screen.

RIGHT

Striking a poised curve in a jade-green cheongsam, Nancy Kwan channels 1960s East-meets-West glamor—her iconic *Flower Drum Song* elegance in full modern swing.

ABOVE

Nancy Kwan rose to fame with *The World of Suzie Wong* (1960), breaking Hollywood barriers as one of the first Asian actresses to gain international stardom in Western cinema.

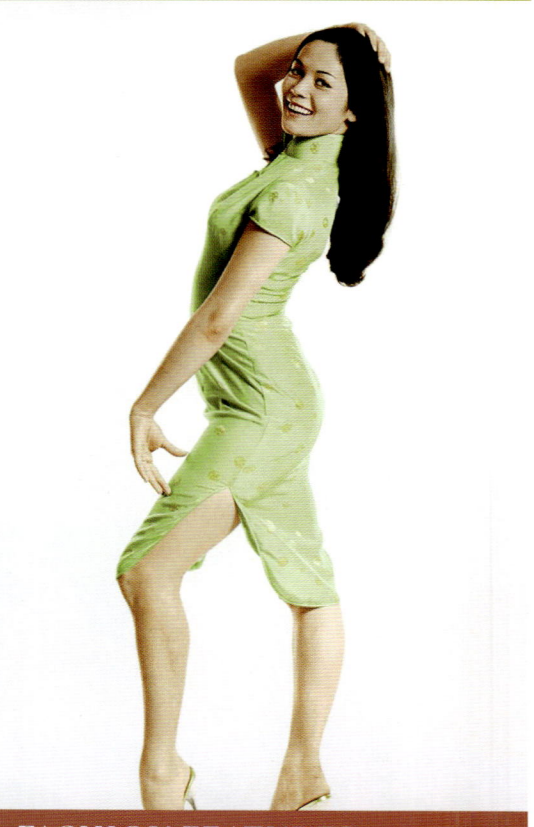

FASHION FEATURES

THE WORLD OF SUZIE WONG (1960)
FLOWER DRUM SONG (1961)

The Kwan Look

Feminine and striking, often blending Eastern elegance with Western glamor, Nancy Kwan's style radiated confidence, cultural fusion, and timeless screen charisma.

- Sleek updos
- Cheongsam dresses
- Delicate eye makeup
- Bold yet refined silhouettes

SHIRLEY MACLAINE

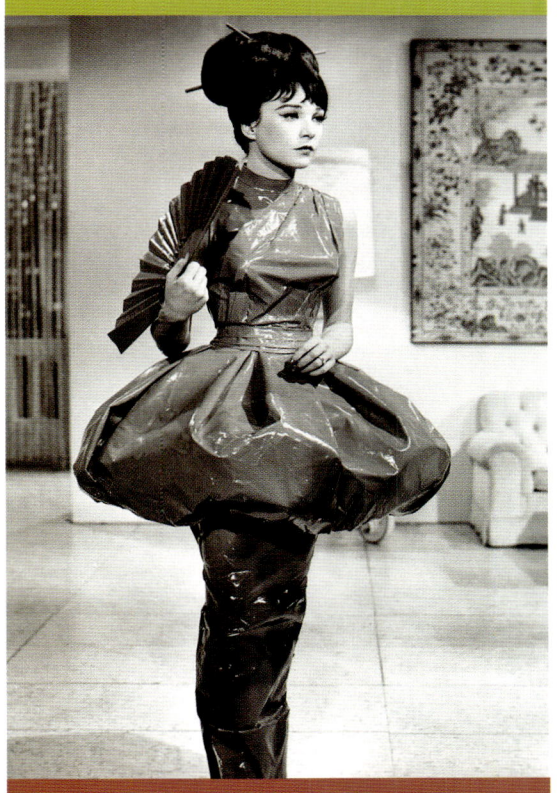

FASHION FEATURES

SOME CAME RUNNING (1958)
THE APARTMENT (1960)
IRMA LA DOUCE (1963)
SWEET CHARITY (1969)
TERMS OF ENDEARMENT (1983)

The MacLaine Look

Her style combined playful sophistication with relaxed glamor—think sleek silhouettes, mod lines, and expressive accessories that mirrored her fearless on-screen energy.

• Short shag haircut
• Bold-colored dresses
• Mod coats and go-go boots
• Eye-framing lashes and soft pink lips

Spirited, smart, and endlessly versatile, Shirley MacLaine brought humor, heart, and honesty to every role—and carved a path all her own in Hollywood.

MacLaine (born 1934) rose to prominence in the 1950s and quickly established herself as one of the most dynamic and unconventional actresses of her generation. Born Shirley MacLean Beaty in Richmond, Virginia, she began as a dancer, studying ballet before shifting to musical theater. Her big break came when she understudied Carol Haney in Broadway's *The Pajama Game* and was discovered by a film producer. MacLaine made her film debut in *The Trouble with Harry* (1955), directed by Alfred Hitchcock, and was soon cast in a string of successful roles that showcased her wit, emotional depth, and offbeat charm.

By the 1960s, MacLaine was a major star. Performances in *The Apartment* (1960) and *Irma La Douce* (1963) earned her widespread acclaim and multiple Oscar nominations. Her ability to oscillate between comic and dramatic roles made her a fixture in films that explored working women, romance, and self-discovery. MacLaine was never afraid to take creative risks or play characters that defied traditional norms of femininity. Beyond acting, she became known for her outspoken views on spirituality, reincarnation, and politics, further distinguishing her public persona.

A gifted performer with an unmistakable voice and presence, MacLaine left an indelible mark on Hollywood—one that continues to evolve with each new generation.

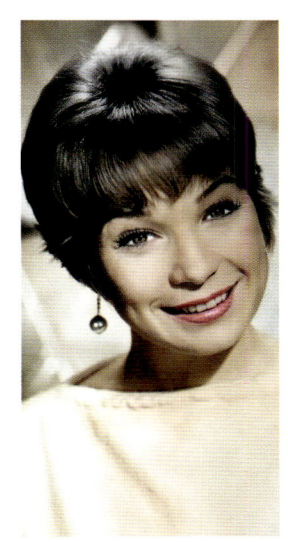

ABOVE

Shirley MacLaine stunned audiences with her bold pixie cut and breakout role in *The Apartment* (1960).

LEFT

MacLaine wore this avant-garde vinyl outfit in *What a Way to Go!* (1964), a musical comedy showcasing seven extravagant costume changes.

LEADING MEN
STEVE MCQUEEN

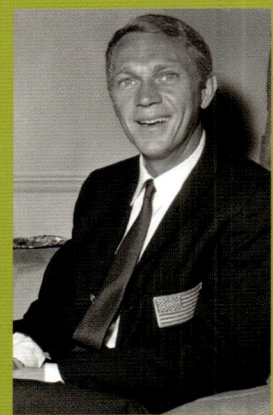

Steve McQueen (1930–1980) was an American actor known for his tough, understated screen presence and rebellious off-screen persona. Born in Beech Grove, Indiana, he had a troubled youth that included time spent in reform school and service in the U.S. Marine Corps. After studying acting at New York's Neighborhood Playhouse, he debuted on Broadway in 1955.

McQueen gained fame through the TV series *Wanted: Dead or Alive* (1958–1961) and transitioned to film with standout roles in *The Magnificent Seven* (1960), *The Great Escape* (1963), *The Sand Pebbles* (1966), *Bullitt* (1968), and *Le Mans* (1971). His performance in *The Sand Pebbles* earned him his only Academy Award nomination. Known for his preference to perform stunts himself, McQueen often played characters defined by resilience and cool defiance.

By the 1970s, he was the highest-paid actor in Hollywood. Films such as *The Getaway* (1972) and *The Towering Inferno* (1974) cemented his star status. He later took a break to pursue racing and returned in *An Enemy of the People* (1978).

Diagnosed with mesothelioma in 1979, McQueen died in 1980 at age 50. His image—jeans, leather jacket, and quiet confidence—continues to define effortless cool on and off screen.

ABOVE

McQueen, pictured on 24 August 1964 in London, prepares to compete in the International Six-Day Trial in East Germany—cool and composed, merging Hollywood stardom with true off-screen grit.

RIGHT

McQueen, with Shirley Anne Field on the set of *The War Lover* (1962), exuding quiet authority in flight gear—his signature blend of rugged charm and simmering intensity already firmly in place.

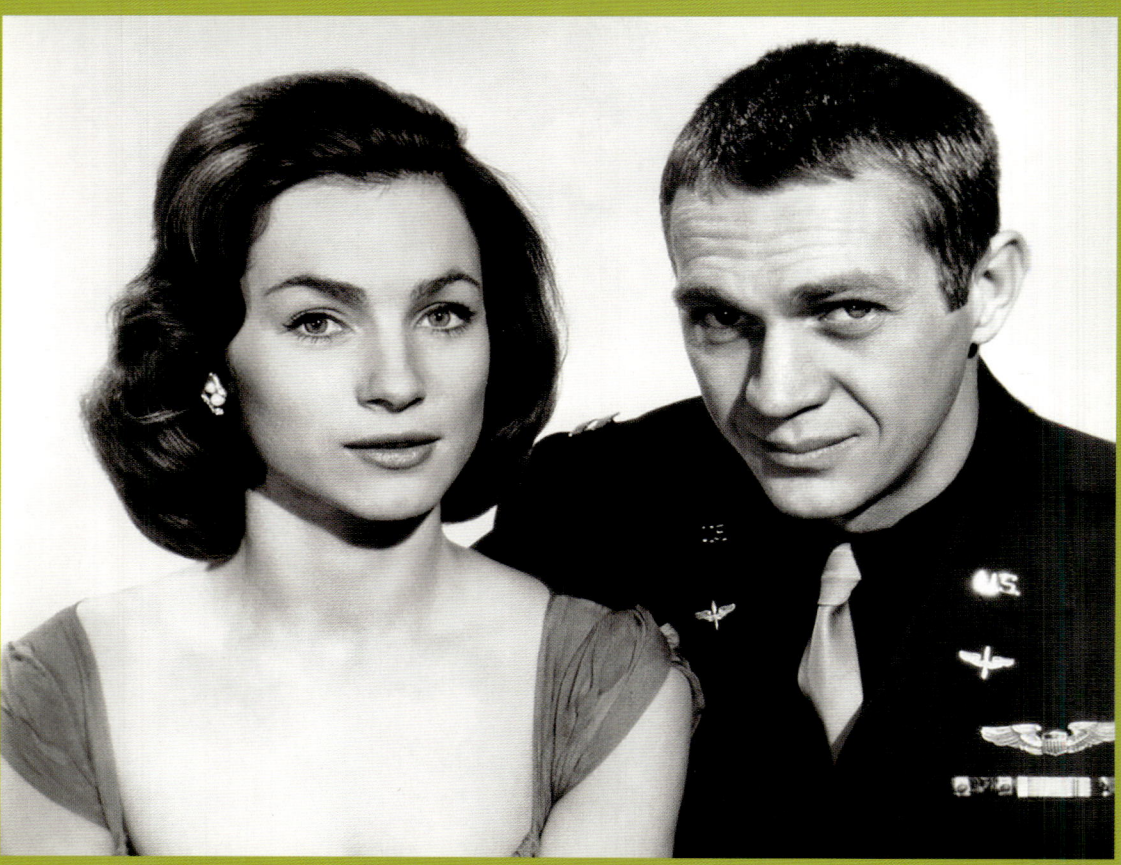

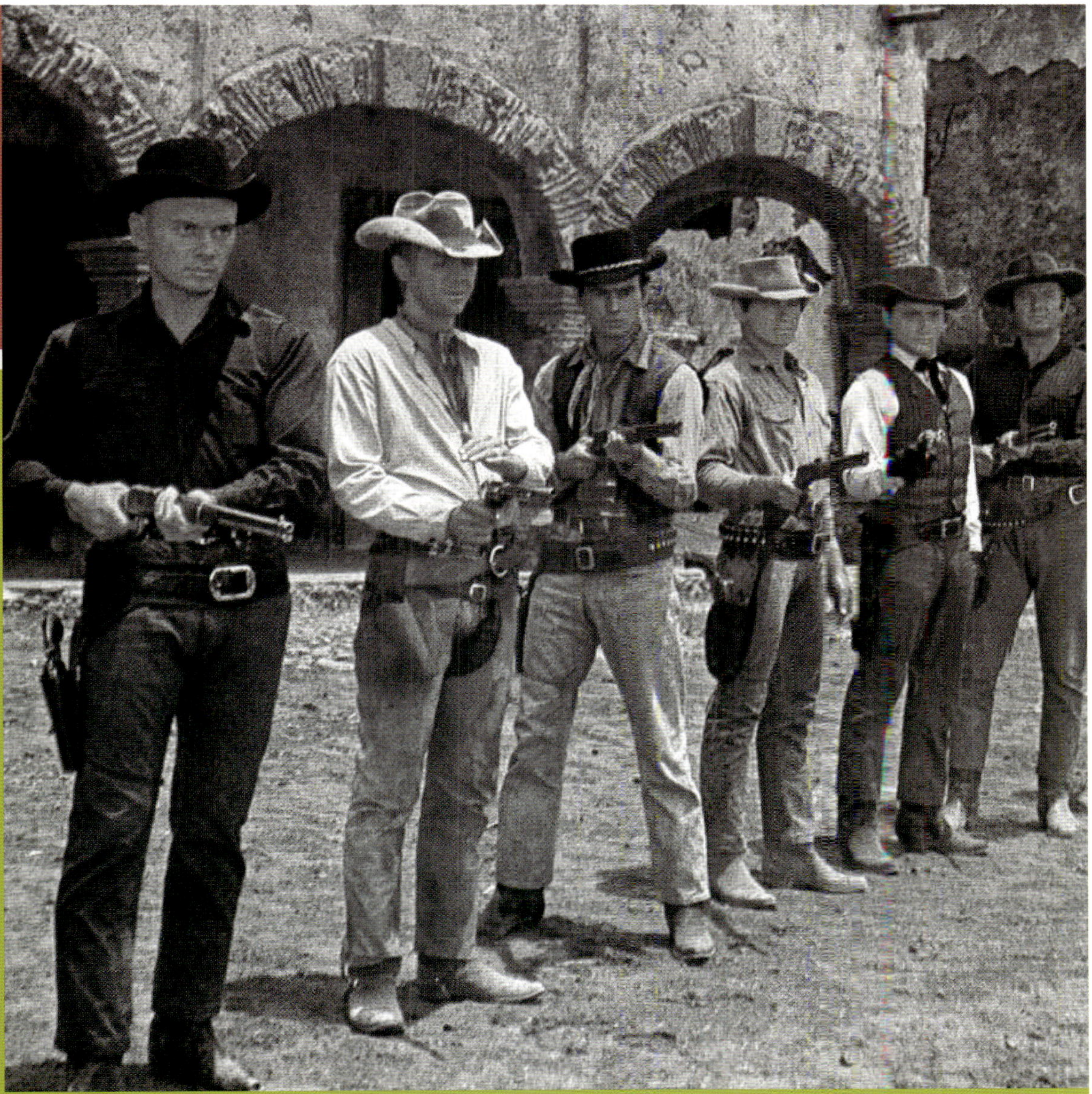

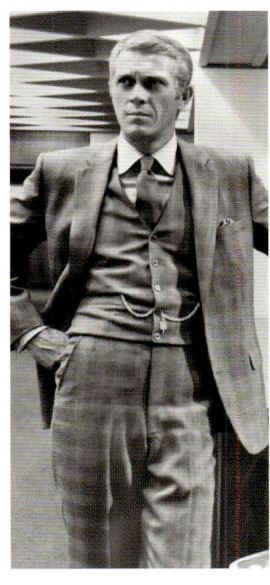

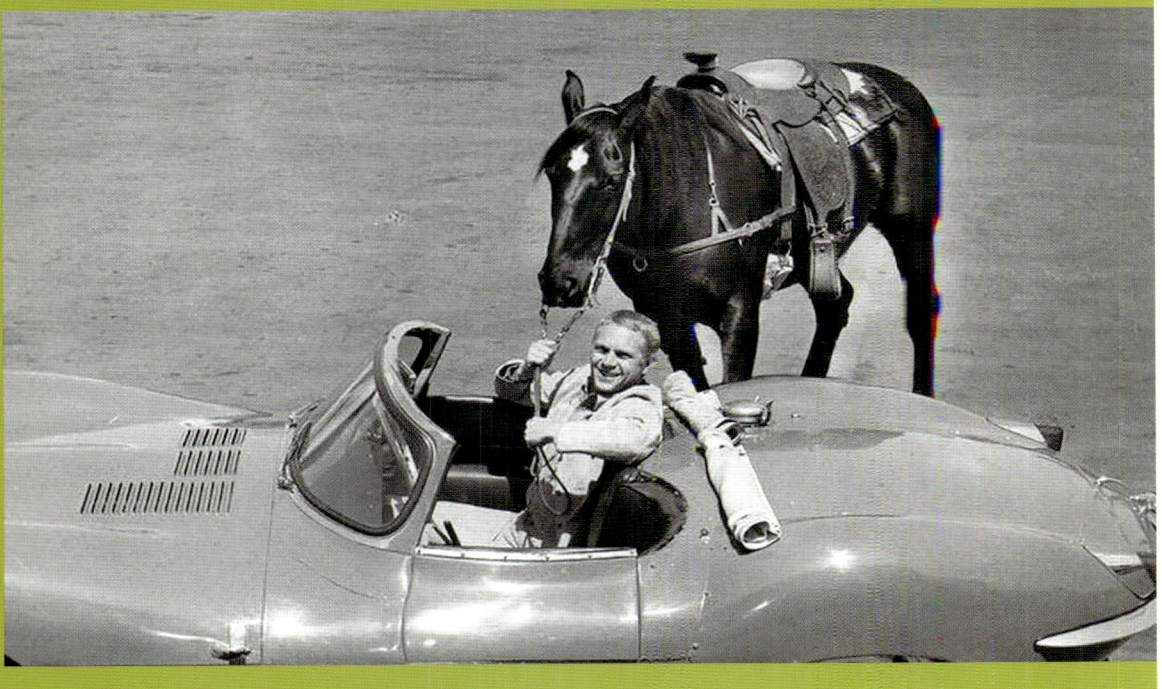

TOP LEFT

The Magnificent Seven (1960):
Yul Brynner, Steve McQueen,
and a powerhouse cast bring
sharp style and steely resolve
to John Sturges' legendary
Western.

TOP RIGHT

In a 1968 publicity still for *The
Thomas Crown Affair*—coolly
composed in a tailored suit,
Steve McQueen embodies
the effortless style and quiet
intensity that defined his
screen legacy.

LEFT

McQueen photographed in the
1960s, holding the reins of a
horse while seated in a Jaguar
XKSS—an image that perfectly
captures his dual passions for
speed and *The Wild West*.

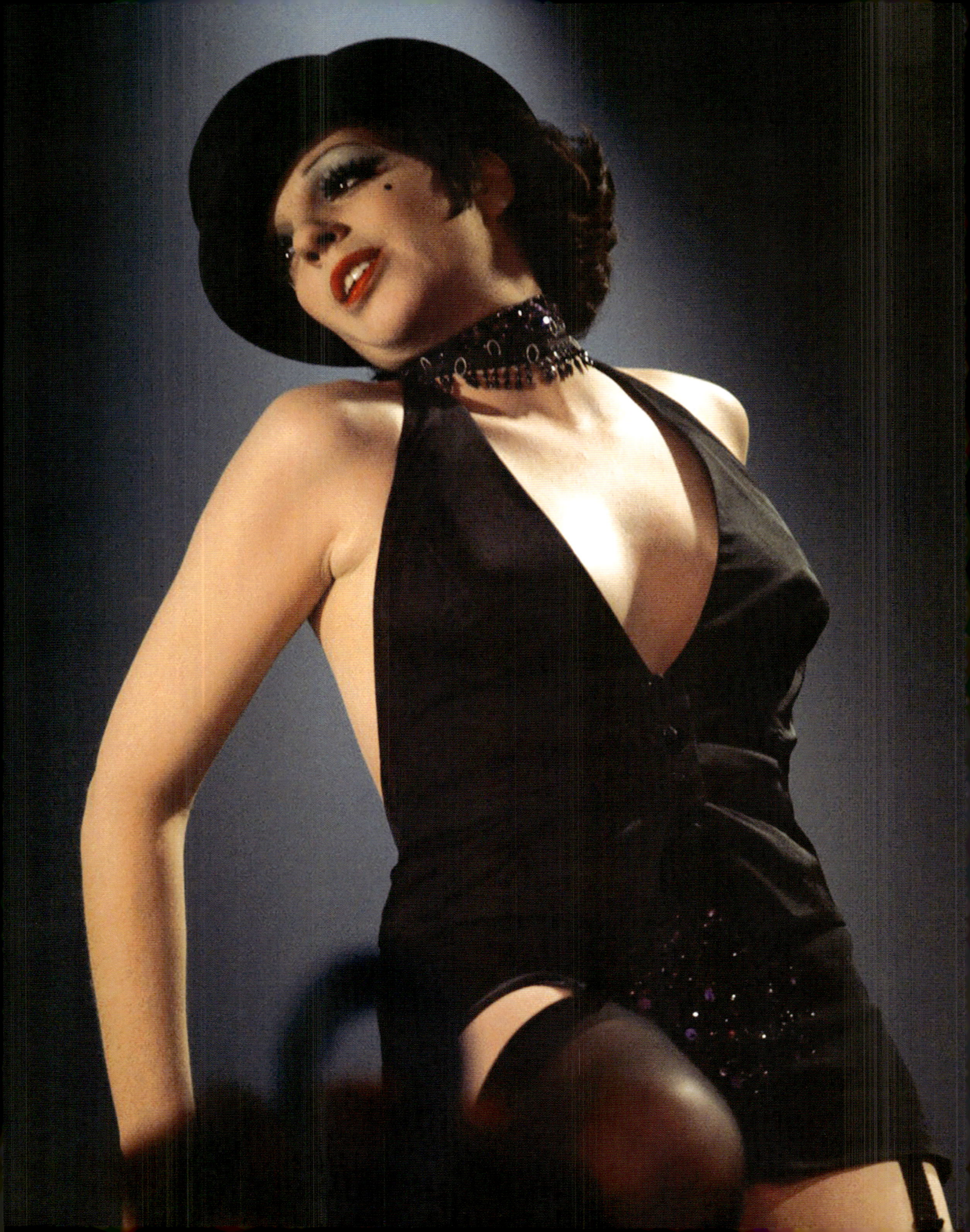

NINETEEN SEVENTIES

The 1970s reshaped American cinema, ushering in a bold era of innovation and storytelling unlike any that had come before. With the decline of the studio-controlled system and a shift in audience expectations, filmmakers began to explore more personal, politically charged, and unconventional narratives. This was not a time for formulaic plots or polished endings—Hollywood underwent significant growth and transformation in the 1970s, and its films reflected a country grappling with war, civil unrest, and generational change.

A wave of fresh talent—directors such as Robert Altman, Sidney Lumet, Hal Ashby, and Roman Polanski—delivered sharp, character-driven stories that challenged social norms and cinematic rules. Movies such as *Network* (1976), *All the President's Men* (1976), *Klute* (1971), and *The Last Detail* (1973) examined everything from media corruption to sexual politics. Meanwhile, auteur-driven passion projects such as *Apocalypse Now* and *Annie Hall* broke genre expectations and redefined what a movie could be.

Simultaneously, new technologies and marketing strategies led to the rise of commercial cinema. *Jaws* and *Star Wars* weren't just hits—they were game-changers, giving rise to the era of summer blockbusters.

Costume design embraced realism and individuality, moving away from Hollywood glamor toward styles that reflected the people watching—flared pants, leather, knits, and street-inspired fashion. In every way, the 1970s pushed boundaries, laying the foundation for modern American filmmaking.

JILL CLAYBURGH

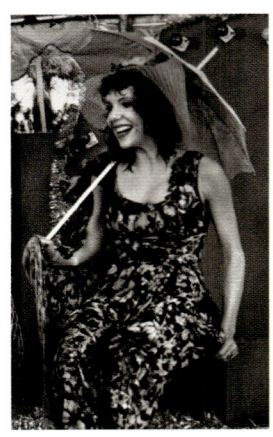

A fearless trailblazer of 1970s cinema, Jill Clayburgh brought a fresh realism to the screen—portraying women not as ideals, but as intelligent, emotional, and evolving human beings

Jill Clayburgh, born in New York City in 1944, was raised in a cultured, liberal household and studied drama at Sarah Lawrence College, where her passion for acting took root. Her career began on stage and television, where she developed a reputation for thoughtful, emotionally rich performances. But it was in film that Clayburgh would make her most enduring mark. With her luminous presence and subtle emotional intelligence, she redefined the female lead, breaking away from Hollywood's narrow archetypes.

Her breakthrough role in *An Unmarried Woman* (1978) showcased her as Erica, a woman rediscovering herself after divorce. The film resonated deeply with audiences and critics alike, earning Clayburgh an Academy Award nomination and establishing her as a voice for a new kind of cinematic woman—independent, imperfect, and real.

She continued this exploration in *Starting Over* (1979) and *First Monday in October* (1981), portraying characters with wit, intellect, and emotional complexity. Clayburgh brought honesty and restraint to each role, portraying vulnerability without weakness and confidence without arrogance.

Although later seen in more supporting roles, her influence never waned. Clayburgh's legacy is one of courage, authenticity, and a fearless commitment to portraying women's truths on screen.

ABOVE

Jill Clayburgh, perched with a parasol above the dunk tank in *An Unmarried Woman* (1978), captures a playful pause in a story of strength, change, and self-discovery.

RIGHT

Bathed in studio light, Clayburgh and James Brolin (as Carole Lombard and Clark Gable) channel true Hollywood glam—his stylish sports jacket and her soft curls and dark blazer capturing the appeal of this beloved screen couple in *Gable and Lombard* (1976).

FASHION FEATURES

AN UNMARRIED WOMAN (1978)
STARTING OVER (1979)
SILVER STREAK (1976)

The Clayburgh Look

Understated and modern, Clayburgh favored relaxed silhouettes, rich textures, and effortless ensembles that echoed the grounded strength of her characters.

- Windswept curls
- Tailored blazers and slacks
- Soft, natural fabrics
- Minimalist jewelry with bold accents

CATHERINE DENEUVE

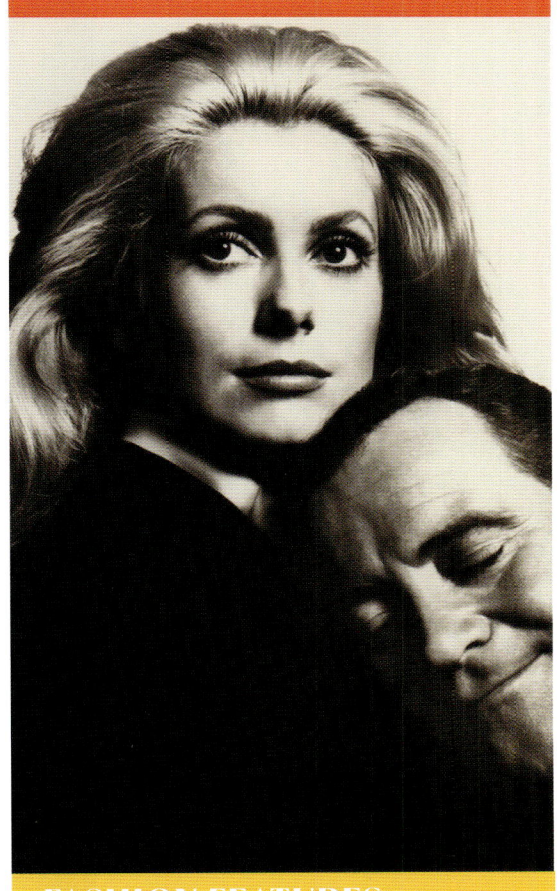

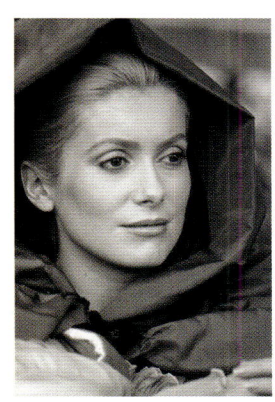

With her cool elegance and porcelain beauty, the Catherine Deneuve look defined a generation of understated glamor. She made elegance feel effortless—less about trend, more about quiet command and curated restraint.

From the moment she stepped into the spotlight, Deneuve's style was both unmistakable and impossible to imitate. Her screen presence in films like *Belle de Jour* and *La Chamade* set a visual tone for the modern French woman: minimal but never plain, sensual but never exposed. With Yves Saint Laurent as her trusted collaborator and couturier, Deneuve perfected a wardrobe of crisp trench coats, structured dresses, silk blouses, and pencil skirts—uniforms of polish that left room for mystery.

Accessories were chosen with surgical precision: black leather gloves, oversized sunglasses, a slim handbag. Hair was perfectly set, often in a soft blowout or chignon, and makeup was subtle but sculpted—nude lips, lined eyes, porcelain skin. She rarely ventured into the extravagant; instead, her elegance came from balance and confidence, from knowing what not to wear.

Off-screen, Deneuve maintained the same poise. Whether attending a film festival or photographed at home, she favored classic tailoring and neutral tones, always exuding a cool detachment that only heightened her allure. Her style was not performative; it was armor—an elegant shield for a fiercely independent woman navigating the male-dominated worlds of cinema and fashion.

Today, "The Deneuve Look" remains shorthand for refined, enduring chic. It's seen in every beige trench slung over a little black dress, every pair of sunglasses worn with quiet intent. Deneuve didn't just follow fashion—she wore it like a second skin, calm and untouchable, a walking embodiment of timeless style.

FASHION FEATURES

BELLE DE JOUR (1967)
LA CHAMADE (1968)
UN FLIC (1972)
THE HUNGER (1983)

The Deneuve Look

- Immaculate trench coats
- Shift dresses with clean lines
- Silk blouses and pencil skirts
- Gloved hands, perfect blowout
- Understated glamor with a cool, aloof edge

ABOVE

In *Tristana* (1970), Catherine Deneuve is the picture of sophisticated poise—her violet coat, silk scarf, and wide-brimmed hat perfectly framing a face as composed and enigmatic as the film itself.

RIGHT

In *The April Fools* (1969), Catherine Deneuve exudes statuesque serenity beside a smitten Jack Lemmon—her sculpted hair and sleek tailoring capturing late-60s elegance with a hint of modern melancholy.

LEADING MEN
AL PACINO

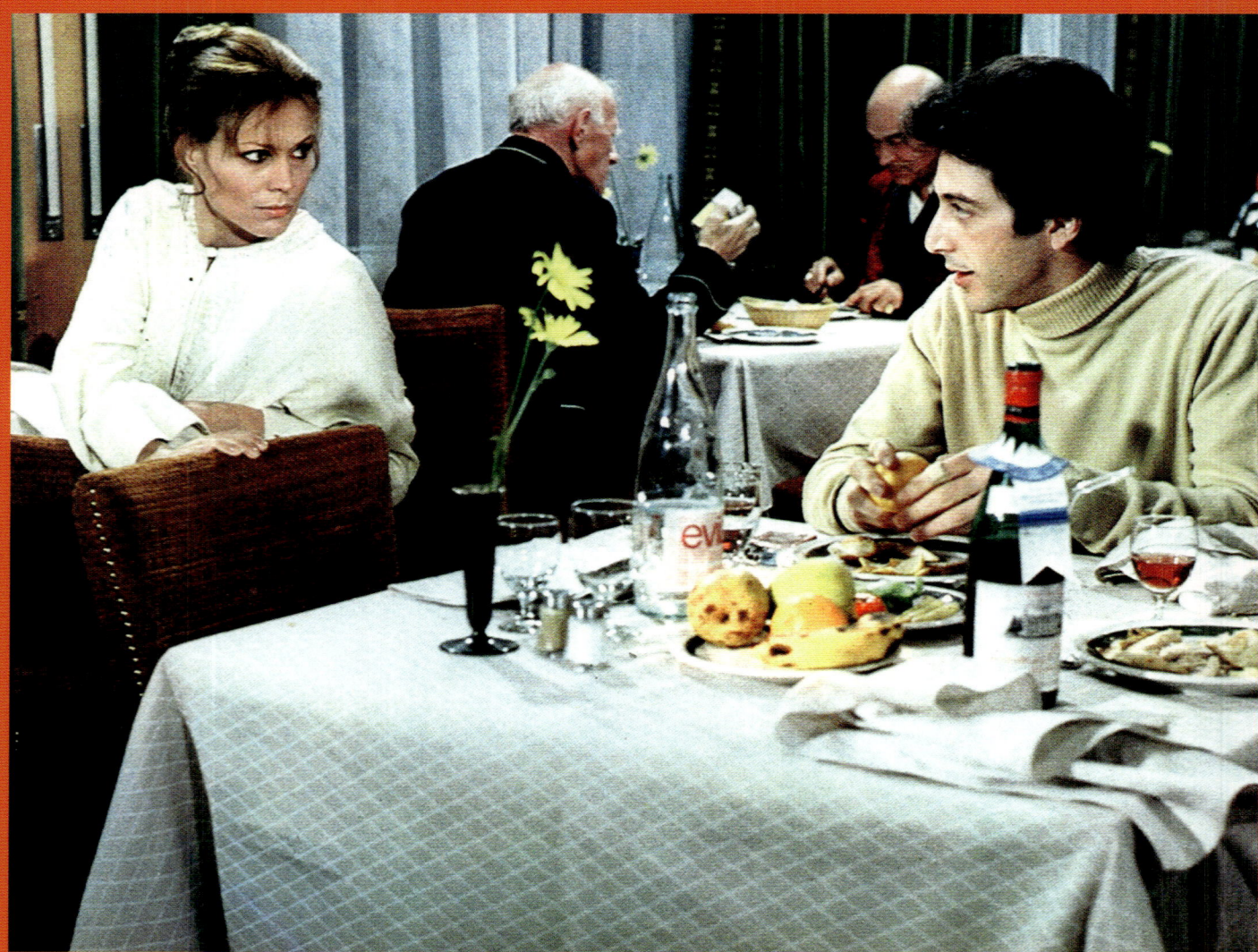

ABOVE
—

In *Bobby Deerfield* (1977), Al Pacino plays a Formula One race car driver who has been spooked by a recent death on the track. Here, co-star Marthe Keller catches his gaze at a restaurant, foreshadowing their upcoming romance.

Al Pacino is a legendary American actor known for his intense performances and powerful screen presence. Yet during his long career, he also proved his versatility as a romantic lead, a comedic actor, and even a classical master of Shakespeare.

He began his career on the stage before making his film debut in *Me, Natalie* (1969). His breakthrough came with *The Godfather* (1972), where he portrayed Michael Corleone, a role that became one of the most iconic in film history. Pacino reprised the role in *The Godfather Part II* (1974) and *Part III* (1990), solidifying his place as an actor of great stature.

Throughout the 1970s and 80s, Pacino delivered a series of powerful performances in films like *Serpico*

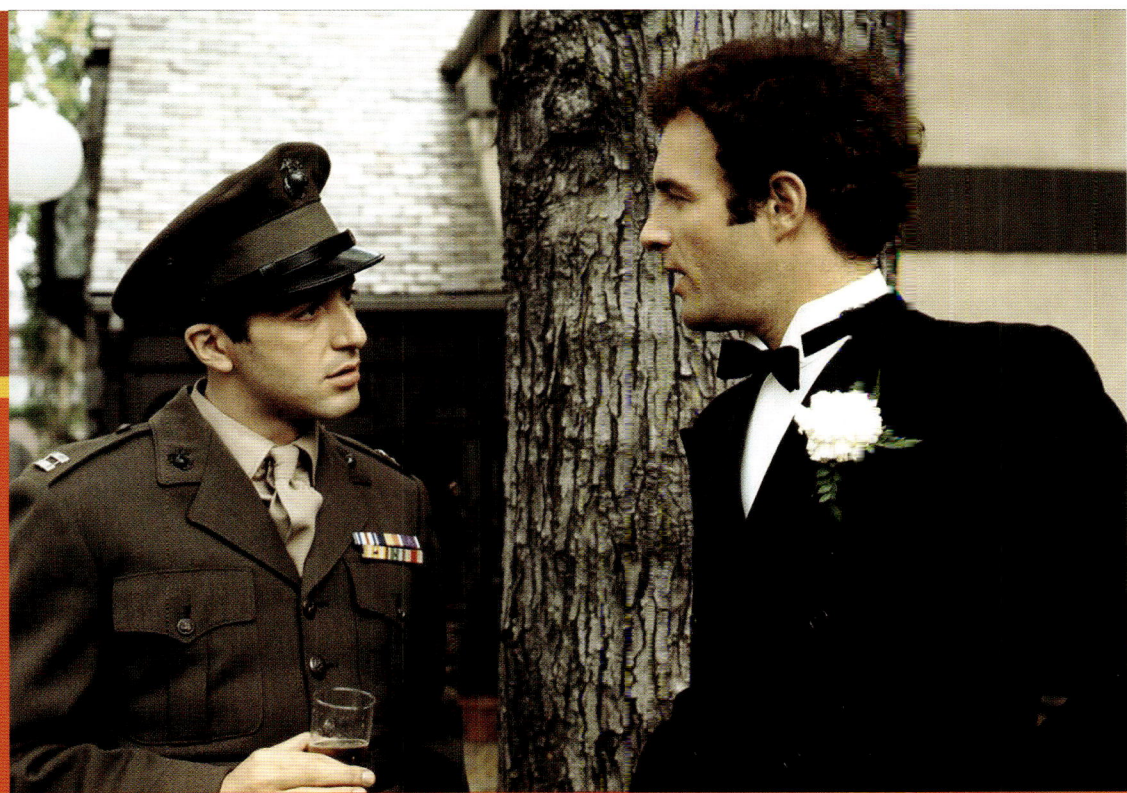

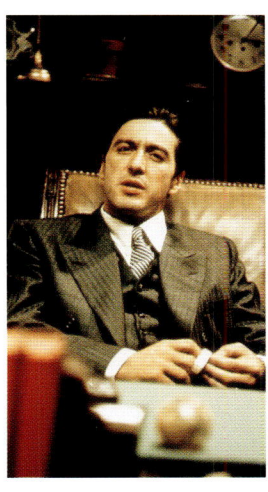

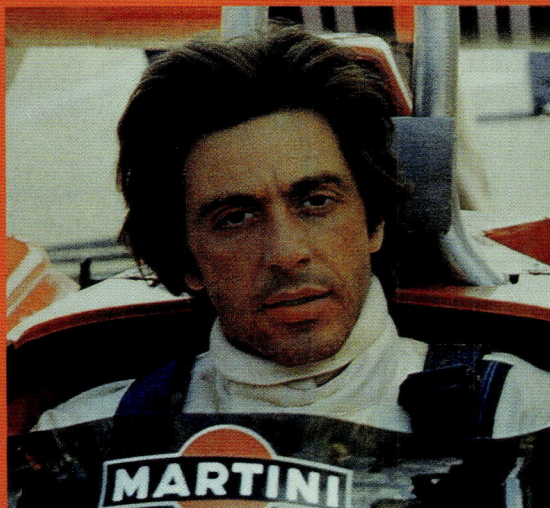

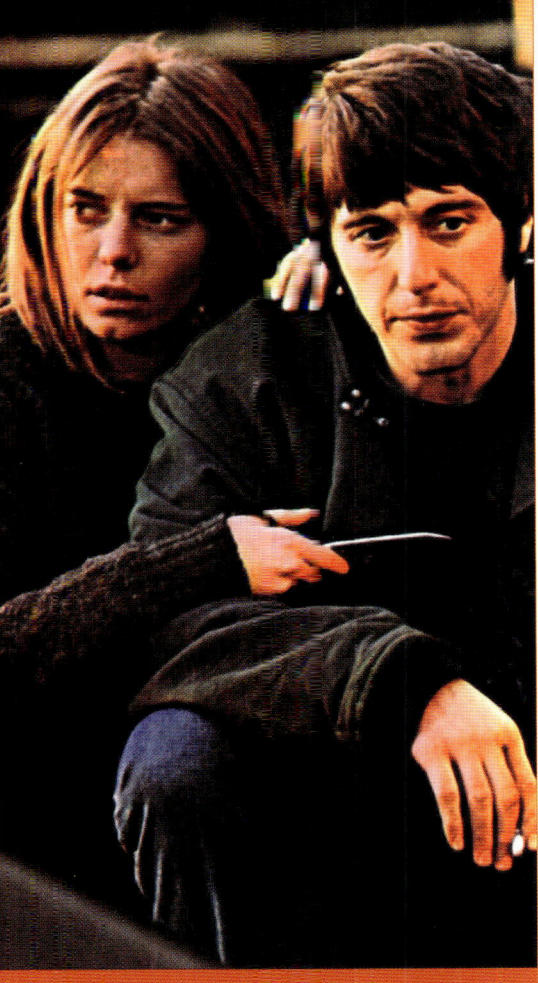

(1973), *Dog Day Afternoon* (1975), and *Scarface* (1983). Known for portraying complex, often morally ambiguous characters, he developed a reputation as one of the greatest method actors of his generation.

In 1992, he won the Academy Award for Best Actor for his role as a blind, retired Army officer in *Scent of a Woman*. Pacino has continued to work across film, television, and stage, with notable later roles in *Heat* (1995), *The Insider* (1999), *Angels in America* (2003), and *The Irishman* (2019).

His career, marked by intensity and depth, has left an indelible impact on American cinema.

ABOVE

Seated behind a desk in a three-piece pinstripe suit, he exudes calculated authority in a pivotal scene from *The Godfather Part II* (1974), where power is measured in silence, and every gesture conceals a decision already made.

LEFT

Perched on a rooftop with tension etched across their faces, Pacino and Kitty Winn express the paranoia of heroin junkies on the lam in *Panic in Needle Park* (1971); their wary glances mirroring the grit and disillusionment of a city closing in.

FAR LEFT

Al Pacino, suited in racing gear, rests inside a Formula One car cockpit, exuding quiet intensity during a promotional still that blends cool detachment with cinematic charisma.

TOP LEFT

Al Pacino, in Marine dress uniform, exchanges a loaded glance with James Caan during the wedding scene in *The Godfather* (1972), a quiet prelude to power and betrayal framed in formality and fraternal tension.

DIANE KEATON

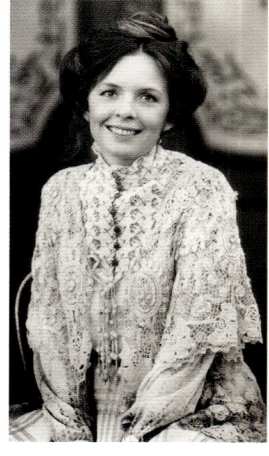

Quirky, fearless, and effortlessly individual, Diane Keaton became a defining presence of 1970s and 1980s American cinema, celebrated for her offbeat charm, nuanced performances, and distinctive personal style.

Diane Keaton (1946–2025) began her career on stage, studying acting in California and appearing in stage productions such as *Hair* before transitioning to film. Her breakthrough film role came as Kay Adams in *The Godfather* (1972), a role she reprised in the iconic trilogy. However, it was her partnership with writer-director Woody Allen that launched her into widespread fame. Keaton earned an Academy Award for Best Actress for her performance in *Annie Hall* (1977), a character that embodied her spontaneous wit, emotional honesty, and effortless style. The film not only redefined romantic comedy but also made Keaton a household name.

She continued to prove her versatility in critically acclaimed roles across genres, including *Manhattan* (1979), *Reds* (1981), for which she received another Oscar nomination, *Marvin's Room* (1996), and *Something's Gotta Give* (2003). Her work consistently showcased a balance of strength and vulnerability.

Beyond acting, Keaton has directed, produced, and authored several books. Off-screen, her menswear-inspired fashion—featuring tailored suits, ties, and signature hats—made her a style icon. Diane Keaton's enduring appeal lies in her fearless originality, quirky charm, and unwavering independence, making her one of Hollywood's most admired and influential figures.

ABOVE

In 1976's period comedy *Harry and Walter Go to New York*—with Elliott Gould, Michael Caine, and James Caan—Keaton plays a newspaperwoman who falls in with two con men. Here, her elaborate lace dress and upswept hair reflect the late 1800s, during which the film takes place.

LEFT

Wearing her iconic menswear-influenced outfit of dark vest and necktie with oversized trousers, Diane Keaton in Woody Allen's *Annie Hall* set the fashion world on its ear . . . and started the very '70s trend for idiosyncratic vintage clothing.

FASHION FEATURES

ANNIE HALL (1977)
MANHATTAN (1979)
SOMETHING'S GOTTA GIVE (2003)

The Keaton Look

Eclectic and androgynous, Keaton embraced menswear silhouettes, layering, and vintage-inspired ensembles that defied trends and defined a generation.

- Wide-brimmed hats
- Ties and vests
- Tailored blazers
- Earth-tone palettes with bold accents

LIZA MINNELLI

FASHION FEATURES

CABARET (1972)
NEW YORK, NEW YORK (1977)
ARTHUR (1981)

The Minnelli Look

Alluring and theatrical, Minnelli favored sequined jumpsuits, dramatic capes, and tailored tuxedos—always with flair and fearless originality.

- Jet-black pixie cut
- Heavy lashes and bold eyeliner
- Sequins and velvet
- Statement accessories

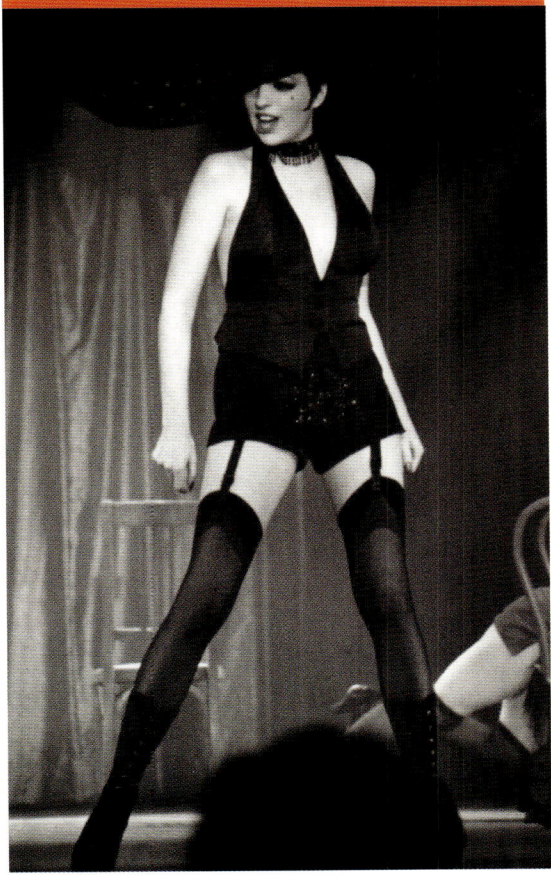

Magnetic, fearless, and unmistakably iconic, Liza Minnelli captivated audiences with her powerhouse performances and bold personal style, becoming one of the most celebrated entertainers of her generation.

Liza Minnelli (born in 1946), the daughter of Hollywood legends Judy Garland and director Vincente Minnelli, seemed destined for stardom since birth. She made her film debut at just three years of age in *In the Good Old Summertime* (1949), appearing briefly alongside her mother. Raised in the spotlight, she quickly proved she was more than just a famous name. Her breakout came with the Broadway musical *Flora, the Red Menace* (1965), where she won a Tony Award at the age of 19, launching a dynamic and eclectic career across stage and screen.

Her defining moment came with *Cabaret* (1972), where she portrayed the irrepressible Sally Bowles. This iconic performance earned her an Academy Award for Best Actress and showcased her distinctive blend of emotional vulnerability and electric charisma. With her rich, expressive voice, dramatic flair, and commanding stage energy, Minnelli became a beloved figure on Broadway, in Hollywood, and Las Vegas, known for her captivating concerts and unforgettable television specials.

Offstage, Minnelli faced personal trials, including serious health challenges and a series of high-profile marriages, yet her enduring resilience and passion for performance only deepened her mystique. She earned an Emmy, a Grammy Legend Award, an Oscar, and multiple Tonys—placing her among the elite few to achieve the EGOT status.

Liza Minnelli remains a dazzling symbol of theatrical brilliance, fearless style, and enduring star power; her legacy a bridge between the glamor of classic Hollywood and the energy of contemporary performance.

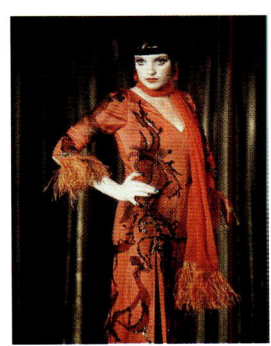

ABOVE

Minnelli in *Cabaret* (1972), striking in red sequins and feathers, embodies bold glamor and the raw allure of Weimar era performance in this iconic moment.

LEFT

Liza Minnelli electrifies the screen in *Cabaret* (1972) as Sally Bowles—under Bob Fosse's direction and the music of Kander and Ebb, she delivers a career-defining performance in this bold, jazz-soaked masterpiece.

ALI MACGRAW

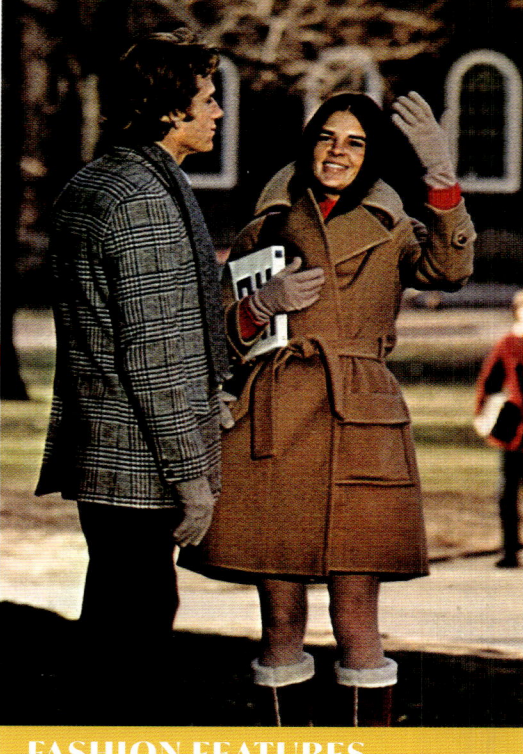

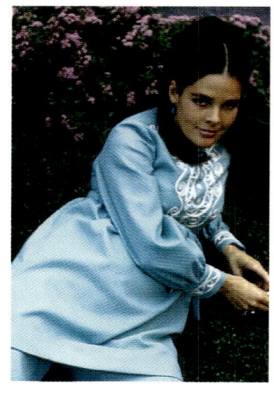

Chic, soulful, and undeniably magnetic, Ali MacGraw became a defining face of 1970s cinema, captivating audiences with her down-to-earth glamor and raw emotional depth.

Born Elizabeth Alice MacGraw in 1939 in the artsy enclave of Pound Ridge, New York, she didn't follow the conventional path to Hollywood stardom. After earning an art history degree from Wellesley College, MacGraw made her mark behind the camera as a fashion assistant before stepping in front of the lens as a model. She quickly rose to fashion prominence, with her effortless beauty, expressive eyes, and free-spirited charm, becoming a favorite for photographers and gracing the covers of elite magazines such as *Vogue* and *Harper's Bazaar*. Her striking combination of elegance and authenticity made her a natural for the screen, embodying the modern woman of the era with depth and sophistication. Her big break arrived with *Goodbye, Columbus* (1969), a sharp, romantic drama adapted from Philip Roth's novella. Her portrayal of the confident, contemporary Brenda Patimkin earned widespread acclaim and won her the Golden Globe for Most Promising Newcomer. But it was *Love Story* (1970) that transformed her into a full-fledged phenomenon. Playing the clever, self-assured Jenny Cavilleri opposite Ryan O'Neal, MacGraw captivated the world with a performance that was poignant, witty, and heartbreakingly sincere. The role earned her an Academy Award nomination and a second Golden Globe, whereas the film's famous line— "Love means never having to say you're sorry"— cemented her place in pop culture forever.

MacGraw's screen presence felt different from other leading ladies of the time: she was grounded yet luminous, stylish, and emotionally raw. Her appeal wasn't just in her looks—it was the vulnerability and strength she projected on screen. She followed *Love Story* with *The Getaway*

FASHION FEATURES

GOODBYE, COLUMBUS (1969)
LOVE STORY (1970)
THE GETAWAY (1972)

(1972), co-starring Steve McQueen. Their crackling chemistry drew critical and public praise, and spilled into real life, resulting in a high-profile romance and marriage that captivated tabloids for years.

Although her film roles were few, each one felt distinct, often reflecting her evolution. MacGraw walked away from the height of stardom to focus on her private journey. In her deeply revealing memoir *Moving Pictures* (1991), she wrote candidly about fame, addiction, heartbreak, and self-discovery, connecting with readers through her honesty and resilience.

Later in life, she shifted her energy toward spiritual growth, yoga, and activism. Settling in Santa Fe, New Mexico, MacGraw became an advocate for animal welfare, the environment, and mindful living. She also participated in charitable theater work and remained engaged in causes close to her heart. Her devotion to simplicity and authenticity became her new trademark, just as admired as her onscreen persona.

To this day, Ali MacGraw is celebrated not just as a star of her era but as a woman of enduring influence, inner strength, and timeless allure—a Hollywood icon who followed her path, both in front of the camera and far beyond it.

ABOVE

Reclining on a summer lawn in a powder-blue tunic set, Ali MacGraw captures the effortless poise of late 1960s style—her serene gaze and sculpted half-up hair echoing the quiet elegance of a rising Hollywood icon.

TOP RIGHT

Ali MacGraw, wrapped in a camel belted coat and shearling boots, shares a teasing campus moment with Ryan O'Neal in *Love Story* (1970)—conveying a budding collegiate romance that enthralled countless readers and filmgoers.

FULL PAGE

Twirling beneath sun-dappled trees, MacGraw channels early 70s Bohemia in an embroidered blouse, gypsy skirt, coin-fringed belt and crimson boots, a vision of carefree elegance steeped in folk-inspired glamor.

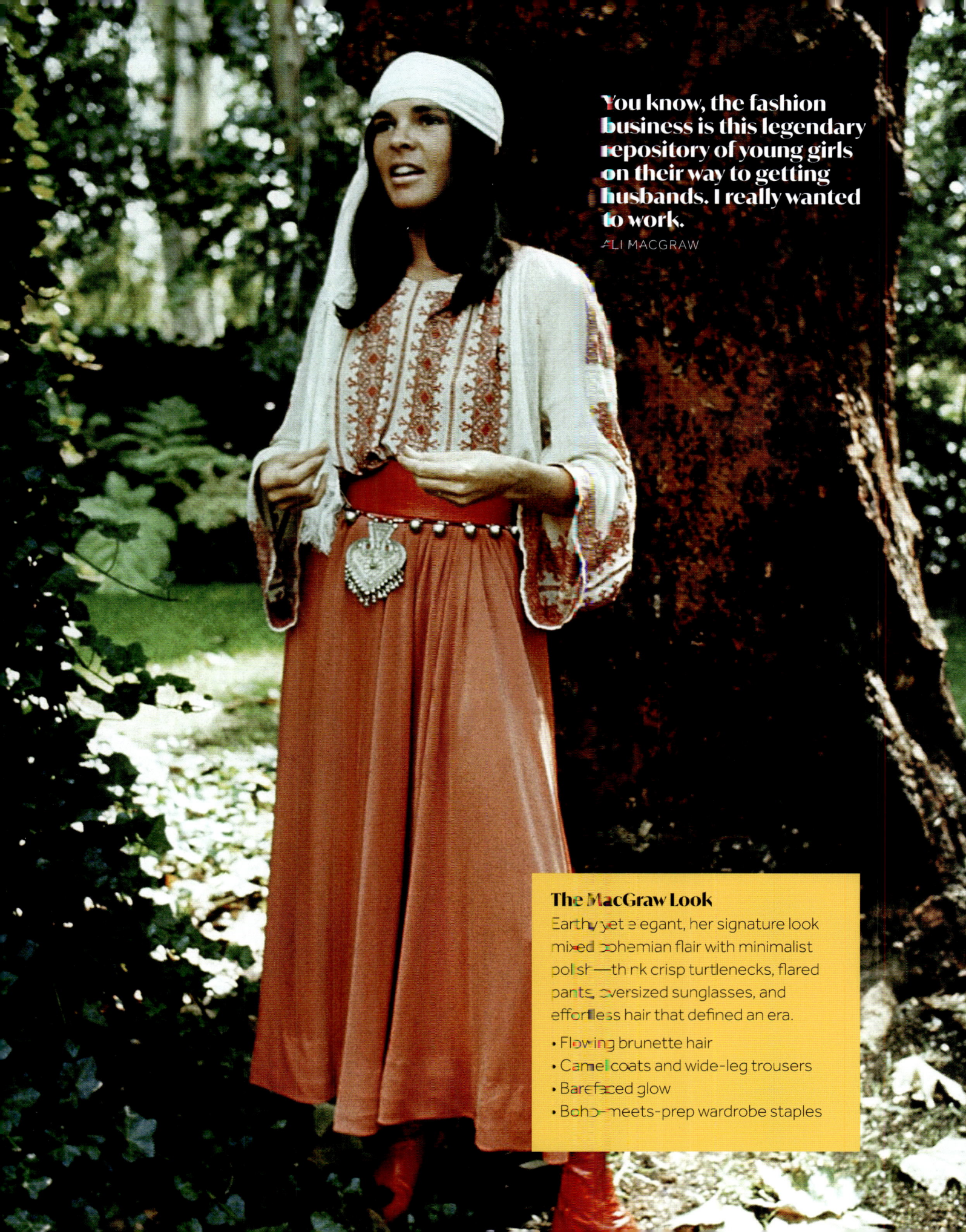

You know, the fashion business is this legendary repository of young girls on their way to getting husbands. I really wanted to work.
— ALI MACGRAW

The MacGraw Look

Earthy yet elegant, her signature look mixed bohemian flair with minimalist polish—think crisp turtlenecks, flared pants, oversized sunglasses, and effortless hair that defined an era.

• Flowing brunette hair
• Camel coats and wide-leg trousers
• Barefaced glow
• Boho-meets-prep wardrobe staples

LEADING MEN
ROBERT REDFORD

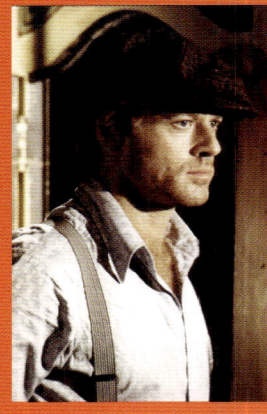

Robert Redford was a celebrated American actor, director, and producer whose career spanned over six decades. He rose to prominence in the 1960s and 70s, becoming one of Hollywood's most iconic leading men. With his thick shock of blond hair and All-American good looks, he quickly became a style-setter as well, frequently being photographed in Western wear or classic preppy separates.

Redford's breakout role came with *Butch Cassidy and the Sundance Kid* (1969), in which he starred with action veteran Paul Newman. The charismatic duo took Hollywood—and fans—by storm. So it was not surprising the two actors paired up again for the *The Sting* (1973). This was followed by the thrilling *Three Days of the Condor* (1975) with Faye Dunaway, *All the President's Men* (1976) with Dustin Hoffman, and *The Way We Were* (1973), where he wooed activist Barbra Streisand. Known for his natural charm and on-screen intelligence, Redford often portrayed thoughtful, independent characters.

A skilled rider, he often found himself in the saddle in films, playing a down-and-out former rodeo star in the *Electric Horseman* (1979) with Jane Fonda and working with actual horse trainers while filming the *Horse Whisperer* (1998), which also featured Kristin Scott Thomas and a young Scarlett Johansson.

In addition to his acting, Redford made a significant impact behind the camera. His directorial debut, *Ordinary People* (1980), won four Academy Awards, including Best Picture and Best Director. He continued to direct critically acclaimed films such as *A River Runs Through It* (1992) with Anthony Hopkins and Brad Pitt, and *Quiz Show* (1994) with Ralph Fiennes.

Beyond film, Redford was a passionate environmentalist and founder of the Sundance Institute, which supports independent filmmakers and hosts the renowned Sundance Film Festival each year in Park City and Salt Lake City, Utah. Sundance has even branched out into fashion and now offers a catalog of carefully curated Bohemian styles and artisanal jewelry.

Redford's contributions to cinema and culture earned him numerous accolades, including a Presidential Medal of Freedom in 2016. Redford reunited with three-time costar Jane Fonda for the film *Our Souls at Night* (2017), both of them playing lonely seniors who find love and comfort. Redford retired from acting in 2018 with *The Old Man & the Gun*, leaving behind a legacy defined by artistic integrity and social consciousness.

> ## A lot of what acting is, is paying attention.
> ROBERT REDFORD

ABOVE

Wearing a newsboy cap, open collar, and suspenders, con artist Redford stands poised for action—an emblematic image from *The Sting* (1973).

ABOVE RIGHT

Redford, in denim and shades, rests on a Yamaha motorcycle while filming *Little Fauss and Big Halsy* in 1970. The comedy-drama, which embodied the restless spirit of the early '70s, also featured Lauren Hutton and Michael J. Pollard.

BELOW RIGHT

Robert Redford, in a velvet jacket and ribbon tie, arrives at a 1970s Hollywood gala beside his flower-crowned wife, Lola.

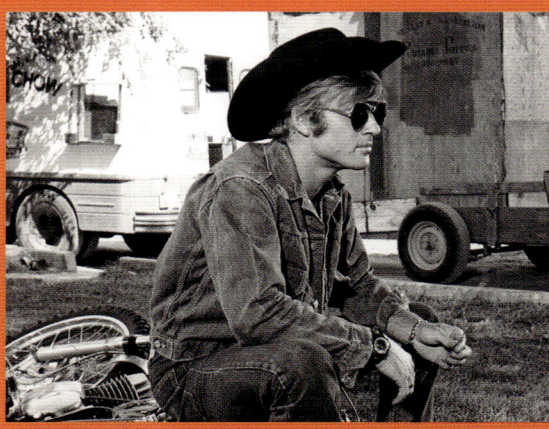

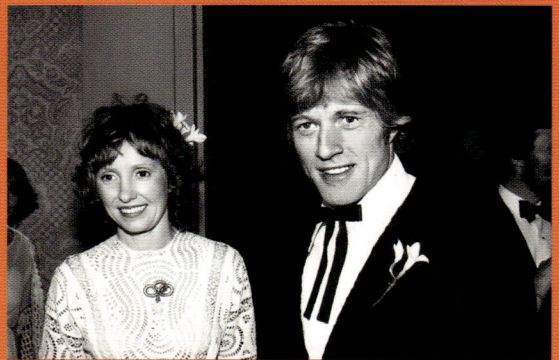

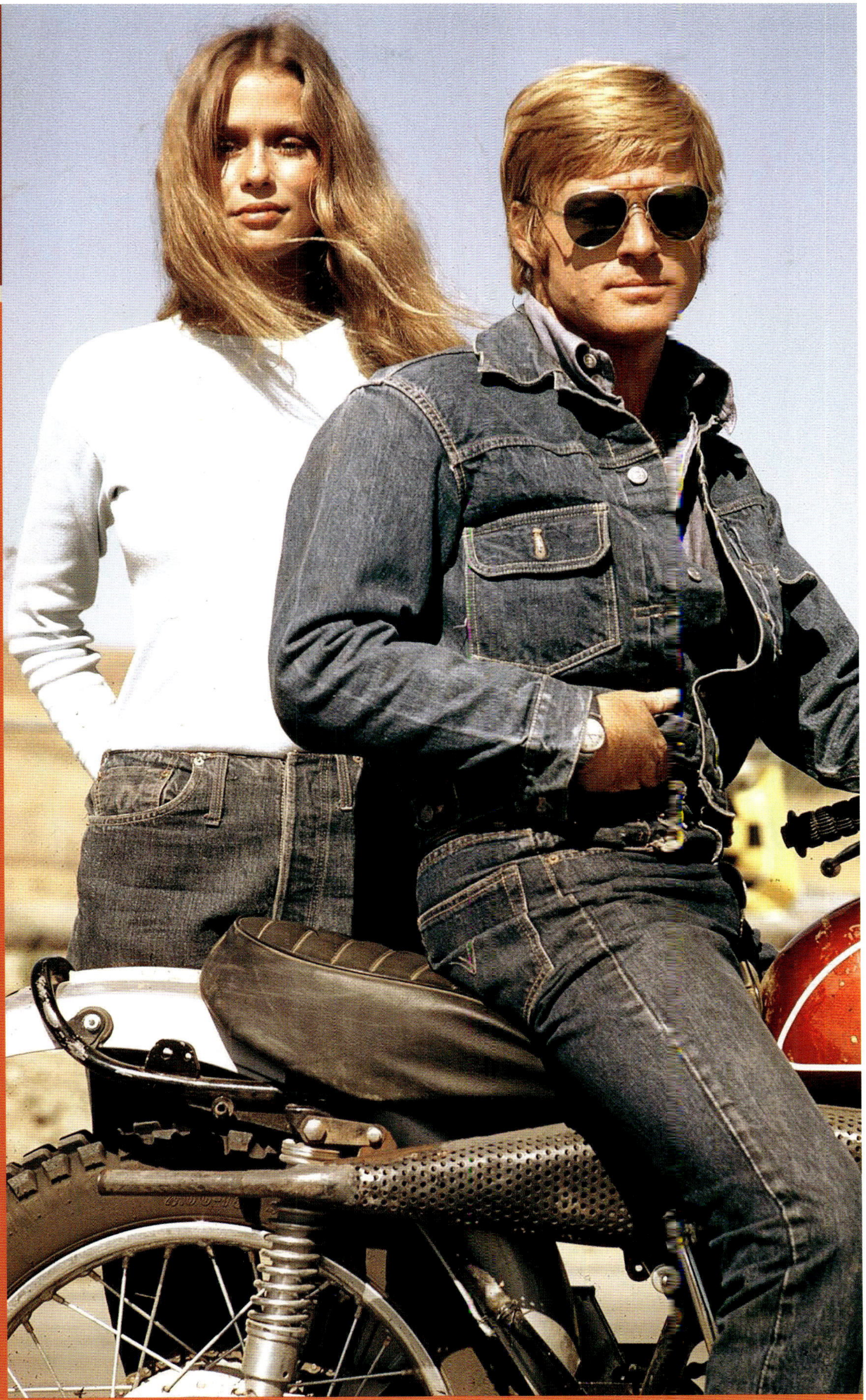

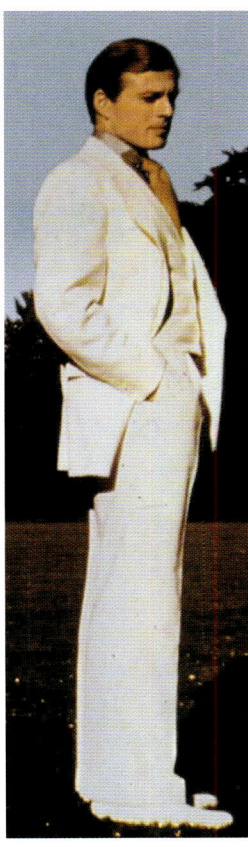

ABOVE

Dressed in an ivory suit with a golden tie, Redford, as enigmatic tycoon Jay Gatsby, stands apart from the opulent mansion behind him—a solitary figure of yearning and illusion in *The Great Gatsby* (1974). The film brought flapper fashions and elegant, formal suiting again to the fore.

LEFT

Redford, shown here with co-star Lauren Hutton, plays a dirt bike racer in the comedy-drama *Litte Fauss and Big Halsy*. His double denim outfit, also known as the "Canadian tuxedo," was one of the most popular casual looks of the decade.

DIANA ROSS

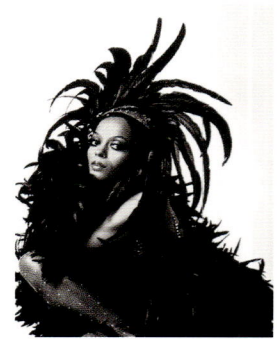

"I love fashion, or should I say I love style."

DIANA ROSS

ABOVE

Cocooned in a flourish of feathers and rhinestone fishnets, Ross gazes into the lens with quiet intensity, her showgirl regalia evoking the glamor and theatrical precision of a stage icon in her dazzling prime.

ABOVE RIGHT

Diana Ross commands the spotlight in a dramatic white gown with an opulent feathered train and matching hat, making a regal entrance at the 2025 Met Gala.

RIGHT

Bathed in stage lights, a luminous Ross raises her arms, showcasing in a metallic fringed capelet and matching bell bottoms that shimmer from gold to emerald, a dazzling emblem of 1970s soul and showmanship.

Poised, glamorous, and passionately driven, Diana Ross reshaped the sound of American music and set the standard for pop stardom with her velvety voice, commanding stage presence, and trailblazing influence across decades.

Diana Ross (born in 1944), raised in Detroit, Michigan, began her rise to fame as the lead singer of The Supremes, Motown's most successful act of the 1960s. Under the guidance of Berry Gordy, Ross and The Supremes topped the charts with timeless hits such as "Stop! In the Name of Love," "Baby Love," and "You Can't Hurry Love," becoming the first U.S. group to have five consecutive number-one singles. Their music, style, and poised television appearances helped bring Motown to mainstream audiences, and Ross' radiant stage presence made her a defining voice of the era. As a Black woman leading one of the most successful musical acts of the decade, Ross broke barriers in a segregated industry, becoming a symbol of elegance, talent, and progress.

In 1970, Ross embarked on a solo career that was just as impactful. Her debut solo single, "Ain't No Mountain High Enough," topped the Billboard Hot 100 and showcased her distinctive vocal phrasing. Throughout the 1970s and 1980s, she released a series of hits, including "Touch Me in the Morning," "Love Hangover," and "Upside Down." Ross also proved her range as an actress, earning an Academy Award nomination for her portrayal of Billie Holiday in *Lady Sings the Blues* (1972), followed by memorable performances in *Mahogany* (1975) and *The Wiz* (1978).

Ross, a fashion trailblazer, became known for her glamorous gowns, full hair, and high drama on and off stage. She was inducted into the Rock and Roll Hall of Fame with The Supremes in 1988 and awarded the Presidential Medal of Freedom in 2016. Diana Ross remains a symbol of empowerment, artistry, and enduring star power.

FASHION FEATURES

LADY SINGS THE BLUES (1972)
MAHOGANY (1975)
THE WIZ (1978)

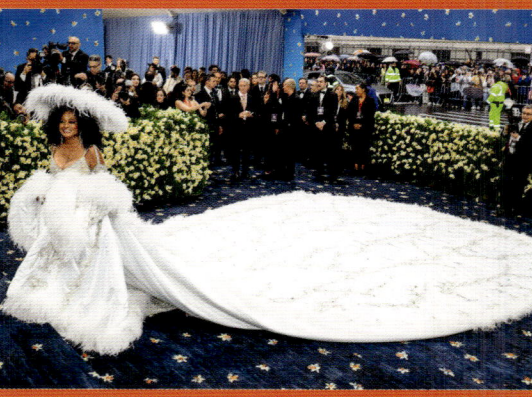

The Ross Look

Dramatic and diva-worthy, Ross embraced sequins, capes, and sleek silhouettes that emphasized her status as a global superstar.

- Feathered or full-volume hair
- Glamorous gowns
- Bold eye makeup
- Statement accessories

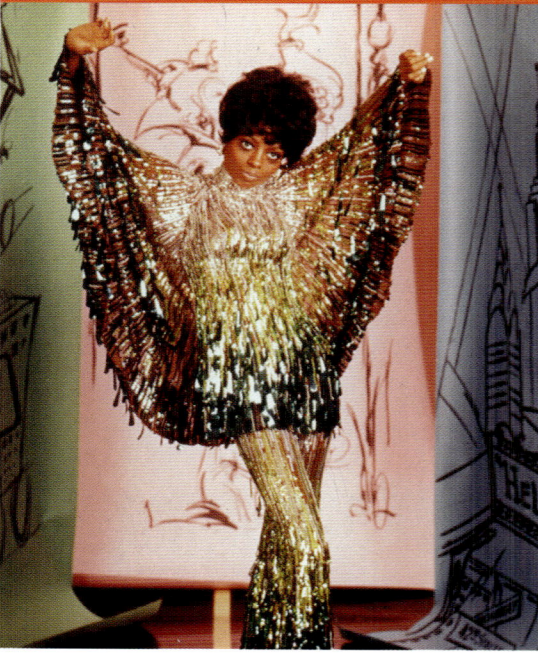

SUSAN SARANDON

FASHION FEATURES

THE HUNGER (1983)
THELMA & LOUISE (1991)
DEAD MAN WALKING (1995)

The Sarandon Look

Her red-carpet style leans toward confident glamor—structured suits, plunging necklines, and luxe fabrics that emphasize her rebellious sophistication.

- Auburn curls
- Statement sunglasses
- Bold, sculptural gowns
- Effortless elegance with a provocative edge

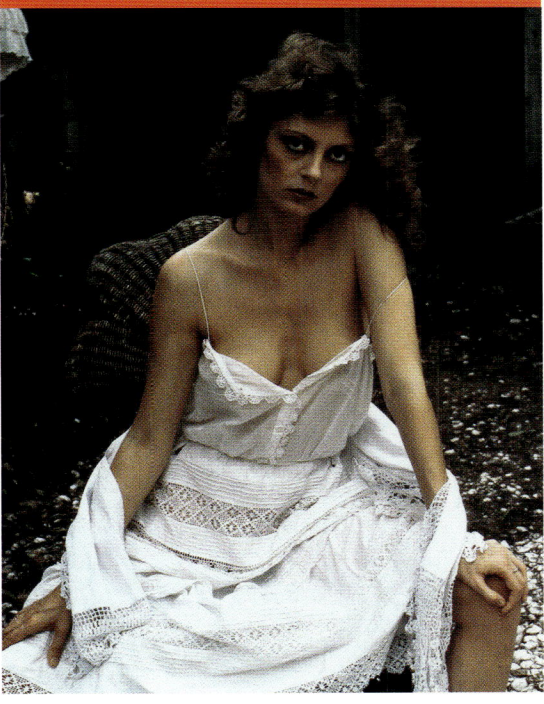

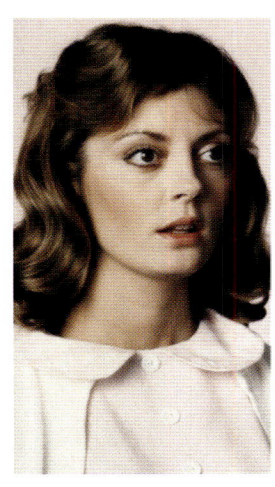

Commanding, candid, and constantly evolving, Susan Sarandon has etched her name into the fabric of American film with performances that challenge convention and exude fierce authenticity.

Susan Abigail Tomalin, born in 1946 in New York City, discovered her passion for acting during her studies at The Catholic University of America. Her screen debut in *Joe* (1970) marked the beginning of a dynamic and unpredictable career. A few years later, she caught the public's attention with her role as Janet Weiss in the genre-defying musical *The Rocky Horror Picture Show* (1975), a performance that hinted at her attraction to complex offbeat characters. That early spark of unconventional charisma became a throughline in her career, setting her apart from her contemporaries.

Sarandon's true ascent came with *Atlantic City* (1980), earning her widespread acclaim and her first Oscar nomination. She went on to deliver powerful, era-defining roles in *Thelma & Louise* (1991), *Lorenzo's Oil* (1992), and *Dead Man Walking* (1995)—the last earning her an Academy Award for Best Actress. Her work often explores the resilience of women facing moral or emotional crossroads, portrayed with raw conviction and layered sensitivity. Her characters are rarely passive; they question, challenge, and evolve—mirroring her real-life persona.

Away from film sets, Sarandon has never shied from controversy or cause. Her activism—ranging from opposition to war and inequality to environmental advocacy—has become inseparable from her public identity. Whether speaking at protests or lending her voice to humanitarian efforts, she demonstrates the same fearlessness that characterizes her acting.

Across decades, genres, and generations, Susan Sarandon has remained a formidable presence—bold in her choices, grounded in principle, and endlessly compelling. She is not just a performer but a force of nature in Hollywood and beyond.

ABOVE
—

In the cult classic *The Rocky Horror Picture Show* (1975), Sarandon gained fame playing Janet Weiss, a naive virgin wearing a pale pink dress with a Peter Pan collar and tiny white buttons and a white cardigan.

LEFT
—

Susan Sarandon in *Lovespell* (1981), luminous in a white lace gown, sits poised against a bleak, rustic backdrop—an ethereal figure of passion and tragedy in this medieval tale of doomed love.

BARBRA STREISAND

FASHION FEATURES

FUNNY GIRL (1968)
HELLO DOLLY! (1969)
ON A CLEAR DAY YOU CAN SEE FOREVER (1970)
THE WAY WE WERE (1973)
THE MIRROR HAS TWO FACES (1996)

ABOVE

Barbra Streisand in *Hello, Dolly!* (1969), dazzling in a gold-beaded gown with plume-topped headpiece and opera gloves—commanding the screen in one of the film's most iconic musical moments.

RIGHT

In a sheer, polka-dot ensemble trimmed with magenta marabou, she strikes a playful pose in her cluttered apartment set from *The Owl and the Pussycat* (1970), mixing seduction and satire with signature 1970s flamboyance.

FULL PAGE

Barbra Streisand in *On a Clear Day You Can See Forever* (1970), directed by Vincente Minnelli. Her costume—a heavily embellished gown with matching turban and choker—is detailed with silver beading and embroidery that reflects the film's blend of period style and 1970s fantasy. It's a striking look that captures the film's theme of identity across time, with Streisand's presence grounded, poised, and visually unforgettable.

Barbra Streisand, originally named Barbara Joan Streisand, entered the world on April 24, 1942, in Brooklyn, New York. She rose from modest beginnings to become one of the most celebrated and multifaceted entertainers of all time. Her talents as a singer, actress, director, and producer have earned her a rare place in the entertainment industry, where few have achieved success across several fields.

Streisand began her career singing in New York nightclubs, captivating audiences with her unique vocal style and emotional intensity. Her big break came in 1962 when she was cast in the Broadway musical *I Can Get It for You Wholesale*. The performance drew critical acclaim and introduced her as a rising star. Her debut album, *The Barbra Streisand Album* (1963), won two Grammy Awards, including Album of the Year, and launched her recording career, which would go on to span decades and cross genres.

Her film debut came with *Funny Girl* (1968), where she reprised her Broadway role as Fanny Brice. The performance won her an Academy Award for Best Actress and made her an international star. She followed with roles in *Hello, Dolly!* (1969), *The Owl and the Pussycat* (1970), *What's Up, Doc?* (1972), and *The Way We Were* (1973), further proving her versatility on screen. In 1976, she starred in and produced *A Star Is Born*, winning an Oscar for Best Original Song for "Evergreen."

In 1983, Streisand made history with *Yentl*, becoming the first woman to write, produce, direct, and star in a major Hollywood film. Her work on the project won critical praise and marked her transition into directing. She went on to direct *The Prince of Tides* (1991) and *The Mirror Has Two Faces*

(1996), both of which received Academy Award nominations.

As a musician, Streisand is one of the best-selling recording artists of all time, with over 150 million albums sold globally. Her musical catalog includes *People* (1964), *Guilty* (1980), and *The Broadway Album* (1985), showcasing her ability to evolve with changing musical styles while staying true to her vocal roots. She is one of the few performers to achieve an EGOT status, having won Emmy, Grammy, Oscar, and Tony Awards. Additional honors include the Kennedy Center Honors, the National Medal of Arts, and the Presidential Medal of Freedom, which was awarded to her in 2015.

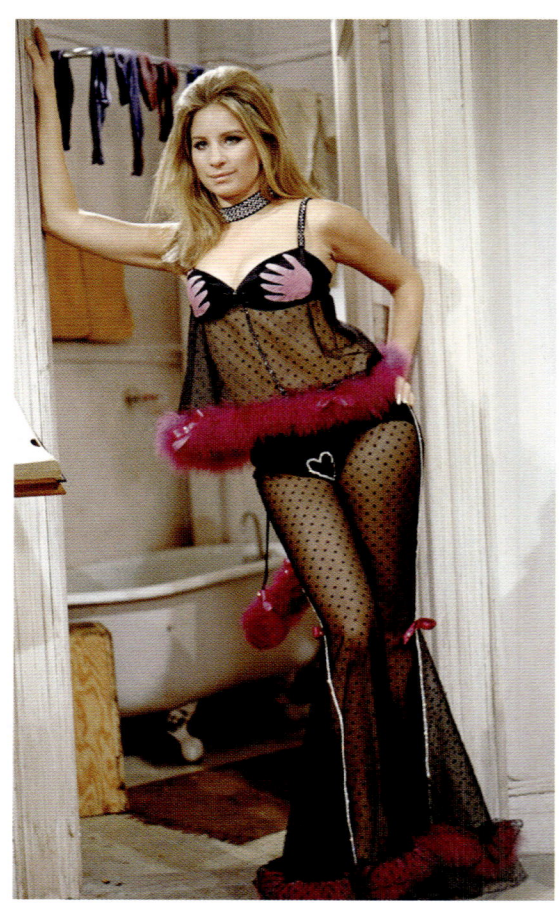

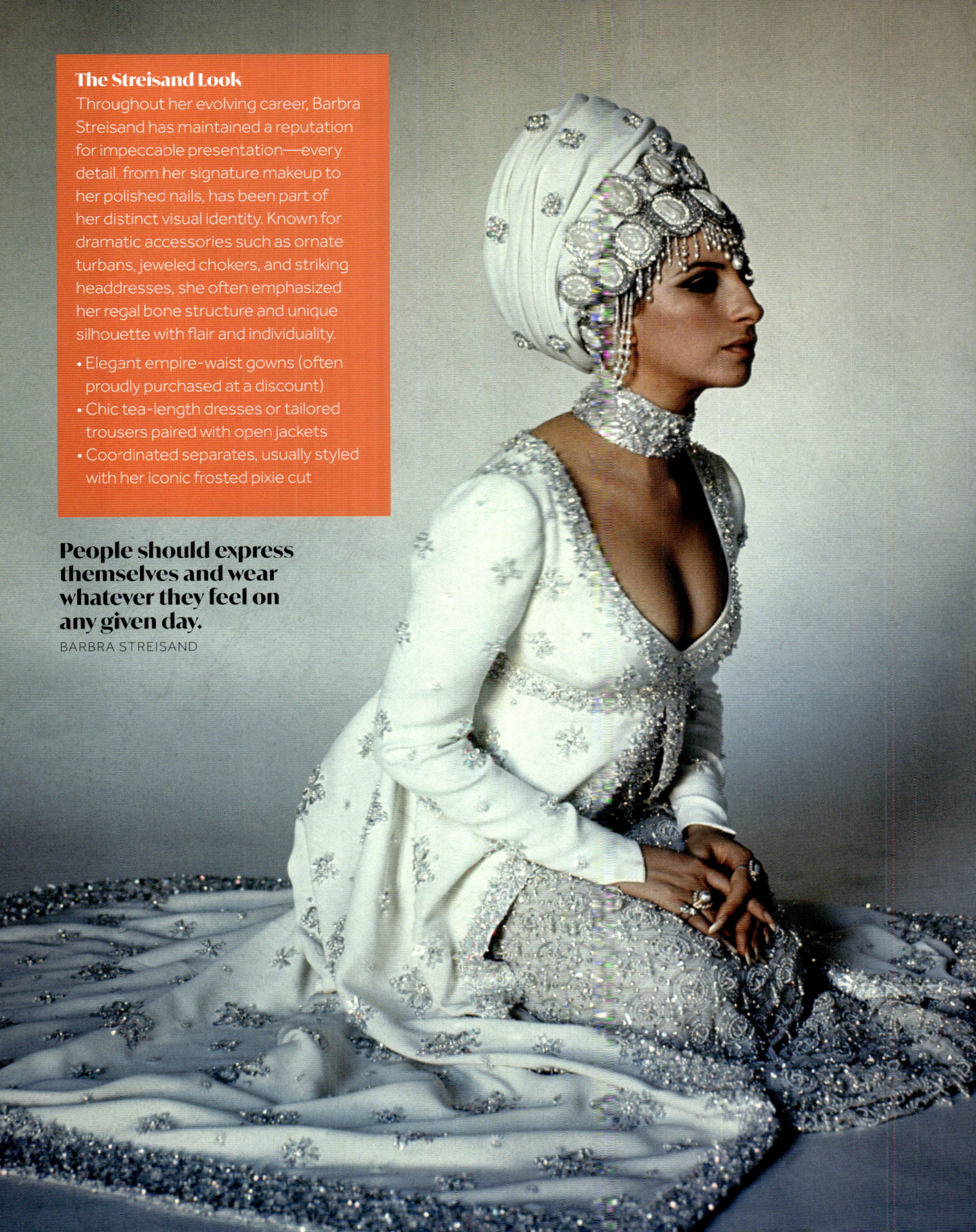

The Streisand Look

Throughout her evolving career, Barbra Streisand has maintained a reputation for impeccable presentation—every detail, from her signature makeup to her polished nails, has been part of her distinct visual identity. Known for dramatic accessories such as ornate turbans, jeweled chokers, and striking headdresses, she often emphasized her regal bone structure and unique silhouette with flair and individuality.

- Elegant empire-waist gowns (often proudly purchased at a discount)
- Chic tea-length dresses or tailored trousers paired with open jackets
- Coordinated separates, usually styled with her iconic frosted pixie cut

People should express themselves and wear whatever they feel on any given day.

BARBRA STREISAND

CHARLOTTE RAMPLING

FASHION FEATURES

THE NIGHT PORTER (1974)
MAX, MON AMOUR (1986)
SWIMMING POOL (2003)
THE LOOK (2011)

Charlotte Rampling (born on February 5, 1946 in Essex, England) rose to prominence in the 1970s as one of cinema's most intriguing and unconventional stars. Known for her commanding presence and emotionally restrained performances, she made a lasting impact with roles in films such as _The Night Porter_ (1974), _Zardoz_ (1974), and _Farewell, My Lovely_ (1975). Her characters often carried a sense of mystery and intelligence, setting her apart from traditional leading ladies of the era.

Rampling's fashion in the 1970s echoed her on-screen persona: sleek, subtle, and striking.

She favored structured blazers, fluid silk shirts high-waisted trousers, and minimalist gowns. Her palette leaned toward muted earth tones and monochromes, often accented by sharp tailoring. Frequently seen in Yves Saint Laurent and menswear-inspired pieces, she embodied an androgynous, modern elegance that stood in quiet contrast to the decade's louder trends. More than just an actress, Rampling became a symbol of understated sophistication. Her fashion choices didn't chase attention but commanded it. Cool, cerebral, and always composed, she became a favorite of designers, photographers, and directors alike. In both film and fashion, she defined a new kind of femininity—strong, stylish, and completely her own.

ABOVE
—
Charlotte Rampling reclines in gleaming satin and pearls, her eyes intense beneath softly sculpted waves—an unforgettable vision of 1970s noir elegance and commanding screen presence.

RIGHT
—
Rampling in _Angel Heart_ (1987) exudes eerie sophistication, playing a mysterious figure cloaked in shadows and ambiguity—her cool composure and penetrating gaze heightening the film's dark, psychological tension.

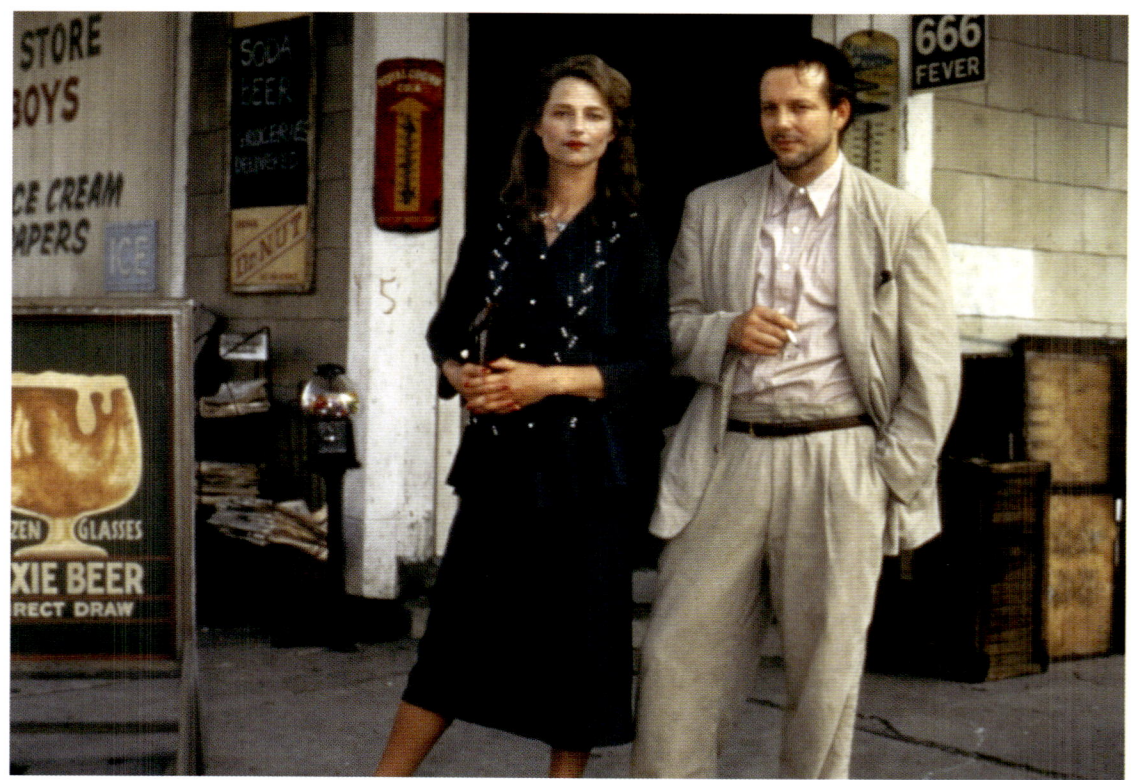

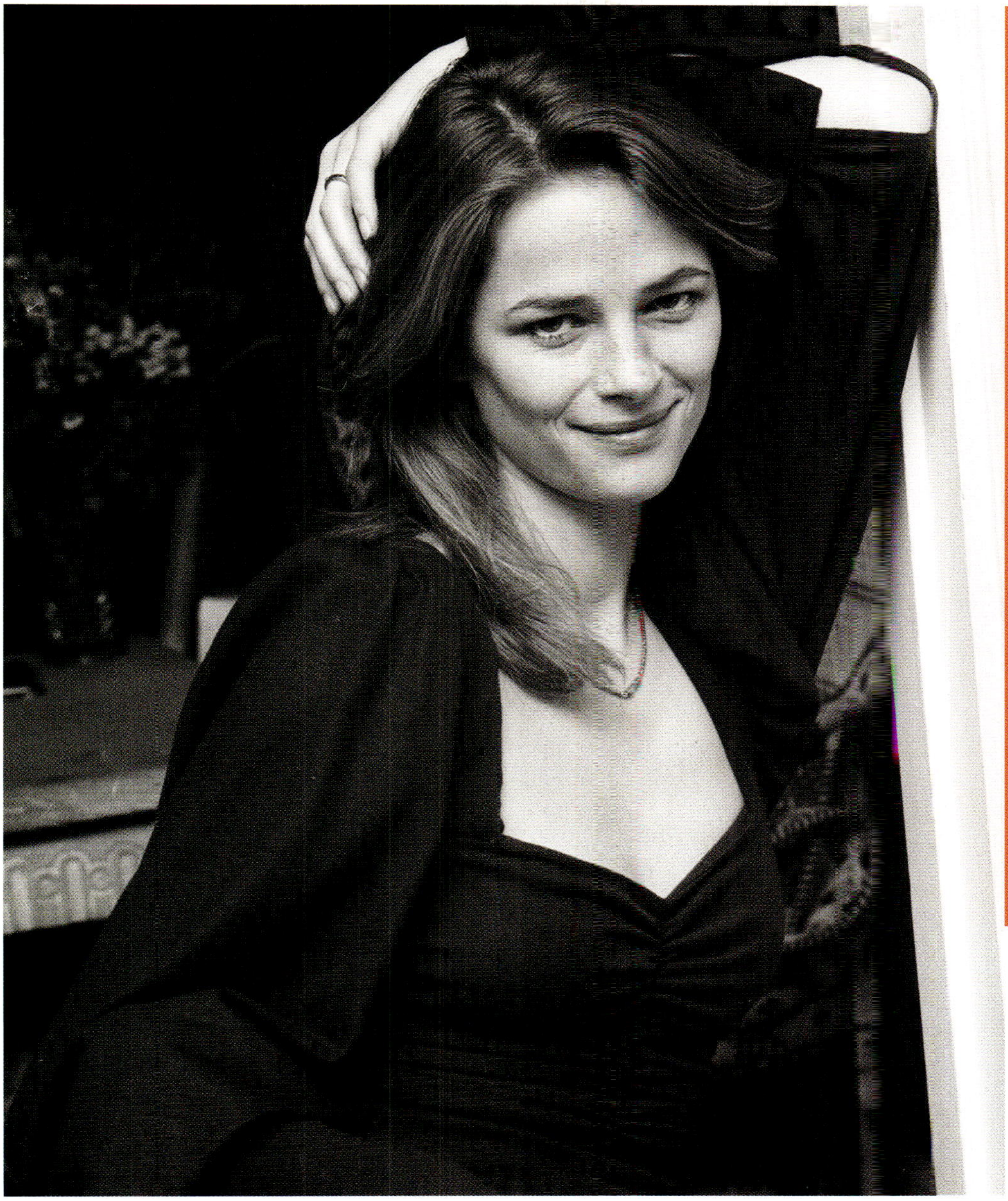

The Rampling Look

Charlotte Rampling's style is minimalist, cerebral, and quietly commanding. Eschewing flash, she favors pieces that project intellect over spectacle— always elegant, never obvious. Her wardrobe leans on precise tailoring, muted tones, and sculptural silhouettes that age gracefully with her.

- Crisp white shirts
- Structured black blazers
- Narrow trousers and midi skirts
- Clean lines, no excess
- Dark neutrals, occasional jewel tones
- Minimal makeup and natural hair

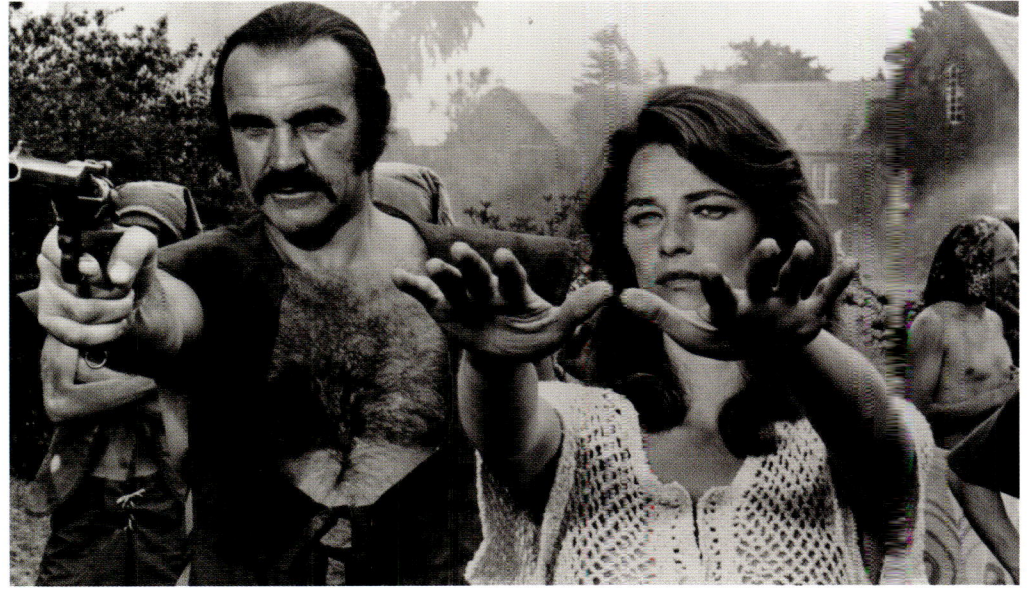

TOP

Charlotte Rampling at her London home, January 4, 1973—effortlessly composed in a relaxed pose, she captures the cool, understated style and introspective charm that defined her presence both on and off-screen.

BOTTOM

Charlotte Rampling and Sean Connery in *Zardoz* (1974), a surreal sci-fi odyssey blending dystopian vision with bold, unconventional style—Rampling's piercing gaze and ethereal presence anchoring the film's futuristic mystery.

161

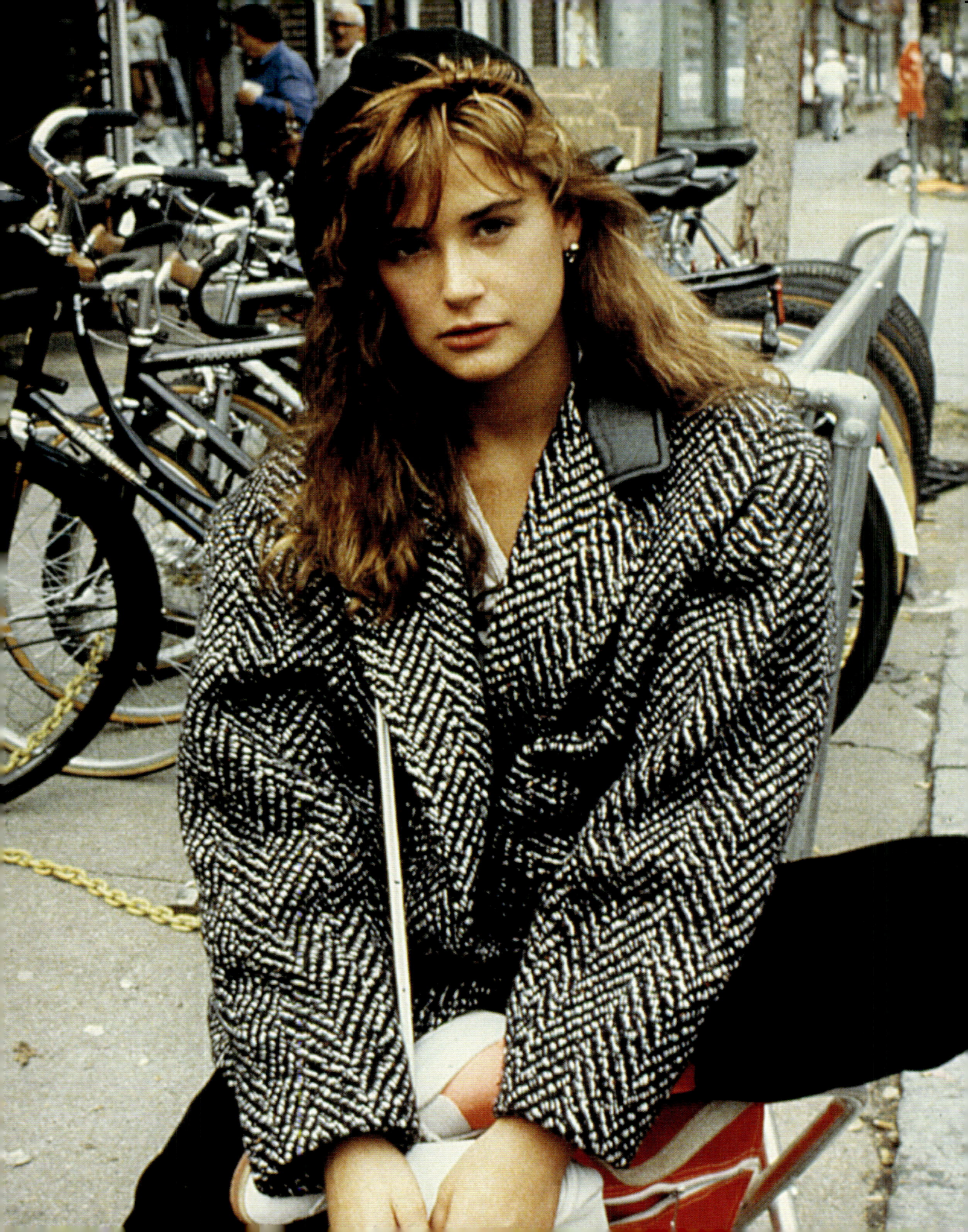

NINETEEN EIGHTIES

The 1980s were a decade of bold reinvention in Hollywood fashion. Gone were the understated palettes of the 1970s—this was an era defined by excess, power dressing, and unapologetic glamor. On screen and off, stars embraced dramatic silhouettes, high-octane chic, and expressive individuality. Hollywood's leading women wore sharply tailored suits, strong shoulder pads, sequined gowns, and body-conscious dresses that reflected a new kind of empowered femininity. Designers such as Bob Mackie, Nolan Miller, and Donna Karan became household names thanks to their influence on celebrity wardrobes and television costume design.

Blockbuster actresses such as Meryl Streep, Jessica Lange, Kathleen Turner, and Demi Moore commanded the screen in looks that balanced strength and seduction. TV dramas such as *Dynasty* and *Dallas* made an impact too, with Joan Collins and Linda Evans setting fashion trends with plunging necklines, shimmering fabrics, and sculptural hairdos. Men leaned into clean-cut minimalism or flashy opulence, from sleek Armani suits to rock-star leather and denim.

Music videos and red-carpet appearances further blurred the line between screen style and street fashion. Hollywood's fashion in the 1980s wasn't just about looking good—it was about making a statement. Confidence, extravagance, and attitude were woven into every look.

KIM BASINGER

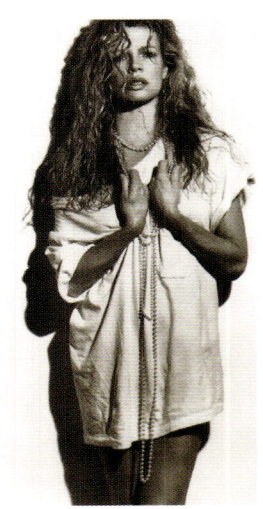

Kim Basinger (born December 8, 1953, in Athens, Georgia) is an American actress whose blonde good looks and comedic skills made her a top movie star in the 1980s.

She began her career as a model before transitioning to acting in the late 1970s. Basinger gained prominence with her role as Bond girl Domino Petachi in *Never Say Never Again* (1983), and further established her status with performances in *The Natural* (1984) and *9 ½ Weeks* (1986). Her portrayal of photo journalist Vicki Vale in Tim Burton's *Batman* (1989) was a commercial success and remains one of her most recognized roles.

In 1997, Basinger won the Academy Award for Best Supporting Actress for her role as Lynn Bracken in *L.A. Confidential*, a performance that also earned her a Golden Globe and a Screen Actors Guild Award. She continued to take on diverse roles in films such as *I Dreamed of Africa* (2000), *8 Mile* (2002), and *The Door in the Floor* (2004). Her later work includes appearances in *The Nice Guys* (2016) and *Fifty Shades Darker* (2017).

Basinger's personal life has been marked by high-profile relationships, including marriages to makeup artist Ron Snyder (1980–1989) and actor Alec Baldwin (1993–2002). She has a daughter with Baldwin, Ireland Baldwin. Beyond her acting career, Basinger is known for her activism, particularly in animal rights. She has posed for anti-fur advertisements and has been involved in efforts to protect farm animals.

Throughout her career, Kim Basinger has demonstrated a remarkable ability to navigate both commercial blockbusters and critically acclaimed dramas, solidifying her place in Hollywood history.

ABOVE

Bathed in stark contrast and shadow, Kim Basinger redefines minimalism in GAP's 1989 "Power" campaign—pearls, tousled waves, and a pocket tee radiating unfiltered allure.

RIGHT

Kim Basinger stuns in monochrome scarlet—polka-dot gloves, sculptural hat, and sleek blonde hair—during a scene from *The Marrying Man* (1991), blending glamor with vintage whimsy.

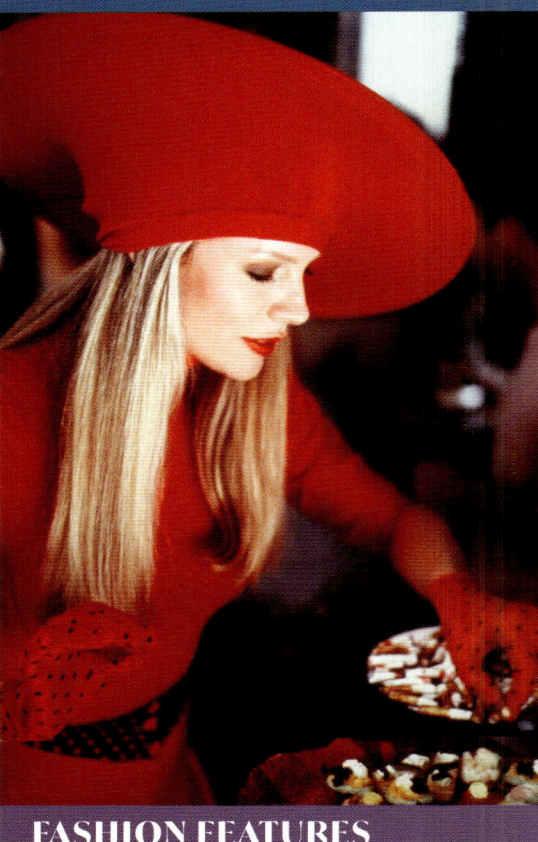

FASHION FEATURES

THE NATURAL (1984)
THE MARRYING MAN (1991)
L.A. CONFIDENTIAL (1997)

The Basinger Look

With her platinum-blonde beauty and timeless elegance, Kim Basinger has been a style icon since her early modeling days as a "Breck Girl." Her fashion choices blend glamor with sleek sophistication.

• Elegant black or white evening gowns
• Slouchy off-the-shoulder knits
• Refined, polished separates

CHER

FASHION FEATURES

MOONSTRUCK (1987)
THE WITCHES OF EASTWICK (1987)
TEA WITH MUSSOLINI (1999)

The Cher Look

Even before her film debut, Cher was a bold fashion icon—evolving from boho glam to dazzling, daring Bob Mackie ensembles. Her style has always been fearless, dramatic, and unforgettable.

- Sleek black hair or bold, theatrical wigs
- Sheer, figure-hugging gowns
- Slouchy off-the-shoulder tops and sweaters

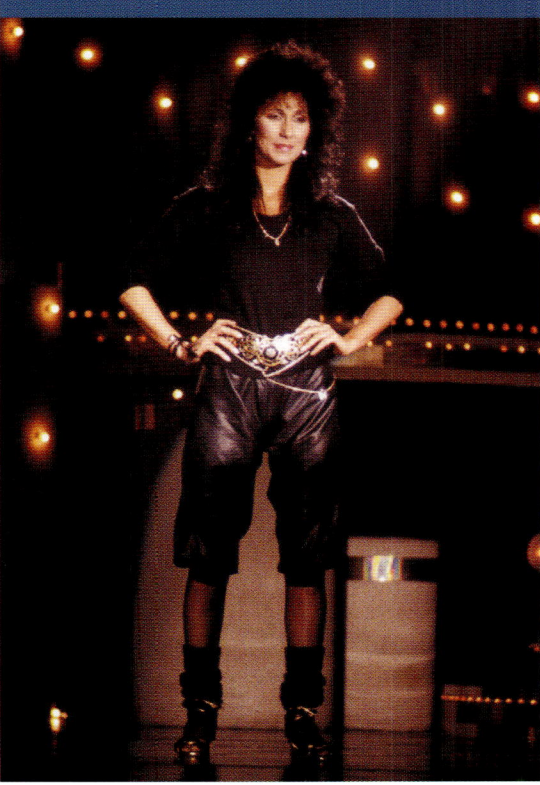

Cher (born Cherilyn Sarkisian on May 20, 1946, in El Centro, California) is an American singer, actress, and television personality renowned for her distinctive contralto voice and enduring presence in the entertainment industry.

She rose to fame in the 1960s as part of the duo Sonny & Cher, achieving major success with the hit single "I Got You Babe" in 1965. The pair's popularity extended to television with *The Sonny and Cher Comedy Hour* (1971–74), showcasing their musical talents and Cher's unique fashion sense.

Embarking on a solo career, Cher released chart-topping songs such as "Gypsys, Tramps & Thieves" (1971), "Half-Breed" (1973), and "Dark Lady" (1974). Her acting prowess was recognized with an Academy Award for Best Actress for her role in *Moonstruck* (1987), following acclaimed performances in *Silkwood* (1983) and *Mask* (1985).

In 1998, Cher's single "Believe" became a global hit, notable for its pioneering use of Auto-Tune, and earned her a Grammy Award. She continued to captivate audiences with albums such as *Living Proof* (2002) and her Las Vegas residency from 2008 to 2011. Her versatility was further displayed in films such as *Burlesque* (2010) and *Mamma Mia! Here We Go Again* (2018).

Cher's contributions to music and film have been recognized with numerous accolades, including an Emmy Award, a Grammy Award, an Academy Award, and three Golden Globe Awards. Her ability to reinvent herself has solidified her status as a pop culture icon across multiple generations.

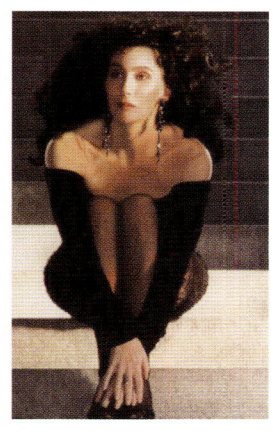

ABOVE

Cher, draped in black velvet and cascading curls, evokes fierce elegance in this 1989 *Uninhibited* fragrance campaign—her gaze defiant, her presence unmistakably iconic.

LEFT

Cher commands the stage in leather culottes, bold belt, and voluminous curls—an electrifying vision from her 1987 Las Vegas residency, blending rock edge with theatrical flair.

LEADING MEN
HARRISON FORD

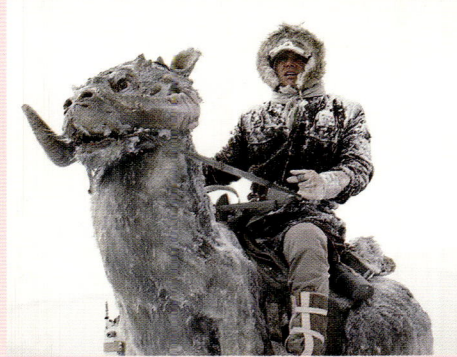

Harrison Ford (born July 13, 1942, in Chicago, Illinois) is an American actor who rose from humble beginnings to become one of the most iconic and highest-grossing film stars in Hollywood history. Known for portraying rugged, principled heroes with wit and grit, Ford's career spans more than five decades and includes some of cinema's most beloved franchises.

He began acting in the 1960s after studying English and philosophy at Ripon College in Wisconsin. Ford initially signed a contract with Columbia and then Universal, appearing in bit parts in television shows such as *Gunsmoke*, *The F.B.I.*, and *Ironside*. Frustrated by the limited scope of his early roles and concerned with providing for his family, Ford turned to carpentry. His skills took him into the homes and offices of key Hollywood figures, including George Lucas, who would become a pivotal influence on his career.

In 1973, Ford was cast in Lucas's nostalgic coming-of-age film *American Graffiti* as Bob Falfa. Although a small role, it marked the beginning of a fruitful collaboration. Just four years later, Lucas cast him as the cocky, endearing smuggler Han Solo in *Star Wars* (1977), a role that would change Ford's life and establish him as an international star. He reprised the role in four additional *Star Wars* films spanning nearly four decades.

In 1981, Ford debuted as Indiana Jones in *Raiders of the Lost Ark*, directed by Steven Spielberg and produced by Lucas. His portrayal of the whip-cracking archaeologist solidified his action-hero persona and led to four sequels, the most recent being *Indiana Jones and the Dial of Destiny* (2023).

Ford's talent extended far beyond science fiction and action. He received an Academy Award

ABOVE

Bundled in frostbitten gear atop a Tauntaun, Harrison Ford rides through the icy planet Hoth as Han Solo in *The Empire Strikes Back* (1980)—sci-fi survival redefined.

RIGHT

Harrison Ford, rugged in a torn tropical shirt and weathered glasses, tinkers with invention in *The Mosquito Coast* (1986)—a portrait of brilliance descending into obsession.

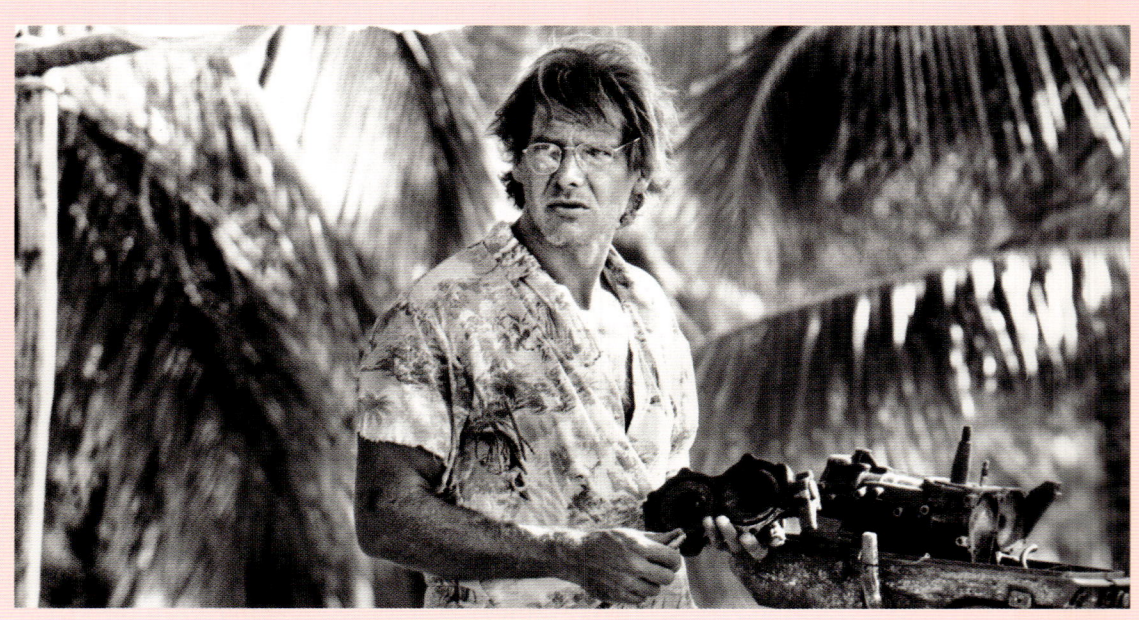

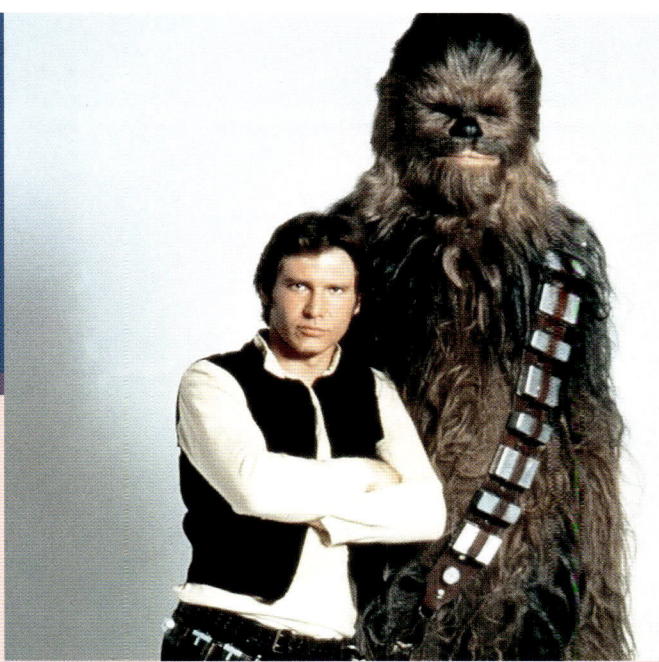

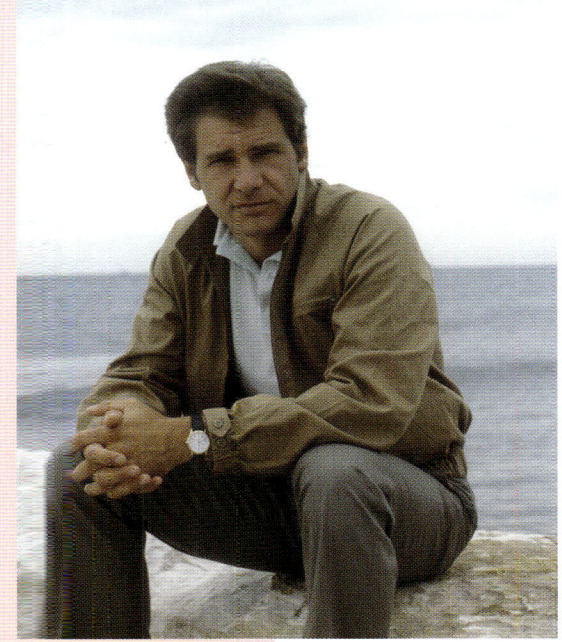

nomination for *Witness* (1985), in which he played a detective hiding among the Amish. He followed with critically acclaimed roles in *The Mosquito Coast* (1986), *Frantic* (1988), and *Presumed Innocent* (1990). He also headlined thrillers such as *The Fugitive* (1993), *Clear and Present Danger* (1994), and *Air Force One* (1997), often portraying men of integrity under siege.

In 1982, he starred in *Blade Runner* as Rick Deckard, a futuristic "blade runner" hunting rogue androids—a role he revisited in *Blade Runner 2049* (2017). Known for his understated charisma, Ford avoided overexposure and embraced privacy, preferring to let his work speak for itself.

Beyond acting, Ford is a licensed pilot, a dedicated environmentalist, and vice chair of Conservation International. Despite surviving multiple aviation accidents, he continues to fly and advocate for the planet. Honored with the American Film Institute Life Achievement Award (2000) and the Cecil B. DeMille Award (2002), Ford remains a legend whose career combines commercial success with timeless cultural resonance.

In addition to his film work, Ford played supporting roles in documentaries, voiced animated characters, and made occasional television appearances. His enduring popularity also led to appearances in video games, pop culture tributes, and fan conventions worldwide.

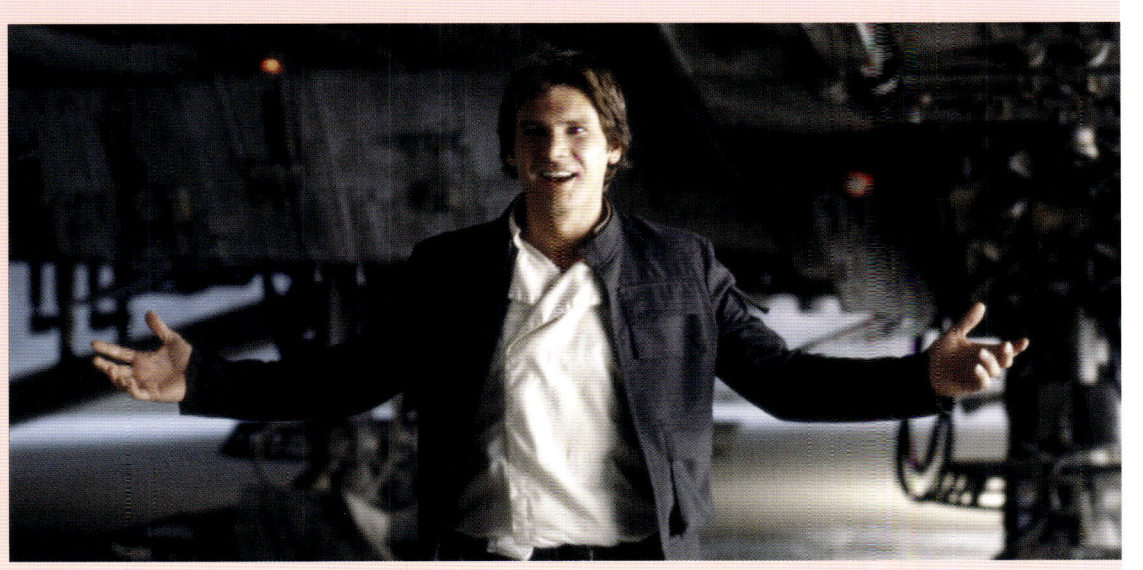

TOP LEFT

Eternally cool, Harrison Ford as Han Solo stands alongside Peter Mayhew as Chewbacca in *Star Wars* (1977)—a legendary movie etched in science fiction cinema history.

TOP RIGHT

Harrison Ford, in a tan windbreaker and contemplative gaze, pauses seaside during the 1980s—a candid moment between blockbuster movie roles.

LEFT

Arms outstretched beneath the Millennium Falcon, Harrison Ford embodies Han Solo's swagger in *The Empire Strikes Back* (1980)—a rebel rogue etched in cinematic legend.

WHOOPI GOLDBERG

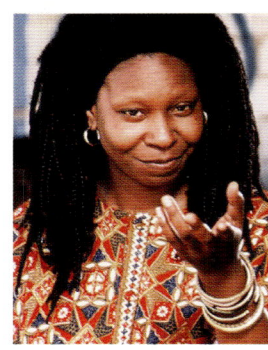

Whoopi Goldberg (born Caryn Elaine Johnson on November 13, 1955, in New York City) is an American actress, comedian, author, and television personality celebrated for her versatility and barrier-breaking career. Known for her candid humor, socially conscious roles, and commanding presence, Goldberg emerged as a groundbreaking figure in entertainment, becoming one of the few performers to win an Emmy, Grammy, Oscar, and Tony Award— collectively known as an EGOT status.

Goldberg gained early acclaim for her one-woman Broadway show in 1984, which showcased her sharp wit and ability to portray a range of characters. This led to her breakthrough role in *The Color Purple* (1985), directed by Steven Spielberg. Her performance as Celie earned her an Academy Award nomination and launched her film career. She later won the Academy Award for Best Supporting Actress for her role as the eccentric psychic Oda Mae Brown in *Ghost* (1990), further cementing her star status.

Throughout the 1990s, Goldberg starred in popular films including *Sister Act* (1992), *Sister Act 2: Back in the Habit* (1993), and *The Lion King* (1994), in which she voiced the hyena Shenzi. She also played Guinan in *Star Trek: The Next Generation*, becoming a fan favorite in the science fiction genre.

Off-screen, Goldberg has been an outspoken advocate for civil rights, women's issues, and LGBTQ+ rights. Since 2007, she has co-hosted *The View*, contributing her signature directness and humor to daytime television. Goldberg's enduring legacy lies in her ability to navigate comedy and drama while challenging norms and amplifying underrepresented voices.

ABOVE

Goldberg has remained a proponent of ethnic patterns and fashions throughout her career; here, from 1992's *Sarafina!*, she wears a traditional South African-style dress, bangle bracelets, and dreadlocks.

RIGHT

In 1990's *Ghost*, Goldberg, in a vivid cherry red dress suit with feathered toque, played a fake medium who discovers she really does have psychic powers.

FASHION FEATURES

GHOST (1990)
SARAFINA! (1992)
MADE IN AMERICA (1993)

The Goldberg Look

Whoopi Goldberg is known for her bold, culturally inspired fashion. She blends African and Caribbean influences with standout jewelry and dramatic fabrics Her look is expressive, untraditional, and always authentic.

• Long dreadlocks
• Ethnic-inspired layers
• Rich, flowing gowns

MELANIE GRIFFITH

The Griffith Look

Playful yet polished, Griffith's style has ranged from 1980s power suits to sleek evening gowns, always reflecting her blend of boldness and warmth.

- Tousled blonde hair
- Smoky eyes and nude lips
- Bold shoulder silhouettes
- Fitted dresses with feminine flair

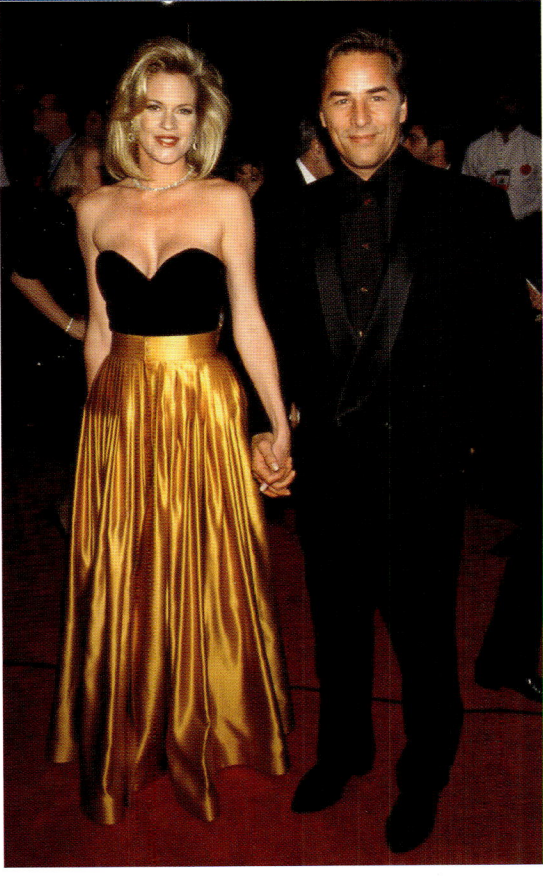

Charismatic, vulnerable, and quietly resilient, Melanie Griffith built a multifaceted acting career that bridged mainstream stardom and deeply personal character work.

Born in 1957 in New York City, to actress Tippi Hedren and advertising executive Peter Griffith, Melanie Griffith was introduced to the world of film at an early age. She made her screen debut as a teenager in *The Harrad Experiment* (1973) and gained wider attention for her daring performance in *Night Moves* (1975). However, it was her role in *Body Double* (1984), where she played a complex, bodacious adult film actress, that marked her true breakthrough and established her as a spirited, fearless performer.

Griffith reached her career peak with *Working Girl* (1988), playing the determined, street-smart Tess McGill. Her performance earned critical acclaim and numerous award nominations, including an Academy Award nomination for Best Actress and a Golden Globe win. Her portrayal of a woman navigating the corporate world with wit and heart became a defining moment in 1980s cinema.

Throughout the 1990s, Griffith continued to work across genres with roles in *Pacific Heights* (1990), *Shining Through* (1992) and *Crazy in Alabama* (1999), directed by her then-husband Antonio Banderas. She also pursued theater work, earning praise for her Broadway debut in *Chicago* (2003).

Despite personal struggles and fluctuating career visibility, Griffith remains a symbol of tenacity and transformation. Her unique voice, expressive eyes, and openness on- and off-screen have earned her a lasting place in Hollywood's evolving story.

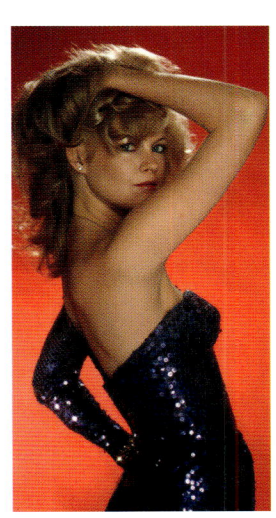

ABOVE

Melanie Griffith strikes a sculptural pose in a sequined midnight-blue gown—an emblem of 1980s glamor— during a publicity shoot at the height of her rising stardom.

LEFT

Melanie Griffith stuns in a velvet bodice and molten-gold satin skirt, arriving hand-in-hand with Don Johnson at the 1997 Academy Awards— Hollywood elegance, rekindled.

JESSICA LANGE

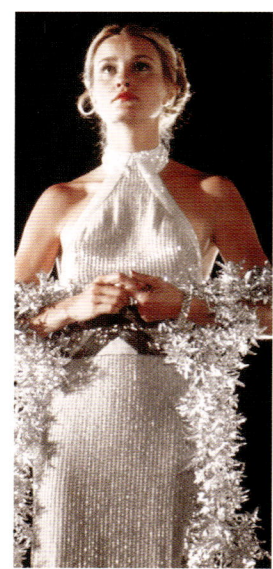

Fierce, fearless, and remarkably versatile, Jessica Lange has built a career defined by emotional depth, magnetic screen presence, and a remarkable ability to transform into every role she plays.

Born in 1949 in Cloquet, Minnesota, Lange studied art before shifting her focus to acting. Her first major break came when she was cast in the 1976 remake of *King Kong*, a debut that introduced her to wide audiences. Although the film received mixed reviews, Lange's striking presence stood out and set the stage for a career that would evolve well beyond beauty and spectacle.

Throughout the 1980s and 1990s, Lange solidified her reputation as one of the most gifted actresses of her generation. She earned critical acclaim for *Frances* (1982), portraying troubled actress Frances Farmer, and won her first Academy Award for *Tootsie* (1982). Her second Oscar came for *Blue Sky* (1994), in which she played the complex, unpredictable wife of a military officer. Her performances in *Country* (1984), *Sweet Dreams* (1985), and *Music Box* (1989) further showcased her dramatic range.

In later years, Lange earned renewed attention for her powerful work on television, particularly in *American Horror Story* and *Feud: Bette and Joan*. She has also received accolades for her stage work and photography.

Jessica Lange's career is a testament to longevity, reinvention, and fearless artistry—qualities that continue to captivate audiences across generations.

ABOVE

Jessica Lange simmers in a sequined halter gown while awaiting her "date" in her debut film—*King Kong* from 1976.

RIGHT

With a gleaming jacket, gingham blouse, and soft bouffant curls, Jessica Lange portrays country music legend Patsy Cline in 1985's *Sweet Dreams*.

FASHION FEATURES

FRANCES (1982)
TOOTSIE (1982)
SWEET DREAMS (1985)
BLUE SKY (1994)
AMERICAN HORROR STORY (2011–2014, 2018)

The Lange Look

Timeless and understated, Lange favors clean silhouettes, elegant tailoring, and subtle detailing that reflect both poise and power.

• Soft, flowing hair
• Classic red lips
• Structured gowns
• Chic, minimal accessories

JAMIE LEE CURTIS

FASHION FEATURES

PERFECT (1985)
A FISH CALLED WANDA (1988)
TRUE LIES (1994)

The Curtis Look

Jamie Lee Curtis brought fitness-inspired fashion to the spotlight in the 80s, especially in *Perfect* (1985). Her style blends confidence and clean lines, often showcasing her toned legs and curves with sleek, structured outfits.

- Edgy, cropped hairstyles
- Clean-cut skirts with waist emphasis
- Ankle-strap heels for a sharp finish

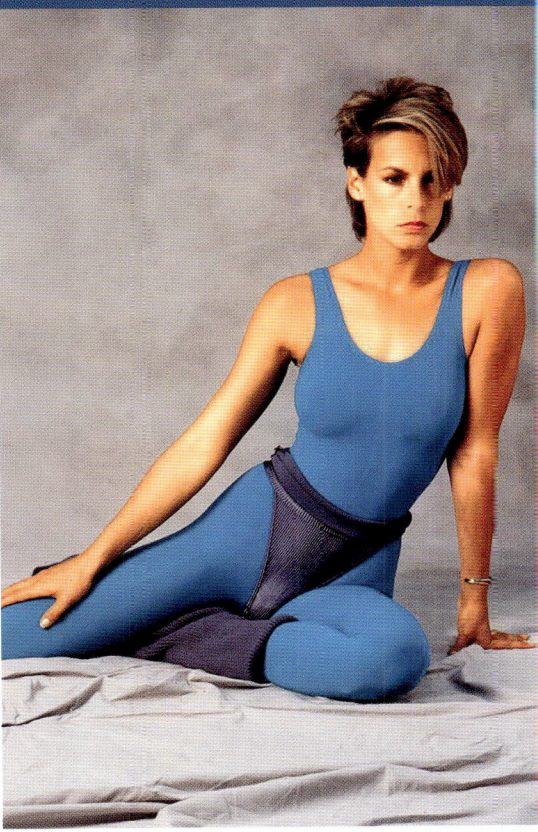

Jamie Lee Curtis (born November 22, 1958, in Los Angeles, California) is an American actress and author known for her iconic roles in horror films and her versatile performances in both comedy and drama. The daughter of legendary actors Tony Curtis and Janet Leigh, she made her film debut in John Carpenter's *Halloween* (1978), which became a massive success and established her as a defining "scream queen" of modern horror.

She went on to star in several horror sequels and thrillers, including *The Fog* (1980), *Prom Night* (1980), and *Halloween II* (1981). Curtis later broadened her range, delivering acclaimed comedic performances in *Trading Places* (1983) and *A Fish Called Wanda* (1988), both of which highlighted her timing and charisma. Her role in *True Lies* (1994) earned her a Golden Globe Award for Best Actress in a Musical or Comedy.

In addition to acting, Curtis is a bestselling children's book author and a public advocate for health-related causes, including addiction recovery and body positivity. Her later work includes reprising her role as Laurie Strode in several *Halloween* sequels and winning the Academy Award for Best Supporting Actress in *Everything Everywhere All at Once* (2022), marking a career pinnacle in a remarkable decades-long journey.

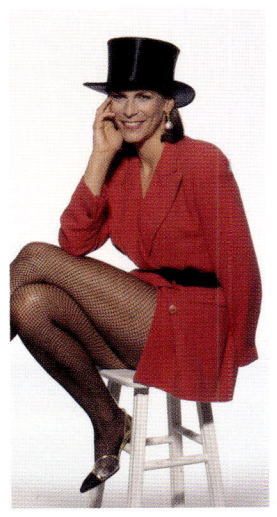

ABOVE

Effortlessly poised in a crimson blazer and top hat, Jamie Lee Curtis merges cabaret glamor with 80s power dressing in this striking, theatrical portrait.

LEFT

Jamie Lee Curtis, clad in electric blue Lycra with ribbed accents, epitomizes 1980s fitness chic—captured in a promotional still for *Perfect* (1985), where aerobics met allure.

SETTING TRENDS
WORKOUT CLOTHES

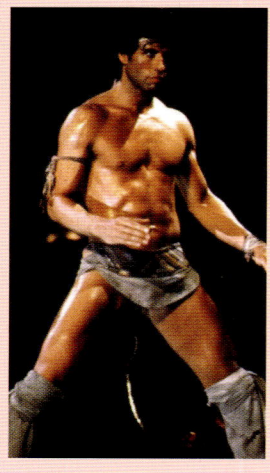

By the late 1970s and early 1980s, American culture had developed a new obsession—fitness. As gyms, health clubs, and aerobics studios popped up across the country, the fashion industry responded by transforming athletic wear into a booming, body-conscious trend. Workout clothes, once reserved for sports professionals or serious athletes, became mainstream. Suddenly, people began wearing leotards, leggings, and leg warmers not only for exercise but also for coffee runs and casual outings. Films such as *Perfect* (1985), *Flashdance* (1983), and *Fame* (1980) helped popularize the aesthetic of dance-inspired athletic wear, turning the sweaty gym look into a form of self-expression.

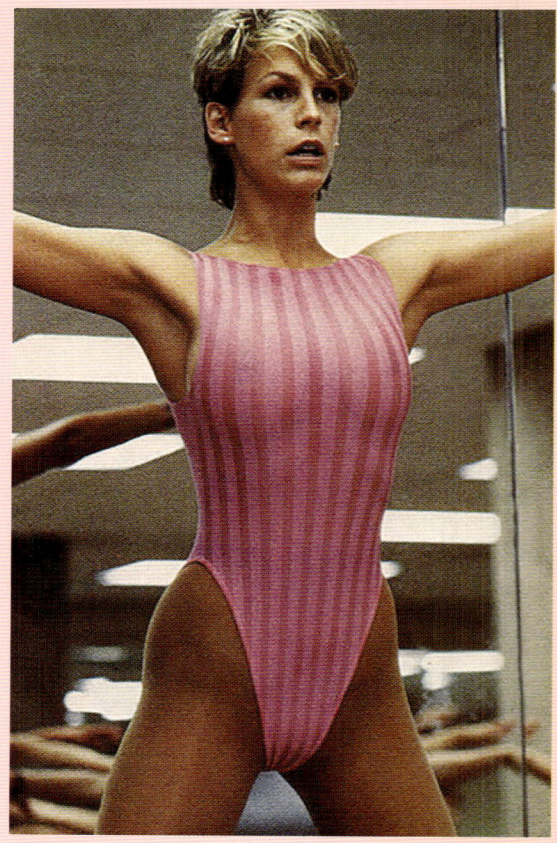

Jane Fonda's wildly successful workout videos—released throughout the 1980s—made fitness routines fashionable, especially among suburban women. Her brightly colored unitards, belted leotards, and scrunched socks helped set a national trend. Stretch fabrics such as Lycra and Spandex were seen everywhere suddenly, hugging the body and showcasing the toned silhouettes that health-conscious Americans were working hard to achieve. Neon became a signature palette, and layering was key—tank tops over crop tops, sweatshirts over leotards, and tights under shorts. The "no pain, no gain" mantra extended to the mirror, where fashion was as important as form.

Off the screen, stars such as Olivia Newton-John, with her "Physical" music video, and pop icons such as Madonna helped blur the line between fitness fashion and streetwear.

ABOVE

John Travolta, bronzed and sculpted, strikes a primal pose in *Staying Alive* (1983)—a fantasy ballet climax blending Broadway bravado with 80s body aesthetics and theatrical heat.

TOP RIGHT

Jamie Lee Curtis, poised in a candy-striped leotard, commands the mirror-lined studio in *Perfect* (1985)—where fitness, fame, and sensuality collide in glossy 80s rhythm.

BOTTOM RIGHT

Mikhail Baryshnikov and Leslie Browne in *The Turning Point* (1977), in classic ballet studio wear—tank top and tights for him, sheer wrap skirt and leotard for her.

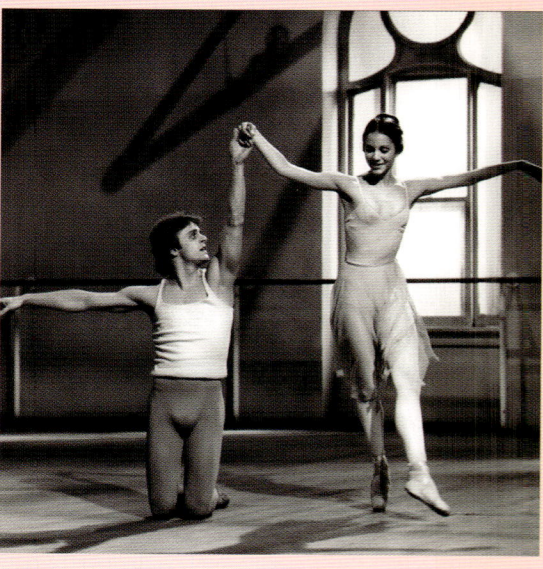

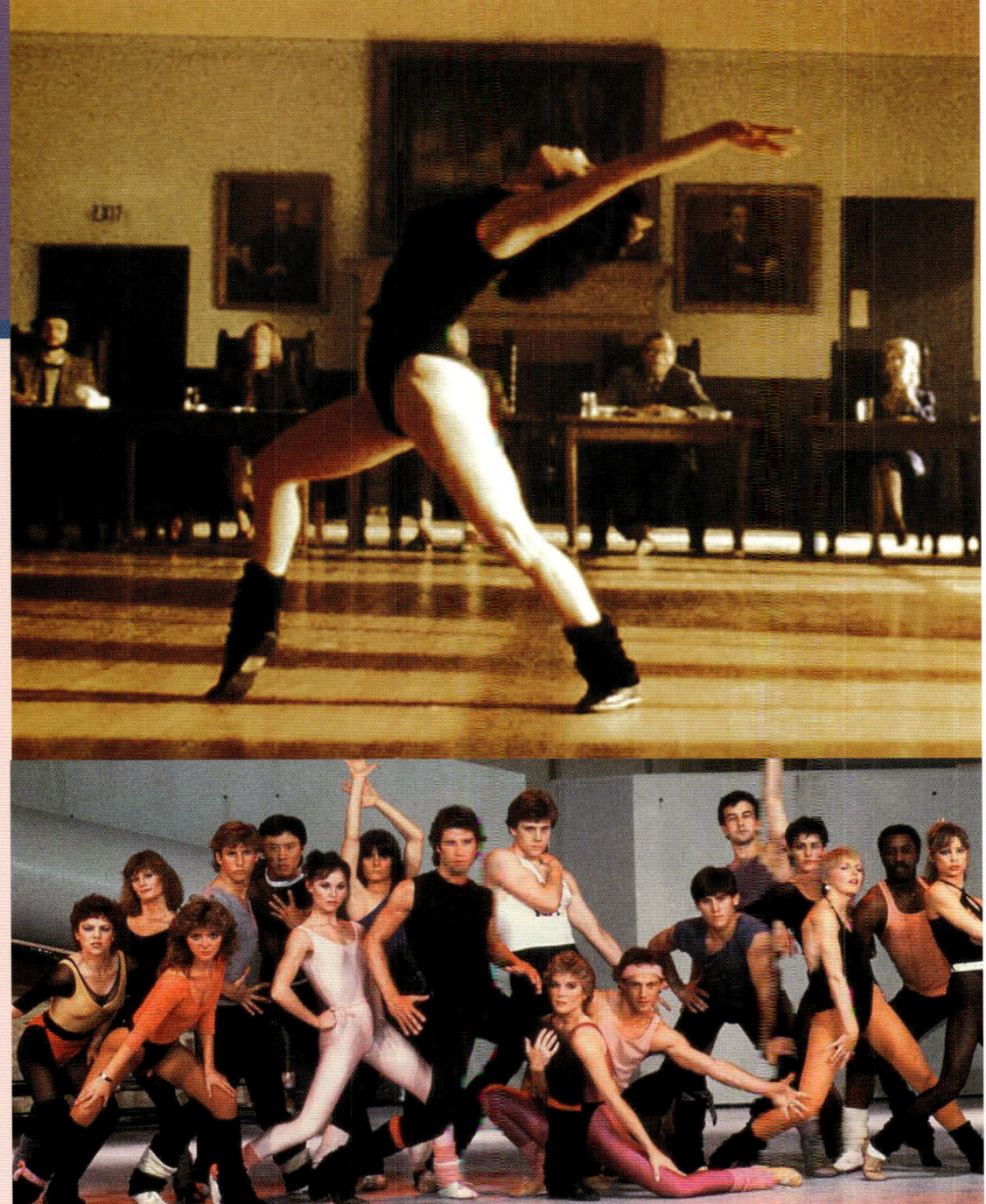

I wanted to dance on tabletops during math class with leg warmers.

NAOMI WATTS

Headbands, wristbands, and high-top sneakers became accessories for everyday wear, not just workouts. Even men got in on the trend, sporting gym shorts, muscle tees, and tracksuits in public. Designers such as Norma Kamali and brands such as Adidas and Reebok capitalized on the craze, creating collections that could go from gym to street.

What began as a niche fashion subculture soon became an enduring part of American style. Athleisure, the modern-day descendant of the workout wear boom, owes much of its legacy to this era. The idea that fashion should be functional, flattering, and flexible was born in the aerobics studio—and never really left. From the dance floor to the weights room and the grocery store, workout clothes redefined comfort and confidence. And in Hollywood, where appearance and physicality often went hand in hand, the fitness look became yet another way for stars to shape trends and turn heads.

TOP LEFT

In *Flashdance*, Jennifer Beals played a working-class young woman determined to gain entry to dance school. Here she goes all out to impress the school's committee.

BOTTOM LEFT

John Travolta leads a fiercely posed ensemble in *Staying Alive* (1983)—a high-gloss sequel to *Saturday Night Fever* steeped in sweat, spandex, and Broadway ambition beneath glimmering 80s lights.

MADONNA

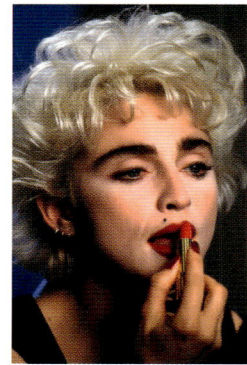

Explosive, irreverent, and unshakably stylish, Madonna defined the look and attitude of the 1980s. She didn't follow fashion—she weaponized it, making every outfit a challenge, a message, a moment. She blurred lines between streetwear and couture, sacred and profane, femininity and defiance. Madonna didn't just wear clothes—she wielded them to provoke, transform, and control the narrative around her. In doing so, she redefined what it meant to be a woman in pop culture, leaving a legacy that still echoes through fashion, music, and visual media.

At a time when most pop stars were polished and packaged, Madonna arrived with a raw, DIY sensibility. Her early "Like a Virgin" look— lace gloves, rosaries, bustiers, bows—was instantly iconic. Teen girls copied her, designers scrambled to catch up, and a generation of "Madonna wannabes" was born.

She was a master of reinvention. From *Desperately Seeking Susan*'s Boy Toy styling to "Material Girl's" Monroe homage and "True Blue's" platinum-punk aesthetic, Madonna used fashion to tell stories. Jean Paul Gaultier's cone bras became emblematic of her daring.

But Madonna's style wasn't about trends—it was about control. In an industry that tried to define women, she defined herself. By decade's end, she wasn't just a star. She was a style archetype—rebellious, theatrical, fearless. She didn't follow the fashion curve; she bent it to her will.

FASHION FEATURES

DESPERATELY SEEKING SUSAN (1985)
EVITA (1996)
TRUTH OR DARE (1991)

The Madonna Look
Unapologetically bold and endlessly imitated, Madonna's 1980s style was a curated chaos of rebellion and glamor.
• Lace gloves
• Layered rosaries
• Tousled bleached hair
• Bustiers and mesh
• Crucifix jewelry
• Bold brows and red lips
• Attitude above all

ABOVE
—
Studio still from *Who's That Girl* (1987): Madonna applies a slick of red lipstick, her platinum curls, beauty mark, and arched brows evoking a punked-up Marilyn Monroe with unmistakable '80s attitude.

RIGHT
—
Madonna as Susan in *Desperately Seeking Susan* (1985): Street-style rebellion defined—lace top, stacked bangles, studded boots, and a tousled bow-tied updo. She's every inch the downtown New York icon.

DEMI MOORE

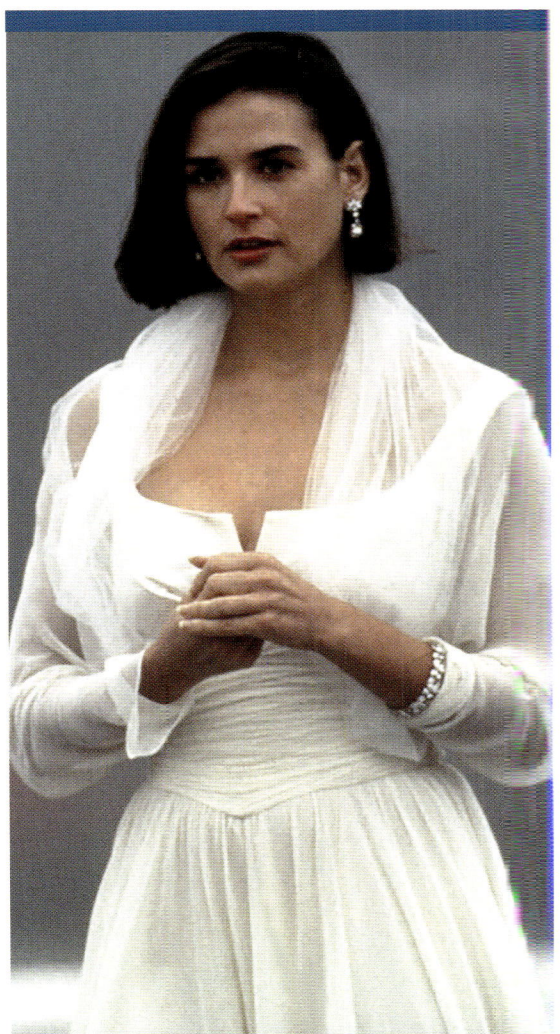

Daring, edgy, and unafraid to reinvent herself, Demi Moore rose to stardom in the 1980s and 1990s as one of Hollywood's most bankable and influential actresses.

Born in 1962 in Roswell, New Mexico, Moore began her career as a model and soap opera actress before gaining attention with roles in coming-of-age films such as *St. Elmo's Fire* (1985), which helped establish her as part of the "Brat Pack." Her breakthrough role came in *Ghost* (1990), where her emotional performance opposite Patrick Swayze became a cultural phenomenon and solidified her place as a dramatic lead.

In the 1990s, Moore took on increasingly daring roles in *A Few Good Men* (1992), *Indecent Proposal* (1993), and *Disclosure* (1994). She made headlines for shaving her head in *G.I. Jane* (1997), further showcasing her commitment to physical and emotional transformation. Off-screen, she became known for her high-profile marriage to Bruce Willis and later Ashton Kutcher.

Moore's striking looks, trendsetting fashion choices, and an ability to balance vulnerability with strength made her one of the defining stars of her era.

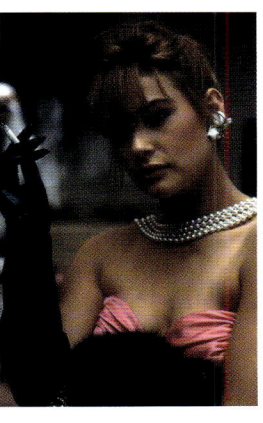

I don't like to take my clothes off.

DEMI MOORE

The Moore Look

Minimalist and sleek, Moore's style embraced clean lines, dark tones, and tailored sophistication that mirrored her confident screen presence.

- Glossy dark hair
- Smoky eyes and nude lips
- Strong-shouldered gowns
- Monochrome and minimalist ensembles

FASHION FEATURES

GHOST (1990)
A FEW GOOD MEN (1992)
INDECENT PROPOSAL (1993)
G.I. JANE (1997)

ABOVE

Demi Moore smolders in satin pink, opera gloves, and pearls in *No Small Affair* (1984), capturing the raw allure of youthful ambition dressed in vintage glamor.

LEFT

Moore, veiled in white chiffon and ocean mist, delivers quiet intensity as Diana Murphy in *Indecent Proposal* (1993)—a portrait of beauty entangled with moral ambiguity.

MICHELLE PFEIFFER

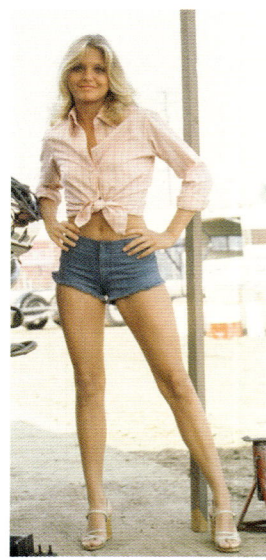

Michelle Pfeiffer (born April 29, 1958, in Santa Ana, California) is an American actress celebrated for her beauty, versatility, and compelling performances across a diverse array of film genres.

She began her acting career in the late 1970s, gaining early attention with roles in *Grease 2* (1982) and *Scarface* (1983).

Pfeiffer's breakthrough came with *Dangerous Liaisons* (1988), earning her an Academy Award nomination for Best Supporting Actress. She followed this with acclaimed performances in *The Fabulous Baker Boys* (1989) and *Love Field* (1992), both of which garnered her Best Actress Oscar nominations. Her portrayal of Catwoman in *Batman Returns* (1992) remains one of her most iconic roles.

Throughout the 1990s, Pfeiffer showcased her range in films such as *The Age of Innocence* (1993), *Dangerous Minds* (1995), and *What Lies Beneath* (2000). After a brief hiatus, she returned with notable performances in *Hairspray* (2007), *Stardust* (2007), and *The Wizard of Lies* (2017). In recent years, she has taken on roles in the Marvel Cinematic Universe, portraying Janet van Dyne in *Ant-Man and the Wasp* (2018) and its sequel.

Beyond acting, Pfeiffer advocated for environmental causes and children's health, for which she was recognized. She has been married to television writer and producer David E. Kelley since 1993. With a career spanning over four decades, Pfeiffer continues to captivate audiences with her talent and dedication to her craft.

ABOVE
———
Michelle Pfeiffer stands sunlit in cutoff denim and a tied blouse beside a V8 engine—capturing 1970s Americana with effortless charm and mechanical cool.

RIGHT
———
Bathed in soft studio light, Michelle Pfeiffer poses in a flowing blouse—her voluminous waves and serene gaze capturing the poised allure of early 1980s Hollywood stardom.

FASHION FEATURES

SCARFACE (1983)
THE FABULOUS BAKER BOYS (1989)
BATMAN RETURNS (1992)
THE AGE OF INNOCENCE (1993)

The Pfeiffer Look

Whether playing a sultry singer or an inner-city teacher, Michelle Pfeiffer understands the power of clothing to define a character. Her style combines classic glamor with understated confidence, seamlessly blending sophistication with edge.

• Red carpet gowns in black, metallic, or neutral tones
• Feminine staples such as pencil skirts and stiletto heels
• Long, loose, softly waved blonde hair

MOLLY RINGWALD

> I do regret...the time that I shaved off half of my eyebrows thinking that I could draw them in better—and they would grow back anyway.

MOLLY RINGWALD

FASHION FEATURES

SIXTEEN CANDLES (1984)
THE BREAKFAST CLUB (1985)
PRETTY IN PINK (1986)

The Ringwald Look

Youthful and eclectic, Ringwald's 1980s look featured layered outfits, oversized blazers, florals, and chunky accessories.

- Auburn bob haircut
- Pearl earrings and vintage touches
- Layered skirts and boots
- Soft makeup with pink hues

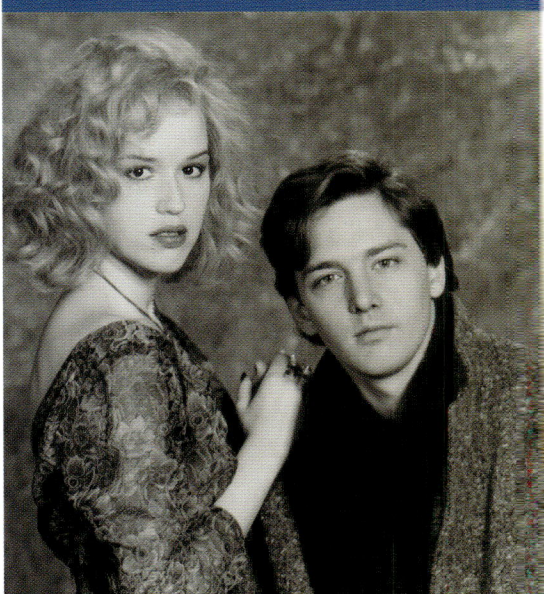

Bright, relatable, and effortlessly expressive, Molly Ringwald became the face of 1980s teen cinema, leaving an unforgettable mark on pop culture through her collaborations with director John Hughes.

Born in 1968 in Roseville, California, Ringwald began her performing career at a young age, appearing in theater and television, including *The Facts of Life*. Her big break came when she was cast as the lead in Hughes' coming-of-age classic *Sixteen Candles* (1984), playing the awkward but endearing Samantha Baker. The film's success catapulted her into teen stardom and cemented her as a voice for adolescent experience.

Ringwald followed this with two more John Hughes hits, *The Breakfast Club* (1985) and *Pretty in Pink* (1986), where she portrayed smart, sensitive, and independent girls navigating friendship, romance, and social pressure. These roles struck a chord with young audiences and helped redefine the teen genre with honesty and emotional depth.

Although her fame waned in the 1990s, Ringwald continued to act in film, television, and theater, and later found success as a writer and singer. She also experienced a resurgence with roles in *The Secret Life of the American Teenager* and *Riverdale*, appealing to a new generation.

Molly Ringwald's legacy is tied not only to her era-defining roles but also to her authentic portrayals of adolescence that made countless viewers feel seen.

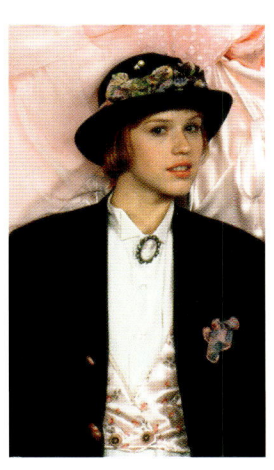

ABOVE

Molly Ringwald, in floral-trimmed vest and vintage brooch, defines teen individuality as Andie Walsh in *Pretty in Pink* (1986)—a style icon of heartfelt rebellion.

LEFT

Wearing floral chiffon and soft curls, Molly Ringwald stands beside Andrew McCarthy in a promotional still for *Pretty in Pink* (1986)—a defining image of 80s teen romance.

LEADING MEN
RICHARD GERE

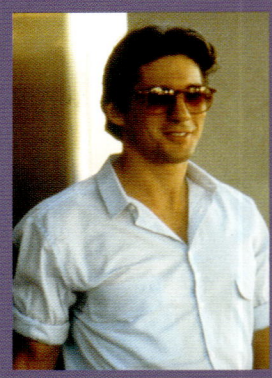

In the 1980s, Richard Gere emerged as a Hollywood fashion icon, defining masculine elegance with a cool, minimalist edge. His breakthrough role in *American Gigolo* (1980) famously featured a wardrobe designed by Giorgio Armani, launching both Gere and the designer into international fame. The film's sleek, unstructured suits became the blueprint for the modern "power look," influencing men's fashion throughout the decade. Gere's style was marked by tailored silhouettes, open-collared shirts, and effortless charm—he made simplicity look seductive. Off-screen, he maintained the same understated sophistication, often seen in neutral tones, casual blazers, and crisp, classic fits.

In his semi-autobiographical reflections and interviews, Gere has spoken more about his spiritual journey and activism than fashion, but he acknowledges that *American Gigolo* shaped public perception. Although he has never written a full autobiography, Gere's perspectives have been shared in various profiles and interviews where he emphasizes inner peace over appearances. Still, in the 1980s, his fashion influence was undeniable—he wasn't just a leading man; he was a style movement. Through his roles and personal aesthetic, Richard Gere helped redefine what modern masculinity looked like, blending softness and strength with quiet confidence and timeless tailoring.

ABOVE

In rolled sleeves and aviators, Richard Gere strolls coolly through *American Gigolo* (1980)—a sunlit study in West Coast swagger and sharply understated sensuality.

TOP RIGHT

Richard Gere, bare-chested beneath a tailored suit, leans into shadowed brick with effortless cool—an early 1980s portrait blending street realism with rising star allure..

BOTTOM RIGHT

Clad in dress whites atop a Triumph, Richard Gere delivers an unforgettable exit in *An Officer and a Gentleman* (1982)—a moment of romance, redemption, and cinematic triumph.

RIGHT

Drenched and determined, Richard Gere wades through murky bayou waters alongside Kim Basinger in *No Mercy* (1986)—a neo-noir tableau of grit, pursuit, and perilous romance.

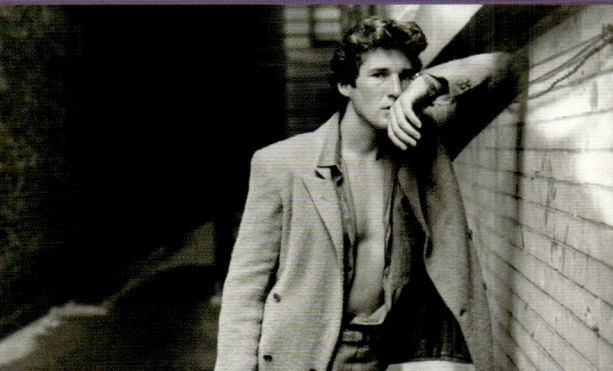

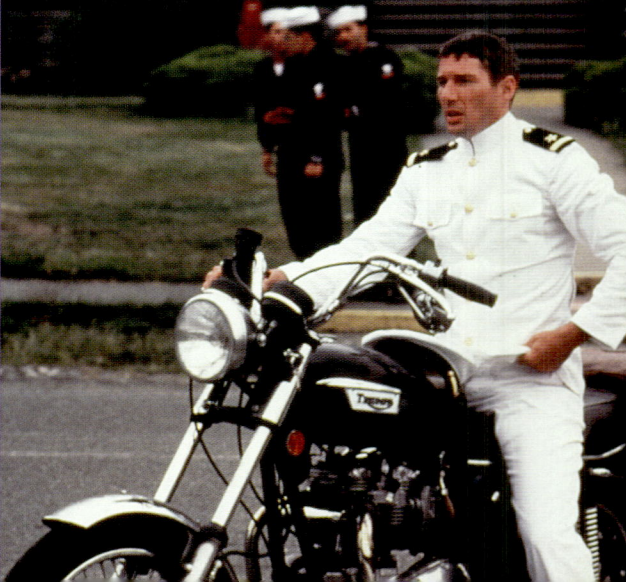

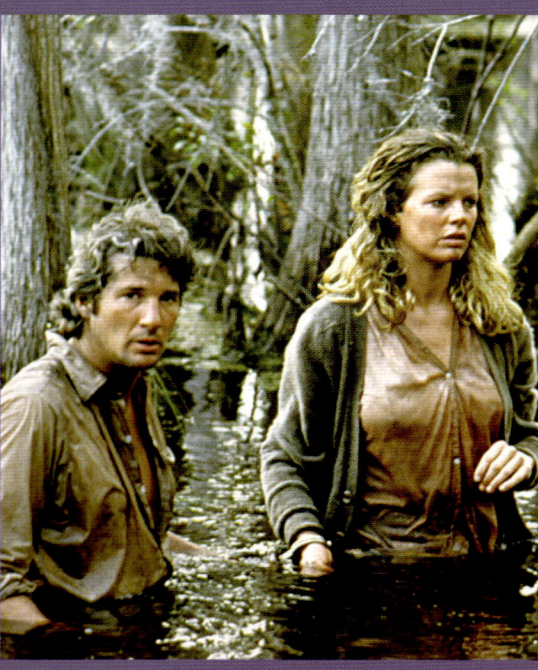

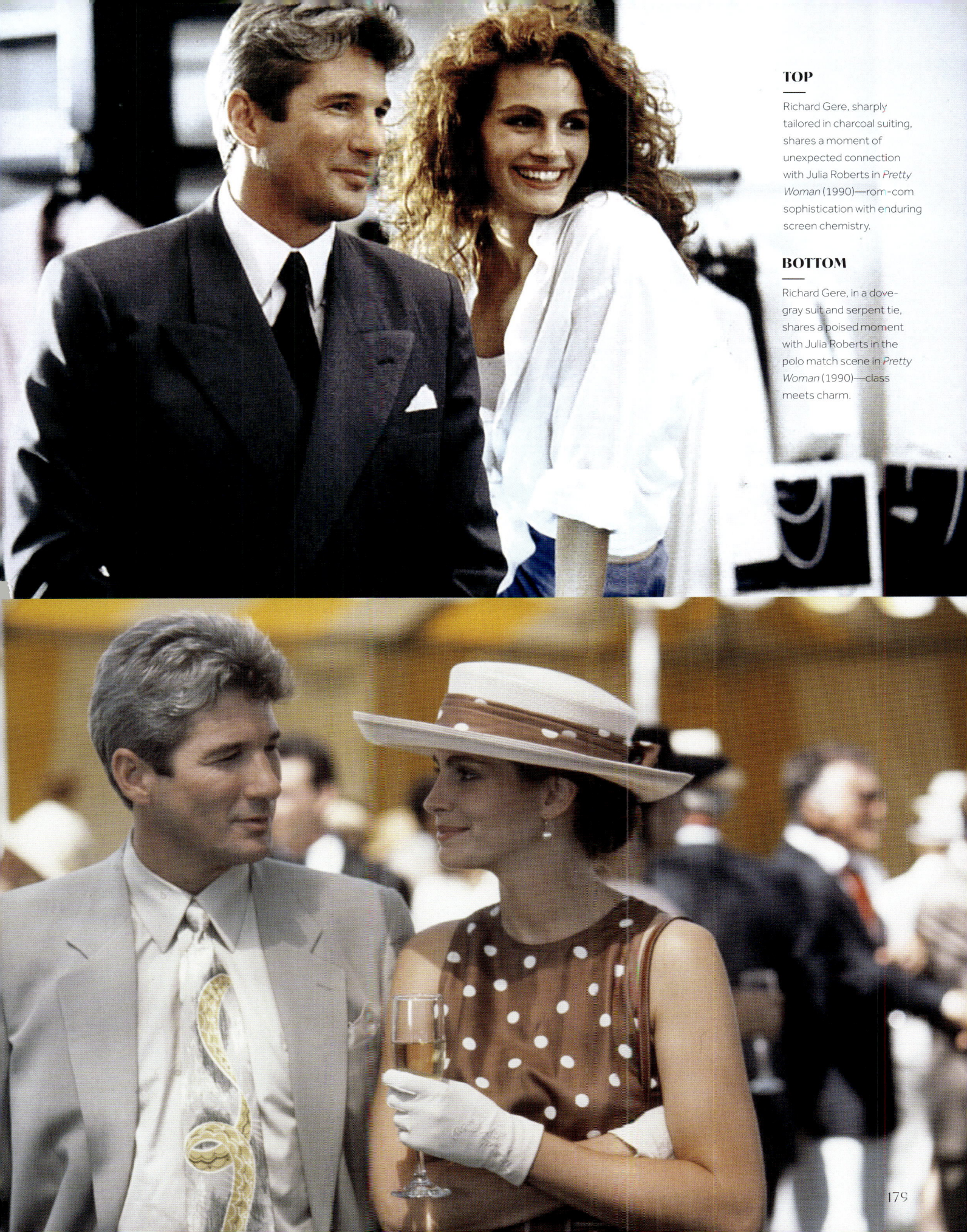

TOP

Richard Gere, sharply tailored in charcoal suiting, shares a moment of unexpected connection with Julia Roberts in *Pretty Woman* (1990)—rom-com sophistication with enduring screen chemistry.

BOTTOM

Richard Gere, in a dove-gray suit and serpent tie, shares a poised moment with Julia Roberts in the polo match scene in *Pretty Woman* (1990)—class meets charm.

WINONA RYDER

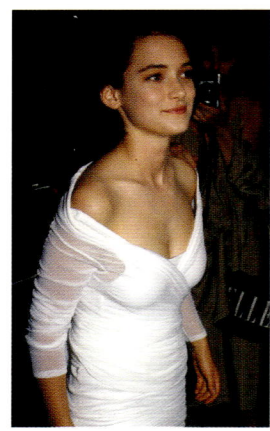

Winona Ryder (born Winona Laura Horowitz on October 29, 1971, in Winona, Minnesota) is an American actress renowned for her portrayals of intelligent and unconventional characters. She gained early acclaim with roles in *Beetlejuice* (1988) and *Heathers* (1988), establishing herself as a distinctive presence in Hollywood.

Ryder's versatility was evident in films such as *Edward Scissorhands* (1990), *Mermaids* (1990), and *Bram Stoker's Dracula* (1992). Her performance in *The Age of Innocence* (1993) earned her a Golden Globe Award and an Academy Award nomination. She received another Oscar nomination for her role as Jo March in *Little Women* (1994).

In the late 1990s, Ryder continued to take on diverse roles in films such as *Alien Resurrection* (1997) and *Girl, Interrupted* (1999), the latter of which she also executive produced. After a brief hiatus in the early 2000s, she returned to the screen with performances in *Star Trek* (2009) and *Black Swan* (2010).

Since 2016, Ryder has starred as Joyce Byers in the critically acclaimed Netflix series *Stranger Things*, earning nominations for both Golden Globe and Screen Actors Guild awards. Her enduring career reflects her ability to navigate both mainstream and independent cinema with equal finesse.

ABOVE

Winona Ryder turns heads in ruched white mesh at a 1989 premiere—radiating minimalist elegance as Hollywood's rising ingénue under the glare of paparazzi flashbulbs.

RIGHT

Winona Ryder, in layered ruffles and tousled curls, captures outsider charm as Veronica Sawyer in *Heathers* (1989)—a darkly iconic vision of teen rebellion and wit.

FASHION FEATURES

HEATHERS (1988)
EDWARD SCISSORHANDS (1990)
THE AGE OF INNOCENCE (1993)

The Ryder Look

Winona Ryder has captured the spirit of youth subcultures through her roles, from goth aesthetics in *Beetlejuice* to preppy rebellion in *Heathers* and grunge minimalism in *Reality Bites*. Her fashion often echoes these influences—moody, minimalist, and effortlessly cool.

- Tousled, cropped dark hair
- Black or muted-toned separates
- Simple, tailored dresses with minimal accessories

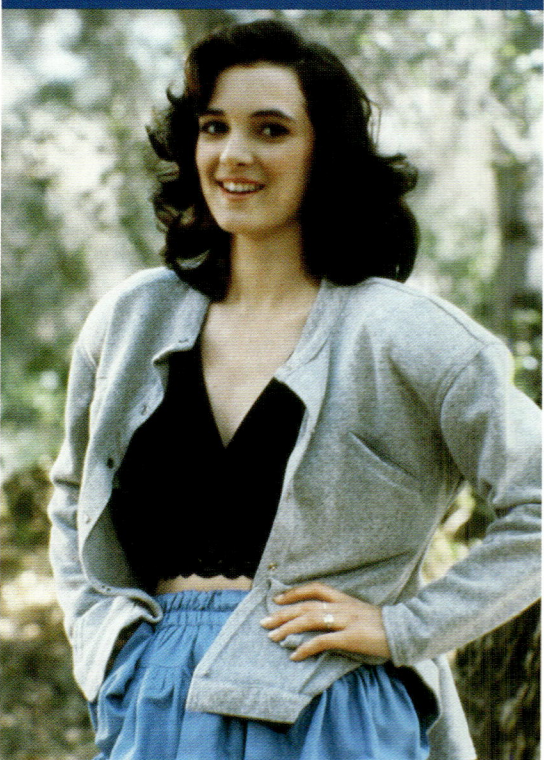

MERYL STREEP

FASHION FEATURES

KRAMER VS. KRAMER (1979)
SOPHIE'S CHOICE (1982)
OUT OF AFRICA (1985)
THE IRON LADY (2011)
THE DEVIL WEARS PRADA (2006)

The Streep Look

Refined and resolute, Streep favors timeless silhouettes, tailored pieces, and subtle elegance that mirror her thoughtful and authentic screen presence.

- Natural makeup and soft waves
- Elegant long coats and blazers
- Monochrome palettes
- Statement eyewear and minimalist jewelry

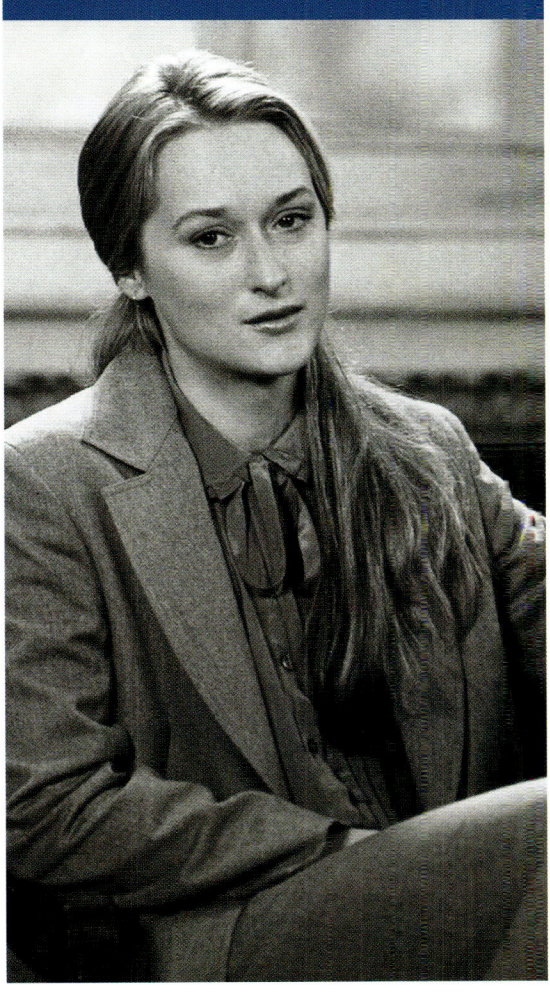

Universally hailed as one of the greatest actresses of all time, Meryl Streep is renowned for her transformative performances, exceptional range, and unwavering commitment to her craft.

Born Mary Louise Streep in Summit, New Jersey, in 1949, Streep studied drama at Vassar College and later earned a Media Federation Award from the Yale School of Drama. She began her professional career on stage in the early 1970s before transitioning to film. Her breakthrough role came with *The Deer Hunter* (1978), which earned her the first of many Academy Award nominations. She followed it with a powerful performance in *Kramer vs. Kramer* (1979), winning her first Oscar for Best Supporting Actress.

Throughout the 1980s and beyond, Streep earned a reputation as a master of character work, particularly in films such as *Sophie's Choice* (1982), for which she won the Best Actress Oscar, and *The French Lieutenant's Woman* (1981). She became known for her meticulous preparation, including mastering accents and immersing herself fully in each role. Her performances span historical drama, comedy, romance, and musicals, with acclaimed turns in *Out of Africa* (1985), *The Bridges of Madison County* (1995), and *Doubt* (2008). She portrayed Margaret Thatcher in *The Iron Lady* (2011), which earned her a third Oscar.

Streep's more recent work includes crowd-pleasing performances in *Mamma Mia!* (2008), *The Devil Wears Prada* (2006), and *Big Little Lies* (2019). A recipient of numerous awards and honors, including the Presidential Medal of Freedom, Streep continues to inspire generations of performers with her integrity, intelligence, and unmatched talent.

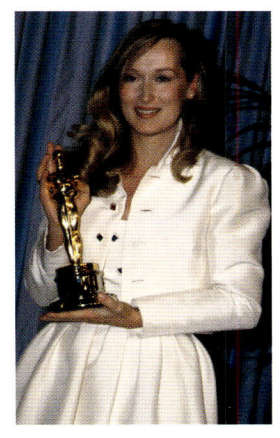

ABOVE

In ivory pleats and soft waves, Meryl Streep accepts her 1983 Oscar for *Sophie's Choice*, radiating poise in a moment that defined cinematic excellence.

LEFT

In a tailored suit and loosely tied blouse, Meryl Streep embodies courtroom composure as Joanna Kramer in *Kramer vs. Kramer* (1979), a role that redefined onscreen motherhood.

KATHLEEN TURNER

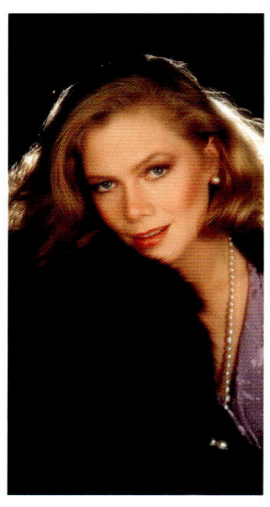

Sultry, sharp-witted, and fiercely commanding, Kathleen Turner emerged in the 1980s as one of Hollywood's most dynamic leading ladies, known for her husky voice, magnetic screen presence, and powerful versatility.

Born in 1954 in Springfield, Missouri, Turner spent much of her youth abroad due to her father's diplomatic career. She studied theater at the University of Maryland and began her acting career on stage before transitioning to television and film. Her breakthrough came with the steamy thriller *Body Heat* (1981), in which she played a seductive femme fatale. The role made her an overnight sensation and launched her as a new icon of cinematic sensuality.

Throughout the 1980s and early 90s, Turner proved she was more than just a screen siren. She displayed strong comedic chops in hits such as *Romancing the Stone* (1984), *The Jewel of the Nile* (1985), and *Peggy Sue Got Married* (1986), the latter earning her an Academy Award nomination. Her voice work as Jessica Rabbit in *Who Framed Roger Rabbit* (1988) became instantly legendary.

In the 1990s, Turner returned to the theater and continued working in television, despite battling rheumatoid arthritis, which affected her mobility and career momentum. Nevertheless, her commanding performances and unmistakable voice have left an indelible mark on stage and screen.

ABOVE

Bathed in soft light, Kathleen Turner channels classic noir allure in fur, pearls, and lilac silk—an image echoing her smoldering 1980s screen persona.

RIGHT

Draped in emerald veils and quiet intensity, Kathleen Turner captivates in *The Jewel of the Nile* (1985), embodying desert intrigue with Old Hollywood mystique.

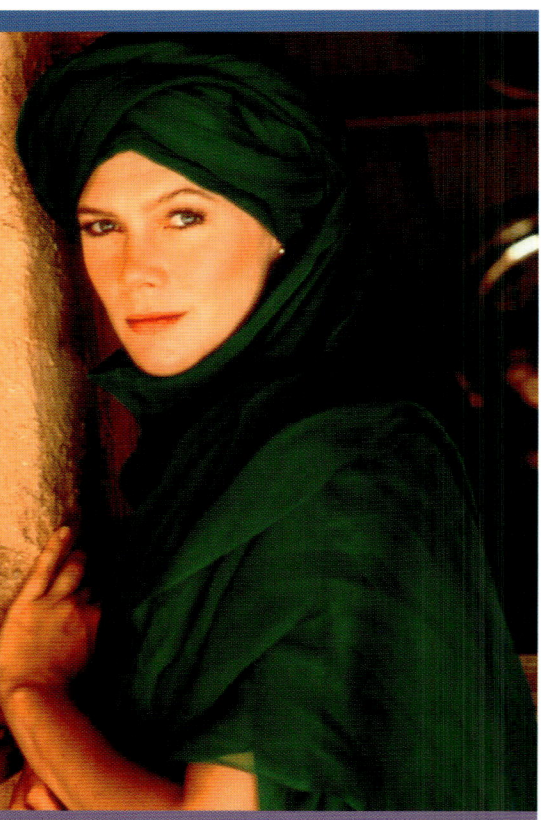

FASHION FEATURES

BODY HEAT (1981)
ROMANCING THE STONE (1984)
PEGGY SUE GOT MARRIED (1986)
WAR OF THE ROSES (1989)
WHO FRAMED ROGER RABBIT (1988)

The Turner Look

Classic and audacious, Turner embraced strong silhouettes, vibrant colors, and sultry gowns that reflected her fierce, empowered screen image.

• Wavy, shoulder-length hair
• Bold lips and smoky eyes
• Fitted power suits and wrap dresses
• Statement jewelry and heels

SIGOURNEY WEAVER

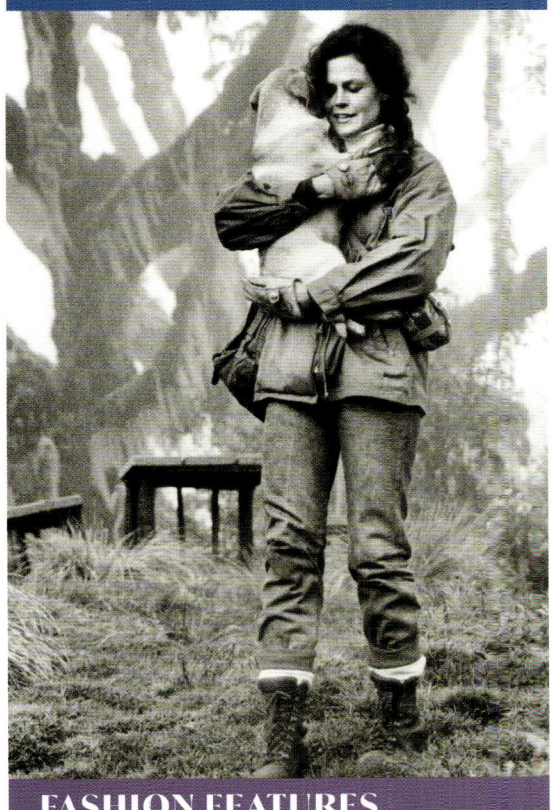

Sigourney Weaver (born October 8, 1949, in New York City) is an American actress renowned for her portrayals of strong, independent women in film. She gained prominence with her role as Ellen Ripley in Ridley Scott's *Alien* (1979), a performance that redefined female protagonists in science fiction. Weaver reprised this role in three sequels, earning an Academy Award nomination for *Aliens* (1986).

Her versatility is evident in films such as *Gorillas in the Mist* (1988), where she portrayed primatologist Dian Fossey, and *Working Girl* (1988), both performances earning her Academy Award nominations. Weaver's other notable works include *Ghostbusters* (1984), *The Ice Storm* (1997), and *Avatar* (2009) where she played Dr. Grace Augustine. In the sequel, *Avatar: The Way of Water* (2022), she portrayed Kiri, Dr Augustine's 14-year-old Na'vi daughter, utilizing technologies that slow down the aging process and Computer-Generated Imagery.

Beyond film, Weaver has appeared in television and stage productions, earning accolades including Golden Globe and British Academy of Film and Television Arts awards. Her enduring career and impactful roles have solidified her status as a trailblazer in the entertainment industry

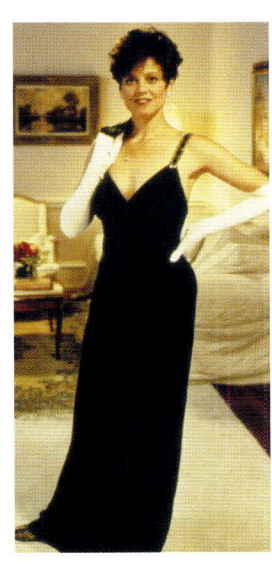

FASHION FEATURES

ALIEN (1979)
THE YEAR OF LIVING DANGEROUSLY (1982)
GHOSTBUSTERS (1984)
DAVE (1993)

The Weaver Look

With her striking features, towering presence, and graceful frame, Sigourney Weaver brings elegance and power to any look—whether in utilitarian space gear or refined red carpet fashion. Her style blends strength and sophistication with timeless appeal.

• Voluminous dark curls
• Sleek, structured suits
• Elegant, understated gowns

ABOVE

Sigourney Weaver exudes Old Hollywood elegance in a midnight gown and opera gloves for *Working Girl* (1988)—boardroom power recast in satin, poise, and cinematic glamor.

LEFT

Amid fog-draped foliage, Sigourney Weaver cradles a pup on the set of *Gorillas in the Mist* (1988)—a tender pause within a story of courage and conservation.

LEADING MEN
DECADE OF DECADENCE

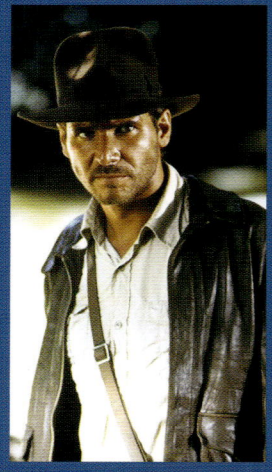

The 1980s ushered in a heroical transformation in men's fashion—one defined by excess, color, and rule-breaking style. This was a time when traditional boundaries dissolved, giving rise to flamboyant trends: bright hues, shoulder-length hair, designer suits worn with sneakers, and even makeup entered the male fashion vocabulary.

An American Original

Richard Gere launched the decade with a smoldering appeal in *American Gigolo* (1980). His sleek wardrobe of Giorgio Armani suits and the hypnotic rhythm of Blondie's "Call Me" made both actor and aesthetic instantly iconic.

Miami Vice Effect

TV show *Miami Vice* influenced men everywhere to adopt the pastel palette of South Beach. White or light-toned suit jackets were worn open over tropical T-shirts—relaxed, yet strikingly stylish.

Power Dressing Emerges

Gordon Gekko's declaration that "greed is good" in *Wall Street* (1987) was matched by his prominent sartorial choices—pinstripes, suspenders, gold watches, and high-contrast collars. The power suit became a corporate essential.

Music and Edge

Michael Jackson's *Thriller* (1982) video revolutionized fashion with its slim, red

leather jacket. The look evolved further in films such as *The Lost Boys* (1987), where leather jackets were studded, slashed, and worn open to project rebellion.

A Preppy Comeback

Michael J. Fox championed a return to clean-cut prep in *Back to the Future* and *Family Ties*. This style leaned into IZOD polos, plaid trousers, khakis, suspenders, argyle sweaters, and loafers. Pullovers tossed over the shoulders became a uniform of collegiate cool.

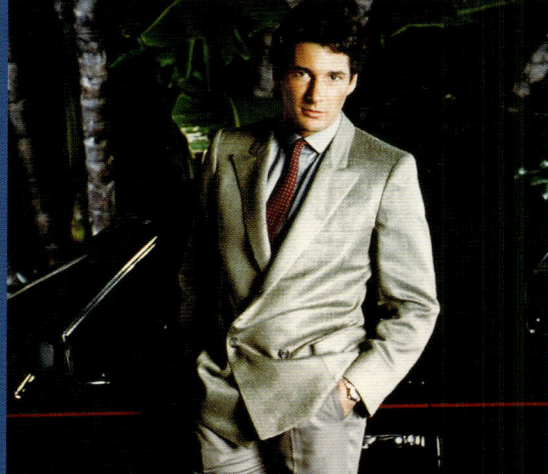

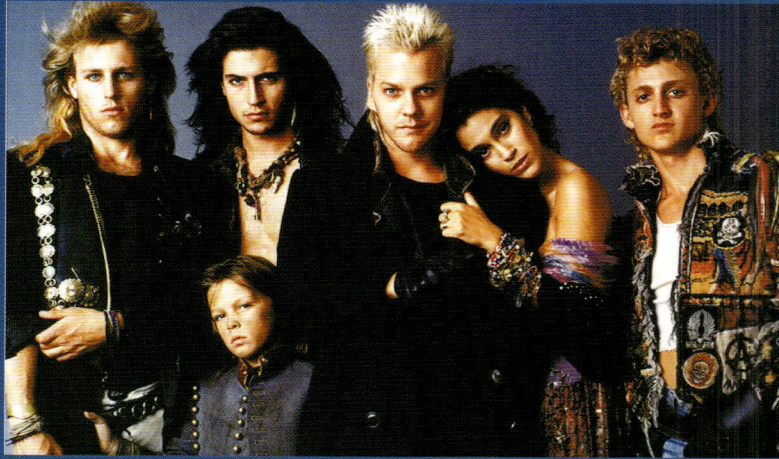

ABOVE

Harrison Ford, sweat-dusted and resolute in fedora and leather, defines cinematic adventure as Indiana Jones in *Raiders of the Lost Ark* (1981)—a modern myth forged in motion.

TOP RIGHT

Richard Gere displays the new attitude in men's suits—relaxed lines, muted colors, and sleek, elegant fabrics—in *American Gigolo* (1980).

BOTTOM RIGHT

The Lost Boys (1987), led by Kiefer Sutherland (center), evoked the rising Goth and New Romantic fashions inspired by Michael Jackson and Prince; hair was either a punk-style mullet or the flowing locks of MTV's heavy-metal bands.

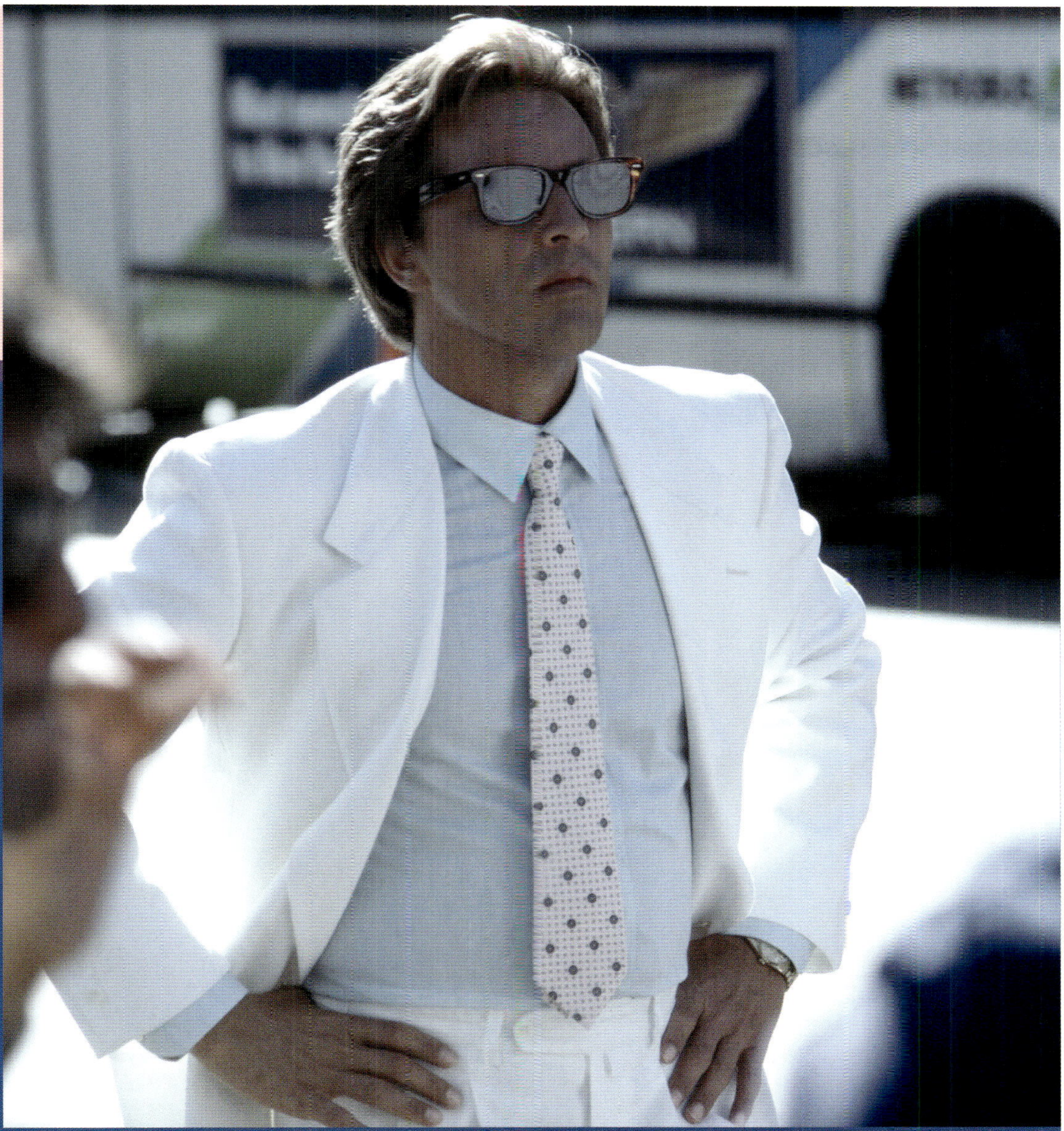

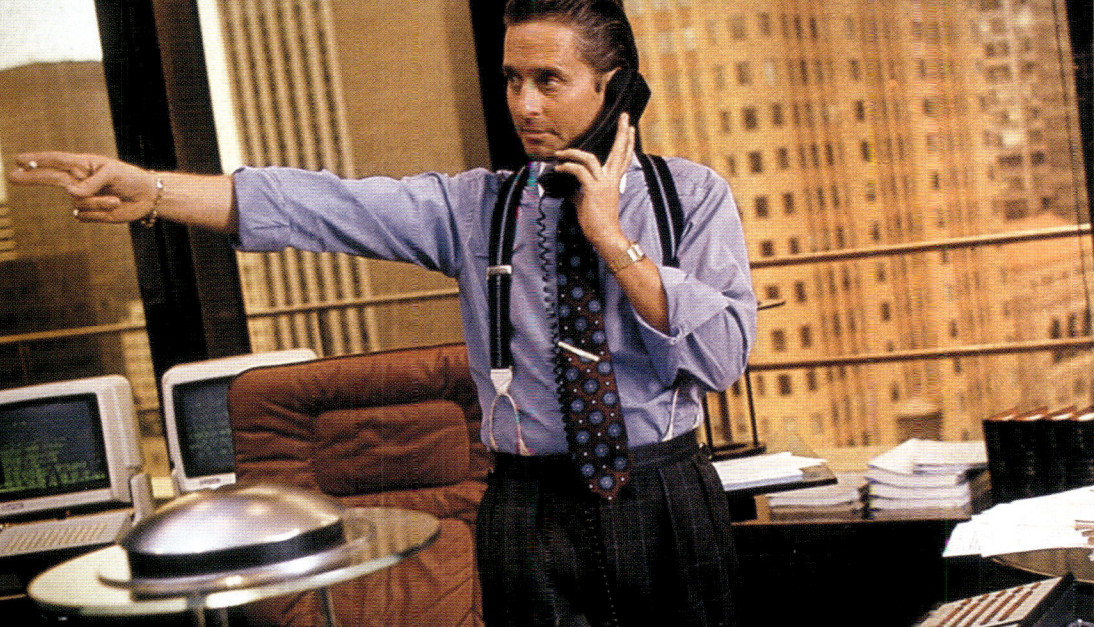

STYLE SIGNIFIERS

- Armani jackets layered over graphic or plain tees
- Ray-Ban Wayfarers and Tom Cruise-style aviators
- Acid-washed jeans and denim jackets
- Indiana Jones-inspired bomber jackets
- Flannel shirts with chunky hiking boots
- A permanent five o'clock shadow

The secret of my success is my hairspray.

RICHARD GERE

TOP LEFT

Don Johnson, in crisp white linen and mirrored shades, epitomizes *Miami Vice* cool—an emblem of 1980s style and swagger on the sun-drenched streets of television history.

BOTTOM LEFT

Michael Douglas in *Wall Street* (1987), as Gordon Gekko—power-dressed in bold suspenders, patterned tie, and slicked-back hair, defining the sharp-edged excess of 80s corporate style.

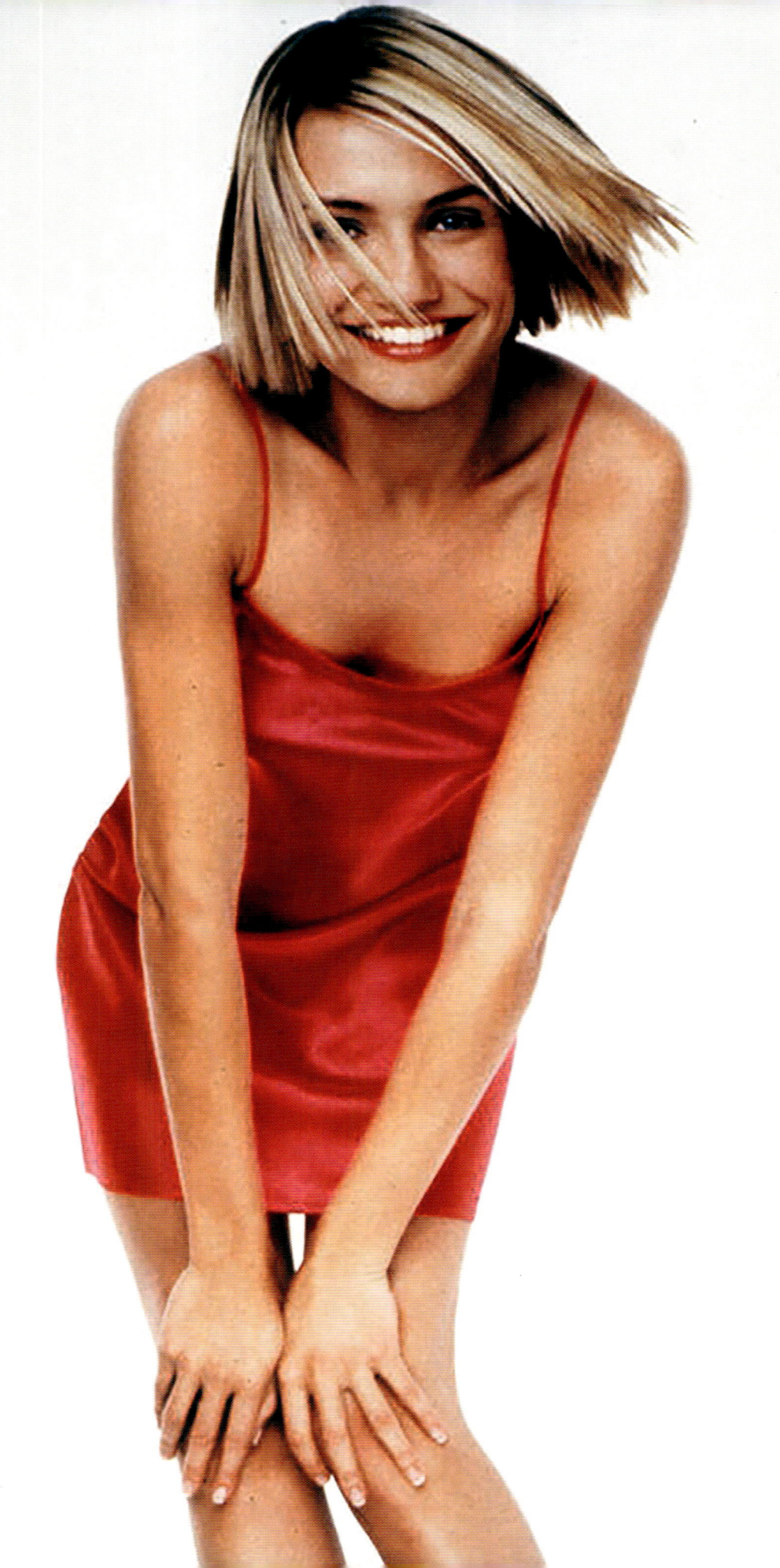

NINETEEN NINETIES

It was only the 1990s that brought a shift away from the extravagant, heavily styled looks of the previous decade. Fashion in Hollywood embraced a cooler, more minimalist attitude, often drawing on streetwear, grunge, retro glamor, and global influences. Actresses favored sleek silhouettes, natural makeup, and simpler fabrics such as silk, jersey, and matte satin. The slinky slip dress became an icon, often paired with bare skin and tousled hair, whereas vintage revival styles from the 30s and 70s emerged on red carpets.

The era also saw a rise in alternative beauty standards, with stars such as Winona Ryder and Uma Thurman redefining elegance with their individuality. Supermodels transitioned into film, bringing fashion-forward sensibilities onto the screen. Meanwhile, Jennifer Lopez, Julia Roberts, and Sharon Stone fused sex appeal with confidence, often mixing menswear-inspired pieces with glamorous cuts.

Menswear evolved too—relaxed tailoring replaced stiff suits, and designers such as Tom Ford introduced a sensual, refined masculinity. Leather jackets, dark denim, and layered neutrals became staples.

By the decade's end, designers blurred the line between Hollywood and high fashion. Red carpet events became major style platforms, and celebrity stylists rose in influence. The 1990s demonstrated that confidence along with reinvention was the best accessory.

DREW BARRYMORE

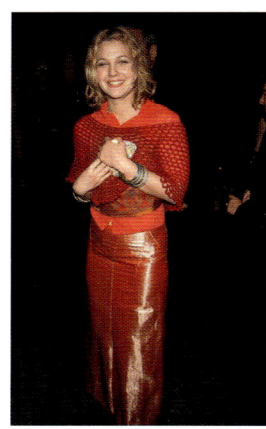

Drew Barrymore has grown up in the spotlight, evolving from a child star to influential producer, director, author, and talk show host. Born on February 22, 1975, in Culver City, California, she comes from the legendary Barrymore family of actors. At just seven years of age, she captured hearts worldwide with her performance as Gertie in *E.T. the Extra-Terrestrial* (1982) and made history that same year as the youngest person to host Saturday Night Live.

Despite early fame, Barrymore faced personal struggles during her adolescence, including substance abuse, which she candidly documented in her 1990 memoir *Little Girl Lost*. In the 1990s, she reclaimed her career with bold roles in *Poison Ivy* (1992), *Guncrazy* (1992), and *The Amy Fisher Story* (1993).

In 1995, she co-founded Flower Films, producing and starring in beloved films such as *Never Been Kissed* (1999), *Charlie's Angels* (2000), and *50 First Dates* (2004). She earned a Golden Globe and Screen Actors Guild Award for *Grey Gardens* (2009) and made her directorial debut with *Whip It* the same year.

Barrymore starred in Netflix's *Santa Clarita Diet* (2017–2019) and launched *The Drew Barrymore Show* in 2020. She also founded Flower Beauty and authored *Wildflower* (2015). A UN World Food Programme Ambassador, she was named one of *Time* magazine's 100 most influential people in 2023.

ABOVE
———
Drew Barrymore's fearless 1990s style blended boho spirit with Hollywood edge, mirroring her evolution from child star to indie fashion icon.

RIGHT
———
Drew Barrymore transitioned from child star to rom-com queen, winning hearts with her relatable charm in films such as *The Wedding Singer* and *Never Been Kissed*.

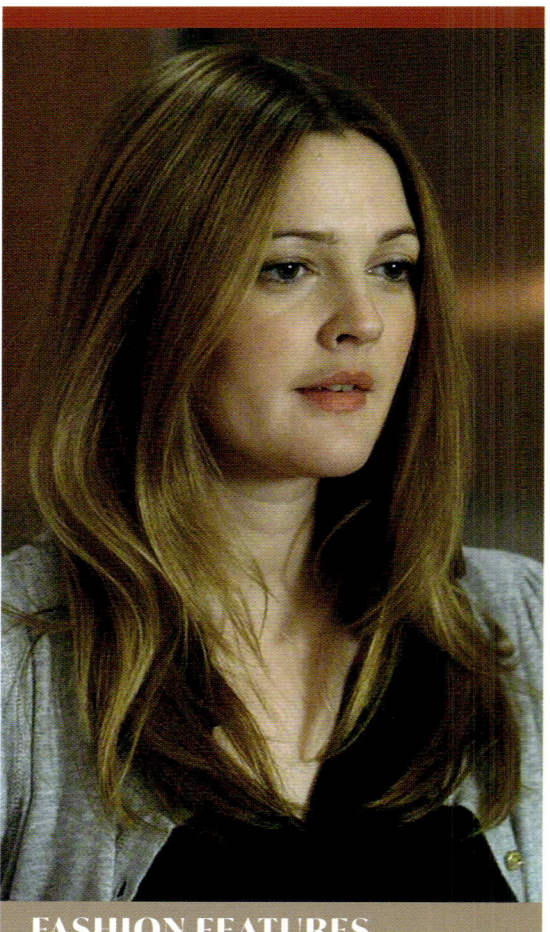

FASHION FEATURES

CHARLIE'S ANGELS (2000)
50 FIRST DATES (2004)
FEVER PITCH (2005)
MUSIC AND LYRICS (2007)

The Barrymore Look

Since 2009, she has been modeling for Cover Girl cosmetics and remains a much sought-after celebrity spokeswoman.

• Long, tousled, ombre-effect hair
• Boho separates in bold patterns
• Draped, feminine gowns

HALLE BERRY

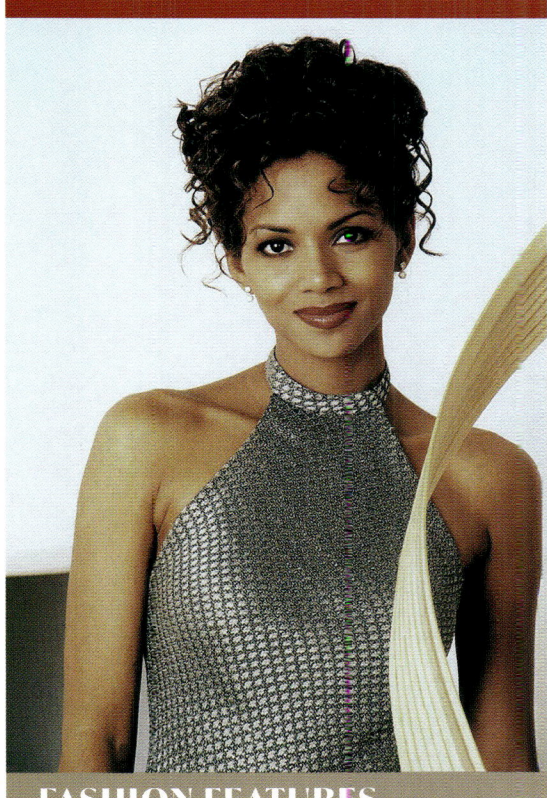

FASHION FEATURES

SWORDFISH (2001)
DIE ANOTHER DAY (2002)
CATWOMAN (2004)
CLOUD ATLAS (2012)

The Berry Look

The face of Revlon Cosmetics for many years, Berry possesses a natural beauty that seems to owe little to cosmetics or trendy clothes. Yet even when dressed down, she remains a favorite with the paparazzi.

• Short, wispy, razor-cut hair
• Loose-fitting tops with tight jeans
• Big sunglasses, ethnic scarves, and couture handbags

Halle Berry has carved a powerful path in Hollywood as both a trailblazing actress and a symbol of resilience and talent. Born on August 14, 1966, in Cleveland, Ohio, she began her public career in beauty pageants, placing as the first runner-up in Miss USA and sixth in Miss World in 1986. Her charisma soon led her to modeling and eventually to acting, debuting in _Jungle Fever_ (1991), and gaining her wider attention with roles in _Boomerang_ (1992) and _The Flintstones_ (1994).

In 2002, Berry made history by becoming the first Black woman to win the Academy Award for Best Actress for her performance in _Monster's Ball_. She went on to headline major studio films, including the _X-Men series_ (2000–2014), _Die Another Day_ (2002), and _Gothika_ (2003), establishing herself as a dynamic action and dramatic lead.

Berry expanded into television with the sci-fi series _Extant_ (2014–2015) and stepped behind the camera to direct _Bruised_ (2020), also starring in the film. A longtime Revlon ambassador and advocate for women's health and domestic violence awareness, she continues to use her platform for social impact.

Her accolades include an Oscar, a Golden Globe, and an Emmy, underscoring her enduring influence in entertainment.

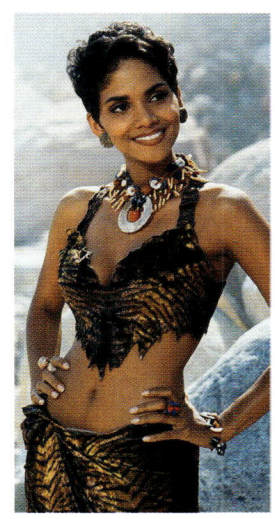

I'm not the girl for superhigh fashion because I don't have the right body.

HALLE BERRY

ABOVE

Halle Berry played a memorable role as the glamorous "Sharon Stone" in _The Flintstones_ (1994), showcasing early star power and playful screen presence.

LEFT

Halle Berry became the first Black woman to win Best Actress at the Oscars in 2002 for _Monster's Ball_, making history.

CATE BLANCHETT

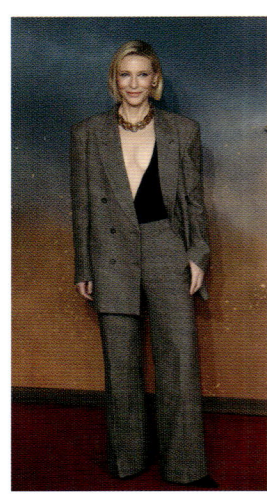

Only a few performers possess the transformative power and critical acclaim that define Cate Blanchett's career. Born on May 14, 1969, in Melbourne, Australia, Blanchett originally studied fine arts and economics at the University of Melbourne before shifting to acting at the National Institute of Dramatic Art, from which she graduated in 1992.

Blanchett launched her career on the Australian stage, quickly earning recognition for her performances with the Sydney Theatre Company in productions such as *Kafka Dances*, *Oleanna*, and *Top Girls*. Her international breakthrough came with *Elizabeth* (1998), where she played Queen Elizabeth I—a role that earned her a Golden Globe and her first Academy Award nomination.

She gained further recognition portraying the elf queen Galadriel in *The Lord of the Rings* trilogy (2001–2003), returning to the role in *The Hobbit* series. Blanchett won her first Oscar for Best Supporting Actress for her portrayal of Katharine Hepburn in *The Aviator* (2004) and her second, for Best Actress, in *Blue Jasmine* (2013).

She has also starred in *Notes on a Scandal* (2006), *I'm Not There* (2007), *Carol* (2015), and *Tár* (2022), which earned her widespread acclaim as a fictional orchestra conductor facing personal and professional turmoil.

Her television credits include *Mrs. America* (2020), where she portrayed conservative activist Phyllis Schlafly. Blanchett also served as co-CEO and artistic director of the Sydney Theatre Company from 2008 to 2013.

Outside of her artistic achievements, Blanchett advocates for humanitarian and environmental causes. She has served as a UNHCR Goodwill Ambassador since 2016 and received the Crystal Award at the World Economic Forum in 2018.

Blanchett's dedication to craft and conscience makes her one of modern cinema's most influential and respected artists.

ABOVE

Cate Blanchett exudes modern elegance in a tailored grey suit with a plunging neckline at the world premiere of *The Lord of the Rings: The War of the Rohirrim* in London, December 2024.

RIGHT

Cate Blanchett in *Carol* (2015), wrapped in a sweeping fur coat with a silk blouse and cinched belt—her poised elegance and 1950s sophistication captured in a moment of quiet resolve.

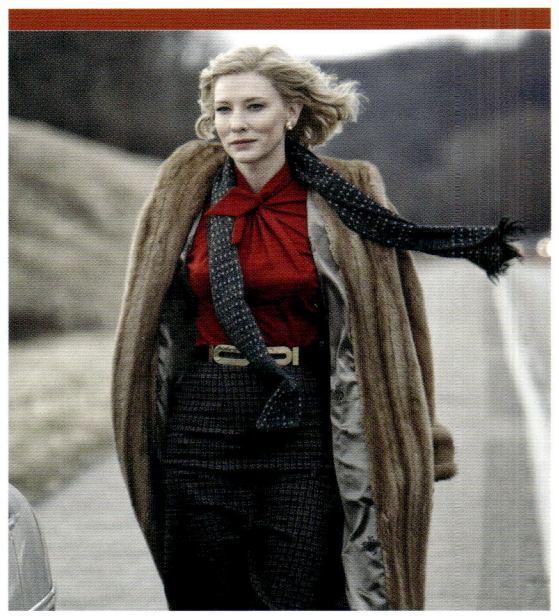

FASHION FEATURES

ELIZABETH (1998)
LORD OF THE RINGS TRILOGY (2001)
THE AVIATOR (2004)
THE CURIOUS CASE OF BENJAMIN BUTTON (2008)
CAROL (2015)

The Blanchett Look

A red-carpet favorite, Blanchett likes gowns with a little oomph—ruffles, embroidery, trains, or unusual necklines. Out of the public eye, she prefers a more relaxed look for her frequent travels with her playwright husband, Andrew Upton, and their four children.

- Gowns with lavish skirts or eye-catching embroidery
- Suede or leather jackets
- High boots and jeans

SANDRA BULLOCK

FASHION FEATURES

MISS CONGENIALITY (2000)
TWO WEEKS NOTICE (2002)
THE PROPOSAL (2009)
THE BLIND SIDE (2009)

The Bullock Look

The actress has always preferred flattering, feminine separates and classic, unfussy evening gowns.

- Voile or chiffon tops
- Pastel or neutral-colored gowns with natural lines
- Tailored suits with feminine blouses

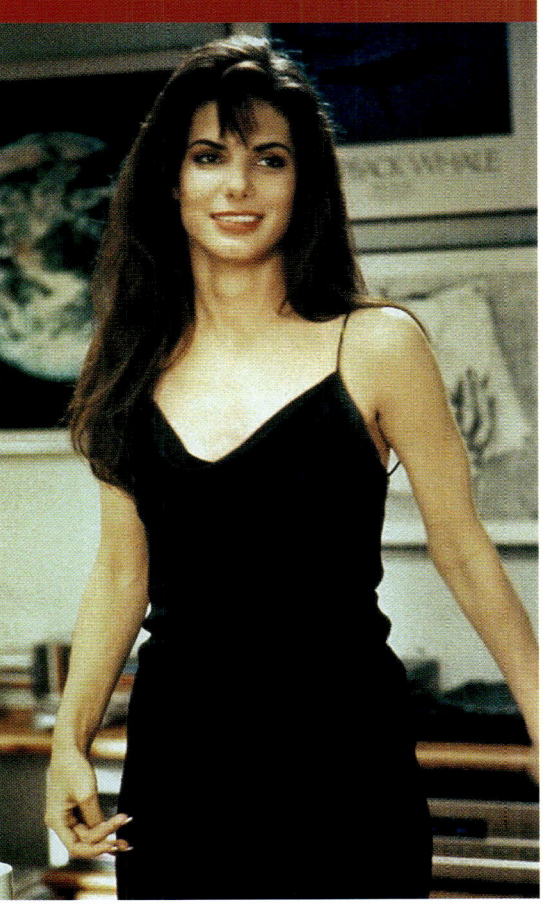

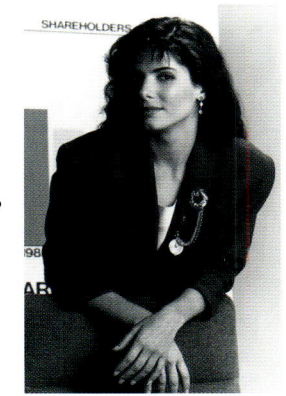

With charm, resilience, and comedic brilliance, Sandra Bullock has carved out a lasting image in Hollywood. Born on July 26, 1964, in Arlington, Virginia, she spent part of her childhood in Nürnberg, West Germany, performing in operas alongside her mother, a voice teacher and opera singer. After studying drama at East Carolina University, Bullock pursued acting more seriously at New York's Neighborhood Playhouse, eventually landing roles on stage and in small film and television projects.

Her film debut came with *Hangmen* (1987), but it was her breakout performance in the action blockbuster *Speed* (1994) that made her a household name. She followed this success with standout roles in *While You Were Sleeping* (1995), *A Time to Kill* (1996), and *Hope Floats* (1998), showcasing her talent in both drama and romantic comedy.

Bullock continued her rise with hits such as *Miss Congeniality* (2000), *Two Weeks Notice* (2002), and *The Proposal* (2009). Her performance in *The Blind Side* (2009) as Leigh Anne Tuohy earned her the Academy Award for Best Actress. In *Gravity* (2013), she delivered a gripping performance that earned her another Oscar nomination.

Outside of acting, Bullock founded Fortis Films and served as producer on several of her projects. Her philanthropic work includes major donations to disaster relief efforts and support for children's and education charities.

Recognized for her versatility, down-to-earth persona, and wide-ranging performances, Bullock earned a star on the Hollywood Walk of Fame in 2005 and remains one of the industry's most beloved talents.

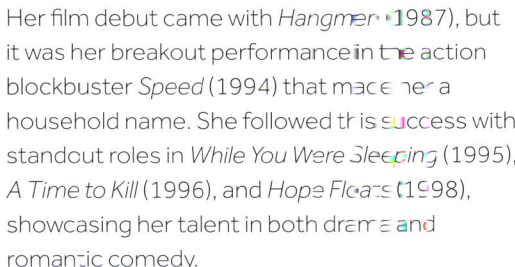

ABOVE

Sandra Bullock's breakout role came in *Speed* (1994), where she starred opposite Keanu Reeves. The film's massive success launched her into stardom and established her as a leading lady in Hollywood.

LEFT

Sandra Bullock's waiflike appeal in her early films was accentuated by her wardrobe choices of feminine, slightly mismatched separates and man-tailored outerwear.

LEADING MEN
KEANU REEVES

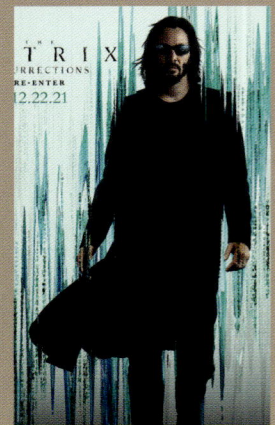

In the 1990s, Keanu Reeves rose from indie obscurity to global fame, becoming one of the most intriguing and stylish figures in Hollywood. Although his fashion choices may not have screamed red-carpet glamor, his offbeat, understated style made him a quiet icon of the decade. Often dressed in worn-in denim, beat-up boots, flannel shirts, and simple black tees, Reeves effortlessly channeled the grunge spirit that defined the early 90s. He was never one for showy designer labels—instead, he favored comfort, authenticity, and pieces that looked lived-in. Whether photographed with his band Dogstar or promoting blockbuster films, he stayed true to his unpretentious look.

During press tours and premieres, Reeves occasionally cleaned up in minimalist suits, often in charcoal, brown, or classic black, pairing them with a modest tie or none at all. His shoulder-length hair and brooding gaze became signature features, contributing to a sense of effortless cool. In contrast to the flashy excesses of other '90s stars, Keanu's fashion presence was refreshingly grounded and relatable. He made normcore look cinematic.

Born in Lebanon in 1964 and raised in Toronto, Reeves began acting in Canadian television before breaking into film. His breakthrough role came with *Bill & Ted's Excellent Adventure* (1989), but the '90s cemented his stardom with hits such as *Point Break* (1991), *Speed* (1994), and *The Matrix* (1999). The decade showcased his versatility, moving from action to indie dramas such as *My Own Private Idaho* (1991), where he starred opposite River Phoenix.

ABOVE

Keanu Reeves returns as Neo in *The Matrix Resurrections* (2021), cloaked in digital code and destiny—long-haired, trench-clad, and striding through the glitch of myth and memory.

TOP RIGHT

Keanu Reeves performs with Dogstar, 2023—bearded, tousled, and introspective, gripping a weathered bass under festival lights, blending grunge-era authenticity with enduring rock-star mystique.

BOTTOM RIGHT

Keanu Reeves flashes a carefree grin as Ted in *Bill & Ted's Bogus Journey* (1991)—center-parted hair, layered flannel, and the enduring charm of slacker optimism.

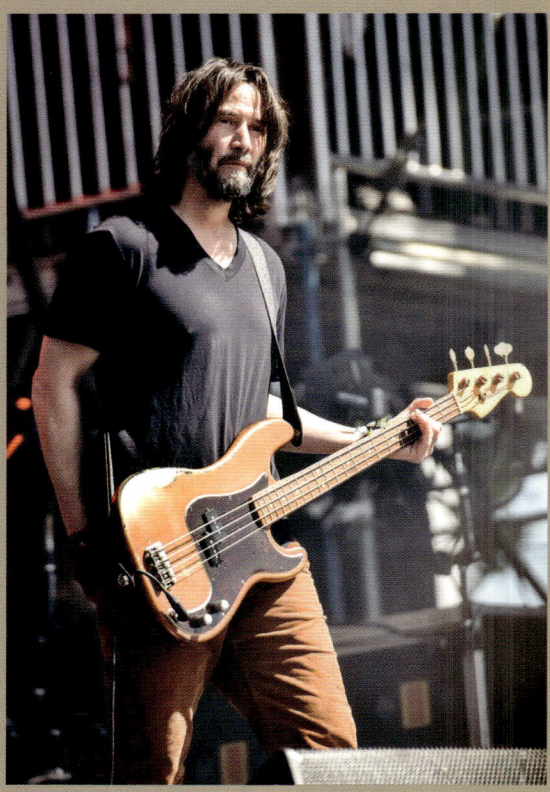

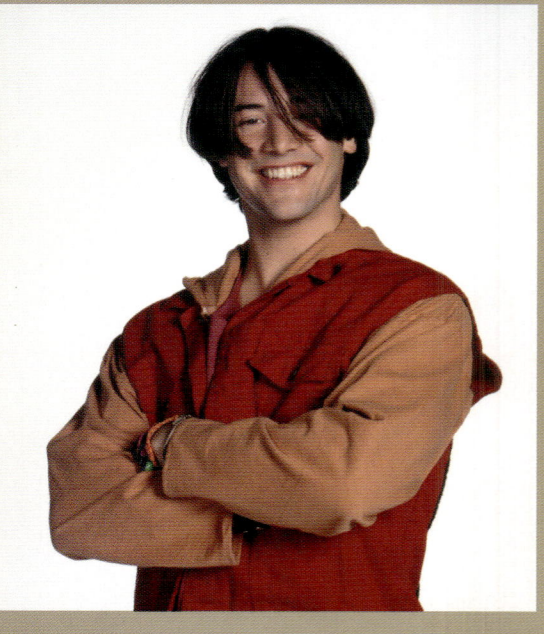

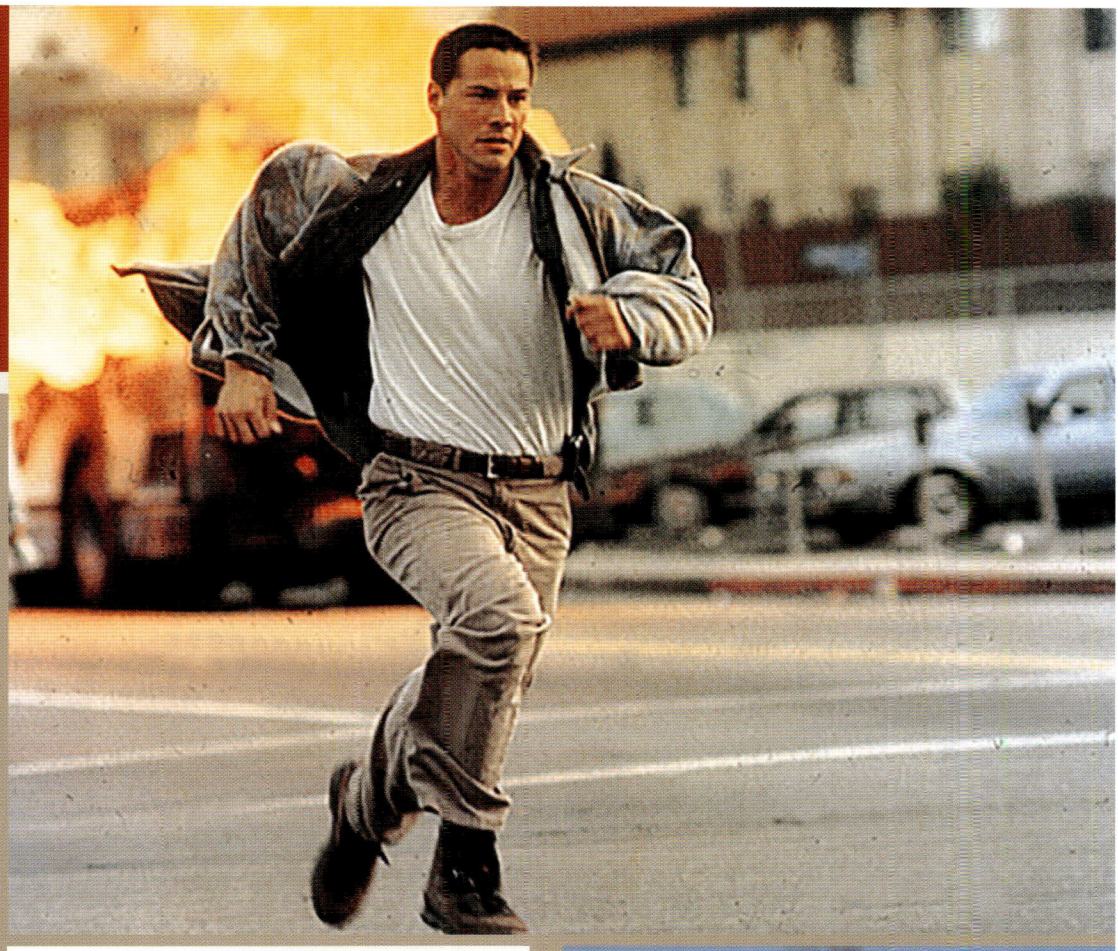

Luxury is the opportunity to experience quality, be it a place, a person or an object.

KEANU REEVES

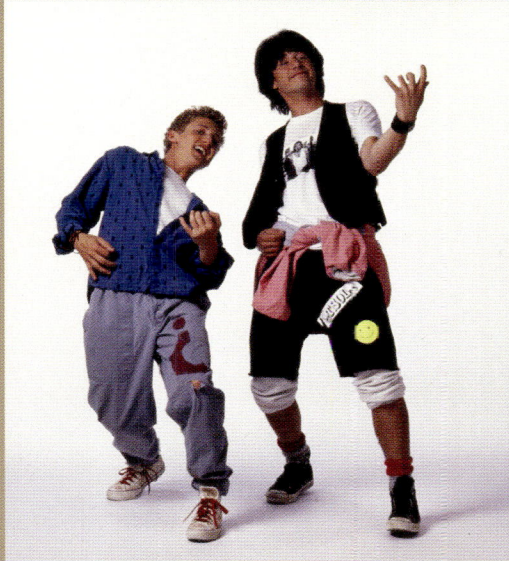

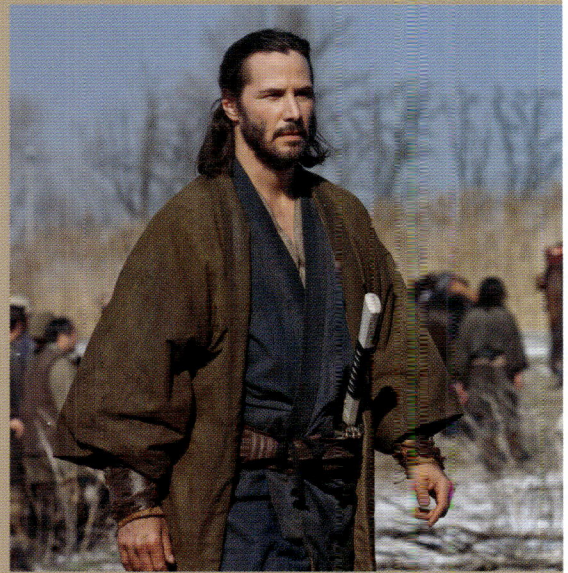

Despite his fame, Reeves remained elusive, avoiding the celebrity spotlight and maintaining a reputation for humility and generosity. Tragedy marked his personal life, including the stillbirth of his daughter and the loss of his longtime partner, Jennifer Syme, in 2001. Yet through hardship, his quiet resilience only deepened his public appeal.

Reeves has never released a traditional autobiography, but glimpses into his life have been shared through interviews, biographies, and documentaries. His enigmatic charm, coupled with a distinct sense of style rooted in sincerity rather than spectacle, made him a defining figure of 1990s Hollywood—both on-screen and on the sidewalk. In an era of excess, Keanu Reeves made simplicity a statement.

TOP LEFT

Keanu Reeves sprints from a fiery explosion as Jack Traven in *Speed* (1994)—white tee, tactical boots, and raw adrenaline in a pulse-pounding action classic.

BOTTOM LEFT

Keanu Reeves as Ted "Theodore" Logan in *Bill & Ted's Excellent Adventure* (1989)—slouchy, smiley-stickered, and air-guitaring his way into Gen X cult stardom.

BOTTOM RIGHT

Keanu Reeves as Kai in *47 Ronin* (2013), robed and resolute, strides through frost-dusted fields—an outsider samurai etched in mythic quietude and cinematic stoicism.

CAMERON DIAZ

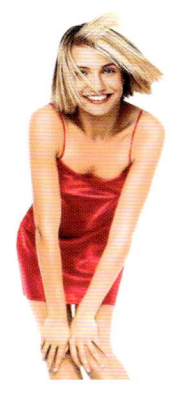

I'm like every other woman: a closet full of clothes, but nothing to wear. So I wear jeans.

CAMERON DIAZ

Cameron Diaz became one of Hollywood's most bankable stars through her blend of comic timing, radiant charm, and versatility. Born on August 30, 1972, in San Diego, California, she was raised in Long Beach and began modeling at 16, landing campaigns for major brands such as Calvin Klein and Levi's through Elite Model Management.

At 21, without prior acting experience, Diaz made a striking debut opposite Jim Carrey in *The Mask* (1994), a performance that catapulted her into stardom. She followed with standout roles in *My Best Friend's Wedding* (1997) and *There's Something About Mary* (1998), the latter earning her a Golden Globe nomination and cementing her status as a comedic lead.

Proving her range, Diaz took on edgier roles in *Being John Malkovich* (1999), *Any Given Sunday* (1999), and *Vanilla Sky* (2001). She voiced Princess Fiona in the hugely successful *Shrek* series (2001–2010), broadening her global appeal.

Her diverse credits also include *Charlie's Angels* (2000), *Gangs of New York* (2002), *The Holiday* (2006), and *Bad Teacher* (2011). After stepping away from acting in 2014, Diaz focused on wellness, co-authoring two health books and co-founding Avaline, an organic wine label.

In 2022, she announced her comeback in *Back in Action* (2025). Diaz is married to musician Benji Madden and is a mother of two.

ABOVE
———
Cameron Diaz became a breakout star with *There's Something About Mary* (1998), redefining romantic comedy with effortless humor.

RIGHT
———
Cameron Diaz starred in *My Best Friend's Wedding* (1997), earning praise for her comedic timing and refreshing take on the runaway bride trope.

FASHION FEATURES

THE MASK (1994)
MY BEST FRIEND'S WEDDING (1997)
CHARLIE'S ANGELS (2000)
IN HER SHOES (2005)

The Diaz Look

Whether she is glamming it up in couture gowns and designer shoes in a *Vogue* feature, or clomping around Hollywood in her Ugg boots, sweater, and jeans, Diaz seems to have discovered the fountain of youth.

• Solid-color gowns, especially black, red, dove gray, and nude
• Ankle boots or high leather boots
• Statement earrings and long scarves

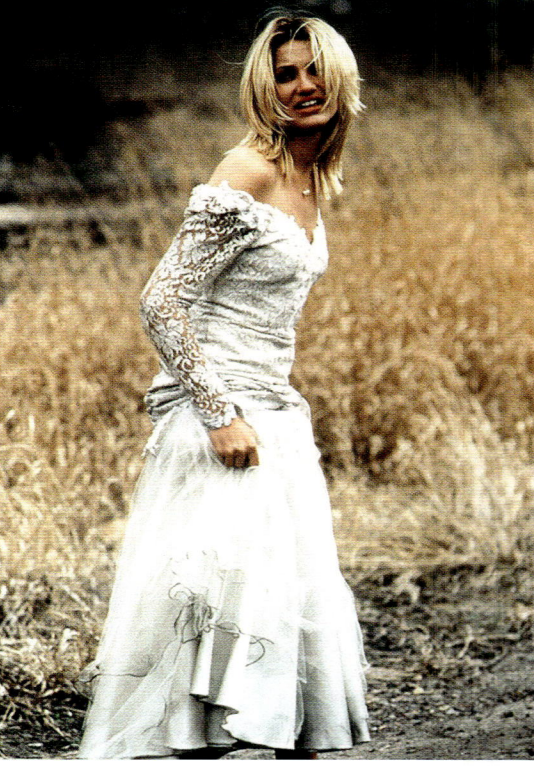

NICOLE KIDMAN

FASHION FEATURES

BATMAN FOREVER (1995)
THE PORTRAIT OF A LADY (1996)
MOULIN ROUGE! (2001)
AUSTRALIA (2008)
QUEEN OF THE DESERT (2015)

The Kidman Look

The camellia-skinned redhead varies her look between masses of natural curls and sleek upsweeps.

- Sheath gowns, often with an ethnic twist
- Lacy, feminine dresses
- Tailored jackets with boyish trousers

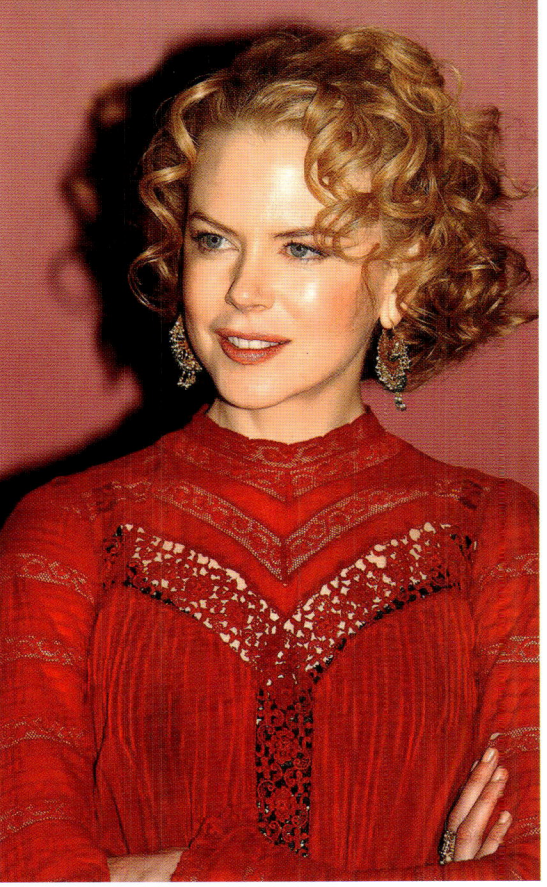

Nicole Kidman's ability to inhabit a wide range of characters has made her one of the most distinguished actresses in international cinema. Born on June 20, 1967, in Honolulu, Hawaii, to Australian parents, she was raised in Sydney, where she began acting as a teenager. Early roles in *Bush Christmas* and *BMX Bandits* (both 1983) marked her screen debut, but it was her chilling performance in *Dead Calm* (1989) that signaled her pivotal role. She soon gained international attention through the miniseries *Bangkok Hilton* and her Hollywood debut in *Days of Thunder* (1990) alongside Tom Cruise.

Kidman's filmography spans genres, earning her acclaim in both commercial hits and arthouse projects. She won critical praise for *To Die For* (1995) and achieved widespread recognition with *Moulin Rouge!* (2001) and *The Others* (2001). In 2002, she received the Academy Award for Best Actress for her portrayal of Virginia Woolf in *The Hours*. Her notable later roles include *Cold Mountain* (2003), *Lion* (2016), and *Being the Ricardos* (2021).

On television, Kidman starred in and produced acclaimed series such as *Big Little Lies* (2017–2019), *The Undoing* (2020), and *Nine Perfect Strangers* (2021), which earned her two Primetime Emmys.

She co-founded the production company Blossom Films and serves as a Goodwill Ambassador for UNICEF and UN Women, advocating for children's rights and gender equality.

In 2024, Kidman became the first Australian to receive the American Film Institute Life Achievement Award, a testament to her global influence, artistry, and enduring legacy in film and television.

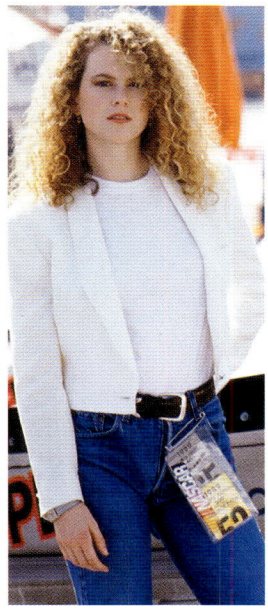

You don't have to be naked to be sexy.

NICOLE KIDMAN

ABOVE

Nicole Kidman gained widespread recognition for her role in *Days of Thunder* (1990), where she starred alongside future husband Tom Cruise.

LEFT

Nicole Kidman, in crimson lace and cascading curls, attends the *Cold Mountain* premiere (2003)—a vision of Victorian romance reimagined through contemporary glamor and restrained theatrical poise.

JENNIFER LOPEZ

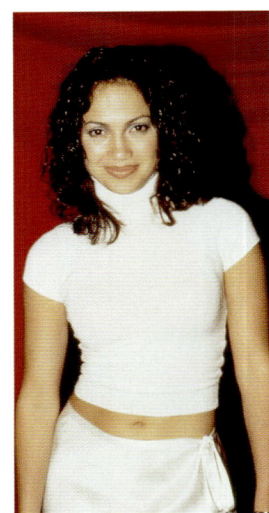

A powerhouse of talent and ambition, Jennifer Lopez rose from humble beginnings in the Bronx to become one of the most influential multi-hyphenate entertainers in the world. Born on July 24, 1969, to Puerto Rican parents, Lopez showed early passion for the performing arts, training in singing, dancing, and acting. Her first major exposure came in 1991 as a "Fly Girl" dancer on the hit sketch comedy show _In Living Color_.

Lopez transitioned into film with roles in _Jack_ (1996) and _Blood and Wine_ (1997), but it was her portrayal of the beloved Tejano singer in _Selena_ (1997) that marked her breakthrough. The role earned her a Golden Globe nomination and positioned her as a rising star. She went on to appear in action and romantic comedies, including _Anaconda_ (1997), _Out of Sight_ (1998), and _The Wedding Planner_ (2001).

Parallelly, Lopez launched a hugely successful music career. Her debut album, _On the 6_ (1999), produced hits such as "If You Had My Love," and in 2001, she became the first woman to have a No. 1 film and album in the same week. Subsequent albums such as _This Is Me..., Then_ (2002), and _Love?_ (2011) solidified her status as a global pop icon.

Beyond entertainment, Lopez built a fashion and fragrance empire and continues to be involved in philanthropy through the Lopez Family Foundation. Her acclaimed role in _Hustlers_ (2019) and Super Bowl halftime performance in 2020 further cemented her status as a cultural force with a lasting impact.

ABOVE

Jennifer Lopez made history in 2001 as the first woman to have a number one album and film simultaneously.

RIGHT

Jennifer Lopez broke through with her role in _Selena_ (1997), becoming the first Latina actress to earn $1 million for a film.

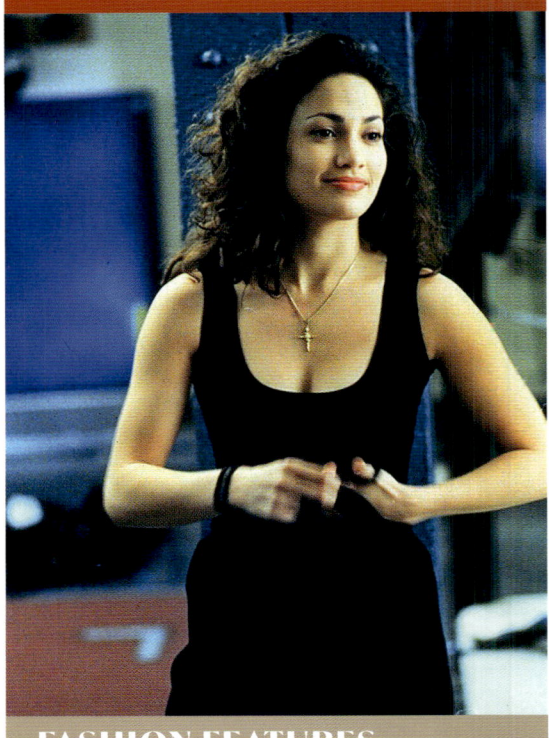

FASHION FEATURES

OUT OF SIGHT (1998)
THE CELL (2000)
THE WEDDING PLANNER (2001)
MAID IN MANHATTAN (2002)
SHALL WE DANCE (2004)
THE BACK-UP PLAN (2010)

The Lopez Look

This Latina icon is proud of her womanly curves and likes showing them off in eye-popping outfits. Lopez has her own clothing, accessory, and perfume line and has inspired the look of other performers for years.

- Plunging necklines
- Form-fitting workout suits with couture labels
- Sexy, sky-high heels

GWYNETH PALTROW

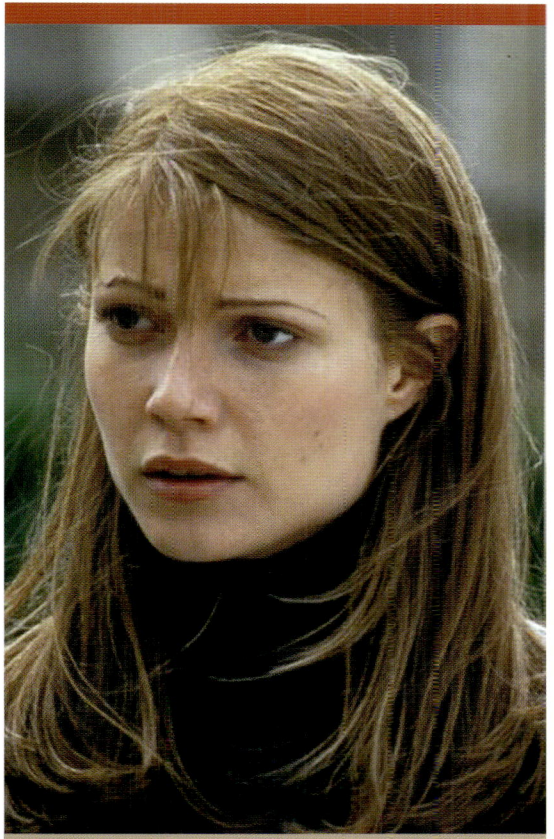

FASHION FEATURES

EMMA (1996)
SHAKESPEARE IN LOVE (1998)
THE TALENTED MR. RIPLEY (1999)
THE ROYAL TENENBAUMS (2001)
POSSESSION (2002)
IRON MAN (2008)

The Paltrow Look

The actress enjoys showing off her shapely legs, and frequently wears micro-minidresses with stiletto heels.

- Simple, unadorned dresses and trouser suits
- Classic high heels
- Long, straight, ash-blonde hair

Gwyneth Paltrow has successfully navigated a multifaceted career as an Oscar-winning actress, lifestyle entrepreneur, and pop culture icon. Born on September 27, 1972, in Los Angeles, California, she was immersed in the entertainment industry from an early age—her mother, Blythe Danner, is an acclaimed actress, and her father, Bruce Paltrow, was a respected producer and director.

Paltrow began acting on stage at 18 and gained early recognition with film roles in *Flesh and Bone* (1993) and *Se7en* (1995). Her landmark performance came in *Emma* (1996), and she solidified her star status by winning the Academy Award for Best Actress in *Shakespeare in Love* (1998).

She continued her momentum with roles in *The Talented Mr. Ripley* (1999), *The Royal Tenenbaums* (2001), and *Proof* (2005). In 2008, she joined the *Marvel Cinematic Universe* as Pepper Potts, a role she reprised through *Avengers: Endgame* (2019), earning international fan acclaim.

That same year, Paltrow launched Goop, a wellness and lifestyle brand that grew into a major business enterprise. Although often controversial, Goop positioned itself as a leading voice in modern wellness culture.

She shares two children with her ex-husband Chris Martin and married TV producer Brad Falchuk in 2018. Today, Paltrow balances her creative work with entrepreneurial ventures, continuing to influence both Hollywood and the wellness world.

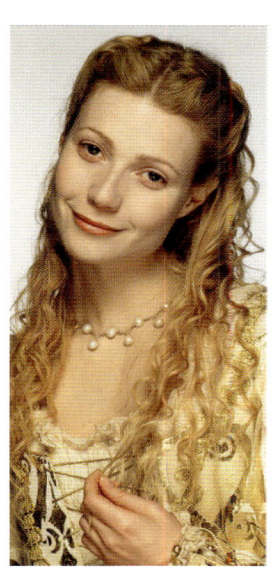

ABOVE

Gwyneth Paltrow won the Academy Award for Best Actress for her role in *Shakespeare in Love* (1998), captivating audiences with wit and elegance.

LEFT

Gwyneth Paltrow gained critical acclaim for *Sliding Doors* (1998), where her dual-role performance explored fate, timing, and alternate realities with minimalist 90s fashion to match.

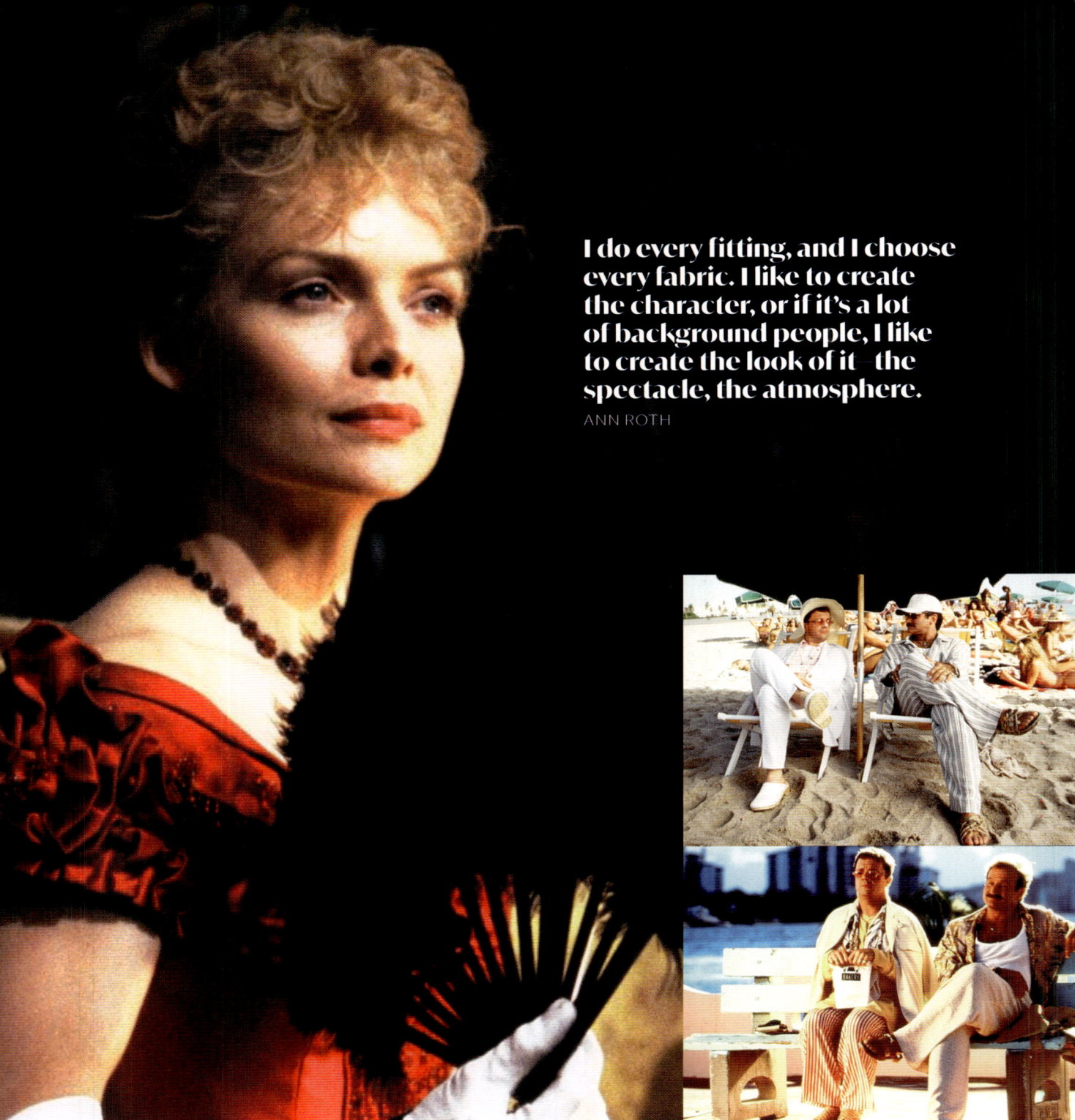

> **I do every fitting, and I choose every fabric. I like to create the character, or if it's a lot of background people, I like to create the look of it—the spectacle, the atmosphere.**
> ANN ROTH

FULL PAGE

Michelle Pfeiffer in *The Age of Innocence* (1993), wearing a richly detailed scarlet gown designed by Ann Roth. The off-the-shoulder bodice, full skirt, and white opera gloves evoke the rigid elegance of Gilded Age society. With a black feather fan and restrained expression, the look captures the constraint of a woman navigating social exile.

TOP RIGHT INSERT

In *The Birdcage* (1996), Ann Roth costumes Robin Williams and Nathan Lane in sun-bleached resortwear—striped linen, crisp white suiting, and camp accessories channeling Palm Beach theatricality with tailored precision.

BOTTOM RIGHT INSERT

Ann Roth's costume design in *The Birdcage* (1996) radiates Florida flair—bold stripes, layered linens, and pastel prints capturing queerness, comfort, and quiet rebellion in sunlit symmetry.

Academy Awards

Roth won the Oscar for *The English Patient*, and was nominated for *Places in the Heart*, *The Talented Mr. Ripley*, and *The Hours*.

Fashion Legacy

- Costumes for sex workers, con artists, and drifters
- Rigorous attention to detail
- Forensic approach to researching period clothing

DESIGN SENSE
ANN ROTH

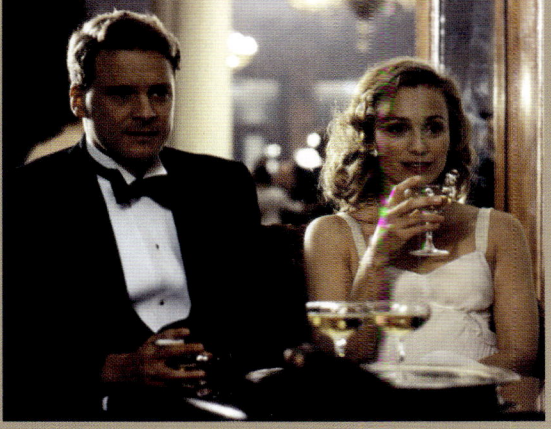
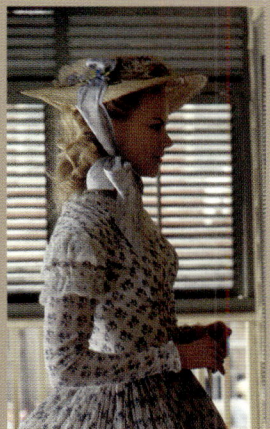

Ann Roth is someone who uses fabric, silhouette, and detail to convey a character's tale before even a single word is spoken. Born on October 30, 1931, in Hanover, Pennsylvania, Roth has become a towering figure in the world of costume design, celebrated for her unmatched ability to infuse clothing with narrative purpose. Her career, which spans over six decades, has redefined how costumes shape character and deepen storytelling in both film and theater.

Originally trained in scenic design at Carnegie Mellon University, Roth shifted to costume work after an apprenticeship with iconic designer Irene Sharaff. She began her career in earnest with *The World of Henry Orient* (1964) and went on to collaborate with some of cinema's most respected directors, including Mike Nichols, Martin Scorsese, Anthony Minghella, and Stephen Daldry.

Roth's cinematic highlights include *Midnight Cowboy* (1969), *Silkwood* (1983), *The English Patient* (1996), *The Hours* (2002), *Cold Mountain* (2003), and *Ma Rainey's Black Bottom* (2020). She earned her first Academy Award for *The English Patient* and, at age 89, won her second for *Ma Rainey's Black Bottom*, making her the oldest woman ever to win an Oscar.

Her influence extends beyond the screen. In the theater, Roth has designed for more than 100 Broadway and Off-Broadway productions, including *The Odd Couple, Hurlyburly, The Book of Mormon,* and *Shuffle Along.* Her work has earned her multiple Tony Award nominations and lasting admiration from the stage community, further cementing her place among the most influential figures in American theater.

What distinguishes Roth is her method: intensive research, emotional intuition, and precise craftsmanship. She selects every element—from buttons to hems—with an eye toward historical authenticity and psychological truth. To Roth, costume design is never decoration—it's essential storytelling.

Roth continues to work well into her nineties, mentoring young designers and shaping the next era of visual storytelling through her wisdom, discipline, and boundless creativity.

With a legacy that bridges generations and mediums, Ann Roth continues to inspire designers and captivate audiences. Her work remains a masterclass in how clothing can speak volumes without saying a word.

MOST FASHIONABLE DESIGNS

MIDNIGHT COWBOY (1969)
KLUTE (1971)
THE BIRDCAGE (1996)
THE ENGLISH PATIENT (1996)
THE TALENTED MR. RIPLEY (1999)
THE HOURS (2002)

ABOVE RIGHT

In *Cold Mountain* (2003), Ann Roth's costume design captures 1860s Southern restraint—floral calico, lace cuffs, and bonneted elegance reflecting Ada's vulnerability and rural transformation.

ABOVE LEFT

In *The English Patient* (1996), Ann Roth's refined costuming—silk slip, bow-tied tuxedo—elevates this candlelit moment into a study of wartime elegance and aching restraint.

JULIA ROBERTS

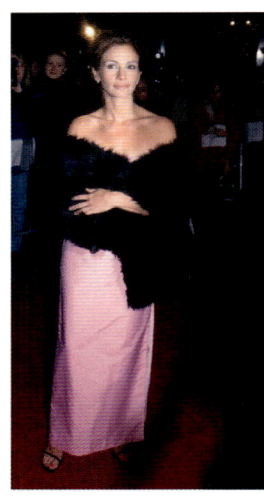

Gifted with a dazzling smile and adept at playing both drama and comedy, Julia Roberts has become one of the most recognizable and enduring stars in Hollywood. Born Julia Fiona Roberts on October 28, 1967, in Smyrna, Georgia, she was raised in a creative household and moved to New York to pursue acting after high school. She made her screen debut in the late 1980s, capturing attention with her role in *Mystic Pizza* (1988). A year later, she earned critical acclaim and an Academy Award nomination for Best Supporting Actress in *Steel Magnolias* (1989).

Her career skyrocketed with *Pretty Woman* (1990), where her portrayal of Vivian Ward charmed audiences worldwide and earned her a second Oscar nomination. Throughout the 1990s, Roberts became a household name, starring in hits such as *Sleeping with the Enemy* (1991), *The Pelican Brief* (1993), *My Best Friend's Wedding* (1997), *Notting Hill* (1999), and *Runaway Bride* (1999).

In 2000, she won the Academy Award for Best Actress for her role in Erin Brockovich, a performance praised for its depth and conviction. She continued to take on diverse roles in *Ocean's Eleven* (2001), *Closer* (2004), *Charlie Wilson's War* (2007), *Eat Pray Love* (2010), and *August: Osage County* (2013), which earned her another Oscar nomination.

Roberts has also worked in television, starring in *Homecoming* (2018) and *Gaslit* (2022). A devoted philanthropist, she supports causes such as UNICEF and Conservation International. Married to Daniel Moder since 2002, she is a mother of three and remains a beloved Hollywood icon.

ABOVE

Julia Roberts, radiant in blush satin and a black fur stole, graces the red carpet circa late '90s—timeless elegance framed by flashbulbs and effortless star magnetism.

RIGHT

Julia Roberts, in cutout mini and thigh-high boots, strides into cinematic legend as Vivian Ward in *Pretty Woman* (1990)—a pop-culture silhouette of boldness, grit, and charm.

FASHION FEATURES

PRETTY WOMAN (1990)
NOTTING HILL (1999)
CHARLIE WILSON'S WAR (2007)
EAT PRAY LOVE (2010)

The Roberts Look

This "*Pretty Woman*" conveys a relaxed style that incorporates touches of preppy classics mixed with slightly boho touches.

- Feminine Indo-Asian separates with ethnic jewelry
- Pastel twin sets
- Form-fitting gowns in rich fabrics

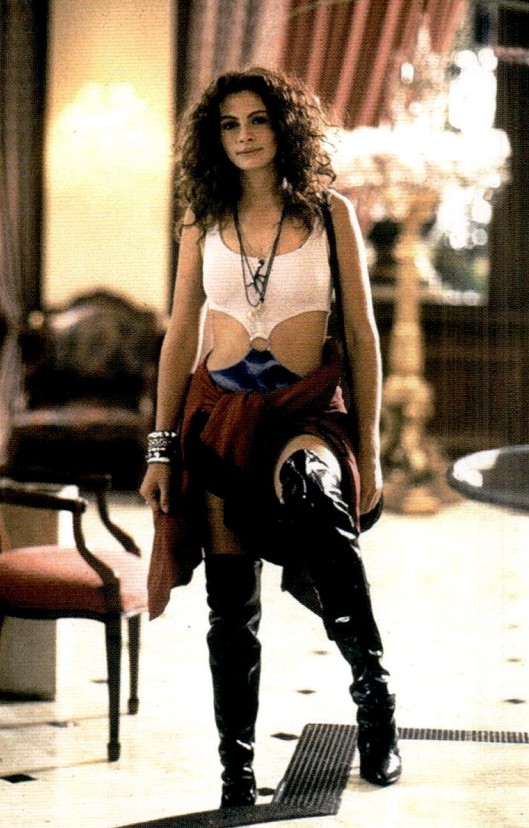

MEG RYAN

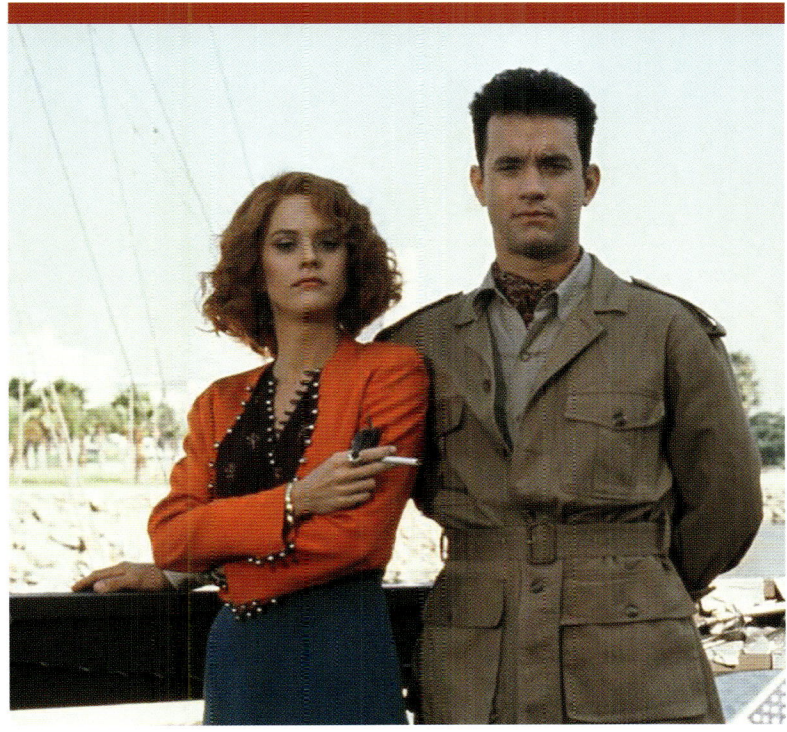

Often dubbed "America's sweetheart," Meg Ryan became the face of romantic comedies in the late twentieth century with her warm charm and expressive performances. Born on November 19, 1961, in Fairfield, Connecticut, she began acting in the early 1980s, appearing in commercials, soap operas, and supporting film roles.

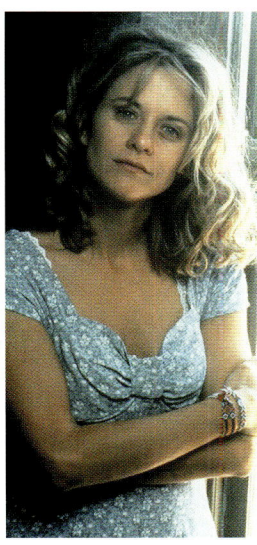

FASHION FEATURES

WHEN HARRY MET SALLY ... (1989)
SLEEPLESS IN SEATTLE (1993)
FRENCH KISS (1995)
THE WOMEN (2008)

The Ryan Look

Her loosely preppy style layers classic pieces—cardigans or wool blazers—over more casual separates such as jeans, ethnic skirts, and T-shirts.

- Short, scrunched blonde hair
- Tailored khakis with sweaters
- Severely plain, form-fitting evening gowns

Her breakthrough came with *When Harry Met Sally...* (1989), a career-defining performance that earned her a Golden Globe nomination and positioned her as a beloved leading actress. The 1990s saw Ryan headline a series of popular romantic comedies including *Sleepless in Seattle* (1993), *French Kiss* (1995), and *You've Got Mail* (1998), often portraying independent, witty women with emotional depth. Her recurring collaborations with Tom Hanks became iconic.

Ryan also starred in dramas such as *Courage Under Fire* (1996) and *City of Angels* (1998). She stepped behind the camera in 2015 to direct *Ithaca*, in which she also acted, and returned to both directing and acting with *What Happens Later* (2023).

Ryan shares a son, actor Jack Quaid, with former husband Dennis Quaid, and adopted a daughter, Daisy True, in 2006.

ABOVE

Meg Ryan became America's sweetheart in the 1990s with hits like *When Harry Met Sally...*, *Sleepless in Seattle*, and *You've Got Mail*, becoming one of Hollywood's top-grossing romantic comedy actresses.

LEFT

Meg Ryan starred alongside Tom Hanks for the first time in *Joe Versus the Volcano* (1990), where she impressively played three different characters, showcasing her versatility and comedic charm.

SETTING TRENDS
OUR FAVORITE
BRUNETTES

They've played spies and temptresses, exotic sirens and glamorous divas, fiery rebels, loyal friends, and steadfast wives.

Always captivating—sometimes smoldering, often bold—Hollywood's most celebrated brunettes have brought intelligence, style, and presence to every role. Their appeal reaches well beyond Hollywood too, with dazzling talents from around the world defining strength and sophistication on screen.

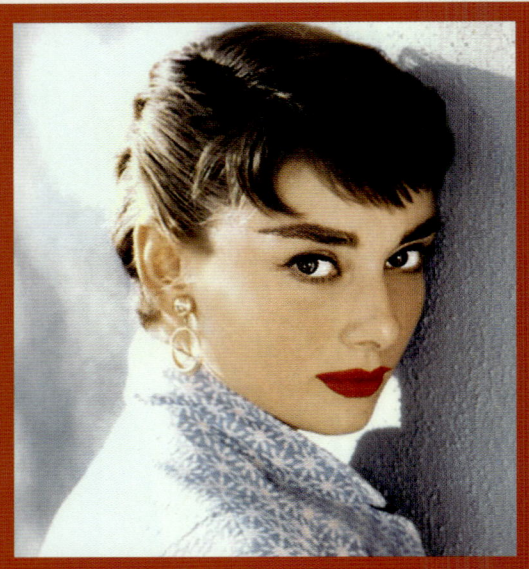

TOP RIGHT

Audrey Hepburn's dark pixie cut became as iconic as her little black dress. Her understated brunette style embodied intelligence, wit, and quiet confidence.

BOTTOM LEFT

Julia Roberts' chestnut hair and radiant charm made her one of Hollywood's most recognizable leading women. Her warmth and wit brought a modern edge to classic screen glamour.

BOTTOM RIGHT

Anne Hathaway's dark hair and expressive features evoke the classic studio-era brunette—but with a modern, accessible warmth that makes her instantly real.

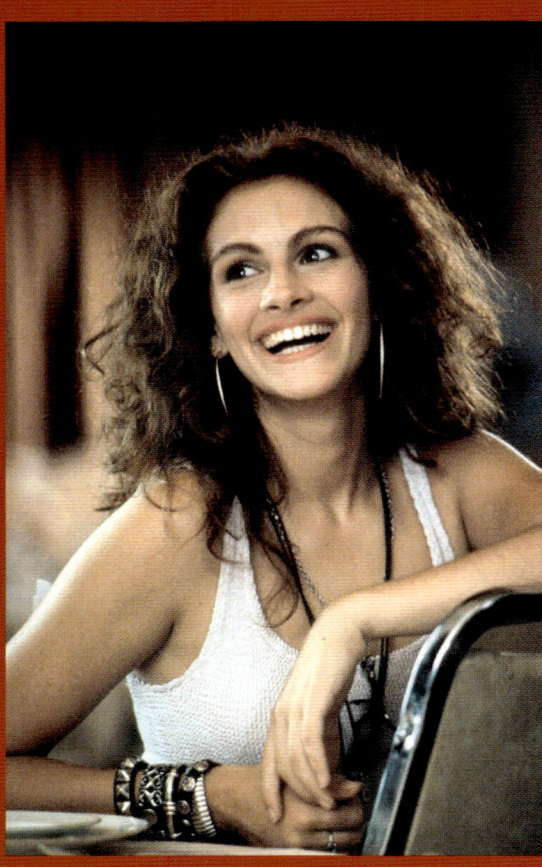

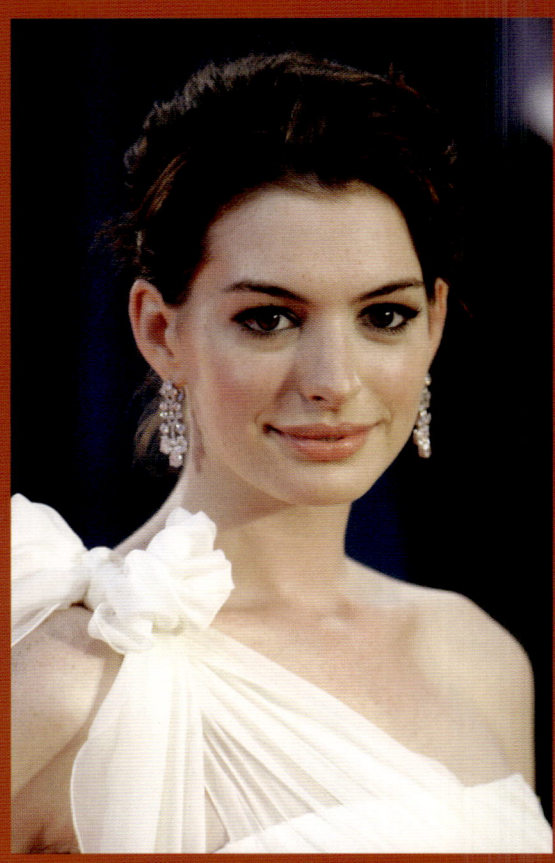

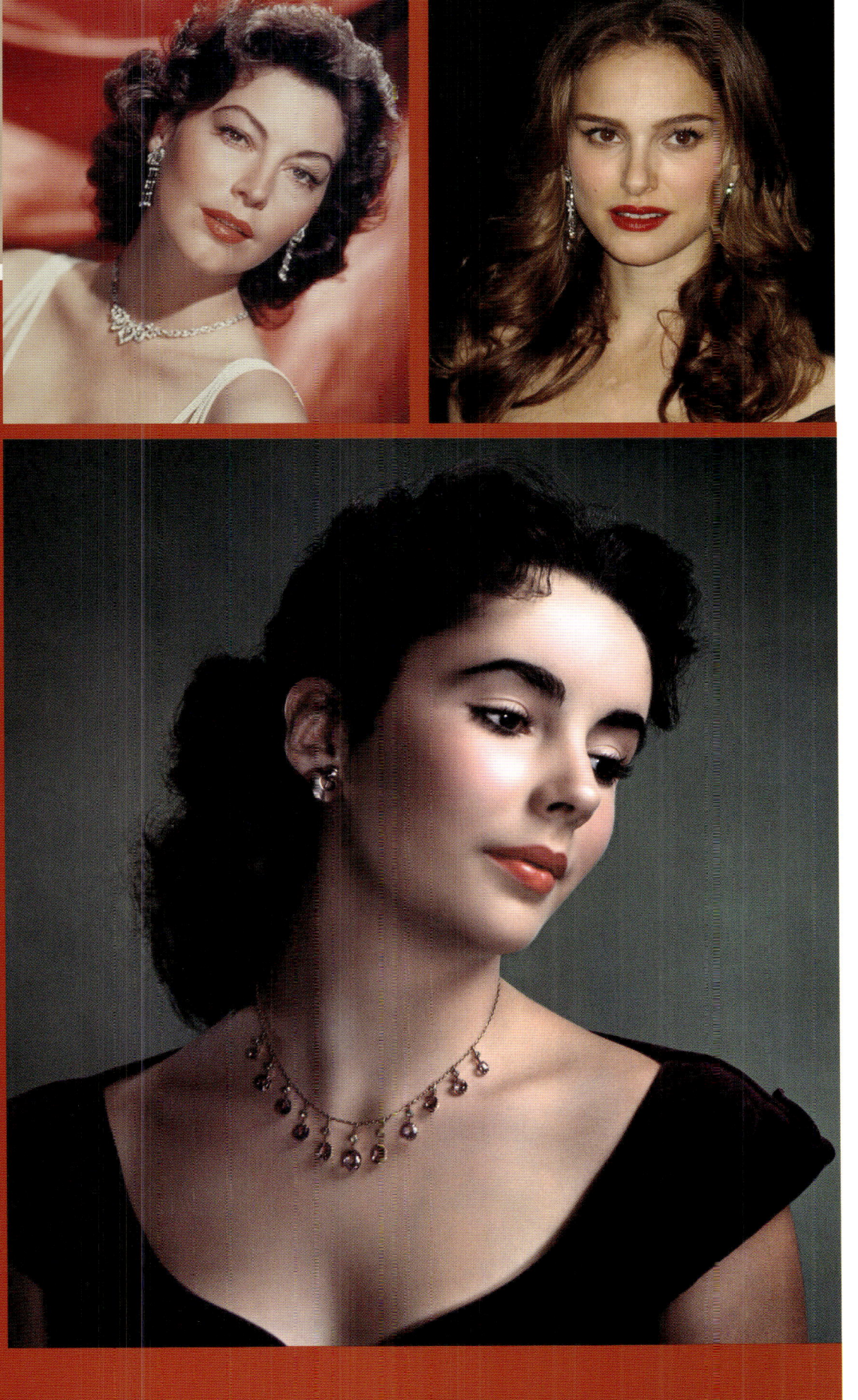

Gentlemen prefer blondes... but gentlemen marry brunettes.

ANITA LOOS

TOP LEFT

Ava Gardner's deep, glossy waves framed a face made for Technicolor. She brought heat and vitality to the brunette archetype, transforming it into something earthy and electric.

TOP RIGHT

Her natural brunette look gives Natalie Portman an honesty that grounds even her most complex roles. She carries intelligence and empathy without artifice.

LEFT

With her rich dark curls and unmistakable presence, Elizabeth Taylor proved that brunettes could radiate as much glamour as any blonde. Her dramatic power and striking beauty redefined Hollywood allure.

SHARON STONE

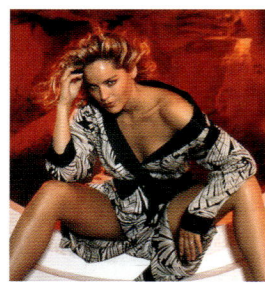

Renowned for her sharp intellect and magnetic screen presence, Sharon Stone became one of the most iconic actresses of the 1990s. Born on March 10, 1958, in Meadville, Pennsylvania, she began her career as a fashion model before pursuing acting in the early 1980s. Her early film appearances included roles in *Irreconcilable Differences* (1984) and *Above the Law* (1988), but true stardom arrived with her bold and unforgettable portrayal of Catherine Tramell in *Basic Instinct* (1992). The role earned her a Golden Globe nomination and transformed her into an international symbol of allure and complexity.

Throughout the decade, Stone starred in major films, including *Sliver* (1993), *The Specialist* (1994), and *The Quick and the Dead* (1995), working across multiple genres. Her most acclaimed role came in Martin Scorsese's *Casino* (1995), where her performance as Ginger McKenna won her a Golden Globe and an Academy Award nomination.

Stone continued her momentum with *Diabolique* (1996), *Sphere* (1998), and *The Muse* (1999), and later transitioned into television with success, earning an Emmy for her guest role on *The Practice* (2004). She also appeared in *Mosaic* (2017) and *Ratched* (2020).

Outside of acting, Stone is a dedicated humanitarian. She has worked extensively to raise awareness about HIV/AIDS and was awarded the Peace Summit Award in 2013 for her activism and advocacy.

ABOVE

Sharon Stone smolders in geometric silk and tousled waves on the *Total Recall* (1990) set—femme fatale styling against the fiery surrealism of Verhoeven's Martian dreamscape.

RIGHT

Sharon Stone, in a slinky champagne mini and stilettos, channels icy allure in a promotional portrait for *Basic Instinct* (1992)—cool seduction etched in noir modernism.

FASHION FEATURES

BASIC INSTINCT (1992)
CASINO (1995)
THE MUSE (1999)

The Stone Look

The actress still turns heads on the red carpet and can mix couture with menswear in a pinch.

- Monochromatic black or white ensembles that showcase her ash-blonde hair
- Combining menswear white shirts with couture evening skirts
- Lately seen in 1920s'-style vintage dresses, coats, and cloche hats

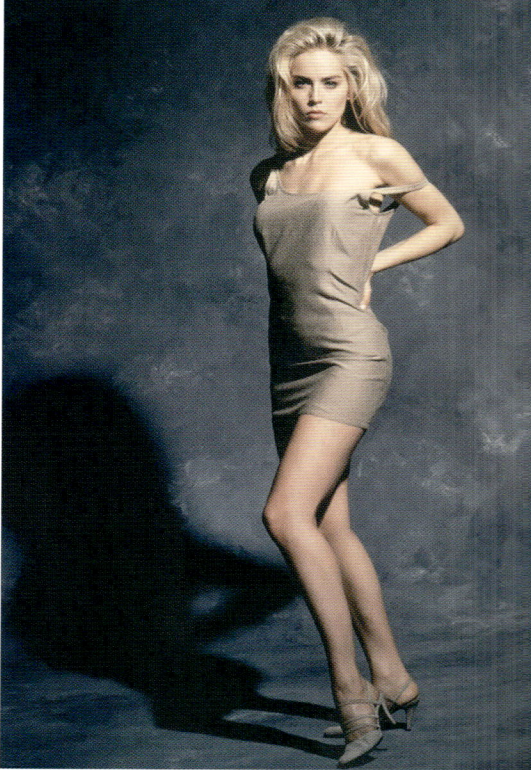

KATE WINSLET

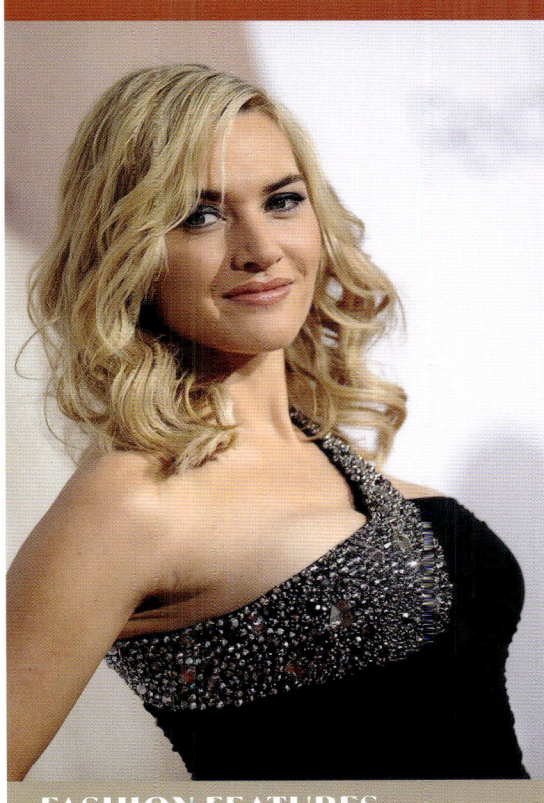

FASHION FEATURES

SENSE AND SENSIBILITY (1995)
TITANIC (1997)
ETERNAL SUNSHINE OF THE SPOTLESS
MIND (2004)
REVOLUTIONARY ROAD (2008)

The Winslet Look

After her success in *Titanic*, the softly rounded actress became a fashion inspiration for women with "average" figures. She continues to be a red carpet favorite.

- Lace or draped fitted evening gowns
- Crop pants and flats worn with an oversized sweater
- Jeans tucked into suede boots

Kate Winslet has built a remarkable career portraying emotionally complex, independent women in both period dramas and modern films. Born on October 5, 1975, in Reading, Berkshire, England, she grew up in a theatrical family and began acting in childhood, appearing in stage productions and British television. Her breakout role came in *Heavenly Creatures* (1994), directed by Peter Jackson, where she portrayed a teenager swept into a disturbing fantasy world. A year later, she earned her first Academy Award nomination for *Sense and Sensibility* (1995) for playing the passionate Marianne Dashwood.

Winslet rose to global fame in *Titanic* (1997), starring as Rose DeWitt Bukater in James Cameron's historical epic. The film's massive success solidified her reputation as a leading actress. She continued to explore challenging roles in films such as *Eternal Sunshine of the Spotless Mind* (2004), *Little Children* (2006), and *The Reader* (2008), which earned her the Academy Award for Best Actress.

Beyond films, Winslet has made a significant impact on television. She won Emmy Awards for her work in *Mildred Pierce* (2011) and *Mare of Easttown* (2021), showcasing her range on the small screen. She also received a Grammy Award for narrating *Listen to the Storyteller* (1999).

She was appointed a Commander of the Order of the British Empire (CBE) in 2012 in recognition of her contributions to drama. Continuing to challenge herself, Winslet returned to blockbuster cinema in *Avatar: The Way of Water* (2022), affirming her versatility and enduring appeal across genres.

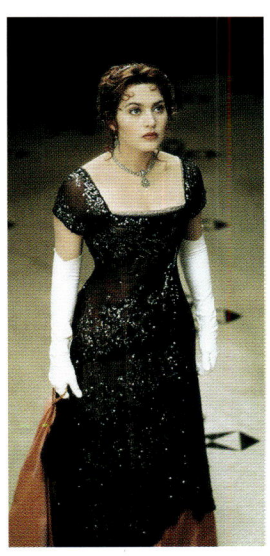

ABOVE

Kate Winslet wore over 30 different costumes in *Titanic* (1997), each meticulously designed to reflect her character Rose's transformation and social status throughout the epic historical romance film.

LEFT

Kate Winslet, radiant in a crystal-studded black gown and soft curls, arrives at the *Revolutionary Road* premiere (2008)—poised between elegance and emotional intensity.

LEADING MEN
RUGGED REBELS

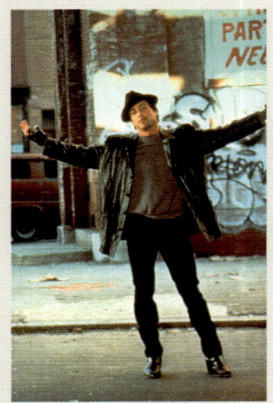

In the 1990s Hollywood, tough guys weren't just action stars—they were fashion icons of brute force and effortless edge. Quentin Tarantino's *Pulp Fiction* (1994) redefined criminal cool with John Travolta's Vincent Vega—dressed in a slim black suit, bolo tie, and greasy ponytail, exuding ironic charm and silent menace.

Arnold Schwarzenegger's *Terminator 2: Judgment Day* (1991) look—leather jacket, sunglasses, and steel-eyed silence—became a global symbol of indestructibility. His cybernetic swagger made biker gear iconic, blending machine-like power with cinematic presence. Sylvester Stallone tackled rugged terrain in *Cliffhanger* and dystopian justice in *Demolition Man*, favoring tactical vests, utility belts, and muscle-hugging tops. Jean-Claude Van Damme brought martial arts intensity to the screen in *Timecop* and *Hard Target*, his style rooted in sleeveless tees, denim, and physical bravado.

Bruce Willis personified the battered antihero in *Die Hard with a Vengeance* (1995)—his sweat-stained tank top, worn jeans, and visible frustration mirrored a man pushed beyond his limits. Meanwhile, Nicolas Cage tore through *The Rock*, *Con Air*, and *Face/Off*, pairing explosive energy with sleeveless shirts, leather, and chaos-tinged charisma.

These men weren't just taking down villains—but were shaping a masculine aesthetic defined by grit, gear, fearless attitude, and relentless, adrenaline-fueled appeal.

ABOVE
—
Sylvester Stallone, arms wide in leather and wearing a fedora, embodies underdog defiance as Rocky Balboa in *Rocky III* (1982)—a street-hardened icon forged in grit and glory.

TOP RIGHT
—
Arnold Schwarzenegger, in tactical black and leather holster, strikes a hardened pose as Harry Tasker in *True Lies* (1994)—spy thriller bravado with blockbuster brawn.

BOTTOM RIGHT
—
Actor Mickey Rourke sports a pinstripe suit and gold tie with rebellious flair at the Hollywood premiere of *The Rainmaker* (1997), embodying his signature blend of rugged edge and unconventional style.

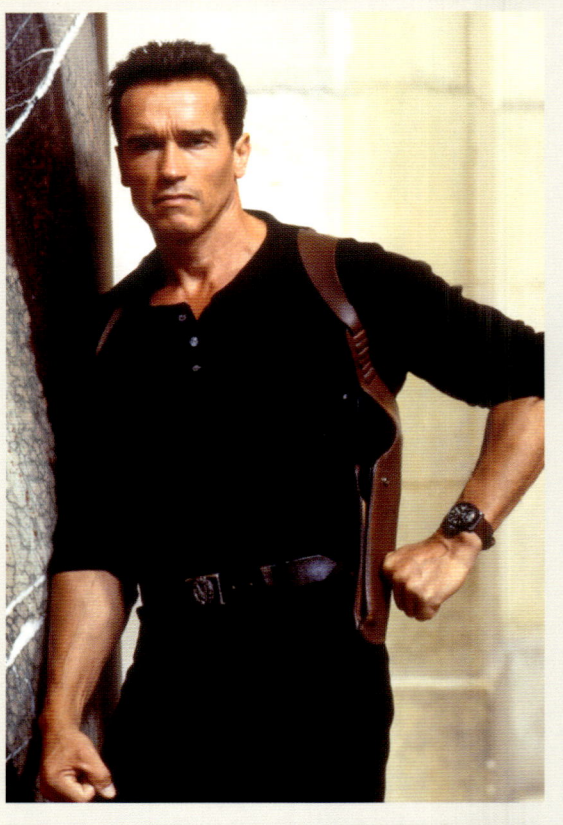

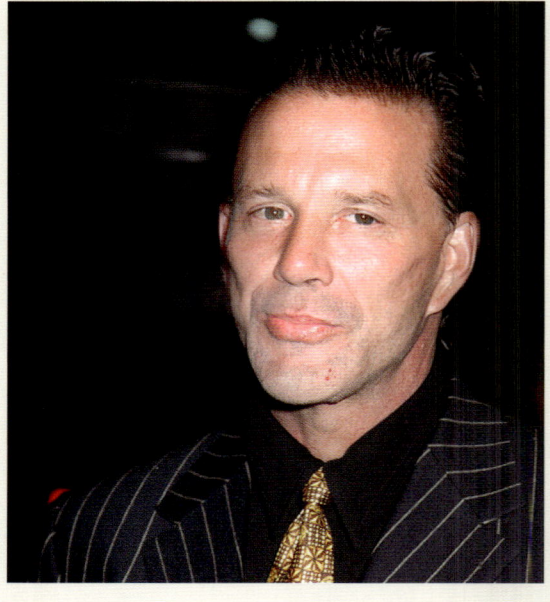

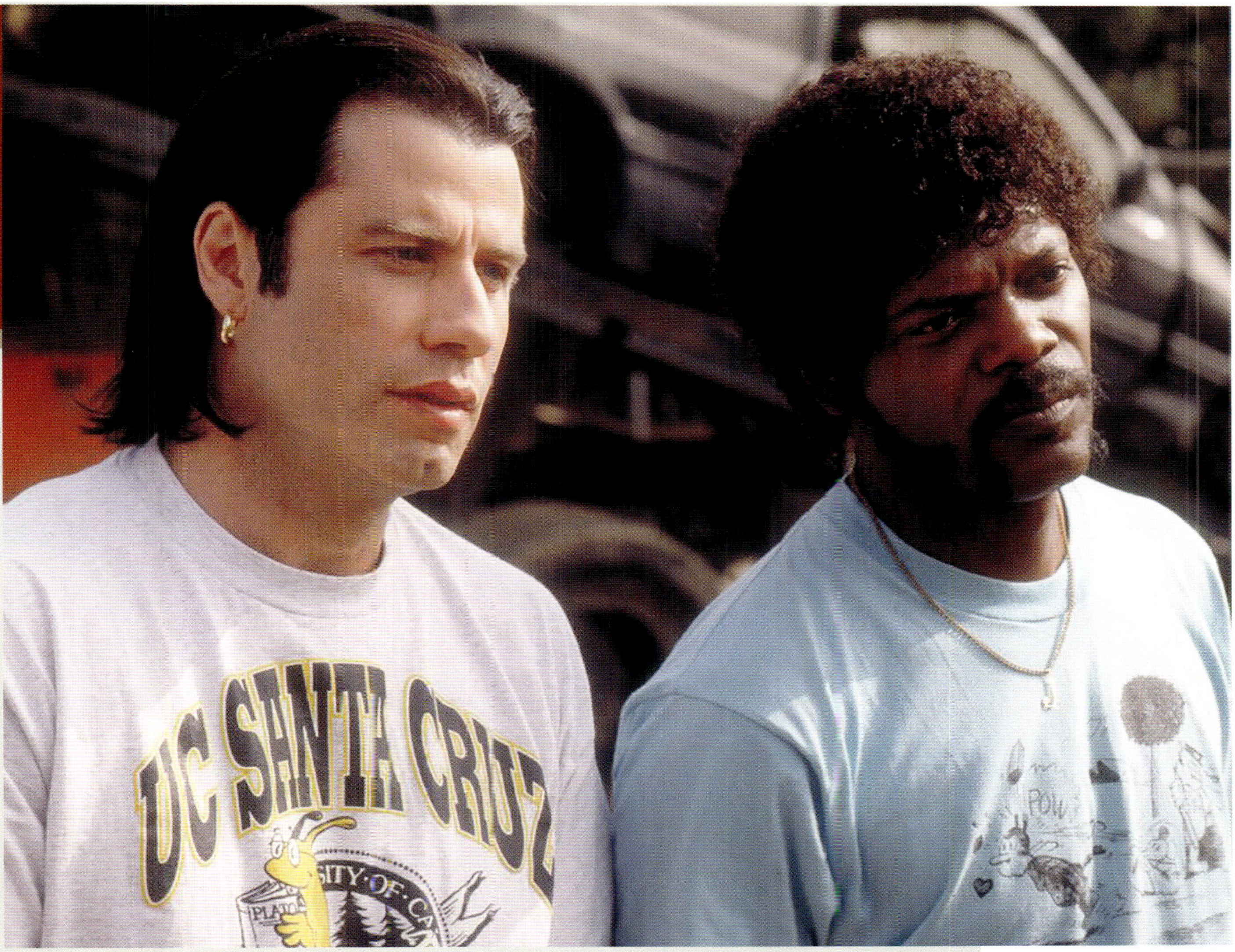

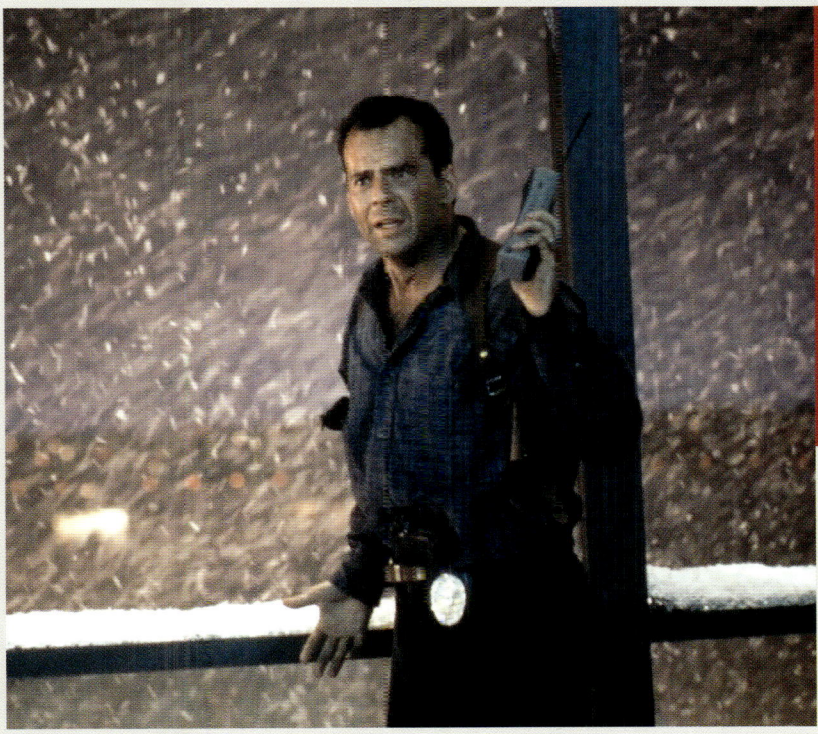

Key Men's Fashion Trends of the 1990s:

- Leather jackets
- Combat boots
- Tactical vests
- Muscle tees
- Black suits
- Distressed denim

TOP

John Travolta and Samuel L. Jackson, in post-hitman casuals, brood beneath L.A. sun in *Pulp Fiction* (1994)— Tarantino's cult classic meets ironic Americana in sharp repose.

LEFT

Bruce Willis, bloodied and resolute in flannel and snow, radios through chaos as John McClane in *Die Hard 2* (1990)— the everyman hero tested in frozen, airborne peril.

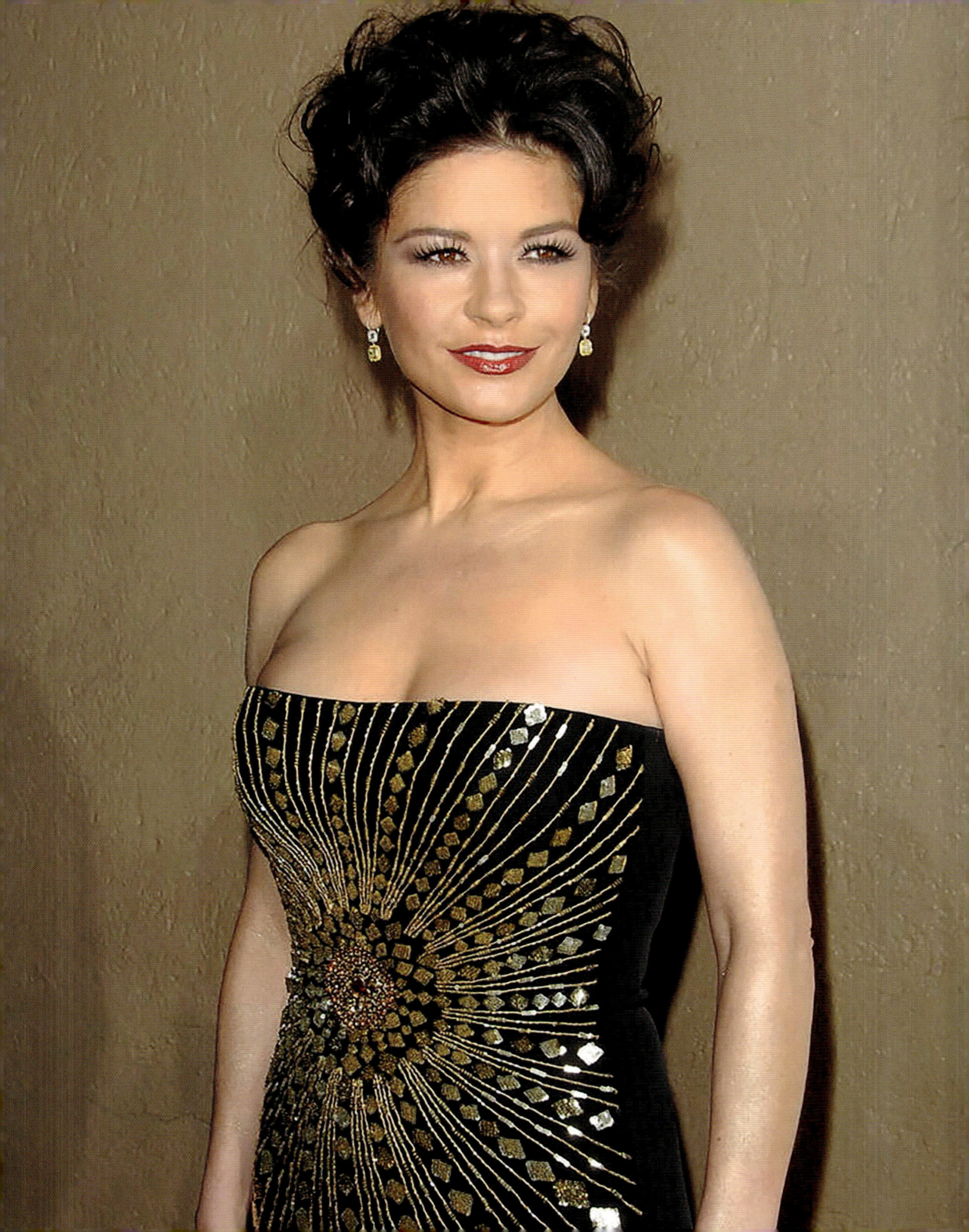

NEW
MILLENNIUM

The early 2000s saw Hollywood embrace fantasy franchises like *Harry Potter* and *The Lord of the Rings*, sparking a wave of big-budget sequels. In contrast, fashion turned inward, recycling past styles instead of chasing the avant-garde. Following 9/11, bold experimentation felt out of step with the cultural mood. Designers favored nostalgia, practicality, and subdued tones, reflecting a collective desire for familiarity and comfort during uncertain times.

Yet couture was by no means dead in Hollywood. Anne Hathaway in *The Devil Wears Prada* went from drab to fab... and sent sales of knee-high boots and designer handbags soaring. *The Sex and the City* movie had women craving those Blahniks, Louboutins, and Jimmy Choos. And fashionable coeds and working girls got wardrobe inspirations from stylish young blondes such as Reese Witherspoon.

By the 2010s, some trendspotters claimed Hollywood was no longer inspiring fashion choices, but then came the mighty Marvel incursion. Tony Stark's preppy CEO in *Iron Man*, both Thor's long golden locks and his retro mullet, Peter Quill's steampunk space pirate in *Guardians of the Galaxy*, and *Black Panther's* sleek futuristic uniform all borrowed from past films but offered something new as well—superhero pizzazz. Not to be outdone, DC Comics gave us a *Wonder Woman* for the ages...with beautiful period costumes.

Only time will tell what future fashion trends will be inspired by movies yet to be made... or what hip streetwear will wind up being glorified in film.

ANNE HATHAWAY

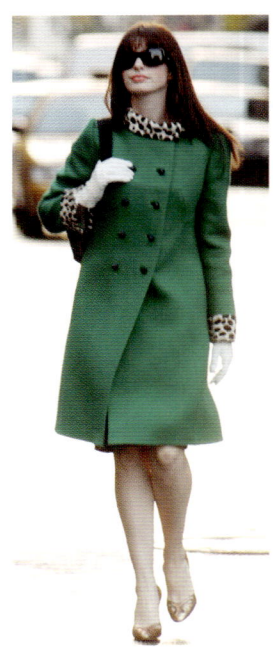

Anne Hathaway, born November 12, 1982, in Brooklyn, New York, is an American actress renowned for her versatility across genres, from fairy tales to intense dramas. Raised in Millburn, New Jersey, she was inspired by her mother, a stage actress, and began acting at a young age. Her early training included studies with New York's Barrow Group, leading to her first television role in *Get Real* (1999–2000).

Hathaway's breakthrough came with Disney's *The Princess Diaries* (2001), where she portrayed Mia Thermopolis, a teenager discovering her royal heritage. She transitioned to more mature roles with performances in *Brokeback Mountain* (2005) and *The Devil Wears Prada* (2006), showcasing her range and earning critical acclaim.

In 2012, Hathaway delivered a lauded performance as Fantine in *Les Misérables*, earning her the Academy Award for Best Supporting Actress. That same year, she portrayed Selina Kyle/Catwoman in *The Dark Knight Rises*, further cementing her status in Hollywood.

Her subsequent roles span various genres, including *Interstellar* (2014), *The Intern* (2015), and *Ocean's 8* (2018). In 2022, she starred in the miniseries *WeCrashed*, and in 2024, she led the romantic comedy *The Idea of You*.

Beyond acting, Hathaway is an advocate for gender equality, serving as a UN Women Goodwill Ambassador. She is married to actor and businessman Adam Shulman, with whom she has two children.

ABOVE

Anne Hathaway finally struts her stuff after her runway magazine makeover in *The Devil Wears Prada* (2006), transforming from timid assistant to high-fashion force in a sleek coat, stilettos, and blunt bangs.

RIGHT

At the Oscars, Anne Hathaway wears a crimson, one-shoulder gown adorned with sculpted rosettes, her long hair swept back in a soft and paired with teardrop diamond earrings.

FASHION FEATURES

THE PRINCESS DIARIES (2001)
ELLA ENCHANTED (2004)
THE DEVIL WEARS PRADA (2006)
ALICE IN WONDERLAND (2010)

The Hathaway Look

The actress laments that she has a small face with large features, but no one else is complaining. Her aura of great robustness and charming playfulness is reflected in her sporty-yet-feminine fashion choices. In January 2008, Hathaway became the face of the Lancôme fragrance, Magnifique.

• Romantic, retro gowns
• Feminine blouses with tweed skirts and jackets
• Simple, monochromatic separates

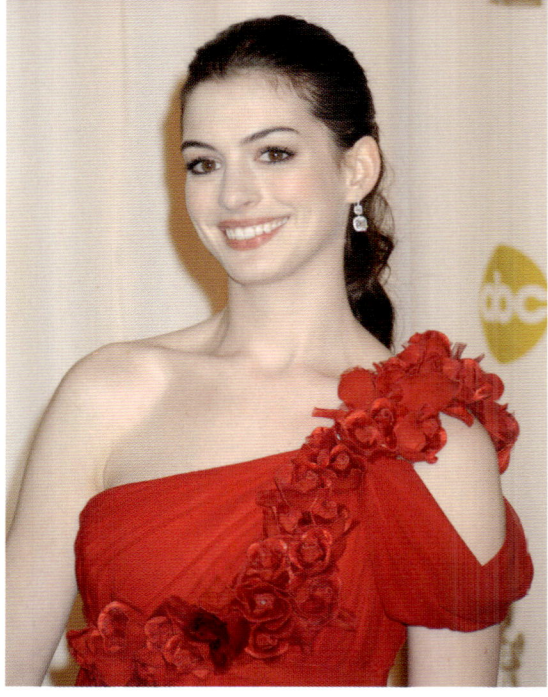

ANGELINA JOLIE

FASHION FEATURES

ORIGINAL SIN (2001)
MR. & MRS. SMITH (2005)
THE TOURIST (2010)

The Jolie Look

Considered by many to be the most beautiful woman in Hollywood, Jolie's fashion choices are often obscured by her overall aura of glamor.

- Dramatic couture gowns
- Sleek, dark, upswept hair with striking earrings
- Sexy, yet understated daywear

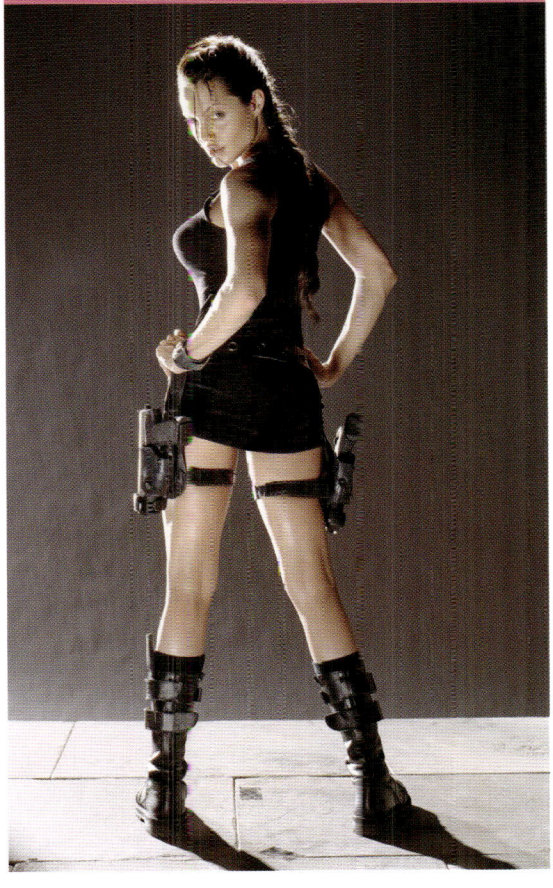

Angelina Jolie's multifaceted career and humanitarian endeavors have solidified her status as a prominent figure in both the entertainment industry and global advocacy.

Born on June 4, 1975, in Los Angeles, California, to actors Jon Voight and Marcheline Bertrand, Jolie embarked on her acting journey in the early 1990s. Her breakthrough came with the television films *George Wallace* (1997) and *Gia* (1998), the latter earning her a Golden Globe Award. She achieved critical acclaim and won an Academy Award for Best Supporting Actress for her role in *Girl, Interrupted* (1999).

Jolie's filmography showcases her versatility, with notable performances in action-packed films such as *Lara Croft: Tomb Raider* (2001), *Mr. & Mrs. Smith* (2005), and *Salt* (2010), as well as dramatic roles in *A Mighty Heart* (2007) and *Changeling* (2008), the latter earning her an Academy Award nomination for Best Actress. She also lent her voice to the *Kung Fu Panda* franchise (2008–2016) and portrayed the titular character in Disney's *Maleficent* (2014) and its sequel.

Transitioning behind the camera, Jolie directed and wrote several films, including *In the Land of Blood and Honey* (2011), *Unbroken* (2014), and *First They Killed My Father* (2017). Her directorial work often focuses on themes of conflict and human rights

Beyond her cinematic achievements, Jolie is renowned for her humanitarian efforts. Appointed as a UNHCR Goodwill Ambassador in 2001 and later as a Special Envoy, she has undertaken numerous field missions to advocate for refugees and displaced individuals. She established the Maddox Jolie-Pitt Foundation, focusing on community development and conservation in Cambodia. In recognition of her humanitarian work, she received the Jean Hersholt Humanitarian Award in 2013.

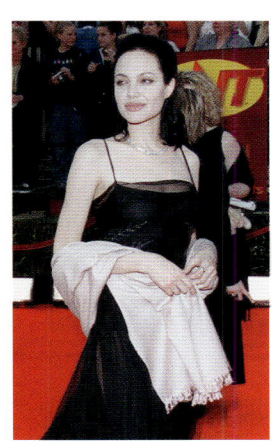

ABOVE

Angelina Jolie pauses on the red carpet in a sheer black gown with delicate straps, her hair swept back and a diamond necklace accenting the minimalist look.

LEFT

Angelina Jolie's Lara Croft look in *Tomb Raider*—combat boots, utility shorts, and dual holsters—became an action-icon uniform, blending video game fantasy with fierce, functional fashion.

KEIRA KNIGHTLEY

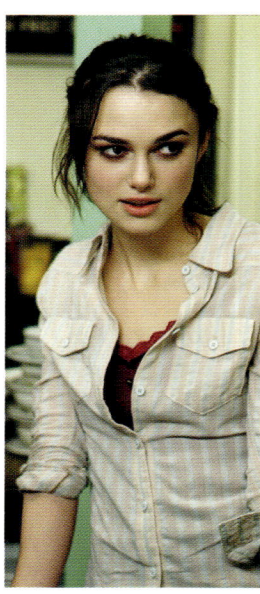

Keira Knightley has built a dynamic and enduring career through her versatility and depth as an actress. Raised in Teddington, England, in a creative household—her father an actor and her mother a playwright—Knightley was immersed in storytelling from an early age. By six, she had secured an agent and began appearing in television and film, including a supporting role in *Star Wars: Episode I—The Phantom Menace* (1999) as Sabé, the queen's decoy.

She rose to prominence with *Bend It Like Beckham* (2002), portraying a young woman breaking gender norms through football. This role led to her iconic performance as Elizabeth Swann in *Pirates of the Caribbean* (2003–2017), establishing her as a global star.

Knightley is particularly known for her work in period dramas. Her portrayal of Elizabeth Bennet in *Pride & Prejudice* (2005) earned her an Academy Award nomination. She followed with acclaimed roles in *Atonement* (2007), *The Duchess* (2008), and *Anna Karenina* (2012).

She has also taken on contemporary roles, including *Begin Again* (2013) and *The Imitation Game* (2014), the latter earning her a second Oscar nomination. In 2024, she starred in Netflix's *Black Doves*, playing a spy, a role that brought her a Golden Globe nod.

Knightley has also earned praise on stage in *The Misanthrope* (2009) and *Thérèse Raquin* (2015). In 2018, she was named an Officer of the Order of the British Empire for her services to drama and charity. Married to musician James Righton, she balances family life with a passion for compelling, diverse storytelling.

ABOVE

Keira Knightley in *Domino* (2005), in a striped shirt and lace camisole, channels grit and attitude with effortless, edgy charm.

RIGHT

Keira Knightley's emerald green gown in *Atonement* became instantly iconic—its flowing silk and daring cut capturing both 1930s elegance and cinematic sensuality in one unforgettable look..

FASHION FEATURES

PIRATES OF THE CARIBBEAN: THE CURSE OF THE BLACK PEARL (2003)
ATONEMENT (2007)
THE DUCHESS (2008)
ANNA KARENINA (2012)

The Knightley Look

Even when she isn't wearing period gowns and beribboned bonnets, this actress frequently gets dolled up for red-carpet and charity events.

- "Barely there" gowns
- Designer daywear dresses
- Hip-hugger, skintight jeans with trendy tops

SARAH JESSICA PARKER

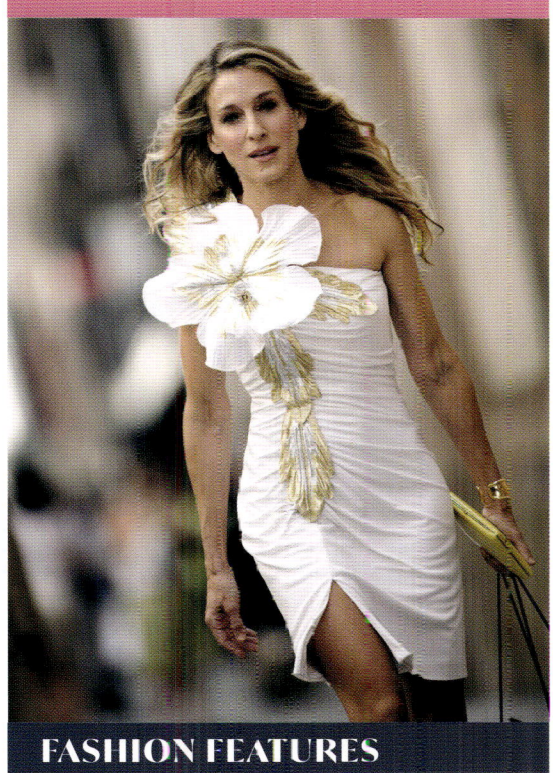

FASHION FEATURES

MIAMI RHAPSODY (1995)
THE FAMILY STONE (2005)
SEX AND THE CITY (2008)

The Parker Look

Whereas TV's Carrie managed to combine ballet tutus, Hawaiian shirts, tube tops, and 3D purses, the real SJP opts for a more glamorous tone. In 2007, SJP launched her line of clothing, Bitten. Her three signature fragrances are Covet, Lovely, and SJP NYC.

- Cinch-waisted short dresses
- Strapless evening gowns with pouf skirts
- Endless supply of high-heeled designer shoes

From Broadway beginnings to global stardom, Sarah Jessica Parker's journey reflects her versatility and enduring influence in entertainment and fashion.

Born on March 25, 1965, in Nelsonville, Ohio, SJP was one of eight children in a blended family. Her early exposure to the arts led her to New York City at age 11, where she secured the lead role in Broadway's *Annie* in 1979. She transitioned to screen acting with roles in *Square Pegs* (1982–83) and films such as *Footloose* (1984) and *Girls Just Want to Have Fun* (1985).

SJP's portrayal of Carrie Bradshaw in HBO's *Sex and the City* (1998–2004) catapulted her to international fame, earning her multiple Emmy and Golden Globe Awards. The character became a cultural icon, leading to two feature films and the sequel series *And Just Like That...* (2021–2025).

Beyond acting, SJP has made significant contributions as a producer through her company Pretty Matches, developing content for HBO and other networks. She is also recognized for her influence in the fashion industry, launching the SJP Collection footwear line and collaborating on various fashion ventures.

In her personal life, SJP married actor Matthew Broderick in 1997, and they have three children. The family resides in New York City. SJP continues to balance her roles in film, philanthropy, and as a mother, leaving an indelible mark on both the entertainment industry and global humanitarian efforts.

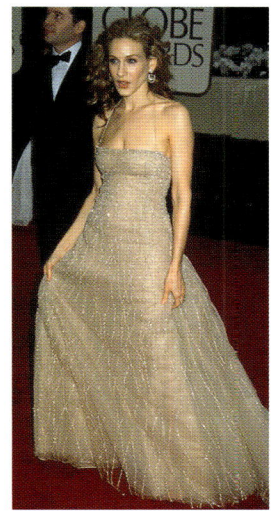

But there are no rules with Pat when it comes to fashion. It's liberating.

SARAH JESSICA PARKER ON WORKING WITH *SEX AND THE CITY* DESIGNER PATRICIA FIELD

ABOVE

Parker arrives at the Golden Globe Awards in a nude beaded gown, her voluminous curls and poised stance capturing the era's red carpet glamor.

LEFT

Sarah Jessica Parker turns the sidewalk into a runway in *Sex and the City*, wearing a sculptural white dress crowned with an oversized flower—an iconic Carrie Bradshaw moment in maximalist fashion.

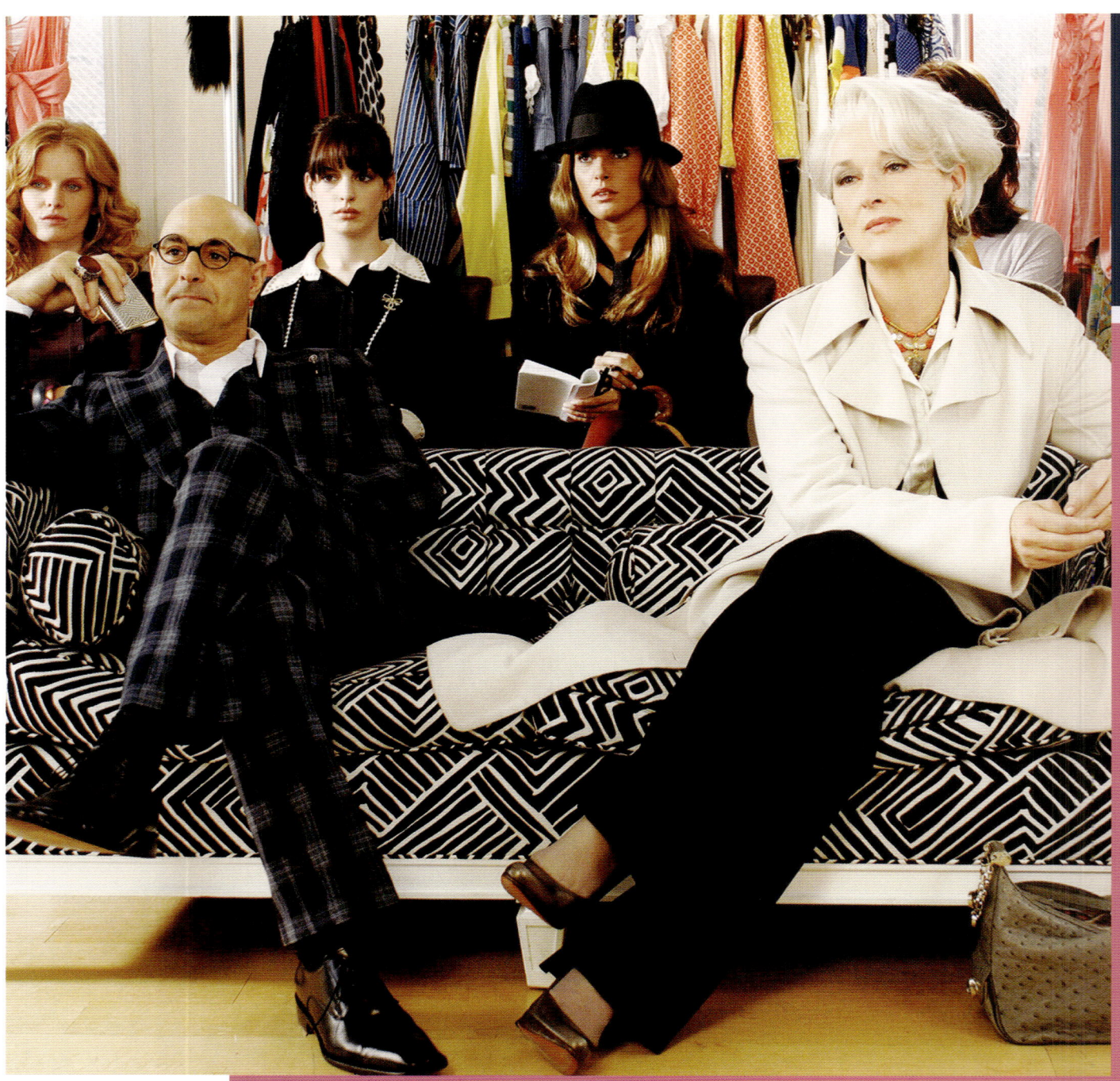

The way you dress yourself is a form of self-expression and a way of communicating to others who you are. But style is broader than just fashion—it's not only the way you dress, but also how you decorate your home, and the books you read. It all runs together.

ABOVE
—
Field culled the best of the current couture collections for the fashions in 2006's *The Devil Wears Prada*. Here, magazine publisher Meryl Streep, in a classic trenchcoat, conveys her displeasure during a fashion preview as her art director, Stanley Tucci, pulsating with plaid, looks on.

Fashion Legacy
- Ballet tutus reimagined as streetwear
- Credited with introducing modern leggings to Europe in the 1970s
- Oversize floral pins as statement pieces
- Iconic gold nameplate necklaces

DESIGN SENSE
PATRICIA FIELD

Style is more than fashion—it's a deeply personal language of self-expression. From the clothes you wear to the décor in your home and even the books on your shelves—it all speaks volumes about who you are. For Patricia Field, style is a powerful form of communication. The more ways one expresses themselves, the more nuanced and impactful the message becomes.

Movie and television designer Patricia Field (1941–) is often labeled a visionary for her ability to spot a style trend or take a tiny ripple in the fashion industry and turn it into a tsunami. The child of a Greek father and Armenian mother, she grew up in Astoria, Queens. Her career as a designer began with the opening of her Greenwich Village boutique in 1966, which for more than four decades would remain the fashion mecca for hip celebrities who wanted something quirky or memorable to wear.

Field won her first Emmy in 1990 for Shelley Duvall's *Mother Goose Rock n' Rhyme* and was likewise honored for *Sex and the City*. She also won five Costume Designers Guild Awards, four for *Sex and the City* and one for *Ugly Betty*.

In 1995, while designing costumes for the film *Miami Rhapsody*, Field worked with actress Sarah Jessica Parker. It would prove to be a fortuitous meeting—Parker was impressed with Field's clothing collection, and the two became friends. When Parker was cast as Carrie Bradshaw in HBO's *Sex and the City*, she turned to Field, a born and bred New Yorker, to give her heroine a distinctive "look." Field was soon designing or styling outfits for all the characters on the hit show; she became known for her ability to put together eclectic or vintage elements and make them contemporary and chic.

Nominated for an Oscar in 2006 for *The Devil Wears Prada*, Field admits that in this film she was more of a "style wrangler," putting together ensembles from couture designers rather than creating costumes from scratch.

With her signature bright red hair and outsized personality, the openly lesbian Field is a high-profile presence at many fashion events. She also appeared as the first guest judge during the inaugural year of *Project Runway*. She is currently working on U by Kotex to "ban the bland" and add color to feminine protection products. Field has also designed a line of inexpensive but fashionable shoes, boots, and bags for Payless.

> **Style has become very important, the whole idea of style, what your personal style is. It's your identity**
>
> PATRICA FIELD

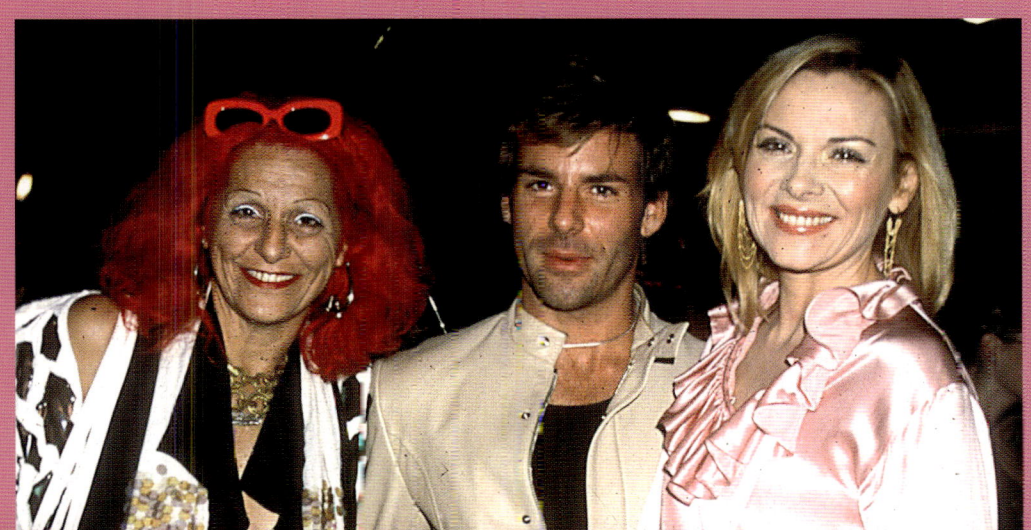

LEFT

At a fashion event the red-haired Field poses with some fellow attendees, including Kim Cattrall, who played Samantha on *Sex in the City*, here dolled up in pink satin.

NATALIE PORTMAN

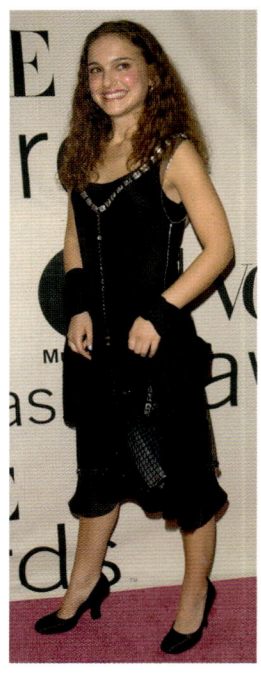

Few actors have navigated the transition from child prodigy to acclaimed adult performer as seamlessly as Natalie Portman. Born Natalie Hershlag on June 9, 1981, in Jerusalem, she moved to the United States at a young age and soon found herself in the spotlight. Her breakthrough came at just 13 years old in *Léon: The Professional* (1994), where her haunting portrayal of Mathilda captivated critics and audiences alike.

Portman's international fame soared when she took on the role of Padmé Amidala in George Lucas's *Star Wars* prequel trilogy (1999–2005). Despite the global frenzy surrounding the franchise, she remained committed to her education, earning a degree in psychology from Harvard University in 2003—a testament to her intellectual drive.

She quickly established herself as a leading actress in adult roles, earning a Golden Globe for *Closer* (2004) and receiving widespread recognition for *V for Vendetta* (2005). In 2010, her intense and physically demanding performance in *Black Swan* won her the Academy Award for Best Actress, solidifying her position as one of the era's most talented performers.

Natalie continued to explore diverse characters, portraying Jacqueline Kennedy in *Jackie* (2016), a role that earned her another Oscar nomination. She also entered the Marvel Cinematic Universe as Jane Foster in the *Thor* films, returning in *Thor: Love and Thunder* (2022) as the Mighty Thor.

Off-screen, she is an outspoken advocate for environmental causes, animal rights, and women's empowerment. She co-founded MountainA, a production company dedicated to female-driven stories, producing *May December* (2023) and *Lady in the Lake* (2024). With a career marked by intelligence, bold choices, and artistic integrity, Portman remains a defining figure in contemporary cinema.

ABOVE

At the 2000 *Vogue* Fashion Awards, Natalie Portman embraced youthful edge in a black beaded slip dress, pairing soft curls and a sheer shawl with playful confidence on the early-2000s pink carpet.

LEFT

Natalie Portman's haunting transformation in Black Swan is immortalized by her eerie makeup, blood-red eyes, and sculpted crown—fashion and madness entwined in balletic perfection.

FASHION FEATURES

CLOSER (2004)
MY BLUEBERRY NIGHTS (2007)
THE OTHER WOMAN (2009)
BLACK SWAN (2010)

The Portman Look

This actress is not above experimenting with her clothing choices. She sometimes opts for trendy or modern on the red carpet, but usually relies on timeless glamor.

- Ruffled or draped gowns
- Balloon skirts
- Man-tailored daywear worn with girly shoes

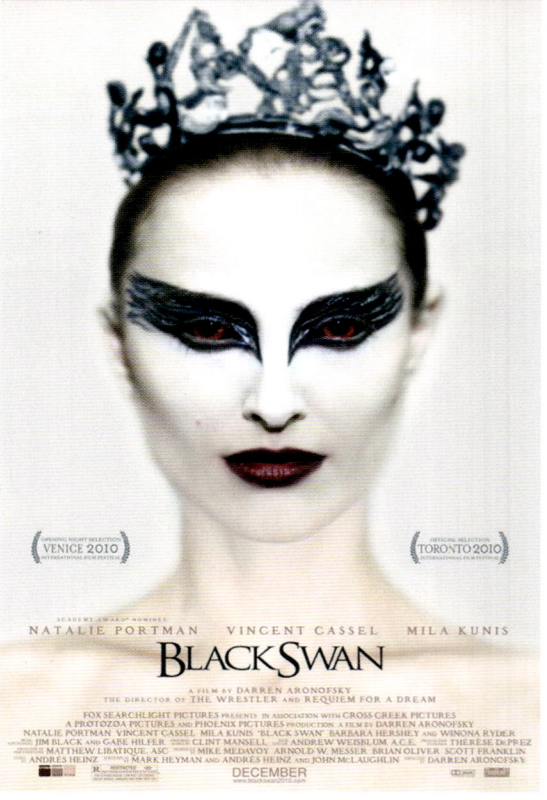

UMA THURMAN

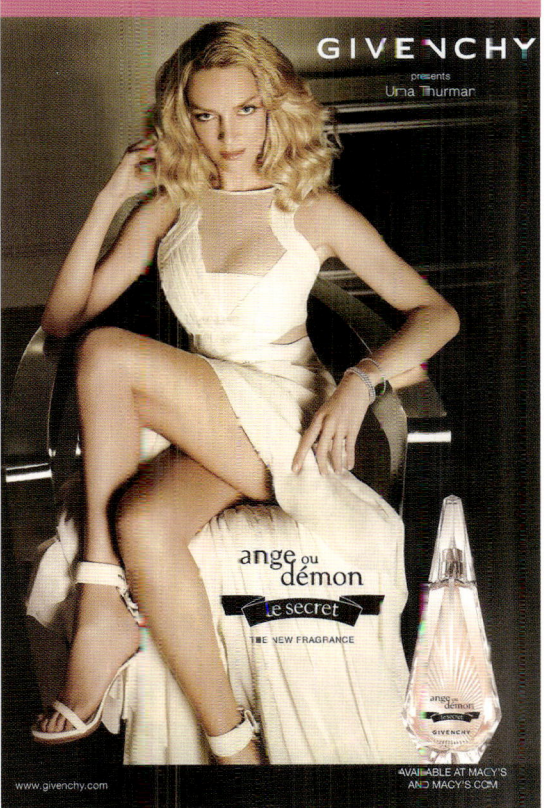

With a commanding presence and eclectic filmography, Uma Thurman has become one of Hollywood's most intriguing actresses. Born on April 29, 1970, in Boston, Massachusetts, she was raised in a culturally rich household—her father was a renowned Buddhist scholar, and her mother a former high-fashion model. These global influences shaped her early exposure to the arts and literature.

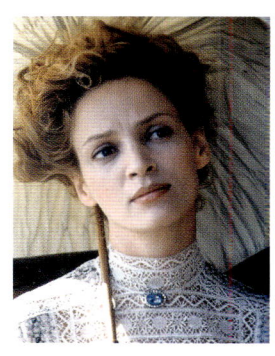

Thurman began her career as a fashion model, gracing the covers of British *Vogue* before transitioning to film. She made her screen debut in *Kiss Daddy Goodnight* (1987) and gained recognition with her role in *Dangerous Liaisons* (1988). However, it was her unforgettable performance as Mia Wallace in Quentin Tarantino's *Pulp Fiction* (1994) that made her a global star and earned her an Academy Award nomination.

She later portrayed memorable roles in *Gattaca* (1997), *Les Misérables* (1998), and as the deadly Beatrix Kiddo in *Kill Bill: Vol. 1* (2003) and *Vol. 2* (2004). Her work spans stage and screen, including TV appearances in *Smash* (2012) and *Suspicion* (2022) and Broadway's *The Parisian Woman* (2017).

Mother of actress Maya Hawke, Thurman remains admired for her daring roles, intense screen presence, and enduring versatility.

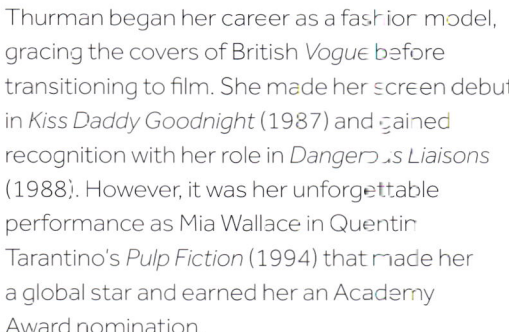

ABOVE

Uma Thurman as Grace in *The Golden Bowl* (2000), framed in Edwardian lace and a pale parasol, channels quiet unrest beneath refined elegance in this Merchant Ivory period adaptation of Henry James's final novel.

LEFT

Thurman fronts Givenchy's *Ange ou Démon: Le Secret* campaign, poised in ivory silk with sculpted waves and a sidelong gaze—an image of 2000s elegance shaped for fragrance, allure, and cinematic mystique.

REESE WITHERSPOON

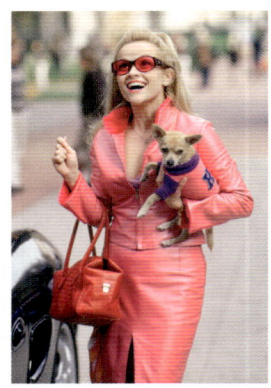

Reese Witherspoon's career is a powerful blend of talent, resilience, and entrepreneurship. Gaining early attention with roles in films such as *The Man in the Moon* (1991), she rose to stardom with her iconic performance as Elle Woods in *Legally Blonde* (2001), redefining the modern female lead with wit and determination. Her portrayal of June Carter Cash in *Walk the Line* (2005) earned her an Academy Award for Best Actress, showcasing her emotional depth and range.

She continued to pursue challenging roles in films such as *Wild* (2014), which brought her another Oscar nomination, and expanded her influence as a producer. Witherspoon's production company, Hello Sunshine, has been instrumental in bringing strong, women-centered narratives to the screen, including the critically acclaimed series *Big Little Lies* (2017–2019), for which she earned an Emmy as a producer.

Beyond film and television, she launched Reese's Book Club to highlight works by women authors and founded the fashion label Draper James, inspired by her Southern heritage. Witherspoon's commitment to storytelling, advocacy for gender equality, and sharp business acumen have positioned her as a transformative force in Hollywood. She continues to inspire through performances and projects that empower and engage audiences worldwide.

"It's funny that it all becomes about clothes. It's bizarre. You work your butt off, and then you win an award, and it's all about your dress. You can't get away from it."

REESE WITHERSPOON

ABOVE

Reese Witherspoon's fashion-obsessed Elle Woods makes a bold impression in *Legally Blonde*, strutting Harvard Yard in head-to-toe hot pink—proof that fashion can be fierce, fun, and unapologetically smart.

RIGHT

Reese strikes a playful pose at the 47th CMA Awards, wearing a lace one-shoulder black gown—balancing Old Hollywood flair with a touch of cheek on Nashville's most-watched red carpet.

FASHION FEATURES

LEGALLY BLONDE (2001)
VANITY FAIR (2004)
WATER FOR ELEPHANTS (2011)

The Witherspoon Look

With her willowy figure, blue eyes, and honey-blonde hair, the actress does justice to clothing from any period—but especially today's casual "rich-girl" choices.

- Ultrafeminine dresses and gowns
- Classy cardigan or pullover sweaters with high boots
- Big scarves over fitted jackets and blazers

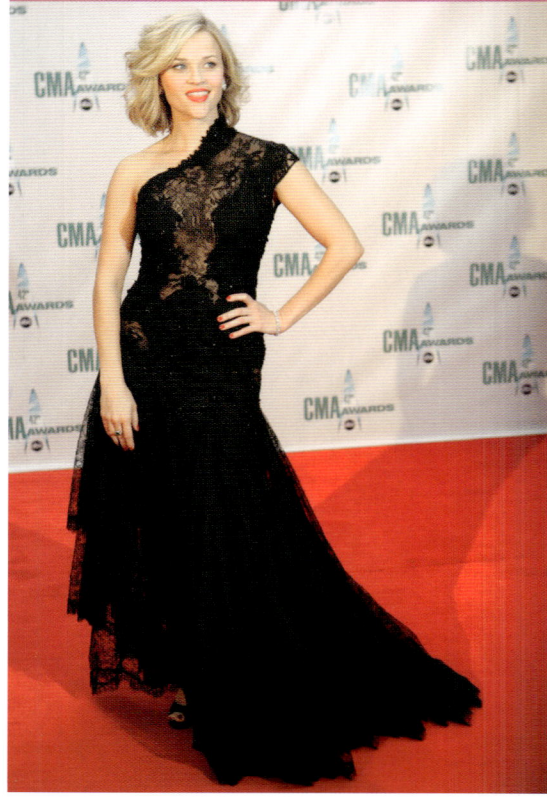

CATHERINE ZETA-JONES

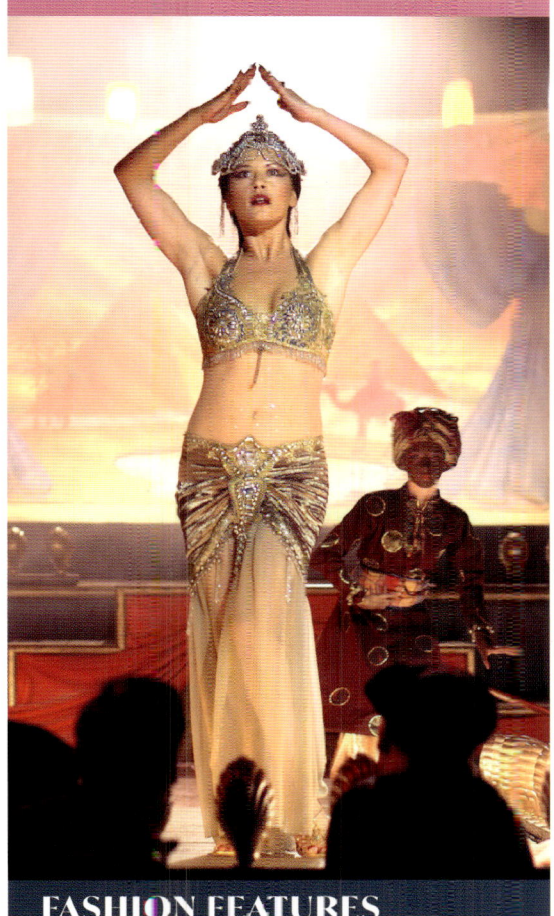

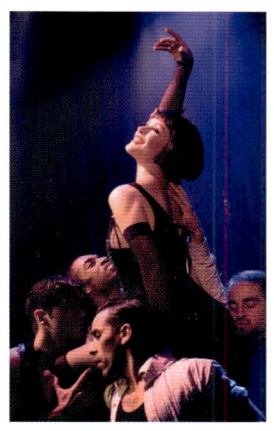

Catherine Zeta-Jones rose from a small Welsh town to become one of Hollywood's most captivating stars. Born on September 25, 1969, in Swansea, Wales, she displayed a flair for performance from a young age, studying dance and acting and joining the theater stage in her teens. Her early break came in London's West End, where she starred in musicals such as *42nd Street*, showcasing her natural charisma and musical talent.

Zeta-Jones gained widespread attention in the UK for her role in the popular television series *The Darling Buds of May* (1991–1993), which brought her into the national spotlight. Eager to expand her career internationally, she moved to Los Angeles and secured a breakout role in *The Mask of Zorro* (1998), followed by *Entrapment* (1999), which highlighted her elegance and action-star potential.

Her critically acclaimed performance in *Traffic* (2000) was followed by her Oscar-winning role as Velma Kelly in *Chicago* (2002), where she blended sharp acting with dazzling musical prowess. She continued her Hollywood success with *Intolerable Cruelty* (2003), *Ocean's Twelve* (2004), and *The Terminal* (2004).

Jones married actor Michael Douglas in 2000, and they have two children. The couple's high-profile relationship often draws media attention, but Zeta-Jones remains known for her professionalism and privacy. After a brief hiatus, she returned to the screen with acclaimed performances in *Feud* (2017) and Netflix's *Wednesday* (2022).

Effortlessly graceful and intensely talented, Zeta-Jones has secured her place as a beloved and enduring figure in global cinema.

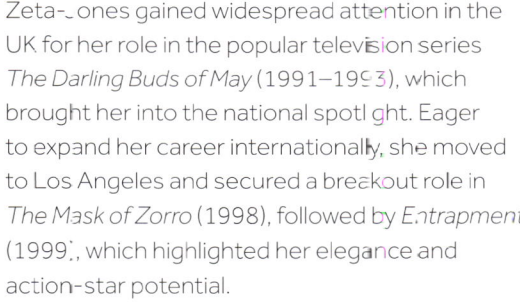

FASHION FEATURES

THE MASK OF ZORRO (1998)
ENTRAPMENT (1999)
CHICAGO (2002)

The Zeta-Jones Look

Like most Hollywood royalty, Zeta-Jones prefers richly embellished fabrics for evenings and classy separates for daytime.

- Strapless gowns in jewel tones
- Knee-length dress and coat ensembles
- Tailored, feminine skirt suits

ABOVE

Catherine Zeta-Jones dazzles in a sultry, sequined black dress as Velma Kelly in *Chicago*—a defining look of 1920s-inspired Hollywood glamor.

LEFT

Zeta-Jones stuns in jeweled regalia as Mata Hari in *Dad's Army* (2016)—a dazzling homage to espionage mystique and stagecraft wrapped in vintage spectacle.

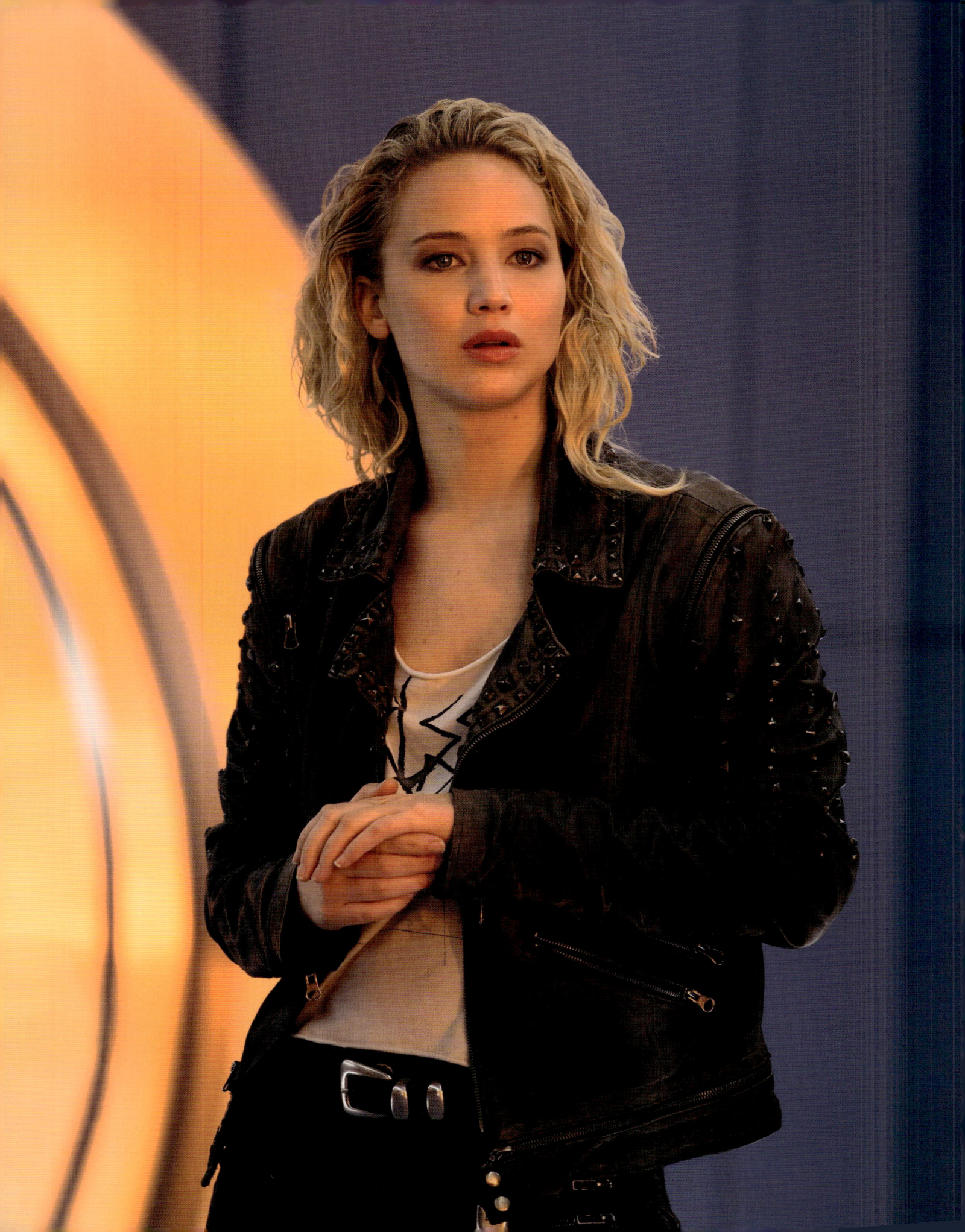

TWENTY TENS

The 2010s ushered in a dynamic and eclectic era for Hollywood fashion, marked by a fusion of nostalgia, innovation, and bold individuality. As social media transformed red carpet moments into global phenomena, style became more immediate and democratic. Stars embraced risk-taking looks that ranged from high-octane couture to streetwear influences, reflecting the decade's blurring of luxury and casualwear.

Actresses like Lupita Nyong'o, Zendaya, and Cate Blanchett became style icons, celebrated for their ability to oscillate between avant-garde silhouettes, power tailoring, and romantic gowns. Meanwhile, the "naked dress" trend—sheer fabrics, strategic cutouts, and body-con fits—dominated headlines as stars like Jennifer Lopez and Kim Kardashian-West embraced hyper-feminine sensuality with unapologetic confidence.

Menswear, too, evolved with figures like Timothée Chalamet and Harry Styles redefining red-carpet dressing through gender-fluid fashion, luxurious textures, and unexpected color palettes. Designers including Alessandro Michele at Gucci and Virgil Abloh at Louis Vuitton injected a sense of playfulness and subversion, making their mark on celebrity wardrobes.

By decade's end, sustainability became a talking point, with stars opting for vintage pieces and ethical brands. The 2010s proved that Hollywood style was no longer confined to rules; it celebrated reinvention, inclusivity, and personal expression as the ultimate markers of glamor.

DIANA AGRON

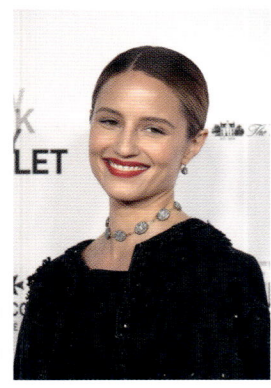

Diana Agron is one of Hollywood's most quietly stylish figures—an actress whose fashion choices reflect as much thought and artistry as her onscreen performances. Her look is defined by contrast: romantic yet restrained, vintage in tone but never stuck in time. Whether in sculptural couture or an understated sheath, Agron dresses with a sensibility that nods to Old Hollywood, but always with a knowing, modern edge. She is not a slave to trends; instead, she curates a wardrobe that communicates elegance, character, and quiet power.

Agron first came to prominence in *Glee*, but she has since forged a parallel reputation as a red carpet sophisticate. She gravitates toward designers like Valentino, Miu Miu, and Ulyana Sergeenko—names known for their flair for the feminine, the gothic, and the whimsical. Her silhouettes tend to be structured yet fluid, favoring high collars, defined waists, or diaphanous sleeves. Agron often plays with textures—lace, velvet, brocade—and her color palette leans toward classic jewel tones, inky blacks, and ethereal neutrals.

She has appeared at festivals and premieres in ensembles that feel almost literary in mood: a satin gown with puffed shoulders and opera gloves; a sharply tailored brocade jacket over silk palazzo pants. She wears fashion like a narrative device— each outfit part costume, part poetry. In an era of statement dressing and social media saturation, Agron's quiet confidence and cinematic sense of style stand out all the more. She is, in many ways, the thinking woman's fashion muse.

ABOVE

Diana at the New York City Ballet 2023 Fall Gala in Manhattan, wearing an embellished navy ensemble with tonal embroidery and a structured neckline—elegant, timeless, and true to her vintage-inflected red carpet signature.

RIGHT

Diana Agron channels refined bohemian glamor at the La Mer by Sorrenti campaign launch in New York, pairing a softly structured animal-print dress with sharp black accessories. With her loose waves, sleek boots, and sculptural clutch, Agron balances playfulness with polish.

FASHION FEATURES

I AM NUMBER FOUR (2011)
BARE (2015)
BERLIN, I LOVE YOU (2019)

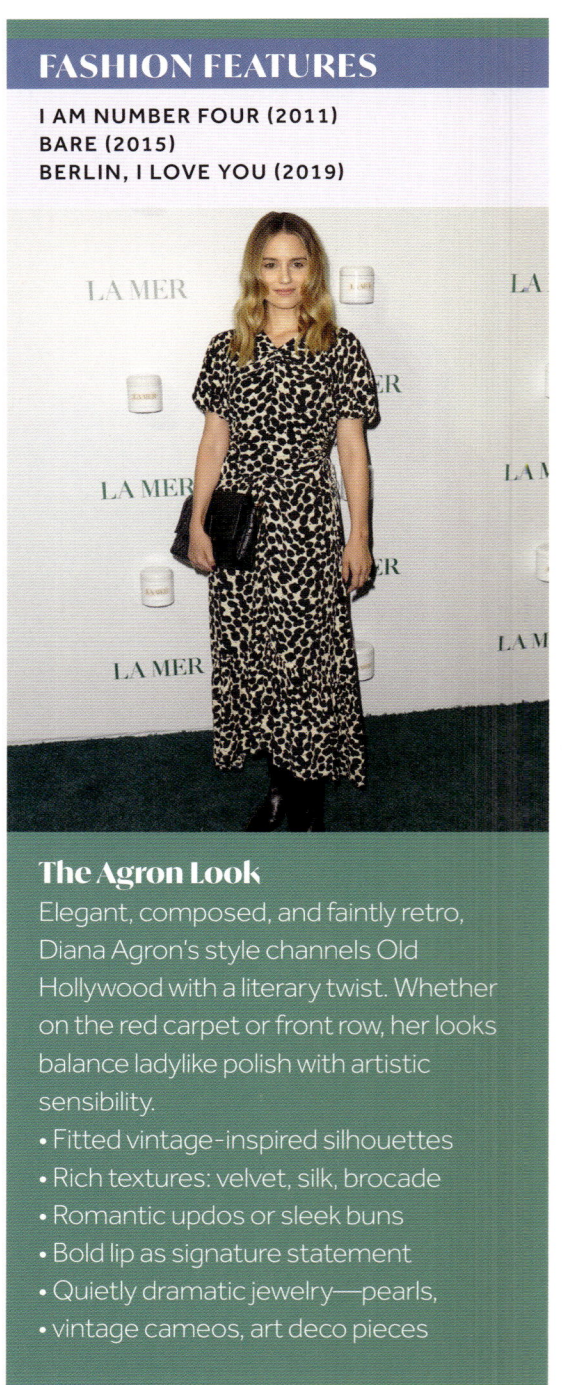

The Agron Look
Elegant, composed, and faintly retro, Diana Agron's style channels Old Hollywood with a literary twist. Whether on the red carpet or front row, her looks balance ladylike polish with artistic sensibility.
- Fitted vintage-inspired silhouettes
- Rich textures: velvet, silk, brocade
- Romantic updos or sleek buns
- Bold lip as signature statement
- Quietly dramatic jewelry—pearls,
- vintage cameos, art deco pieces

SCARLETT JOHANSSON

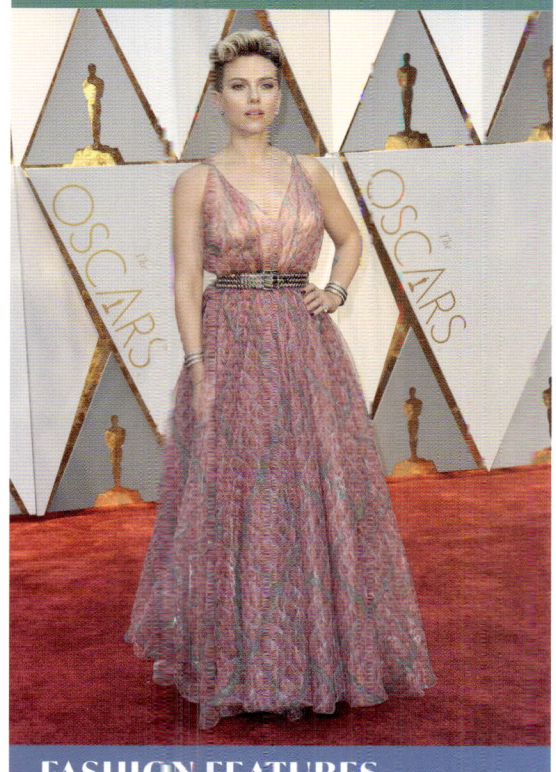

With a presence that blends Old Hollywood glamor and modern edge, Scarlett Johansson has long been one of cinema's most fashion-forward stars. From her teenage breakout years to her reign as a red-carpet favorite, she has proven a master of reinvention. Whether channeling Marilyn Monroe's sensuality or embodying sleek contemporary minimalism, Johansson's style reflects her versatility as an actress and a cultural icon.

On red carpets, she exudes effortless sophistication, balancing daring necklines and sculptural gowns with a cool, unfussy attitude.

A vivid yellow satin Calvin Klein dress at the 2004 Met Gala announced her as a bold new presence. Over the years, she has embraced sultry lace, dramatic cutouts, and architectural silhouettes— her 2017 Oscars look in a flowing Alaïa gown being a standout. Equally striking are her moments of pared-down chic, such as a structured Prada shift at a 2009 film festival, where she let her sharp bob and red lips steal the show.

Johansson's film roles have also allowed her fashion sensibilities to shine. In *Lost in Translation*, her delicate slip dresses became emblematic of the early 2000s aesthetic. As a 1950s starlet in *Hail, Caesar!*, she leaned into vintage glamor with coiffed hair and cinched waists, while *Match Point* showcased a sultry, sophisticated wardrobe in moody tones.

Johansson's style mixes vulnerability with power, yielding a wardrobe as multifaceted as her screen persona: timeless yet contemporary, soft yet undeniably strong

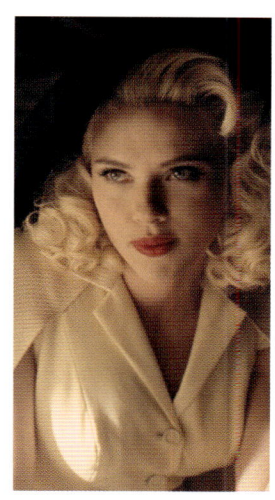

FASHION FEATURES

LOST IN TRANSLATION (2003)
MATCH POINT (2005)
LUCY (2014)
HAIL, CAESAR! (2016)

The Johansson Look
A study in modern glamor, Scarlett Johansson's style combines bold femininity with subtle strength:

- Sculptural gowns with daring necklines or cinched waists
- Old Hollywood waves paired with smoky eyes and a bold lip
- Sleek minimalism offset by unexpected textures and details
- A knack for balancing timeless elegance with avant-garde edge

ABOVE

On-screen in *Hail, Caesar!* (2016), Johansson channels Marilyn Monroe with platinum waves, red lips, and structured tailoring, exuding pure mid-century screen siren allure.

RIGHT

At the 2017 Academy Awards, a flowing Alaïa gown in dusky pink, cinched at the waist with a studded belt, showcases her love for fluid silhouettes and statement details.

JENNIFER LAWRENCE

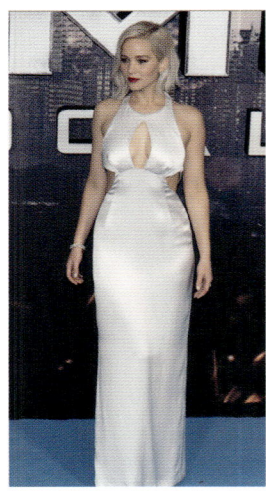

Jennifer Lawrence brings a rare, compelling duality to the red carpet: an ease that suggests she's slightly amused by the pomp, paired with a knack for high-voltage glamor that never feels forced. From her breakout years promoting *The Hunger Games* **to her transformation into a Dior muse, Lawrence's fashion journey has been defined by fearless choices and a sense of authenticity.**

Whether she's gliding past flashing cameras in frothy couture or striking an insouciant pose in a sleek column gown, she retains an air of grounded confidence—a "take it or leave it" attitude that has endeared her to both fashion critics and fans.

Her style evolution reflects a maturing artistry. Early appearances showcased youthful experimentation: playful prints, bold colors, and the occasional misstep. But as her career soared, so did her sartorial instincts. Aligning with Dior in 2012 marked a pivotal shift, as Lawrence embraced a more refined palette of minimalist gowns, architectural tailoring, and occasional nods to vintage Hollywood. Yet even at her most elegant, there's always a trace of the girl who once tripped up the Oscars stairs: unpretentious, self-aware, and unafraid of taking risks.

Off-duty, Lawrence favors a breezy uniform of slouchy knits, maxi skirts, and oversized sunglasses—channeling Californian cool with an underlying polish. This balance of glamor and relatability makes her a modern-day style icon: the rare actress equally at ease in couture and casuals.

ABOVE

At the *X-Men: Apocalypse* fan screening in 2016, she delivered minimalistic sophistication in a figure-hugging satin gown by Dior, featuring cut-out details and a soft sheen that reflected the blue carpet's cool tones.

RIGHT

For the London premiere of *The Hunger Games: Mockingjay – Part 2*, Lawrence turned heads in a navy blue Dior dress with scattered gold motifs, its flowing shape perfectly balancing drama and refinement.

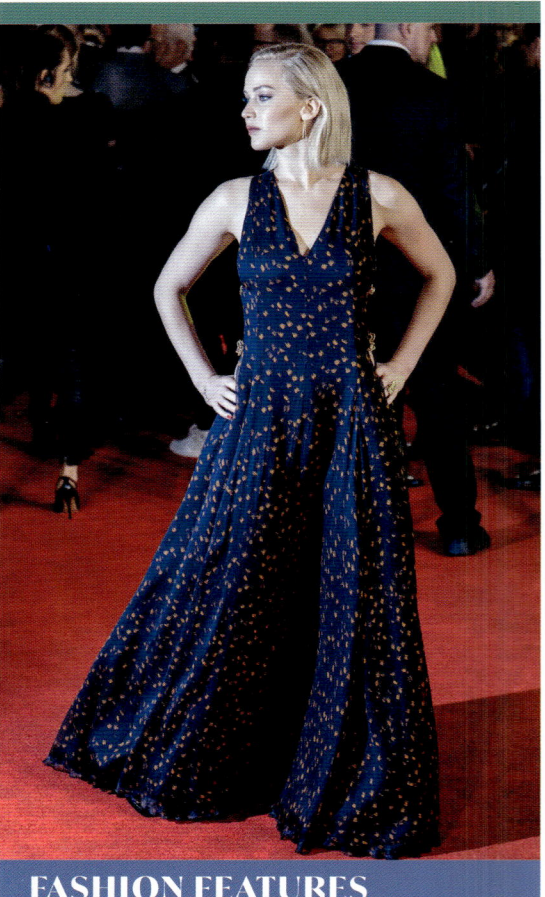

FASHION FEATURES

AMERICAN HUSTLE (2013)
SERENA (2014)
X-MEN: APOCALYPSE (2016)
MOTHER! (2017)

The Lawrence Look
Effortless glamor infused with a playful edge.

- Sleek gowns with daring cuts
- Muted palettes punctuated by jewel tones
- Relaxed, understated daywear
- A knack for blending modernity with classic Hollywood poise

LUPITA NYONG'O

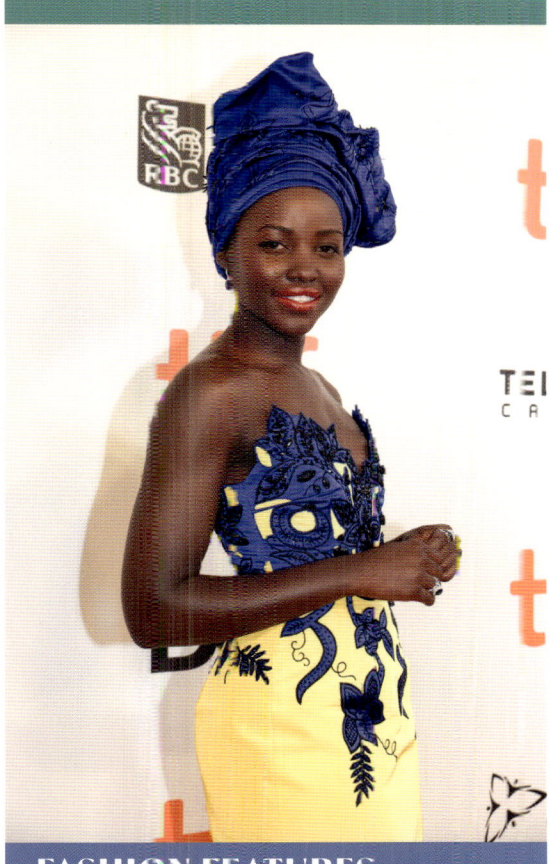

FASHION FEATURES

QUEEN OF KATWE (2016)
BLACK PANTHER (2018)
US (2019)

The Nyong'o Look

The actress' taste ranges from classic looks such as surplice dresses and wide-leg dress pants to African-influenced fashions. She doesn't shy away from bright colors or bold prints, but also looks stunning in neutrals and pastels.

- Short, natural hair
- Trousers look
- Ethnic prints and head wraps

Lupita Nyong'o's journey from behind-the-scenes roles to international acclaim is a testament to her talent and determination. After earning a bachelor's degree in film and African studies from Hampshire College in 2007, she worked on productions such as *The Constant Gardener* and *The Namesake*. Her passion for acting led her to the Yale School of Drama, where she obtained a master's degree in 2012.

Nyong'o's breakout role came in 2013 with *12 Years a Slave*, where her portrayal of Patsey earned her an Academy Award for Best Supporting Actress. This performance marked her as the first Kenyan and Mexican actress to win an Oscar. She continued to showcase her versatility in films such as *Non-Stop* (2014), *Queen of Katwe* (2016), and *Us* (2019), where her dual role received critical acclaim.

In the Marvel Cinematic Universe, Nyong'o portrayed Nakia in *Black Panther* (2018) and its sequel, *Black Panther: Wakanda Forever* 2022). She also lent her voice to characters such as Maz Kanata in the *Star Wars* sequel trilogy and Raksha in *The Jungle Book* (2016)

Beyond film, Nyong'o made her Broadway debut in *Eclipsed* (2016), earning a Tony Award nomination. She authored the children's book *Sulwe* (2019), addressing themes of colorism and self-love, which became a *New York Times* bestseller.

An advocate for women's rights and historic preservation, Nyong'o continues to use her platform to inspire and effect change. Her multifaceted career reflects a commitment to storytelling that resonates across cultures and generations.

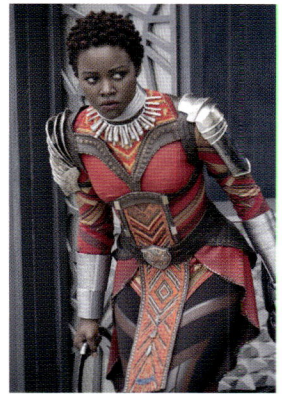

It's great to have something to dress up for...I spent three years in slacks at drama school, so now I like putting dresses on.

LUPITA NYONG'O

ABOVE

In this scene from 2018's *Black Panther*, Nyong'o wears the uniform of the all-female Wakandan guard, the Dora Milaje. The blockbuster's costumes were designed by Ruth E. Carter, the first Black woman to win an Oscar for Costume Design.

LEFT

At the *Queen of Katwe* premiere, Lupita Nyong'o dazzles in a bold yellow-and-blue gown with intricate African-inspired embroidery, crowned by a regal cobalt headwrap—celebrating heritage with red carpet grace.

LEADING MEN
TIMOTHÉE CHALAMET

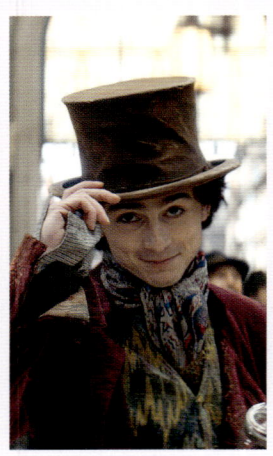

ABOVE
—
A whimsical twist on vintage flair: velvet, pattern clash, and a towering top hat—Timothée Chalamet's Wonka look blends charm, eccentricity, and timeless confectionery style.

RIGHT
—
Timothée Chalamet brings his signature flair to the *A Complete Unknown* premiere photocall in Rome, January 2025. Dressed in a velvet two-piece with exaggerated stitching and a rich plum tone, he layers on a vibrant green scarf and beaded accessories for a look that's eclectic, textured, and completely his own.

FULL PAGE
—
Timothée Chalamet in *A Complete Unknown* embodies Bob Dylan's early mystique—suede, denim, and disheveled charm capturing the raw style of a rising icon on the cusp of legend.

Timothée Chalamet has swiftly ascended to prominence as one of the most versatile and captivating actors of his generation. His breakthrough role came in 2017 with *Call Me by Your Name*, where his portrayal of Elio Perlman garnered critical acclaim and an Academy Award nomination for Best Actor, making him the third-youngest nominee in that category.

Following this success, Chalamet demonstrated his range with performances in films such as *Lady Bird* (2017), *Beautiful Boy* (2018), and *Little Women* (2019). In *Beautiful Boy*, his depiction of a young man battling addiction earned him nominations for both BAFTA and Golden Globe awards. His foray into major franchises began with his role as Paul Atreides in Denis Villeneuve's *Dune* (2021) and its sequel *Dune: Part Two* (2024), solidifying his status as a leading man in blockbuster cinema.

In 2023, he took on the iconic character of Willy Wonka in *Wonka*, a musical fantasy film that showcased his singing abilities and earned him a Golden Globe nomination. The following year, Chalamet portrayed Bob Dylan in the biographical drama *A Complete Unknown*, a role that required him to perform over 40 songs live. His performance was met with widespread acclaim, earning him his second Academy Award nomination and a Screen Actors Guild Award for Best Actor.

Beyond acting, Chalamet has made significant strides in the fashion industry. He became the face of Chanel's men's fragrance, Bleu de Chanel, in 2023, and made history as the first solo male cover star of British *Vogue* in 2022. His personal life has also garnered attention. Since 2023, he has been in a relationship with Kylie Jenner, with

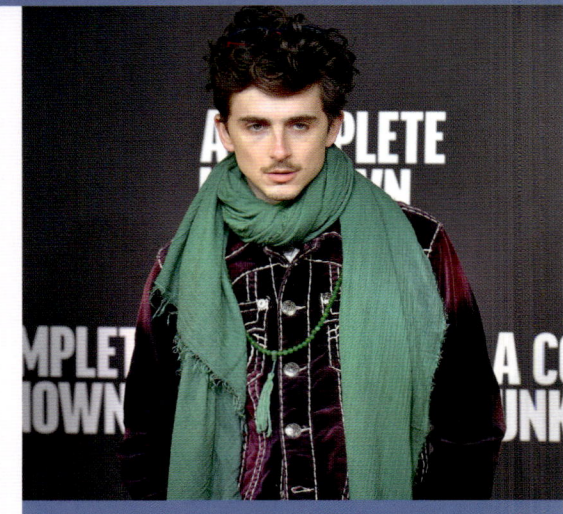

The Chalamet Look
Bold, boundary-pushing, and gender-fluid, Timothée blends sharp tailoring with daring, fashion-forward pieces.

- Slim suits in bold shades
- Backless tops and harnesses
- Statement jewelry
- Tousled hair and minimal fuss

the couple making several public appearances together.

With a career marked by diverse roles and critical acclaim, Timothée Chalamet continues to captivate audiences worldwide, solidifying his place as a defining actor of his generation. In addition to his acting and fashion influence, he is fluent in French and maintains dual U.S.–French citizenship. He studied at Fiorello H. LaGuardia High School of Music & Art and Performing Arts in New York, where he honed his craft. Known for his thoughtful approach to fame, he supports various youth- and arts-focused initiatives.

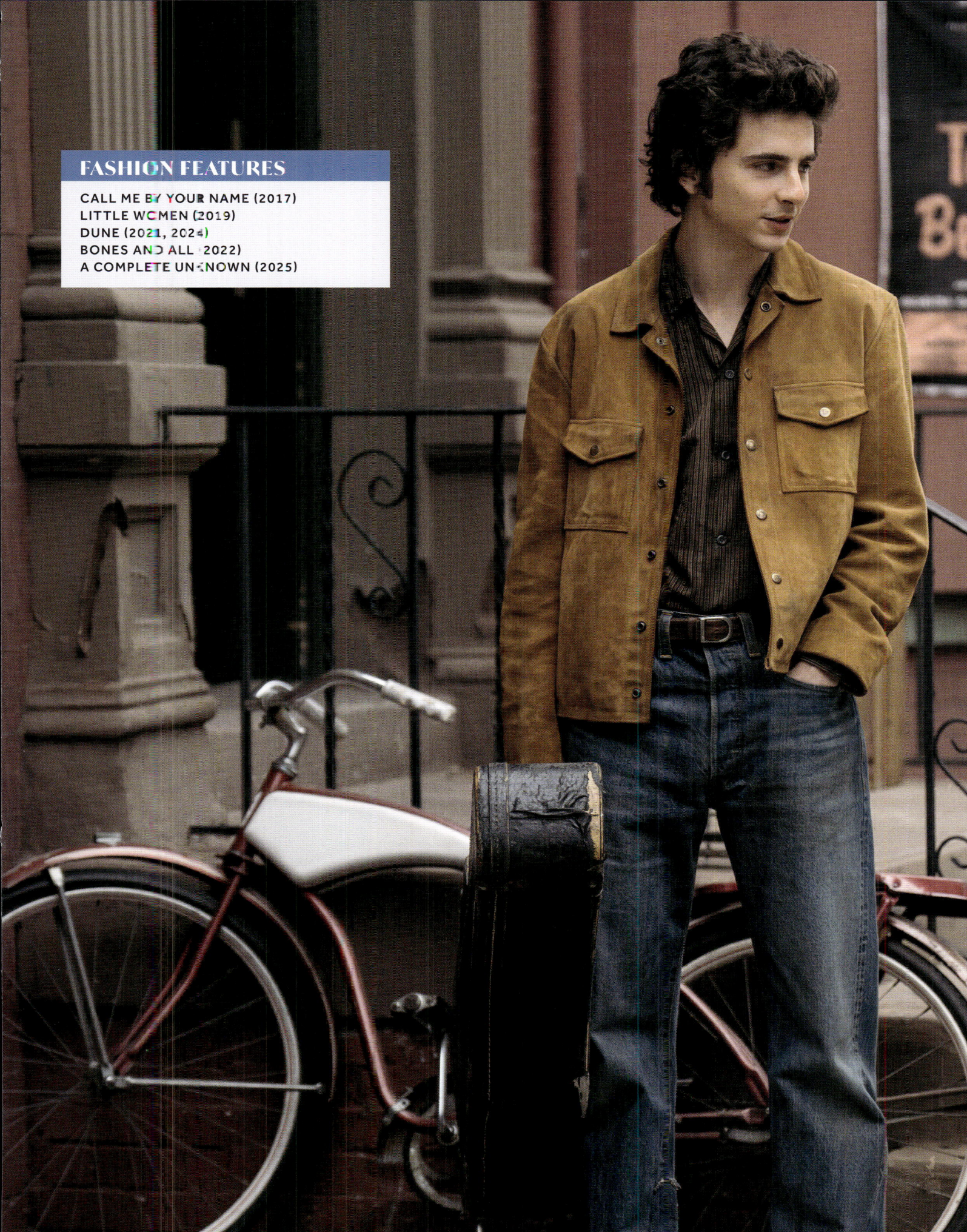

FLORENCE PUGH

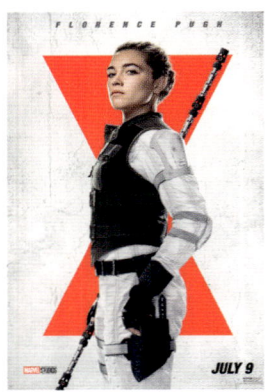

Florence Pugh has swiftly become one of the most dynamic and admired actresses of her generation, known for tackling emotionally intense and varied roles with remarkable ease. Her breakthrough came in 2019 with three critically acclaimed performances. She brought humor and warmth to her portrayal of WWE wrestler Paige in *Fighting with My Family*, then stunned audiences with her raw, haunting performance as Dani in the psychological horror *Midsommar*. Later that year, her portrayal of Amy March in Greta Gerwig's *Little Women* earned her an Academy Award nomination for Best Supporting Actress.

Pugh's ability to shift seamlessly between indie dramas and blockbuster franchises sets her apart. She joined the Marvel Cinematic Universe as Yelena Belova in *Black Widow* (2021), winning praise for her fierce yet humorous performance. She reprised the role in the Disney+ series *Hawkeye*.

In 2022, she starred in *Don't Worry Darling* and *The Wonder*, further proving her dramatic range. She followed this with a standout performance as Jean Tatlock in Christopher Nolan's *Oppenheimer* (2023) and took a leading role in *A Good Person*, which she also co-produced and contributed music to.

Her dedication to her roles is evident—she shaved her head for *We Live in Time* (2024), in which she plays a chef facing terminal illness. Outside of acting, Pugh is a vocal advocate for body positivity and self-acceptance, challenging beauty standards with her confident, unfiltered presence on and off the red carpet. With bold choices and powerful performances, Pugh continues to shape modern cinema on her terms.

RIGHT
———
Florence Pugh at the *Thunderbolts* European premiere in Leicester Square, turning heads in a daring sheer black gown with intricate beading and floral appliqué. Slicked-back hair and bold orange eye makeup amped up the drama, blending gothic glamor with a modern edge.

ABOVE
———
Florence Pugh suits up as Yelena Belova in *Black Widow*, wearing a sleek white tactical ensemble with utility straps and twin batons—blending function and fierce attitude in Marvel's next-gen spy style.

FASHION FEATURES

LADY MACBETH (2016)
MIDSOMMAR (2019)
LITTLE WOMEN (2019)
DON'T WORRY DARLING (2022)
THUNDERBOLTS (2025)

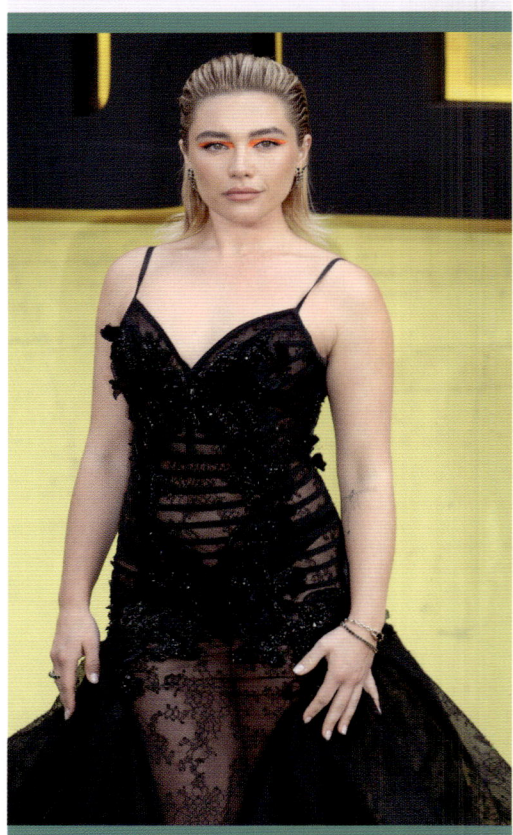

The Pugh Look

Florence Pugh's style is bold and theatrical, mixing sheer fabrics, strong silhouettes, and romantic touches with a punk edge. She's known for turning heads in daring couture with fearless flair.

• Sheer gowns with corset details
• Sculpted mini dresses
• Leather ensembles with bold accessories
• Platinum blonde pixie or spiky hair
• Statement jewelry and smoky eye makeup

MARGOT ROBBIE

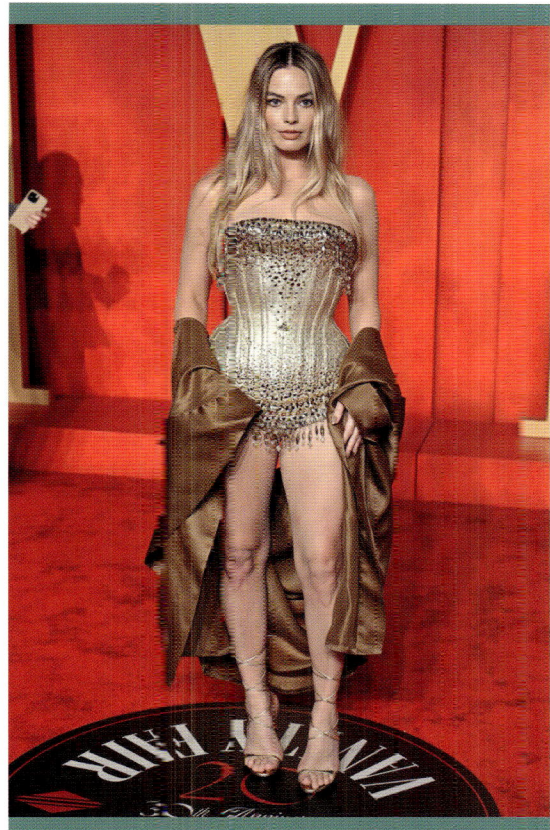

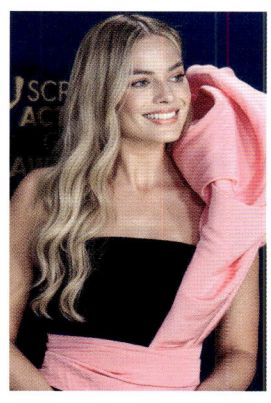

Margot Robbie has mastered the art of Hollywood style evolution. From sun-kissed ingénue to red carpet risk-taker, she blends classic beauty with modern glamor. Whether channeling Old Hollywood or tapping into playful fashion storytelling, Robbie never looks like she's trying too hard—her style feels effortless, intelligent, and curated. She understands the power of image, and each look she wears feels like an extension of the role she's chosen to play.

As a longtime ambassador for Chanel, Robbie has leaned into polished, feminine silhouettes—bouclé skirt suits, sleek column gowns, and delicate embellishments—but she's also proven unafraid to break the mold. Her press tour for *Barbie* (2023) marked a fashion masterstroke: an inspired homage to Mattel doll looks spanning decades, recreated with high-fashion precision and a wink of irony. From sparkling pink minidresses to dramatic opera gloves and polka-dot vintage chic, she turned each appearance into a fashion event.

Robbie balances her bombshell allure with clever restraint. She often chooses clean lines, soft palettes, and sleek tailoring, letting her natural presence do the work. Yet when the occasion calls for it, she embraces drama—structured gowns, bold color, or statement accessories that add personality to polish.

Above all, Margot Robbie dresses with a sense of self-awareness. Her fashion is aspirational, yes—but never out of touch. She's the rare modern icon who can play Barbie, wear Chanel, and still feel entirely original.

The Robbie Look

- Sculpted golden corset
- Crystallized micro hemline
- Bronze satin opera coat
- Barely-there stilettos
- Tousled blonde hair
- Ultra-feminine power glamor redefined

FASHION FEATURES

THE LEGEND OF TARZAN (2016)
ONCE UPON A TIME IN HOLLYWOOD (2019)
BABYLON (2022)
BARBIE (2023)

LEFT
———

Margot Robbie attending the 2024 Vanity Fair Oscar Party in Beverly Hills, California. Wearing a sparkling, gold beaded corset mini-dress with a bronze satin coat draped off the shoulders, Robbie evoked Old Hollywood glamor with a futuristic twist. The structured silhouette and crystal fringe channeled red carpet decadence while showcasing her bold, body-confident style.

ABOVE
———

Margot Robbie wearing Schiaparelli FW20 Couture at the 30th Annual Screen Actors Guild Awards, held at the Shrine Auditorium and Expo Hall in Los Angeles on February 24, 2024. The sculptural blush-pink shoulder swirl channeled high drama with a sense of fun—echoing the spirit of Barbie, while the sleek black bodice grounded the look in modern elegance.

LEADING MEN
TOM CRUISE

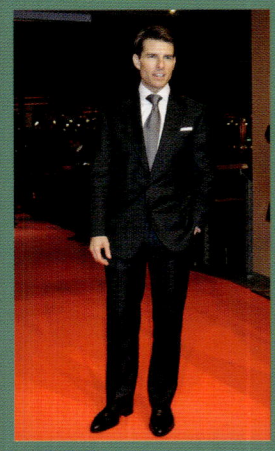

In the 2000s, Tom Cruise transitioned from Hollywood heartthrob to global icon, and his fashion sense evolved to reflect that shift. Whereas the 80s saw Cruise introducing bomber jackets and aviators to a generation in Top Gun, and the 90s solidified his everyman appeal, the new millennium saw Cruise embrace a more refined, tailored, and mature aesthetic. His style in the 2000s mirrored his career's progression–precise, polished, and subtly commanding.

Cruise became a master of understated elegance, favoring classic silhouettes over fleeting trends. Whether walking red carpets or promoting blockbuster hits such as *Minority Report* (2002), *The Last Samurai* (2003), *War of the Worlds* (2005), and *Mission: Impossible III* (2006), he consistently chose sleek suits in neutral tones—grays, blacks, and midnight blues. These looks, often crafted by designers such as Giorgio Armani or Tom Ford, spoke volumes without shouting. The fit was always flawless: slim, never tight, with clean lines that accentuated his lean physique.

What stood out most in Cruise's 2000s wardrobe was his attention to detail. He rarely wore anything overly embellished or experimental. Instead, he mastered the art of minimalism with confidence. A perfect example is his penchant for crisp white shirts under single-breasted jackets, usually paired with black leather shoes and the occasional narrow tie. It was a no-nonsense, leading-man look—an ensemble that communicated charm, professionalism, and gravitas in equal measure.

For more casual appearances, Cruise favored smart-casual looks that struck a balance between youthful and mature. Slim-fit jeans, leather jackets, and polo shirts became go-to staples. He'd often be seen off-duty in darkwash jeans paired with suede boots or classic sneakers, layering with neutral-toned crewnecks or jackets. His approach to casual fashion emphasized structure, simplicity, and timelessness—clothing that wouldn't look out of place a decade later.

One accessory that remained a constant in Cruise's wardrobe through the 2000s was his eyewear. His affinity for aviator sunglasses—most famously tied to his *Top Gun* legacy—continued to define his off-screen persona. The Ray-Ban aviators became his signature, reinforcing an air of coolness that never felt contrived.

ABOVE

Tom Cruise stands on the red carpet at the Berlinale premiere of *Valkyrie* (2009), dressed in a dark tailored suit and tie, exuding leading-man poise in a moment of international cinematic diplomacy.

RIGHT

In *Top Gun* (1986), Tom Cruise as Lt. Pete "Maverick" Mitchell gives a thumbs-up from the cockpit, framed by an American flag backdrop—an enduring pose that defined a generation of aviation-fueled bravado.

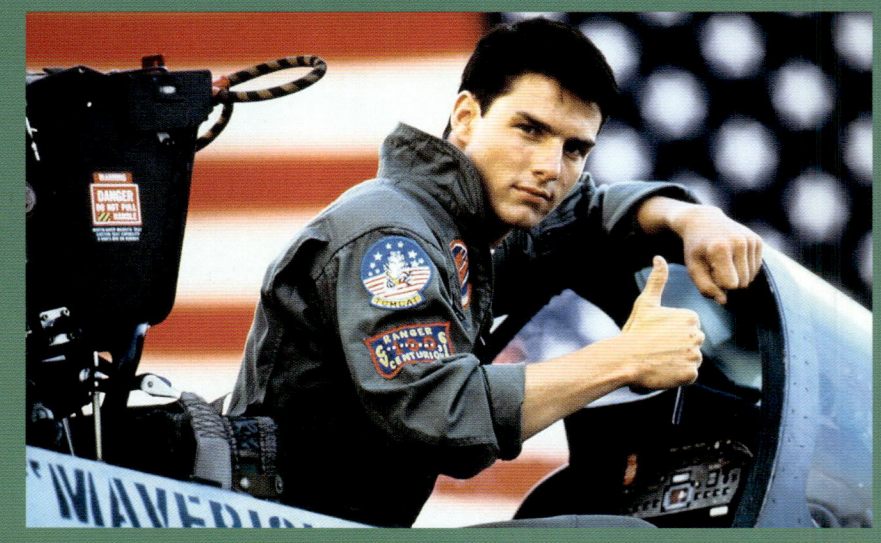

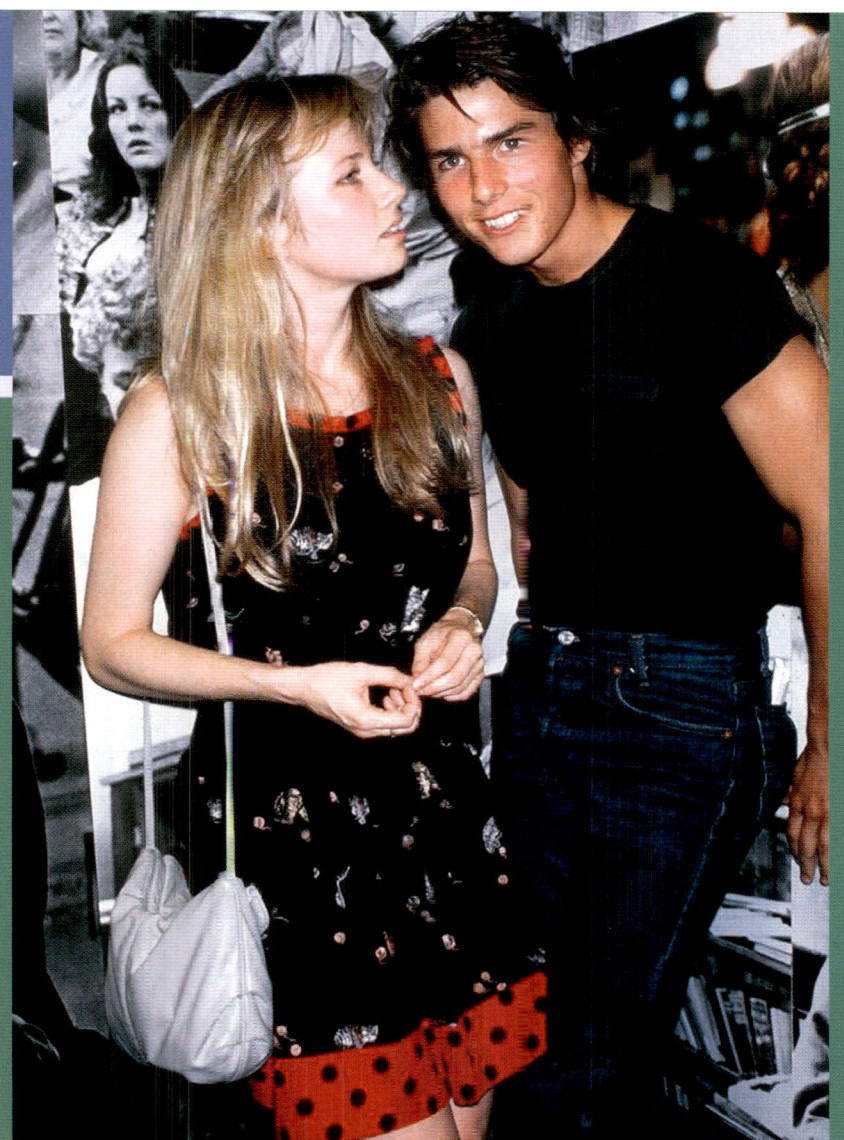

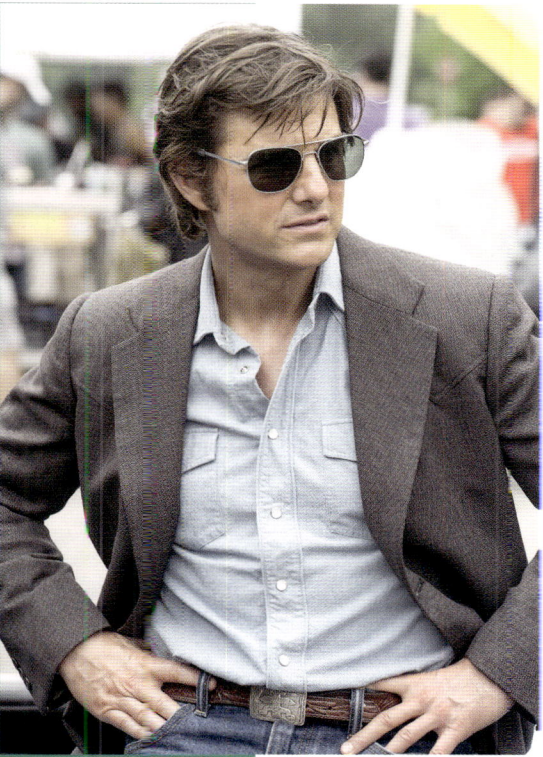

Notably, Cruse's fashion sense during this era also aligned closely with his public image as a meticulous, high-performing actor. Every appearance seemed calculated to reinforce his brand: dependable, driven, and undeniably stylish. Although he never pushed avant-garde boundaries such as some of his peers, he didn't need to—his consistency and confidence made him a fashion icon in a more classical sense.

By the end of the decade, Tom Cruise had become a symbol of how to age gracefully in Hollywood. His fashion choices in the 2000s weren't about chasing trends—they were about mastering timeless menswear with finesse. Cruise showed that you could be both a movie star and a style role model without ever looking like you were trying too hard.

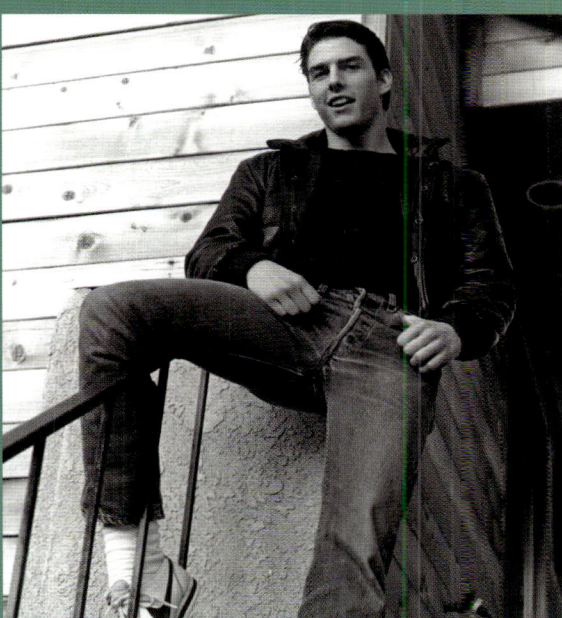

ABOVE

On the set of *American Made* (2017), Tom Cruise channels Barry Seal in aviators, denim, and a sport coat—hands on hips, leaning coolly on a car, caught mid-scene in a tale of risk and ambition.

TOP LEFT

A young Tom Cruise poses with Rebecca de Mornay in a fitted tee and jeans at a 1980s film event, his early charisma already apparent. The backdrop of cinematic legends echoes the ascent of a rising Hollywood star.

LEFT

In another portrait from the early 1980s, a young Tom Cruise in denim, leather, and sneakers leans effortlessly against a stair rail. His star was already on the rise with that of Hollywood's next generation of leading men.

ZOË SALDAÑA

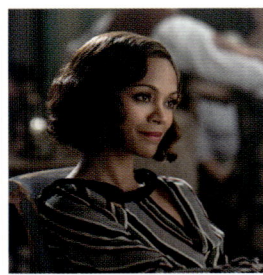

God as my witness, I am going to try to do everything I can to keep this ass together for as long as I possibly can— without going against nature.

ZOË SALDAÑA,
ON PLASTIC SURGERY

Zoe Saldaña's career is a testament to her versatility and enduring appeal in Hollywood. Raised in Queens, New York, she spent part of her youth in the Dominican Republic, where she studied dance at the Ecos Espacio de Danza studio. Returning to New York at 17, Saldaña began performing with youth theater groups, leading to her first film role as a ballet dancer in *Center Stage* **(2000).**

Her early work included roles in *Crossroads* (2002) and *Drumline* (2002), but it was her portrayal of Anamaria in *Pirates of the Caribbean: The Curse of the Black Pearl* (2003) and an immigration officer in *The Terminal* (2004) that garnered wider attention. In 2009, Saldaña achieved a career breakthrough with two iconic roles: Nyota Uhura in *Star Trek* and Neytiri in James Cameron's *Avatar*. Both films were major hits, with *Avatar* becoming the highest-grossing film of all time at its release.

Saldaña continued to captivate audiences as Gamora in Marvel's *Guardians of the Galaxy* (2014) and its sequels, as well as in *Avengers: Infinity War* (2018) and *Avengers: Endgame* (2019). She reprised her role as Neytiri in *Avatar: The Way of Water* (2022). In 2024, her performance in *Emilia Pérez* earned her critical acclaim and several awards, including an Academy Award for Best Supporting Actress.

Beyond film, Saldaña has taken on television roles, starring in the Netflix miniseries *From Scratch* (2022) and the Paramount+ series *Special Ops: Lioness* (2023—), where she plays a CIA operative. Her contributions to science fiction and action genres have solidified her status as a leading actress in Hollywood.

ABOVE

Zoe Saldana channels vintage elegance in *Live by Night*, with soft finger waves and a striped silk blouse that evoke the sultry glamor of 1920s noir.

RIGHT

Zoë Saldaña at the 2013 Vanity Fair Oscar Party, wearing a black halter gown with delicate pleats and a scalloped edge. Her sleek updo, bold red lip, and elegant drop earrings complete a look that's both polished and playful.

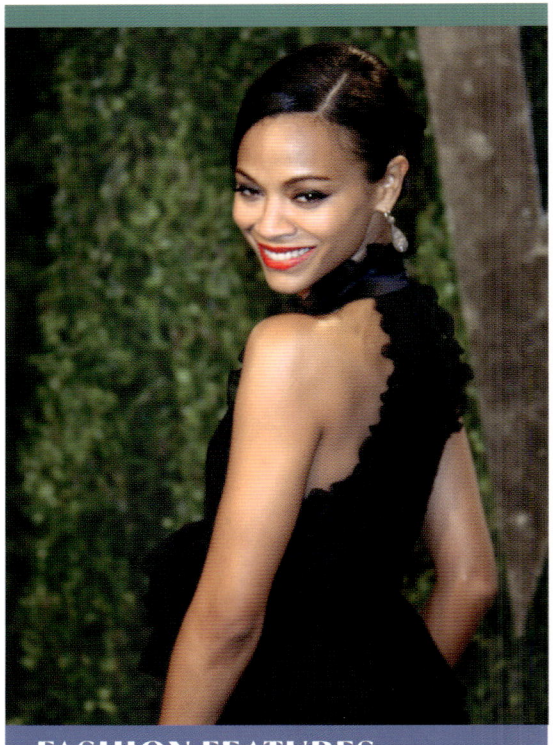

FASHION FEATURES

CENTER STAGE (2000)
AVATAR (2009)
STAR TREK (2009)
GUARDIANS OF THE GALAXY (2014)
NINA (2016)
LIVE BY NIGHT (2016)

The Saldaña Look

An acknowledged style icon, Saldaña believes that she knows what looks best on her body type. For nights out, she prefers pencil skirts or flirty miniskirts, and for the red carpet, she chooses form-fitting or mermaid-style gowns, typically in red, black, or white.

• Jeggings or leggings with short jackets
• High heels
• Long, wavy hair and smudged eyes

EMMA STONE

The Stone Look

Emma's style both on and off the screen is classic, feminine, and sometimes flirty. It has sometimes been described as "accessible." Stone is a favorite on evening talk shows, where she displays crisp comic timing and a throaty laugh.

- Soft dressing
- Minimal make-up and sleek hair
- "Big" coats and jackets

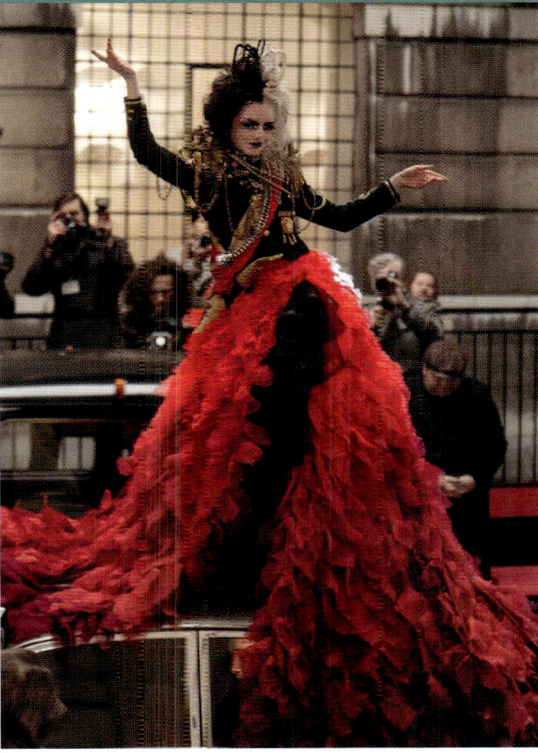

Emma Stone's ascent in Hollywood is marked by her remarkable versatility, magnetic screen presence, and a unique blend of humor and emotional depth. Her breakout role came in 2010 with the teen comedy *Easy A*, where she portrayed a high school student navigating rumors and reputation, earning her a Golden Globe nomination and establishing her as a leading actress.

Stone continued to showcase her range with performances in *Crazy, Stupid, Love* (2011) and *The Help* (2011), both of which were commercial and critical successes. Her portrayal of Gwen Stacy in *The Amazing Spider-Man* (2012) and its 2014 sequel expanded her appeal to blockbuster audiences. In 2014, she earned her first Academy Award nomination for Best Supporting Actress for her role in *Birdman*.

A defining moment in her career was her performance in *La La Land* (2016), where she played an aspiring actress in Los Angeles. The role garnered her an Academy Award, a British Academy Film and Television Arts Award, and a Golden Globe for Best Actress. She continued to take on challenging roles, such as Abigail Masham in *The Favourite* (2018), earning another Oscar nomination.

In 2023, Stone starred in and produced *Poor Things*, a fantasy film that earned her a second Academy Award for Best Actress. She also appeared in the satirical series *The Curse* (2023), receiving critical acclaim.

Beyond acting, Stone co-founded the production company Fruit Tree with her husband, Dave McCary, producing films such as *When You Finish Saving the World* (2022) and *A Real Pain* (2024). Her career reflects a commitment to diverse storytelling and a continuous evolution as an artist.

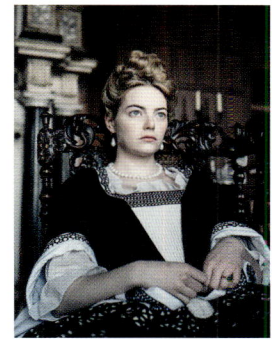

What sets you apart can sometimes feel like a burden and it's not. And a lot of the time, it's what makes you great.
EMMA STONE

ABOVE

Stone plays the scheming cousin of the Duchess of Marlborough in 2018's *The Favourite*. The film showcased lavish period costumes from the early eighteenth century from British designer Sandy Powell.

LEFT

Emma Stone's Cruella in a theatrical ensemble: a fitted military jacket dripping in gold chains atop a billowing train of layered red ruffles—anarchic couture that captures the rebellious spirit of fashion's fiercest antihero.

233

SAOIRSE RONAN

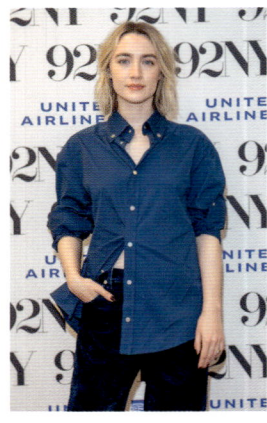

ABOVE
———
At a 92NY discussion event in New York, Saoirse Ronan keeps it sharp yet relaxed in a deep blue button-down with rolled sleeves and velvet trousers. The crisp shirt and undone styling strike a balance between intellect and ease—perfectly suited to the literary setting. Her tousled bob and minimal makeup add polish to a look that whispers confidence without theatrics.

RIGHT
———
Ronan channels sleek modernism in a sculptural white column gown with high neckline and cinched waist, adorned with eyelet detailing. The minimalist silhouette and sharp tailoring echo her signature fashion-forward aesthetic—elegant, intelligent, and quietly subversive. With slicked-back hair and minimal makeup, the look feels both futuristic and timeless, proving once again that Ronan's red carpet style is as considered as her performances.

From precocious talent to red carpet authority, Saoirse Ronan has carved out a singular space in Hollywood—both on screen and in style. With an affinity for fashion that's as intelligent and unpredictable as her roles, she consistently balances classic refinement with modern edge. Never one to chase trends, Ronan has emerged as a muse for designers who value narrative, restraint, and exquisite construction.

Ronan's fashion evolution reflects her acting journey—elegant, cerebral, and subtly subversive. As she transitioned from breakout roles in *Atonement* and *The Lovely Bones* to complex leads in *Lady Bird* and *Little Women*, her red-carpet style matured into a showcase of polished risk-taking. Working frequently with stylist Elizabeth Saltzman, Ronan became a darling of fashion houses like Gucci, Valentino, and Erdem—labels known for storytelling through silhouette and textile.

She's known for embracing vintage-inflected cuts, high necklines, strong shoulders, and painterly prints, often nodding to her Irish heritage with soft romanticism or Celtic minimalism. Whether clad in a sharp houndstooth suit or a fluid embroidered gown, Ronan favors fashion with intent. Her approach is never loud but always resonant—each look seems rooted in purpose, character, and restraint.

Off-duty, Ronan keeps her style pared back and sustainable, favoring ethical designers and understated tailoring. Her quiet fashion authority has earned her the respect of critics and couturiers alike. In a landscape often dominated by spectacle, Ronan offers something rarer: timeless intelligence dressed in silk and structure.

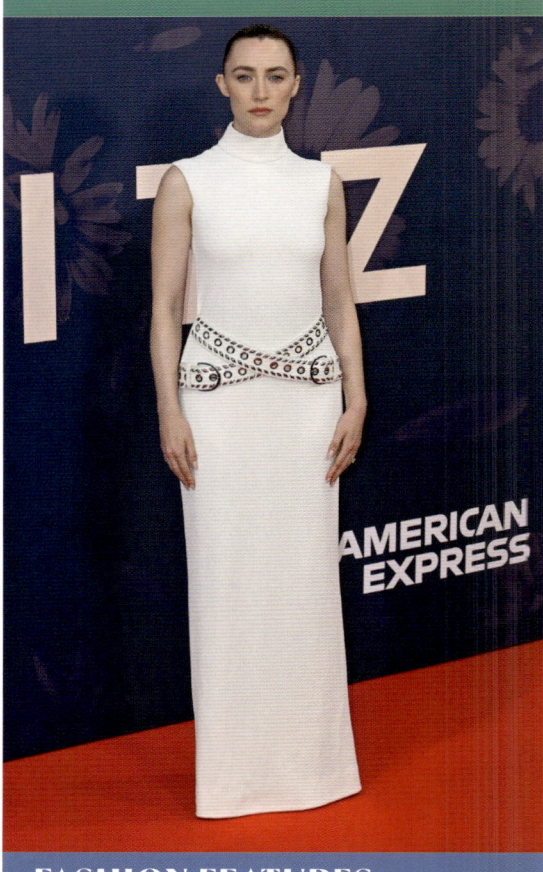

FASHION FEATURES

THE GRAND BUDAPEST HOTEL (2014)
BROOKLYN (2015)
AMMONITE (2020)
SEE HOW THEY RUN (2022)

The Ronan Look
Ladylike polish meets literary depth
• Vintage silhouettes with modern cuts
• Demure necklines and strong tailoring
• Soft florals, embroidered tulle, or sharp suiting
• Understated makeup, sleek buns or loose waves
• Elegant, intelligent, and editorial-ready

CHARLIZE THERON

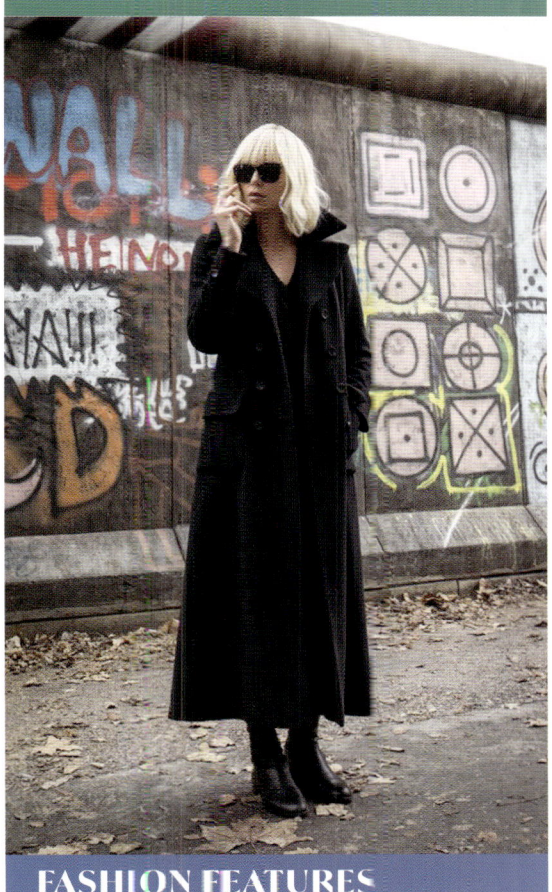

From ballet studios to blockbuster sets, Charlize Theron has carved a remarkable path in entertainment. Born on August 7, 1975, in Benoni, South Africa, she was raised on a farm near Johannesburg and initially pursued a career in ballet. After training at a performing arts boarding school, she moved to Milan at 16 to model, eventually settling in New York City to study at the Joffrey Ballet School. A knee injury ended her dance aspirations but opened the door to acting.

Theron's Hollywood breakthrough came with *The Devil's Advocate* (1997), which led to key roles in *Mighty Joe Young* (1998) and *The Cider House Rules* (1999). Her transformative performance as serial killer Aileen Wuornos in *Monster* (2003) earned her the Academy Award for Best Actress, making her the first South African to win an Oscar for acting.

She followed with acclaimed roles in *North Country* (2005), *Young Adult* (2011), *Mad Max: Fury Road* (2015), *Tully* (2018), and *Bombshell* (2019), which earned her a third Oscar nomination. Known for her willingness to undergo bold physical and emotional changes, Theron is celebrated for her fierce, nuanced performances.

Beyond acting, she is the founder of Denver and Delilah Productions, promoting strong female-led stories. A committed humanitarian, she launched the Charlize Theron Africa Outreach Project to support youth health in Africa and was named a UN Messenger of Peace in 2008.

Now a dual citizen of South Africa and the U.S., Theron remains a vocal champion of gender equality and LGBTQ+ rights worldwide.

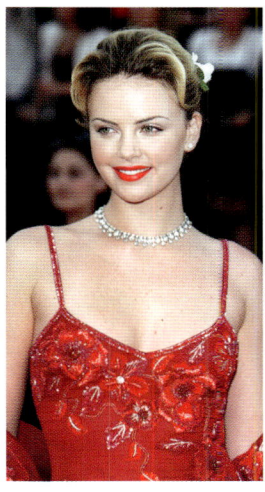

Hey, I'm a girl, and we like to play dress-up.

CHARLIZE THERON

FASHION FEATURES

THE CIDER HOUSE RULES (1999)
THE ITALIAN JOB (2003)
ÆON FLUX (2005)
SNOW WHITE AND THE HUNTSMAN (2012)

The Theron Look

Besides being the face of Dior's J'Adore fragrance, the actress is a red-carpet darling. Off-screen, she prefers trendy separates.

- Sexy black or white evening gowns
- Pencil jeans with masculine jackets and fedoras
- Leather pants with oversized tops

ABOVE

Theron stuns in a red beaded gown with floral embroidery, accented by a diamond necklace and a single flower tucked in her swept-up hair.

LEFT

Charlize Theron exudes icy cool in *Atomic Blonde*, pairing a platinum bob with a sweeping black trench and boots—espionage chic with a punk Berlin edge.

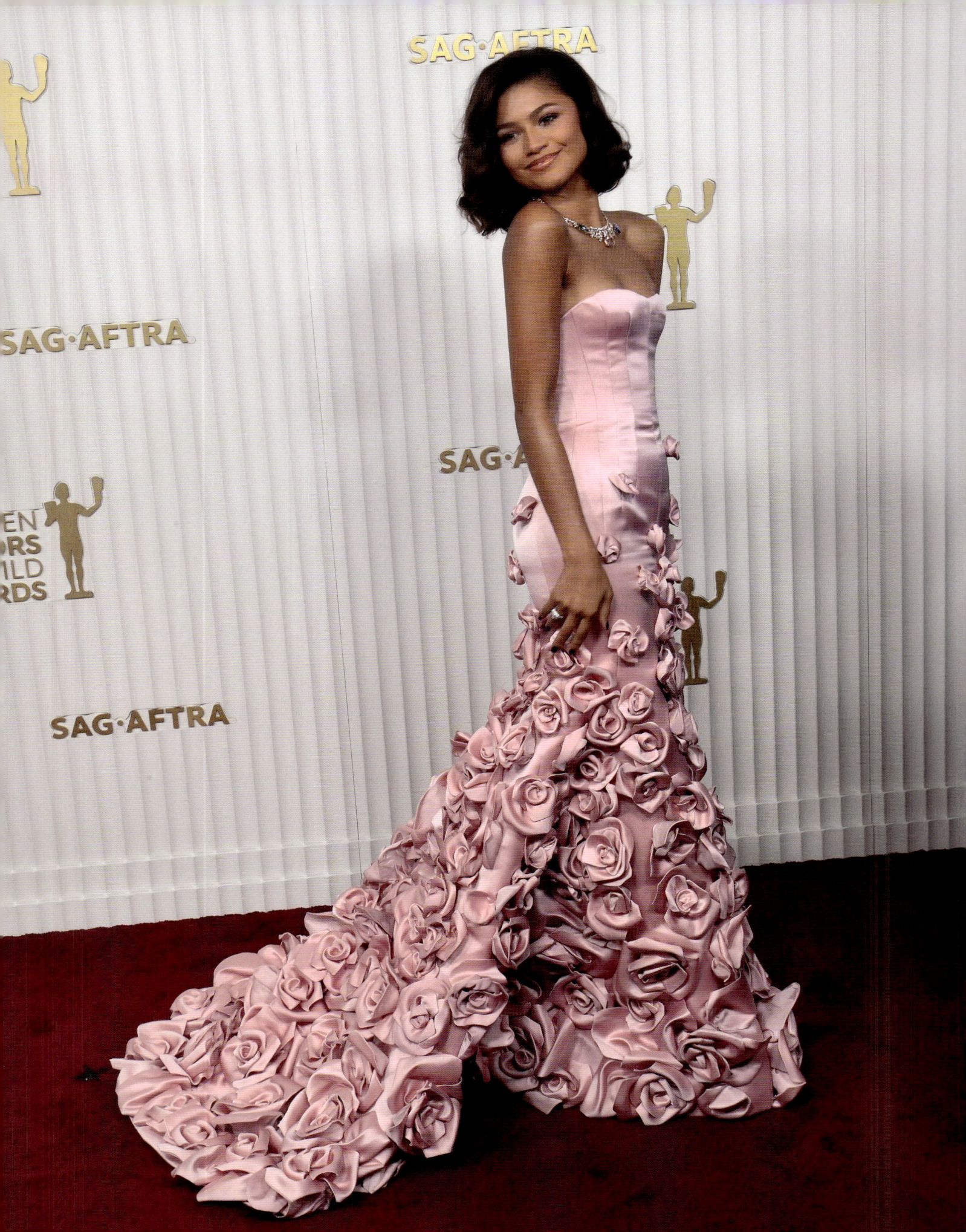

TWENTY TWENTIES

The 2020s began with seismic shifts in both entertainment and fashion. As streaming platforms surged in popularity, actors found new global audiences, and with them came a new era of visibility and influence. Stars such as Timothée Chalamet, known for his fluid fashion sense and red carpet risks, blurred traditional style boundaries. His looks—often custom-made by designers such as Haider Ackermann and Louis Vuitton—helped redefine what modern menswear could be.

Harry Styles further pushed those limits, embracing pearls, sheer blouses, and tailored skirts with confidence, inspiring gender-fluid fashion across generations. Simultaneously, Asian actors and musicians, such as BTS and *Squid Game's* Lee Jung-jae, cemented their positions as global icons, bringing K-fashion to mainstream prominence with clean lines, oversized tailoring, and bold accessories.

Costume design also adapted, reflecting a more inclusive, expressive world. Shows such as *Euphoria* and *Bridgerton* emphasized personal style, from futuristic sparkle to Regency elegance. Meanwhile, superhero and sci-fi franchises such as *The Batman* (2022) and Marvel's Phase 4 introduced darker tones, tactical layering, and stylized armor—all of them trickled into everyday fashion.

Social media accelerated trend cycles and allowed fans to adopt or remix celebrity looks in real time. Red carpet events saw more individuality, less formality, and rising eco-conscious fashion, with stars opting for vintage or sustainably crafted pieces. The 2020s style landscape continues to evolve, driven by digital influence, cultural crossover, and the celebration of authenticity.

PAMELA ANDERSON

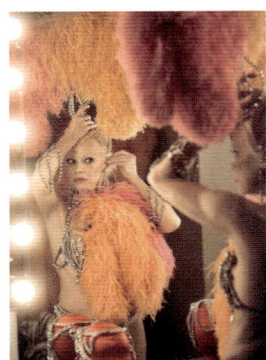

I just want to flip the script; I want to challenge beauty.

PAMELA
ANDERSON

Pamela Anderson has continually reinvented herself, evolving from pop culture icon to acclaimed actress, writer, and activist. She gained widespread recognition in the 1990s through *Baywatch*, but her recent work has earned her renewed critical acclaim. In 2024, Anderson starred in *The Last Showgirl*, portraying Shelly Gardner, a retired Las Vegas performer navigating reinvention and self-discovery. Her performance earned Golden Globe and SAG Award nominations, marking a significant milestone in her acting career.

FASHION FEATURES

BAYWATCH (1992–1997)
RAW JUSTICE (1994)
BARB WIRE (1996)
VIP (1998–2002)
THE LAST SHOWGIRL (2024)

The Anderson Look
From 90s bombshell to modern minimalist, Pamela now favors clean lines, neutral tones, and timeless elegance.

- Monochrome outfits
- Soft curly bob
- Natural makeup
- Simple, classic accessories

ABOVE
Pamela Anderson backstage in her well-reviewed *The Last Showgirl* (2025)— a riot of sequins, satin, and sherbet-toned feathers. The bejeweled bra and towering headdress channel vintage Vegas glam with unapologetic flair, capturing the nostalgia and spectacle of a vanishing world. Lit by mirror bulbs and memory, the look is pure theatrical decadence.

RIGHT
Pamela Anderson reinvents herself in understated glamor at the 2025 Met Gala, wearing a long-sleeved silver gown and barefaced makeup—embracing quiet luxury and redefining red carpet elegance in her 50s.

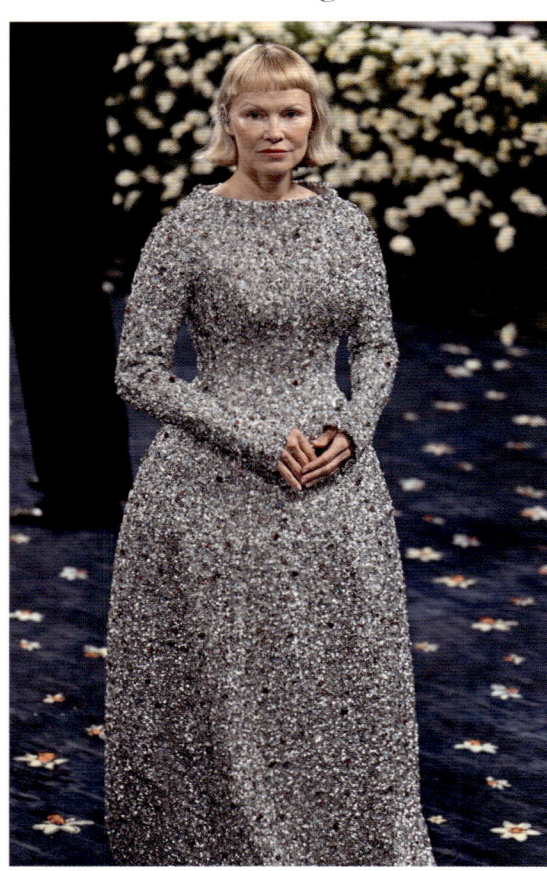

Anderson also embraced a passion for plant-based cooking and healthy living. She launched *Pamela's Cooking with Love*, a vegan culinary series on Canada's Flavour Network, and released the cookbook *I Love You: Recipes from the Heart* (2024), which was nominated for a James Beard Award. A long-time animal rights advocate, she continues to work closely with PETA and other organizations promoting ethical living.

In 2023, Anderson took control of her narrative through the memoir *Love, Pamela* and the Netflix documentary *Pamela, a Love Story*, both of which offered an unfiltered look at her life, fame, and resilience. Rejecting media sensationalism, she has embraced authenticity—often appearing makeup-free at public events as a statement of self-acceptance.

Now living in her hometown of Ladysmith, British Columbia, Anderson focuses on gardening, advocacy, and creativity, proving her legacy extends far beyond the red swimsuit.

JENNA ORTEGA

The Ortega Look

Jenna Ortega's style is a masterclass in gothic glamor. She seamlessly blends vintage references with modern edge often incorporating dark palettes, structured silhouettes, and bold accessories. Her fashion choices reflect a fearless approach to style, making her a standout on red carpets and at fashion events alike.

- Dark, structured ensembles
- Platform heels and statement accessories
- Sleek, dark hairstyles
- Minimalist makeup with bold accents

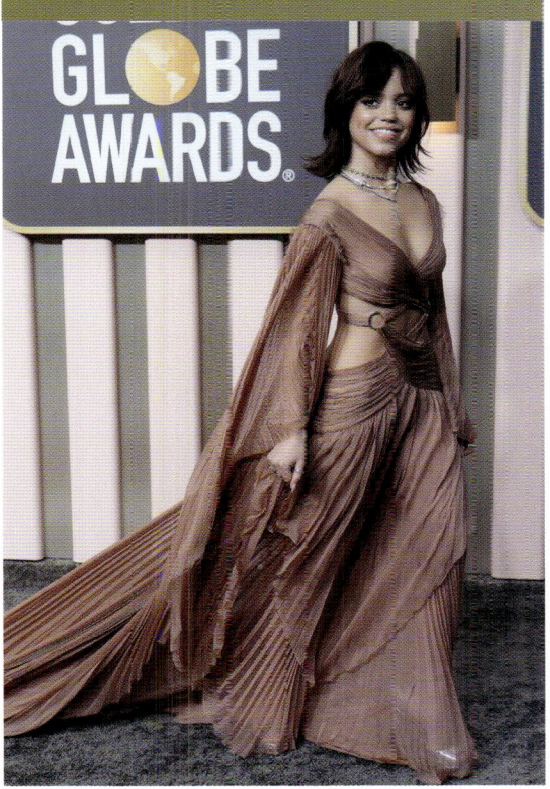

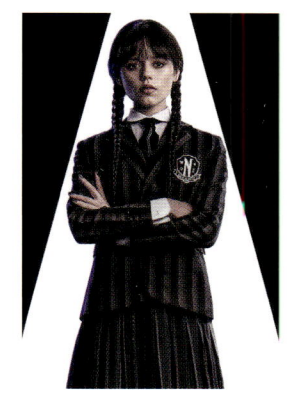

Jenna Ortega has rapidly emerged as one of Hollywood's most compelling young talents, captivating audiences with her versatility and depth across a range of genres. Her career began with notable roles in television, including a recurring part as young Jane in *Jane the Virgin* (2014–2019) and a leading role as Harley Diaz in Disney Channel's *Stuck in the Middle* (2016–2018), for which she received an Imagen Award.

Transitioning into more mature roles, Ortega starred as Ellie Alves in the second season of Netflix's thriller series *You* (2019), earning praise for her performance. She continued to showcase her range with roles in films such as *The Fallout* (2021), where she portrayed a high school student dealing with the aftermath of a school tragedy, and *Yes Day* (2021), a family comedy that highlighted her comedic timing.

Ortega's portrayal of Wednesday Addams in Netflix's *Wednesday* (2022–) marked a significant breakthrough, earning her nominations for a Golden Globe, Primetime Emmy, and Screen Actors Guild Award. Her performance was lauded for bringing a fresh perspective to the iconic character.

In the horror genre, Ortega has been dubbed "Gen Z's scream queen," with standout performances in *Scream* (2022), *X* (2022), and *Scream VI* (2023). Her ability to convey vulnerability and strength has resonated with audiences and critics alike.

Beyond acting, Ortega has ventured into production, serving as an executive producer for the romantic drama *Winter Spring Summer or Fall* (2024), in which she also stars. She continues to expand her creative horizons with projects such as *Death of a Unicorn* (2025), a dark fantasy comedy where she stars alongside Paul Rudd.

ABOVE

Jenna Ortega redefines gothic schoolgirl chic in *Wednesday*—a razor-sharp pleated skirt, striped blazer, and signature braids merge moody minimalism with macabre sophistication.

LEFT

Jenna Ortega sweeps through the 2023 Golden Globe Awards in pleated Gucci chiffon, her tousled bob and cutout gown channeling 1970s glamor with avant-garde poise.

LEADING MEN
COLMAN DOMINGO

> **I'm inspiring generations of men to be like, "Yeah, I want to put that shit on too."**
>
> COLMAN DOMINGO

Colman Domingo has emerged as one of the most dynamic and multifaceted talents in contemporary entertainment, seamlessly bridging theater, film, and television with his distinctive presence and storytelling prowess.

After graduating from Temple University with a degree in journalism, Domingo transitioned into acting, beginning his career on stage in San Francisco. He gained early acclaim for his performances in productions such as *Passing Strange* and *The Scottsboro Boys*, earning nominations for both Tony and Olivier Awards. His autobiographical solo play, *A Boy and His Soul*, showcased his depth as a playwright and performer, winning a Lucille Lortel Award.

Domingo's film career features a range of impactful roles. He portrayed civil rights leader Ralph Abernathy in *Selma* (2014), and appeared in *If Beale Street Could Talk* (2018) and *Ma Rainey's Black Bottom* (2020). His portrayal of Bayard Rustin in the biopic *Rustin* (2023) earned him nominations for the Academy Award, BAFTA, and Golden Globe for Best Actor, marking a significant milestone as the first Afro-Latino and openly gay American to receive an Oscar nomination for playing a gay character. In *Sing Sing* (2024), he delivered a compelling performance as an incarcerated man finding redemption through theater, further solidifying his reputation for powerful character work.

On television, Domingo is widely recognized for his role as Victor Strand in AMC's *Fear the Walking Dead* (2015–2023) and as Ali in HBO's *Euphoria*, a performance that earned him a Primetime Emmy Award in 2022. His recent work includes leading roles in Netflix's *The Madness* (2024) and voicing Norman Osborn in Marvel's animated series *Your Friendly Neighborhood Spider-Man* (2025).

RIGHT

Colman Domingo makes a bold statement at the 97th Academy Awards in a striking red double-breasted jacket with black lapels and a matching sash belt. Paired with wide-leg black trousers and gold accessories, the look blends classic tailoring with theatrical flair.

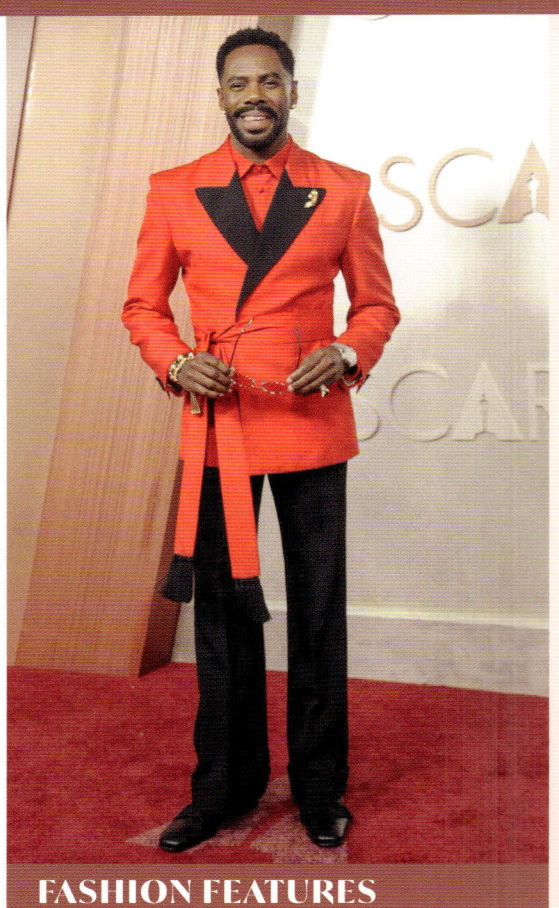

FASHION FEATURES

RUSTIN (2023)
SING SING (2024)
THE COLOR PURPLE (2023)
ZOLA (2021)
MA RAINEY'S BLACK BOTTOM (2020)

The Domingo Look

Confident and expressive, Colman blends classic tailoring with bold colors and high-fashion flair.

• Vibrant suits
• Dramatic outerwear
• Statement accessories
• Sharp, unique tailoring

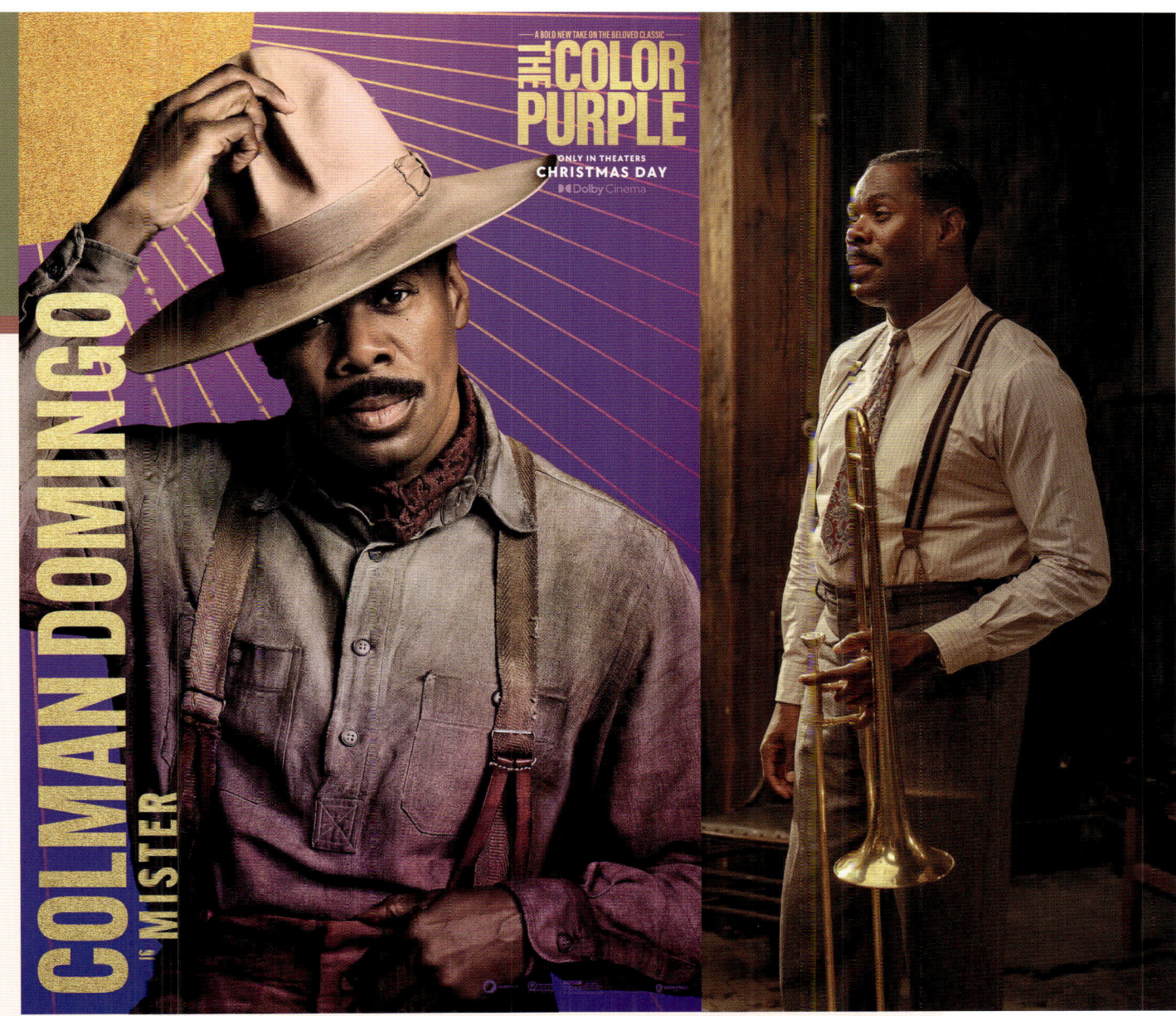

A BOLD NEW TAKE ON THE BELOVED CLASSIC

THE COLOR PURPLE

ONLY IN THEATERS
CHRISTMAS DAY
Dolby Cinema

COLMAN DOMINGO

IS MISTER

Beyond acting, Domingo is a prolific writer and director. His plays, such as *Dot* and *Wild with Happy*, have been produced at esteemed venues such as The Public Theater and the Vineyard Theatre. He co-wrote the Broadway musical *Summer: The Donna Summer Musical* and is set to direct and star in an upcoming Nat King Cole biopic. Through his production company, Edith Productions, he continues to develop projects that amplify diverse voices and stories.

Domingo's contributions have been recognized with numerous accolades, including a Primetime Emmy Award, multiple NAACP Image Awards, and honors from film festivals and critics' associations. In 2024, *Time* magazine named him one of the 100 most influential people in the world, acknowledging his impact on the arts and culture.

Openly gay and an advocate for LGBTQ+ representation, Domingo's personal and professional journey reflects a commitment to authenticity, resilience, and the transformative power of storytelling.

In addition to his work in entertainment, Colman Domingo is a passionate educator and mentor. He has taught acting and playwriting at institutions such as the University of Texas at Austin and has spoken widely on representation in media. Actively involved in advocacy, he supports numerous initiatives focused on diversity, mental health awareness, and uplifting marginalized voices through the arts.

ABOVE

Colman Domingo in *Ma Rainey's Black Bottom* exudes 1920s elegance—pinstripes, suspenders, and a paisley tie meet the soulful weight of jazz, bringing style and history into perfect harmony.

TOP LEFT

Colman Domingo commands the screen in *The Color Purple* with rugged charisma—earth-toned workwear, worn suspenders, and a wide-brimmed hat evoke a timeless masculinity shaped by hardship and pride.

LEADING MEN
CHANNELING THE GOLDEN ERA

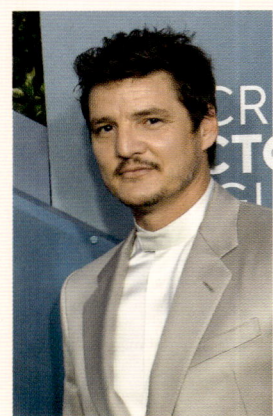

The Golden Age of Hollywood never really ended—it just went undercover. In an age of red carpet experimentation and streetwear ubiquity, a certain breed of leading man continues to draw from the classic style playbook: structured tailoring, open collars, cigarette trousers, polished loafers, and that intangible mix of charm and cool that once belonged to Cary Grant, Sidney Poitier, Paul Newman, and Alain Delon. Their secret isn't nostalgia—it's restraint. These men understand that old-school elegance still holds power, especially when filtered through modern sensibilities.

The hallmarks remain recognizable: suits that hang just so, sunglasses that whisper rather than shout, hair that's styled but never sprayed stiff. It's a look that communicates confidence through understatement. And while the style may originate from mid-century ideals, today's leading men bring with them new codes of masculinity—queer, global, quietly defiant. The cut might be softer, the accessories more playful, but the silhouette still says one thing clearly: movie star.

Actors like Andrew Scott and Riz Ahmed bring a relaxed intelligence to their looks—swapping bow ties for buttonless knits, favoring fabric over flash. Others, like Daniel Craig and Brad Pitt, have evolved their style alongside their careers, toggling between rugged and refined, classic and directional. The influence of Europe is palpable too: think Italian sprezzatura, French minimalism, and the effortless cool of contemporary British tailoring.

What unites these men isn't uniformity—it's conviction. Whether in sharp monochrome or soft neutrals, vintage denim or summer suiting, they dress as if they know who they are. It's a far cry from costume or homage. The influence of the golden era lingers not as mimicry, but as a mood—of precision, of polish, of presence. Where once tuxedos ruled, now we see slouchy suits with attitude, tonal layering, and the return of quietly decadent fabrics: silk, velvet, linen worn like armor and air.

The most stylish leading men today understand what their forebears did: that great clothes don't scream, they speak. They set the stage before the actor even says a word. They gesture to legacy while leaning forward. And they know that a well-cut lapel, like a well-delivered line, can steal the scene.

ABOVE

Pedro Pascal at the 2023 SAG Awards, clad in dove-gray tailoring and clerical collar—an emblem of modern masculinity tinged with quiet, cinematic defiance.

RIGHT

Brad Pitt and Leonardo DiCaprio bring effortless Old Hollywood charm to Cannes, echoing the camaraderie and cool of Newman and Redford, sporting tailored classics, sunglasses, and swagger.

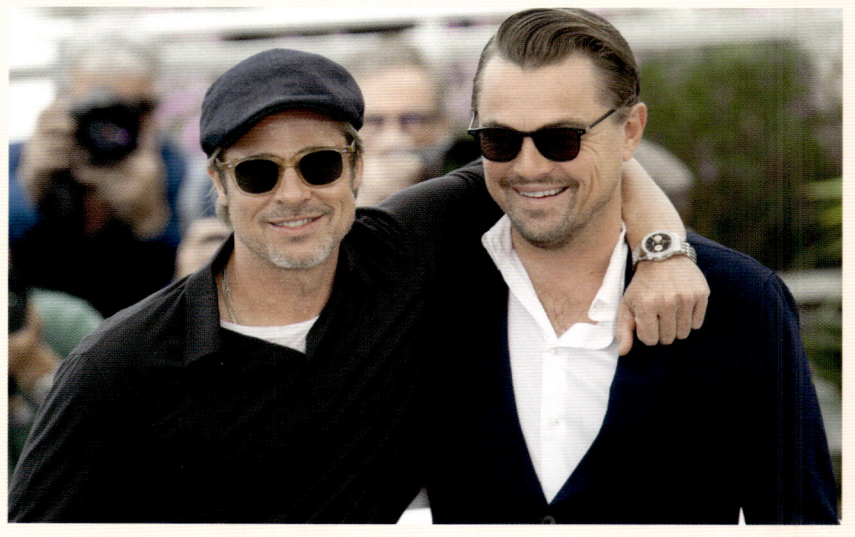

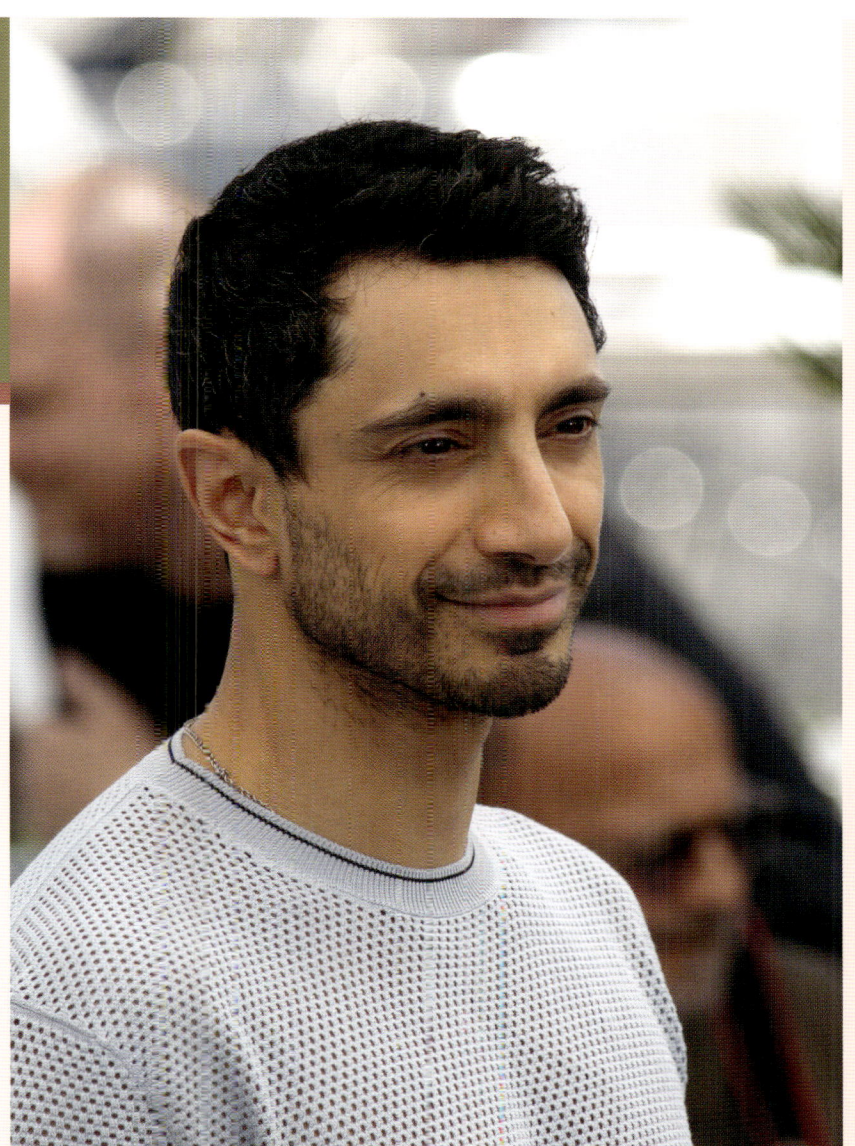

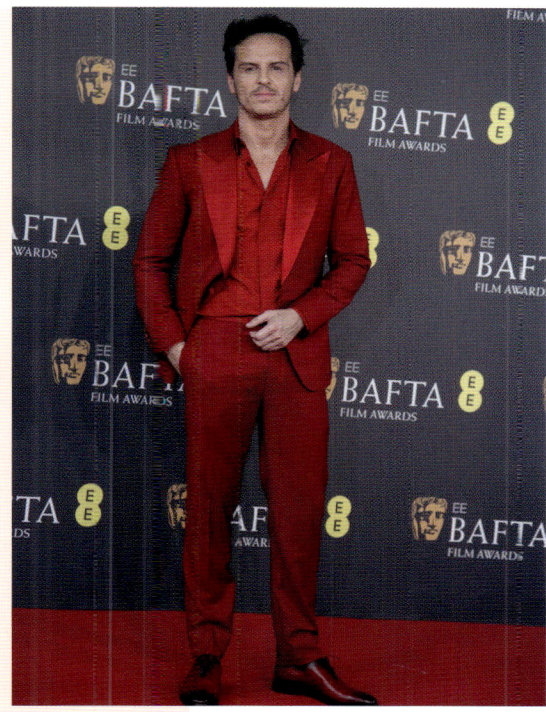

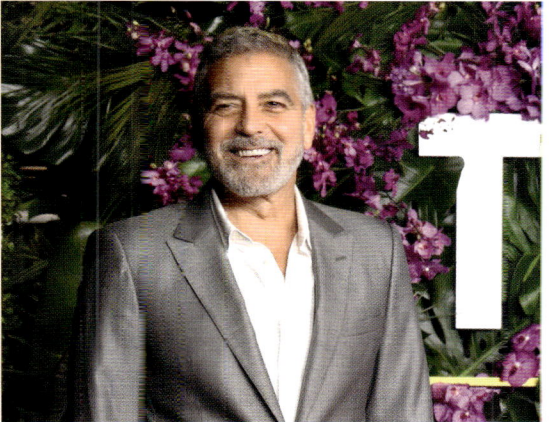

This isn't about dressing like it's 1949. It's about dressing like you know it's the 2020s—and choosing elegance anyway. In the right hands, a suit still sings. And in the right light, even the past feels like the future.

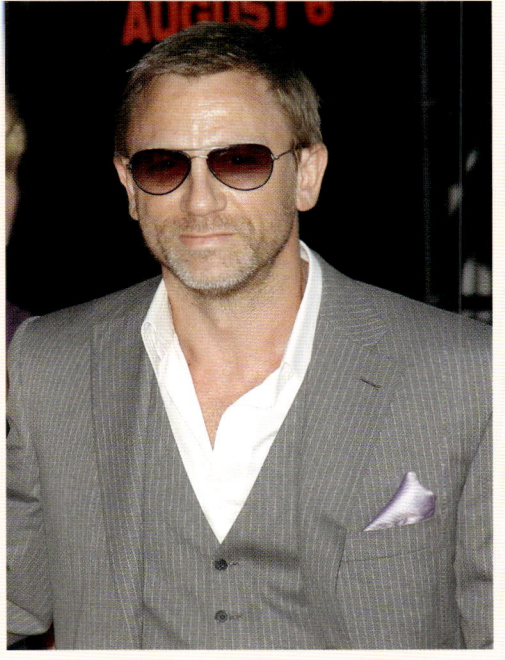

ABOVE

Riz Ahmed redefines laid-back elegance at Cannes 2025, pairing a textured knit with quiet confidence, proving that subtle style can speak volumes on the world stage.

RIGHT

Daniel Craig softens the sharp edges of suiting at the *Pineapple Express* premiere with a pinstripe vest, open collar, and lavender pocket square—evoking Rat Pack cool with a modern, Bond-worthy twist.

TOP

Andrew Scott turns up the heat in a crimson-tone tuxedo with matching shirt and shoes at the 2024 BAFTA Film Awards, giving classic tailoring a bold, monochrome twist.

ABOVE

George Clooney channels old-school charm with effortless ease, pairing a silver sheen suit with an open white shirt, he radiates the timeless allure of a modern-day Cary Grant.

HUNTER SCHAFER

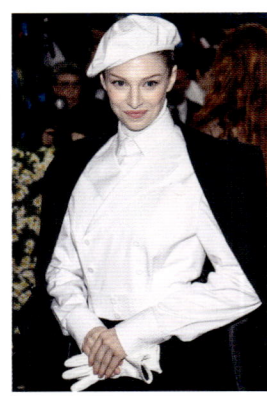

In a landscape often defined by tradition and conformity, Hunter Schafer has carved out a space all her own—one that fuses fashion, identity, and cinematic presence. A model, actress, and activist, Schafer has emerged as one of Hollywood's most daring style icons of the 2020s. Her red carpet appearances defy gendered convention, playing instead with theatrical silhouettes, sharp tailoring, and sculptural form. She brings a rare synthesis of high fashion and avant-garde expression to every look, reflecting a new generation's embrace of fluidity, rebellion, and individuality.

From the moment she stepped into the spotlight, Schafer has used fashion as both a shield and a beacon. Whether wrapped in whimsical Iris van Herpen gowns or precise Thom Browne tailoring, she evokes a fearless elegance that feels at once futuristic and deeply personal. Her partnership with major fashion houses—Dior, Prada, Mugler—has become symbiotic, with designers tailoring pieces specifically to her lithe, statuesque frame and expressive persona.

But Schafer's influence is more than visual. Her presence at industry events and on film sets alike signifies a reshaping of beauty standards and gender expectations. In Euphoria, she didn't just wear costume—she inhabited it, turning clothing into narrative. And offscreen, she has remained a vocal advocate for LGBTQ+ rights, bringing authenticity to every public appearance.

Hunter Schafer doesn't simply follow trends— she helps write them. With a sense of style that is sculptural, cerebral, and consistently bold, she represents a new frontier in Hollywood fashion: one where self-expression, politics, and aesthetics walk hand in hand.

RIGHT

Hunter exudes sleek glamor in a liquid gold gown with dramatic feathered train at the 2025 Vanity Fair Oscar Party in Beverly Hills, pairing 1930s sensuality with futuristic attitude.

ABOVE

Schafer channels androgynous elegance in a sculptural Thom Browne ensemble at the 2025 Met Gala, reimagining classic tailoring with futuristic poise for the "Superfine: Tailoring Black Style" theme.

FASHION FEATURES

THE HUNGER GAMES: THE BALLAD OF SONGBIRDS & SNAKES (2023)
BELLE (2023)
CUCKOO (2024)
MOTHER MARY (2025)

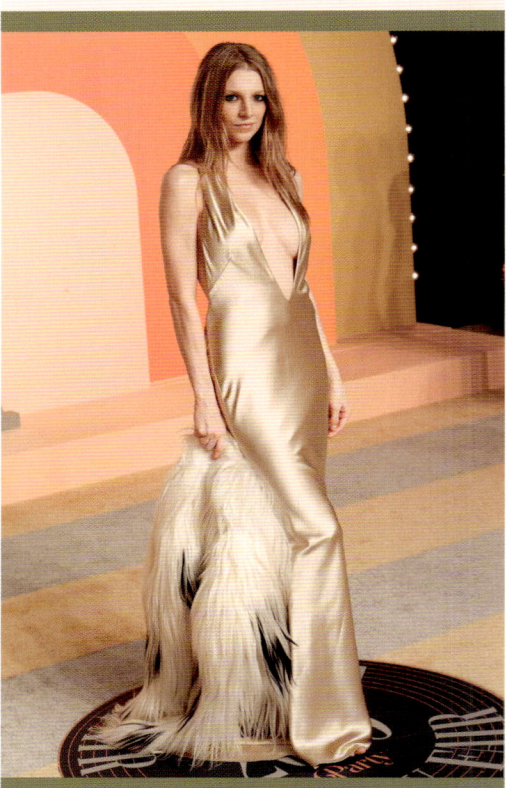

The Schafer Look

Hunter Schafer's style is bold, cerebral, and boundary-breaking— where fashion meets futurism and form becomes statement.

• Sculptural silhouettes
• Androgynous tailoring
• Ethereal makeup
• High-concept couture
• Metallics and mesh
• Anime and sci-fi influences
• Sleek platinum hair
• Experimental textures
• Custom pieces by Loewe, Prada, and Thom Browne
• A fearless fusion of fashion, identity, and art

NAOMI SCOTT

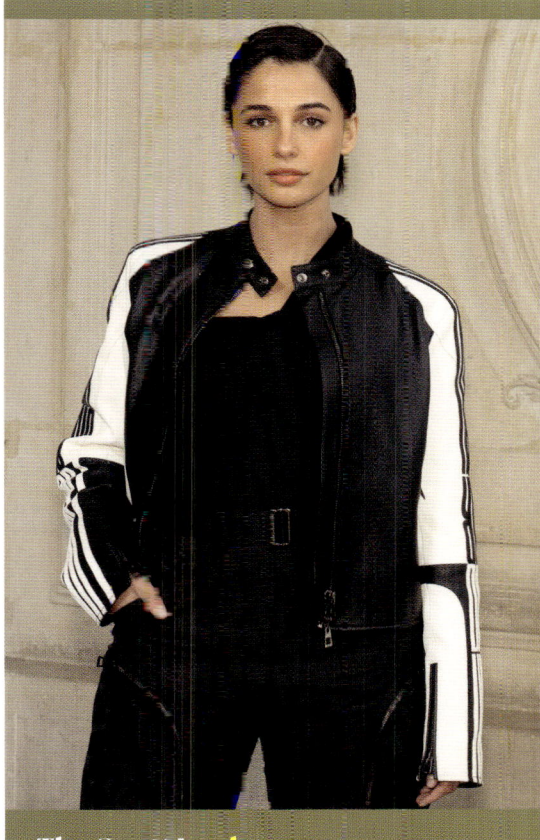

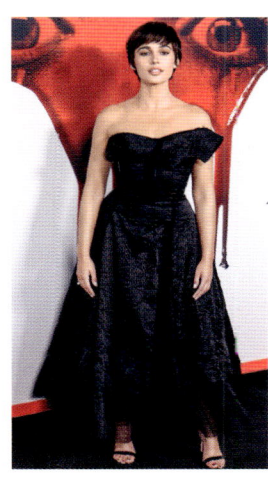

Naomi Scott is a modern fashion chameleon—elegant, edgy, and always unexpected. With a background in music and film, she brings both theatricality and cool restraint to the red carpet. Whether channeling old-Hollywood glamor or opting for minimalist futurism, her style is never stagnant. Scott dresses with an intelligent intentionality, using fashion to express both strength and softness, presence and play. Every look feels considered, contemporary, and just a little bit bold.

Catapulted into the spotlight with her role as Princess Jasmine in *Aladdin* (2019), Scott quickly established herself as a fashion force. She has since cultivated a red carpet identity defined by architectural tailoring, rich textures and a fearless use of structure. She favors brands like Burberry, Valentino, and Givenchy—labels known for clean lines and modern luxury—but often selects looks with asymmetry, sharp shoulders or dramatic silhouettes that reflect her sharp creative instincts.

Scott's style plays with contrasts: masculine vs. feminine, sleek vs. romantic, bold color vs. muted monochrome. A scarlet power suit might be followed by a soft lilac gown with sheer panels and delicate embroidery. Her hair and makeup, often understated, allow the fashion to speak—but a strong lip or slicked-back style can add punctuation when needed.

In an industry saturated with fashion moments, Naomi Scott delivers fashion statements. Her looks command attention but quietly, with elegance and impact.

The Scott Look

Elegant yet modern, Naomi Scott blends classic silhouettes with contemporary edge.

- Sculptural tailoring
- Off-shoulder gowns
- Monochrome palettes
- Statement necklines
- Futuristic textures
- Sleek minimalism

FASHION FEATURES

ALADDIN (2019)
CHARLIE'S ANGELS (2019)
ANATOMY OF A SCANDAL (TV, 2022)
DISTANT (2024)

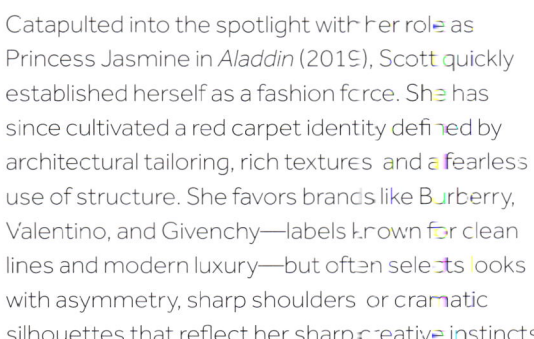

LEFT

Scott brings monochrome elegance with a sporty twist to the Christian Dior Haute Couture Spring–Summer 2025 show in Paris, pairing structured tailoring with a sleek zip-up silhouette and understated hair.

ABOVE

Naomi channels gothic romance at the *Smile 2* premiere in Los Angeles, pairing a sculptural black strapless dress with sheer tulle underlay and a chic pixie cut for dramatic modern elegance.

ANYA TAYLOR-JOY

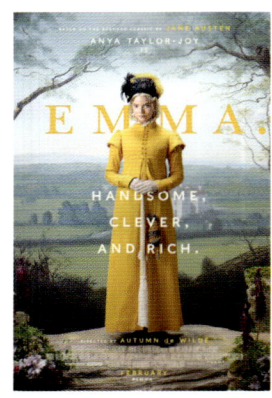

Anya Taylor-Joy has swiftly emerged as one of the most captivating and versatile actors of her generation, known for her distinctive screen presence and transformative performances. Her breakthrough role came in Robert Eggers' 2015 horror film _The Witch_, where she portrayed Thomasin, a young Puritan girl facing supernatural forces in 17th-century New England. The film's critical success spotlighted Taylor-Joy's talent, earning her the Empire Award for Best Female Newcomer.

Building on this momentum, Taylor-Joy took on diverse roles that showcased her range. In M. Night Shyamalan's _Split_ (2016) and its sequel _Glass_ (2019), she played Casey Cooke, a teenager confronting a man with dissociative identity disorder. Her performance in _Thoroughbreds_ (2017) further demonstrated her ability to delve into complex characters.

In 2020, Taylor-Joy starred as Emma Woodhouse in _EMMA._, a film adaptation of Jane Austen's novel. Her portrayal brought a fresh perspective to the classic character, earning her a Golden Globe nomination.

It was, however, her role as Beth Harmon in Netflix's _The Queen's Gambit_ (2020) that catapulted her to international stardom. As the orphaned chess prodigy battling personal demons, Taylor-Joy delivered a nuanced performance that garnered her a Golden Globe Award and a Screen Actors Guild Award.

Taylor-Joy continued to take on challenging roles, such as her performance in _The Menu_ (2022), where she played a young woman navigating a high-stakes dining experience. In _The Northman_ (2022), she portrayed Olga, a Slavic sorceress, reuniting with director Robert Eggers.

RIGHT

Anya Taylor-Joy brings vintage glamor to the 82nd Golden Globe Awards in a blush satin gown with a draped neckline and matching shawl. Her platinum hair is swept back to highlight a dazzling statement necklace and bracelet set, evoking old Hollywood elegance.

ABOVE

Anya Taylor-Joy in _EMMA._—a Regency-era vision in marigold yellow, complete with lace gloves, bonnet, and wit as sharp as her silhouette. Period fashion with playful precision.

The Taylor-Joy Look

Elegant and daring, Anya blends vintage Hollywood glamor with modern couture edge.

- Sculpted gowns
- Retro-modern flair
- Platinum blonde hair
- Clean makeup with bold details

FASHION FEATURES

EMMA. (2020)
LAST NIGHT IN SOHO (2021)
THE NORTHMAN (2022)
THE MENU (2022)
FURIOSA: A MAD MAX SAGA (2024)

JODIE TURNER-SMITH

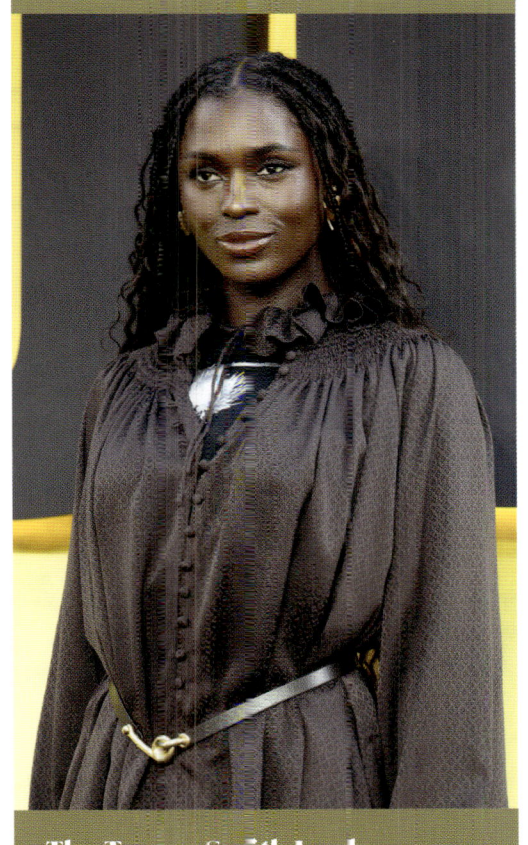

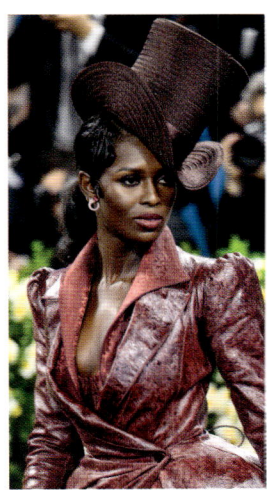

With her statuesque presence and fearless sense of style, Jodie Turner-Smith has become one of the most distinctive fashion voices in Hollywood. Effortlessly blending regal poise with experimental daring, she approaches the red carpet as a canvas—each appearance curated like performance art. From bold color choices to audacious silhouettes, she isn't just following fashion—she's pushing its boundaries, proving that true style means wearing the unexpected with complete conviction.

Since her breakout role in *Queen & Slim*, Turner-Smith has made fashion a central part of her public identity. Whether she's in floor-length Gucci, metallic Balmain, or a boldly sculpted Christopher John Rogers gown, she brings drama with elegance, commanding attention without sacrificing grace. She's known for embracing vivid color—acid greens, highlighter pinks, canary yellow—and wearing them in monochrome glory, often paired with matching eye makeup or statement jewelry. Her looks incorporate rich jewel tones or luminous fabrics that accentuate her luminous complexion.

But what sets her apart isn't just her wardrobe—it's her styling choices and the story she tells with each outfit. A lover of fashion history, Turner-Smith nods to everything from 1970s disco to Elizabethan drama, reimagined through a modern, Afro-futurist lens. Her maternity looks, including a now-iconic golden Gucci gown at the 2022 BAFTAs, redefined pregnancy fashion with strength and glamor. Jodie Turner-Smith doesn't wear clothes—she embodies them.

The Turner-Smith Look
A fearless blend of regal drama and futuristic minimalism.
- Sculptural tailoring
- Head-turning hats
- Jewel tones & metallics
- Natural hair & bold lips
- Confident, couture attitude

FASHION FEATURES

QUEEN & SLIM (2019)
AFTER YANG (2021)
WHITE NOISE (2022)
THE INDEPENDENT (2022)

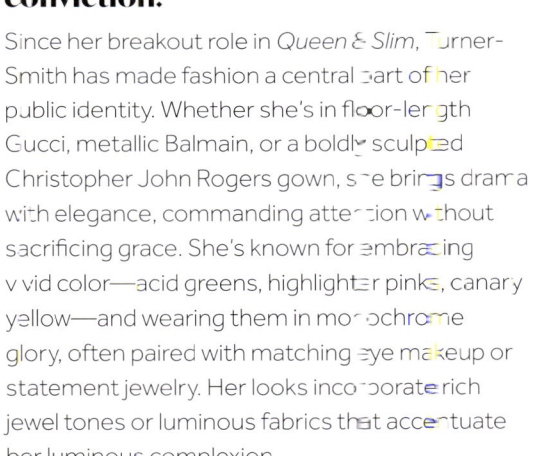

LEFT

At the *Thunderbolts* premiere in London, Jodie exudes understated opulence in a ruffled chocolate-brown gown cinched with a sculptural belt. The textured fabric and high neckline evoke Edwardian elegance, while her natural curls and luminous complexion keep the look resolutely modern. It's a masterclass in quietly powerful tonal dressing.

ABOVE

Jodie Turner-Smith commands the red carpet in sculptural burgundy leather and a towering curled top hat at the 2025 Met Gala, embodying avant-garde drama with fearless, high-fashion precision.

ZENDAYA

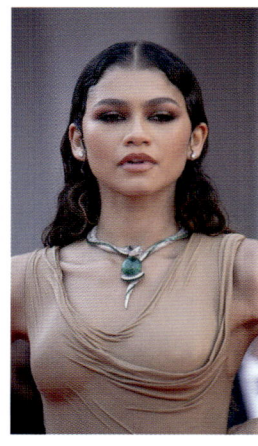

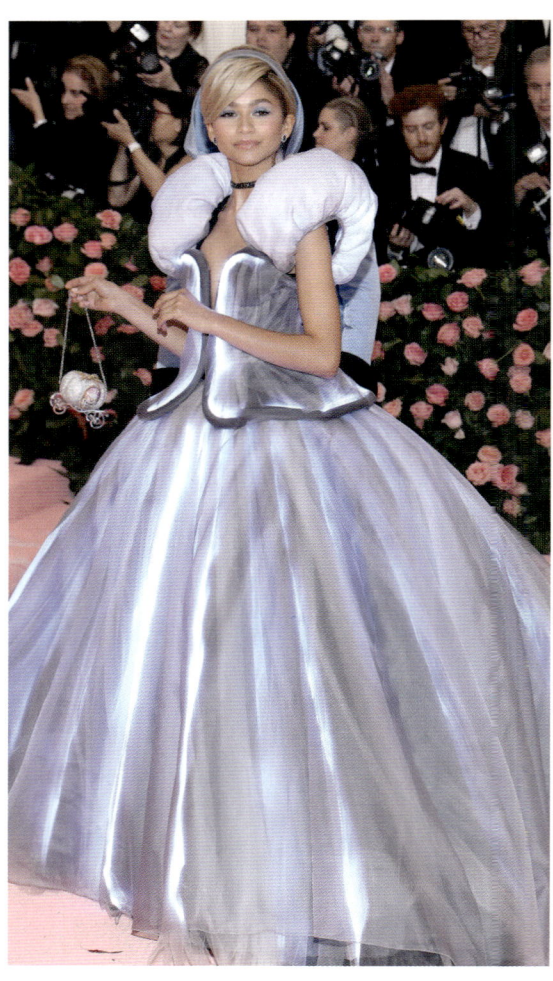

Zendaya has emerged as one of the most influential and multifaceted talents of her generation, seamlessly transitioning from a child star to acclaimed actress, singer, fashion icon, and producer. Her journey began in Oakland, California, where she cultivated her passion for performance through dance and theater, eventually leading to her breakout role as Rocky Blue in Disney Channel's *Shake It Up* (2010–2013). This early success paved the way for her lead role in *K.C. Undercover* (2015–2018), where she also served as a co-producer, showcasing her behind-the-scenes acumen.

ABOVE

Zendaya at the 2021 Venice Film Festival, statuesque in wet-look Balmain and Bulgari serpent emeralds—evoking a modern mythic siren cast in cinematic bronze.

RIGHT

Zendaya channels a techno-Cinderella at the 2019 Met Gala in a light-up Tommy Hilfiger gown—fairy-tale fantasy reimagined through the lens of theatrical futurism.

FULL PAGE

Zendaya in futuristic couture, wearing a custom chrome armor bodysuit that channels sci-fi elegance with warrior edge—an interstellar fashion moment worthy of *Dune's* red carpet.

Expanding her artistic repertoire, Zendaya ventured into music, releasing her debut single "Swag It Out" in 2011, followed by her self-titled album in 2013, which featured the hit song "Replay." Her musical talents further shone in the 2017 film *The Greatest Showman*, where she performed "Rewrite the Stars" alongside Zac Efron, contributing to the film's multiplatinum soundtrack.

Zendaya's transition to mainstream cinema was marked by her portrayal of MJ in the Marvel Cinematic Universe's *Spider-Man* series, beginning with *Spider-Man: Homecoming* (2017) and continuing through its sequels. Her performance as Rue Bennett in HBO's *Euphoria* (2019–present) garnered critical acclaim, earning her two Primetime Emmy Awards for Outstanding Lead Actress in a Drama Series, making her the youngest recipient of this honor.

Beyond acting, Zendaya has made significant strides in the fashion industry. In 2019, she collaborated with designer Tommy Hilfiger on the Tommy x Zendaya collection, celebrated for its inclusivity and diversity, featuring models of various ages and backgrounds. Her distinctive style earned her the CFDA Fashion Icon Award in 2021, solidifying her status as a trendsetter.

Zendaya's recent film endeavors include her role as Chani in *Dune* (2021) and its sequel *Dune: Part Two* (2024), as well as her performance in *Malcolm & Marie* (2021), which she also co-produced. In 2024, she starred in and produced the romantic sports drama *Challengers*, directed by Luca Guadagnino, further demonstrating her versatility and commitment to complex roles.

Off-screen, Zendaya is an advocate for various social causes, including racial justice, gender equality, and mental health awareness. She has supported organizations such as Convoy of Hope and UNICEF, using her platform to inspire positive changes.

Zendaya's multifaceted career and dedication to authenticity continue to resonate with audiences worldwide, establishing her as a formidable force in contemporary entertainment.

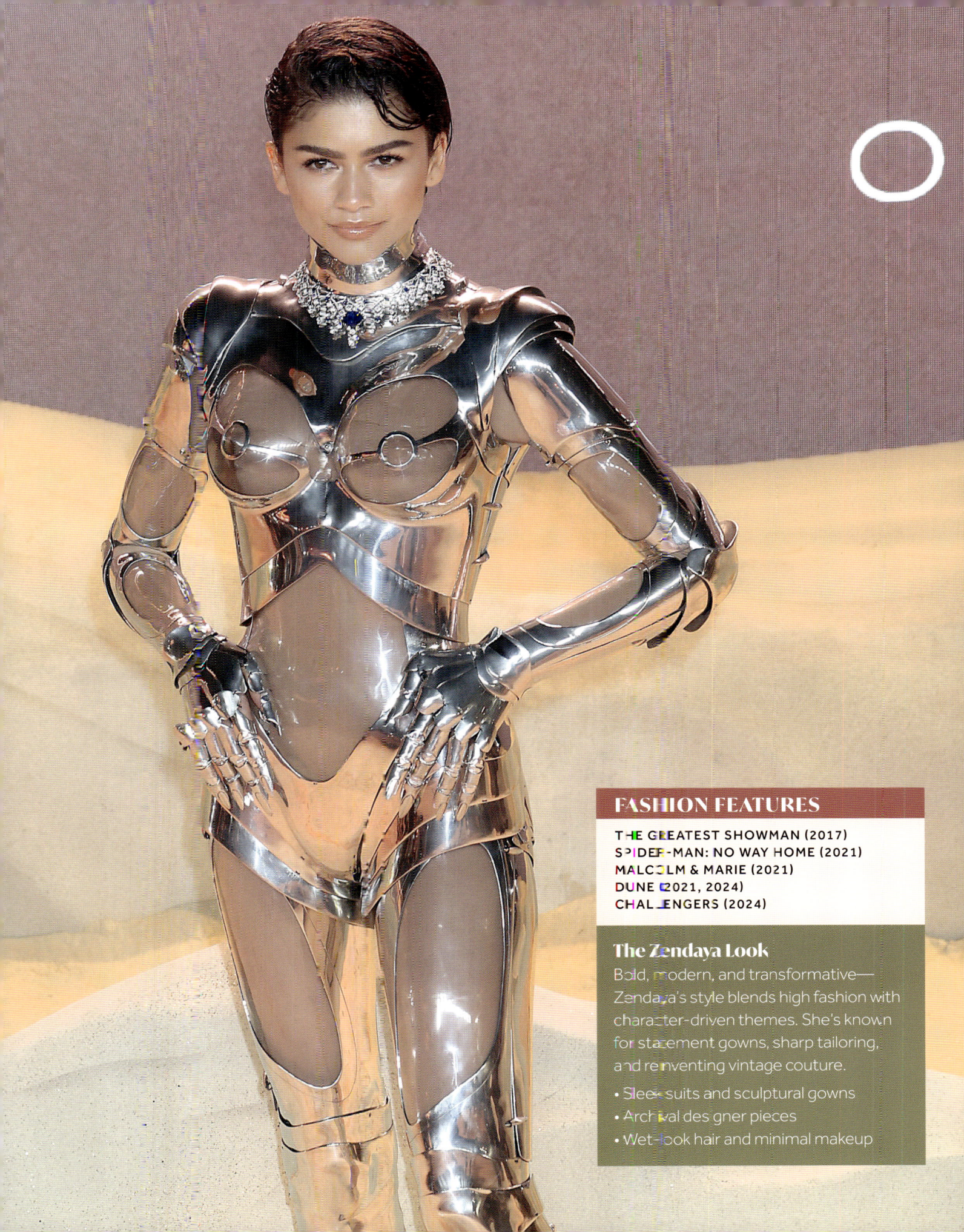

FASHION FEATURES

THE GREATEST SHOWMAN (2017)
SPIDER-MAN: NO WAY HOME (2021)
MALCOLM & MARIE (2021)
DUNE (2021, 2024)
CHALLENGERS (2024)

The Zendaya Look

Bold, modern, and transformative—
Zendaya's style blends high fashion with
character-driven themes. She's known
for statement gowns, sharp tailoring,
and reinventing vintage couture.

• Sleek suits and sculptural gowns
• Archival designer pieces
• Wet-look hair and minimal makeup

GALLERY OF STYLE

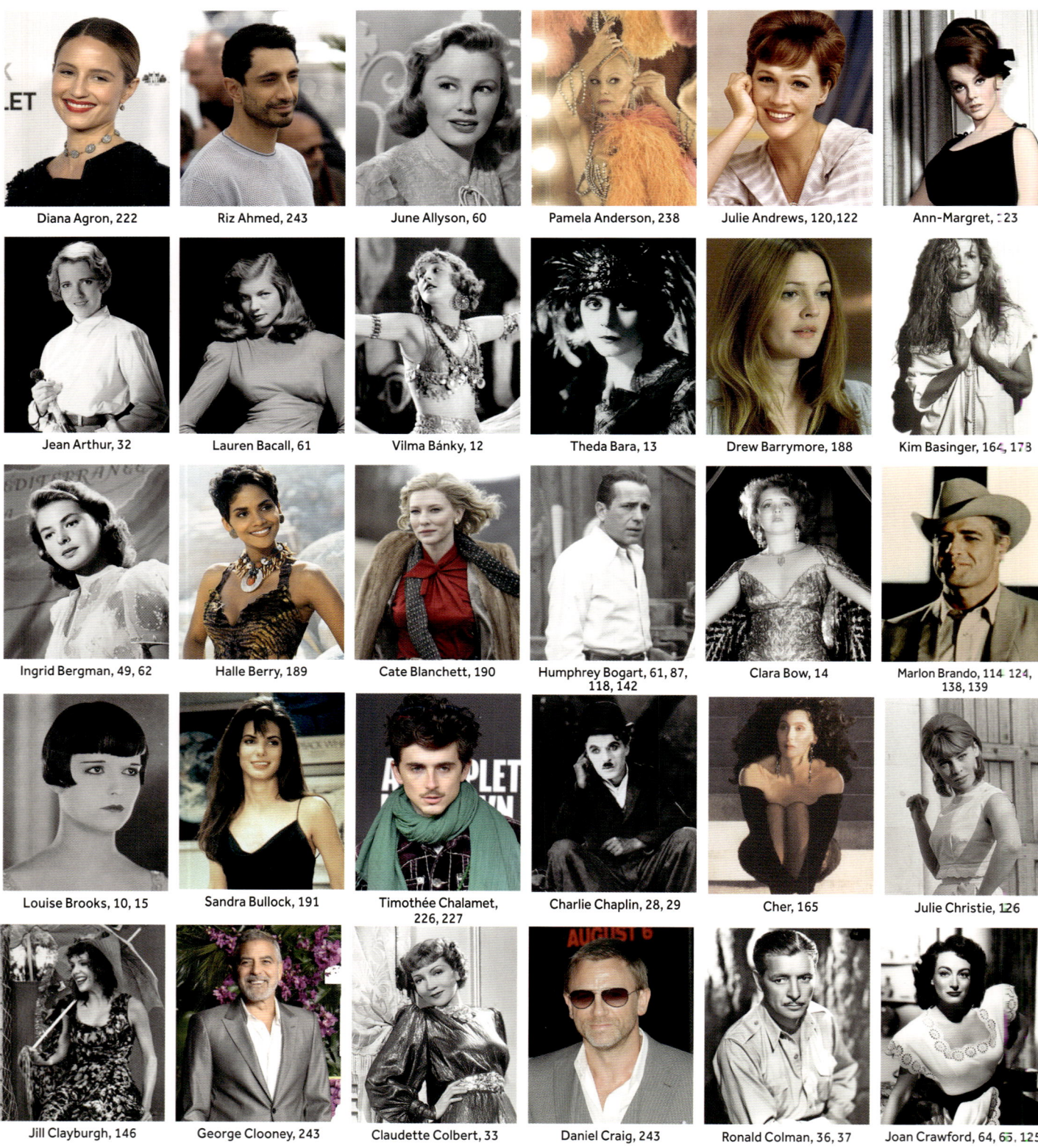

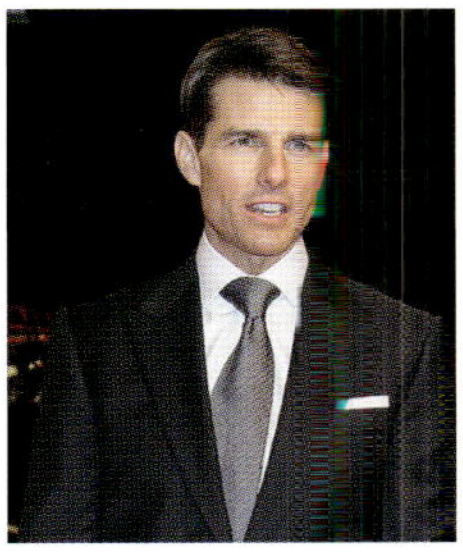

Tom Cruise, 230, 231

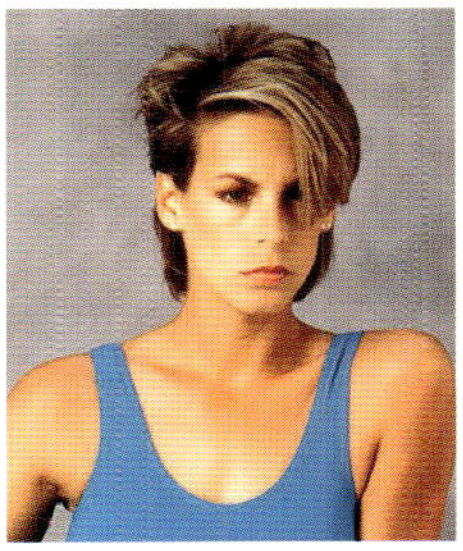

Jamie Lee Curtis, 171, 172

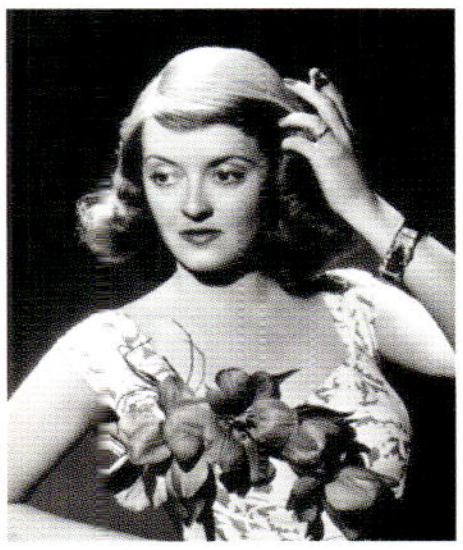

Bette Davis, 68, 69, 124

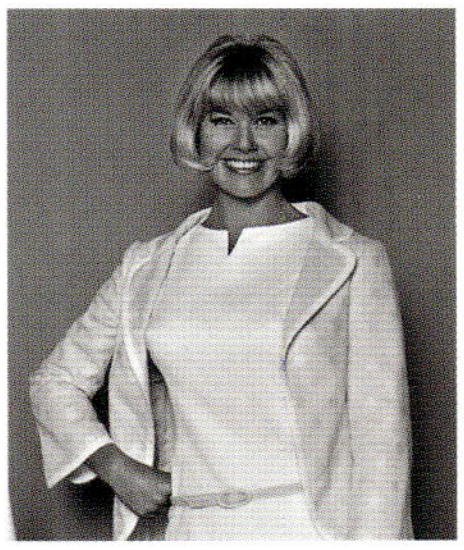

Doris Day, 108, 127

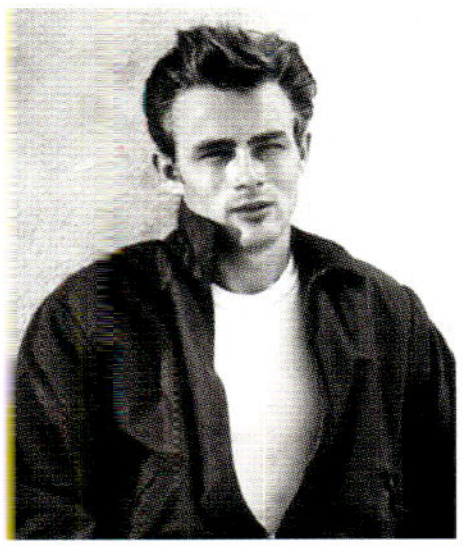

James Dean, 92, 93

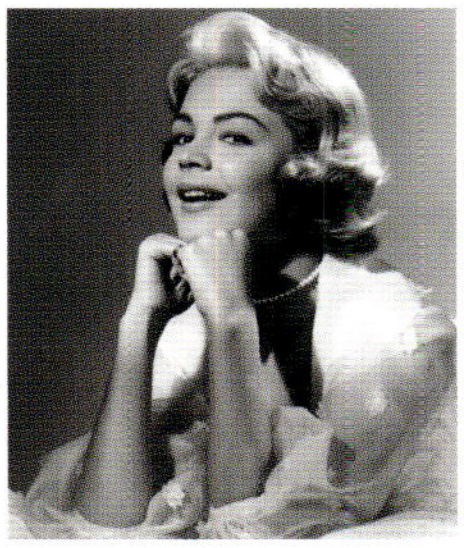

Sandra Dee, 90

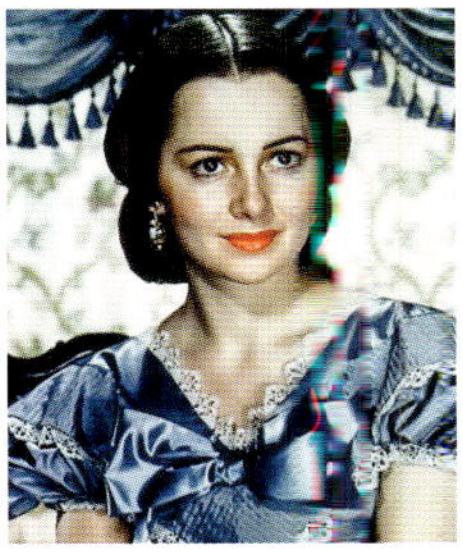

Olivia de Havilland, 97, 123

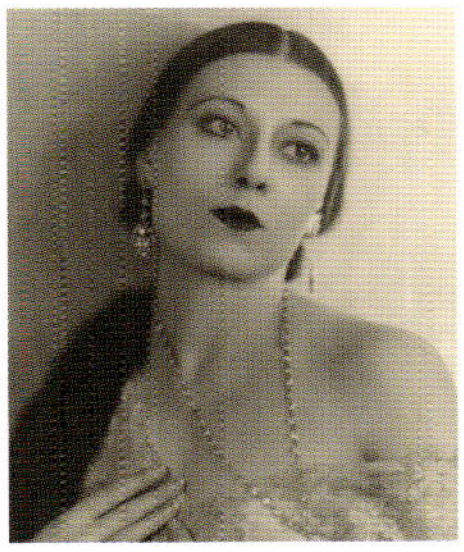

Dolores del Río, 18

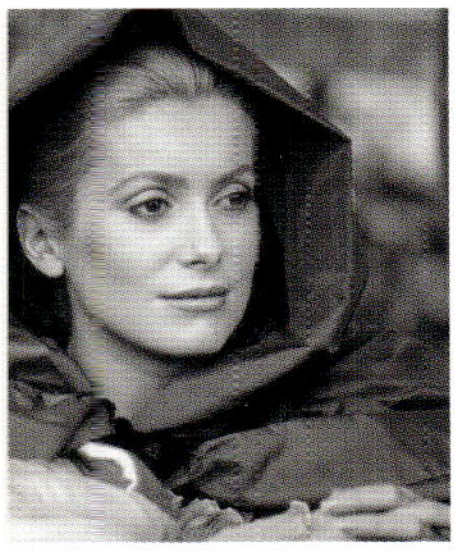

Catherine Deneuve, 147

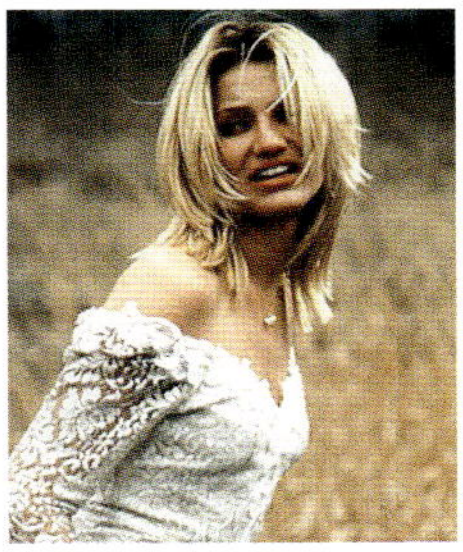

Cameron Diaz, 186, 194

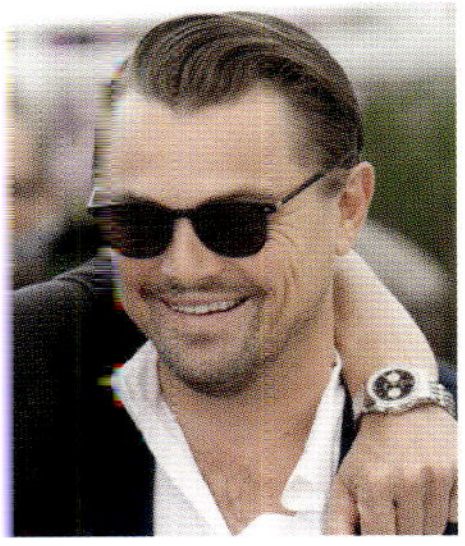

Leonardo DiCaprio, 129, 242

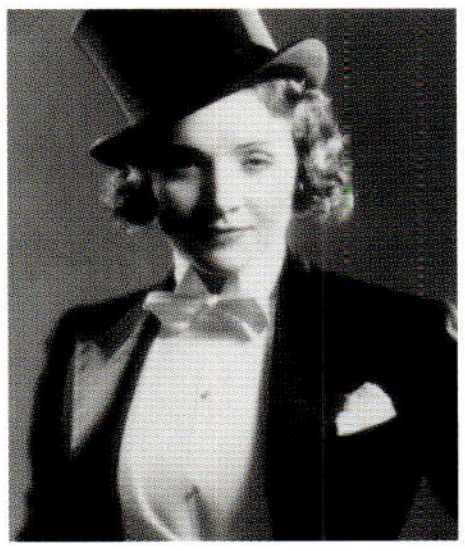

Marlene Dietrich, 34, 38, 39, 49

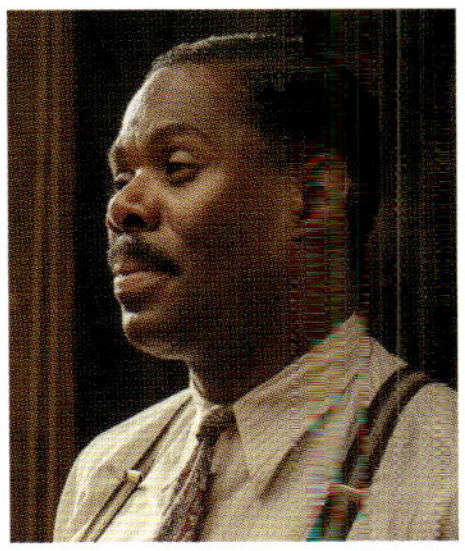

Colman Domingo, 240, 241

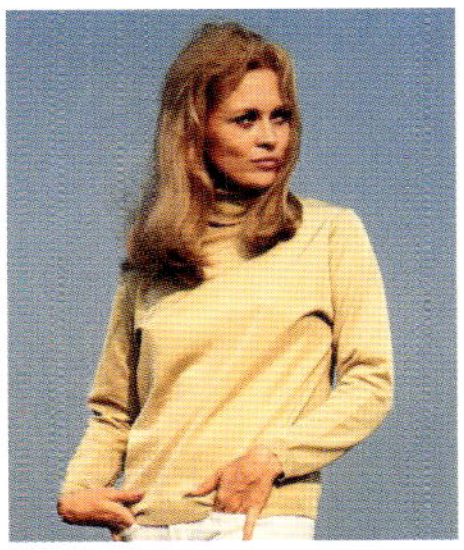

Faye Dunaway, 130

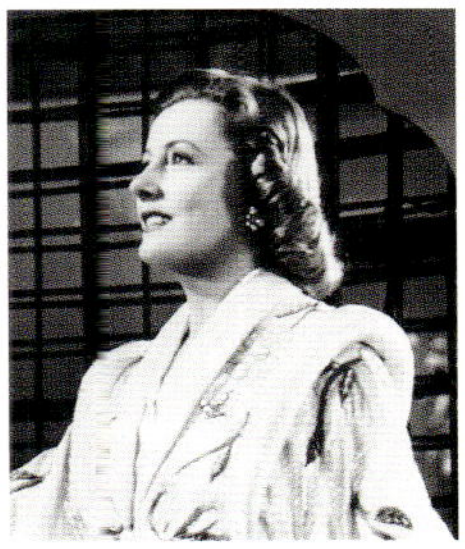

Irene Dunne, 63

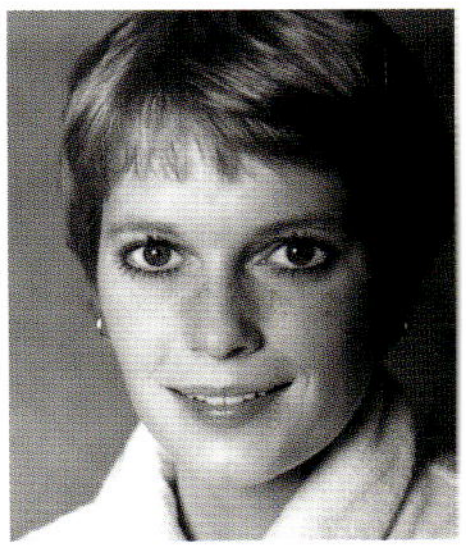

Mia Farrow, 131

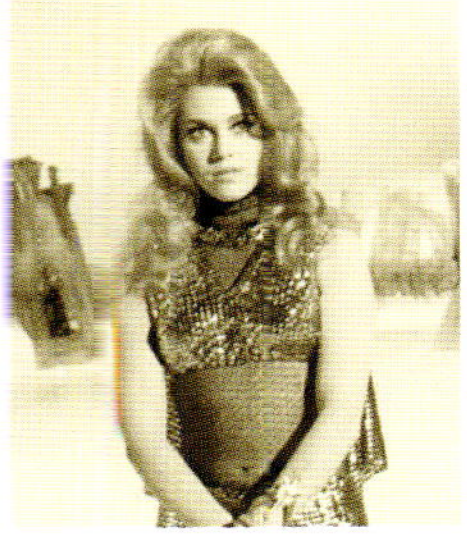

Jane Fonda, 132

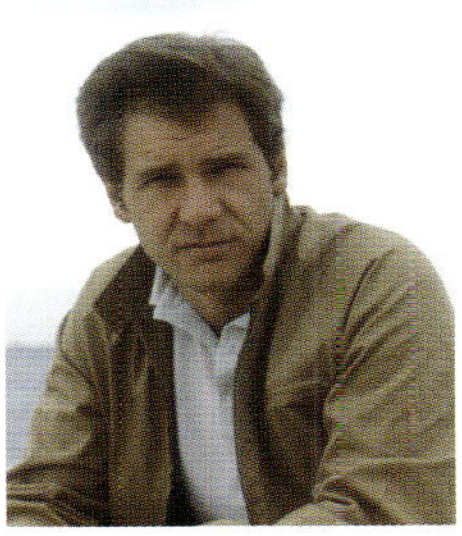

Harrison Ford, 166, 167, 184

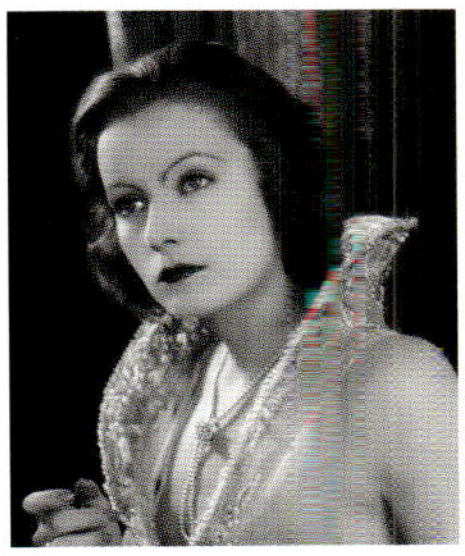

Greta Garbo, 20, 21, 22, 23

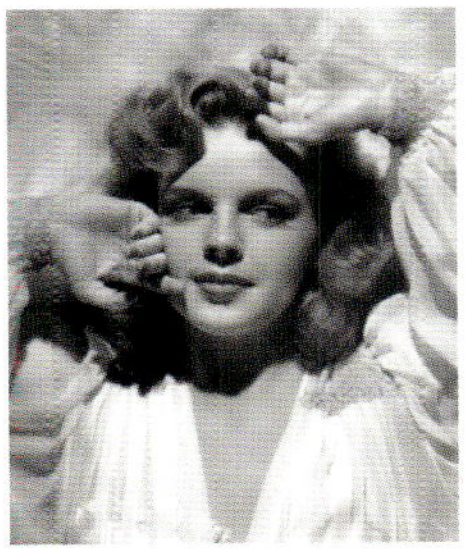

Judy Garland, 70, 71

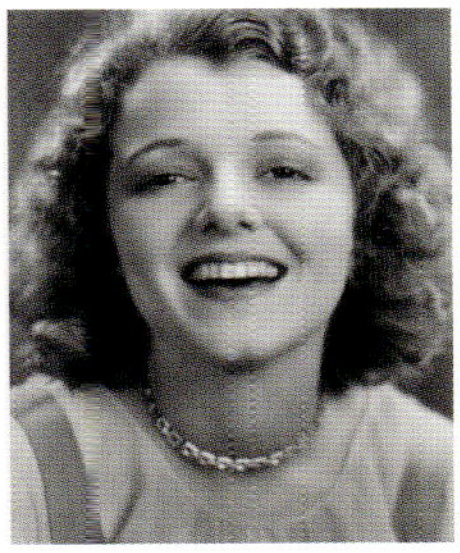

Janet Gaynor, 19

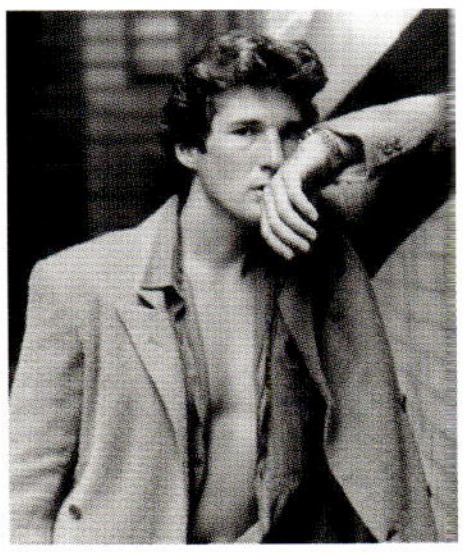

Richard Gere, 178, 179, 184

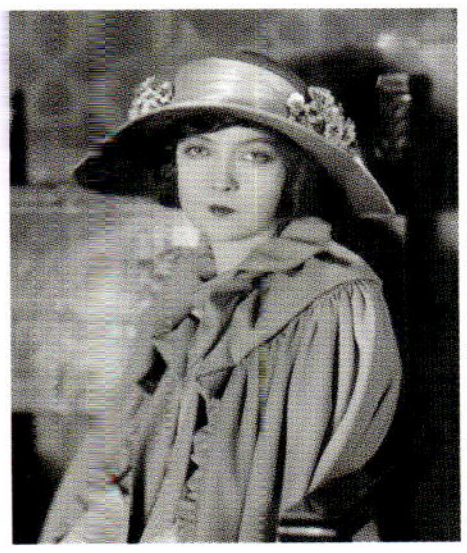

Lillian Gish, 24

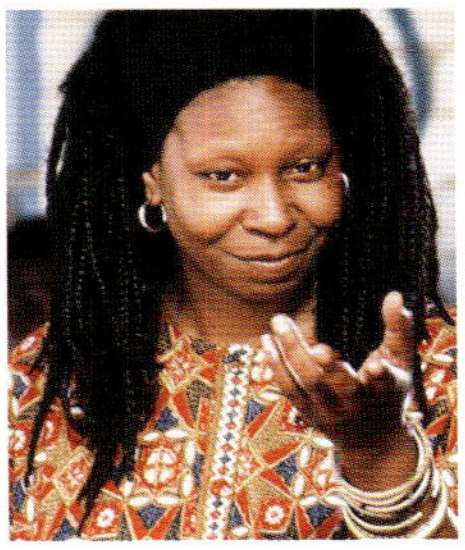

Whoopi Goldberg, 168

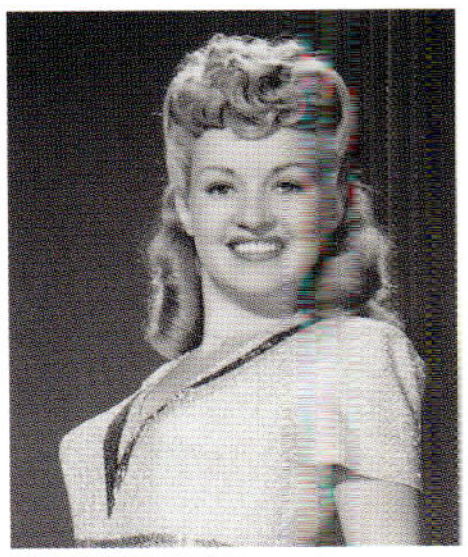

Betty Grable, 72

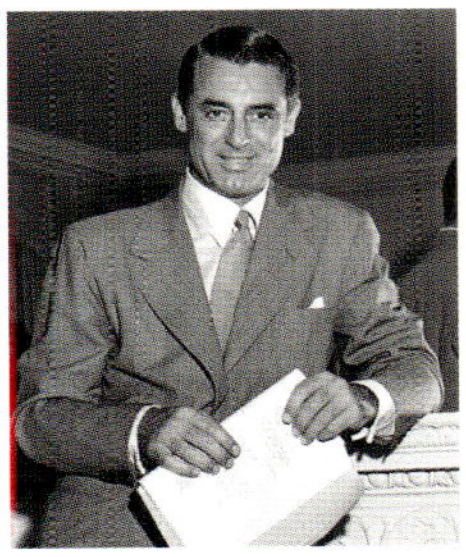

Cary Grant, 55, 87, 98, 99, 117

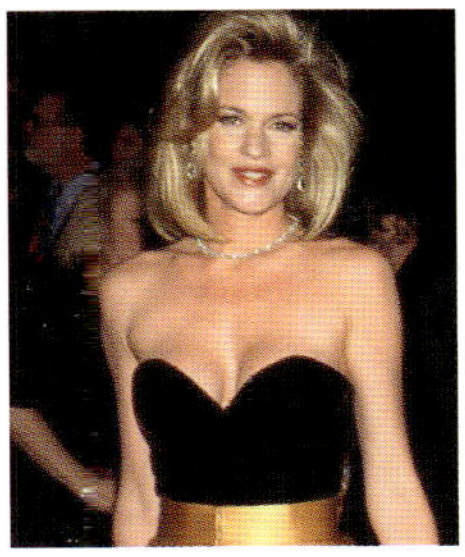

Melanie Griffith, 169

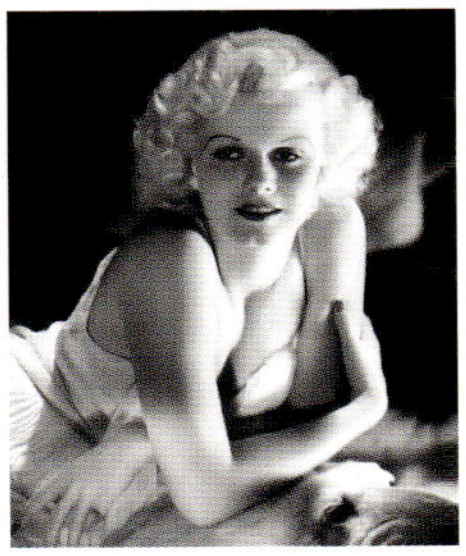

Jean Harlow, 30, 42, 43

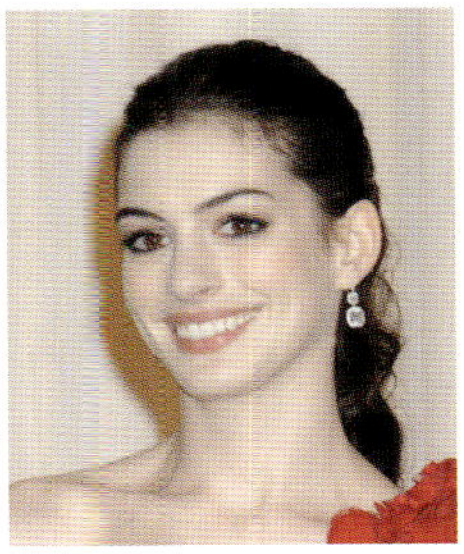

Anne Hathaway, 210, 214

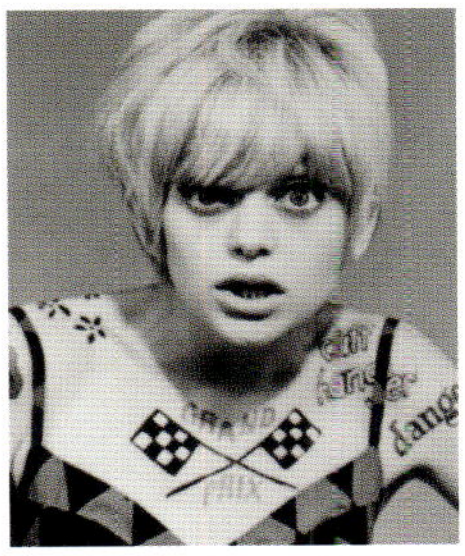

Goldie Hawn, 133

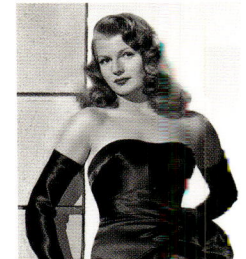

Rita Hayworth, 73

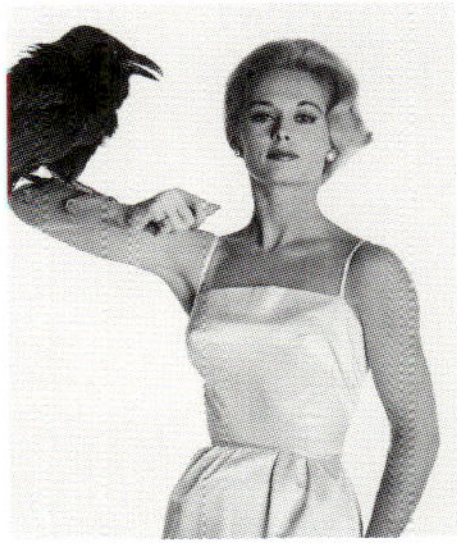

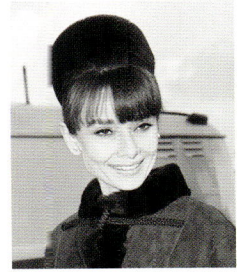

Tipi Hedren, 41

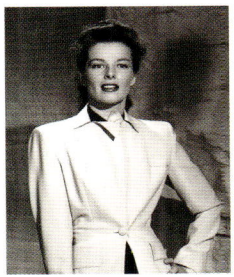

Audrey Hepburn, 136, 137

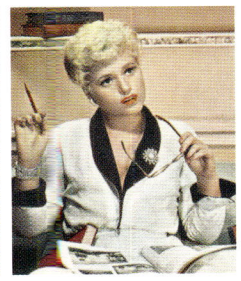

Katherine Hepburn, 58, 59, 83, 97

Judy Holliday, 100

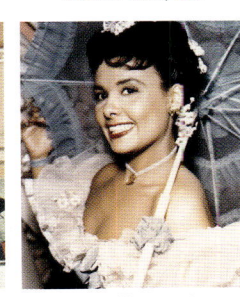

Lena Horne, 76

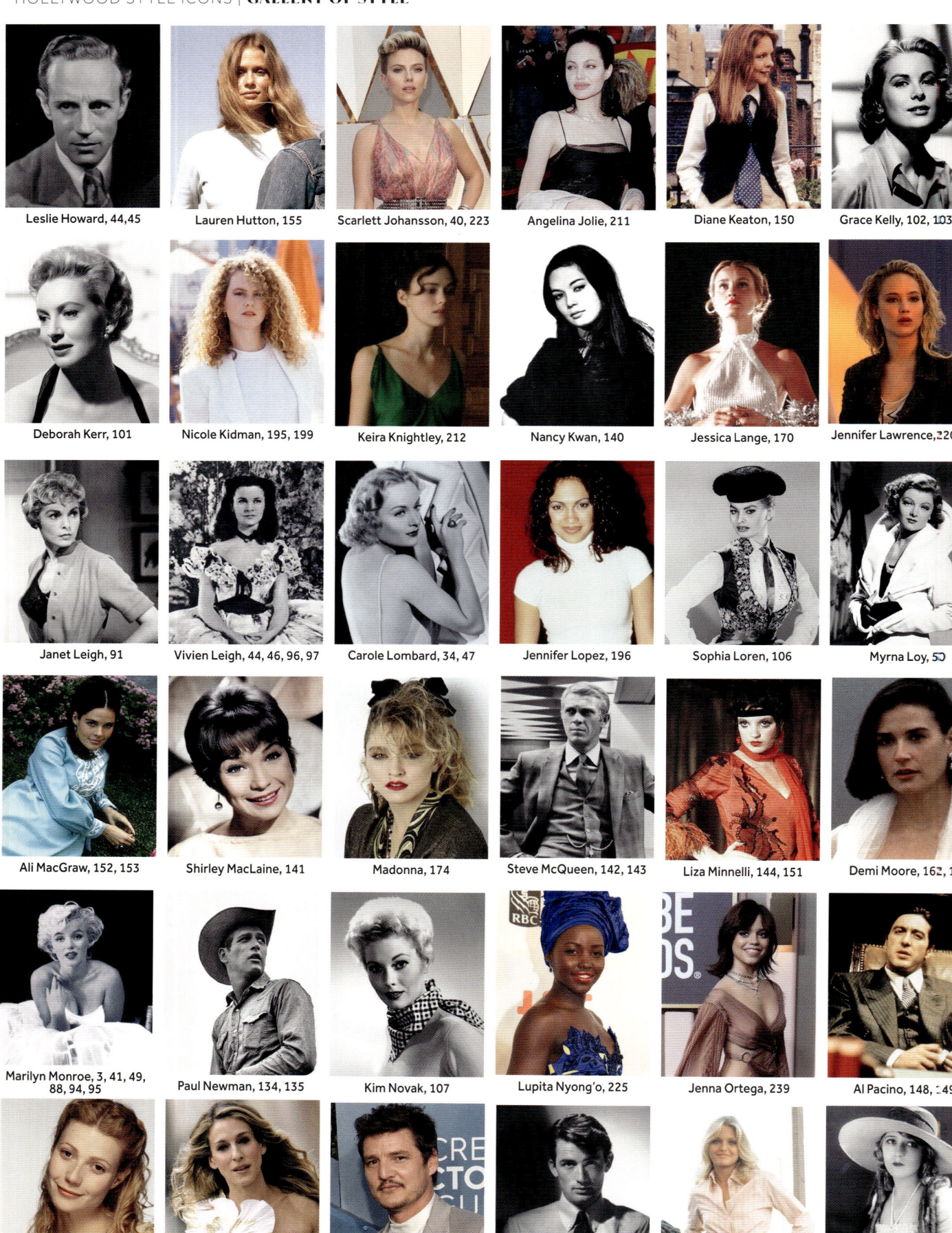

Leslie Howard, 44,45

Lauren Hutton, 155

Scarlett Johansson, 40, 223

Angelina Jolie, 211

Diane Keaton, 150

Grace Kelly, 102, 103, 109

Deborah Kerr, 101

Nicole Kidman, 195, 199

Keira Knightley, 212

Nancy Kwan, 140

Jessica Lange, 170

Jennifer Lawrence, 220, 224

Janet Leigh, 91

Vivien Leigh, 44, 46, 96, 97

Carole Lombard, 34, 47

Jennifer Lopez, 196

Sophia Loren, 106

Myrna Loy, 50

Ali MacGraw, 152, 153

Shirley MacLaine, 141

Madonna, 174

Steve McQueen, 142, 143

Liza Minnelli, 144, 151

Demi Moore, 162, 175

Marilyn Monroe, 3, 41, 49, 88, 94, 95

Paul Newman, 134, 135

Kim Novak, 107

Lupita Nyong'o, 225

Jenna Ortega, 239

Al Pacino, 148, 149

Gwyneth Paltrow, 197

Sarah Jessica Parker, 213

Pedro Pascal, 242

Gregory Peck, 74, 75

Michelle Pfeiffer, 176, 198

Mary Pickford, 25

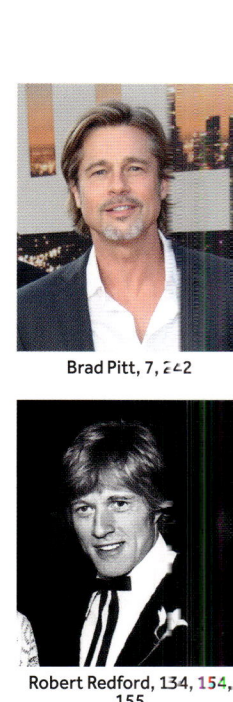

Brad Pitt, 7, 242

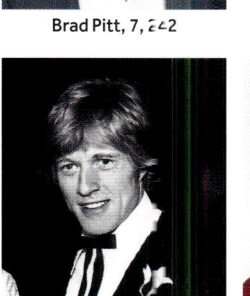

Sidney Poitier, 114

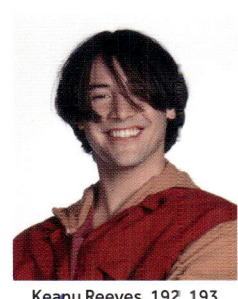

Natalie Portman, 216

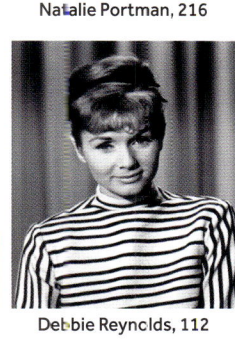

Elvis Presley, 105

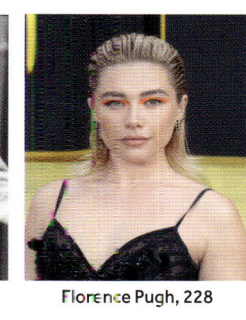

Florence Pugh, 228

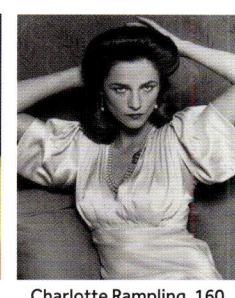

Charlotte Rampling, 160, 161

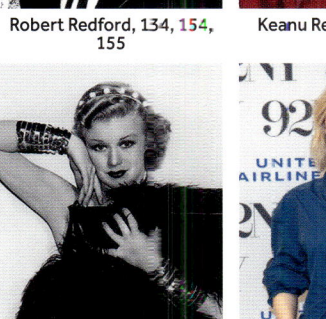

Robert Redford, 134, 154, 155

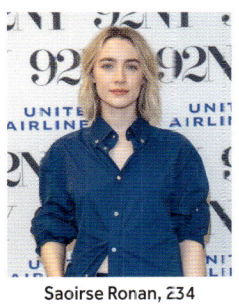

Keanu Reeves, 192, 193

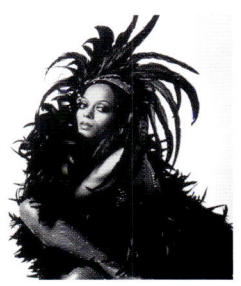

Debbie Reynolds, 112

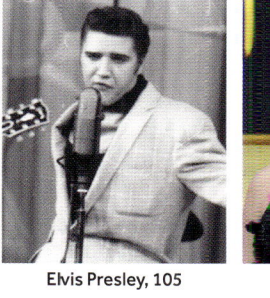

Molly Ringwald, 177

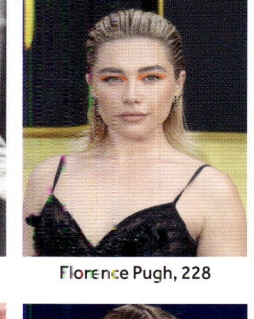

Margot Robbie, 229

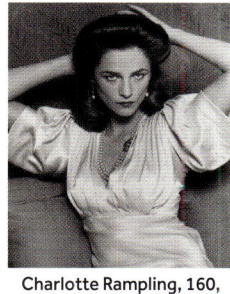

Julia Roberts, 179, 200, 202

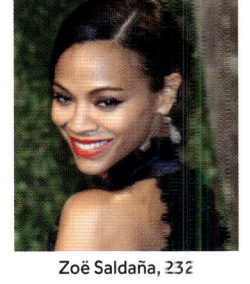

Ginger Rogers, 51

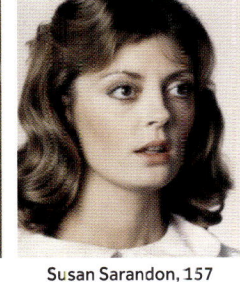

Saoirse Ronan, 234

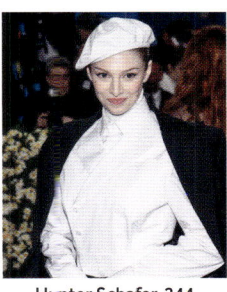

Diana Ross, 156

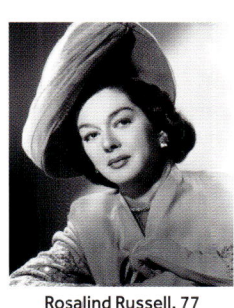

Rosalind Russell, 77

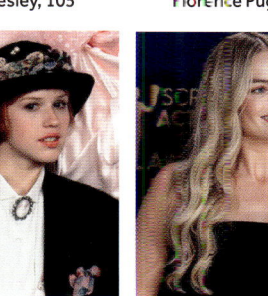

Meg Ryan, 201

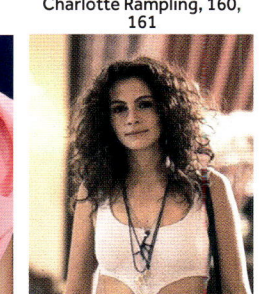

Winona Ryder, 180

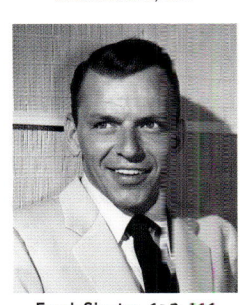

Zoë Saldaña, 232

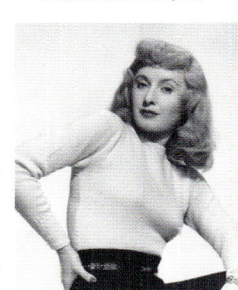

Susan Sarandon, 157

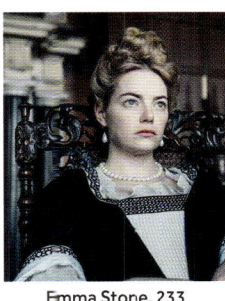

Hunter Schafer, 244

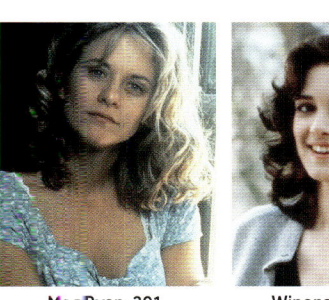

Andrew Scott, 243

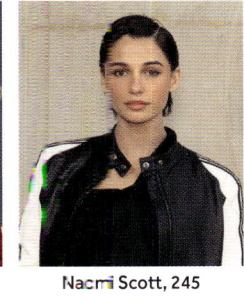

Naomi Scott, 245

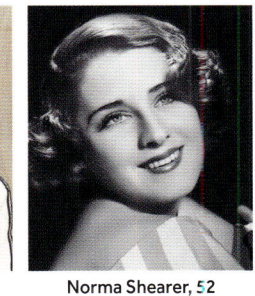

Norma Shearer, 52

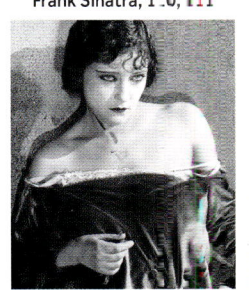

Frank Sinatra, 110, 111

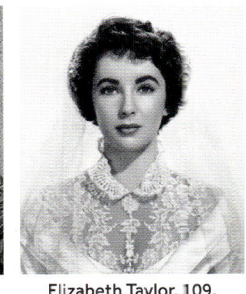

Barbara Stanwyck, 80, 82

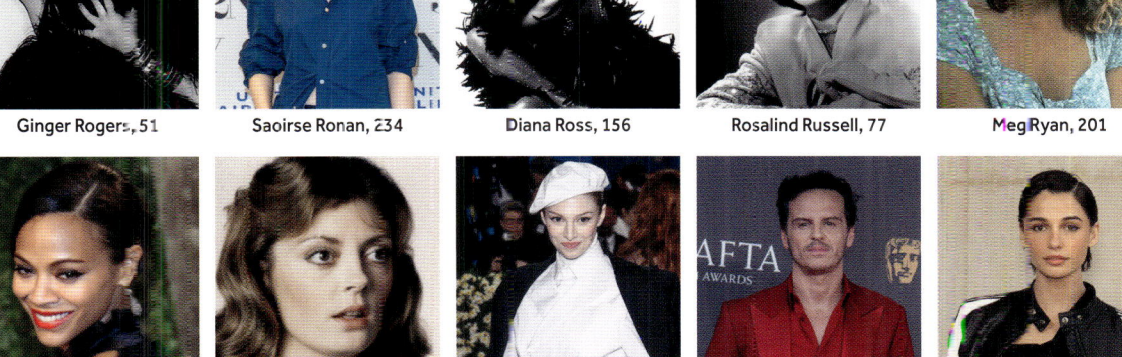

Emma Stone, 233

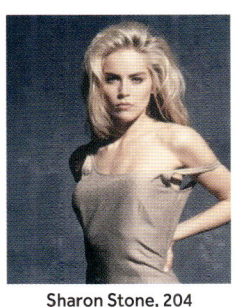

Sharon Stone, 204

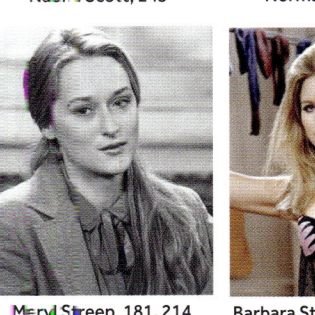

Meryl Streep, 181, 214

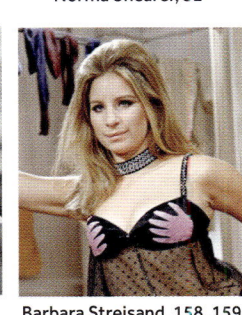

Barbara Streisand, 158, 159

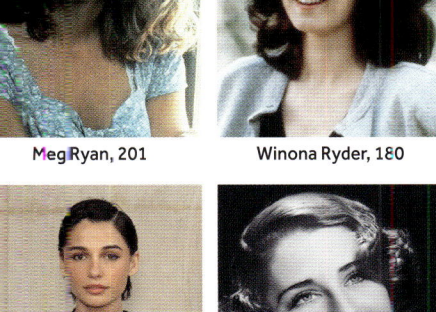

Gloria Swanson 8, 9, 26

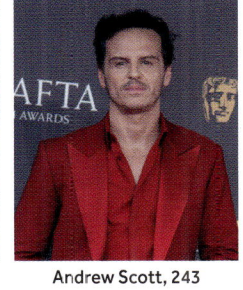

Elizabeth Taylor, 109, 116, 117

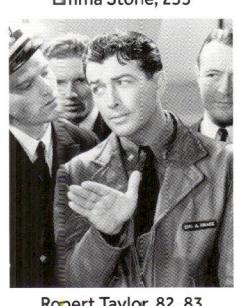

Robert Taylor, 82, 83

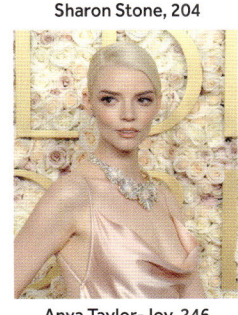

Anya Taylor-Joy, 246

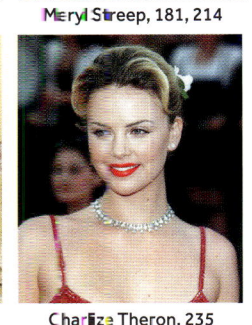

Charlize Theron, 235

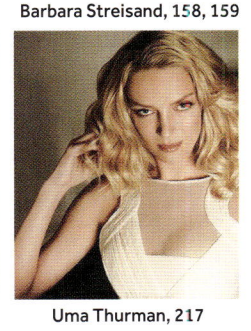

Uma Thurman, 217

253

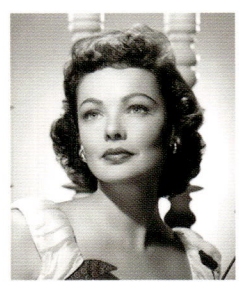
Gene Tierney, 81

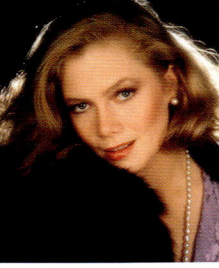
Kathleen Turner, 182

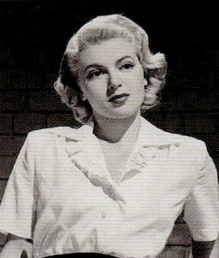
Lana Turner, 56, 83, 84

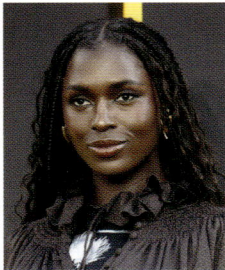
Jodie Turner-Smith, 247

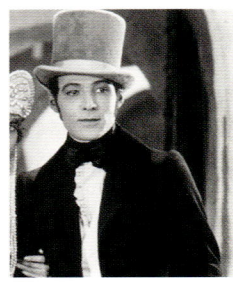
Rudolph Valentino, 16,17

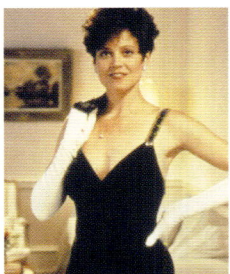
Sigourney Weaver, 183

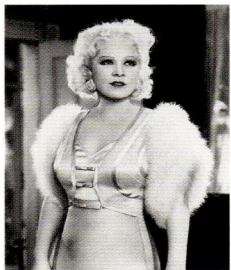
Mae West, 53

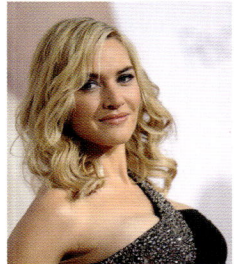
Kate Winslet, 205

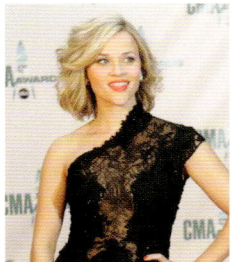
Reese Witherspoon, 218

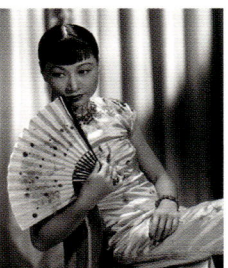
Anna May Wong, 27, 34

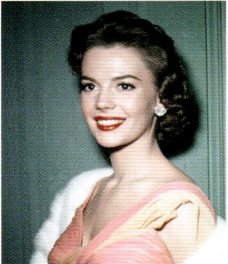
Natalie Wood, 113

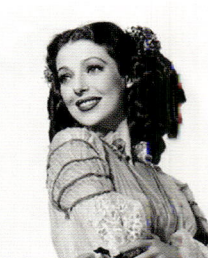
Loretta Young, 85

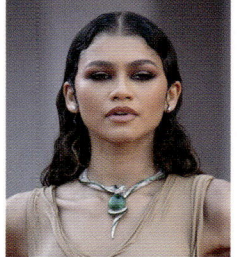
Zendaya, 236, 248

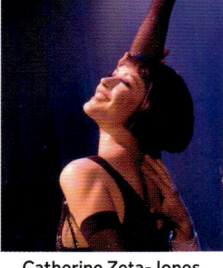
Catherine Zeta-Jones, 208, 219

COSTUME DESIGNERS

OSCARS FOR COSTUME DESIGN

This award, voted on by the costume designers in the Academy of Motion Picture Arts and Sciences, did not always reflect the most influential or outstanding costuming, but rather the costumes that voters felt best served each film.

1948
B&W: *Hamlet*, Roger K. Furse
Color: *Joan of Arc*, Dorothy Jeakins and Barbara Karinska

1949
B&W: *The Heiress*, Edith Head, Gile Steele
Color: *Adventures of Don Juan*, Marjorie Best, Leah Rhodes, William Travilla

1950
B&W: *All About Eve*, Edith Head, Charles LeMaire
Color: *Samson and Delilah*, Edith Head, Dorothy Jeakins, Elois Jenssen, Gile Steele, Gwen Wakeling

1951
B&W: *A Place in the Sun*, Edith Head
Color: *An American in Paris*, Orry-Kelly, Walter Plunkett, Irene Sharaff

1952
B&W: *The Bad and the Beautiful*, Helen Rose
Color: *Moulin Rouge*, Marce Vertes

1953
B&W: *Roman Holiday*, Edith Head
Color: *The Robe*, Charles LeMaire and Emile Santiago

1954
B&W: *Sabrina*, Edith Head
Color: *Gate of Hell*, Sanzo Wada

1955
B&W: *I'll Cry Tomorrow*, Helen Rose
Color: *Love Is a Many-Splendored Thing*, Charles LeMaire

1956
B&W: *The Solid Gold Cadillac*, Jean Louis
Color: *The King and I*, Irene Sharaff

1957
Les Girls, Orry-Kelly

1958
Gigi, Cecil Beaton

1959
B&W: *Some Like it Hot*, Orry-Kelly
Color: *Ben-Hur*, Elizabeth Haffenden

1960
B&W: *The Facts of Life*, Edith Head, Edward Stevenson
Color: *Spartacus*, Arlington Valles

1961
B&W: *La Dolce Vita*, Piero Gherardi
Color: *West Side Story*, Irene Sharaff

1962
B&W: *What Ever Happened to Baby Jane?*, Norma Koch
Color: *The Wonderful World of the Brothers Grimm*, Mary Wills

1963
B&W: *8½*, Piero Gherardi
Color: *Cleopatra*, Renié Conley, Vittorio Nino Novarese, Irene Sharaff

1964
E&W: *The Night of the Iguana*, Dorothy Jeakins
Color: *My Fair Lady*, Cecil Beaton

1965
E&W: *Darling*, Julie Harris
Color: *Doctor Zhivago*, Phyllis Dalton

1966
B&W: *Who's Afraid of Virginia Woolf?*, Irene Sharaff
Color: *A Man for All Seasons*, Elizabeth Haffenden, Joan Bridge

1967
Camelot, John Truscott

1968
Romeo and Juliet, Danilo Donati

1969
Anne of the Thousand Days, Margaret Furse

1970
Cromwell, Vittorio Nino Novarese

1971
Nicholas and Alexandra, Yvonne Blake and Antonio Castillo

1972
Travels with My Aunt, Anthony Powell

1973
The Sting, Edith Head

1974
The Great Gatsby, Theoni V. Aldredge

1975
Barry Lyndon, Milena Canonero and Ulla-Britt Soderlund

1976
Fellini's Casanova, Danilo Donati

1977
Star Wars, John Mollo

1978
Death on the Nile, Anthony Powell

1979
All That Jazz, Albert Wolsky

1980
Tess, Anthony Powell

1981
Chariots of Fire, Milena Canonero
Gandhi, Bhanu Athaiya and John Mollo

1983
Fanny and Alexander, Marik Vos

1984
Amadeus, Theodor Pistek

1985
Ran, Emi Wada

1986
A Room with a View, Jenny Beavan and John Bright

1987
The Last Emperor, James Acheson

1988
Dangerous Liaisons, James Acheson

1989
Henry V, Phyllis Dalton

1990
Cyrano de Bergerac, Franca Squarciapino

1991
Bugsy, Albert Wolsky

1992
Bram Stoker's Dracula, Eiko Ishioka

1993
The Age of Innocence, Gabriella Pescucci

1994
The Adventures of Priscilla, Queen of the Desert, Tim Chappel and Lizzy Gardiner

1995
Restoration, James Acheson

1996
The English Patient, Ann Roth

1997
Titanic, Deborah Lynn Scott

1998
Shakespeare in Love, Sandy Powell

1999
Topsy-Turvy, Lindy Hemming

2000
Gladiator, Janty Yates

2001
Moulin Rouge!, Catherine Martin and Angus Strathie

2002
Chicago, Colleen Atwood

2003
Lord of the Rings: The Return of the King, Ngila Dickson and Richard Taylor

2004
The Aviator, Sandy Powell

2005
Memoirs of a Geisha, Colleen Atwood

2006
Marie Antoinette, Milena Canonero

2007
Elizabeth: The Golden Age, Alexandra Byrne

2008
The Duchess, Michael O'Connor

2009
The Young Victoria, Sandy Powell

2010
Alice in Wonderland, Colleen Atwood

2011
The Artist, Mark Bridges

2012
Anna Karenina, Jacqueline Durran

2013
The Great Gatsby, Catherine Martin

2014
The Grand Budapest Hotel, Milena Canonero

2015
Mad Max: Fury Road, Jenny Beavan

2016
Fantastic Beasts and Where to Find Them, Colleen Atwood

2017
Phantom Thread, Mark Bridges

2018
Black Panther, Ruth E. Carter

2019
Jojo Rabbit, Mayes C. Rubeo

2020
Little Women, Jacqueline Durran

2021
Ma Rainey's Black Bottom, Ann Roth

2022
Cruella, Jenny Beavan

2023
Black Panther: Wakanda Forever, Ruth E. Carter

2024
Poor Things, Holly Waddington

2025
Wicked, Paul Tazewell

ANNALEE HODGES

Author Annalee Hodges grew up just outside Manhattan, where she developed a love for Broadway theater that quickly expanded to Hollywood movies. Her other titles include guides to gardening, nature, and health. She has also written on crime, pop music idols, and the American cultural experience.

CREDITS